Teaching the Mentally Retarded Student

Teaching the Mentally Retarded Student
CURRICULUM, METHODS, AND STRATEGIES

Richard L. Luftig

Miami University
Oxford, Ohio

Allyn and Bacon, Inc.

Boston • London • Sydney • Toronto

Library of Congress Cataloging-in-Publication Data

Luftig, Richard L., 1949-
    Teaching the mentally retarded student.

    Bibliography: p.
    Includes index.
    1. Mentally handicapped children—Education (Elementary)
—United States. 2. Mentally handicapped children—
Education (Elementary)—United States—Curricula.
3. Curriculum planning—United States. I. Title.
LC4603.3.L84   1987   371.92'8   86-26467
ISBN 0-205-10262-X

Series editors: John Coleman, Martin Connor
Production coordinator: Helyn Pultz
Editorial-production service: Custom House Publishing Services
Cover coordinator: Linda K. Dickinson
Cover designer: Christy Rosso

Printed in the United States of America

10 9 8 7 6 5 4 3 2 1   90 89 88 87 86

To Amy and David, who had to share Daddy with this book and who are shared with readers throughout this text. I love you both. And to my wife Diane, who encouraged, loved, and cajoled me when I believed that I simply couldn't write another word, all my love. This one's for you.

Contents

9. Arithmetic Instruction 259

10. Social Studies and Science Instruction 309

Preface

This book has grown out of almost a decade of teaching a course in curriculum methods for teaching mildly mentally retarded learners, as well as supervising both practicum and student teaching experiences. In the years that I have taught the course, I have been struck with a number of impressions. First, it became clear to me that prospective special education teachers (and, for that matter, practicing teachers) are extremely weak in the theoretical underpinning of teaching in general and the core academic areas in particular. That is, students and teachers have little or no understanding of the information processing, learning, and memory processes involved in the schooling process; nor do they understand how children learn to accomplish such tasks as reading, arithmetic, spelling, and written expression.

Second, I became aware that the majority of the prospective special education teachers with whom I came into contact do not have any unified conceptualization of teaching. Rather, they tend to see teaching of subject matter to mildly mentally retarded children throughout the school day as a series of isolated events without any connecting "thread" to draw them all together and make them meaningful for the learner. Finally, I was struck with the fact that students are much concerned about classroom management and control (they call it *discipline*) but possess precious little information about physically and psychologically structuring a learning environment in order to optimize the probability of learning while decreasing inappropriate student behavior.

As I continued to teach the course, I also continued to be dissatisfied with the inability of available texts to handle these issues. Often, such texts are little more than "cookbooks" that provide students with litanies of activities for students but little or no understanding of such processes as reading, arithmetic, and spelling, or specific information as to how best to structure and sequence core area curricula. Likewise, these texts tend to treat each subject matter as a separate event with little or no information about making the curriculum a coherent "whole" to exceptional students on the basis of relevance and importance to the normalization process. Finally, I perceive available texts to be extremely weak in explaining the newest (and highly exciting) research and developments in the areas of information processing, learning, and memory as well as classroom management and effective teaching.

It is my intent to remediate in this book what I propose to be weaknesses in others. For example, the initial chapters deal at length with the information processing, learning, and memory processes and how this information applies specifically to mildly mentally retarded learners. From there the text moves to specific information on writing good instructional objectives at differing levels of complexity using Bloom's Taxonomy of Objectives. Only after the reader has mastered understanding of these important processes is instruction in teaching specific core academic areas covered.

A key aspect of this text is that it adopts a long-term instructional unit approach to teaching. In this approach a central, well-conceived thematic topic becomes the umbrella under which all curriculum core areas are taught during the school day. Teaching under such a topical umbrella provides a focus or theme for the learner in which content becomes topical rather than fragmented. Such thematic teaching has proven to be facilitative in the learning of mentally retarded learners, and the prospective teacher (i.e., the reader of this text) is taken step-by-step through the unit writing process. Additionally, there is a section in each chapter dealing with teaching a core academic area in that subject within a long-term unit.

Besides the teaching of academic content, this book also attempts to give prospective teachers information on setting up both the physical and psychological classroom environments. It discusses different physical classroom structures and their effects on learning as well as psychological environmental structures that facilitate a warm, motivating framework in which to teach and learn. Finally, there are sections on classroom management and behavioral change.

It is difficult in a short book to cover everything there is to know about effective teaching for mildly mentally retarded learners. Such a book probably has never been written and surely this text falls short in that attempt. Nevertheless, the key to effective teaching is to understand *what* you are trying to teach, *how* it might best be taught, and *why* you should (or should not) teach it the way you currently do. This book is an attempt to help students understand how mildly mentally retarded individuals learn as well as give information as to sound teaching methods, materials, and activities for helping them learn. Finally, it is an attempt to help the reader to become a warm, effective teacher rather than an adversary for children to avoid. If I have helped the prospective teacher achieve these goals, then this book has proven successful beyond my greatest expectations.

I would like to thank the following reviewers for their helpful comments and suggestions during the development of this book: Paul Bates, Southern Illinois University at Carbondale; Jack C. Dinger, Slippery Rock State College; Earle Knowlton, University of Kansas; David A. Powers, East Carolina University; Scott Sparks, Ohio University; and Anthony Van Reusen, University of Arizona. I would also like to thank Mary Manion, Lynn Welty, and Jennifer Wolfe for contributing their long-term instructional units.

PART I

The Learner

1

The Nature of Mildly Mentally Retarded Learners and the Special Education Curriculum

My first year as a teacher in a classroom for mildly mentally retarded learners (EMH)* was a mixture of anxiety and satisfaction, of an intense desire to run away and do something else for a living and the feeling that I was performing the most important job in the world. I was hired on an emergency basis—the school system was forced to open a classroom due to overflow conditions in another school, and they had a very short time in which to accomplish their goal. The good news was that they interviewed me on a Friday and gave me the job the same day. The bad news was that I was to start the following Monday! And what they didn't tell me was that it would be a while before I got even the most basic equipment—paper, pencils, books, and other supplies. We would have to wait for these things to come from other school buildings or to be ordered. Students, on the other hand, I had *lots* of. Fifteen EMH children between the ages of nine and eleven. After that first day on the job, things were so bad that I wanted to quit and run away.

Yet somehow, things began to turn around. Once I learned what was important in my student's lives, they began to become interested in what I had to say and offer. And the parents of my students, many of whom had failed in school themselves, also began to warm up to me when they learned that I wasn't ashamed to travel to their homes, their 'turf', to ask for their help. I guess, what made it all worthwhile for me, was the note one of those parents sent into school scribbled on the back of a paper bag. "Elmer and I both like you real good," the letter said. "You have did more for our boy than any body has. You welcome any time."

*Synonyms for mildly mentally retarded students are numerous. Some people still refer to them as educable mentally retarded learners or EMH despite the fact that the American Association on Mental Deficiency (AAMD) discourages this term. Other states and school systems refer to such students as developmentally handicapped (DH). For the purposes of this book, such students will be referred to as mildly mentally retarded.

I've kept that letter and I read it every time I question why it is I teach these children. I plan on teaching and reading that letter for a long time.
—*Diane, a teacher in rural Upper Michigan*

I didn't begin teaching mentally retarded children until later in life—I was over forty years old when I went back to school, gained my degree, and began teaching. I now teach in an inner-city school, to tough, street-wise minority kids who at first seemed to go out of their way to antagonize me and make me angry. After awhile though, I realized that they really weren't so tough, that they were often hurting inside. What they were seeking with their attention-getting behavior was someone to accept them for who they were with no strings attached. As I grew to know them and like them, I learned that what I had first considered disrespectful behavior, calling me grandma and things like that, were their ways of accepting me and showing affection.

It was a wonderful journey through the school year as I watched them improve their grades and actually *learn*. They began taking pride in themselves and gained a stronger self-concept as they learned that they weren't just a bunch of "dummies" but valued persons who could learn and achieve.

I guess just how much they grew to care for me became apparent when I went into the hospital for some minor surgery. Almost the entire class descended on the hospital intent on visiting me in my room. I guess the hospital staff became really frightened—they were convinced that there was going to be a gang war right there in the hospital lobby! But they had come only to visit their teacher and wish her well. I believe that their visit had more to do with making me better than any medicine in the world.
—*Jane, a teacher in an urban school district*

Look, don't let anybody talk you into believing that teaching mentally retarded children is going to be easy. There's all kinds of reasons for going into the field; you think you're going to save these poor kids from themselves or that the hours are good, or that you're suddenly going to make kids "nonretarded." None of these reasons are the right ones. The hours are longer than you think, and the kids are going to learn notoriously slow—that's why the kids are in your class in the first place. And the pay? You could make more money working for the post office! When you get right down to it, there's only one reason for teaching these children. You do it because you like them and you think that your teaching skills might help them learn better. Maybe that reason doesn't sound very romantic or good enough. But when a child who previously hasn't learned and thinks he's dumb beams up into your face and exclaims "I did it teacher!" that reason will suffice a lifetime.
—*Grace, a teacher in a suburban school district*

WHAT MAKES AN EFFECTIVE TEACHER?

☐ ☐ Teaching is not easy. Teaching handicapped learners is even harder. Some teachers have a major influence on the lives of their students, while others make a negligible difference. Some teachers are able to present material in orderly, interesting ways to increase the probability of learning by mentally retarded students, while others seem to talk until they are "blue in the face" with no significant increase in the learning performance of their students. Thus, the question can (and should) be asked: What constitutes good teaching?

Unfortunately, the answer to this question is not straightforward. If it were, there would assuredly be more effective teachers in special education classrooms. Nevertheless, there do appear to be some clues as to what makes a good teacher (Ausubel, Montemayor & Svajian 1977). These attributes include selecting, sequencing, and organizing segments of instruction, skills of presentation, and the human/social skills of patience, fairness, and empathy while managing learning activities (Sass-Lehrer 1983; Sass-Lehrer & Wolk 1985; Serwatka, Venn & Shreve 1984; Sindelar, Smith, Harriman & Hale 1985). In short, the teacher's job is one of active decision making about choice and sequence of what is to be learned (curriculum), how it is to be presented (instruction), and how the learning environment is to be structured (management). Such a job description implies that good teaching is not restricted to competency in one area but encompasses knowledge and skill in several areas of responsibility (Sass-Lehrer & Wolk 1985).

THE SPECIAL EDUCATION TEACHER AS ACTIVE DECISION MAKER

☐ ☐ Michael Graham was perplexed. A teacher in a senior high classroom for mildly mentally retarded learners, Michael had a student, Floyd, who simply refused to learn. In fact, Floyd refused to even participate in any classroom activities, whether English, arithmetic, or social studies. He complained in class repeatedly that school was boring, that it was stupid, that it didn't teach him 'nothin', and that he was going to drop out just as soon as he turned sixteen. Michael was concerned about Floyd. He knew that by dropping out of school, Floyd was destined to a life of unemployment or underemployment, and a cycle of despair and unhappiness. If Floyd was to have any chance of making it in the world, he needed all of the education that he could get. What could Michael do to get Floyd to change his mind, stay in school, and apply himself?

As Joan Mayberry read over the reading activities in the teacher's manual of her basal reader, she frowned in discouragement. Over Joan's objections, the school reading committee had chosen a basal reading series for her eleven- and twelve-year-old mentally retarded learners. The material, although supposedly at her students' third-grade reading level, was not in any way related to the interests of Joan's students. To Joan, the stories seemed immature. She was also concerned that the authors assumed the readers would possess certain reading skills and expertise that Joan suspected her mentally retarded students lacked. Joan wanted her students to have a positive reading experience in her class; they had suffered from enough failure in their academic lives. What should Joan do?

Susan Lacy was confused. None of what she had learned in college about behavior modification seemed to be working with her junior-high level, mentally retarded learners. Susan was especially concerned about Robby, a disruptive student in her class. In her behavior modification course, Susan had learned about extinguishing inappropriate behavior by ignoring (not reinforcing) such behaviors while concurrently reinforcing appropriate behavior. Susan decided to try this approach with Robby. She ignored his disruptive behavior and effusively praised his in-seat, on-task performance. To her consternation, however, Robby began to act even more disruptively. He also acted in a rejecting way to Susan's praise. What was going on? What should Susan do?

Decisions. Decisions. Each of these teachers is faced with difficult choices—decisions that nevertheless must be made. Michael Graham must come up with a way to make the curriculum relevant and important to a student. He must convince the student that what he is learning in school will have direct applicability in his life. Michael must make a decision regarding curriculum choice.

Joan has a dual problem. First, she is convinced that the reading material authorized for her students is inappropriate in terms of interest level and will have no motivational value. Second, Joan believes that the authors assume her students possess prerequisite skills which they may not have and that the materials will therefore inhibit their learning. Joan has problems of curriculum and instruction.

Then there is Susan. She wants to apply principles of behavior modification learned in college and does not understand why these principles are not working. What Susan does not realize is that her strong praise of Robby's school-appropriate behavior runs directly counter to his peer group's norms about the value of school. Robby is being accused by his friends of being the teacher's pet and runs the risk of being ostracized by peers. To get Susan to stop praising him and save his status with his friends, Robby feels he *has* to act disruptive in class, the more disruptive the better. Susan has a problem of classroom management.

Teachers are faced with hundreds of daily educational problems ranging from why Johnny can't read to how to deal with disruptive and possibly dangerous behavior. In general, educational decisions will be made in four main areas: what to teach (curriculum), how to teach it (instructional methods), how to structure and maintain the learning environment (management), and how to evaluate the extent to which learning takes place (evaluation) (Garguilo & Pigge 1979; Sass-Lehrer & Wolk 1984, 1985). Figure 1.1 shows the relationship among these areas in terms of their order of occurrence in the educational process.

One way or the other these educational decisions must be made. Such

FIGURE 1.1   Sequence of Events in Educational Programming for Mentally Retarded Students

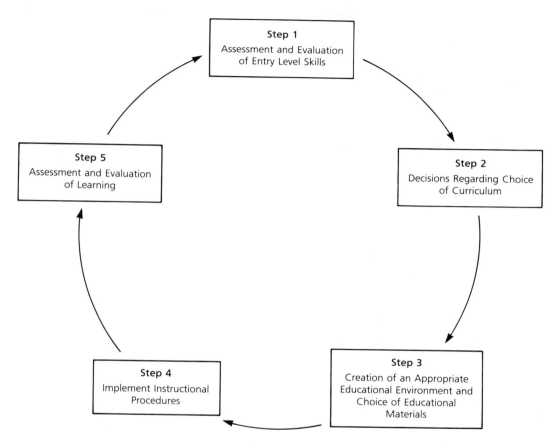

decisions can be made on the basis of sound educational and psychological theory and research, or they can be made on the basis of belief, supposition, and invalid reasoning. For example, Michael could decide that Floyd must either conform to the curriculum or drop out of school. Joan could hope her mentally retarded students pick up the prerequisite reading skills on their own during their daily reading sessions. Finally, Susan could decide that behavior modification simply does not work and return to a traditional, and punitive, way of controlling student behavior. Although these decisions could be made, they would be inappropriate according to sound educational and psychological theory. The implications of such choices would probably prove disastrous for teacher and student alike, but would not be apparent to the naive teacher at the time of decision making. Only later, after students began to suffer the consequences of the teacher's choices, would the inappropriateness of the decisions become apparent.

THE PURPOSE OF THIS TEXT

□ □ The purpose of this text is to help prospective teachers in the educational decision-making process. Many decisions need to be made in the areas of curriculum, instructional methods, and creation of useful and appropriate learning environments for mildly mentally retarded learners. This text will thus attempt to reach four objectives. First, it will discuss mildly mentally retarded students as processors and learners of information; that is, as individuals who must take in, process, interpret, and recall information in order to learn effectively. Second, this text will discuss the academic subject-matter areas typically taught to mildly mentally retarded learners. These subjects will be discussed both in terms of their processes and skill areas and in terms of effective assessment of achievement in these areas. Third, the chapters dealing with the academic subject areas will offer teaching ideas and suggestions in terms of choice of curricular material to-be-covered and activities for effectively teaching that material. Finally, this text will offer suggestions for modifying a student's physical and psychological learning environment in order to increase the probability of meaningful learning. In addition, each chapter dealing with teaching an academic subject area will discuss diagnosis and assessment of that area. Such assessment is vital to understanding the child's current operating levels as well as measuring the effectiveness of teaching. However, it must be pointed out that educational assessment and diagnosis is a complex subject in its own right and deserves an in-depth treatment beyond the scope of this text. For this reason, the interested reader is directed to additional textbooks and coursework designated for in-depth coverage of educational assessment for mildly handicapped learners.

THE MENTALLY RETARDED CHILD AS LEARNER

□ □ The concept of the mildly mentally retarded child as an active learner and processor of information is of great importance in understanding how and under which circumstances such children learn best. To create an educationally sound curriculum and set of instructional methods and procedures, a teacher must possess a precise understanding of how children learn and remember. The mentally retarded learner will be presented as a processor of information, a person who takes in, selects, organizes, and eventually learns and remembers information (Bray 1985; Glidden 1979; Meador & Ellis 1985). A breakdown may occur at any point in this process (Cherkes-Julkowski, Gertner & Norlander 1985; Ellis & Meador 1985; Spitz 1979; Zeaman & House 1979) and it is the teacher's responsibility to identify just where such difficulties are taking place as well as to prescribe remedial activities designed to compensate for them. Thus, this text contains a section on the learning and processing attributes of memory including a strong emphasis on strategy learning, transfer, and generalization by mentally retarded learners. Understanding these processes will prove important for successful teaching to mentally retarded students who are typically deficient in these areas (Brown 1978; Borkowski & Cavanaugh 1979; Cherkes-Julkowski et al. 1985).

☐ Curriculum

Curriculum deals with what you are planning to teach. Mentally retarded children will need to learn materials in a variety of core academic areas which include reading, arithmetic, written expression, and spelling. Additionally, such learners will also need to gain exposure in the areas of art, music and creativity, career education, social studies, health, and science. Each of these curricular areas contains its own knowledge and concepts—material which will need to be learned and mastered if mildly mentally retarded students are to be successful in adult life. A major portion of this text deals with the major curricular academic areas and the material contained within those areas which are appropriate for learning by mildly mentally retarded students.

☐ Instruction

Another purpose of this text is to discuss proposed sequences of learning in each of the academic core areas. It is not enough to know what to teach within a given core area; the teacher must know how to teach the material. If the teacher does not develop a sequenced model of skills within each skill area and does not teach those skills in a sequenced, logical fashion, learning by mildly mentally retarded students will be virtually impossible. Thus, it will be important for the teacher to know not only what to teach but how to teach it.

TWO VIEWPOINTS OF MENTALLY RETARDED LEARNERS

☐ ☐ In recent years, a debate has been taking place in special education as to whether mental retardation is a *quantitative* or *qualitative* phenomenon (Telford & Sawrey 1981; Hallahan & Kauffman 1982). The quantitative viewpoint holds that mentally retarded children develop in the same general way as their nonretarded peers, they just progress through those stages at a slower rate (Zigler 1973). Hence proponents of the quantitative viewpoint have advocated referring to mentally retarded learners as "developmentally delayed." They argue that the same methods and materials used with nonretarded children are applicable with mentally retarded learners. The key, as proposed by quantitative proponents, is to teach at a slower rate.

The qualitative viewpoint on the other hand holds that mentally retarded and nonretarded students are different in ways others than just degree. These advocates argue that the two groups are radically and functionally different and that what works for one group will not work with the other.

There appears to be a danger in full adoption of either viewpoint. For example, if one takes the qualitative point of view, one is admitting, at least tacitly, that mentally retarded learners are so different, so unlike their nonretarded peers that they do not develop and learn in the same ways as everyone else. Rather, they are "a breed apart" because they are functionally different. This viewpoint, in the author's view, is dangerous and potentially injurious to mentally retarded children and their hopes of becoming accepted members of society. The validity of this viewpoint is also probably largely untrue.

However, there is also danger in adopting a purely quantitative viewpoint. Such a viewpoint holds that since mentally retarded children are merely developmentally delayed, all one has to do is teach slower and mentally retarded learners will eventually learn. Such a method of teaching slower and repeating things to students in the same fashion simply does not work. Mentally retarded children will require a specialized learning environment which contains specialized materials and instructional sequences. This is what special education is all about.

Rather than taking a strictly qualitative or quantitative viewpoint, teachers should probably take a more *eclectic* approach. That is, while it is true that mentally retarded children are more like their nonretarded peers than they are unlike them, it is also true that mentally retarded children do demonstrate significant deficits in the ways that they process, organize, learn, and remember information (Borkowski & Wanschura 1974; Bray, Goodman & Justice 1982; Campione & Brown 1977; Ellis 1979; Justice in press; Zeaman & House 1979). If such deficits and differences in the curriculum planning for mentally retarded students are not taken into account, educational intervention for these students will be an abysmal failure. Simply teaching more slowly and/or repeating material will not work. Special education is more than just slowing down instruction. Successful teaching requires knowledge of the ways that mentally retarded individuals learn, knowledge about available educational technology and materials, and teacher expertise in designing curriculum and instruction. The purpose of this text is to help the reader learn and develop these skills.

WHO ARE THE MENTALLY RETARDED LEARNERS?

□ □ Who are the mentally retarded students you are likely to meet in your classroom and what characteristics do they possess? The purpose of this discussion is not to offer a composite of the typical mentally retarded learner. Such a composite does not exist, and to offer one would underplay the diversity of the students whom you are likely to encounter in your classes. However, while each child in your class will be a unique individual, a significant proportion of students designated as mildly mentally retarded do display common characteristics. Over the years some patterns have emerged which seem to be representative of many mildly mentally retarded pupils. This section attempts to identify some of those patterns.

The accepted (and traditional) method of describing the characteristics of mentally retarded students is to use the definition devised by the American Association on Mental Deficiency (Heber 1959), and subsequently revised in 1961, 1973, 1977, and 1983. The 1983 definition states: "Mental retardation refers to significantly subaverage general intellectual functioning resulting in or associated with concurrent impairments in adaptive behavior and manifested during the developmental period" (Grossman 1983, 11). This definition includes a number of terms which need to be clearly understood in order to fully grasp the requisite behaviors which must be demonstrated before a child can be considered to be mentally retarded. These terms include

General Intellectual Functioning: Defined as results obtained through assessment with one or more individually administered, standardized intelligence tests.

Significantly Subaverage: Defined as a measured IQ of 70 or below based on a standardized test of intelligence. This upper limit is intended as a guideline and could be extended to 75 or higher especially in settings where behavior is believed to be impaired due to deficits in reasoning and judgment. As the IQ upper limit is increased, more individuals would be considered to be mentally retarded.

Impairments in Adaptive Behavior: Defined as significant limitations in an individual's effectiveness in meeting the standards of maturation, learning, personal independence, and/or social responsibilities that are expected for the individual's age level and cultural group.

Developmental Period: Defined as the period between conception and the eighteenth birthday. Developmental deficits are typified by slow, arrested, or incomplete development (Grossman 1983).

This definition of mental retardation differs from earlier definitions in that a child considered mentally retarded must demonstrate both deficits in intellectual functioning and adaptive behavior. In other words, simply possessing a deficit in one area would not be sufficient for an individual to be identified as mentally retarded. Likewise, a key word in the new definition is the word *associated*. This means that mental retardation must be associated with or result in adaptive behavior deficits. Figure 1.2 shows the possible combinations of intellectual functioning and adaptive behavior deficits. Notice in only one of the four conditions can a classification of mental retardation correctly occur.

FIGURE 1.2 Decision Matrix on Defining Students as Mentally Retarded or Not Mentally Retarded Based on Intellectual Functioning and Adaptive Behavior

Intellectual Functioning

	High	Low
Adaptive Behavior — Low	**Not** Mentally Retarded	Mentally Retarded
Adaptive Behavior — High	**Not** Mentally Retarded	**Not** Mentally Retarded

MEASURING MENTAL RETARDATION

☐ ☐ As the AAMD definition states, there are two areas which need to be measured in order to determine whether individuals are mentally retarded. These two areas are intelligence and adaptive behavior. As we have seen, individuals must possess deficits in both areas in order to be determined to possess mental retardation. Thus, accurate intellectual and adaptive behavior assessment is extremely important in identifying mentally retarded learners.

☐ Intelligence Tests

The AAMD definition states that the child must be tested with an individual, standardized intelligence test. Two commonly used tests to assess intelligence are the Wechsler Intelligence Tests and the Stanford-Binet Intelligence Test. There are three tests in the Wechsler series: the Wechsler Intelligence Test for Children—Revised (WISC—R), the Wechsler Preschool and Primary Scale of Intelligence (WPPSI), and the Wechsler Adult Intelligence Scale (WAIS). The Wechsler tests are intended to measure both verbal and performance aspects of intelligence as well as yielding a full-scale IQ. The Stanford-Binet measures the full-scale IQ.

IQ, or intelligence quotient, is determined by dividing *mental age* by chronological age and multiplying the quotient by 100. Mental age represents the age level at which the person is functioning on mental tasks and is measured by the norms of the intelligence test being used. Thus, a 10-year-old child who is functioning at a mental level of 8 years will have a measured IQ of 8/10 × 100 = 80.

Even though IQ tests are highly reliable, valid, and useful, there are still problems with them. For example, it has been demonstrated that a child's IQ can change dramatically, especially during the formative years of schooling (McCall, Appelbaum & Hogarty 1973; Robinson & Robinson 1976). In fact, it has been found that the younger the child being given the IQ test, the more changeable that child's IQ will be over time. Finally, it has been well demonstrated that IQ tests are culturally biased to some extent (Mercer 1973b; Mercer & Lewis 1978; Perrone 1977). Thus, children from minority groups are at a significant disadvantage when taking such tests.

☐ The System of Multicultural Pluralistic Assessment (SOMPA)

Sociologist/psychologist Jane Mercer (1973b) has asserted for some time that intelligence tests are culturally unfair to minority children. Her beliefs led her to develop the System of Multicultural Pluralistic Assessment (SOMPA) to eliminate as much as possible cultural bias from intelligence testing (Mercer & Lewis 1978). The basis of Mercer's belief is that there are two distinct cultural groups in the United States, the white majority and minority groups. She argues that these groups are comparable in innate intellectual ability but because of experiential advantages, the majority children score better on IQ tests than minority children. For this reason, Mercer devised a formula for converting the child's WISC—R IQ score to an estimated learning potential (ELP) score based on factors which include the child's ethnic group, family size, income, and parental background. While the SOMPA has drawn heavy criticism based on its scientific credibility (Brown 1979; Goodman 1979; Oakland 1979), it does represent a first step in attempting to correct cultural unfairness in IQ tests.

☐ Assessing Adaptive Behavior

The measurement of adaptive behavior is not as well defined, reliable, or advanced as that of intelligence testing. This should not be surprising when one considers that while intelligence testing and research has been going on for the better part of a century, measurement of adaptive behavior only began in the 1950s.

There are a variety of different scales to measure adaptive behavior. One of the newest instruments is the Adaptive Behavior Inventory for Children (Mercer & Lewis 1977). The ABIC is part of the SOMPA and is used to gain information about the individual in the areas of family, community, peer relations, nonacademic school roles, earner/consumer, and self-maintenance. Many professionals believe that the ABIC is the best adaptive behavior assessment instrument available for school-age learners. Among other adaptive behavior scales commonly

FIGURE 1.3 Major Areas Assessed by the AAMD Adaptive Behavior Scale—Public School Version

Part I	*Measures*
Physical Development	Physical Development
Cognitive Development	Language
	Number and Time Concepts
Functional Skills	Independent Living
	Economic Skills
	Vocational Skills
Volitional Domains	Self-Direction
	Responsibility
Socialization	Socialization

Part II	*Measures*
Social Maladaptation	Violent and Destructive Behaviors
	Antisocial Behavior
	Rebellious Behavior
	Untrustworthy Behavior
Personal Maladaptation	Odd Mannerisms
	Eccentric Habits
	Odd Speech Patterns
	Self-Abusive Behavior
	Hyperactive Behavior

used are the AAMD Adaptive Behavior Scale (Nihira, et al. 1974), the AAMD Adaptive Behavior Scale—Public School Version (Lambert, Windmiller, Cole & Figueroa 1975), the Balthazar Scales of Adaptive Behavior (Balthazer 1971), the Cain-Levine Social Competency Scale (Cain, Levine & Elzey 1963), and the Vineland Social Maturity Scale (Doll 1953). Of this group, perhaps the scale most useful for assessing the adaptive behavior of school-age, mildly mentally retarded children is the AAMD Adaptive Behavior Scale. Figure 1.3 contains the major areas this scale measures.

LEVELS OF MENTAL RETARDATION

□ □ Mental retardation exists at different levels of severity; that is, while some individuals possess mental retardation at mild levels (i.e., possess mild intellectual and adaptive behavior deficits), others possess mental retardation at more severe and debilitating levels. The AAMD has identified four levels of mental retardation ranging from mild to profound (Grossman 1983). Table 1.1 contains the levels of mental retardation identified by the AAMD with the IQ ranges for each level.

TABLE 1.1 Levels of Retardation as a Measure of IQ Range as Obtained from the AAMD Classification Scale (Grossman 1983)

Retardation Level	Suggested IQ Range
Mild	50-55 to ca. 70
Moderate	35-40 to 50-55
Severe	20-25 to 35-40
Profound	Below 20 or 25

EDUCATIONAL SERVICES FOR MENTALLY RETARDED LEARNERS

☐ Mildly Mentally Retarded Learners

Different educational services and programs are typically offered to individuals at different levels of mental retardation. The typical programs for mildly mentally retarded individuals focus on academic skills such as reading, arithmetic, language, and vocational training in order to prepare the person for independent living. The educational experiences for such learners have been traditionally divided into preschool classes, elementary/primary classes, intermediate classes, and secondary school classes.

Preschool Classes

Preschool experiences for mildly mentally retarded learners are primarily concerned with readiness skills. Readiness skills represent the prerequisite skills the child will need for later learning. These include skills in language and communication, following directions and attending, discriminating auditory and visual information, self-help skills, and acquiring fine and gross motor coordination.

Evidence suggests that a strong preschool experience can improve the mildly retarded child's intellectual functioning and help insure a more successful academic future (Hayden & Dmitriev 1975; Hayden, Morris & Bailey 1977; Jordan 1976; LaCrosse 1976). Such research demonstrates not only the usefulness of establishing preschool programs for mentally retarded learners but also the cost effectiveness and efficiency in terms of the child's later academic success.

Primary Classes

Children in primary classes for mildly mentally retarded children typically have chronological ages from six to ten years and mental ages from four to six years. To a great extent, the curriculum of primary classes extends the preschool curriculum of readiness skills with additional instruction in the main academic areas of reading, writing, and arithmetic when the children are ready.

There has also been a growing trend toward inclusion in the primary curriculum of social training and *social intelligence* (Goldstein 1975; Greenspan 1979). Such training includes such topics as getting along with peers, appropriately "reading" social situations, and acquiring the general social expertise needed to succeed in social settings. Social expertise is crucial for later successful life-functioning in society (Greenspan 1979).

Intermediate Classes

Children in intermediate classes for the mildly mentally retarded typically are about nine to thirteen years old with corresponding mental ages from six to nine years. Academics are strongly stressed in intermediate classroom with readiness skills becoming less of a curricular focus. The children usually receive instruction in all the main academic areas plus art, music, physical education, and health. Many intermediate programs stress prevocational instruction to prepare students for the world of work.

Secondary School Classes and Work-Study

Secondary school training usually refers to training given the mentally retarded individual who is of late-junior-high-school or high-school years. In secondary school, the mildly mentally retarded learner receives instruction mostly in academic areas that relate to vocational training and eventual employment. Academics are also tied to life skills such as reading a newspaper, following written directions, and completing functional math.

Work-study training is often a part of the high school experience for mildly mentally retarded learners. The premise of work-study is a close association between what the student is learning in school and vocational training for a specific job. Students typically are placed on jobs in the community in the afternoons after attending class in the morning. A professional from the school usually operates as liaison between school and employer, preparing a smooth transition from school to job after the student graduates.

☐ Moderately Retarded Learners

The education of moderately mentally retarded persons generally focuses on the development of self-help and survival skills as well as adequate communication and social skills to allow for semi-independent living. Typically, the education of moderately mentally retarded learners is generally broken down into six main areas (Patton, Payne & Beirne-Smith 1986). These areas include

1. **Self-help skills:** Helping the learner to take care of everyday needs. Self-help areas include toileting, dressing, and grooming.

2. **Communication skills:** Include speech, language, listening, and non-speech communication.
3. **Personal-social skills:** Instruction with getting along with other children. Include learning and accepting social responsibility.
4. **Perceptual-motor skills:** Include visual, auditory, and tactile perception and training.
5. **Functional academic skills:** Here the term functional is stressed. Only those academics which will directly contribute to independent living (e.g., reading signs, functional counting, etc.) are stressed.
6. **Vocational skills:** Training in work and vocational skills which will allow the individual typically to work semi-independently in environments such as workshops, or under direct supervision.

Severely/Profoundly Retarded Learners

A strong emphasis on the education of severely/profoundly mentally retarded persons, with a movement toward deinstitutionalization, has occurred during the last two decades (Blatt, Ozdins & McNally 1979; Snell 1981; Wolfensberger 1972, 1976). However, with the impact of deinstitutionalization has come the responsibility of education and care of severely/profoundly retarded persons (Switzky, Haywood & Rotatori 1982). Today, the emphasis of educational services for this population is daily living skills in the areas of physical development, self-care, language training (including training in non-speech systems), and social behavior. Included in such a curriculum is the elimination of undesirable behaviors such as rocking, self-abusive behavior, or hand-banging through behavior modification procedures (Balthazar 1975; Foxx & Azrin 1973). The reader interested in the area of educational programming for severely/profoundly retarded individuals is referred to the writings of Martha Snell and her associates (Snell 1983; Snell & Gast 1981).

PREVALENCE OF LEVELS OF MENTAL RETARDATION

☐ ☐ Although the actual number of mentally retarded individuals is not precisely known, currently accepted estimates place the prevalence from 1 to 2 percent of the general population (Berdine 1985; Birch, Richardson, Baird, Horobin & Illsley 1970; Tarjan, Wright, Eyman & Keeran 1973). While some investigators have estimated the incidence of mental retardation at 3 percent, this estimate is based on a one-dimensional definition of retardation (i.e., intelligence) rather than the multidimensional definition advocated by the AAMD (Mercer 1973). With a 1 to 2 percent prevalence rate and a United States population of approximately 220 million people, we would expect between 2.2 and 4.4 million people in the United States to be classified as mentally retarded.

Traditionally, the ratio of mildly mentally retarded to moderately and severely/profoundly retarded individuals has been approximately 75:20:5 (Berdine 1985). This means that for each one hundred persons identified as mentally retarded, we would expect seventy-five to be mildly mentally retarded, twenty to be in the moderate range, and five to be severely/profoundly mentally retarded. Translated into population numbers, if we estimate a population of approximately three million mentally retarded persons in the United States, we would expect 2.25 million of them to be in the mild mental retardation range. For this reason, the majority of the educational services provided to mentally retarded learners are geared to the mildly retarded.

EDUCATIONAL OPTIONS FOR MENTALLY RETARDED LEARNERS

☐ ☐ A variety of educational options are available for mentally retarded learners. For example, Figure 1.4 contains a "cascade" or continuum of services (Deno 1973) which range along the continuum from least restrictive to most restrictive. You will notice in the series the restrictiveness of the educational placement increases as the severity of the child's retardation increases.

FIGURE 1.4   Continuum of Special Education Placements

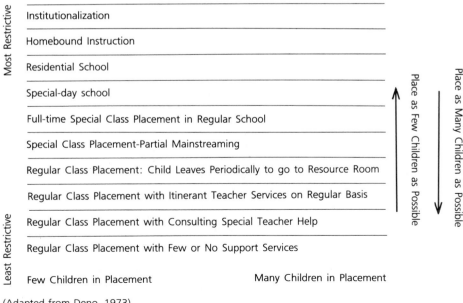

(Adapted from Deno, 1973)

When an appropriate educational placement for a child is decided upon by the educational team, a number of considerations should be kept in mind. First, it is essential to remember that the educational placement should be based on the child's needs, not what is best or most convenient for the school system. Second, the child should be placed in the least restrictive educational environment. This means that not every child should be mainstreamed. Mainstreaming may be the most appropriate placement for some mentally retarded children; for others the self-contained classroom may be the least restrictive placement. Finally, placement should not be "written in stone." It should be flexible enough that a child can be moved into a different setting as soon as he or she is capable of functioning appropriately in that setting.

Following is a short description of the educational service options available to mentally retarded learners ranging from mild to severe/profound retardation. Typically, mildly mentally retarded students will not be placed into the more restrictive environments but will be placed either in the regular classroom or the special class.

☐ The Regular Classroom

The educational trend for mildly mentally retarded learners is toward placement in a regular classroom with nonretarded peers. However, it is not enough to place these children in regular classrooms and then forget about them. Placed in that situation, students are destined to fail. Rather, special teachers and staff, such as a resource room or itinerant teacher, need to work with the retarded child and give extra help in the curricular areas in which the child is experiencing difficulty.

☐ The Special Class

For some mildly mentally retarded students placement in the special class is most facilitative. Such a placement is usually in a self-contained class in a regular school. Special class placement is usually of two types: part-time or full-time placement. Part-time placement is one in which the student spends part (or most) of the school day in the special class but is mainstreamed as appropriate into the regular class setting. Full-time placement precludes mainstreaming. Where mainstreaming occurs, it is probably best for the student to remain in the special class for the core academic areas and be mainstreamed into non-technical subject areas such as physical education, driver education, art, music, or industrial education. For most mildly mentally retarded learners, mainstreaming is usually preferable over full-time special class placement. Full-time placement is probably only warranted when the child possesses extremely poor adaptive behavior and social skills in addition to problems in the academic areas.

☐ **The Special School**

Often, moderately mentally retarded students will attend special day schools. These are self-contained classes in self-contained schools for the moderately retarded. Such placements are only appropriate for those children who cannot function in less restrictive settings. Even in such schools, the trend has been toward busing students to regular schools for some supervised social contact with nonretarded individuals.

☐ **Characteristics of Mildly Mentally Retarded Learners**

There are certain characteristics of mentally retarded learners which you may find in your students as you begin to teach. These characteristics are based less on formal definitions and more on the environments in which many mildly mentally retarded often live and learn. For example, most mildly mentally retarded students will be of the *cultural-familial type* (Hallahan & Kauffman 1982). This means that for at least 80 percent of all mildly mentally retarded students, the primary cause of their mental retardation will not be due to injury or trauma but rather to a series of cultural and environmental circumstances which has affected their lives and the lives of their families. A significant proportion of mildly mentally retarded students may be found in inner-city or rural environments with proportionately less students being found in suburban, middle class placements. The students you may find yourself working with are likely to be relatively poor.

In fact, Mercer (1973, 1979) found that one of the greatest predictors of placement into classes for the mentally retarded was socio-economic class and cultural difference. As such, many mentally retarded children in your class can be expected to come from culturally different and, in many cases, financially impoverished environments. A large proportion of these students can be expected to come from single parent homes, usually with the mother or some other female functioning as the primary caretaker. Many of these families will be struggling just to psychologically and economically survive and will not possess the time or resources to devote to their children's education. Finally, you will probably be dealing with children and families in which cognitive, speech, and social interaction patterns will be different from the majority culture. In summary, the mildly mentally retarded children you encounter in your class may think, talk, and behave differently from what you might initially expect. These special learning and cultural characteristics will necessitate adoption of special teaching strategies and materials in order to facilitate learning.

LEARNING CHARACTERISTICS

☐ ☐ One of the most obvious defining characteristics of mentally retarded learners is their difficulty in learning. Compared to their nonretarded peers of the same chronological age, mildly mentally retarded students typically learn at a significantly slower rate. Thus, an understanding of the different learning and memory characteristics of mentally retarded learners is important for the prospective teacher.

It is important for the reader to realize, however, that this discussion refers only to mildly mentally retarded learners as a *group*. Each individual mentally retarded student learns and remembers material in ways similar or different in degree to the group composite. Thus, there is a great deal of variability in the way that a given mentally retarded child will learn and remember.

☐ Attention

Mentally retarded children typically experience problems of attention (Zeaman & House 1979). This attentional deficit usually occurs in two ways. First, it appears that mentally retarded individuals have a narrower breadth of attention. That is they do not attend to as many stimuli as their nonretarded peers (Krupski 1981; Zeaman & House 1963, 1979). Second, they do not appear to differentiate well the important things to which they should attend; that is, they are not very good at differentiating relevant from irrelevant task dimensions (Lovaas et al. 1971; Zeaman & House 1979). The attentional processes of mentally retarded learners and the educational implications of these findings are expanded upon in chapter 2, which deals with learning and memory processes.

☐ Learning Strategies

Strategies are procedures for processing pieces of information and transforming this information into usable knowledge. Available research indicates that mentally retarded learners are extremely poor in learning and spontaneously using learning strategies (Bray 1985; Butterfield & Belmont 1977; Butterfield & Ferretti 1985). Research supports the contention that mentally retarded persons possess both *mediational* and *production* deficiencies (Flavell & Wellman 1977). Mediation deficiencies occur when the child has not learned a proper strategy for acquiring information while production deficiencies occur when the child has learned the strategies but does not use them spontaneously. The issue of production and mediational strategy deficiencies and their implication for curriculum and instruction of mildly mentally retarded learners are discussed in chapter 2.

☐ Memory

Mentally retarded learners often perform poorly on memory tasks. This may be due less to a lack of the biological equipment required to remember and more to a lack of requisite memory strategies needed to remember effectively (Brown, Campione, Bray & Wilcox 1973; Butterfield & Belmont 1977; Butterfield & Ferretti 1985; Ferretti & Butterfield 1983). For example, mentally retarded individuals do not appear spontaneously to rehearse (Belmont & Butterfield 1971; Butterfield, Wambold & Belmont 1973), cluster items into categories (Jensen & Frederickson 1973), or recognize patterns of to-be-remembered material (Spitz 1973, 1979). Many of the deficits in memory of mentally retarded individuals seem to respond to training and educational intervention. The educational implications of memory strategy training are discussed in subsequent sections of this text.

☐ Generalization and Transfer

The ability to generalize and transfer recently learned material to a new situation or problem is crucial for life success. Nevertheless, this appears to be a problem area for many mentally retarded individuals (Borkowski, Levers & Gruenenfelder 1976; Butterfield & Belmont 1977; Campione, Brown & Ferrara 1982). Helping mentally retarded learners to see the similarity or differences between two problem situations and to generalize learned material to the new problem is a key skill which must become an integral part of the special educational curriculum.

☐ Language

Language problems are frequently encountered by mentally retarded children. This is unfortunate because adequate language development and usage is a key component in cognitive development (Inhelder & Piaget 1958). Mentally retarded children are typically deficient in the areas of sentence complexity and length, speech and sound discrimination, and number of nouns in vocabulary (Bowerman 1976). Adequate language development is of course crucial for life success. Chapter 6 deals with teaching language to mentally retarded learners.

THE LONG-TERM THEMATIC UNIT

☐ ☐ A key aspect of this text is to sanction the adoption of long-term thematic units in the teaching of school material to mildly mentally retarded learners. As outlined by Meyen (1971, 1981), units are long-term programs of instruction which are based on a single thematic topic which permeates every academic core area presented to students during the school day. For example, a typical unit topic for a primary mildly mentally retarded group might be "Dressing Appropriately for the Weather." In this unit, everything that is presented to the students in each academic subject ranging from language arts though arithmetic to even music and art is weather-related. Likewise, a unit designed for a secondary group of mildly mentally retarded students, "Using Transportation Safely in the Community" would be the topic of every lesson in every academic area presented to these high school students for at least a two-week period.

As we shall see in chapter 5, the long-term thematic unit addresses itself to many of the learning, memory, cognitive, and information-processing deficits of mentally retarded students. It encourages organization through its use of redundancy and heavy emphasis on sequential presentation in all core areas by the teacher. It encourages learning and memory through its use of active rehearsal by its constant repetition of the thematic topic. And finally, since the thematic topic must pass a test of relevancy to the student's lives, it is salient, interesting, and topical.

This text proposes that use of the thematic long-term unit as a teaching tool can greatly facilitate the learning of relevant academic material by mentally retarded learners. Additionally, it argues that learning will be unified when a single unified topic is presented and applied in each core academic area. Thus, each academic core area presented in this text is discussed, at least in part, as a member of a "team", the "captain" of which is the theme picked for the unit.

ORGANIZATION OF THIS BOOK

☐ ☐ This text is divided into four main sections: the learner, the educational process, curriculum and instruction, and classroom environment and management. In addition, a variety of sample instructional units are included at a variety of instructional levels and topics.

Section I deals with attributes of mentally retarded learners. One cannot design and implement meaningful instruction for mildly mentally retarded learners if one does not understand their intellectual, behavioral, and cognitive attributes. To that end, Section I includes a discussion of the cognitive, learning, and memory functioning of mentally retarded students, including where they are deceptively strong and where they typically possess deficits. Such information will prove useful when the teacher takes into account the creation of material and the sequencing and presentation of that material.

Section II deals with the educational process. This includes the things that teachers do before beginning to teach material to mentally retarded learners to help insure both the probability of learning and the relevance of academic content. To that end, chapter 3 examines diagnostic/prescriptive programming and assessment in educational programming for the mildly mentally retarded learner. Chapter 4 covers writing and using instructional objectives at different taxonomic levels, while chapter 5 deals with writing long-term instructional units for mentally retarded learners. Creation of sound instructional objectives at various taxonomic levels is crucial to sound programming for mentally retarded learners while creating good long term, instructional units will be a major focus of this text.

Section III covers curriculum and instruction in the various core areas.

Chapters 6–12 explore the areas of language, reading, spelling and written expression, arithmetic, career education, science and social studies, and art and creativity. In each chapter there is a theoretical overview of the area, followed by a section on assessment. Also included are sections on curricular planning in each area as well as instructional tips and techniques. Finally, each chapter contains a section on available materials in that core area for teachers as well as a brief discussion of the use of microcomputers when applicable.

The final section deals with creating a sound physical and psychological environment as well as managing behavior in the classroom. Chapter 13 handles creating the physical classroom environment designed to facilitate learning. Chapter 14 covers creating a sound psychological environment as well as techniques for managing and modifying student behaviors.

In summary, this text will provide the prospective teacher with information designed both to facilitate good teaching and to increase the probability of meaningful learning by mentally retarded students. A goal of this text is to provide teachers with knowledge and skills that will allow them to become enthusiastic as well as effective. Mentally retarded students *can* learn and *can* become interested in school and learning. Unfortunately, schools have been failing them for too long and then blaming them for not learning. It is the author's sincere hope that this text can help break the cycle of bad teaching and bad learning.

2

Learning and Memory Processes

Key Concepts

- ☐ Information Processing
- ☐ Perception of Input Information
- ☐ Iconic and Echoic Memory
- ☐ Central Processor—Selective Attention
- ☐ Short-Term and Long-Term Memory
- ☐ Rehearsal, Input Organization, and Clustering
- ☐ Learning—Incidental and Intentional
- ☐ Concept Formation and Critical Attributes
- ☐ Long-Term Memory and Recall Processes
- ☐ Metacognition—Learning and Memory Strategies
- ☐ Mediational versus Production Deficits

Most teachers of mildly mentally retarded children probably would say that the education of such children can be an exasperating affair. Teachers tend to complain that these students often seem to forget material or misapply learned information in real-life problem-solving situations.

Why do mentally retarded persons sometimes act in these ways? After all, to nonretarded adults, it seems so *obvious* what must be done to solve a problem or apply some bit of acquired information. Why can't mentally retarded persons think and solve problems efficiently?

In the not too distant past, the answers to these questions were often phrased in terms of problems of native intelligence. It was explained that mentally retarded individuals did not possess the same cognitive abilities as nonretarded persons and it was this lack of native ability which caused retardation. This deficiency in cognitive ability was advanced as the explanation for inefficient learning, adaptive, and problem solving behaviors by mentally retarded persons.

The past two decades have seen a shift from an emphasis on native intelligence as an explanation of mental retardation to one on *structural features* and *control processes* (Atkinson & Shiffrin 1969; Belmont & Butterfield 1977; Butterfield & Ferretti 1985). Structural features are the native abilities, the cognitive "hardware" which people bring into learning and memory situations. Control processes, on the other hand, represent the ways in which structural features are used. To use a computer analogy, structural features represent the computer which we purchase, while control processes represent the software which makes that equipment useful.

This shift in explaining learning and memory deficiencies of mentally retarded persons from one of native intelligence to one of structural features and control processes is educationally important. No longer is it adequate to describe children by some inexact attribute such as intelligence or problem solving ability. Such summarizations of individuals do little to further our understanding of how children learn and remember. Instead, learners are described in terms of their precise behaviors in areas such as perception, information processing, and the strategies which they use to learn and apply information efficiently. By better understanding how mentally retarded and nonretarded children engage in these processes, the educational professional can do a better job in efficiently designing prescriptive measures for remedying deficiencies (Flavell & Wellman 1977).

This chapter deals with the cognitive learning and memory functioning of mentally retarded persons. It draws heavily from the learning and information processing theory of Broadbent (1970) and Atkinson and Shiffrin (1969) which describe how individuals take in, learn, modify, and remember information. Information processing theory views the learning process as beginning with perception and ending with behavior based upon what has been remembered and applied. Learning and memory is treated in a computer analogy of data input, information modification within the system, and final output in the form of behavior.

An even newer aspect of information processing theory which has generated interest among educators and psychologists is that of strategy acquisition. Strategies are procedures used for processing pieces of information and solving problems (Borkowski & Cavanaugh 1979; Butterfield & Ferretti 1985; Weed, Ryan & Day 1984). People use these strategies in order to organize information for meaningful learning and to recall and use this information when it is needed. Examples of strategies would include clustering information by groups or categories, separating relevant from irrelevant information, and actively rehearsing information in order to keep it in working memory.

This chapter also discusses *metacognition*. Metacognition refers to a person's knowledge of when and how to use cognitive strategies. It is concerned with the ways in which the person uses, or in the case of many mentally retarded individuals, does not use strategies in order to aid learning and memory. Research indicates that mildly mentally retarded persons typically do not acquire strategies easily (Belmont & Butterfield 1977; Butterfield & Ferretti 1985; Luftig 1983a; Paris, Newman & McVey 1982). Likewise, they also exhibit marked deficiencies in appropriately and spontaneously using the strategies which they do learn (Borkowski & Cavanaugh 1979; Borkowski & Krause 1985; Borkowski, Johnston & Reid in press; Pressley, Borkowski & O'Sullivan 1984). Thus a key concern of the special education teacher will be in aiding mildly mentally retarded students to learn and spontaneously transfer strategies to real-life situations.

AN INFORMATION PROCESSING MODEL OF LEARNING AND MEMORY

☐ ☐ In the past, learning and memory were considered to be distinct entities. Professionals interested in memory did not study learning and researchers interested in learning did not concern themselves too much with memory. This fractional manner of viewing human cognition was drastically changed by the work of Donald Broadbent and his associates (Broadbent 1958, 1970; Broadbent & Gregory 1963, 1965). Broadbent conceptualized a continuum of information flow from initial sensory input through learning, memory, and behavioral output calling the process *information processing*. Broadbent and his associates argued that to understand the cognitive abilities of the individual, one had to view the entire process. Trying to understand components of the information processing continuum in isolation was not appropriate. Figure 2.1 shows the information processing continuum Broadbent hypothesized. The continuum contains the following components:

1. **The Sensory Apparatus:** This contains the components of perception. Information from the environment enters the system at this stage.
2. **Sensory Memory:** The information taken in through the sensory apparatus is held very briefly in a buffer or "memory store" and is either passed on or lost. Separate buffers exist for the different perceptual modalities such as seeing, hearing, and touch.

FIGURE 2.1   Information Processing Model

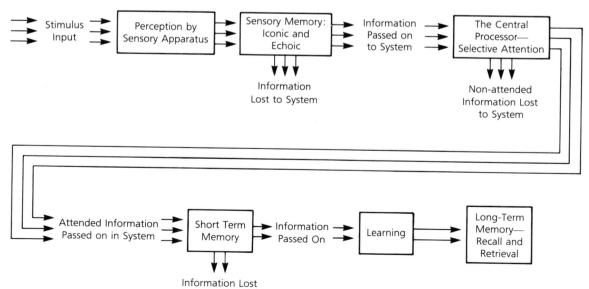

Reprinted with permission from D.E. Broadbent, *Perception and Communication*, copyright 1958, Pergamon Press.

3. **The Central Processor:** This is the "executive decision maker." It decides which information to attend to and which to ignore. Ignored information is dropped from the system.
4. **Short-Term Memory (STM):** Also known as "working memory." The STM keeps information in consciousness for a short period of time. It allows the person to consciously work and modify information.
5. **The Learning Phase:** Information is modified, given meaning, and attached to the person's existing knowledge.
6. **Long-Term Memory (LTM):** LTM is permanent memory. It allows for recall and retrieval of previously learned information.

Let us look at each of these components of the information-processing system in somewhat greater depth to see how they affect the learning and memory of mentally retarded learners.

PERCEPTION OF INPUT INFORMATION

□ □ According to the information processing model, information cannot be learned and remembered unless it is first perceived. Thus the first step in the information processing continuum which must be monitored to see that it is working properly is the sensory (perceptual) apparatus.

Although there are five channels for sensory input (seeing, hearing, touch, taste, and smell), most school-related information is taken in through the visual and auditory channels. Additionally, some information is taken in through the kinesthetic/tactile (touch) channel. For this reason, one of the first screening tests which should be carried out by the special educational professional is that of sensory assessment.

Sensory handicaps are perhaps more prevalent than some people believe. For example, it is estimated that 8 percent of the United States population or approximately 17.4 million Americans possess a hearing difficulty serious enough to affect speech and/or learning (Punch 1983). Similar studies conducted by the National Center for Health Statistics (1982) estimate a prevalence rate of 7.64 percent or 16.2 million Americans with hearing losses. Table 2.1 shows a breakdown of the prevalence rates by chronological age groups. It shows that a significant number of children possess a hearing loss serious enough to affect their education.

Visual impairment, although not as common as hearing impairment, is also significantly represented in the general population. It is estimated that approximately 0.1 percent of school-age children are either legally blind or partially sighted (Caton 1985; Jones & Collins 1966). If we consider the percentage of those individuals who possess a noncorrected visual deficit serious enough to affect their school success or life adjustment, the rate of prevalence becomes significantly higher.

TABLE 2.1   Prevalence of Hearing Loss by Chronological Age Group (1977)

Age	Number of Students	Percentage
Below 5	96,034	0.64
5-14	592,595	1.63
15-24	922,012	2.32
25-34	1,380,760	4.29
35-44	1,344,130	5.82
45-54	2,269,974	9.79
55-64	3,095,322	15.35
65-74	3,430,852	24.10
75-	3,087,095	
All	16,218,774	7.64

Source: National Center for Health Statistics, 1982. Reprinted from W. Berdine & A. Blackhurst (1985).

The prevalence of sensory impairments among mentally retarded individuals has been found to be much higher than in the general population (Bensberg & Sigelman 1976). For example, most studies conducted in schools for the deaf have found a 10–15 percent prevalence rate of mental retardation. As Lloyd (1973) has pointed out, the problems of sensory impairment (e.g., hearing difficulties) seriously compound the already difficult learning problems of mentally retarded students.

The implications of this discussion on the importance of sensory functioning on the entire information processing continuum should be evident for special education professionals. Screening and early identification of sensory problems are important for all students but they are particularly crucial for mentally retarded learners. Hearing and vision must be vigorously, systematically, and frequently assessed with the goal being early diagnosis and intervention. Children simply cannot learn what they do not perceive.

ICONIC AND ECHOIC MEMORY

□ □ During the early 1960s, George Sperling, a graduate student, conducted a series of interesting experiments (Sperling 1960). Sperling displayed an array of letters to subjects for only 50 milliseconds (50/1000 of a second). He then asked his subjects to report as many of the letters as they could remember. After looking at Sperling as if he was a madman, the subjects agreed to try. On the average, they could recall about four of the twelve letters.

Sperling then tried a modification of the experiment. This time he instructed subjects to pay attention to a designated row of letters as they flashed on the screen. He found that when he asked the subjects to report the letters in the row, recall was almost 100 percent. However, if they were asked to report letters in an adjacent row, recall was almost zero. From these results, Sperling hypothesized a visual short-term "buffer" or memory which is able to store information briefly. He believed information in this memory system was quickly lost if not passed on further in the information processing chain. This buffer system was termed *iconic memory* (Neisser 1967), and it was argued that people had only 250 milliseconds (¼ second) in which to do something with the information. After this time, the information was dropped and lost. From the discovery of the iconic memory, it was not long until a comparable memory system for the auditory system was advanced (Broadbent 1958; Neisser 1967) and termed *echoic memory*. Experiments indicate that the auditory memory can hold information for as long as two seconds.

It appears that mentally retarded and nonretarded individuals do not differ significantly in iconic and echoic memory functioning. Likewise, it appears that modifications or improved functioning in the systems cannot occur through training or practice. Thus, the perceptual buffers probably should not be a major concern of special educators.

THE CENTRAL PROCESSOR—THE EXECUTIVE DECISION MAKER

□ □ Next we come to a crucial point in the information processing system, the *central processor*. The central processor influences what is learned and it appears that strong differences exist in the efficiency of central processor functioning between mentally retarded and nonretarded individuals. Also known as the executive decision maker, the central processor functions like a bridge keeper in deciding which information will pass through for further processing and which information will be discarded and lost. In short, the central processor is the key decision maker for the system. What is learned and remembered by the person and what will be discarded and forgotten is determined here.

The central processor makes its decisions by using *selective attention*. Selective attention is the phenomenon that some stimuli are attended and responded to by the learner while other stimuli are selectively ignored (Zeaman & House 1963, 1979). Consider, for example, the dozens of stimuli impinging on you at this very moment, all competing for your attention. There is light impinging on your eyes, environmental noise in the background, distracting thoughts, the feeling of your clothing, the sound of your own heartbeat, room temperature, and dozens of other stimuli. There is no way that you can pay attention to all of these stimuli at once, so you make a decision. Since the other stimuli do not seem very important or life-threatening you ignore them while paying attention (hopefully) to the words and thoughts of this text.

Imagine, however, that the temperature in the room in which you are studying begins to rise dramatically. Your central processor would most likely drop the attention which you have been giving to this text and divert your attention to the heat in the room. You would probably find your attention toward the book waning as you attend to the discomfort caused by the heat.

The process of selective attention has been shown to be central to the learning of mentally retarded individuals (Friedman 1978; Lorsbach & Gray 1985; Tarver, Hallahan, Kauffman & Ball 1976; Zeaman & House 1979). Effective learning requires that the person process relevant information while simultaneously rejecting irrelevant information. In order to do this the individual must engage in the following behaviors (Zeaman & House 1963, 1979):

1. Maintain a level of arousal (sensitivity) in order to attend to stimuli.
2. Scan the entire field of available stimuli. Decide upon the relevant stimuli and attend to such stimuli.
3. Constantly make decisions upon what constitutes relevant stimuli. Attend to different sets of stimuli as relevancy dimensions change (e.g., the room grows warmer).
4. Maintain attention over extended periods of time.

It appears that while mildly mentally retarded individuals usually take in as much information through their sensory apparatus as their nonretarded peers, they are markedly deficient in selectively attending to relevant information (Fisher & Zeaman 1973; Luftig & Greeson 1983; Luftig & Johnson 1982; Zeaman & House 1979). Mentally retarded learners typically are drawn toward and attend to interesting but nevertheless unimportant information. This usually leads to either partial learning or learning of the wrong information.

☐ Implications of Selective Attention for Mentally Retarded Learners

The importance of selective attention and the nature of the central processor holds implications for professionals involved in the education of mildly mentally retarded students. Since these learners are susceptible to the competitive aspects of interesting but unimportant information, every effort must be made by the teacher to:

1. Highlight relevant information in presentations to mentally retarded learners. Make sure that you present relevant information in exciting, salient ways so as to grab the attention of mildly mentally retarded students.
2. Play down the interest level of irrelevant information. Try to make sure that you are not inadvertently making unimportant information highly interesting and attention getting.

In addition, Zeaman and House (1963, 1979) suggest the following techniques be followed in directing selective attention toward important information:

1. Reward attention to relevant information while selectively not rewarding attention to unimportant information. Use behavioral techniques to reinforce appropriate selective attention.
2. Try to make the relevant information contained within your lesson fresh, novel, and interesting. Frequently change your manner of presentation, materials, and activities to keep student attention high. Many mentally retarded students may begin to lose interest in an activity after ten or fifteen minutes so keep your presentation concise and brisk.
3. As you plan a lesson, decide on the most important or relevant points. Then present these points as forcefully as you can. Keep potentially distracting and irrelevant stimuli to an absolute minimum. Make sure that the most important information is presented in the early parts of lessons when interest and attention are highest.

Incidently, mentally retarded persons are not the only individuals who are easily drawn toward interesting but irrelevant information. Kintsch and Bates (1977) conducted a study with college undergraduates to see what was remembered from lectures—important information, less important details, or irrelevant jokes and announcements. They tested students weeks and months after the lectures. Jokes and announcements were remembered best. Selective attention, it seems then, is an important variable for all individuals, not just mentally retarded persons.

SHORT-TERM MEMORY

□ □ Once the central processor makes its decisions based on selective attention, one of two things happens when information enters. Either the information is nonselected and is dropped, or it is passed on along the information processing system. Information passed on is next sent to the *short-term memory* (STM) system.

STM is sometimes called primary or working memory. It allows us to keep information in consciousness so that we can work with it, use it, or change it in some way. To use a computer analogy, STM is the information file which we are currently using at any given time the computer is operating.

STM has limitations. First, it appears that STM has a definite size capacity and that capacity is reached at about seven to nine pieces (or chunks) of information (Miller 1956; Simon 1974). It seems that after seven to nine pieces or chunks have been taken into STM, information begins to fall out in the inverse order in which they entered (first chunks in, first chunks out). The second limitation of STM is the length of the time material can survive in STM. It appears the upper limit of survival time in STM is about 30 seconds. However, this upper limit can be extended significantly if certain things are done to keep the material in consciousness (Keppel & Underwood 1962; Reitman 1971). Figure 2.2 shows how quickly material fades from STM; memory drops from almost 100 percent to about 10 percent in only 18 seconds.

As stated above, the STM has a capacity for about seven to nine pieces or chunks of information. However, what constitutes a chunk, and what a chunk's size is, can be modified. Simon (1974), for example, conducted an interesting experiment regarding information chunking. Simon presented himself with the following words

Lincoln
Milky
Criminal
Differential
Address

FIGURE 2.2   Loss of Information in STM over Time

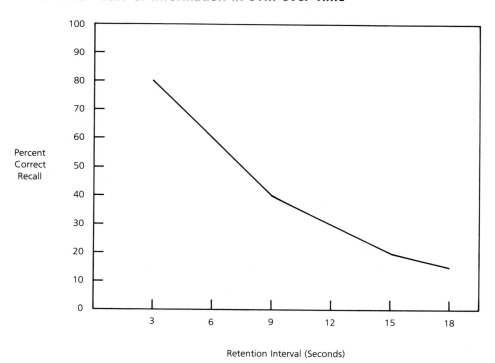

From L.R. Peterson & M.J. Peterson (1959). Short-term retention of individual verbal items. *Journal of Experimental Psychology, 58.* Copyright 1959 by the American Psychological Association. Reprinted by permission of the authors.

Way
Lawyer
Calculus
Gettysburg

After one presentation, Simon found he could not remember all of the words. STM capacity had been reached. However, after combining or rearranging the words so they read

Lincoln Gettysburg Address
Milky Way
Criminal Lawyer
Differential Calculus

Simon found he had no trouble remembering the words. They had been arranged in bigger chunks but the number of chunks had decreased to four, thus leaving room in STM for more chunks of information. It appears that a strategy which encourages clustering of information by category or association value (e.g., Milky Way) can increase the storage capacity of STM.

The question of the rapid decay (forgetting) of material in STM also poses a problem. How might the material be sustained so that it can be effectively learned and placed in long-term memory (LTM)? Research has indicated that material can be kept in STM for longer periods of time without decay by using the process of *rehearsal*. Rehearsal is the continual repetition of material by the learner in a way that keeps the material in the forefront of consciousness (Flavell & Wellman 1977; Hagen & Stanovich 1977). For example, if you wish to keep the phone number of someone you just met at a party in memory, you repeat the telephone number over and over (either verbally or subvocally) until you can write it down. As long as you continue to rehearse the phone number, you keep it in STM, thus postponing decay of the information for as long as you wish.

☐ Implications of STM Functioning for Mentally Retarded Students

Available evidence suggests that mildly mentally retarded pupils are typically quite deficient in organizing and clustering material in order to increase chunk size as well as in rehearsing material in order to keep it in STM (Belmont & Butterfield 1977; Baumeister & Brooks 1981; Butterfield, Wambold & Belmont 1973; Detterman 1979). These persons typically do not categorize or chunk information in STM but rather attempt to remember the information in the order it entered the system. An example is in Figure 2.3. As can be seen, while Student A attempted to reorganize information by categories, thus allowing more information to be processed in STM, Student B did not. The available space to process additional information by Student B is therefore severely restricted.

FIGURE 2.3   Categorical and Non-categorical Clustering by Two Students

	Input Stimuli	Output Responses
Student A	Bear, Football, Table, Cow, Shoe, Golf, Knife, Duck, Touchdown, Dish	Bear, Cow, Duck = animals = Chunk 1 Football, Golf, Touchdown = sports = Chunk 2 Table, Knife, Dish = eating utensils = Chunk 3 Shoe = 4

Chunks Remaining in STM = approximately 3
Approximate remaining Space in Each Chunk
Chunk 1 = 4
Chunk 2 = 4
Chunk 3 = 4
Chunk 4 = 6

Student B	Bear, Football, Table, Cow, Shoe, Golf, Knife, Duck, Touchdown, Dish	Bear, Football, Table, Cow, Shoe, Golf, Knife. Responses End. STM Storage Space Filled.

Mildly mentally retarded pupils also typically do not rehearse material (Belmont & Butterfield 1977; Detterman 1979; Flavell, Beach & Chinsky 1966). However, in situations where these students have been trained to cluster and rehearse, STM performance increases dramatically (Baumeister & Brooks 1981; Borkowski & Cavanaugh 1979; Butterfield & Ferretti 1985; Campione & Brown 1979). In such training situations, mentally retarded students are taught to name and/or find, group, or physically manipulate stimuli with the result being improved STM functioning and hence better learning (Borkowski & Cavanaugh 1979; Dugas 1975; Detterman 1979; Spitz & Webreck 1972). Since a great deal of information is typically lost by mentally retarded individuals in STM because of failures to organize and rehearse material, organizational and rehearsal strategies should become a part of the special education curriculum. The following classroom techniques may prove helpful in improving STM functioning by mentally retarded pupils:

1. Present new material categorically. That is, organize materials so that it is presented to students by categories which will aid STM. For example, if you were teaching a unit on "Getting Around Your Community," you might present all means of transportation first, followed by the major streets and avenues in town, followed by major bus routes, etc. It is crucial in the organization of material that the categories chosen be *meaningful* and *relevant* to the lives of the mentally retarded pupils. Otherwise they will be meaningless and will not be used by the students.
2. Practice and drill material in categorical learning. Have students group objects by categories and make such categorical drill and practice a part of the daily curriculum. Practice papers and exercises should reinforce student efforts to categorize and cluster. Figure 2.4 contains a sample

work paper which requires that students categorize and cluster information.

3. Encourage (and require) students to recall information categorically. That is, students' oral responses to teacher questions should be clustered and given by categories.

4. Students should be encouraged to rehearse material. Training should move from vocal rehearsal (where the teacher can listen to students), to subvocal rehearsal (silently moving the lips), to silent rehearsal. During the silent rehearsal stage, the teacher can check whether rehearsal is occurring by having the student switch to vocal rehearsal on demand (Barclay 1979; Kellas, Ashcraft & Johnson 1973).

5. Allow students to manipulate objects physically. What are the different ways in which objects can be moved in order to group them by category? Encourage creativity in grouping.

FIGURE 2.4   Sample Workpaper to Aid in Clustering

Circle all the *wild animals* in *red*.
Circle all the *furniture* in *blue*.
Circle all the *boys' names* in *green*.

Sofa	Lion	Steven
Tiger	Table	Oscar
Chair	Robert	Bed
Andy	Elephant	Chair

Which of these words go with *touchdown*? Why?

Eat
Quarterback
Elephant
Football
Sing
Team
Arithmetic

Which of these words *do not* belong? Why?
Eggs
Steak
Breakfast
Basketball
Food
Automobile

LEARNING PROCESSES

☐ ☐ As we have seen, STM is a temporary holding store, information is kept there briefly and then it is either lost or learned in order to be retained permanently. Learning and remembering constitute the final portions of the information-processing model. Learning and long-term memory functioning of mentally retarded pupils are the topics of the remainder of this chapter.

There are different types and levels of learning. Gagné (1977) has identified eight types of learning which differ in complexity and abstractness. Gagné argues that these types of learning occur in a fixed order and that the lower levels must be learned first before higher levels are mastered. The eight levels of learning are

1. **Signal Learning:** This corresponds to Pavlov's classical conditioning. A stimulus acts as a signal for an involuntary response, much like Pavlov's dog salivating at the sound of the bell.
2. **Stimulus-Response Learning:** This corresponds to operant conditioning. A stimulus leads to a deliberate response by the learner (e.g., the rat pressing the bar for a pellet of food).
3. **Chaining:** This involves the linking and learning of two or more stimulus response (S-R) associations, For example, a child wants a drink but does not know the word. He does know the association between pointing at the sink (Stimulus 1), and getting a drink (Response). When he receives the drink from Mother, she says "drink" (Stimulus 2). In the future, the child will be able to go from pointing at the sink and saying "drink" to simply saying "drink" and receiving a reward for the verbalization. This type of learning is particularly important in language acquisition.
4. **Verbal Associations:** Here the child learns words can be associated with other words in parallel meanings. For example, the knowledge that "Christmas" in English means the same as "Noel" in French would be learning at the verbal association level.
5. **Discrimination Learning:** This type of learning involves recognizing distinct events as separate and requiring different responses from the learner. For example, while hugging a friend is an appropriate response, hugging a perfect stranger is not. The learner must be able to discriminate the situation and respond accordingly. This type of learning is important for generalization and transfer of learning to appropriate real-life situations.
6. **Concept Learning:** Involves classifying stimuli in terms of their central or defining attributes and characteristics (e.g., shape, color, size). For example, two separate concepts are truck and man. They are judged to

be separate since they have different defining characteristics. This type of learning is relevant to reading and arithmetic readiness.

7. **Rule Learning:** A rule is formed by two concepts joined by a verb. Thus, "When two vowels go walking (Concept 1), the first one does the talking (Concept 2)" constitutes a rule.

8. **Problem Solving:** This is the ultimate goal of learning. Problem solving involves defining the problem, classifying what the solution should accomplish (the goal), recalling rules to solve the problem, and actually solving the problem. This represents the highest level of learning and is necessary for successful adult living.

☐ Implications of Gagné's Levels of Learning for Mentally Retarded Learners

While mentally retarded students have little trouble mastering learning types 1–4 in Gagné's scheme, they demonstrate considerable difficulty in mastering learning types 5–8 (Cherkes-Julkowski, Gertner & Norlander 1985; Evans & Bilsky 1979; Glidden 1979). For example, mentally retarded pupils often do not perceive diverse situations as being different (discrimination learning) and thus behave in similar ways in markedly different situations (preseveration) (Berndt 1981; Borkowski & Wanschura 1974; Borkowski & Cavanaugh 1979; Bray 1979). Likewise, mentally retarded students possess deficiencies in the areas of concept formation and rule learning with the result being a marked inability in adaptive problem solving (Borkowski & Wanschura 1974; Brown 1977; Campione & Brown 1979). Because of these demonstrated deficiencies, it is suggested that special education teachers include discrimination learning, concept formation, and problem solving in the special education curriculum. More specifically, teachers of mildly mentally retarded pupils should initiate the following instructional strategies:

1. Focus on the central dimensions of concepts. Concepts contain attributes or characteristics. Some of these attributes are critical as they define the concept. Others are not crucial. For example, consider the concept of *dog*. The crucial attributes of *doginess* include canine, meat-eater, four legs, man's best friend while noncritical attributes include size, floppy ears, length of tail. When presenting new concepts to mentally retarded learners, the teacher cannot assume that the students will discover critical attributes on their own. Rather, crucial characteristics of concepts must be organized and intentionally highlighted by the teacher.

2. Adjust to changes in critical attributes as a function of the situation. Consider the horse. It has a large number of characteristics such as size, speed, and strength. But what are considered its critical attributes change

depending on for what purpose the horse is needed: speed for the Kentucky Derby, strength to pull a plow, and so forth. Part of the discrimination process is learning that situations change and that different concept attributes become central as situations become different. Since mentally retarded students typically perform poorly in understanding and responding appropriately to different situations, it will be up to the teacher to continually point out how problems or situations are different from one another and how the situation determines which concept attributes become central.

3. Use concrete examples. Young children and most mentally retarded individuals are tied to the concrete, here and now of what they can experience through their five senses (Ginsburg & Opper 1969; Piaget 1952; Siipola & Hayden 1965). Thus, it is imperative that the special education teacher present concepts as concretely as possible. Bring in real-life examples whenever possible and allow students to have hands-on experience with those examples of the concepts. If real-life examples are not feasible or possible, use charts, graphs, maps, pictures or anything which will make the concept more concrete to mentally retarded learners. Try to stay away from simply verbally describing concepts in abstract, symbolic verbal language.

4. Teach the concepts needed for learning new rules. Perhaps one of the mistakes made most frequently by teachers of mildly mentally retarded students is trying to teach new rules to learners before the concepts upon which the rules are based are acquired. For example, the author once supervised a student teacher who tried to teach a class of young mildly mentally retarded students the rule, "always write your name in the upper left-hand corner of the paper before you begin any assignment." She could not understand why the children looked at her in confusion and did not follow the rule. The reason they could not follow the rule was because they had not yet learned the concepts of left, upper, and corner, all critical concepts needed for understanding the teacher's command. Remember, rules are defined as two or more concepts linked together by a verb. Thus, the special education teacher must intentionally teach the concepts upon which the rule is based.

OTHER TYPES OF LEARNING

☐ Operant Learning

Operant learning is sometimes called instrumental learning or trial-and-error learning (Skinner 1971, 1980). It is based on the notion that all overt (observable) behavior (responses) are the result of preceding stimuli. Furthermore, responses lead to environmental consequences in the form of reward or punishment. Rewarded (positively reinforced) responses increase in strength and frequency. On the other hand, punished (or ignored) responses lose strength and extinguish.

Operant learning is also based on the concept of shaping behavior. Organisms learn responses in pieces or successive approximations. Each approximation of the correct goal behavior must be positively reinforced until the total appropriate behavior appears and is learned. Thus, according to Skinner, behavior is learned on a trial-and-error, gradual basis.

Operant learning theory has had profound effects on the education of handicapped children. These effects include the areas of behavior modification, teaching machines and computers, the sequencing of instruction, and the technology of successful instruction. Operant learning is considered in Part IV in the chapters on classroom management, behavior change, instructional sequencing, and in the appendix in the long-term instructional unit. However, at this time, there are some practical implications of operant learning theory which the prospective teacher should keep in mind, including:

1. Always remain aware that behavior is not random. It is the result of particular stimuli and resulting environmental consequences. Behavior may only seem random because we do not yet understand the particular antecedent stimuli causing it and the consequential environmental rewarding agents which take place after the behavior has occurred.
2. Use positive reinforcement to strengthen the behavior you wish to occur while simultaneously ignoring (extinguishing) inappropriate behavior.
3. Use planned schedules of reinforcement. Know when, how, and how much you are going to reinforce.
4. Reinforcement comes *after* the desired behavior, not before. When the reward comes before the behavior there is no reason for the behavior to occur.
5. In the beginning of a behavior modification program, deliver reinforcement promptly. Reinforcement should follow immediately after the behavior. Do not wait to reinforce at some later time.
6. Use a programmed, systematic approach. Describe the desired goal behavior to the child. Provide feedback and reinforcement when it is approximated.
7. Reinforce even slight approximations of the goal behavior. Do not wait for perfect performance of the behavior before reinforcing. Reward successive approximations.

☐ Observational Learning

Observational learning is the phenomenon in which some skills or behaviors are acquired by imitation after the observation of other persons (Bandura 1969, 1977, 1978). According to Albert Bandura, its chief advocate, observational learning is not shaped, gradual, or trial-and-error but rather occurs "in toto" in one perfect trial. This one-trial perfect learning is accomplished by watching a model exhibit the behavior and then by imitating the model's actions. Such imitation behavior is particularly useful in learning situations, such as medical surgery or learning to drive an automobile, where trial-and-error mistakes would be costly or dangerous.

According to Bandura, there are four processes which must take place in order for successful observational learning to occur. These are

1. **Attentional Processes:** The model "catches" the attention of the learner. The learner selectively centralizes attention on the model while selectively not attending to other stimuli.
2. **Retention Processes:** The learner interprets the model's behavior, and remembers it using a recall/rehearsal strategy.
3. **Motor Reproduction Process:** The learner overtly imitates the model's behavior and receives feedback on the accuracy of the imitation attempt.
4. **Motivational Processes:** The child receives positive reinforcement for imitation. This increases the probability that the imitating behavior will strengthen. The positive reinforcement may be external or the child may be taught self-reinforcement techniques.

Figure 2.5 depicts the four processes in the observational learning sequence.

Since mentally retarded learners are typically sensitive to models (Turnure, Larsen & Thurlow 1976), and often rely on external cues in order to learn (Siegel, Westling & Koorland 1979), they are good candidates to benefit from observational learning instruction. In order to increase the probability of such learning, it is suggested that the teacher keep the following in mind:

FIGURE 2.5   Component Processes of Observational Learning

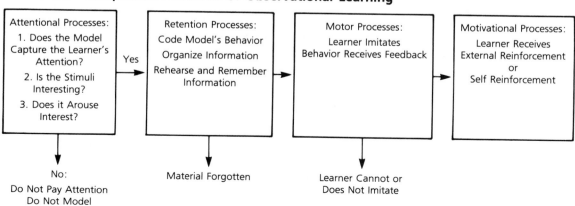

1. The model will not be imitated unless it captures the attention of the learner. Attributes of good models should be novelty, variety, and freshness. A good model is one that just cannot be ignored.
2. The model should possess high status with the learner. It should be someone whom the learner likes and respects. Television characters have been strong role models to children over the years precisely because viewers like and respect them. The higher the status of the model the greater the likelihood that the behavior will be imitated.
3. Make sure that the high-status model is modeling the behavior that you want. Inappropriate behavior is often what is modeled by learners. If possible work with the model and describe precisely what the terminal, modeled behavior should be.
4. A strong component of observational learning is memory and retention. Help learners interpret what they've seen and give them opportunities to commit the model's behavior to memory. Encourage active rehearsal of the model's behavior.
5. Give learners ample opportunity to practice what they have seen. Give feedback on the adequacy of the modeled behavior. This is the time to reinforce and strengthen the newly acquired behavior.
6. Give a reason for the modeled behavior to continue. Give positive reinforcement so that the new behavior will strengthen and increase in frequency. Encourage students toward self-reinforcement for appropriately modeled behavior.

Observational learning is a viable tool for teaching mentally retarded learners (Kauffman, Snell & Hallahan 1976; Mercer & Algozzine 1977). However, it is not meant to be an alternative to operant learning but rather an approach which can be combined with behavior techniques to form a powerful learning plan.

LONG-TERM MEMORY

□ □ After information is learned, it must be remembered; that is, the individual must be able to access and retrieve the learned material when it is needed. We have all experienced the frustration of learning some piece of information only to be unable to recall it at a later time. Learning without recall is useless.

Effective recall depends on the effective organization of material which is to be placed in *long-term memory* (LTM) (Klatzky 1981; Luftig & Johnson 1982; Spitz 1973). Available evidence suggests that mentally retarded students are extremely poor in organizing material for later recall from LTM (Bray 1979, 1985; Justice in press; Turnure & Bray in press). In fact, Spitz argues "a primary difference between educable retardates and normals is the manner in which retardates selectively organize material for storage" (1973, 157–58). On the basis of the problems of stimulus organization as it relates to learning and LTM, it appears important that organization of material be a prime concern of the special education teacher. The following educational suggestions are made regarding the external organization of material by teachers of mentally retarded learners (Baumeister & Brooks 1981; Borkowski & Cavanaugh 1979; Mercer & Snell 1977):

1. Repetition of presented material positively influences organization and learning. A repetition rate of at least 50 percent is suggested for optimal organization, learning, and memory. For example, a sample of presented drill material of addition facts might look like this

   $$1 + 1 =$$
   $$1 + 1 =$$
   $$2 + 2 =$$
   $$3 + 3 =$$
   $$2 + 2 =$$
   $$3 + 3 =$$

2. Prompting, underlining, or other highlighting should be used whenever possible to aid organization of material going into LTM. Eventually these prompts are faded out when material is mastered.

3. Change as few characteristics of the presented stimuli at a time as possible. The ideal set of presented stimuli at one setting is one where only one characteristic or dimension is changed at a time. Examples of changing only one dimension at a time are shown for language arts and arithmetic

   Language arts =   cat, bat, rat, fat

   Arithmetic = $1 + 1 =$ $2 + 1 =$ $3 + 1 =$

4. Simultaneous visual and auditory presentation seems to facilitate organization and learning. Multimodality presentation is, in most cases, superior to unimodal presentation of material.

5. To-be-remembered information should be meaningful and relevant to learners in order to aid recall. Information which is important to the learner is remembered best.

6. Give direct assistance in chunking and categorically organizing material to students. External organization of material optimizes learning and recall for mentally retarded students.

7. Allow opportunity to practice memory strategies such as active rehearsal or organization of material by student. Give adequate feedback and positive reinforcement when students use these strategies.

8. Overlearning of material and constant use of that material is essential to

remembering. Material that is often used is better remembered than material left unused in LTM for long periods of time. Do not teach material and then let it sit unused in classroom activities for months. It will not be remembered by students when it is finally needed.

As with the other main areas of the information processing model (e.g., perception, selective attention, STM, and learning), mentally retarded learners will require specific, intentional, and systematic instruction in the organization of material to be placed in long-term memory for future recall. The importance of such instruction may be demonstrated by the belief of some research experts who claim that nothing ever learned is forgotten. Rather, what occurs is an inability on the part of the learner to access and retrieve information from LTM. This inability occurs because the information was not originally organized and placed in LTM in an efficient manner. Since effective organization of material is so important in the memory process, we cannot expect mentally retarded students to learn such organization incidently. Rather, such instruction will need to be intentional and systematic and should become part of the special education curriculum for mentally retarded learners.

STRATEGY USE AND METACOGNITION

☐ ☐ Learning and memory strategies include selective attention, material organization, clustering, chunking, and rehearsal. However, knowing when to use a given strategy and how to use it is a key to successful learning and remembering in real life.

Suppose you meet someone on the street you have not seen for a long time. You wish to write down the person's telephone number but lack pencil and paper. How would you remember the number until you obtained writing materials? Probably the best way would be by active rehearsal. You would simply say the telephone number over and over until you could write it down.

But do you study for a major examination the same way? Probably not. In studying for an exam, you probably attempt to separate relevant from irrelevant material, attending to what you (or the professor) perceive to be important. You also attempt to categorize and/or organize information some way. Finally, you attempt to place it into bigger, meaningful chunks to aid recall.

These differential strategies probably make perfect sense to you. But how did you know about them and how did you know which ones to use in which situations? Knowing *about* knowing is called *metacognition* (Brown 1974; Flavell & Wellman 1977). Likewise, metacognition includes knowing which strategies to use in which situations (Armbruster, Echols & Brown 1982; Brown 1978; Baird & White 1984). Meaningful learning entails both possessing useful strategies and spontaneously using them in appropriate situations.

Most research indicates that mentally retarded learners possess serious deficits in metacognition (Brown 1978; Borkowski & Cavanaugh 1979; Torgesen 1981). However, Borkowski and Cavanaugh (1979) do hold out hope that mentally retarded students can learn metacognitive strategies and use them appropriately. They suggest the following instructional procedures to facilitate metacognitive functioning of mentally retarded pupils:

1. Teach strategies intentionally. That is, make strategy instruction part of the curriculum. Do not assume that mentally retarded students will acquire and use strategies on their own. They will not.
2. Be consistent in strategy training. Train systematically and keep the situations constant. Only after the strategies have been learned can situations be changed and generalization be worked on.
3. Plan for the fading of any prompts or cues that you use in teaching. Do not fade the prompts and cues until you are convinced that the strategy has been overlearned. They should be faded in the generalization and transfer stages, not during strategy acquisition.
4. Allow for physical manipulation of objects during strategy teaching. Keep examples and materials as concrete as possible. Just describing strategies in abstract language will not be enough for most students.
5. Give strong positive reinforcement and feedback for strategy acquisition and usage.
6. Give strong positive reinforcement and feedback when strategies are used spontaneously in appropriate situations.
7. Make sure that children are not following a rule blindly. Help students learn when a strategy will and will not work.
8. Allow for continual practice and maintenance of strategies.

In summary, the teacher should actively give instruction in strategies. The teaching of metacognitive strategies should be an integral part of the special educational curriculum. In addition, the teacher should strongly provide feedback and reinforcement for the spontaneous and appropriate use of learning and memory strategies in real-life situations. Such usage is a requisite for successful adult living in society.

SUMMARY

☐ ☐ In the past, mental retardation was defined by a lack of native intelligence on the part of individuals. Thus children were retarded if they possessed a deficiency in intelligence and nonretarded if it was judged that they possessed enough of the attribute. In recent years there has been a shift from a native-intelligence explanation of mental retardation to one which describes children's ability to take in, modify, and appropriately act upon information. Termed *information processing,* this model describes cognitive functioning in terms of structural features (hardware) and control processes (software). The information-processing model involves the flow of information beginning with the perception of information through the senses, and then moves in turn through the iconic or echoic buffer, the central processor, the short-term memory, learning process, and finally to long-term memory.

The perceptual processes involve information taken in through the senses. Most school related information comes in through the visual or auditory modality with some information also entering through the kinesthetic/tactile modality. In the past, it was believed that mentally retarded individuals were deficient in the amount of perceptual information absorbed. Available evidence now suggests that while the incidence of sensory impairment among mentally retarded persons is somewhat higher than for the general population, retarded and nonretarded persons typically take in approximately equal amounts of sensory information.

Sensory information is transferred to the iconic or echoic memory buffer. The information is extremely short-lived in these buffers, sometimes lasting only milliseconds. These buffers are not modifiable through training or practice. Information is either lost in the buffers or passed on to the central processor. The central processor is the mechanism of selective attention. Mentally retarded pupils typically possess deficiencies in selective attention and they often attend to irrelevant dimensions of stimuli.

From the central processor, information attended to is passed on to short-term memory (STM). STM possesses limitations in terms of size and the amount of time that it can hold information. However, both of these limitations are modifiable through training and practice. Mentally retarded students are typically deficient in knowledge of strategies which may expand the capabilities of STM memory.

Material passed on from STM must be learned to be retained. There are eight different types of learning existing in a hierarchy of complexity. Mentally retarded students are typically deficient in the higher order levels of learning. Additional types of learning include operant and observational learning.

Information learned must be organized and placed in long-term memory (LTM) so that it can be stored and retrieved for later use. Mentally retarded pupils are typically deficient in organizing material in LTM and thus have difficulties with retrieval of information. It is hypothesized that once material is learned, it is never forgotten. Rather, inability to remember material stems from the inability to access and retrieve information from LTM. This is a particular problem of mentally retarded students.

The ability to acquire and appropriately use learning and memory strategies is known as metacognition. Adequate metacognition is needed for everyday functioning in normal society. Mentally retarded students are typically deficient in acquiring and using learning and memory strategies in real-life situations. Thus learning and using metacognitive strategies should become an integral part of the curriculum for mentally retarded students.

3

Assessment, Diagnosis and Prescription for Mentally Retarded Learners

Key Concepts

- ☐ Public Law 94-142
- ☐ The Diagnostic/Prescriptive Model
- ☐ Assessment: Testing versus Evaluation
- ☐ Diagnosis and Prescription
- ☐ Individual Educational Programs (IEPs)
- ☐ Norm-Referenced versus Criterion-Referenced Tests
- ☐ Group versus Individual Tests
- ☐ Formal versus Informal Tests
- ☐ Speed versus Power Tests
- ☐ Culture-Free Testing

Nearly everyone has taken a test at one time or another. Children are tested almost daily on some teacher-made test, and periodically throughout the school year on more formal, standardized assessment instruments. The educational testing industry today is a multimillion dollar business with thousands of tests available and some test authors receive royalty payments comparable to best selling books. What is done with all of the test information collected? How is it scored, evaluated, and interpreted? Are the tests equally fair to all children? How do test results affect the way the child is treated in school and in later life? The answers to these questions are vital in understanding the importance of assessment in the educational programming for mentally retarded children. They are all relevant to the ability of the special education teacher to provide crucial educational services.

COMPONENTS OF ASSESSMENT AND PROGRAMMING FOR MENTALLY RETARDED STUDENTS

☐ ☐ Assessment does not occur in a vacuum; it is only one component in educational programming for mildly mentally retarded pupils. For assessment to be relevant, it must lead to diagnosis and prescription (see Figure 3.1). All three components—assessment, diagnosis, and prescription—must be understood in order to understand fully the educational programming process.

FIGURE 3.1 Components of Educational Programming for Mentally Retarded Students

```
              ┌─────────────────────────────┐
              │  Screening and Identification │
              └─────────────────────────────┘
                            │
                            ▼
                    ┌──────────────┐
                    │   Referral   │
                    └──────────────┘
                            │
                            ▼
              ┌──────────────┐
         ┌───▶│  Assessment  │
         │    └──────────────┘
         │            │
         │            ▼
         │    ┌──────────────┐
         │    │  Evaluation  │
         │    └──────────────┘
         │            │
         │            ▼
         │    ┌──────────────────────────┐
         │    │  Decision Making and     │
         │    │  Educational Diagnosis   │
         │    └──────────────────────────┘
         │            │
         │            ▼
         │    ┌──────────────────────────┐
         │    │  Program and Instructional│◀──┐
         │    │  Design—Prescription     │   │
         │    └──────────────────────────┘   │
         │            │                       │
         │            ▼                       │
         │    ┌──────────────────────────┐   │
         └────│  Evaluation of Student   │───┘
              │  Learning and Program    │
              │  Design                  │
              └──────────────────────────┘
                            │
                            ▼
                    ┌──────────────┐
                    │ Annual Review│
                    └──────────────┘
```

Reassess if Learning Has Not Taken Place

Reassess Program and Instructional Methods if Learning Has Not Taken Place

Adapted from J.A. McLoughlin & R.B. Lewis (1981). Reprinted by permission of the publisher, Charles E. Merrill.

☐ Assessment

Assessment is the process of measuring and understanding the performance of students as they function in their learning environments (McLoughlin & Lewis 1986; Salvia & Ysseldyke 1985; Wehman & McLaughlin 1981). The purpose of assessment is decision making. Tests and other assessment techniques are administered not just for the purpose of collecting data, but with a definite purpose for how the information will be used (Ysseldyke & Salvia 1974). As such, assessment consists of two related components: *measurement* and *evaluation*.

Measurement entails the collection of data about the child. This information may be collected by using standardized tests or informal procedures such as teacher-made tests, or observation. Whichever information-collection procedures are used, it is crucial that the information be reliable, accurate, and relevant. The entire individual assessment program (IAP) programming model is only as sound as the initial information collected about the child. Evaluation is the interpretation of collected information (Hopkins & Antes 1978). Once the information is gathered, it must be systematically organized, analyzed, and interpreted before it can be of any use.

☐ Diagnosis

Educational diagnosis is a set of behaviorally based conclusions, based on assessment, about the child. These conclusions are specific rather than general (global), and describe precisely the child's psychological, cognitive, and psychomotor skills and weaknesses. It also outlines needed services instead of merely describing a physical defect or handicap. Educational diagnoses are made in terms of educational variables instead of those of pathology or medicine.

Educational diagnosis for mentally retarded pupils assumes *specific skill deficits* rather than *global deficiencies*. In order for educational diagnosis to be useful, it must outline the specific skill deficiencies which the student possesses instead of describing the pupil's problems in general, nonspecific terms. Such generalities possess no real applicability and usefulness for the educational programming for mentally retarded students. Figure 3.2 gives an example of specific versus general diagnosis. The diagnosis of Robert's problems are quite general. It tells little more than that Robert is experiencing problems in reading and possesses problems in decoding. Robert's diagnosis does not give us much information from which to design remediational, instructional procedures. On the other hand, the diagnosis of Steven's reading problems are quite specific. We see not only that he is experiencing problems in decoding, but also the precise areas in which he is experiencing these difficulties. Thus, a teacher can readily design prescriptive educational methods intended to help remediate Steven's reading problems. In the process of diagnosis, reporting specific skill deficits is always more helpful than global, general diagnoses which often are of little or no aid in designing educational programs.

FIGURE 3.2 Diagnoses of Two Students' Reading Difficulties

Student	Evaluation
Robert S.	Robert is two years below grade level. Demonstrates poor decoding and word attack skills. Guesses at words.
Steven P.	Two years below grade level. Demonstrated deficiencies in decoding skills. Particular difficulty in the following areas: Initial Consonants Double Consonants Consonant digraphs Stuctural Analysis Difficulties: Root words Compound words Suffixes

☐ Prescription

Just as assessment leads to specific diagnosis of educational problems, diagnosis should lead to specific curriculum planning and programming designed to reme-diate educational weaknesses of students. Such programming implies both the setting of appropriate learning goals for mentally retarded students and the outlining of educational activities and materials which will be used by the teacher and student to reach those objectives.

Prescriptive teaching implies that curricular and instructional programming for mentally retarded children be chosen on the basis of testing and diagnosis of student strengths and weaknesses, not on the basis of what seems interesting to the teacher or what intuitively appears to the teacher to be important. Likewise, the prescriptive component is individualized for each child since each possesses unique strengths and weaknesses. Prescription is not for the masses; it is for individuals, each one unique and special. Finally, the prescriptive model specifies that the processes of testing and diagnosis occur before curriculum is planned and instructional programming constructed. In the diagnostic/prescriptive model, one does not "jump into teaching"; rather, teaching comes only after careful assessment of the child's strong and weak areas.

PURPOSES OF ASSESSMENT

☐ Referral

Assessment is the process of collecting and evaluating information about the student. The data may suggest a *referral*. Referral decisions seek to answer questions about a child's possible need for special educational services and programming from educational professionals other than the regular classroom teacher. Data indicates that a large number of school children, (approximately 5 percent) are referred each year for special services (Algozzine, Ysseldyke & Christenson 1983a; Ysseldyke & Thurlow 1984). Of this group, approximately 92 percent are further tested and 73 percent are eventually given special educational services.

What types of student behavior are likely to get the pupils referred? Re-search suggests that teachers refer students when behavior consistently annoys the teacher or disrupts the class (Algozzine 1979; Algozzine, Ysseldyke & Chris-tenson 1983b; Ysseldyke & Thurlow 1984). Furthermore, low achieving students with acceptable classroom behavior are less likely to be referred than misbehav-ing students. Thus it becomes evident that there is a need for greater care and specificity in the referral process by teachers for each individual referral.

☐ Screening Decisions

All children do not require in-depth, extensive, and time consuming diagnostic assessment. In fact, if a teacher had to spend hour upon hour administering, scoring, and evaluating numerous in-depth diagnostic instruments, there would be little time left to teach! Luckily, not every child in school requires such an in-depth assessment.

The decision to submit a child to in-depth diagnostic assessment is usually made on the basis of a screening level assessment (Otto, McMenemy & Smith 1973; Salvia & Ysseldyke 1985). Screening tests determine whether a student *might* possess a problem in a given area. Screening assessments are typically given to all children within a given program with the goal of identifying or tagging children as candidates for further, in-depth diagnostic assessment. As such, screening can be thought of as first-level assessment indicating the need for further in-depth assessment or to halt the assessment process.

It is important to realize that every screening test contains a degree of error—it will sometimes misidentify or fail to identify students. Figure 3.3 shows a 2 × 2 factorial design of the different types of decisions which may be made after a screening test has been administered. All students after having their survey test scores evaluated will show up in one of the four boxes of the factorial design. The four results possibilities are as follows:

True Positives: These pupils will show up on the screening test as possessing a learning or cognitive problem. In-depth diagnostic assessment will show they actually possess such deficiencies.

True Negatives: These pupils will show up on the screening test as pos-

FIGURE 3.3 Possible Results of Screening Assessment

Designation of Problem Area	Accuracy of Screening: Accurate	Accuracy of Screening: Inaccurate
No Problem	True Negative	False Negative
Problem	True Positive	False Positive

sessing no problems. In-depth diagnostic assessment will not be carried out. If it were performed, they would demonstrate no learning or cognitive deficiencies.

False Positives: On the screening test, these pupils would appear to possess a learning or cognitive deficiency. Follow-up, in-depth, diagnostic assessment would then ensue. Diagnostic testing would show no such learning or cognitive problem exists.

False Negatives: Upon screening, pupils would demonstrate no learning or cognitive deficiencies. No follow-up, in-depth assessment would ensue. However, the child in this category really does possess such deficiencies but the screening test was not sensitive enough to discover them. The problem thus goes undiagnosed.

Of these four possibilities, the true positive and true negative categories represent accuracy in the screening test. The false positive and false negative conditions represent error in the screening test.

In the false positive category, more pupils will be identified as possessing a problem than will actually have the problem. However, since every child who shows up positive on the screening test will undergo in-depth diagnostic assessment, this latter assessment will indicate that no problem actually exists and will prevent the child from being improperly labeled. Thus, the cost of a false positive error is primarily represented in lost time spent by the teacher and student engaging in an unnecessary in-depth assessment.

On the other hand, the consequences of making a false negative error can be devastating to the child. In the false negative condition, the screening misses students; that is, it fails to identify students who actually possess a deficiency or problem. It tags these pupils as normal and possessing no problems which warrant remediation. Because these students turn up in the no problem category, they do not undergo the in-depth, diagnostic assessment which would indicate the true nature of their problem and overturn the finding of the screening tests. Children who fall into the false negative category may go years before their problems are diagnosed and remedial programming implemented. Years of academic failure and psychological frustration may result.

The implications for the screening assessment of mentally retarded children should now be clear. If screening assessments are going to err, it is much better in terms of human cost to err on the side of identifying too many false positives. In fact, if early intervention of learning and psychological problems of handicapped children is as important as many educators believe, false positive identifications may be the only type of error which we should tolerate from our screening instruments.

☐ Classification Decisions

Classification decisions concern the student's eligibility to receive special services under state or federal guidelines. It is typically much more costly for a child to receive special services than to receive an education in a normal school or class. However, if the child meets eligibility requirements set by the state or federal government, the school system is likely to be reimbursed for a large part of these expenses. Thus classification decisions are concerned with including eligible students while excluding students considered ineligible for special services.

While classification decisions are largely administrative in nature, they *are* important in the lives of students. A child determined not eligible for services will not receive them, even if they are needed. Thus accuracy in these decisions is vital (Gerber & Semmel 1984; Mann, Davis, Boyer, Metz & Wolford 1983; Norman & Zigmond 1980). Unfortunately, whether or not a child receives special services based on assessment is often a function of the state, region, or school system in which the child resides. Consistency and fairness must be attached to the assessment process which helps decide questions of eligibility. Students not allowed to partake of special educational services cannot benefit from those services.

☐ Instructional Decisions

Assessment data can be used to help make decisions about how a student should be taught. These include content decisions of what will be included in the plan of study as well as process decisions of how that component will be taught. The first step in using assessment information for instructional decisions is devising an individualized education program (IEP) for the child. This IEP will then become the master "blueprint" for all of the educational programming which the child receives.

☐ Progress Decisions

Assessment must occur before *and* after instruction. Post-instructional assessment measures the extent to which meaningful learning has taken place. There are two kinds of post-instructional assessment, *summative* and *formative* evaluation. Summative assessment is long-term, final (summation) assessment which occurs after a unit of instruction is complete. It indicates a final degree of learning or achievement. Your grade in this course would be an example of summative evaluation.

Formative assessment, on the other hand, is day-to-day evaluation used to judge periodic progress. Its purpose is to give the teacher and student immediate feedback on the adequacy of instruction and learning so that deficiencies or gaps can be quickly remediated. Ungraded review questions throughout a chapter would be an example of formative evaluation. For adequate progress decisions to occur, both summative and formative evaluation assessment procedures should be carried out by the classroom teacher.

PUBLIC LAW 94-142 AND INDIVIDUALIZED EDUCATION PLANS FOR MENTALLY RETARDED STUDENTS

☐ ☐ In the early days of special education, assessment was often patterned after the medical model of exceptionality. That is, the exceptional student was thought to possess some defect which resulted in predictable symptoms of behavior. Thus, children in the 1940s and 1950s were assessed and classified as brain damaged or dyslexic and these diagnoses, like the diagnoses of pathological diseases, were considered to be self-explanatory.

In 1975, Congress passed the most important, most comprehensive piece of legislation ever written to help handicapped children, Public Law (PL) 94-142. This act provided full educational opportunity to over eight million handicapped children who had previously been denied basic educational services. This legislation provided for the first time the following basic rights to handicapped children:

1. Selection must be by due process guidelines. Students possess basic rights that cannot be violated. Classification and placement cannot be arbitrarily assigned by school system personnel. Parents and students have a right to have a say in what happens in these educational matters.
2. Students are protected against discriminatory testing.
3. Educational placement must be in the least restricted environment (LRE).
4. An individualized educational program (IEP) must be created for each handicapped child.

THE CREATION OF IEPS FOR MENTALLY RETARDED LEARNERS

☐ ☐ One of the most important aspects of PL 94-142 is the mandate to create an individualized educational program for each handicapped student. The IEP is to contain the following components:

1. A statement of the child's level of educational performance.
2. A statement of annual goals, including long-term goals and short-term behavioral objectives.
3. A statement of specific educational services to be provided to the child.
4. The projected date of initiation and duration of these services.
5. The specific criteria and evaluation procedures for determining whether these goals have been reached.

IEPs represent a total program for mentally retarded learners. The programs begin with assessment, include setting goals and objectives, describe instructional procedures, and conclude with assessment of student learning. They represent a statement of what the child is to learn and how the student is going to learn the material.

For the IEP to be useful, it must be at the proper levels of specificity and detail. However, evidence suggests that many IEPs are of little educational value; they tend to be either too specific or too vague (McLoughlin & Kelly 1982; Tymitz 1981; Ysseldyke & Thurlow 1984). For example, Safer and Hobbs (1979) examined hundreds of IEPs and reported that over 20 percent of them contained goals too broad to be of educational value (e.g., the child will improve his reading). On the other hand, they found that 12 percent of the IEPs examined were 11 pages or more with long lists of goals too minute to be adequately covered in the classroom. Thus, the goal of the special education teacher should be writing IEPs which are not too broad and general so as to be useless but at the same time not to get bogged down in detail too technical and minute to be of value. Figure 3.4 contains a sample IEP considered to be at an acceptable level of specificity.

WRITING THE IEP

☐ ☐ A good IEP should contain four major components: current performance levels, annual goal, short-term objectives, and evaluation provisions.

☐ Performance Levels

Performance levels give a summary of the educational levels at which the child is currently operating. They tell where the child currently is. In order to be useful, performance levels must emphasize what the child can do, not what he cannot accomplish. Negative performance levels which describe deficiencies are not useful in IEPs.

Performance levels may take the form of test scores, behavioral descriptions, or performance profiles. These may be used in any combination the teacher deems appropriate. Whichever form of performance level is used, it should be specific enough to give a precise idea of the child's current operating level but concise enough not to bury the reader with needless trivia.

☐ Annual Goals

Annual goals represent long-term aims or objectives which the teacher predicts the child will meet during the academic year. These goals represent the best-guess estimates of the child's achievement levels in the next six to ten months. These estimates are based on the child's chronological and mental ages, current performance levels, as well as academic and learning history.

FIGURE 3.4   Sample IEP: Assessment, Performance Levels, Annual Goals and Short-Term Goals

INDIVIDUALIZED EDUCATIONAL PLAN

PUPIL _____BIRTH DATE _____AGE _____ DATE _____
 Last Name   First Name   Month   Day   Year

HAMILTON COUNTY BOARD OF MENTAL RETARDATION PROGRAM_____LOCATION_____

DISTRICT OF RESIDENCE_____ EXTENT OF PARTICIPATION IN REGULAR EDUCATIONAL PROGRAM _____

Present Level of Educational Performance*

P.L.P. I,A,Level _____	P.L.P. III,A,Level _____	P.L.P. V,A,Level _____
B,Level _____	B,Level _____	B,Level _____
C,Level _____	C,Level _____	C,Level _____
P.L.P. II,A,Level _____	P.L.P. IV,A,Level _____	P.L.P. VI,A,Level _____
B,Level _____	B,Level _____	B,Level _____
C,Level _____	C,Level _____	C,Level _____
D,Level _____		D,Level _____

State of Ohio Curriculum Guide for Moderately Mentally Retarded Learners

PARTICIPANTS IN I.E.P. MEETING				ANNUAL GOALS/SHORT TERM OBJECTIVES
				Annual Goals will be expected to be reached by the end of the school year; they will be evaluated by using an assessment tool through observation of performance. (see attached sheets)
Parent/Guardian				
Classroom Teacher				
School District Representative/Designee				I.E.P. CONFERENCE (FALL)
Other(s)				I have participated in the development of this I.E.P. and the Annual Review Conference.
SUPPORTIVE SERVICES	Check Needs	Expected Duration	Staff Person Providing Services	
Language Development				
Speech Therapy				Parent/Guardian Signature Date
Physical Development				I have reviewed this I.E.P.
Art				
Music				
Pre Vocational Training				Signature Title
Home Living Training				I.E.P. CONFERENCE (SPRING)
Occupational Therapy				I have participated in the Spring Conference to review progress.
Physical Therapy				
Health Services				Parent/Guardian Signature Date
Social Services				I have reviewed this I.E.P.
Home Based Services				
Transportation				Signature Title

(continued)

FIGURE 3.4 (continued)

INDIVIDUALIZED EDUCATIONAL PLAN IMPLEMENTATION RECORD

Pupil: _____ Johnny _____

Teacher: _____ Keyes _____ Specialist: _____ School: _____ School Year: ___ 82-83 ___

Annual Goal(s)—Number Goal(s)

1. To maintain and improve sight word vocabulary, word attack, and comprehension skills.
2. To display improvement in conversation and grammar usage.

```
CODE
I P – In Process
M – Mastered
```

M.P.	No. of Annual Goal	SHORT TERM OBJECTIVES	DATE INIT.	DATE EVAL.	CODE	COMMENTS
	1	Given instruction, Johnny will complete the "Trips and Travel" workbook, record all words in his vocal workbook, and state simple definitions, to teacher approval.	10/11			Comprehension will be oral or written
	1	Given current events, Johnny will copy weekly news from screen, and orally read contents, to teacher approval.	10/11			
	2	Given the daily behavior goal, "I will talk in sentences," Johnny will do so, with 90% accuracy, 30 days consecutively = M.				

INDIVIDUALIZED EDUCATIONAL PLAN IMPLEMENTATION RECORD

Pupil: ___ Johnny ___

Teacher: ___ Keyes ___ Specialist: _____ School: _____ School Year: ___ 82-83 ___

Annual Goal(s)—Number Goal(s)

1. To maintain and improve sight word vocabulary, word attack, and comprehension skills.
2. To display improvement in conversation and grammar usage.

```
CODE
I P – In Process
M – Mastered
```

M.P.	No. of Annual Goal	SHORT TERM OBJECTIVES	DATE INIT.	DATE EVAL.	CODE	COMMENTS
		Given instruction, Johnny will state and write exposed time to 5 minute intervals, with minimal assist, to 90% accuracy.	10/11			
		Given instruction/practical training, Johnny will make coin combinations up to 10¢, combining nickels, pennies, independently, to teacher satisfaction.	10/11			
		Given calculator, Johnny will add 2d + 2d and 3d + 3d w/carry, to 100% accuracy, and record his calculations on worksheet independently, to teacher satisfaction.	10/11			
		Given instruction, Johnny will calculate, on calculator, random amounts of coins up to 30¢, and state findings to teacher satisfaction.	10/11			*Real* money.

Reprinted by permission of the author, Denis Keyes.

Setting accurate goals can be difficult for many teachers. While long-term goal setting skills often come as a function of experience and expertise, Merbler (1978) has devised a formula which helps teachers set realistic long-term goals. This process involves arriving at a compromise between the most optimistic and pessimistic goals. The steps in Merbler's formula are:

1. Based on the child's past progress, make time estimates for learning: optimistic, most likely, and pessimistic time-to-learn.
2. Multiply the most likely time by four and add this product to the optimistic and pessimistic times.
3. Divide the sum of the estimates arrived at in step 2 by six. The resulting number is the projected time-to-learn in the long-term goal.
4. Repeat steps 1–3 for each goal in the IEP.

In writing long-term goals, the statements should be *measurable, positive*, and *student oriented*. Measurable goals are behavioral. They can be measured in terms of observable, finite behavior. They can be seen, measured, and agreed upon. More on measurable behaviors will be included in chapter 4 on writing good instructional objectives.

Positive goals tell us what the child will be able to do, not fail at. Nor should the goals be couched in negative terms. For example, while the statement "staying in his seat for two consecutive minutes" is a positive statement, "not getting out of his seat and bothering other children" represents a negative one. Goals should contain the word *will* not the words *will not*. Finally goals should be student oriented. They should tell what the student will do, not what the teacher or other personnel will do. Describe student behaviors, not materials or teaching methods.

☐ Short-Term Objectives

IEPs should include sequential behavioral statements which describe how the long-term objectives will be reached. Each short-term objective (STO) should describe one step in the learning chain which will ultimately lead to learning the long-term goal. Thus each STO must be sequential and relevant, rather than tangential to the long-term goal.

☐ Evaluation

After a unit of instruction, it is crucial to answer two central questions: What has been learned? and How well? The answers tell both teacher and student the extent to which instruction has been successful. Evaluation in IEPs should be both formative and summative. As such, they should be included in both short-term objectives and long-term learning goals. Each STO should contain criteria for passing and those criteria should be stringent enough to represent real learning. Likewise, long-term goals should contain both criteria for passing and a short description of how learning will be measured. More on criteria is included in chapter 4 on writing instructional objectives.

TYPES OF ASSESSMENT AND ASSESSMENT INSTRUMENTS

□ □ At first glance, the hundreds of different assessment instruments available to teachers can be quite confusing. There are so many tests on the market, each purporting to be unique. It is enough to cause confusion, frustration, and even eventual resignation for using assessment for special needs learners. Understanding assessment instruments is somewhat simpler, however, if one views all tests as falling within a 2 × 2 factorial design with *referencing* being one factor and *specificity* the other (see Figure 3.5a).

FIGURE 3.5a 2 × 2 Design of Assessment Instruments

Specificity of Test

	Global	Diagnostic
Norm Referenced		
Criterion Referenced		

Referencing of Test

FIGURE 3.5b Examples of Global and Diagnostic Tests Appropriate for Mentally Retarded Students in Various Core Academic Areas

	Global	Diagnostic
Reading	California Reading Test Iowa Silent Reading Test	Gates-McKillop Diagnostic Tests Stanford Diagnostic Reading Test Woodcock Reading Mastery Test
Arithmetic	SRA Achievement Series in Arithmetic	Key Math Stanford Diagnostic Arithmetic Test
Spelling	Test of Written Spelling	Lincoln Diagnostic Spelling Test Spellmaster
Written Expression	Comprehensive Tests of Basic Skills	Sequential Test of Educational Progress
	Iowa Test of Basic Skills	Picture Story Language Test

☐ Referencing

Referencing is a comparison of the child's test score. It is a way of making sense out of a score or set of scores. Without such comparisons, interpretation of test results would be impossible (Salvia & Ysseldyke 1985; Worthen & Sanders 1973). Suppose, for example, you took a test and received a score of 68. What would this number mean? Would it be 68 percent out of 100 percent or some other 68? You would want to know how the other test takers did on the test. Were the scores generally higher or lower than 68? Or you might wish to know whether the teacher considered 68 to be a strong or weak score. In short, you would need something to compare your 68 against.

Generally, there are two ways to compare or reference tests. These methods are known as *norm referencing* and *criterion referencing*. Norm referencing is more traditional and has been used more extensively in the past. However, in recent years, criterion-referenced tests have increased in popularity with educators. Both types of referenced tests possess value for the education of mentally retarded learners.

Norm-Referenced Tests

Norm-referenced tests compare an individual's test score against those of peers. This peer group may be other children in the test taker's class or a norm or sample standardization group who took the test when it was first being devised. In either case, the child's test score is placed on a distribution or continuum and compared. Thus, norm-referenced testing can be considered between-people assessment.

Although norm-referenced tests have been severely criticized in recent years, they are useful in certain situations such as screening or program evaluation. Likewise, they are also useful in making placement decisions such as who should receive special services. However, they are not particularly useful or appropriate in assessing a student's learning or achievement after a unit of instruction. In such cases, assessing student learning progress should be a function of the individual's achievement, not an assessment of how much the child has learned in comparison to others. In assessing student learning, criterion-referenced tests should be used. Table 3.1 contains norm-referenced tests commonly used with mildly mentally retarded learners.

Criterion-Referenced Assessment

Criterion-referenced tests measure the child's learning against some objective, criterion, or standard rather than by comparing it to the achievement of others. While norm-referenced testing is relative to peer performance, criterion-referenced testing measures mastery of material against some absolute or standard. Norm-referenced testing asks how Johnny has done in relation to Sally; criterion-referenced assessment asks the extent to which Johnny has mastered the material and how much progress he has made in learning. Table 3.1 contains criterion-referenced tests commonly used with mildly mentally retarded learners.

TABLE 3.1 Commonly Used Norm-Referenced and Criterion-Referenced Tests

Content Area	Name of Test	Reference
Academic Achievement	Brigance Diagnostic Inventory	(C)
	Peabody Individual Achievement Test	(N)
	Wide Range Achievement Test	(N)
	Systems Fore	(C)
Language	Auditory Discrimination Test	(N)
	Goldman-Fristoe Test of Articulation	(N)
	Carrow Elicited Language Inventory	(N)
	Language Sampling	(C)
	Peabody Picture Vocabulary Test	(N)
	Test of Language Development	(N)
Reading	Durrell Analysis of Reading Difficulty	(N)
	Gates-MacGinitie Reading Test	(N)
	Gates-McKillop Reading Diagnostic Test	(N)
	Gray Oral Reading Tests	(N)
	Stanford Diagnostic Reading Test	(N,C)
	Systems Fore	(C)
	Wisconsin Design Test of Reading Skill Development	(C)
	Woodcock-Johnson Psycho Educational Battery	(N)
	Woodcock Reading Mastery Test	(N)
Written Language and Spelling	Test of Written Spelling	(N)
	Spellmaster	(C)
	Basic School Skills Inventory	(N,C)
Arithmetic	KeyMath	(N,C)
	Stanford Diagnostic Mathematics Test	(N,C)
	Basic Educational Skills Inventory-Math	(C)
	Individual Pupil Monitoring Systems-Math	(C)

N = Norm-Referenced
C = Criterion-Referenced

When educational progress is to be assessed, it is best to use criterion-referenced tests. Additionally, many criterion-referenced tests are also *curriculum referenced*. This means that the test items are linked to specific instructional objectives in the child's curriculum so that by evaluating the items the child has missed the teacher can diagnose the student's learning deficiencies. These instructional objectives are then linked to specific remediational activities and instructional material which the teacher can use to help remedy the child's weaknesses. Such curriculum-referenced tests have become very popular with teachers in the last decade.

☐ Specificity

The other variable in the 2 × 2 factorial design of assessment is that of specificity. Specificity refers to the amount of specific information contained in test scores, that is, the degree to which the test provides specific data and information about the child who took the test. A test may give global (general) scores or it may provide specific diagnostic information. Global scores yield unitary pieces of information represented by one or two general numbers (e.g., an IQ or a reading grade level). A diagnostic test, on the other hand, yields a great deal of specific information about not only how a child functions in a given construct (e.g., reading) but also how she or he does on specific skills within that construct.

OTHER VARIABLES UPON WHICH TESTS MAY DIFFER

☐ ☐ There are a variety of other variables which distinguish assessment instruments. These include

1. Group versus individual tests
2. Formal versus informal tests
3. Speed versus power tests

☐ Group versus Individual Tests

Group tests are given to a group of individuals at one time, with the size of the group varying. Individual tests are given to one student at a time with the tester and the test-taker being in a one-to-one relationship. In group tests, instructions are either read by the students themselves or are read to students. Instructions in individual tests may be rephrased or clarified for the test taker.

The characteristics of the test taker often determine the choice between an individual and a group test. The nature of group tests requires that the test taker possess strong reading or listening skills as well as skill in following directions and working independently, skills which mentally retarded students often find difficult. Because of these deficiencies, group tests often penalize mentally retarded students. Interpretation of group test results can be difficult for these learners. Because of these problems with test administration and interpretation, it is best to avoid group tests for mentally retarded students as much as possible.

Individual tests allow the tester to probe student skills in ways not possible with group tests. With individual tests, cues and prompts can be supplied by the tester, as much as the test administration procedures will allow, since the tester and the child are working in a one-to-one relationship. Also, individual tests provide more diagnostic information than group tests, information which can be translated into prescriptive educational programming for learners.

☐ Formal versus Informal Tests

Formal tests are standardized, usually commercially available tests. These assessment instruments are usually appropriate for use nationwide, although there are some formal tests which are designed for regional or statewide use. These tests are appropriate for children over a wide range of geographic areas, socioeconomic levels, and cultural groups. However, there is some debate as to whether these tests are appropriate for such diverse populations.

Informal tests are usually less structured and standardized than formal tests and are usually not national or regional in scope. Rather, informal tests are usually constructed by teachers for use with a given class. These tests are much closer to the day-to-day activities of classrooms. Many teachers prefer informal tests since they believe such tests more directly measure covered material and are thus more valid for use by mentally retarded learners.

☐ Speed versus Power Tests

Have you ever walked out of a test frustrated by the feeling that you knew the material but did not have enough time to finish the exam? If this has ever happened to you then you have experienced the problems of a *speed* test, a test in which there is a limited time to complete the exam. In a severely speeded test, there are many questions, most of them relatively easy and quite answerable. However, severe time constraints do not allow the testee to answer all of the questions in the time allotted.

On the other hand, some instructors, as a regular practice, give students three to four hours, for example, to complete a one-hour exam. The extra time allowance often makes no difference in most persons' test performance. Many students do not finish the exam or else get many questions wrong, not because they do not have enough time to complete the test but because the questions are so difficult. Such a test would be labeled a *power* test, one where the student has adequate time to finish the exam but where the test questions are moderate to severe in difficulty.

Most tests are at least partially speeded in that there is a time limit by which the test must be completed. However, strongly speeded tests should be avoided for mildly mentally retarded students. To be successful on a severely speeded test, one must be a good and fast reader (or fast processor of oral information if the test is read to the test taker). The test taker on a severely speeded test must think quickly, accurately, and unemotionally. All of these traits are ones in which mentally retarded learners typically experience difficulties. Thus, if mentally retarded students do not perform well on severely speeded tests, one cannot know if the poor performance was due to problems with the test content or to difficulties contained within the speeded format of the test.

CULTURAL FAIRNESS IN ASSESSMENT: A PROBLEM FOR MENTALLY RETARDED LEARNERS

☐ ☐ In the last fifteen years, educators have expressed growing awareness that some assessment instruments are unfair to culturally different children. Many tests ask questions which, while within the experience of white, middle class children, are outside the cultural experience of minority and culturally different children (Gamlin & Bountrogianni 1985; Mercer 1975; Yap 1984). Then, when minority children cannot answer culturally loaded questions, they are inferred to be mentally retarded when the only thing that the test actually indicated is that they are culturally different. Statistics show black, Mexican-American, Indian, and poor white children are over represented in classes for mentally retarded students. Current court cases have held the discriminatory nature of culturally biased tests (*Larry P.* v. *Riles*, 1972; *Diana* v. *State Board of Education*, 1972; *Guadalupe* v. *Tempe Elementary School District*, 1971; *Mattie* v. *Holliday*, 1979).

Landmark studies by Jane Mercer have made people aware that mental retardation is often a cultural phenomenon and that many children have been labeled mentally retarded for no other reason than that they are culturally different (Mercer 1973, 1975). This fact was demonstrated to the author when he was teaching in rural Michigan. Most of the students residing in this area were either Native American (Indian) or poor white children. One question asked on a standardized, commonly used intelligence test was, "What are the four seasons?" Many of the students answered "deer, rabbit, trout, and squirrel." Were they wrong? According to their environmental life experiences, their answer was probably more useful than "winter, spring, summer, and fall." However, on this particular, culturally biased test, this answer *was* wrong. And if those children answered enough of the culturally loaded questions "incorrectly," they ended up diagnosed as "mentally retarded".

There are a number of other things teachers of culturally different children might wish to consider in helping to guard against culturally biased assessment. These include:

1. Securing tests which have been translated into the child's native language (Sattler 1974).
2. Finding tests which have been normed to a greater extent on culturally different populations.
3. Having minority professionals administer tests. There is some evidence to suggest that minority children do better on tests where the test administrator shares the culture with the child taking the test (Lefley 1975).
4. Teach minority students the specific skills needed to do well on culturally loaded tests. This solution, however, has been criticized as implying that the child's native culture is somehow inferior. (Alley & Foster 1978).
5. Measure a broad range of information that places the test performance in the perspective of the child's larger culture. Augment traditional assessment procedures with more nontraditional assessment more attuned to the child's culture (Mercer & Lewis 1977).
6. Use specific tests and test procedures developed for minority groups deemed culturally fair (e.g., the BITCH test, Culture-Fair Intelligence Tests, Leiter Intelligence Performance Scale).

None of these solutions totally solves the problem of culture-fair assessment. Perhaps the best thing teachers can do is be vigilant against cultural bias in testing. To that end, professionals suggest checklists for identifying bias in tests as well as checklists for guarding against bias in test interpretation (Turnbull, Strickland & Brantley 1978). Examples of such checklists are in Figure 3.6.

METHODS OF ASSESSING MENTALLY RETARDED STUDENTS

☐ ☐ There are five basic methods for collecting assessment information on children and the environments in which they function (Wehman & McLaughlin 1981). These basic methods are screening tests, structured interviews, norm-referenced tests, criterion-referenced tests, and observations. Each will be discussed briefly in this chapter section.

☐ Sceening Tests

Screening tests occur during the initial stage of assessment. They sort out those children who appear to possess a problem from those who do not. Those children who appear to possess a deficiency in some area of learning or behavior are considered to be at risk and are given additional in-depth assessment.

Screening tests should be administered both in the areas of perceptual functioning (hearing and vision) and academic achievement. Achievement screening tests attempt to identify low-functioning, average, and high-functioning students with the intent of further assessing low-functioning individuals. Most achievement screening instruments compare individuals against their peers (norm referenced). Achievement screening tests may screen students on a single skill or can screen pupils on multiple skills. Table 3.2 contains a list of commonly used achievement screening tests.

☐ Interviews

Once the screening procedure identifies the child as possibly possessing a learning difficulty the professional must begin in-depth assessment in order to understand and diagnose the child's specific problem. The structured interview technique is one method of gaining such insight.

Interviews help gain an understanding of the child's functioning in a variety of environments. They are extremely useful in gathering information about topics and areas not easily accessible or observable by the teacher. For example, a boy was demonstrating extremely disruptive and potentially dangerous behavior in school. The teacher observed that this behavior occurred almost exclusively in the morning just after the children got off the school bus and entered school.

FIGURE 3.6a   Checklist for Detecting Cultural Bias during Scoring and Interpretation of Tests

Name _____ School _____

Examiner _____ Date _____

Examine Child's Score   *A check (✔) indicates potential bias*

_____ Compare them to the adaptive behavior information

_____ Look for characteristics of the child which might bias or influence the results such as:

        _____ native language

        _____ age, health, nutrition

        _____ handicapping conditions

        _____ mode of communication

        _____ sensory and performance modalities

_____ Look for characteristics of the tests and techniques which might bias or influence the results, such as:

        _____ purpose

        _____ communication modalities (a) child-test (b) child-examiner

        _____ norms

        _____ reliability and validity

        _____ type of measure

        _____ relevance of items

        _____ scoring criteria

        _____ type of scores

_____ Look for characteristics of the examiner which might bias or influence the results, such as:

        _____ appropriate training

        _____ communication mode and language

        _____ previous experience

        _____ attitudes

        _____ skills

        _____ knowledge

_____ Look for conditions within the assessment situation which might bias the performance

        _____ time of day

        _____ distractions

        _____ testing materials

        _____ inappropriate use of cues

        _____ length of session

        _____ comfort and accessibility of materials

        _____ order of assessment activities

_____ Look for conditions between the examiners and child which might bias the performance

        _____ rapport

        _____ attending behavior

        _____ initial success or failure

        _____ maintaining responding behavior

        _____ communication

        _____ directors, modeling or demonstrating

        _____ dress and/or mannerisms

_____ Try to determine if the child's performance is representative and/or approximates his/her potential

_____ Compare the results of multiple measures

    From A. P. Turnbull, B. B. Strickland, & J. C. Brantley, developed in conjunction with G. Harbin (1978). *Developing and Implementing IEP's* Columbus, OH: Charles E. Merrill. Used by permission.

FIGURE 3.6b   Checklist for Identifying Cultural Bias During Test Administrations

Name _____   School _____
Examiner _____   Date _____

Potential Examiner Bias   A check (✔) indicates potential bias.

_____ Training (Lack of skills and/or handicapping conditions)
_____ Language/Mode (Lack of language and/or mode of communication needed by the examiner with this child.)
_____ Lack of experiences testing similar types of children: age, cultural group, handicapping conditions
_____ Biased attitude toward particular cultural groups
_____ Knowledge of alternative measures

Situational Interference

_____ Time of day
_____ Distractions
_____ Testing Materials (color, size, etc.)
_____ Inadvertent use of cues such as position cues/position of materials
_____ Length of session
_____ Comfort and accessibility of materials
_____ Order of assessment activities

Interaction between Examiner and Child/Respondent

_____ Lack of rapport
_____ Failure to obtain and maintain attending behavior
_____ Failure to maintain child's optimum effort.
_____ Inadequate communication (mode, manner, language)
_____ Dress and/or mannerisms of examiner (distracting, unique)
_____ Questionable knowledge and candor of interviewee

Checklist for identification of
Potential Bias during Scoring

_____ Ambiguous answers
_____ Unique, creative, unusual answers
_____ Other (describe) _____

Procedural Reminders to Avoid Errors

_____ Check ceiling and basal limits   _____ Check interpolation
_____ Check item credits   _____ Check age
_____ Check addition

From A.P. Turnbull et al. (1978). Reprinted by permission of the publisher, Charles E. Merrill.

Based on this observation, the teacher began to interview the child's parents as well as school bus personnel in order to identify the source of the child's problem. Through these interviews, the teacher was able to determine that a series of events were occurring at the school bus stop and on the bus itself which were greatly upsetting the boy. By modifying this environment, the teacher was able to greatly improve the child's behavior at the beginning of the school day.

The interviewing method, however, suffers from two major flaws. First, interpretation of data collected from interviews can be difficult. For example, an

TABLE 3.2   Screening/Achievement Tests

Skill	Norm Referenced
Reading	Gates-MacGinitie
	Woodcock-Johnson
	Psychoeducational Battery
Language	Peabody Picture Vocabulary Test
General	California Achievement Test
	Metropolitan Achievement Tests
	Wide-Range Achievement Tests
	Peabody Individual Achievement Tests

interviewer might receive conflicting information from two persons interviewed, or may even receive contradictory information from the same person at different times during the same interview. Thus the teacher must use expertise to make sense out of interview information and to reconcile conflicting data when it appears.

The second weakness of the interviewing technique is the fact that information collected is only as good as the reliability, knowledge, and truthfulness of the person from whom the data is collected. It is a fact of life that people do not always know what they are talking about. Likewise, it is probably a universal truism that people wish to cast themselves and their children in as positive a light as possible. For example, a person who is not entirely familiar with the child may nevertheless be happy to supply you with information in an interview about that child while a parent may distort reality a bit when describing what the child can do. This is not to suggest that parents *lie* about their children. Rather, they may unthinkingly distort reality in order to tell the interviewer what they believe the interviewer would like to hear. Thus, the experienced interviewer must be constantly on guard against distortions of reality.

☐ Norm-Referenced Tests

As mentioned earlier, norm-referenced tests are those which allow comparisons of an individual's results against a norm group of age or grade related peers. Norm-referenced tests are heavily standardized; they possess standard procedures for administration, scoring, and interpretation. This helps the teacher know that students are assessed in a systematic fashion and that data collection, scoring, and interpretation are subject to as little variance as possible.

Since the child taking a norm-referenced test is being compared to other children in the norm group, the characteristics of that norm group are all important. How a student fares on a norm-referenced test is a direct result of the characteristics of the group to whom he or she is being compared. Mentally retarded students in particular often suffer on norm-referenced tests because of inappropriate representation of these and culturally different students in test norm groups. The assurance of compatibility of norm group with test taker is a major responsibility of the professional administrating norm-referenced tests.

☐ Criterion-Referenced Tests

Criterion-referenced tests compare a student's performance to some external standard or criterion of the curriculum rather than to the test performance of other students. Criterion-referenced tests are quite useful as diagnostic instruments and possess value in helping the special education teacher in remediational and instructional planning for mentally retarded students.

Just as norm-referenced tests are only as valid as the norm group against which the test taker is being compared, criterion-referenced tests are only as sound as the specificity of the criteria used to measure student mastery of material. In order for a criterion to be useful, it must be written in the form of a performance or behavioral objective (Kaplan & O'Connell 1979). To be effective as an educational tool, such an objective should describe:

1. What the student must do, i.e., the specific behavior which the student must demonstrate.
2. The conditions under which the behavior is to occur.
3. How well the student must perform (level of criterion) in order to pass the objective.

Objectives such as "knowing phonics" or "understanding the reading lesson" have little or no meaning and usefulness against which to measure criterion-referenced performance. Such "fuzzy" or inexact criteria doom a criterion-referenced test to failure. Well constructed criterion-referenced tests, however, can be educationally valuable in programming for mentally retarded students.

☐ Observation

Teachers observe their students all the time. However, when the teacher suspects an educational or behavioral problem on the part of a student, observational techniques used as an assessment tool must be systematic and intentional. Observation allows the teacher to obtain information not readily available through standardized, formal tests. It is particularly useful in assessing social and non-academic variables such as time-on-task, aggression, peer interaction, behaviors often not assessed because of the unavailability of pencil and paper tests.

The first step in systematic observation is precisely defining the behavior to be measured. For example, suppose you were asked to observe and record all instances of disruptive behavior on the part of a given child. What should you observe? To different teachers, a disruption might be giggling, talking, being out of a seat, and/or hitting another child. Some teachers might even consider a child interrupting a lesson to ask a relevant question a disruption. What constitutes a disruption is in the eye of the observer. Consider, however, the behaviors, "being out of one's seat," "hitting or punching another child," or "being within five feet of another child and maintaining eye contact with him." These descriptions are more precise and possess little ambiguity. If asked to observe and record such behaviors, the teacher could do this with little confusion. Thus, it is imperative that the behavior to be observed be defined as precisely as possible.

Teachers interested in systematic observation of students should answer the following questions before such observation is attempted (Stengel 1985):

1. Who will make the observation?
2. Who will be observed?
3. Where will the observation take place?
4. When will the observation take place?
5. How will the observation be recorded?

If any of these questions is answered in an ambiguous fashion, the observation will almost certainly be unsystematic, confusing, and relatively useless for educational programming.

Types of Observation

There are basically three types of observation which the teacher may use: *duration, interval*, and *continuous recording* (Stengel 1985; Wallace & Larsen 1979). In duration recording, the teacher is interested in how long a student engages in a given behavior. This is particularly useful when a student is not demonstrating a behavior frequently but each time the child does exhibit the behavior, it lasts for a long time. For example, suppose that Tommy threw a temper tantrum "only" twice during the school day (the good news) but that each tantrum lasted over thirty minutes (the bad news). If duration recording had not been used, an observer could get the impression that Tommy's tantrum-throwing behavior was not a real problem. Tommy's behavior would appear less serious than it actually is.

Interval recording is useful when the teacher wishes to measure both the frequency and duration of a student's particular behavior. In this type of observation, the teacher would divide the observation period into equal time periods or intervals and record the occurrences of the target behavior during these intervals. For example, Figure 3.7 shows Mary's out-of-seat behavior for a twenty-minute observational period, each period lasting two minutes. Out of a total of ten intervals, she was out of seat eight times for a behavior rate of 80 percent, an extremely high rate of inappropriate behavior.

Finally, continuous recording is the method by which the teacher keeps a complete account of a child's behavior during a brief observational period. Continual observation is sometimes referred to as *anecdotal recording* since the

FIGURE 3.7 Mary's Out-of-Seat Behavior for a Twenty Minute Period Using Interval Recording

10–10:02	10:02–10:04	10:04–10:06	10:06–10:08	10:08–10:10
X		X	X	X
10:10–10:12	10:12–10:14	10:14–10:16	10:16–10:18	10:18–10:20
X	X		X	X

observation approximates a running account of a given child's total behavior. Continuous observation may contribute to the teacher's understanding of patterns in a child's behavior. However, such recording can be cumbersome and time consuming, and it may be open to error since the observer may miss behavior occurring while she/he is hurriedly trying to write it all down. Unless the teacher has a clear purpose in mind, duration and interval recording may prove to be more useful and less subject to errors of observation.

APPLYING ASSESSMENT INFORMATION: PRESCRIPTIVE TEACHING

☐ ☐ The major purpose of educational assessment carried out by teachers is making instructional planning decisions. Known as *prescriptive teaching*, this process involves the creation and implementation of educational programming designed to remediate the weaknesses indicated by diagnostic assessment. While in-depth diagnostic assessment is conducted during a specified time and usually occurs no more than once or twice during the school year, the prescriptive process is ongoing and continuous. This ongoing process contains two key components, deciding *what* to teach and *how* to teach.

☐ Deciding What to Teach

Deciding what to teach is directly related to diagnostic assessment. That is, the in-depth educational assessment which has been conducted leads to the diagnosis of specific educational weaknesses which the child possesses. These weak areas then become the basis of what to teach.

Decisions of what to teach are included in IEPs; those decisions take the form of long-term objectives and short-term goals. Those objectives and goals must be stated in precise behavioral form and the criteria for assuming that the learner has mastered the objectives must be relatively stringent. In fact, many teachers do not assume that learning has taken place unless mastery of the objective occurs at a rate of 85 percent accuracy or higher.

In order to identify the instructional long-term objectives for each student, the teacher may wish to adopt an instructional grouping grid like the one shown

FIGURE 3.8   An Instructional Grouping Grid

			Skills			
Child	Vowels	Blends	Dipthongs	Dolch Words	Compound Words	Reading Rate
Bill	X			X	X	
Sally		X	X			
John			X	X	X	
Tony	X		X		X	
Mike		X	X	X	X	X

From Zigmond/Vallecorsa/Silverman, ASSESSMENT FOR INSTRUCTIONAL PLANNING IN SPECIAL EDUCATION, © 1983, p. 334. Adapted by permission of Prentice-Hall, Englewood Cliffs, New Jersey.

in Figure 3.8 (Zigmond, Vallecorsa & Silverman 1983). On this grid, the teacher would record the long-term instructional priorities for students. Specific skills range across the top of the form while the students who are weak in the given skill areas are listed down the side. By reading across the rows, the teacher can see at a glance the skills which need to be taught. By reading down the side, the teacher can identify particular students who are weak in given skill areas. Such a grid helps the teacher not only plan instruction but also form instructional groups.

☐ **Teaching Short-Term Goals**

Teaching short-term goals involves the process of *task analysis*. This is defined as "the process of isolating, sequencing and describing all the essential components of a task" (Howell, Kaplan & O'Connell 1979, 81). Task analysis consists of three subprocesses: breaking down the task into essential subtasks, arranging these subtasks into a sequential and hierarchical order, and describing each subtask by the use of an instructional objective.

In task analysis, it is crucial that each subtask require one and only one skill (Frank 1973; Myers & Hammill 1976). If the subtask requires the child to engage in two or more behaviors, the skill should be broken down further into additional subtasks. The task analysis procedure involves the *chaining* of subtasks in their proper sequence in order to lead to mastery of the long-term terminal skill (Myers & Hammill 1976; Sulzer-Azaroff & Mayer 1977). If the subtasks are chained out of sequence, critical, building-block skills will be encountered out of sequence with the result being that the terminal objective will not be reached.

Table 3.3 contains a task analysis of a reading skill for a learner (Polloway & Smith 1982). Notice how the terminal skill is broken down to a series of single behaviors, each behavior appearing to come in its proper sequence and each lower subtask being a requisite for the subtasks which come after it. Finally, notice that the last subtask in the task analysis routine represents the terminal behavior itself.

A task analysis approach to prescriptive teaching is vital to successful educational programming for mentally retarded learners because it allows for instruc-

TABLE 3.3 Sample Expressive Language Task Analysis

Task:

Presented with a picture or object and the verbal question, "What is this?", the child is to respond by saying, "This is a _____ ," correctly 90 percent of the time.

Prerequisites:

1. Eye contact
2. Attending behavior (thirty seconds)
3. Imitation of words
4. Identification and repertoire of nouns familiar to the child

Task Component Steps:

1. Child will imitate the last two words of the chain. "This is a _____" when a picture or object is presented.
2. Child will imitate the four words of the chain when a picture or object is presented.
3. Child will answer with a one-word verbal response when presented with a picture or object and the verbal question, "What is this?"
4. Child will verbally answer the last two words of the four-word chain, "This is a _____" when presented with a picture or object and the words "This is."
5. Child will respond with the last two words of the four-word chain, "a _____" when presented with a picture or object and a verbal question, "What is this?"
6. Child will answer verbally the last three words of the four-word chain when presented with a picture or an object and the word. "This . . ."
7. Child will answer with the four-word verbal response. "This is a _____" when presented with a picture or object and the verbal question, "What is this?"

From E.A. Polloway & J.E. Smith, Jr. (1982).

tional sequencing in the presentation of material. By teaching material in small, sequential steps and chunks, the teacher will not confuse the child by presenting more than the child can handle at any one time. Mentally retarded students learn material when they are not overloaded with more material than they can cognitively handle (Edgar, Masen, Smith & Haring 1977). In fact, for most mildly mentally retarded learners, the quality and amount of learning is directly related to the sequential nature of the learning presentation (Blake 1976). For these pupils, the sequencing and task analysis of material to be presented is a crucial variable.

SUMMARY

□ □ An amazingly large amount of assessment information is collected on all school children in the United States every year. Even more is compiled for handicapped children. Today the field of assessment of children in American schools is a multimillion dollar industry.

Public Law 94-142 mandates an individualized education program (IEP) for every exceptional child. This IEP specifies that the child's program will be individualized and will occur in the least restrictive educational environment. Such a program guarantees fair assessment, due process, and efficient educational programming.

The IEP program is a total package which includes assessment, diagnosis, and prescription. Assessment is the process of measuring and understanding the performance of students as they function in their environments. Assessment consists of two components: measurement and evaluation.

Diagnosis entails making educational conclusions regarding the child's strengths and weaknesses on the basis of assessment. Diagnosis assumes specific skill deficits on the part of the child rather than global deficiencies. Diagnosis of deficits of children is an ongoing process rather than one that occurs just once at the beginning of the school year.

Diagnosis leads to prescription, which is the designing and implementing of educational goals for mentally retarded children. Prescriptive measures are always individualized for students. At the end of a unit of instruction, evaluation of the child's learning as well as the effectiveness of the prescriptive program takes place.

There are a variety of assessment instruments, but generally they fall within a 2 × 2 factorial of referencing and specificity. Tests are either norm or criterion referenced and are either global or specific (diagnostic) in nature. Other properties of tests include group versus individual, formal versus informal, and speed versus power tests.

The cultural fairness of tests is a growing concern among special educators. Many mentally retarded students have been diagnosed as mentally retarded for no other purpose than that they are culturally different. The courts have held that any assessment instruments used with mentally retarded learners must be culturally fair and cannot discriminate on the basis of culture. Attempts are continuing to develop culturally fair and valid tests.

There are basically five methods of assessment: screening tests, structured interviews, norm-referenced and criterion-referenced tests, and observation. Screening tests provide an initial assessment of whether or not a child might possess an educational problem. All screening tests produce error, but it is better for them to produce error which identifies too many children who might have a problem (false positives) than for it to miss students who actually possess a problem (false negatives).

Interviews allow the professional to learn information about how the child functions in other environments. Interviews, however, are subject to error; the person being interviewed may not know the child very well, may wish to please the interviewer, or may desire to portray the child in a positive light. The interviewer must be on guard against such interview bias and adjust conclusions accordingly.

Norm-referenced tests measure the child's score against those of a norm group of age or grade related peers. As such, the norm group must be appropriate to the child taking the test or else the assessment is invalid. The teacher must make sure that the norm group is comparable to the cultural group of the test taker.

Criterion-referenced tests compare a student's performance against an external standard or criterion rather than to other students. Criterion-referenced tests are only as good as the soundness or clarity of the external criterion. Criteria should be written in the form of clear, concise, performance objectives. Performance objectives contain a behavior, a condition under which the behavior is to occur, and the criteria for passing the objective.

Observation is a form of informal assessment. It is useful for collecting information not readily available through the use of paper and pencil tests. There are three methods of collecting observational data: interval, duration, and continuous observational recording.

Prescriptive teaching involves the application of assessment information. Such information gives the teacher insight into what to teach and how to teach it. Decisions as to what to teach are predicated on long-term objectives and short-term learning goals. Long-term objectives should be written in behavioral form with criteria stringent enough to require mastery of content. Short-term learning goals must be sequential in order to be effective and should depend on the process of task analysis. Goals are translated into educational programming and such programming is presented to mentally retarded students in a systematic and sequential manner.

PART II

Creating the Curriculum

4

Creating and Using Instructional Objectives

Key Concepts

☐ The Need to Define Behavior in Observable Terms
☐ Fuzzy versus Behavioral Verbs
☐ The Usefulness of Instructional Objectives
☐ The Relationship between Educational Diagnosis and Instructional Objectives
☐ Components of Instructional Objectives: Conditions, Behavior, and Criteria
☐ Mastery Learning
☐ The Cognitive Taxonomy of Objectives
☐ Long-Term and Short-Term Instructional Objectives
☐ Creating a Specifications Chart

Imagine that you are sitting in the teacher's lounge of a large public school. In the lounge with you are two special education teachers discussing the various curriculums and children in their classrooms. One teacher is boasting about the vast improvement these students have made during the school year. According to this teacher, the students have learned functional math, they know about independent living, they understand how to behave socially, and they have an appreciation for reading (quite an accomplishment indeed!).

You listen to all of this conversation, and you decide to enter the discussion. "That's fantastic," you say, "but how do you *know* they've acquired these skills? How do you know they've learned, know about, understand, and have an appreciation for what you've taught them?"

The conversation in the teacher's lounge stops. "Well, I just know," the teacher answers, a little defensively.

"But how?" you insist (knowing when to quit is obviously not your strong suit!) "What specifically can the students do now they couldn't do before? What proves they possess all these new competencies you say they have?"

"Well, they just seem to know," the teacher answers. "They act like they know. What else do you want?" The teacher gets up and leaves the room.

This scenario is not far fetched. Many educators are convinced their students are learning and their curriculums and instructional methods are efficient and effective. However, they are basing these beliefs on little more than "gut feelings" that their students have learned and "know" the material.

Sometimes such gut feelings can lead to problems. For example, the author once taught in a school in which the principal was extremely authoritarian. The day before school opened, this principal gathered the faculty together and informed them that henceforth no "disturbances" would be tolerated in class. That is, any disturbances should be reported immediately to him so that he could mete out appropriate discipline. The teachers all nodded in understanding.

After the meeting, however, the author conducted a little experiment. He informally polled fifteen of the teachers on their definition of a "disturbance." Not surprisingly, he received a diversity of answers. For some teachers, a disturbance was an action which threatened the health and safety of another child or of the teacher. For other teachers, a disturbance was anything a child did in class which bothered or interrupted the teacher. Thus being sent to the office and receiving discipline from the principal was in large part a function of which teacher a given child had!

What caused the confusion for the teachers in the two examples just given? A great deal of the problem can be attributed to the inexactness of the terms used to specify behavior. In the first example, the teacher indicated that he could assess learning in terms such as "to know," "understand," and "appreciate." In the second example, everybody was so sure that they knew what a disturbance was that they were willing to discipline and punish children based on their perceived understanding of the term. However, when the need to operate on such understandings arose, confusion flourished.

□ **Precise Behavioral Verbs**

This text posits that the education of mentally retarded learners can be significantly improved by the use of detailed specification of the exact behaviors and competencies that the teacher wishes students to exhibit (Baine 1982). This precise specification may be contrasted to the common tactic, which Dyer (1967) has coined "word magic," of using terms that describe behavior (e.g., know, understand, appreciate) without giving any real information about what is expected. Table 4.1 contains the "fuzzy, foggy, fifty-five," (Claus 1968a), a set of fifty-five such magic verbs commonly used in education which really have no educational or behavioral meaning.

It is much more preferable to use verbs which precisely specify what the child is to do in order to be judged competent or deficient on a given skill. For example, look at a few of the functional, forceful, four-hundred-fifty-five (Claus 1968b) shown in Table 4.2. Notice how these terms more precisely state what the child is to do. Verbs such as "choosing," "hopping," "adding," "displaying," and "combining" are terms which are *observable, measurable,* and *finite.* They are observable because people can easily agree as to whether or not they have occurred, they are measurable since a quantitative measure can be taken as to the degree or strength of the demonstrated behavior, and they are finite because they have definite points of beginning and ending in time. These parameters of

TABLE 4.1 The Fuzzy, Foggy Fifty-Five Nonbehavioral Verbs to Avoid in Instructional Objectives

Become:	Experience
able to	
acquainted with	Hear
adjusted to	
capable of	Interest
cognizant of	
conscious of	Know
familiar with	
interested in	Listen
knowledgeable about	
mature	Memorize
self-confident	
	Mind
Can't	
	Perceive
Comprehend	
	Realize
Conceptualize	
	Recall
Cover the content	
	Recognize
Create a classroom:	Reduce:
atmosphere	anxiety
climate	immaturity
	insecurity
Evidence a(n):	
appreciation for	Review
attitude of	
awareness of	Satisfy:
comprehension of	drives
enjoyment of	needs
feeling for	
interest in	See
knowledge of	
understanding of	Self-actualize
	Study
Exhibit:	
capacity	Think
depth	
emotional maturity	Understand
intelligence	
purpose	Won't

From C.K. Claus (1968a).

TABLE 4.2 Verbs Stated Appropriately for Instructional Objectives

THE FUNCTIONAL, FORCEFUL FOUR HUNDRED FIFTY FIVE

1. "Creative" Behaviors

Alter	Generalize	Question	Regroup	Re-phrase	Re-write
Ask	Modify	Re-arrange	Rename	Restate	Simplify
Change	Paraphrase	Re-combine	Re-order	Restructure	Synthesize
Design	Predict	Reconstruct	Re-organize	Retell	Systematize
				Revise	Vary

2. Complex, Logical, Judgmental Behaviors

Analyze	Combine	Contrast	Designate	Formulate	Plan
Appraise	Compare	Criticize	Determine	Generate	Structure
Assess	Conclude	Deduce	Discover	Induce	Suggest
		Defend	Evaluate	Infer	Substitute

3. General Discriminative Behaviors

Choose	Describe	Discriminate	Indicate	Match	Place
Collect	Detect	Distinguish	Isolate	Omit	Point
Define	Differentiate	Identify	List	Order	Select
				Pick	Separate

4. Social Behaviors

Accept	Answer	Co-operate	Forgive	Laugh	Reply
Admit	Argue	Dance	Greet	Meet	Smile
Agree	Communicate	Disagree	Help	Participate	Talk
Aid	Compliment	Discuss	Interact	Permit	Thank
Allow	Contribute	Excuse	Invite	Praise	Visit
			Join	React	Volunteer

5. Language Behaviors

Abbreviate	Call	Indent	Punctuate	Speak	Tell
Accent	Capitalize	Outline	Read	Spell	Translate
Alphabetize	Edit	Print	Recite	State	Verbalize
Articulate	Hyphenate	Pronounce	Say	Summarize	Whisper
			Sign	Syllabicate	Write

6. "Study" Behaviors

Arrange	Circle	Diagram	Itemize	Mark	Record
Categorize	Classify	Find	Label	Name	Reproduce
Chart	Compile	Follow	Locate	Note	Search
Cite	Copy	Gather	Look	Organize	Sort
			Map	Quote	Underline

7. Music Behaviors

Blow	Clap	Finger	Hum	Pluck	Strum
Bow	Compose	Harmonize	Mute	Practice	Tap
			Play	Sing	Whistle

8. Physical Behaviors

Arch	Climb	Hit	March	Ski	Swim
Bat	Face	Hop	Pitch	Skip	Swing
Bend	Float	Jump	Pull	Somersault	Throw
Carry	Grab	Kick	Push	Stand	Toss
Catch	Grasp	Knock	Run	Step	Walk
Chase	Grip	Lift	Skate	Stretch	

9. Arts Behaviors

Assemble	Cut	Frame	Mold	Roll	Stamp
Blend	Dab	Hammer	Nail	Rub	Stick
Brush	Dot	Handle	Paint	Sand	Stir
Build	Draw	Heat	Paste	Saw	Trace
Carve	Drill	Illustrate	Pat	Sculpt	Trim
Color	Fold	Melt	Polish	Shake	Varnish
Construct	Form	Mix	Pour	Sketch	Wipe
			Press	Smooth	Wrap

10. Drama Behaviors

Act	Direct	Enter	Imitate	Pantomime	Respond
Clasp	Display	Exit	Leave	Pass	Show
Cross	Enter	Express	Move	Perform	Sit
				Proceed	Turn

11. Mathematical Behaviors

Add	Compute	Estimate	Integrate	Plot	Subtract
Bisect	Count	Extrapolate	Interpolate	Prove	Sum
Calculate	Cumulate	Extract	Measure	Reduce	Tabulate
Check	Derive	Graph	Multiply	Solve	Tally
Circumscribe	Divide	Group	Number	Square	Verify

12. Laboratory Science Behaviors

Align	Conduct	Dissect	Keep	Plant	Set
Apply	Connect	Feed	Lengthen	Prepare	Specify
Attach	Convert	Grow	Limit	Remove	Straighten
Balance	Decrease	Increase	Manipulate	Replace	Time
Calibrate	Demonstrate	Insert	Operate	Report	Transfer
				Reset	Weigh

13. General Appearance, Health and Safety Behaviors

Button	Comb	Eat	Fill	Taste	Unzip
Clean	Cover	Eliminate	Go	Tie	Wait
Clear	Dress	Empty	Lace	Unbutton	Wash
Close	Drink	Fasten	Stack	Uncover	Wear
			Stop	Untie	Zip

14. Miscellaneous

Aim	Erase	Hunt	Peel	Scratch	Store
Attempt	Expand	Include	Pin	Send	Strike
Attend	Extend	Inform	Position	Serve	Supply
Begin	Feel	Kneel	Present	Sew	Support
Bring	Finish	Lay	Produce	Share	Switch
Buy	Fit	Lead	Propose	Sharpen	Take
Come	Fix	Lend	Provide	Shoot	Tear
Complete	Flip	Let	Put	Shorten	Touch
Correct	Get	Light	Raise	Shovel	Try
Crease	Give	Make	Relate	Shut	Twist
Crush	Grind	Mend	Repair	Signify	Type
Develop	Guide	Miss	Repeat	Slip	Use
Distribute	Hand	Offer	Return	Slide	Vote
Do	Hang	Open	Ride	Spread	Watch
Drop	Hold	Pack	Rip	Stake	Weave
End	Hook	Pay	Save	Start	Work

From C.K. Claus (1968b).

observability, measurability, and finiteness are all useful yardsticks by which to assess whether the verb the teacher selects to describe behavior is behavioral or not.

THE USE OF INSTRUCTIONAL OBJECTIVES IN THE SPECIAL EDUCATION CURRICULUM

☐ ☐ By precisely specifying the behaviors which the teacher expects the child to perform in the classroom, you take a giant first step in creating instructional objectives (sometimes referred to as behavioral objectives). These objectives are nothing more than an accurate description of the terminal behavior, the conditions under which it is to occur, and the performance efficiency required to pass the objective (Gagné 1964; Meyen 1981). Instructional objectives are thus a specification of accomplishments with which the learner is to be equipped when exiting a given unit of instruction.

The creation of such instructional objectives is closely linked with the area of educational diagnosis (chapter 3). Diagnosis entails the in-depth assessment of the child's strengths and weaknesses; it identifies area(s) where the child possesses an educational deficiency. But educational assessment information obtained in a vacuum is useless. Once the educators learn where the child's weaknesses lie, they must design (prescribe) educational programming to remediate those weaknesses. The first step is to select and prioritize precise learning goals (Baine 1982). Each of these learning goals is then summarized behaviorally as a series of instructional objectives. Figure 4.1 contains a flowchart of the diagnostic/prescriptive sequence used in creating instructional objectives from assessment information (Baine 1982).

According to Meyen (1981), advantages to using instructional objectives with mentally retarded learners include

1. Allowing for individualization in the planning of educational goals for mentally retarded students. Each objective is geared to the learning abilities and style of each child in the class.
2. Providing to the teacher a ready-made content checklist of material to-be-covered for each child in the special education class.
3. Allowing the teacher to check to see that what has been taught to students is what was specified in the instructional objective.
4. Stating the accepted level of acceptable performance and specifying proficiency needed in order to exit the objective.
5. Allowing an evaluative component to be built into the instructional objectives.
6. Allowing students to understand what is expected of them.
7. Lending themselves easily to use in long-term instructional units (see chapter five).

FIGURE 4.1   Flow of Instructional Programming from Diagnosis (Assessment) to the Creation of Instructional Objectives

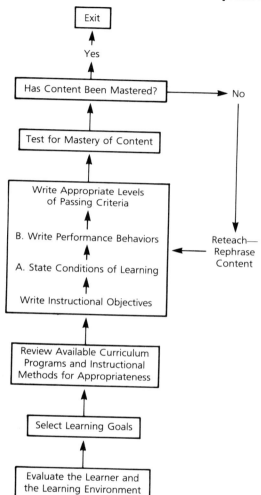

8. Giving to the teacher a clear idea of the types of instructional activities which may be needed in order to reach the child's learning goals.

Perhaps most importantly, instructional objectives lend themselves to *instructional sequencing*. Such sequencing represents the systematic, precise ordering of the curriculum by the teacher in such a way so as to optimize learning (Siegel & Siegel 1977). It allows for the placing of material in its correct order as well as the exclusion of extraneous material which would only confuse the learner and retard or inhibit learning. The creation of well-constructed instructional objectives helps insure that activities designed to teach the objective will be directly related to that objective. Thus, instructional objectives address themselves to the issues of task relevance and task analysis and to the proper identification of the correct skills in their sequential order so as to optimize learning. In short, the use of instructional objectives helps guarantee that curriculum and instruction for mentally retarded learners will be intentional rather than being incidental and left to chance.

STATING THE CONDITIONS OF LEARNING

☐ ☐ In addition to precisely stating the behavior which is to take place, the exact conditions under which that behavior is to occur also must be specified. There are some situations in which a given behavior could be perfectly acceptable in one environment (e.g., physical aggression in the boxing ring) and completely unacceptable in another situation (e.g., physical aggression in the classroom). Thus, in order to avoid ambiguity as to when a given behavior is or is not appropriate, it is important to explicitly state the conditions of behavior.

For teachers and other educators, the conditions of behavior are particularly important since they specify the information, materials, and environment which will be provided to students who are expected to behave in certain ways. Describing the conditions of behavior outlines the environment in which learning and performance is expected to take place. This sometimes is called the "givens" of behavior because it states that given a certain set of stimuli and learning environment, the child will behave in a certain way. Examples of givens which can be included in behavioral objectives are

> **Given** one hour, no manuals, an array of chemicals to choose from and raw glassware
> **Given** a map of the United States with each state outlined and a chalkboard pointer
> **Given** an assortment of United States coins which include at least ten pennies, nickels, dimes, and eight quarters
> **Given** a newspaper story about the space shuttle
> **Given** a list of twenty spelling words orally

The conditions of terminal instructional objectives (as opposed to short-term instructional objectives) should describe the most difficult and/or the most commonly found conditions in which the learner should be required to learn (Baine 1982). This is particularly important for mentally retarded learners who may be taught skills in simplified environments rather than general, more life-like environments in order to cut down on distractions and extraneous material. However, such simplified environmental conditions may actually reduce the mentally retarded student's ability to generalize learning to the larger, more relevant life-situation due to mentally retarded pupils's general inability to spontaneously generalize (Brown 1977; Campione & Brown 1979). For example, the author once was working on functional reading with a group of lower functioning mildly mentally retarded pupils who were taught to read *men* and *women* in relation to reading the signs on public restrooms. These students passed the behavioral objectives when they could read *men* and *women* when shown the door of a public restroom. A field trip to various places in the city followed. The teacher then learned that the various commercial establishments in the city worked overtime in attempting creativity in labeling their restrooms in new and innovative ways. Thus, these students, trained to read *men* and *women* when given the condition of those words printed on a door in the simplified classroom environment, suddenly were faced with *hens* and *roosters, senors* and *senoritas,* and *Johns* and *Janes,* none of which they were trained to read! Behavior cannot take place in a vacuum; rather, it must occur in the real world of stimuli and materials. It is the role of the condition component of instructional objectives to detail those stimuli and materials precisely.

CRITERIA FOR MASTERY

□ □ Suppose a teacher writes the following instructional objective:

Given a map of the United States with the states outlined, the child will point out state capitals.

The teacher has pupils carry out the objective; they come to a map in the front of the room and point out state capitals. One child identifies one state capital correctly, another correctly identifies forty. Suddenly, the teacher realizes a problem: Have both pupils passed the objective? Has one? Has no child passed? What should be done next?

The dilemma occurs largely because this teacher did not specify an acceptable level of passing performance on the instructional objective. The teacher did not include the *criteria* component of the instructional objective and now has no basis for judging the adequacy of student performance. While the behavior component of the objective specifies the *what* and the condition section the *how,* the criteria specify *how much* of the behavior is to occur.

Like the behavior and condition sections of instructional objectives, the criteria must be stated as precisely as possible. For example, look at the four examples of criteria given in Table 4.3. In the first two examples, do you have an absolute understanding of what constitutes passing performance? Probably not. That is because the criteria stated in the first two examples are not criteria at all but rather fuzzy guidelines as to what is going on. Contrast this with the latter two examples given in Table 4.3. These criteria are not ambiguous; they can be measured with exactness to ascertain whether or not the instructional objective has been passed.

TABLE 4.3 Inappropriate and Appropriate Evaluative Criteria Contained in Instructional Objectives

Inappropriate Criteria

1. The student will sing the school fight song nicely.
2. The student will analyze the themes in *Hamlet*.

Appropriate Criteria

1. The student will underline the mistakes with 90 percent accuracy.
2. The student will identify the book authors without error.

☐ Methods of Measuring Criteria in Instructional Objectives

There are a number of ways to measure whether the criteria of an instructional objective has been reached. The traditional method has been to simply tabulate the number or percentage of correct responses. This method, however, may result in the learner meeting the objective's criteria by making a large number of responses even though those responses are punctuated by an equally large number of mistakes. That is, given a large number of responses by a student, at least some of them are bound to be correct just by chance and the objective's criteria could thus be reached. A more effective way to assess the child's competence on a given instructional objective is to tabulate the number of *consecutive* correct responses made. This method insures that the student is responding in a consistently acceptable manner.

Another way of judging the criteria of an instructional objective is by using an upwardly sliding scale of competence. In this method, the degree of competence needed to pass the objective increases on each subsequent day. Thus, while on day one, the child may need only five consecutive correct responses to pass the objective, on day two, she or he may need ten such responses, etc. Such an upwardly sliding scale allows for the realistic expectation of increased competence on a given skill as the learner practices and becomes more proficient.

Finally, performance on an instructional objective can be evaluated as a function of *time* and/or as a function of increased generalization. In time evaluation, it is expected that the learner's responses become more rapid, while remaining accurate, as he or she becomes more proficient. In an evaluation measuring increased generalization, a newly learned skill would become spontaneously generalized to new and life-like environmental situations as the learner becomes more proficient in that skill. The proficient student should be able to generalize responses from the constrained classroom environment to the more diffused, general environment where the child operates for the majority of the time.

☐ Acceptable Criteria for Passing—Mastery Learning

Regarding criteria, the question is often raised as to what constitutes acceptable levels of performance on instructional objectives. Is 65 percent adequate? 70

percent? 80 percent? In the grading systems of many teachers, such different performance levels are possible because the teacher holds time constant while manipulating grades. That is, the children in the class are all given the same specified amount of time to learn the academic material after which they are tested and assigned grades based on the percentage of material learned within that time period. Thus, a grade of 70 percent means that 70 percent of the academic material was learned in the time period specified by the teacher.

But does this method really make sense? Does learning 70 percent of the material have any meaning? Which 30 percent of the material was not learned and how important was it? Would you want to fly on a jet plane in which the pilot scored 70 percent on landings while in flight school or have surgery performed by a doctor who received a grade of B or C+ in medical school? Probably not. Rather, what is probably more appropriate in such learning activities is a solid mastery of the material regardless of how long it takes for the person to master it (Block 1971; Block & Burns 1971; Bloom 1968). In most cases, the *lowest* levels of passing criteria would be at 85–90 percent mastery with some objectives not being considered passed unless 100 percent mastery is indicated.

For mentally retarded children, the mastery learning model makes a great deal of sense. Everything included into the curriculum for mentally retarded pupils must be there due to its relevance and importance to life success and normalization. If the material to be learned is of such crucial importance, shouldn't it be learned at high levels of mastery? What good is acquiring 70 percent proficiency in a critical skill such as money usage? Rather it would seem more appropriate for the child to acquire the material at high levels of expertise and mastery so as to be of greater use in later life. This does not mean, of course, that we must expect perfection (100 percent mastery) of our mentally retarded students. Such expectations of perfection will be impossible to achieve and will prove frustrating to both student and teacher. Rather, levels of mastery beginning at 85–90 percent should be instituted before a given instructional objective is considered passed and the next objective in the instructional sequence attempted.

Figure 4.2 contains a checklist which may be of use in evaluating the adequacy of instructional objectives. This checklist contains guidelines for evaluating the three components of an instructional objective; the condition, behavior, and criteria.

WRITING INSTRUCTIONAL OBJECTIVES AT DIFFERENT DOMAINS AND AT DIFFERENT LEVELS OF COMPLEXITY

☐ ☐ Available evidence suggests a great deal of curriculum material emphasizes trivial or nonimportant behaviors which contain mere rote memorization (Bellack 1976; Gagné 1977; Klausmeier & Ripple 1975). School programs emphasize the learning of facts and ignore generalization and application of learned material to real-life situations. This state of affairs is particularly unfortunate for the education of

FIGURE 4.2   Checklist for Evaluating the Appropriateness of Instructional Objectives

                                                                      Yes   *No*

1. *Conditions of Learning*
   A. The physical or social circumstances under which behavior is to take place
   B. Instructional materials provided
   C. Presentation mode or format
   D. The range of conditions to be accepted
2. *The Behavior*
   A. The *observable, measurable* behavior
   B. The simplest method of demonstrating this behavior
   C. The most acceptable, least stigmatizing form of this behavior
3. *Criteria*
   A. Minimal performance levels
   B. Number of consecutive trials behavior is to be correctly performed
   C. Least number of trials required
   D. Time or rate of response
   E. Acceptable error rate
   F. Acceptable error type
   G. Environmental conditions for successful generalization of performance

mildly mentally retarded children who typically possess deficits in application, generalization/discrimination, and transfer skills. It simply cannot be assumed that mentally retarded students can learn material in rote fashion and, then on their own, apply and use what they have learned in more sophisticated ways. Rather, it is strongly suggested that such higher order learning behavior will never take place unless the mentally retarded child is given specific training and instruction in such higher order processes. Nonretarded children may acquire such skills on their own, but it is most probable that mentally retarded will not acquire higher-order cognitive skills incidently.

A DESCRIPTION OF HIGHER ORDER SKILLS: USING BLOOM'S COGNITIVE TAXONOMY

☐ ☐ What are the higher order cognitive skills which might be learned by children and how might they be described in order to facilitate sound curriculum and instructional intervention? This is a problem facing many educators who realize the shortcomings with the way that information is presented in the schools and who wish to present material at higher cognitive levels. Fortunately, a theoretical hierarchy or scheme was created with the purpose of identifying levels of cognitive functioning in children (Bloom 1956). This scheme is hierarchical in that higher level skills cannot be acquired until each lower skill in the hierarchy is sequentially mastered. Known as the *cognitive taxonomy of objectives*, this hierarchy possesses direct relevance to the ways that instructional objectives should be created for pupils.

Figure 4.3 shows the six levels of the cognitive domain; knowledge, comprehension, application, analysis, synthesis, and evaluation. As you inspect Figure 4.3, keep in mind these skills are hierarchically related; that is, the lower level skills must be mastered by students before higher level skills can be learned. Thus, the taxonomy implies that material presented to students must be task analyzed and sequenced by order of its cognitive complexity.

THE LEVELS IN THE COGNITIVE TAXONOMY

☐ Knowledge

The most basic cognitive level in the taxonomy is *knowledge*. Knowledge level learning refers to the basic operation of retrieval. It is the ability to call into consciousness facts or pieces of information which were learned at an earlier time. As such, knowledge contains a strong component of rote (recall) memory.

According to Bloom et al. (1956), knowledge level conceptualization is the building block for all higher order learning; it is a level of abstraction upon which more complex and abstract forms of knowledge are based. Without knowledge level learning, higher levels of learning, thought, and conceptualization simply cannot occur.

Table 4.4 contains instructional objectives at the knowledge level along with a set of behavioral verbs which would be appropriate to describe knowledge level behaviors. Notice how strongly related to rote, recall memory words like *state, recite*, and *recall* are. In fact, at the knowledge level, students really do not have to do anything or make any cognitive manipulations on material. All they have to do is recall and recite.

☐ Comprehension

The second level in the cognitive taxonomy is *comprehension*. Comprehension involves little more than a basic understanding of the message sent or the material being given. As such, it is represented by the ability to accurately recognize instances of the transmitted information and the ability to differentiate it from non-instances. Comprehension involves recognition of an instance or an example while the knowledge level involves rote recall. For example, multiple choice questions would be considered to be at the comprehension level because they entail the student's ability to pick out or recognize the correct information from a set of incorrect distractors. In comprehension, the information is typically present in its entirety for the student to view. Nothing has to be reproduced by the student. All that needs to be done is recognition and identification.

FIGURE 4.3   Levels of the Cognitive Taxonomy

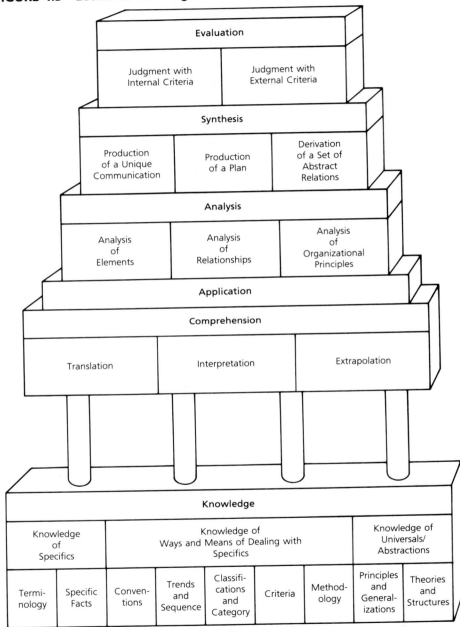

From W.J. Krypsin & J.F. Feldhusen (1974). *Writing behavioral objectives.* Minneapolis, MN: Burgess Publishing Company.

TABLE 4.4   Examples of Instructional Objectives at the Six Taxonomic Cognitive Levels

a) KNOWLEDGE

1. After listening to a lecture on the functions of a bank, the student will list in writing the four functions of the bank with no errors.

2. The student will be able to orally recite all of the notes on the music scale with 100 percent accuracy.

b) COMPREHENSION

1. Given a list of states in the United States, the student will identify four states which border on the Atlantic ocean.

2. The student will in writing match the states to their state capitals with 80 percent accuracy (40 out of 50 states).

c) APPLICATION

1. Given in writing step by step descriptions in baking an apple pie, the student will follow each written instruction without error.

2. Given step by step oral instructions, the student will successfully open a checking account at a local bank.

d) ANALYSIS

1. The student will orally break down a chocolate cream pie into its component ingredients without any omissions of ingredients or inclusion of extraneous ingredients.

2. The student will orally identify the major themes of Hamlet, mentioning at least four themes and including no extraneous themes.

e) SYNTHESIS

1. Given the ingredients with which to make a beef stew, the student will make an acceptable beef stew as judged by the home economics teacher.

2. The student will combine material found around the workshop in order to make a usable and acceptable birdhouse as judged by the industrial arts teacher.

f) EVALUATION

1. Given the standards for a gear design, the students in the industrial arts class will judge whether to accept or reject a sample gear in terms of those standards.

2. When given a sample essay to judge, the senior English class will critique the essay in terms of the criteria given in class as to what constitutes a good essay.

The comprehension objectives in Table 4.4 along with behavioral verbs reflect comprehension level objectives. Notice how comprehension verbs center on words which require recognition like identify, match, or locate. In addition, those behaviors which require students to rephrase, restate, or paraphrase are sometimes included in the comprehension level.

☐ Application

Application is the third level of the cognitive taxonomy and one of the educationally most important for mentally retarded learners. At the application level, the student is expected to be able to use or apply information in order to solve basic problems. This might include using number facts to solve an arithmetic problem, counting out the correct amount of change when given a money figure, or any of hundreds of other behaviors needed for successful life functioning. Application also includes the ability to follow step-by-step directions such as following a cake recipe. Application thus involves the basic operation of putting learning into practice. Information acquired in the knowledge and comprehension stages is used in real world situations.

In application instructional objectives, the verbs *apply*, *use*, or *transfer* represent the ability to put into basic operations the factual knowledge which one has learned. Thus, application involves the processes of generalization/ discrimination, transfer, and higher order usage desired for mentally retarded students. This is the ultimate goal of educational programming for the mentally retarded.

☐ Analysis

The introduction of *analysis* level tasks moves into complex and abstract areas of the cognitive processes. Some special educators assert that these upper levels of the cognitive taxonomy are too abstract for mentally retarded students and that application is all to realistically hope for with these individuals. Evidence suggests however, that this may not be the case and that mentally retarded students can process information at higher levels of abstraction (Borkowski & Cavenaugh 1979). There appears to be no harm in trying to reach the goal of higher cognitive functioning with older mildly mentally retarded students especially since the jury is "still out" on their ability to function at such higher levels. Rather, we should afford mildly mentally retarded students the opportunity to function at such high levels of functioning with the avenue open for easy falling back to more basic, concrete cognitive functioning levels if the situation warrants.

Analysis consists of breaking down of information or products into their component elements or parts. It is the process of dividing the whole into its parts. For example, a chemist analyzing a compound into its constituent elements is performing analysis. Likewise, when a mentally retarded individual relates or divides an apple pie into its individual ingredients and amounts, this too constitutes analysis.

Table 4.4 gives analysis instructional objectives along with a set of behavioral verbs at the analysis functioning level. Notice how words such as "distinguish," "break-down," and "contrast and compare" all refer to dividing the whole into its component parts. This ability to analyze products into their constituent elements is a very important part of critical thinking and problem solving.

☐ Synthesis

Synthesis is the opposite of analysis. Synthesis involves putting together elements or parts in order to form a new whole. It is the creation of something new from available component pieces. For example, a child building a model ship, creating an artistic product, or using available equipment and materials to solve a problem is engaging in synthesis. Synthesis is truly a case of the whole being greater than the sum of its parts.

Table 4.4 contains synthesis instructional objectives as well as a set of verbs appropriate for use in synthesis objectives. In the synthesis objectives, the child creates something or solves some problem alone using the available materials at hand (the givens). Thus synthesis instructional objectives are particularly useful both in the artistic/creativity curriculum area as well as in the self-help part of the curriculum where the child solves real-life, life-experience problems using the means available to him. In this way, synthesis can be particularly useful in the education program for older mentally retarded individuals in testing their ability to generalize solutions to problems in real-life adult daily situations.

□ Evaluation

The final and most complex cognitive process in the taxonomy is *evaluation*. Evaluation involves the making of judgments or the critiquing of products based on sound, objective criteria. Typically, in an evaluation task, the child critiques or appraises products created during the synthesis stage in terms of their appropriateness or worth. This evaluation procedure is a two step process: first the child learns the quantitative and qualitative criteria by which to evaluate products and then uses those criteria in appropriate ways in order to critique the materials, products, or information. In Table 4.4, the evaluation level's behavioral verbs *judge, validate,* and *assess* all indicate the processes of critiquing and evaluation.

USING THE COGNITIVE TAXONOMY

□ □ Instruction at higher levels of cognitive functioning is considered to be important in educational programing for older, mildly mentally retarded students. It has been demonstrated that when properly constructed and integrated into the long-term instructional units of mentally retarded learners (see chapter five), that older mentally retarded students can operate on higher levels of cognitive functioning. Furthermore, by limiting programs of these learners to the lowest cognitive levels we are condemning students to operating on levels not much higher than rote memorization. This method of operating, however, will ultimately prove inappropriate in real-life adult situations.

To demonstrate how a given topic or unit of instruction for mentally retarded pupils might be represented at the six levels of cognitive functioning, Figure 4.4 shows related instructional objectives at the various levels for a unit of instruction. As you read the instructional objectives in Figure 4.4 look at the ways in which the behavioral verbs describe the behavior at the appropriate taxonomic levels. Notice also that while the instructional objectives are at various

FIGURE 4.4   Instructional Objectives from a Unit on Banking

Subtopic 1:   Banks and Banking.

  1A. Using a pamphlet provided by a bank, the student will list, in writing, the seven major functions performed by banks presented in class, omitting no functions. (Knowledge)

  1B. After listening to a lecture and reading a handout on savings accounts, the student will write, word for word, the presented definition of a savings account, leaving out no words. (Knowledge)

  1C. After listening to a lecture and reading a handout on interest, the student will write, word for word, the presented definition of interest leaving out no words. (Knowledge)

  1D. After listening to a lecture and reading a handout on checking accounts, the student will write, word for word, the presented definition for a checking account, leaving out no words. (Knowledge)

  1E. After listening to a lecture and reading a handout on service charges, the student will write, word for word, the presented definition of a service charge, leaving out no words. (Knowledge)

  1F. Given a verbal cue the student will name four out of four of the presented checking accounts. (Knowledge)

  1G. After reading a pamphlet on the Statement Savings account, the student will summarize the benefits of having a Statement Savings account to the teacher's satisfaction. (Comprehension)

  1H. Given a list of possible services available with Jeanie, the student will identify the four that are actual Jeanie functions, with 100 percent accuracy. (Comprehension)

  1I. Following a class discussion the student will recite the five accounts that Jeanie will perform transactions for, with 100 percent accuracy. (Knowledge)

  1J. Given a list of minimum balances and a list of account names, the student will match the account name with its minimum balance, with 100 percent accuracy. (Comprehension)

  1K. Given a worksheet the student will list the major tasks performed by a bank employee, with 100 percent accuracy. (Comprehension)

  1L. Given written cues, the student will identify, in writing, the ten terms introduced in subtopic 1, with 100 percent accuracy. (Comprehension)

Subtopic 2:   The Mechanics of a Savings and Checking Account.

  2A. Following a presentation, the student will *rank order* the steps to opening a bank account, with 100 percent accuracy. (Comprehension)

  2B. Given step by step directions, the student will perform the task of opening a Statement Savings account, omitting no steps. (Application)

  2C. Given step by step directions, the student will perform the task of opening a Now Interest checking account, omitting no steps. (Application)

  2D. Given step by step directions, the student will perform the task of opening a Checking 300 account, omitting no steps. (Application)

  2E. Given step by step directions, the student will perform the task of opening a Regular checking account, omitting no steps. (Application)

  2F. Given step by step directions, the student will perform the task of opening a Special checking account, omitting no steps. (Application)

  2G. Given a list of names for the various slips and pieces of paper involved in bank accounts, the student will match the name to a presented model with 100 percent accuracy. (Comprehension)

  2H. Given a blank check copied on to an 8½″ × 11″ sheet of paper, the student will label the five major lines on the check with 100 percent accuracy. (Comprehension)

2I. Provided with instructions and five checks with all entries, but the amount in symbolic form, the student will enter the indicated number with 100 percent accuracy. (Application)

2J. Given instructions and five checks with all the information provided, except the amount in word form, the student will write out the indicated amount in word form, with 100 percent accuracy. (Application)

2K. Given a list of ten checks that need to be written and step by step instructions, the student will write each check according to the specifications given, with 100 percent accuracy for each of the ten checks. (Application)

2L. Given a sample check register with five transactions entered in it and verbal instructions, the student will write the correct entries in the balance column as they compute the balance using the two line entry format, making no computation errors or entry errors. (Application)

2M. Given the checks from objective 2J and using the two line entry method, the student will enter each of the checks into a check register, omitting the balance column, making no errors. (Application)

2N. Given a check register in which five errors of several different types have been made, the student will locate and correct the five errors using a red pen. (Analysis)

2O. Given a story card and a checking account register to go with the story, the student will locate the missing money and identify the service charge which would account for the missing money, with 100 percent accuracy. (Analysis)

2P. Given step by step instructions and four checking account deposit slips and a listing of four separate amounts of cash to be deposited in a checking account, the student will fill out each of the four slips, omitting no information and making no errors in the amounts listed. (Application)

2Q. Given step by step instructions and a set of three checks to be deposited into a checking account, the student will fill out a deposit slip in which all three checks are entered, with 100 percent accuracy. (Application)

2R. Given a listing of four deposits made up of cash and check combinations and instructions, the student will fill out four deposit slips according to the specifications for each deposit, with 100 percent accuracy. (Application)

2S. Given step by step instructions and a listing of five withdrawals and five deposits for a savings account, the student will fill out a total of ten withdrawal/deposit slips with the appropriate information with 100 percent accuracy. (Application)

2T. Given a demonstration and provided with a sample problem, the student will calculate the interest earned for twenty sample accounts, with 95 percent accuracy. (Application)

Subtopic 3: Managing a savings and/or checking account.

3A. After researching a specific account, the student will outline the major benefits and drawbacks of the account to the teacher's satisfaction. (Analysis)

3B. Given a financial biography of a made up person, the student will state two reasons for choosing a specific account(s) for that person, including both reasons. (Evaluation)

3C. Given a specific account and a list of twenty transactions to perform, the student will write the appropriate checks, fill out the deposit and withdrawal slips, and make entries in an account register, performing each entry or transaction and making no errors of any type. (Synthesis)

3D. Provided with a financial biography, the student will select an appropriate account(s) for that financial biography to the teacher's satisfaction. (Evaluation) levels of abstraction, they all appear to be within the ability levels of many older mentally retarded students. Finally, notice that the cognitive levels which appear first in the presentation of these objectives are at the knowledge and comprehension levels and that there are more of these objectives than of objectives at higher taxonomic levels. Knowledge and comprehension level objectives constitute the knowledge base of whatever is to be taught. They must be in place if higher order cognitive functioning is ever to occur in a given subject matter. For all students, but particularly for mentally retarded students who do not learn incidentally, these building block behaviors must be learned at mastery level performance criteria in order to serve as the basis for all future learning.

LONG-TERM AND SHORT-TERM INSTRUCTIONAL OBJECTIVES

□ □ One of the most useful aspects of instructional objectives is their flexibility. That is, instructional objectives can and should be used in each phase of the development of the individualized education program (IEPs) for mentally retarded learners. As such, they lend themselves quite easily to the development of both long-term and short-term learning goals.

It is crucial that both long-term and short-term objectives be written in behavioral terms. There should be no ambiguity as to exactly which behaviors the student must engage in to pass an objective, the specific criteria for passing that objective, and the conditions under which that behavior is to occur. Such description of long-term and short-term instructional goals described in the instructional objective format will help insure that adequate sequencing of activities and task analysis designed to lead to mastery of the desired behaviors can occur.

SEQUENCING OF INSTRUCTIONAL OBJECTIVES AND TASK ANALYSIS

□ □ Once long-term goals and short-term instructional objectives have been written, the specific skills contained in those instructional objectives must be properly sequenced. Sequencing involves the breaking down of each skill into three or four phases for the purpose of teaching the desired behavior. Each of these phases are then further broken down into a chain of specific, smaller behaviors, the total of which make up the terminal (long-term) instructional objective.

Skill sequencing and *task analysis* are terms which are often used interchangeably, but in reality they are different phases of the learning process (Wehman & McLoughlin 1981; Williams & Gotts 1977). Skill sequencing is the breaking down of a given behavior into a set of manageable phases or segments, each phase appearing in its correct order for reaching the terminal skill. Task analysis is the detailed breaking down of each phase of the task into precise and detailed descriptions of the child behaviors in given instructional situations. Skill sequencing is an intermediate process which falls between the stating of a short-term behavior objective and analysis. It represents the most precise stating of specific behaviors in the instructional process with those detailed skills being rechained to form the terminal skill.

An example of the relationship between instructional objectives, skill sequencing, and task analysis may be seen more clearly in Figure 4.5, which demonstrates the teaching of the terminal objective of appropriately riding a city bus. The task has been broken down into sequences or phases and then each of these phases has been task analyzed. Finally, these chains are relinked in order to reach the desired phase in the sequence and the phases themselves are rechained to achieve the terminal objective.

Appropriate sequencing and task analysis of instructional objectives is useful in the education of mentally retarded students since it presents the material to pupils in small, sequenced chunks. By teaching in this manner, the teacher makes instruction systematic and intentional. For both mildly and more severely mentally retarded pupils, skill sequencing and task analysis of instructional objectives has been shown to facilitate learning (Edgar et al. 1977; Blake 1976). Thus, the prospective teacher is urged to include it in teaching.

CREATING A SPECIFICATIONS CHART FOR YOUR INSTRUCTIONAL OBJECTIVES

□ □ Up to this point, we have discussed how to write sound instructional objectives as well as writing instructional objectives at different levels of cognitive complexity. Now you might be asking: I'm going to be writing so *many* instructional objectives, how am I going to keep track of them all? And how will I know that they're sequenced properly?

There is a teaching aid which can give to you an indication of how your subject matter is organized and whether it is sequenced in a rational matter. This aid is called a *specifications chart* (sometimes called the table of specifications). A specifications chart allows you to view the layout of your subject matter in terms of instructional objectives, the division of the subject matter into appropriate outline subtopics, and cognitive taxonomic levels. It evaluates whether objectives are sequenced properly and if there is representation of objectives at all taxonomic levels.

Table 4.5 shows a typical specifications chart. Going across the horizontal axis are the six cognitive taxonomic levels while going down the vertical axis is a content outline of the materials to be taught. In the individual grids created by the intersections of the two axes appear a nomenclature system which refers to the instructional objectives.

FIGURE 4.5 Skill Sequencing and Task Analysis for Riding a City Bus

Instructional Objective: Given a task requiring the student to ride a bus, the student will be able to ride the appropriate bus with 100 percent accuracy.

Task Analysis of Objective

Phases:

I Teaching *Ss* to ride a simulated city bus in the classroom.

II Teaching *Ss* selected places in the city of Madison, Wis., where food, clothing, opportunities for recreation, and other services could be obtained, and to determine what bus to take in order to reach those places from Capitol Park.

III Teaching *Ss* to ride an actual city bus to and from Capitol Park to obtain the food, clothing, recreation opportunities, or other services listed on bus route cards.

IV Teaching *Ss* to determine what buses to take to places that do not appear on the bus route cards.

Phase I: Teaching *Ss* to ride a simulated city bus in the classroom.

Step 1—*S* tells *T* the differences between a school bus and a city bus and what is meant by the term *destination*.

Step 2—*S* labels the various parts of a Madison Metro bus, recognizes a bus stop, and demonstrates knowledge of the student fare.

Step 3—*S* emits the following behaviors in sequence after *T*'s cues have been faded, using a simulated Madison Metro bus:

a *S* says where he/she wants to go.
b *S* walks to a bus stop.
c *S* waves bus to a stop.
d *S* reads the destination sign on the front of the bus.
e *S* enters the bus by the front door.
f *S* hands the driver the bus route card and says, "Let me off near _____."
g *S* pays the fare.
h *S* sits or stands (varies).
i *S* rings the buzzer and goes to a door on cue from the driver.
j *S* gets off.

Phase II: Teaching *S* selected places in the city of Madison, where food, clothing, opportunities for recreation, and other services could be obtained and what bus to take to reach the destination from Capitol Park.

Step 1—*S* demonstrates the ability to label 9 "sight words" individually presented. (These are words which will appear on individual bus route cards. Each bus route card should be considered a set of 8 words.)

Step 2—*S* points to the 8 words appearing on the bus route card learned in Step 1 on cue from *T*.

Step 3—*S* tells *T* the name of the bus route that would appear on the bus destination sign when traveling between 2 points listed on the bus route card.

Step 4—*T* asks *S* to view a videotape of a bus route and names a destination where *S* should get off. *S* responds by throwing a switch which lights a bulb when the appropriate stop flashes on the monitor.

Phase III: Teaching *Ss* to ride an actual city bus to and from Capitol Park to obtain the food, clothing, recreational opportunities, or other services listed on the bus route cards.

Step 1—*Ss* choose one of the bus routes they have learned. *T* chooses the last stop on this route as *Ss*' destination. Using their bus route cards, *Ss* determine the name of the route leaving and returning to Capitol Park from the destination chosen. *Ss* verbally rehearse the stops along this route. They find the proper bus stop at Capitol Square.

Step 2—Ss, starting at Capitol Park, take the appropriate bus to the destination chosen in Step 1 and return. They travel in a small group with *T*.

Step 3—Same as Step 2, except Ss travel without *T* in a small group.

Step 4—Same as Step 2, except Ss travel alone.

Step 5—Ss perform in the classroom the prerequisite skills necessary to transfer buses.

Step 6—Using their bus route cards in the classroom, Ss gain experience at finding the buses they need to take when transferring.

Step 7—Ss ride a city bus, traveling in a small group with *T*, choose two destinations, and transfer to reach them.

Step 8—Same as Step 7, except Ss travel in small group without *T*.

Step 9—Same as Step 7, except Ss travel alone.

Step 10—Ss perform in the classroom the prerequisite skills for taking a city bus from their houses to Capitol Park and returning home.

Step 11—S chooses a destination, takes a city bus from home, traveling with *T* to Capitol Park, transfers to the destination, and returns home.

Step 12—Same as Step 11, except S rides alone.

   Phase IV: Teaching Ss how to determine what bus to take to places that do not appear on bus route cards.

Step 1—Teaching Ss to label cards with the names of major streets in the city of Madison. (This is done to facilitate labeling addresses in later stages of this phase.)

Step 2—S looks up one of the streets acquired in Step 1 of this phase in the *Street Index* on the back of a map of Madison. S then labels the coordinates listed next to the name of the street located.

Step 3—S gains experience at finding streets on a map of Madison.

Step 4—Teaching Ss how to use the Madison telephone directory to find addresses and phone numbers of places they would like to go to. S also writes down the address and phone number that he/she finds.

Step 5—S calls Directory Assistance to find out the phone number of a place he/she has been unable to locate in the phone book. S then calls the number to find the address.

Step 6—S uses an actual phone to call Directory Assistance to find a phone number. S calls this number and writes down the address.

Step 7—S finds an exact location on a map of Madison using the numerical component of the address.

Step 8—S gains experience at finding exact locations on the map.

Step 9—S is taught the names of various bus routes listed on the map.

Step 10—S gains experience finding bus routes on the map.

Step 11—S learns how to find the closest route to a particular street address he/she has located on the front of the map.

Step 12—S gains experience at finding the appropriate bus route for various addresses using a map of Madison.

Step 13—S looks up an address in the phone book, locates the closest bus route, and rides the bus to the destination with *T* and a small group of Ss.

Step 14—Same as Step 13, except Ss travel in a small group without *T*.

Step 15—Same as Step 13, except S travel alone.

   From P. Wehman & P.J. McLaughlin (1981). *Program development in special education.* New York: McGraw-Hill. Reprinted by permission.

TABLE 4.5   A Table of Specifications (Specifications Chart)

Specifications Chart	*Knowledge*	*Comprehension*	*Application*	*Analysis*	*Synthesis*	*Evaluation*
Sub Topic 1						
The basic four food	1.1	1.4				
groups and the foods	1.2	1.5				
belonging in each	1.3	1.6				
group.	1.9	1.7				
	1.11	1.8				
		1.10				
		1.12				
Sub Topic 2						
The sources for		2.4	2.1	2.5		
nutritious foods and			2.2	2.6		
how these foods effect			2.3	2.7		
growth and			2.10	2.8		
development.				2.9		
Sub Topic 3						
The selection of					3.1	3.6
nutritious foods					3.2	3.7
necessary for planning					3.3	3.8
a well balanced menu.					3.4	3.9
					3.5	

An inspection of Table 4.5 shows how the table works. The first objective which appears (the upper left corner of the table) is objective 1.1 (the first objective of the first content outline subtopic). This objective appears under the taxonomic heading of "knowledge" so expect this objective to deal with some type of recall behavior. Likewise, objectives 1.2 and 1.3 both appear in the same grid as objective 1.1. This means that the first three objectives of the first subtopic (and thus the first three objectives of the unit) are all at the knowledge level. Objectives 1.4 and 1.5 appear at the comprehension level and they follow after the presentation and mastery of the first three instructional objectives.

After all of the objectives of the first subtopic have been written (as well as presented and mastered), the instructional objectives of the second subtopic would be presented. Notice that each subtopic in this specification chart does *not* contain objectives at all of the taxonomic levels. Rather, there is a general linearity to the specifications chart which flows from the upper left to the lower right corner of the table. This linear pattern does not occur by chance nor would it be particular to this specifications chart. Rather, it occurs because while the first subtopic would necessarily deal with basic, building-block concepts of the subject matter (and hence be confined to knowledge/comprehension objectives), the final subtopics would deal with higher order concepts (analysis, synthesis, and evaluation). To the extent that the final subtopic deals with knowledge/comprehension skills, it has failed in providing the student with necessary skills to apply and use in real-life situations.

The specifications chart can help both teacher and student understand what material is going to be covered in the instructional unit and what types of mastery level will be expected. Have you ever been tested over material which was neither covered in your textbook nor in the class lectures? How did you feel after such an event happened? Probably if such a circumstance has happened in one of your classes it occurred because the teacher/professor lost sight of what he/she planned to cover in the course. By using the table of specifications, the teacher can easily check over what has been covered and what remains to be covered, and make sure that evaluation does not occur over material not included in the table.

A specifications chart can give a blueprint for developing a unit of instruction. It will also inform you of what skills are to be taught and in what sequence. Finally, it will tell you which skills are the building blocks which must be mastered before higher order skills are attempted. As a blueprint, it will go far in making sure that what you teach is intentional rather than incidental.

SUMMARY

☐ ☐ Curriculum instruction has often been poor and the education of mentally retarded children has sometimes suffered because teachers did not have a clear-cut idea of the precise learning behaviors in which students were to be engaged. In such cases, teachers expected students to know, understand, or learn material and then were forced to make arbitrary judgments as to whether such goals had been reached.

A better way to define learning goals is through observation of students' overt behaviors. These learning goals are stated in such a way that the behaviors are observable, measurable, and finite. By stating performance in behavioral terms, the ambiguity as to whether learning goals have been reached is greatly reduced.

Instructional objectives represent an attempt to state learning goals in precise, clear-cut, unambiguous terms. Instructional objectives contain three components: performance stated in behavioral terms, the conditions under which behaviors are to occur, and the criteria for acceptable performance. All three components must be appropriately represented for a given instructional objective to be adequate.

Instructional objectives can be written at a variety of complexity and abstractive levels. A cognitive taxonomy has been designed to handle complexity of instructional objectives at cognitive/school-like tasks. This taxonomy is hierarchical in that lower levels of cognitive functioning must be achieved before instructional objectives at higher levels can be attempted. The six levels of the cognitive taxonomy are knowledge, comprehension, application, analysis, synthesis, and evaluation. It has been hypothesized that when properly constructed and sequenced, mentally retarded students can reach high levels of cognitive abstraction. This is important in order to facilitate application and generalization of school material by these students.

Instructional objectives lend themselves to the creation of both long-term and short-term objectives. Long-term objectives, sometimes called annual goals, represent objectives which predict a student's performance at a relatively distant point. Long-term goals represent an attempt to identify and remediate a child's major weaknesses. Short-term goals represent a series of learning behaviors designed to lead to achievement of the long-term goal. They are the day-to-day curriculum objectives which the teacher plans and implements.

Instructional objectives must be properly sequenced and task analyzed for learning to take place. Sequencing represents the breaking down of long-term objectives into phases or sequences while task analysis represents the breaking down of each phase into single, precise, detailed small-step learning behaviors. These small chunks are mastered and then rechained in order to achieve each sequential phase and ultimately mastery of the long-term objective.

A specifications chart is a useful tool for viewing the layout and organization of a set of instructional objectives. A specification chart is laid out by taxonomic levels and thus gives the teacher an idea as to whether a set of instructional objectives are properly sequenced in terms of cognitive complexity. Specification charts are usually constructed after instructional objectives and before the time that the objectives are implemented. Thus, they are planning rather than teaching aids.

5

Curriculum and Instructional Planning for Mentally Retarded Students: The Long-term Unit

Key Concepts

☐ Curriculum versus Instruction: Traditional versus the Modern Viewpoint
☐ Variables in Choosing Curricular Goals
☐ The Long-term Unit Approach to Instruction
☐ Components of the Long-Term Unit
☐ Topic and Subtopic of Long-term Units
☐ Instructional Objectives of a Long-term Unit
☐ Planning Activities in Long-term Units
☐ Using Curriculum Guides

What am I going to teach? How am I going to teach it? These are questions that have confronted and probably panicked every teacher. Deciding what and how to teach carries tremendous responsibilities, especially for the teacher of mentally retarded learners. Choosing what and how to teach are monumental decisions that will affect the present and future of every child in your class. The curricular choices you make for your students must be educationally and psychologically appropriate. Such responsibility, however, may serve only to increase the teacher's fear of making a mistake. After all, there is so much material which may be taught and there are so many ways to teach that material. On what basis should educational decisions such as subject matter and instructional procedures be made?

The purpose of this chapter is to provide the prospective teacher of mentally retarded students with a basis for making such educational, curricular choices. It is designed to provide the teacher with information regarding the basis of curriculum choices for mildly mentally retarded learners as well as information about what such curriculums might contain. Finally, the chapter will provide a framework for designing curriculums and instruction (the long-term instruction unit) as well as examples which may be used in planning content and instruction for mentally retarded learners.

CURRICULUM AND INSTRUCTION IN SPECIAL EDUCATION: THE NEW VIEWPOINT

□ □ You have probably heard the word curriculum used in reference to what goes on in classrooms. People speak of a social studies curriculum in elementary school and a chemistry curriculum in high school. Probably you have also heard the term special education curriculum bandied about regarding the education of exceptional children. What, however, is a curriculum? Are there components to a curriculum or is it nondivisible, a single entity? Finally, if a curriculum can be subdivided into components, how may those components be sequenced in order to optimize learning?

The definition of a curriculum often depends upon the school of thought or frame of reference of the person doing the defining. Currently, there are two basic viewpoints on curriculum, a traditional and a more recent outlook. In the traditional definition, curriculum refers to the sum total of a course of study offered in a given program. Curriculum is the overall set of experiences given to the child in school. Notice that in the traditional definition, curriculum is a nondivisible entity; it encompasses everything that goes on academically in the classroom. Thus teacher objectives, student learning outcomes, and teaching methods would not be specifically isolated and treated separately.

In the newer viewpoint of curriculum, the construct is broken down into components. In this definition, curriculum constitutes *what* is taught while instruction is *how* (teaching methods) information is transmitted to students. In such a definition, academic subject matter defined as precise instructional objectives (see chapter four) constitutes curriculum, while teaching methods, experiences for the student, and activities constitute instruction. Thus, the equation

$$Teaching = Curriculum + Instruction$$

may be constructed.

In this model, both curriculum and instruction are individualized to meet the student's needs. Such individualization meets the requirements for the education of handicapped learners as specified by PL 94-142. Even in cases where a uniform curriculum has been chosen for a group of mentally retarded students (probably an unwise and potentially illegal educational event), the teacher still possesses the responsibility and latitude to implement that curriculum (via instruction) in such a way that the individualization of those learning goals are maximized. In most cases, however, the special education teacher will possess the dual responsibility of creating individualized curricular goals as well as devising instructional procedures for reaching those goals. For these teachers, the potentially intimidating question posed at the beginning of this chapter remains: How may curricula for mentally retarded students be logically and systematically formulated?

CHOOSING CURRICULAR GOALS

☐ ☐ Consider all of the things one could teach given free choice and unlimited access to materials and funds. The curricular choices one could make in such an ideal world are almost limitless. However, we live in a real world, one that limits the choice of an educational curriculum in distinct ways. The question then becomes the identification of the factors which limit curricular choices. There are at least three such limiting factors: the characteristics of the learner, the characteristics of the teacher, and the situational (environmental) variables present in the academic (learning) environment. Each of these factors, considered separately, function to effectively narrow the range of curricular choices from the infinite to the finite. Taken together, the components work to define the curricular goals best suited for each individual student.

LEARNER CHARACTERISTICS

☐ ☐ Each child is unique. There is probably no educator or psychologist who will argue against this statement. But how do children differ? That is, what are some of the characteristics which differentiate children?

☐ Environmental Variables

Children differ in the backgrounds from which they come. They differ in a host of ways including in their culture, their language, and their belief that school is a valuable activity. Such environmental variables constitute the "baggage" which students bring into the learning situation. Teachers who do not appropriately take environmental variables into account in designing curricular goals and instructional methods are destined for problems.

☐ Cognitive/Intellectual Variables

Children differentiate themselves along cognitive and intellectual variables (Flavell 1970, 1977; Piaget 1926; Terman & Oden 1959). Binet was perhaps the first person to substantiate this fact as he assessed school children in Paris, France, in an attempt to identify intellectually subnormal children who were in need of special educational services (Binet & Simon 1916). Cognitive/intellectual variables have long formed the main basis for the definition of mental retardation (American Association of Mental Deficiency 1983). Clearly, some children learn quickly and efficiently while others struggle and labor over material to-be-learned. Cognitive/intellectual variables must be taken into account when considering curricular goals and academic activities.

☐ Developmental Characteristics

Children differ in their developmental history. According to Piaget (1926, 1952, 1968), children differ in their ability to handle abstract and symbolic concepts which appear in much of school learning. Some children are tied to the concrete here-and-now world of the five senses. Abstract and symbolic concepts are difficult, if not impossible, for these children to grasp. Other children can more easily understand the abstract and the purely symbolic; they can deal with the what might be. Such children can hypothesize and can handle purely mental constructs and ideas. Since mentally retarded students cannot handle symbolic, abstract concepts easily (Stephens & McLaughlin 1974; Vernon 1960; Woodward 1979), such concepts must either be avoided or presented in a concrete, hands-on way which allows pupils to actively manipulate their learning environment.

Children also physically develop at different rates. For example, very young children simply do not possess the requisite fine motor and eye-hand skills needed to write well. This often can cause problems for developmentally delayed children who are nevertheless expected to write neatly in school. Physical developmental variables such as these must be taken into account by special education teachers in planning curricula for mentally retarded learners.

☐ Sensory and Perceptual Variables

Not only do children differ on developmental characteristics, but they also differ in the way that they process information through their senses (Bruininks & Clark 1972; Friedes 1974). Some children process information largely through the visual modality. For other children, the optimal sense modality for processing information is aural (hearing) or kinesthetic (touch). Teachers attuned to the sensory modality preferences of their students can facilitate the processing and learning of information (Luftig, Gauthier, Freeman & Lloyd 1980).

☐ Emotional Variables

Children differ in emotional makeup, attention span, and distractibility. Many mentally retarded learners possess difficulties in these areas which further inhibit their learning (Spitz 1979; Zeaman & House 1979). It is important that the special education teacher know the emotional and attentional characteristics of the students in the class. A frustrated or angry student who has lost interest in the material or who is not paying attention is a time bomb waiting to explode. Likewise, the student who is easily distracted and who cannot tolerate potentially distracting stimuli must be treated in a way that will reduce such stimuli to an absolute minimum.

☐ **Health and Physical History**

Teachers need to know the health and physical history of their students so as not to place them in danger or to demand responses which they are not capable of making. Such knowledge on the part of the teacher can avert a negative emotional response by the student who is being asked to make an unrealistic response and allows the teacher to develop instructional activities congruent with the child's physical abilities and possible limitations.

However, a word of warning. The teacher must be careful not to view the child's physical or health situation as a handicap or disability. Children, even children with physical limitations, will often surprise teachers with what they can do if only given a chance. Try not to allow your knowledge about a student's health and physical history lead you to make presuppositions about that child's ability to participate in the learning process and learn subject matter material.

TEACHER CHARACTERISTICS

☐ ☐ Teachers bring their unique characteristics and attributes into the learning situation. These characteristics include teacher expertise and enthusiasm about the subject matter. It cannot be assumed that all teachers possess the same degree of expertise and experience in a given field. Some teachers are turned on to math and science, others become anxious whenever they have to deal with those areas. Some people are not handy or mechanically inclined. Such persons typically possess little knowledge of tools and their use, lack perceptual/spatial abilities, and do not enjoy mechanical/spatial situations. Individuals of this type probably would not possess a great deal of enthusiasm for teaching industrial education. Conversely, the author has also met (and been amazed by) people who have a distinct knack for making and fixing things. They can diagnose mechanical problems and can remediate those problems efficiently in a minimum amount of time. Such persons, if they become teachers, greatly enjoy teaching industrial educational and mechanical-type classes.

The author once met a teacher who was so interested in the Civil War that he did almost nothing but teach and discuss the Civil War with his special education students. This teacher, as dedicated as he was to mentally retarded children, did not understand that the Civil War may have been irrelevant to the lives of his students. After all, to him, the Civil War was so interesting.

There is a lesson in this story. A teacher's interest in a given subject matter, no matter how deep, cannot be the sole reason for teaching that subject. Teachers should be interested in what they teach, but should not teach the subject matter simply because they are interested in the topic.

Likewise, just because a teacher is not extremely interested and/or talented in a subject is *not* reason to exclude the subject from the curriculum of mentally retarded students. Teachers must honestly assess their interest and ability in a given academic core area. If the subject matter is relevant to the lives of their students then the teacher must generate enthusiasm for the topic as well as gain the necessary expertise in order to teach the subject matter well. What is needed is the teacher's honest appraisal of personal abilities and the realization that weaknesses in teaching interest and expertise in relevant subject matter areas need to be remediated.

SITUATIONAL VARIABLES

☐ ☐ There are two immediate, situational variables which the teacher must consider when designing curriculum and instruction: Is it possible to teach the subject matter at this point in time? Do I possess the necessary resources in order to present the curriculum effectively? The best curriculum in the world is useless if it is not feasible. Suppose that you need five microcomputers priced at $2,000 each to implement your curriculum effectively. What are the chances that your school system will allocate $10,000 for classroom materials for your students? Or suppose that you wish to teach ice hockey to your class in southern Mississippi during the month of June? What are your chances of finding an available place to play and practice? Curriculums which are not feasible in terms of resources, materials, or time must either be abandoned or modified. In either case, situational variables must necessarily contribute to the final decision of what subject matter to teach.

A CORE CURRICULUM FOR MILDLY MENTALLY RETARDED LEARNERS

☐ ☐ While it is true that the curriculum for mildly mentally retarded learners needs to be individualized to fit their specialized needs, it does not necessarily follow that teachers must invent an entirely new curriculum for students. Rather, over the years, a relatively standard curriculum has developed for mildly mentally retarded students which takes into account the skills needed by students for successful and independent adult living. Figure 5.1 contains a brief outline of these skills as they would be taught at the elementary, intermediate (junior high), and secondary (high school) levels. Figure 5.1 subdivides such a curriculum into the core academic subject components of reading, handwriting/written expression/ spelling, arithmetic, social studies/social skills, health, and career education. Secondary curricular areas not included in the core curriculum but also usually presented during the school day for mentally retarded learners include science, art/music/creativity, and physical education.

Keep in mind that the skills included in the core curricular areas (Figure 5.1) should be used as a guide. They represent skills which the consensus of

FIGURE 5.1 A Sample Core Curriculum for Mildly Mentally Retarded Learners by Three Age Levels

Reading

Elementary Level

Auditory and Visual Discrimination Skills
Reading Readiness Skills
Basic Word-Attack and Phonics Skills
Basic Sight Word Skills
Basic Sentence Comprehension Skills
Literal Comprehension
Oral Reading Skills and Reading Rate

Intermediate Level

Continued Phonics Skills
Structural Analysis Skills
Higher Level Comprehension Skills
Continued Sight Word Development
Introduction to Literature

Secondary Level

Life-Word Skills
Making Inferences
Following Written Directions
Life-Sucess Reading for Adult Living

Arithmetic

Elementary Level

Arithmetic Readiness Skills
Numerals and Numbers
Comparing and Ordering Sets
Basic Operations

Intermediate Level

Number Systems (place value, fractions, decimals)
Measurement (linear, money, time, temperature)
Basic Consumer Mathematics

Secondary

Advanced Consumer Mathematics
Making Purchases and Using Money
Arithmetic for Successful Adult Living

Spelling

Elementary Level

Sound-to-Letter Analysis
Phoneme-to-Grapheme Analysis
Spelling of Elementary Level Words

(continued)

FIGURE 5.1   (cont.)

Intermediate Level

Spelling of Intermediate Level Words
Rule Learning
Rule Generalization
Integrating Spelling in Written Composition

Secondary Level

Using Spelling in Written Composition
Dictionary Use and Reference Material

Writing Skills

Elementary Level

Pre-Writing Skills (categorizing words, describing sequences, organizing ideas
Handwriting
Writing Words
Learning Grammatical Word Forms
Learning Elementary Grammar
Writing Elementary Sentences

Intermediate Level

Intermediate Grammar
Writing Cogent Paragraphs

Secondary Level

Writing Notes from Reference Materials
Writing Outlines
Writing Reports and Advanced Compositions
Functional Writing for Successful Adult Living

Social Skills and Health

Elementary Level

Care for Oneself in the Environment
Dealing with the Environment
The Family
Self-Care
Self-Concept Development

Intermediate Level

Accepting Authority
Dealing with the Peer Group
Chemical and Alcohol Abuse
Getting Along with Others
Self-Concept Development
Beginning Health
Ethical Behavior
Expressing Feelings

(continued)

FIGURE 5.1 (cont.)

Secondary Level

Government and Law
Group Activities
Independent Work
The Work Ethic
Quality of Work
Responsible Sexual Behavior
Living Successfully in the Community

professionals in special education regard as important for successful and independent living by mildly mentally retarded learners. However, these skills are meant to be an outline, a skeleton of suggestions which the curriculum for a given mentally retarded learner may be built around. Within this outline, the instructional techniques and materials used to teach these skills need to be individualized for students. Likewise, teachers should feel free to add component skills to the list as the educational needs of individual students become apparent.

THE ROLE OF THE STUDENT'S ENVIRONMENT IN PLANNING INSTRUCTION FOR MENTALLY RETARDED LEARNERS

☐ ☐ Many people think instruction is teaching. It is the magic which teachers do which initiates and causes that wonderful process which we call learning. Instruction represents the focal point between ignorance and knowledge, the process which leads to acquisition and application of information. For the purpose of this discussion, we will define instruction as: the experiences provided the learner in an educational setting as a means of implementing a curriculum.

Notice that the key word in this definition is "provided." It has been almost universally accepted that mentally retarded individuals do not learn material incidentally (i.e., on their own), nor are they particularly proficient in focusing and organizing information (Evans & Bilsky 1979; Minsky, Spitz & Bessellieu 1985; Zeaman & House 1979). Rather, the educational experiences which will hopefully facilitate learning by mentally retarded students must be specifically structured and organized for these students. Nonretarded students may sometimes learn in spite of poorly organized instruction or insufficient academic learning experiences. They may somehow pick up the necessary experiences and organize them on their own. This, however, will not be the case for mentally retarded learners. Rather, these pupils will "sink or swim" based on the adequacy of the special education teacher's planning, organizational, and teaching skills. Simply put, there is little margin for bad teaching when it comes to the education of mentally retarded students.

What experiences should be provided to mildly mentally retarded students in order to promote learning? How might the special education teacher insure that these educational experiences will be meaningful to pupils? To appropriately answer these questions, we must briefly return to the earlier discussion of the child's environment and its relationship to learning.

☐ Two Environments and the Mentally Retarded Child

Children spend about six hours per day in school for each of approximately 180 school days. This totals to 1,080 hours a year in the classroom, certainly a great deal of time. But how much time do students spend out of school, away from the academic environment? For the 180 school days, approximately 3,240 hours are spent outside school. Additionally, however, there are approximately 185 days of the year in which the student spends no time at all in school. Multiplied by 24 hours per day, this figures to 4,440 away from school. The total time spent in school as compared to total time spent out of school figures to 1,080:7,680 or a ratio of about 1:7. It should thus become clear that what is needed to succeed in life outside the school should be the major basis for deciding the school curriculum and instructional activities which will prove meaningful to the child.

This chapter posits that to the extent that academic materials, methods, modes of instruction, and organization of content are in agreement (congruence) with the mentally retarded child's outside environment, school curriculum and instruction will be successful. Conversely, to the extent that what is done in school is at odds with the mentally retarded child's outside environment, curriculum and instruction will be unsuccessful and learning will not take place.

Perhaps an example of this necessary congruence between the child's outside environment and the school curriculum might help. A teacher of inner-city school children who had just completed a college course in behavior modification, had a child in her class who did not complete school assignments and generally was unresponsive in class. This student was not particularly disruptive; he simply was content to academically remove himself from most classroom learning situations. The teacher decided to use behavior modification with this child. She devised a program by which the child would receive teacher praise and occasional warm physical contact as a reward for making academically appropriate responses. Inappropriate behavior would be ignored. The teacher was initially pleased to see a significant increase in the child's school behavior. He was participating more and even completed some academic assignments. Here was behavior modification in action! By the second week, however, things were beginning to go awry. The child was engaging in more inappropriate behavior as a consequence of the reinforcement program. In fact, where the child was once well behaved in class (while nevertheless being an academic nonparticipant), he was now going out of his way to cause classroom disturbances. What was happening?

It took a while for the teacher to get to the bottom of the problem, but when she did, the child's behavior made perfect sense. It turned out that in this inner-city environment, school was looked upon as a useless endeavor. In fact, students who valued school and who performed well academically experienced peer group difficulties. Suddenly, this student, who had been engaging in academic behavior acceptable to his peer group, began to receive special teacher attention which, through no fault of his own, began to cause emotional and social problems in the outside environment. It was not surprising at all that he was doing everything in his power to get things back to the way they were.

This example emphasizes that curriculum and instructional activities, if they are to be successful, must be consistent with the child's outside environment; that is, they must tie in with what is important to the child's life outside of the classroom. School does not and should not take place in a vacuum. Rather, everything the child is and knows is brought to the classroom learning situation. The purpose of curriculum and instruction is to facilitate and accelerate learning. This will not occur if the school curriculum and the outside environment are working at cross purposes.

PLANNING CURRICULUM AND INSTRUCTION THROUGH THE UNIT APPROACH

□ □ Assume you decide the curriculum you consider vitally important and relevant to the future life success of your students is not being appropriately covered. Likewise, you analyze the learner, teacher, and situational variables and decide what you wish to teach is appropriate and feasible. How might you design curriculum and instruction for your mentally retarded students based upon the following pieces of empirical information

1. Mentally retarded children are highly unlikely to learn content material incidentally.
2. Mentally retarded pupils are unlikely to learn content material unless it is highly structured and organized, the material is presented repeatedly but in a variety of new and interesting ways, and the content to be presented is highly sequenced and related.
3. Mentally retarded students generally do not generalize what they learn to new situations.

You are faced with a situation in which you wish to teach, and you feel that what you have to teach is important and vital. However, you are somewhat pessimistic about your mentally retarded students' ability to appropriately learn and transfer the information. The key question then becomes: How might you optimize learning and transfer of essential to be learned material by mentally retarded pupils?

One solution to the problem may be found in adoption of the curriculum and instructional unit approach. Meyen (1981) defines the instructional units as long-term, integrated, and sequential instruction of topical subject matter content which includes all of the basic core subject areas and which optimizes probability of appropriate transfer of learning through experientially based objectives. Consider one attribute at a time and a clear picture of the uniqueness of the unit approach emerges.

1. Units are long-term. The average lesson lasts anywhere from ten to thirty minutes. Perhaps if it is an unusually involved lesson, it might even last a few hours. A long-term instructional unit lasts a series of *days*, usually from one to three school weeks. This means that your unit must be broad enough and contain enough content so that it doesn't "run out of steam" and become exhausted after a few short lessons.

2. Units are thematic. There is a central theme to the unit topic; an underlying motif determines what the unit is about. It is believed that the thematic nature of units provide mentally retarded students with the central or unifying structure needed to integrate and recall important information.

3. Units are integrated. Everything that goes on in the unit is related and integrated to the central topic. When teaching a unit, no instructional activity occurs in the classroom which is not related to that unit topic. It becomes the teacher's responsibility to intentionally point out to students how each instructional activity relates to the unit theme. It is through the redundancy (as opposed to fragmented and/or incidental learning) of the central unit theme that the probability of learning by mentally retarded students is increased.

4. Units are sequential. Material is not taught incidentally or haphazardly in the obscure hope that material will be self-organized by the student. Mentally retarded students have been shown to be notoriously poor at information organization and self-learning. In the unit approach, learning is not left to chance. Rather, it involves a sequenced process of integrated, intentional steps.

5. Units encompass the basic core areas. Language arts, mathematics, social studies, science, health, vocational skills, and art should all be based on the theme of the units.

6. Units increase transfer. Suppose you taught a student about money. After your instruction, the student could count money, make change, etc. There was, however, one slight problem. Your student could only perform these behaviors in the classroom environment where he was taught. Outside the classroom in the real world, the student was completely incapable of handling money appropriately. Such behavior would show a clear lack of transfer by this student.

Transfer of learning is crucial for the life success of mentally retarded learners. If learning cannot be transferred to new situations, it is virtually useless to the student. Through the use of instructional objectives, the long-term instructional unit approach helps insure that the transfer of learning will take place.

INTEGRATING THE CORE CURRICULUM INTO LONG-TERM UNITS

☐ ☐ The curriculum in Figure 5.1 represents the skills necessary for successful independent living in society by mentally retarded learners. At any given time in school, it can be assumed that students will be working on a variety of these skills in the given core areas, moving through a sequence of lower-to-higher skill mastery in each subject.

Such skill learning in the various core academic areas would also go on in the long-term instructional unit approach to curriculum and instruction. That is, while studying with a given thematic unit, the student would continue to learn key subject matter in each of the core and secondary academic areas. The only difference between the unit method of teaching and more traditional approaches to special education would be that each skill would be taught within the theme of the long-term unit. For example, if the theme of a unit was "Making Purchases Wisely," the core arithmetic skills of multiplication might be taught within the framework of calculating total number of installment payments times the principle and interest amount of each payment on a credit purchase. Likewise, the skill of reading comprehension might include being able to read and understand a purchase agreement or product warranty. The sample units contained in the appendix include more ways core curriculum areas would be incorporated into the theme of a long-term instructional unit.

COMPONENTS OF THE INSTRUCTIONAL UNIT

☐ ☐ A unit, like other academic material can be broken down into curricular and instructional components. Curriculum refers to what you are going to teach and includes the planning groundwork which includes the creation of instructional goals. The instructional component of a unit involves how you plan to teach the curricular materials. Instruction is described by the lesson plans and activities of the unit.

Units consist of eight basic components which are constructed in a predetermined order. These components are

1. Description of the population of students to be taught (population parameters).
2. The topic and subtopics of the unit.
3. The rationale of the unit topic and subtopics.
4. The general objectives of the topic and subtopics.

5. Prerequisite skills needed to enter the unit.
6. Instructional objectives written at various levels of cognitive complexity and taxonomic levels.
7. A specification chart of instructional objectives (table of specifications).
8. Lesson plans and activities.

Each of these components will be discussed in detail. In addition, in order to aid readers in the possible construction of long-term instructional units, a sample unit in its entirety is included in the Appendix. This unit is an actual product written by a prospective special education teacher enrolled in a curriculum methods course for teaching mentally retarded learners prior to her student teaching experience. The unit is designed for an elementary/intermediate population.

□ Population Parameters

Teachers often actually know little about their students. Students are more than just names and test scores. Each child brings to the school environment many factors which will affect how and if the child will learn. Data which help you to know your students are

1. The chronological and mental ages of your students. What is the spread or range of your students? The wider the spread, the more diverse your student population.
2. The cultural and environmental backgrounds of your students. Are you primarily dealing with inner city children? Rural children? Children from a suburban setting? Are they Anglo or minority, rich or poor? The more you know about the cultural and environmental lives of your students, the more relevant your unit will become. Of course, your students will not be homogeneous. That is, you can expect that children in your class will come from different backgrounds. Even in cases where children's backgrounds are similar, differences between individual children will exist. Nevertheless, knowing about your student's cultural heritage and environmental experiences will be useful in understanding student behavior and designing appropriate unit curriculum and instructional methods.
3. The family history of your pupils. Are you dealing with a majority of students from broken homes? Are there a large number of siblings in the families of your students? Is the student going through a time of family trauma and anxiety? Knowledge of the family backgrounds and histories of your students can be helpful in understanding students' behavior which is occurring in your classroom and how that behavior will affect the planning of your long-term instructional unit.

4. The developmental and cognitive history of your students. Would you attempt to teach calculus to a three-year-old? Wouldn't a sixteen-year-old find instruction in learning colors boring? Choosing inappropriate unit themes and materials can stem from the teacher not knowing in depth the cognitive and developmental aspects of individual students. The choice of unit topics, subtopics, and instructional material must be appropriate to the developmental level of mildly mentally retarded students for the unit to be relevant to their lives.
5. What interests your students and what is relevant in their lives.

☐ Topic

What is the topic of the unit? Answering this question may be more difficult than it first appears. In fact, to adequately answer this question we must pose another: What do we expect our mentally retarded students to do at the end of the unit which they cannot do now? The answer to such a question requires a behavioral phrase which specifically describes the unit terminal behavior. Thus, the unit topic should be stated in appropriate behavioral terms which succinctly summarize what the unit is all about.

Compare, for example, the possible unit topics:

1. bicycle safety.
2. nutrition.

with their behavioral counterparts:

3. getting around town safely on a bicycle.
4. planning a daily nutritious menu.

Statements 3 and 4 are more behavioral and more accurately sum up what the students are expected to do at the end of the unit than statements 1 and 2. Thus the latter two statements are appropriate unit topics while the former two statements are not.

☐ Unit Subtopics

As stated earlier, one of the requisites of a good unit topic is that it be broad enough to sustain curriculum and instruction for days or weeks. But this poses a problem in terms of unit organization. How should a broad topic such as "Planning a Nutritious Menu" or "Getting Around Town Safely on a Bicycle" be broken down and sequenced in order to best facilitate learning? As we have seen, such sequencing is crucial in insuring the high probability of learning of the unit material by mentally retarded students.

FIGURE 5.2   Sample Unit Topics and Component Subtopics

Topic: Using a Bicycle Safely in the Community

I. Places of interest and relevance in the community
II. Rules of the road: Using your bicycle safely
III. Getting around the community safely on your bicycle

Topic: Dressing Appropriately for the Weather

I. Types of weather we find in our community
II. Clothing we often wear and their purposes
III. Different clothing for different seasons and weather conditions
IV. Establishing a program for dressing appropriately for the weather

Topic: Applying and Interviewing for a Job

I. Types of jobs in your community
II. How to find out about job openings
III. Getting information and applying for a job
IV. The job interview

Topic: Planning and Maintaining a Nutritional Diet

I. The four basic food groups and the six basic nutrients
II. Planning and preparing a well-balanced meal
III. Planning and maintaining a nutritional diet

In organizing a unit topic, the division of the topic into related subtopics has been shown to be an extremely useful technique. Subtopics may be viewed as a hierarchical organization of related material which moves from the concrete to the abstract, from the basic building blocks of knowledge to the higher order levels of the cognitive taxonomy. By hierarchical, it is meant that students cannot succeed at higher subtopic levels until they have mastered the more basic material contained in the earlier presented subtopics.

How many subtopics should there be and how should they be written? An inspection of Figure 5.2 as well as the subtopics contained in the sample unit contained in the appendix may prove helpful. Figure 5.2 contains four topics which have been broken down into three or four component subtopics. A good rule to follow is that if your unit topic does not unfold easily into at least three subtopics, your topic is too narrow and is probably actually a subtopic of some other, larger topic (e.g., "The Knife," "The Fork," "The Spoon" subtopics may be combined into a subtopic titled "Eating Utensils"). On the other hand, if you have five or more subtopics in your unit, your unit topic is too broad (e.g., "The World Around Us").

Perhaps a good way to define unit subtopics is to begin at the two ends and work toward the middle. For example, look at the last subtopic for each of the topics defined in Figure 5.2. Notice that the last subtopic is stated exactly how the unit topic itself is stated. The logic of the unit approach dictates that the last major behavior in which the student engages should be what the unit is all about.

Thus if the goal of the unit is getting around town safely on a bicycle, then it stands to reason that the terminal behavior of the unit should be getting around town safely on that form of transportation. The unit terminates when this behavior is mastered.

Now, move to the beginning of the unit. The logic of teaching a unit is that initial content should contain the basic building blocks of knowledge which will allow students to advance to more sophisticated behaviors. For example, look at the unit topic on planning a nutritious menu. Before planning a menu, a student must know about foods, food groups, vitamins, etc. Thus, whatever you teach in the first subtopic of your unit must contain basic building block knowledge that students can use to build upon as they learn higher-order, more abstract material.

That leaves us with the intermediate subtopics. Basically, these subtopics may be viewed as bridges which span between the basic building block material and the terminal behaviors which occur at the end of the unit. Examine the second subtopic of the nutrition unit. This is an intermediate subtopic which bridges the gap between types of food and planning a menu on your own. This subtopic might cover material such as representing each of the four food groups in a meal and picking representative foods from the food groups in order to make an attractive and tasty meal.

These intermediate subtopics are very important. If these intermediate subtopics do not bridge the gap between basic knowledge and complex terminal behavior, the academic leap between material will be too great and the student will not see the connection between the material. If this happens, students will be unable to transfer or apply information. As we have seen, academic material given to mentally retarded students which cannot be transferred and applied is virtually useless.

☐ The Unit Rationale

The rationale is the reason for teaching the unit. It is a justification for the unit's existence. It is essential that every unit contain a rationale. Basically, a rationale consists of three questions which must be satisfactorily answered before future planning of the unit commences.

1. What is the topic of the unit?
2. Why is this topic important, relevant, and vital to the lives of the mentally retarded students in your class?
3. Why should your students be learning the unit material at this time in their academic careers?
4. Can the material be made interesting to students?

The second question in the rationale refers to stating why the unit topic is relevant. It is essential that you be able to defend to anyone why the topic being planned is vital and relevant to the current and future lives of your mentally

FIGURE 5.3   Sample Unit Topics

Elementary Level

Getting Around Successfully in Your Neighborhood
Using Community Helpers
Dressing Appropriately for the Weather
Being a Good Family Member

Intermediate Level

Getting Around Safely on a Bicycle
Planning and Preparing a Nutritious Menu
Taking Care of Your Personal Health Needs

Secondary Level

Getting a Driver's License
Finding and Keeping a Job
Using the Services of a Bank
Demonstrating Appropriate Sexual Behaivor

retarded students. A logical, reasoned analysis as to why the topic is vital to your students' life experience is necessary. Figure 5.3 contains a variety of unit topics which have been used for mildly mentally retarded students at elementary, intermediate, and secondary school levels.

You will also need to consider why your students should be experiencing instruction in this topic at this time. Once again, think of the unit topic of getting around the community safely on a bicycle. This is certainly a relevant topic for students. But when should it be taught? One might argue that for mentally retarded students probably the best time to teach this unit would be from about ten or eleven years up to about fifteen years. Prior to ten years of age, children are probably restricted as to where they can go with their bicycles. Conversely, at about the age of sixteen, many adolescents are eager to graduate from the bicycle to the automobile as the principal form of transportation. Thus, children are motivationally, cognitively, and developmentally ready to learn about bicycles at a certain age range. Teach it too late and the students will be bored and unmotivated; teach it too early and it will have little or no meaning for students. In teaching, like love, the right moment is everything.

Finally, you will need to ask whether you can make the topic and material interesting to students? Can you make the material come alive for your students? Is it a subject which is so important to students, so interesting to them that they would do anything to be included in the unit? For example, driver education instructors will tell you that they have very few discipline problems in their classes. Why? Because all the instructor has to do is threaten the teenager with loss of driving privileges (something very interesting and important to the student) and inappropriate classroom behavior will promptly cease. Likewise, athletic coaches also have learned that threatening to not play an athlete loafing during practices is ample motivation to get the athlete practicing hard again. The goal of your unit topic is to get the student so interested in the subject matter that they will strive to stay in the unit, not act inappropriately in order to escape the academic material.

☐ Prerequisite Skills

Prerequisite skills represent the basic, entry-level skills which students need to possess to be able to enter into your unit and be successful. Such skills might include but would not be restricted to basic reading and math, social skills (e.g., cooperation and paying attention), and physical and manual dexterity. The prerequisite skills needed for sample units may be seen in the appendix.

The basic logic of prerequisite skills is that they would be assessed in a yes-no manner. This is, children who possessed prerequisite skills would gain entry in the unit while pupils who did not would enter another unit of instruction until the prerequisite skills were attained. However, in outlining prerequisite skills, the teacher should be careful to define competencies in such a way that the maximum number of students may enter into the unit. After all, the reason that you are teaching the unit in the first place is because you are convinced that it is crucial for the future life success of your mentally retarded students. If a given prerequisite skill (e.g., a relatively sophisticated level of reading) is barring a significant portion of your students from entering the unit, it may be necessary to reduce this prerequisite skill somewhat (e.g., present more material orally or pictorially) in order to allow more students to enter the unit.

Because of students' differing learning levels, it is probable that not all learners in a class will possess the prerequisite skills needed to enter a given unit at any one time. This means that there may be two or three units going on in a class at any one time. This is perfectly acceptable and, in reality, fairly easy for the classroom teacher to manage. Students at the same learning level would be temporarily grouped and "travel" through a unit together until unit mastery was reached. Students would then enter into the next unit when they were ready to do so. Thus, the class would be divided into two or three ability groups with each group in their own unit. With a class of twelve to fifteen students and two or three units per class, student per unit size would be four to six members.

More than two or three units going on in the class at once would be unwieldy and difficult to control and plan. In such a situation, it is probable that the teacher is too restrictive in creating unit prerequisite skills and thus excluding students from unit inclusion. When this happens, the teacher should attempt to create a unit with less restrictive prerequisite skills so that the number of students allowed to enter the unit is maximized.

☐ Unit and Subtopic Objectives

The construction of the unit objectives is probably the most complex and involved section of unit creation and planning. In order to create these objectives, two vital concepts presented extensively in chapter 4 are needed: instructional objectives and writing instructional objectives at different levels using Bloom's *Taxonomy of Cognitive Objectives.*

When you identified your topic and subtopics, you created a rough curriculum for your instructional unit. However, you did not outline what you were going to teach in each subtopic, nor did you behaviorally specify your curriculum. Finally, you did not sequence any of your material or write specific curricula for all of the major core areas.

In the creation of your unit instructional objectives, you will do all of these things. First, instructional objectives will break down each subtopic into component skills in each academic core area with the final objective of each subtopic culminating in terminal subtopic behavior. Second, the given skills contained in each subtopic (e.g., money identification) will be task analyzed (see chapter 4) into component skills and will be written as separate instructional objectives to be linked together (identifying pennies, then nickels, then dimes, etc.). Finally, the instructional objectives in each subtopic will be written at the appropriate level of cognitive complexity with the building block levels (knowledge and comprehension) appearing in the first subtopic, the middle levels (application and perhaps analysis) appearing in the second subtopics, and the highest levels (synthesis and evaluation) appearing in the final, summary subtopic.

Perhaps inspection of the instructional objectives as well as the specification charts of the sample units contained in the appendix will help illuminate these three points. First, notice that in each of the subtopics, the instructional objectives take in a number of core areas (language arts, math, social studies, etc.) That is, the first subtopic does not include only reading, the second only arithmetic and so on. Since each subtopic will last a number of days, we would expect that during each day, students would receive their usual instruction in all the academic areas. We would not expect a school day to occur in which the student received only language arts or arithmetic instruction. The only difference in the unit approach is that the instruction which students receive in the various core areas is related to the unit theme. Thus, instructional objectives within any subtopic include all of the basic core areas.

Second, inspection of the unit instructional objectives contained in the sample units will reveal that many of the skills have been broken down into subskills; that is, they have been task analyzed. Some instructional objectives, particularly in the first, building block subtopic, are repetitive or circular with the only difference in some objectives being that the child is expected to learn each skill in the chain. The final objective in the chain is the relinking or rechaining of those subskills. This is particularly important in learning basic skills like money equivalences or learning the basic foods of the four food groups.

Finally, inspection of the objectives and the specification charts will show that at each subtopic, the objectives cluster around certain taxonomic levels. For both units, the first subtopic contains almost exclusively knowledge- and comprehension-related instructional objectives. These represent the factual, basic building block skills which the student must master in order to move into higher-order, more abstract behaviors. The second subtopic contains mostly application and analysis objectives, the ability to transfer in a basic way what has been learned and to break down products into their component parts. Finally, in the last subtopic we expect our students to perform some complex tasks, to create products, and to evaluate those products based on sound, objective criteria. Thus, there is a linear movement in our unit from the concrete to the abstract, from the basic to the complex. This linearity must be reflected in the unit's instructional objectives for it to be successful.

☐ Creating the Specifications Chart

After the instructional objectives have been written, it is a good idea to place them in a specifications chart. Recall from chapter 4 that the specifications chart is a grid system with the six taxonomic levels along the horizontal axis and the subtopics down the vertical axis. Each instructional objective for each subtopic is then placed in its appropriate box or grid on the chart. By placing each objective in its correct place, the unit author can quickly see whether any objectives are out of sequence in terms of their taxonomic level. Such knowledge helps insure that the unit will progress from the basic building block level to higher abstract/ symbolic levels and that it is sequenced in a logical, progressive order. An example of a specifications chart for a unit may be seen in Table 4.5 and the appendix.

☐ Writing Unit Lesson Plans

By identifying your topic and subtopics and creating instructional objectives at various taxonomic levels, you have completed the curriculum of your unit. You have identified what you are planning to teach; however, you have not yet identified how you plan to teach the curriculum. In short, the instructional phase of your unit still needs to be constructed.

The instructional component of the unit is created when the teacher makes lesson plans. Such lesson plans necessarily include the instructional objective to be mastered, activities which the teacher plans to utilize, the materials which will be needed to complete the lesson, and the evaluation procedures which the teacher will use to assess whether the instructional objective has been reached. Finally, a good lesson plan will contain the estimated duration of the lesson and the academic core area which the lesson encompasses. The appendix contains a set of lesson plans for the sample unit.

☐ Activities

Instructional activities represent the "magic" which you perform in order to get the child to reach mastery of the instructional objective. It is teaching. Before your lesson, your students could not do something. Then based on your teaching, they can now perform what was previously impossible. Thus, the appropriateness of your instructional activities is one of the key components of effective teaching.

There are some basic guidelines for constructing strong instructional activities. First, the goal of the activity is to reach mastery of the instructional objective or objectives (more than one objective may be included in a given lesson plan). Activities should not be chosen because they are cute or interesting. Rather, the overriding reason to include activities in your teaching should be based upon their relevance to the instructional objectives. Hopefully, however, your activities will be interesting as well as relevant.

Second, instructional activities need to be at an appropriate ability level of the mentally retarded students in your class. Choose activities below the students' capabilities and they will reject them as babyish. Choose activities too difficult or abstract for your students and you'll be the recipient of confusion, chaos, and misfollowed directions.

Finally, students must themselves see the relevancy of what you teach. They need to realize the applicability of the subject matter to their current life circumstances. Why do we have to learn this? is a common question asked by students. The teacher should have a strong answer ready, one designed to demonstrate relevancy and applicability, or students will quickly lose motivation to actively participate in the learning process. Motivation to learn can also be increased by allowing students input into the choice of learning activities. People participate more fully in activities and enjoy such activities more when they can have active input into what and how they are going to learn.

☐ Materials

A good teacher knows the materials needed to teach a lesson and has all these materials handy and organized before the lesson gets underway. Probably nothing can kill the effectiveness of a lesson quicker than the teacher who must stop and hunt for materials halfway through the lesson. Likewise, disaster is probably awaiting the teacher who does not attempt at least one dry run using lesson materials prior to teaching the lesson. Wise indeed is the teacher who takes the time to read manuals, instructions, and plans in order to become familiar with materials prior to teaching the lesson.

The teacher must also judge appropriateness of materials when planning lessons. How expensive are the materials? Are they appropriate for a school setting? Are they toxic or dangerous? Are they cleanable if there is an accident? A little forethought on appropriateness regarding lesson materials can avert a disaster later on.

☐ Evaluation

The teacher needs a way to assure that the criteria of an instructional objective are reached. If the objective has been mastered, the student then may move on to a new (and more complex) objective in the unit sequence. If the objective has not been reached, then it is the teacher's job to devise new instructional activities, or alternatively, to modify the set of objectives.

Evaluative procedures for lessons may be simple or complex. Usually, they are teacher-made and refer specifically to the lesson just taught. Evaluative materials may consist of, but are not limited to, creative questioning by the teacher, having students perform sample behaviors, and indicating mastery by using pencil-and-paper measures. Regardless of the evaluative procedures used, they should satisfactorily measure without ambiguity whether or not the criterion of the instructional objective has been reached. Evaluation should immediately follow lesson presentation.

USING CURRICULUM GUIDES IN DESIGNING LONG-TERM INSTRUCTIONAL UNITS

☐ ☐ Curriculum guides are programs of study devised by school system personnel for use in that system's special education program. Such guides usually present the curriculum for a given set of pupils in terms of long-term and short-term instructional objectives. Additionally, guides provide ideas for activities and materials to use in order to teach the curriculum.

Curriculum guides help the teacher create objectives and lessons for long-term instructional units. Many guides are written in unit form and the teacher need only modify them to the students in the classroom. Even when the curriculum guide is not written in unit form, the teacher may wish to modify and include individual objectives or instructional procedures contained in the guide in the long-term unit.

There are a larger variety of curriculum guides available at a variety of educational (i.e., elementary, intermediate, and secondary) levels for mildly mentally retarded learners. These guides can be easily obtained either through a university library, curriculum center or through a state or county special education material resource center. They are also often available from school systems themselves for little or no charge. Such guides have been developed by most large and midsize school districts so it should not be difficult to obtain at least one locally for the age level of mildly mentally retarded students which you are going to teach.

Minimal criteria have been developed for judging the adequacy of curriculum guides (Cegelka 1978). These include

1. The guide should specify the age-level of the student for whom it has been designed.
2. It should specify and be organized by severity of mental retardation (mild, moderate, and/or severe).
3. It should be based on sound educational and psychological theory and should identify and delineate that theory.

4. It should contain behaviorally stated instructional objectives at both the long-term and short-term levels.
5. Long-term objectives should be follwd by short-term objectives and these short-term objectives should be task organized and sequenced hierarchically.
6. Activities and material should be well described. When commercially available materials are described the cost of these materials should be included.
7. That evaluation procedures be described. Such procedures should describe evaluation of mastery of instructional objectives as well as evaluation of the learning program itself.

SUMMARY

☐ ☐ What to teach and how to teach it has always been a central question for teachers. In the past, when educators have referred to curriculum, they have meant the total sum of academic experiences which a child receives in school or the total sum of experiences received in a given academic core area. A more modern viewpoint of curriculum is: what the teacher plans to teach. It refers to content, while instruction refers to the way (methods) in which the teacher plans to get the content across to students.

There are a number of variables which influence the choice of curriculum. These include student characteristics, teacher variables, and situational variables. Student characteristics include the cultural, environmental, cognitive, and developmental history—as well as the health and emotional characteristics—of the child. Teacher variables include the teacher's skill and interest in teaching a subject matter. However, teacher expertise and/or interest or disinterest should not be a prime factor in choosing not to teach a relevant subject or for teaching an irrelevant one. Student characteristics, teacher variables, and situational variables serve to limit curriculum for mentally retarded learners from the finite to the relevant.

Curriculum for mentally retarded learners must be relevant and vital for the future life success of the learners in question. Likewise, instruction for mentally retarded learners must be systematic, intentional, and sequential. One way of insuring the adequacy of both curriculum and instruction for mentally retarded learners is through the instructional unit approach. The long-term instructional unit is thematic in scope covering two to three weeks. The thematic nature of the unit helps to insure its relevancy while the long-term nature as well as the covering of all academic core areas in terms of the thematic topic insures redundancy and helps to insure application of material. Long-term instructional units facilitate learning for mildly mentally retarded students.

Instructional units consist of a number of components. These include precise definition of the population to be taught; the division of the topic into component, hierarchical subtopics; a rationale of the topic and subtopics; defining prerequisite skills for entry into the unit; the creation of a set of instructional objectives at a variety of cognitive taxonomic levels; creation of a specification chart; and creation of lesson plans. The lesson plans represent the instructional component of the unit and outline how the curriculum is to be taught. Lesson plans necessarily contain the instructional objective to be taught, activities, materials to be used, and a method for measuring that mastery of the instructional objective has been reached.

Curriculum guides can be useful aids to teachers by giving them ideas about curriculum and instruction for mildly mentally retarded learners. Such guides may already be in long-term unit form or may contain objectives and activities which may be incorporated into thematic long-term units. In either case, a curriculum guide should not be adopted whole but should be modified to meet the needs of individual students. Criteria for judging the adequacy of curriculum guides have been created and they should be used before any particular curriculum guide is adopted for classroom use.

PART III

The Special Education Curriculum and Instructional Methods

6

Language and Communication

Key Concepts

- ☐ Referential versus Egocentric Communication
- ☐ Conventionality and Displacement in Language Usage
- ☐ Phonology and Phonemes
- ☐ Morphology and Morphemes
- ☐ Syntax and Semantics
- ☐ Receptive and Expressive Language
- ☐ Assessment Procedures in Language and Communication
- ☐ Commercially Available Language Programs
- ☐ Communication Programming for Mentally Retarded Learners
- ☐ Creating a Facilitative Environment for Communication

Almost all people learn language to a greater or lesser degree. However, the fact that language acquisition is close to universal often causes us to take language learning for granted and overlook the magic and mystery of the process. Stop for a moment and think about it. A tiny child, limited both physically and cognitively, in a short period of no more than two or three years, manages to make sense out of the babble and clatter of human sound and acquires language. This same child, with little or no formal instruction, also will learn the grammatical rules of language culture demands. And in five or six years, society will consider this small child to be a full-fledged member, a distinct human being ready to enter school and use language on the lifelong journey of future learning. Surely, this acquisition and use of language by the child in order to communicate and learn is one of the mysteries of being human.

Unfortunately, the almost universal nature of language acquisition and usage often hides the fact that for a significant minority of individuals, language learning and usage is a difficult process. For these persons, language often develops incompletely or, in extreme cases, not at all. While such severe language handicaps are fortunately relatively rare and restricted to the most severely handicapped of individuals, many mildly mentally retarded children in school may still suffer from communication deficiencies because of factors ranging from intelligence to cultural difference and lack of environmental opportunities (Luftig 1983; Polloway & Smith 1982).

The ability to use language appropriately has long been associated with what is considered intelligent behavior (Piaget 1926, 1952; Piaget & Inhelder 1969, 1973; Binet & Simon 1916). For example, Piaget (1926) has asserted that the ability to handle abstract symbolic and verbal concepts represents the highest form of human thought. Likewise, the major intelligence tests (e.g., Stanford-Binet, the Wechsler Intelligence Test for Children, the Otis-Lennon Mental Abilities Test) all contain subcomponents which to a large extent define intelligence in terms of vocabulary, language usage, and verbal reasoning. Mildly mentally retarded individuals have been found to include persons who have acquired language in much the same fashion as the normal population but at a significantly slower pace and who possess gaps or deficits in both concept (vocabulary) acquisition and effective communication (Goh & Hanson 1984; Lancy, Goldstein & Rueda 1984; Wheldall 1976). Across the entire spectrum of mental retardation, estimates regarding deficiencies in language have ranged from 55 percent (President's Committee on Mental Retardation) to 70 percent (Fristoe & Lloyd 1979; Bensberg & Sigelman 1976).

Based on these estimates of high prevalence of language difficulties in mentally retarded learners, it seems imperative that any curriculum for mentally retarded learners contain language instruction. Such instruction will necessarily be tailored to the individual needs of students and will range from vocabulary acquisition to articulation therapy and instruction in language usage. This language instruction, to be effective, will need to be ongoing, systematic, and intentional. Since the appropriate use of language is closely tied with school performance as well as future vocational success (Gray 1978; Kokaska & Brolm 1985; Lazarus 1985; Phelps & Lutz 1977; Vellutino 1979), language instruction should be a central component of the curriculum for mentally retarded learners.

This chapter contains four main areas. First, it contains a brief discussion of the components of language, that is, what constitutes language and language usage. Second, it discusses how the language of mentally retarded students is assessed by teachers and language therapists. Third, it discusses the language development program as well as materials and activities designed to facilitate language usage among students. Finally, it includes ways to create a physical and psychological classroom environment conducive to good communication and thereby enhance language acquisition and communication expertise by mentally retarded learners.

EFFECTIVE COMMUNICATION: THE PURPOSE OF LANGUAGE

□ □ The purpose of language is effective communication (Phillips, Durham, Brubaker & Butt 1970; Donahoe & Wessells 1980). Through communication a person makes wants, wishes, and ideas known and a listener responds or comments on the speaker's message. The adequate sending and receiving of communication constitutes a communication loop which forms the basis of effective communica-

FIGURE 6.1   The Communication Feedback Loop

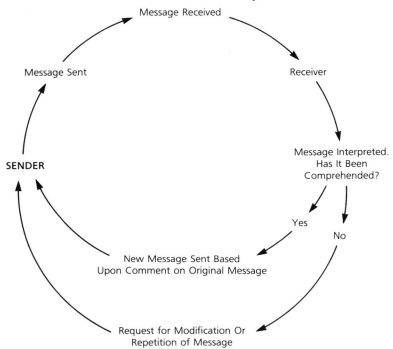

tion. Such a loop may be seen in Figure 6.1. Language users constantly switch roles from senders to receivers and back to senders again in loop fashion. Such switches occur when the receiver of the original message comments on whether it has been understood and sends back a message.

☐ **Egocentric versus Referential Communication**

What might interfere with a child's effectively using language in order to be a good encoder and decoder of communication? One such interfering variable has been shown to be whether or not the child can appropriately take another's perspective, that is, whether the child can go in another's shoes. Being able to take another's perspective, known as *referential communication*, is related to the ability to revise and adjust communication for maximum efficiency. The opposite of the ability to take another person's perspective is known as *egocentric communication* and takes place when the child cannot appropriately adjust language and modify the message in order to facilitate communication (Flavell, Botkin, Fry, Wright & Jarvis 1975; Glucksberg, Krauss & Higgins 1975; Maratsos 1973; Piaget 1926). For example, a child engaging in egocentric communication would not be able to slow down the message or modify vocabulary depending on the competency of the listener (e.g., if the listener was adult or child, normal or mentally retarded). A person communicating in an egocentric manner typically fails to realize that personal experiences are not the same as everyone else's and that different experiences yield different ways of viewing the world. Thus, a child using language egocentrically will not be either an effective message sender or receiver. (Cooper 1972).

An example of dialogue between two four-year-old children best illustrates how egocentric language patterns may interfere with effective communication (Glucksberg, Krauss & Higgins 1975). Two children participated in an experiment. Seated on opposite ends of a screen, they could not see each other nor could they see what the other child was viewing. In front of each child were a set of identical pictures. The speaker's job was to get the listener to guess the picture the speaker was viewing. Their dialogue went like this.

Speaker: It's a bird.
Listener: Is this it?
Speaker: No.

Although egocentric languge patterns begin to fade at about age four or five in nonretarded children, there is strong evidence to suggest that egocentric communication is more pervasive and lasts longer with mentally retarded children (Diaz 1984; Houssiadas & Brown 1967; Monson, Greenspan & Simeonsson 1976; Rubin & Orr 1974). It appears that the inappropriate usage of language as a communication medium caused by poor perspective taking often lasts through middle childhood for mentally retarded children. Thus intentional instruction in using language to communicate effectively is probably warranted and should become part of the curriculum for these students. Such instruction may take the forms of intentional role taking in communication by students as well as specific training in encoding and decoding techniques.

☐ Conventionality and Displacement

Two other skills which children need in order to use language effectively are *conventionality* and *displacement* (Harrell, Bowers & Bacal 1973). Conventionality refers to the fact that virtually everyone within a given culture uses the same words (symbols) to describe given concepts as well as the same word order (grammar) to express ideas. Words are nothing more than agreed-upon symbols for concepts. However, when a person begins to use highly idiosyncratic words for concepts, effective communication ceases. For example, one of the author's children decided during early language development that *aten* meant *thank you, ya-ya* was *Daddy*, and *mambu* was *cookie*. These idiosyncratic words worked fairly well with the child's family—that is the words took on conventional characteristics with the child's parents and siblings. Suffice it to say however, that the child experienced a certain amount of frustration when he tried out his new vocabulary with the uninformed babysitter! These symbols suddenly became idiosyncratic and incomprehensible.

Articulation difficulties can also interfere with the conventionality of words. That is, even though a child is using conventional words, those words may appear unconventional due to a child's problems in articulating sounds correctly. Since it is estimated that a majority of young mentally retarded children possess at least some articulation deficits (Fristoe & Lloyd 1979), the question of conventionality of a message becoming more idiosyncratic due to articulation errors difficulties becomes important.

Displacement refers to the child's ability to refer to objects not physically present or to events which have occurred in the past or which will occur in the future. The ability to handle displacement is a key component of intelligence (Piaget 1952). Young children often cannot handle past and future in their language functioning. To them, everything in the past is yesterday while all future events will be tomorrow. Likewise, these children experience difficulty in referring to concepts not immediately in their environment. The inability to displace by the time the child enters schools represents a serious language deficiency and must be addressed. It appears that such deficiencies usually are restricted to only the most language handicapped of individuals.

THE COMPONENTS OF LANGUAGE

☐ Phonemes

Appropriate oral communication begins with the production of speech sounds. Speakers must move their lips and tongues and produce sound across their vocal chords which are meaningful to the listener. The study of the speech sounds of oral language and their relationship to language and communication is known as *phonology* (de Villiers & de Villiers 1978; Clark & Clark 1977; Lenneberg 1967).

All spoken languages consist of basic sounds known as *phonemes*. It is estimated that adult humans can produce about one hundred basic sounds and that the English language contains approximately forty-five phonemes. Considering that the major languages of the world range in phoneme number from fifteen to about eighty-five, English falls about midway on the continuum of phoneme complexity.

The most basic division of phonemes in English is between vowels and consonants. Vowels are typically classified two ways: by the height of the tongue as the sound is produced and by the part of the tongue involved in forming the vowel (Clark & Clark 1977). Consonants differ along three dimensions: place of articulation in the mouth, manner of articulation, and whether the consonant is voiced or unvoiced.

Phoneme acquisition takes place gradually over a series of months or years. For developmentally delayed children such as the mentally retarded, it is expected that appropriate acquisition and usage of phonemes would take even longer. Such a hypothesis might help explain the high degree of articulation errors found in the speech of mentally retarded school children and would hold implications for the importance of phonetic (articulation) intervention for mentally retarded pupils by special education teachers.

Phoneme acquisition appears to be both systematic and invariant (occurs in the same order among children). In terms of acquisition, it appears that phonetic *stops* (*b*, *g*, and *d*) are learned first followed by *fricatives* (e.g., *f* and *s*) (Smith 1974). *Liquids* (*l* and *r*) and *glides* (*w* and *y*) emerge later in phoneme development and often are not fully in place and used appropriately even by age four or five (e.g., the common practice of the child saying *wed* for *red*). By age eight, most children can produce all of the basic phonemes of English and can use them appropriately without error. However, the development and appropriate usage of all of the speech sounds of English would be expected to be slower in mentally retarded children.

☐ Morphemes

Language sounds do not appear usually in isolation. Rather, they are combined in order to make meaningful sound strings which we interpret as words. The smallest unit of speech which contains linguistic meaning is the *morpheme* (Clark & Clark 1977; Slobin 1979). As an example of what constitutes morphemes, consider the word *dog*. The speech sounds which constitute *dog* (*d*, *o*, and *g*) contain linguistic meaning when those sounds are combined. This sound contains no linguistic meaning. It is simply a sound with no linguistic meaning of itself. Thus *dog* is a morpheme which cannot be broken down or parsed into any subcomponent morphemes. However, the word *dogs* contains two morphemes, *dog* which means mammal-canine and the suffix *s* which means more than one. The letter *s* (or *es*) when placed on the end of a word always carries the meaning of plural. Thus it is a morpheme since it contains a unit of meaningful sound.

While phoneme instruction represents articulation intervention, instruction in morphemes represents vocabulary training (Clark & Clark 1977; Phillips et al. 1970). Children learn the basic morphemes of language as well as learn that prefixes and suffixes may be added to root words thus modifying root words in systematic and consistent ways. Morphemic rule learning and vocabulary acquisition hold implications for the efficiency of language instruction for mentally retarded learners.

☐ Syntax

Syntax is the glue which holds language together. Syntax is the arrangement or order of words in an utterance which are formed into phrases and sentences. In the study of syntax, the key question that is asked is: How is the phrase structured? To answer this question, one must possess a knowledge of the rules of grammar of language. Without grammar, no systematic syntax can exist.

The conventional use of syntax and grammar is essential for communication between people to be easily understood. This is why grammar is studied in school. Since human information processing capacity is severely limited (Broadbent 1958; Broadbent & Gregory 1963, 1965; Gray & Wedderburn 1960), attention which must be devoted to deciphering the syntax of grammatically incorrect utterances takes away from processing capacity which a listener could more efficiently spend attaching meaning to a message. Thus, conventionality of syntax and grammar is important in the curriculum of students.

☐ Semantics

Probably the most important level of language is that of *semantics* which refers to the meaning or content of an utterance. The key question regarding semantics is: What is the meaning of a particular message?

The meaning of an utterance is referred to as the deep structure as opposed to surface (syntactic) structure (Chomsky 1957, 1965, 1975; Lakeoff 1971; Sachs 1967). Often the deep structure of utterances is ambiguous even though the surface structure is relatively straightforward. For example, consider the sentence

"Did you see the nudist play?"

While the surface structure of the sentence is relatively straightforward, the deep structure can be interpreted on two quite different (but interesting) levels. The key to effective communication is to insure that the semantic meaning of the message is straightforward and unambiguous.

RECEPTIVE AND EXPRESSIVE LANGUAGE

☐ ☐ Communication requires both a sender and a receiver. These two requirements are reflected in two different types of language: *receptive* and *expressive*. Receptive language is the understanding of a message. It entails two processes: the reception of stimuli through the sense organs and the ability of the person to gain understanding from sensory experience (Smith 1974). Expressive language entails the effective translation of ideas into vocal or motor expression. It is the sending of a message.

Of the two types of language, receptive language is developed first. Examples of receptive language include following directions (both single and complex directions) as well as indicating comprehension of spoken messages. Expressive language is reflected in the child's adequate verbal expression of wants and needs. Both types of language are crucial to the life success of children and should thus become part of the curriculum for mentally retarded learners.

CULTURAL DIFFERENCES VERSUS LANGUAGE DEFICIENCIES

☐ ☐ In the past, some children have been considered to possess a language deficit primarily because they use different vocabulary or use different language patterns than children of the dominant culture. Since in the United States, the dominant culture is middle class white (Anglo), children who are not members of this cultural group may be considered to possess a language "problem."

There is strong evidence to suggest that culturally different children in the United States not only may use different or modified vocabulary than their Anglo counterparts but also may differ in syntax, semantics, and voice intonation (Kachuck 1978; Mims & Camden 1984; Wood 1976). However, what is defined as a language deficit may only occur when the child is forced to communicate with individuals of the dominant culture (Shriner 1971).

Some educators argue that the language of some culturally different groups are deficient when it comes to learning basic concepts (Becker, Englemann & Thomas 1971; Osborn 1968; Berieter & Englemann 1966). They argue that since culturally different children will spend most of their adult lives interacting with persons of the dominant culture, they should learn how to effectively communicate within that culture. Other professionals argue that while culturally different children may differ from dominant children in vocabulary and syntax, the language of culturally different children is not inferior in handling life's basic concepts (Committee on the Status of Racial Minorities 1983; Di Vesta 1974; Hart & Risley 1974; Mims & Camden 1984). These professionals assert that it is improper for the majority culture to demand that their language standards be adopted by minority cultural groups.

There is evidence to suggest that most culturally different children possess the ability to switch back and forth from the minority to the dominant language as the social and linguistic situation demands (Mims & Camden 1984; Woods 1976). For example, the author once met a four-year-old girl from Iceland who could quickly and effortlessly switch back and forth almost in mid-sentence from English to Icelandic depending upon whether she was speaking to her family or her American friends. This child demonstrated great bilingual expertise and obviously was not language deficient.

Teachers of mentally retarded/culturally different children would do well to help such students switch from one code to another as situations warrant. This would include instruction in specific social and linguistic situations and which manner of language might be the best way of making a response. Such instruction would include but would not be limited to role playing different situations as well as making forays into the real world outside the classroom to investigate the most optimal ways to handle language situations which arise in the child's environment. In this type of learning environment, the child would receive instruction in using the language pattern which the receiver of the message would understand the best.

Only in those situations where speech and language differs significantly from the norms of the child's own culture would that child's communication skills be considered deficient. Only if the child's language and communication is lagging significantly behind cultural peers should language remediation and/or therapy be considered. Thus, the focus of comparison should be switched from an inspection of the child's minority language in relation to the dominant culture to the child's language in relation to other children in the child's own cultural group.

THE ROLE OF THE SPEECH AND LANGUAGE THERAPIST IN LANGUAGE ASSESSMENT AND INTERVENTION

□ □ The special education teacher is not alone in trying to remediate the language and communication deficiencies of mentally retarded children. Rather, at the teacher's disposal are the expertise, resources, and assessment capabilities of the speech and language therapist. This individual has been specifically trained in assessment of speech, language, and communication difficulties, as well as in the areas of articulation training, speech therapy, and the designing of communication programming of children. Usually, the speech and language therapist is an itinerant person traveling from school to school and classroom to classroom working either with small groups of children or with individual pupils. The therapist conducts formal language and communication assessments and makes programmatic suggestions to teachers regarding classroom remediational activities and materials designed to enhance children's speech and language functioning.

Children usually come to the attention of the speech and language therapist through referral by the classroom teacher. In the referral process, the teacher can be most helpful by keeping a log designed to answer the following questions (Hallahan & Kauffman 1982):

1. How much and how often does the child speak? Does the student appear to be comfortable talking one-on-one? In small groups? In front of larger groups?
2. How do other children react to the child's speech? Is the individual ignored, ridiculed, or mimicked?
3. How well does the child listen to others? Is the child a good receiver of information? Does information often have to be repeated or modified to the child?
4. Does the child modify a message to others as communication situations demand?

5. How intelligible is the child's speech? Does it contain more articulation errors than other children the child's age? How serious are the articulation errors? Does it make the child's message relatively unintelligible?

6. How rapidly does the child speak? Is the child dysfluent? Are there repetitions, hesitations, or problems of rhythm?

7. How does the child modulate voice? How is the pitch and loudness of the child's voice?

8. How well does the child express thoughts? Is the child's vocabulary adequate to make wants and wishes known? Does the child use proper syntax and grammar? Does the child's message make sense?

THE ASSESSMENT OF LANGUAGE

☐ ☐ The need for language mastery and the fact that mentally retarded children often possess language acquisition deficits, make language assessment particularly important (Howell & Kaplan 1980; Serapiglia 1980; Stephens, Hartman & Lucas 1982). Information regarding the degree of communication expertise of mentally retarded children is necessary in order to determine where gaps exist (diagnosis), and the extent instructional intervention is required in order to remediate these deficiencies (prescription).

Assessment of a child's language should occur in all four components of language, beginning with acquisition of basic phonemes. To evaluate articulation, the teacher assesses phonetic ability in the child's everyday speech (Howell & Kaplan 1980). There are a number of commercially available, standardized assessment instruments which may be used to measure the child's ability to make the basic speech sounds. Table 6.1 contains a partial list and a short description of their major attributes and uses.

☐ Assessment of Articulation

The speech and language therapist often conducts articulation assessment after referral by the classroom teacher. However, if a speech and language professional is not readily available or cannot fit the child into the schedule, articulation therapy may be carried out by the teacher. As Table 6.1 indicates, there are a number of standardized, commercial articulation tests available which includes the Goldman-Fristoe Test of Articulation (Goldman & Fristoe 1972) and the Auditory Discrimination Test (Wepman 1975). Both of these tests measure the child's ability to hear and adequately reproduce basic phonemes at different positions of words.

Especially in cases where commercial articulation assessment instruments are not available, the teacher or speech therapist may choose to conduct an

TABLE 6.1 Listing of Commonly Used, Commercially Available Language Assessment Tests

Area	Name	Reference	Level
Articulation	Auditory Discrimination Test	Norm-Referenced	Ages 5–8
	Goldman-Fristoe Test of Articulation	Norm-Referenced	Age 6–Adult
	Goldman-Fristoe-Woodcock Auditory Skills Battery	Norm-Referenced	Ages 3–Adult
	Templin-Darley Tests of Articulation	Norm-Referenced	Ages 3–8
Morphology and Syntax	Carrow Elicited Language Inventory	Norm-Referenced	Ages 3–8
	Developmental Sentence Analysis	Norm-Referenced	Ages 2–7
	Northwestern Syntax Screening Test	Norm-Referenced	Ages 3–7.4
	Test of Auditory Comprehension of Language	Norm-Referenced	Ages 3–7
Semantics and Meaning	Ammons Full-Range Picture Vocabulary Test	Norm-Referenced	Ages 2–Adult
	Boehm Test of Basic Concepts	Norm-Referenced	Grades K–2
	Peabody Picture Vocabulary Test	Norm-Referenced	Ages 2.5–Adult

informal articulation assessment. One method is to have the child recite a list of words. The child is shown pictures of words which are within the vocabulary and life experiences of young children. These words would contain a large sample, if not all, of the forty-five English phonemes as they appear in various positions in words (Goldman & Fristoe 1972). As the child recites the words, the teacher or speech therapist notes the phonemes which are misarticulated along with the positions in the words which the phonemes are missed. Such information is then used to create an articulation profile for the child and aids in designing articulation intervention.

Another method of informally assessing articulation difficulties is to tape record a running sample of the child's speech. Since the errors that a child makes in natural speech may be different and more plentiful than those made when the child is slowly reciting words from pictures, samples of spontaneous speech may be a more valid method for assessing articulation difficulties (McLean 1976). However, it should be pointed out that in cases where articulation errors are severe or especially numerous, it may prove difficult or impossible to determine just what sounds are being made by the child in spontaneous speech as the teacher attempts to review the tape recording of the child's speech at a later date.

For these children, the word recitation method may prove to be more reliable for accurately diagnosing and assessing phoneme production difficulties.

Regardless of whether articulation assessment is formal or informal, certain procedures are suggested to safeguard the validity of the assessment (Johnson et al. 1967). These procedures include

1. Obtaining a carefully controlled sample of the child's spontaneous (running) speech rather than using the word recitation method alone (if the child's speech is at least understandable).
2. Using a checklist or some other data recording instrument which will keep accurate track of the child's articulation errors.
3. Checking the validity of the assessment results by obtaining information about the child's articulation from other sources including anecdotal records, parents, other professionals, and language samples gathered from a number of naturalistic environments.
4. Determining whether the child makes the same errors in spontaneous speech as in tests of isolated words and sounds.

□ Assessment of Morphology and Syntax

Assessment procedures in the area of morphology include the study of vocabulary as well as that of grammatical markers used in language to specify concepts such as plural, verb tense, or a shift from adjective to adverb (Klein 1981; Myers & Hammil 1976). Likewise, assessment of syntax surveys the child's ability to organize morphemes into phrases using grammatical rules (Lamberts 1979). Just as assessment in morphology gauges how well the child can combine phonemes to make words, the essence of syntactical assessment lies in the child's ability to produce conventional combinations of words in different language situations in order to produce grammatically acceptable utterances (Crystal, Fletcher & Garman 1976).

Many of the commercially available tests on the market measure both morphology and syntax. Table 6.1 gives a short list of these tests. Such tests may be receptive or expressive in nature and generally test the child's ability to create morphemes and then combine these morphemes into simple and conventionally grammatical messages (Lamberts 1979).

A child's understanding of morphology and syntax may be measured in a number of ways. For example, Berko (1958, 1961) has developed a technique for testing a child's understanding of morphology which is useful with both mentally retarded and nonretarded children. The child is shown figures with fictitious names attached (e.g., zug). After learning the names of the items, the child is given a test which assesses understanding of twenty-seven common morphemes including plurals, tense, and possessions. Likewise, Carrow (1973) has developed a procedure in which the child has only to point (rather than verbalize as in the

Berko technique) to examples of morphemes and grammatical constructions. Since Carrow's procedure is receptive in nature, it may be used to assess the language functioning of nonspeaking children or children who are experiencing severe articulation difficulties. This procedure is useful for both mildly and more moderately mentally retarded individuals (Lamberts 1979).

Two other useful methods for testing morphology and syntax usage with mentally retarded students are the object-manipulation approach (Bellugi-Klima 1968) and the sentence-imitation procedure (Anastasiow & Hanes 1974; Menyuk 1963, 1964). In the object-manipulation approach, the child is given two dolls and is asked to play-act certain grammatical constructions (e.g., the boy is washing the girl; the boy is washed by the girl). The child's knowledge of vocabulary and syntax is inferred by the ability to carry out via the objects the sentences provided by the tester. Of course, this technique would not be appropriate for children who possess motoric disabilities severe enough to impede successful manipulation of the objects. In the sentence-imitation method, the child is asked to reproduce sentences which contain grammatical forms normally found in language. The key criterion of the test is whether the child reproduces the sentence using requested syntactical forms. For example, given the sentences

Stephen is here.
Robert is there.

and the required form of *conjunction*, the child should imitate the sentence as

Stephen is here and Robert is there.

Sentences imitated in this method of assessment would range in syntactical complexity from simple to expanded to complex.

□ Semantics

Tests of semantics assess the child's ability to use vocabulary in an appropriate and efficient manner for the purpose of communicating messages (Lamberts 1979). Tests of semantics assess the child's ability to use words in sentences and ideas rather than in isolation (Howell & Kaplan 1980; Serapiglia 1980).

One method used to assess the child's ability to use the semantic basis of language is to test the child's receptive comprehension of sentences and passages (Englemann 1967). In this procedure, the child is read a prose passage and is then asked a series of comprehension questions using a multiple choice picture format. A child who can correctly answer these literal and inferential comprehension questions is assumed to possess adequate semantic language skills. However, such a procedure possesses a strong memory component, and if the child does not do well on the procedure, one cannot be sure if failure was caused by semantic or memory deficiencies. In assessment terms, this testing procedure confounds memory with semantic abilities.

Another method of assessing semantic language abilities is that of paraphrasing. This procedure involves giving the child passages, usually in written form, and having the child restate the message in the individual's own words. Paraphrasing constitutes a form of expressive semantics and requires that the child possess expressive language skills in order to interpret the central theme or message of the passage and then convert that message into parallel terms.

Regardless of the method of semantic assessment used, assessment of the child's discourse vocabulary as well as ability to use language in order to effectively communicate should test certain basic skills (Serapiglia 1980). A listing of these skills can be found in Figure 6.2. It should be pointed out that the skills listed in these tables are not hierarchical; that is, they do not necessarily need to be mastered in a predetermined order. However, it is assumed that most if not all of these skills will need to be mastered if the child possesses appropriate semantic skills.

FIGURE 6.2 Semantic Skills Needed by Children

1. Body Parts
2. Clothing
3. Classroom Objects and Environment
4. Family Members
5. Household Objects
6. Outdoor Objects
7. Animals, Pets, and Insects
8. Food and Drink
9. Occupations
10. Colors
11. Community
12. Grooming and Hygiene
13. Vehicles and Transportation
14. Money
15. Gender-related Words
16. School
17. Toys and Playthings
18. Time: Calendar
19. Holidays and Celebrations
20. Spatial Concepts
21. Numbers and Quantitative Concepts
22. Shapes
23. Tools
24. Music and Sounds
25. Opposites and Categories
26. Sensory Verbs
27. Idioms and Figures of Speech

LANGUAGE INSTRUCTIONAL PROGRAMS

□ □ A variety of commercially available language programs are appropriate for use with mildly mentally retarded students. These programs are designed both as a daily instructional program and for remediation of specific language deficits in one or more of the language component areas. These programs usually take the form of kits and contain all of the materials needed to implement a language program including instructional materials and activities. Figure 6.3 contains a brief listing of the commonly used kits as well as the target population for whom they have been designed. Some of the more popular programs include:

Peabody Picture Vocabulary Kits (PPVK) (Dunn, Horton & Smith—Revised 1982). This is one of the most popular programs on the market. The PPVK is a multi-level language stimulation kit designed for preschool through upper elementary years. There are a number of different levels of the kits designed for chronological and mental ages. The kits stimulate receptive and expressive language as well as enhance school-like vocabulary and speech. The kits contain stimulus pictures of environmental objects and situations, hands-on materials, records, tapes, puppets, reinforcement chips, and many manipulative materials. The kits are used primarily in small group instruction. The PPVK appears to be a highly motivating program for younger mildly mentally retarded pupils and is popular with both students and teachers.

Direct Instruction for Teaching Arithmetic and Reading (DISTAR) (Engelmann & Osborn 1972, 1976). Originally designed to remediate language deficiencies of culturally different children, DISTAR kits are highly sequenced, structured, and organized programs. There are three kits in the DISTAR series. DISTAR I stresses language used in the elementary classroom environment while DISTAR II stresses language analysis skills. DISTAR III is concerned primarily with sentence form and the language skills needed for higher level school work. Some critics complain the kits are so structured they are unspontaneous and unmotivating. The kits rely heavily on drill and a teacher-questioning format which may prove uninteresting to some students. Skills in the DISTAR programs are sequenced and outlined in detailed step-by-step fashion. Activities include seat-work to reinforce presented skills. Positive reinforcement and immediate feedback are important parts of the program.

Developing Understanding of Self and Others (DUSO) (Dinkmeyer 1972). Appropriate for grades K–4, the DUSO program is designed to increase both language skills and social interaction. It is predicated on the assumption that language is a social process and thus language training should be accomplished with the purpose of facilitating social interaction between people. The key aim to the DUSO program is to

FIGURE 6.3 Commonly Used, Commercially Available Language and Communication Kits Suitable for Use with Mildly Mentally Retarded Students

Name	(Author of Kit)	Target Population
Developmental Language Lessons Levels 1 and 2	(Mowery and Replogle, 1977, 1980)	Language delayed; other handicapped
Developmental Syntax Program Revised Edition	(Coughran and Liles, 1979)	Ages 3-10 who need syntactic remediation
DISTAR I, II, III	(Engleman and Osborn, 1970, 1973, 1975)	Preschool up
Fokes Sentence Builder Kit	(Fokes, 1975)	Learning disabled, deaf, hard of hearing, borderline to mild mentally retarded
Fokes Sentence Builder Expansion		Same
GOAL: Language Development—Games Oriented Activities for Learning	(Karnes, 1976a)	Normal to moderately handicapped
Karnes Early Language Activities	(Karnes, 1976a)	All mentally handicapped
Language Rehabilitation Program Levels 1 and 2	(Hain and Lainer, 1980)	Aphasic; mentally retarded; hard of hearing
Monterey Language Program	(Programmed Conditioning for Language) (Gray and Ryan, 1972)	All children needing help on language
MWM Program for Developing Language Abilities	(Minskoff, Wiseman, and Minskoff, 1972)	Ages 3 to 11 with evidence of language deficits
Peabody Language Development Kits	(L.M. Dunn, J.O. Smith, & L. Dunn, 1981; L. M. Dunn, L. Dunn, and J. O. Smith, 1981; L. M. Dunn, Horton, & J. O. Smith, 1981; L. M. Dunn, J. O. Smith, & D. Smith, 1982)	All children
Project MEMPHIS	(Quick, Little, and Campbell, 1973)	Mild to severely handicapped
SYNPRO (Syntax Programmer)	(Peterson, Brener, and Williams, 1974)	All ages with mild problems
Visually Cued Language Cards	(Foster, Giddan, and Stark, 1975)	Normal to profoundly retarded
Wilson Initial Syntax Program	(Wilson, 1973)	Those with syntax problems, especially TMR

Adapted from D.D. Hammill & N.R. Bartel (1982).

increase the child's receptive and expressive skills and to improve referential communication within the feedback loop.

DUSO consists of two separate kits which contain activities and lessons designed to increase language usage sophistication. An important component of the kits is the teacher's ability to lead flexible, group discussions so the teacher should analyze personal skills in this area before DUSO is presented to students. Each kit provides all of the lessons and materials needed for an academic year.

Games Oriented Activities for Learning (GOAL) (Karnes 1972) This program is based on the skills outlined in the Illinois Test of Psycholinguistic Abilities (ITPA). It uses a games format which appears to be quite motivating for young learners (mental age 3–5 years). GOAL creates and specifies mastery levels for a series of objectives before new activities are attempted.

GOAL contains 337 sequential lessons with activities designed to teach each skill. Materials in the program include picture cards, situation pictures, picture puzzles, games, and templates. Checklists of guidelines facilitate ongoing (formative) language assessment.

Fokes Sentence Builder (Fokes 1976) This is actually two kits: the basic kit and an expansion kit for somewhat older students who have mastered the objectives and activities of the basic kit. The kits are designed for mildly handicapped students which include the mildly mentally retarded. The kits teaches syntactic and grammatical rules through a structured but non-rote, non-drill approach. The kits appear to be motivating and stimulating for the populations for whom they are intended.

The MWM Program for Developing Language Abilities (Minskoff, Wiseman & Minskoff 1972) This program is also based on the skills outlined in the ITPA. It includes an inventory of learning abilities, comprehensive language screening device, six manuals, and five workbooks. The activities tend to be highly structured and drill oriented but sequenced at different levels of students thus leading to individualization. MWM may be used either as a daily language facilitation program or as a means of remediating specific language deficits.

UTILIZING LONG-TERM INSTRUCTIONAL UNITS IN LANGUAGE INSTRUCTION

☐ ☐ In the language and communication curriculum, the long-term instructional unit approach is particularly useful for including thematically related speech and language topics. In this approach, the language and communication activities relate directly to the theme of the long-term unit. (See Figure 6.4) Vocabulary ties in to the unit topic as well as speech and language activities directly relate to what the

FIGURE 6.4 Language and Communication Activities for Older Mildly Mentally Retarded Students Taken from Unit Lesson Plans

Knowledge/Comprehension

4 Lesson Learning and recognizing sounds made by the phone Core Area Language Arts Time 15-20 minutes

Objectives	Activities	Materials	Evaluation	Notes

When asked by the teacher the students, as a group, will be able to recall three different sounds a telephone makes, with 100% accuracy. (Knowledge)
 	
When listening to a tape recording of a telephone ringing, a busy signal, and a dial tone, the students, as a group, will be able to identify all 3 sounds, with 100% accuracy.
	1. Initiate class discussion about different sounds a telephone makes when you make a call.
	  a) dial tone
	  b) ringing
	  c) busy signal
	
	2. Teacher gives different situations when you hear one of these sounds.
	
	Students take turns answering.
	
	Example: when you first pick up the phone, before you dial, what sound do you hear?
	
	3. Play tape recording and have students identify the three sounds.
		Tape Recorder & Tape Recording of dial tone ringing busy signal	Although these tasks are relatively simple, I will evaluate these tasks very carefully. I will make sure that each student understands by asking individual questions.	

Comprehension

5 Lesson _____ Core Area Language Arts Time 25 minutes

When the teacher asks where to locate a telephone number of an individual or business in the telephone book, the students will correctly choose either the white pages or the yellow pages, with 100% accuracy.	1. Initiate class discussion about the telephone book, talk about both white pages and yellow pages. 2. Give each student a copy of the Middletown telephone book to examine. (approx. 5 minutes)	Middletown telephone book	I will evaluate this by grading each student's worksheet individually. If students complete 90% of the multiple choice questions correctly, the activity will be considered mastered. This summative evaluation will be recorded in grade book.	For those students scoring less than 90%, an additional worksheet will be given to the student. The extra practice may help obtain mastery.

FIGURE 6.4   (cont.)

Comprehension

Objectives	Activities	Materials	Evaluation	Notes
	3. Ask students if they can tell me difference between white pages & yellow pages.			
	4. Give students a multiple choice ditto with names of individuals and businesses and have them choose the correct place to look in the telephone book.	Teacher made worksheet		

Core Area: <u>Social Studies</u> Time: <u>done throughout unit so every child can interview</u>

| F—Given the assignment develop a school lunch menu, the student will interview 4 students outside classroom to determine what foods other students like to eat for lunch, to satisfaction of the teacher | 1. During a student's free time he is allowed to enter a nearby class to interview students about school lunch.

2. The students will develop 3 questions to ask the other students and have them written on paper.

3. Using the tape recorder he will interview 4 students with his 3 questions.

4. Afterwards, he will listen to the tape recording and write his results to be added to the other students. | Paper
Pencil
Tape recorder w/tape
Microphone | Teacher sees the students suggestions written on his interview sheet. | |

Core Area: <u>Science/Health</u> Time: <u>30-45 minutes</u>

| IG—Given other students' ideas the student will develop a school lunch menu for one week which would fulfill the needed requirements and students' choices 100% | 1. Teacher will read the suggestions made by other students.

2. During class discussion lead by the teacher, as a group they will develop the weekly menu.

3. The teacher will write it on a master sheet to be returned to the kitchen staff. | Master menu
Student responses | Menu fulfills daily nutritional requirements and student's choices | |

students do in the unit. It is suggested that the teacher of mildly mentally retarded students, particularly older students, consider relating language curriculum and activities to the long-term unit.

ACTIVITIES AND PROGRAMMING IDEAS FOR THE LANGUAGE CURRICULUM

□ □ Table 6.2 lists books and guides which contain a large and varied source of activities designed to enhance the language functioning of mildly mentally retarded students. Additionally, this chapter examines some proven, interesting, and motivating language activities for such students.

□ Elementary Age Learners

Word Lotto
Use picture cards made from tagboard. Children have game cards like bingo cards that contain pictures similar to the pictures which the teacher possesses. As the picture cards are presented by the teacher, the child identifies the picture name and places it on his game card if the picture is represented on the card.

This is an activity useful in phonology and morphology. But what pictures should be used? This would depend on the curriculum being studied by the class. The class, for example, might be studying a unit on animals. In that case, the lotto pictures would consist of animals. Likewise, if the unit of study was transportation, modes of transportation would be depicted on the lotto cards. In short, the curriculum would determine the subject matter of the pictures and game cards.

Finish the Story
Show students large, interesting action pictures with ambiguous or inconclusive endings. Have each child in the class orally provide a plausible ending to the picture story. Students should be encouraged to use complete sentences as well as appropriate syntax and vocabulary.

Weatherperson
Children take turns acting as class weatherperson and report to the class the day's weather conditions as well as the implications of the day's weather on dress needs as well as class activities such as gym, recess, or field trips.

Shopping for Prizes
Set up a small store in the class where students may purchase items with points earned for appropriate language usage in class. Items which may be purchased include penny candy, magazines, or small cosmetics. Children exchanging points

TABLE 6.2   Sources of Books, Ideas, and Materials for Language and Communication Instruction for Mildly Mentally Retarded Learners

Title	Publisher	Level
Alike and Not Alike	Mafex	Primary
Art Experiences for Young Children (Pile)	Teacher's Publishing	Primary
Auditory Closure Cards	Mafex	Primary
Bank Street College Inter-Act Materials	Constructive Playthings	Primary
Basic Materials Resource Kit	Teaching Resources	Primary
Bowmar Artworlds Develops Verbal and Visual Fluency (Mandlin)	Bowmar	Primary-Secondary
Bowmar Language Stimulus Program (Allinson, Allinson, and McInnes)	Bowmar	Primary
Classification Play Tray Card Sets	Interstate	Primary
Colors Everywhere	Special Learning	Primary
Community Worker Puppets (Set of 4 puppets) Available in white or black.	J. L. Hammett	Primary
Developmental Skills for Early Childhood	T. S. Denison	Primary
Developmental Syntax Program (Coughman and Liles)	Learning Concepts	Primary-Intermediate
Early Childhood Series (Curry, Jaynes, Crume, and Radlauer)	Bowmar	Primary
Early Language Activities (Karnes)	Childcraft	Primary
Emerging Language 2 (Halton, Gomen, and Lent)	Communication Skill Builders	Primary
Everyday Language Skill Charts Twenty colorful charts display essential oral and written language skills.	Beckley Cardy	Primary
Flannel Board Aids Opposites Story Kits Build a Story	Milton Bradley	Primary-Intermediate
Fokes Sentence Builder (Fokes) Comprehensive oral-language program.	Teaching Resources	Primary-Secondary
Goal: Level 1 Language Development	Milton Bradley	Primary

(continued)

TABLE 6.2 (continued)

Title	Publisher	Level
Goal: Level 2 Language Development	Milton Bradley	Primary-Intermediate
Handwriting Programs (Prices Variable)	Zaner-Blosner	Intermediate-Secondary
Ideal Rhyming Puzzles	Ideal School Supply	Primary-Intermediate
Informal Dramatics: A Language Arts Activity for the Special Pupil	Stanwix	
Instructo Activity Kits (Summer, Spring, Winter, Fall) Sequence opposites: beginning sounds, farm animals, zoo community helpers, creating stories.	Beckley Cardy	Primary
Instructo Flannel Board Aides: safety, family, party. Halloween: original story set.	Beckley Cardy	Primary
Instructo Language Arts	Beckley Cardy	Primary
Language Association Boards Prepositions Verbs Adjectives	Modern Education Corp.	Primary-Intermediate
Language Big Box	DLM	Primary
Language Building Cards (Flowers) Matching and Serial Speech	Interstate	Primary
Language Development: "See How You Feel Card Set" "Prepositions" "Spatial Relationship Concept Cards" "Why Because Card Set" "Opposites Concept Cards" "Action Cards"	Lakeshore	Primary-Secondary
Language Development Phonics Transparencies	Noble and Noble	Primary-Secondary
Language Structure Simplified (Millstein) Sentence formulation and syntax development	Educational Activities	Primary-Secondary
Language Through Play Acting (Betty Mintz)	Mafex	Primary
On Stage: Wally, Bertha, and You Multimedia Kit focusing on self-confidence, personal awareness, and oral expression.	Encyclopedia Britannica	Primary

(continued)

TABLE 6.2 (continued)

Title	Publisher	Level
Parts of Speech (Brown) (Language development cards.)	Teaching Resources	Primary-Secondary
Peabody Language Development Kits	American Guidance	Primary-Intermediate
Level P (3-5)		
Level 1 (4½-6½)		
Level 2 (6-8)		
Level 3 (M.A. 7½-9½)		
(Self-contained kit designed to stimulate oral language—materials, plus lesson plans.)		
People, Places, and Things	Teaching Resources	Primary
Phonetic Drill Cards	Milton Bradley	Intermediate-Secondary
Scenes Around Us Story Posters	Milton Bradley	Primary-Intermediate
SEARCH: Structured Environmental Activities for the Rehabilitation of the Communicatively Handicapped. (Wilmot, Bober, A'skew)	Learning Concepts	Primary
See Quee Sequence Boards	Judy Co.	Primary-Intermediate
four piece		
six piece		
twelve piece		
Sequence Pictures for Storytelling (Parker)	Whitehaven	Primary-Intermediate
Shape and Size Perception Materials (Prices Variable)	Constructive Playthings	Primary
Size Sequencing Cards	DLM	Primary-Intermediate
Sound Out: Listening Skills Program	Mafex	Primry
Storytelling with the Flannel Board	Constructive Playthings	Primary
TAD Kit: Toward Affective Development. Program of lessons, activities, and materials designed to stimulate psychological and affective development.	AGS	Primary
Talking with Mike	Special Learning	Primary-Secondary
Designed to help the child who speaks one of the nonstandard American dialects acquire the standard American English dialect.		
The Learning Well (Inseland Edson)	Educational Activities	Primary

(continued)

TABLE 6.2 (continued)

Title	Publisher	Level
The MWM Program for Developing Language Abilities (Minskoff, Wiseman, and Minskoff)	Childcraft	Primary-Secondary
Think, Tell, and See	Mafex	Primary
Touch and Tell Identifying and Describing Textures.	Ideal School Supply	Primary
Traffic Signs (set of four)	J. L. Hammett	Primary
TRY: Experiences for Young children	Noble and Noble	Primary
Verb Puzzles	DLM	Primary-Intermediate
Vinel Family Hand Puppets Set of five puppets—white or black.	J. L. Hammett	Primary
Visual Motor Teaching Materials Kit Complete kit including puzzles, geometric forms, size shapes (games—not available). Various visual motor kits are available, each includes some of the above materials.	Teaching Resources	Primary-Secondary

From: R.J. VanHattum, DEVELOPMENTAL LANGUAGE PROGRAMMING FOR THE RETARDED. Boston: Allyn and Bacon, 1979.

for items would be expected to use appropriate vocabulary, syntax, and semantics in making purchases.

Lying for Dollars

The purpose of this game is for students to tell the biggest "whoppers" that they can. Students must tell syntactically and semantically appropriate stories which possess absolutely no truth to them. A panel of classmates act as judges selecting the most outrageous and inventive lie which has been communicated appropriately.

Grocery Story

This is a variation on the shopping for prizes theme. A small grocery store is set up in a classroom with common store items stocked. Students acting as customers must come in and communicate their needs to the grocer in coherent and syntactically appropriate sentences. The grocer must then communicate to the customer where the item may be found. The key to this activity is to encourage good referential communication between grocer and customer with both people taking the roles of encoder and decoder.

Where's My Ending

Teacher makes up root words on cards as well as cards with prefixes and suffixes. The children take a root word out of the word pile and a card for the prefix/suffix pile. The student must then place the prefix/suffix in the correct place in relation to the root word, define the new word, and use it appropriately in a syntactic and semantic context.

Telephone

Students are separated by a screen. Their task is to converse by telephone, or walkie-talkie. Each child communicates the message received to a new person until each child in the class has had an opportunity to receive and transmit the message. The final message is then compared to the original message for accuracy.

☐ Adolescent Age Learners

Oral Reports

Tiedt and Tiedt (1978) have identified more than 150 topics of interest for oral reports by students. These interesting topics are arranged into fifteen categories such as hobbies, pets, nature, and amusements (see figure 6.4). Each student in the class chooses a topic of interest and presents a five to ten minute talk either previously prepared or impromptu. Students may also prepare visual or audio aids for their talks.

The Television Interview

Have a student pretend to be a television news reporter or anchorperson. A big story has just broken and the reporter's job is to interview the people involved and report the news on the air. Roles can be played by other class members. Have students in the audience critique the reporter's interviews and reporting.

Plays

Have students read a short story or play of high interest.[1] Students then take the different roles in the story or play and act it out using appropriate language. Such acting should be largely improvisational with students filling in their lines as they go along.

Role-Playing Interviews

In order to give students experience in seeking, obtaining, and succeeding in job interview situations, have students role-play job interview situations. This should begin with students finding out about jobs and calling for information. They then telephone for an interview and prepare for that interview. Finally, they would go to the job interview and meet the prospective employer. Afterward, the student's

[1] One of the best sources of plays is the magazine *Plays Inc.* available in most school libraries.

FIGURE 6.5 Categories and Topics Suitable for Developing Oral Communication Reports and Discussions

Amusements

1. Reading the Sunday funnies
2. Playing hide and seek
3. Popsicle from the ice cream truck
4. Chinese checkers with a friend
5. Swinging in a hammock
6. Going to a movie
7. Watching a kitten play
8. Riding a Ferris wheel
9. Playing in the sand
10. Going to a school dance

Hobbies

1. Photographing wildflowers
2. Hobbies are relaxing
3. Profitable hobbies
4. My hobby helped me meet people
5. Building strange kites
6. Sharing a hobby
7. Inexpensive hobbies
8. Outdoor hobbies
9. Collectors' items
10. Animals are interesting

Education

1. Why Government?
2. A good teacher
3. More schooling or work?
4. The value in experience
5. A well-rounded education
6. Does business want bright students?
7. A practical education
8. The value of art and music
9. Preparing for responsibility
10. Education for fun

Manners

1. Going out to eat
2. Waiting for a man to open the door
3. Manners at home
4. Are good manners needed?
5. Courtesies are appreciated
6. Remembering a sick friend
7. What are good manners?
8. How manners can make a difference
9. A time when *please* helped me
10. Things I am thankful for

Nature

1. What is a biologist?
2. Classifying wildflowers
3. Understanding ecology
4. Dolphins and porpoises
5. Underwater creatures
6. Growing a garden
7. Hiking in the forest
8. Edible plants
9. Bee language
10. Mountain trout fishing

Occupations

1. I want to be a pilot
2. Going on a job interview
3. Work can be fun
4. Working with people
5. Scientific research
6. Working in a foreign country
7. I like the outdoors
8. My career is marriage
9. My paper route
10. Teaching is rewarding

Organizations

1. What is a Democrat?
2. Charitable organizations
3. Are unions necessary?
4. Businessmen's groups
5. Wildlife preservation
6. Social clubs
7. I'm a nonconformist
8. Senior citizens
9. Religious membership
10. Magicians

Pets

1. Animals have personalities
2. Training a dog
3. Cats are night creatures
4. Parakeets are clowns
5. Dogs can be protective
6. Problems in raising exotic pets
7. Unusual pets
8. Keeping your pet healthy
9. Annual visitors
10. Trust and wild animals

(continued)

FIGURE 6.5 (continued)

Customs

1. Prayers at mealtime
2. Saluting the flag
3. Celebrating holidays
4. Shaking hands
5. Honking horns after a wedding
6. Learning new dances
7. Ladies carrying purses
8. Sunday drive
9. Birthdays
10. Shopping on Saturday

Home

1. Picking out a new house
2. Wedding in the spring
3. Family discussions
4. Sharing experiences
5. Planning for a holiday
6. A new brother or sister
7. Home-making as a full-time job
8. Father likes to go to the beach
9. Mother enjoys working
10. Learning responsibilities

Friends

1. Friends for life
2. I wonder what happened to . . .
3. The beauty of friendship
4. So comfortable to be with
5. We're on the same wavelength
6. A friend in need
7. The art of being a friend
8. The friends I miss the most
9. She never gave advice unasked for
10. My dog, Scottie, is always there

Sports

1. Women in sports
2. Enjoying the Olympics on TV
3. Jogging
4. I'd rather go sailing
5. Bicycle trips
6. Understanding football
7. Water ballet
8. Tennis fanatics
9. Archery for the whole family
10. Sportsmanship

Morals

1. Cheating on tests
2. My personal philosophy
3. Respect for law and order
4. Gambling problems
5. Being self-reliant
6. What is an honor code?
7. Morals in the business world
8. Are chaperones needed?
9. Attending church
10. Is honesty the best way?

Reading

1. My favorite stories
2. Reading for recreation
3. Learning from biographies
4. Story hour at home
5. Appealing adventure stories
6. Books my teacher read
7. My favorite character
8. Magazines on newsstands
9. Comic book collections
10. Funny and sad poems

Travel

1. Discovering new cultures
2. Exploring America
3. Coastal cruises
4. Historical American Indian dwellings
5. Trips for camera buffs
6. Sailing the Mediterranean Sea
7. Hazards of traveling
8. Communication problems
9. Hitchhiking through Europe
10. A good traveling companion

From S. Tiedt & I. Tiedt (1978). *Language activities for the classroom.* Boston: Allyn and Bacon.

interview behavior is assessed by the teacher and other students. This activity fits nicely into long-term units dealing with finding and keeping jobs.

Analyzing Public Statements

Have students analyze public statements such as political statements or television commercials. What part of such statements are fact and what opinion? Where are statistics used? Were they used clearly and fairly? Should the statements be believed? Such analysis of public statements will help students become better consumers.

CREATING AN ENVIRONMENT FOR LANGUAGE USAGE

☐ ☐ This chapter has discussed how language develops in children, the basic components of language and communication, and the methods by which these components may be assessed so as to discover gaps or deficiencies in the language functioning of mentally retarded children. Now it explores what the special education teacher can do in terms of intervention, curriculum, and instruction in order to help remediate language deficits of mentally retarded children. The teacher of mildly mentally retarded children should consider the following questions regarding the communication interaction between teacher and student.

1. How may I modify the classroom environment in order to promote language usage and increased communication between students?
2. How sensitive am I in my language interactions with children in creating a psychological atmosphere conducive to increased communication?
3. How good am I at coping with speech and language deficiencies of my students?
4. What kind of stimuli and instructional activities do I offer my students in order to encourage language and communication?

The ways that the teacher answers these four questions will go far in determining the efficiency of language intervention in the special education classroom.

☐ The Classroom Environment

Look at the typical classroom sketched in Figure 6.6a. One of the striking things in such a typical classroom is its high structure. It seems that everything is ordered to the point of appearing unspontaneous. What does the high amount of structure in the classroom (i.e., straight rows of desk all facing the same way) tell students about their relationships with each other and with their teacher in terms of communication patterns? It should be readily apparent that the classroom depicted in Figure 6.6a is not designed to elicit maximum language inter-

FIGURE 6.6   Classroom Physical Environments and Their Effect on Students' Communication

a. The Traditional Classroom Structure

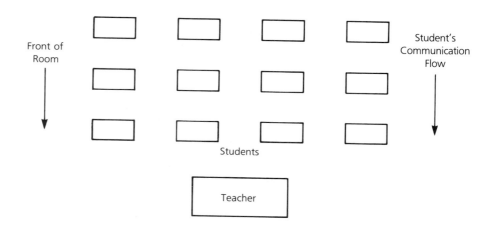

b. A Classroom Structure Designed to Foster Communication

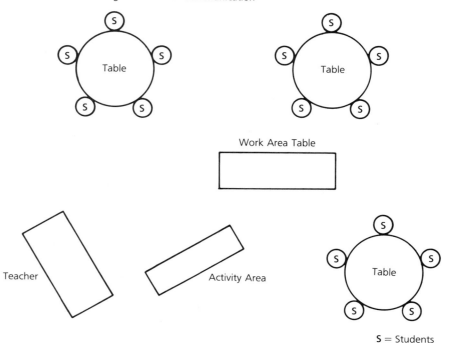

action and stimulation among children. In fact, such a classroom probably would inhibit language between children by indicating to students that communication was to flow only from and toward the teacher who was centered at the front of the room.

Now examine the classroom depicted in Figure 6.6b. This classroom, with its interest and learning centers and its lack of centralization is one in which the teacher-student-teacher flow of centralized language has been diffused. This classroom is a student-controlled language situation which encourages child interactions, environmental explorations, and self-expression (Cohen & Plaskon 1980).

The teacher interested in fostering language development in children should keep the following considerations in mind when creating the physical classroom environment (Cohen & Plaskon 1980):

1. Multiple opportunities should exist for children to engage in nonformal language and communication.
2. The classroom environment should allow for easy modification in order to allow novel presentations of material and instructional methods.
3. Freedom should exist for students to move about the room as topics and activities dictate.
4. The environment should allow for easy interactions of other adults and student visitors as situations warrant.

Teachers often give scant attention to the physical structuring of the classroom in order to facilitate language and communication (Blackburn & Powell 1976). However, many educators and psychologists believe that teachers who wish to improve the language and communication skills of children should give consideration to the physical environment of the classroom. To the extent that the classroom inhibits the free flow of communication and crushes the child's desire to explore the environment, language intervention for children will become increasingly more difficult.

☐ Teacher Sensitivity to Student Language

Suppose you are sitting in a college lecture course in a subject matter which you find difficult. There comes a point in the teacher's lecture which you simply do not understand. It might be a relatively simple or straightforward point, obvious to the other students, but to you it is opaque. It just does not make any sense. Meekly, you raise your hand and ask your question. Your professor, after a long, scornful glare in your direction, says, "Why are you bothering us with such a trivial question? Anybody with any sense at all could look up the answer in the beginning of the textbook. Now please don't bother us again with such drivel."

How would you feel if such comments had been directed at you or another member of your class? Would you be apt to participate in class again or ask another question? Probably not.

Children communicate best in an atmosphere in which they feel valued and comfortable. Nothing will shut off a child's language faster than a teacher's or parent's nonresponsiveness. Teachers sometimes stifle language and communication even when they do not mean to because they are busy with something else. For example the author knew of an inner city student who came to school about ten minutes late just as the teacher was bogged down in the opening ritual of taking attendance, collecting lunch money, and checking permission slips. The child had a lump of coal which he had found. He tried to tell the teacher how pretty it was, that it reflected light, and could show different colors depending on how you viewed it. In fact, he told the teacher, he could even write with it. But this particular teacher was far too busy and annoyed by the hassles of the morning to sit through a child's speech on the beauty of coal. "You're late," she snapped. "Did you get a late slip from the office? And throw away that dirty lump of coal. It's all over your hands. Now I'll have to write you a pass to go to the bathroom to wash up."

A glorious language opportunity lost, and given enough of this nonreinforcement for engaging in language this child may eventually become withdrawn and sullen in school. Strong evidence indicates vocabulary growth among children occurs in classrooms where teachers are judged to be warm and supportive. Authoritarian teachers tend to discourage student communication and language (Donmoyer & Kidd 1984; Orazco 1980; Roth 1984). Teachers must guard against communicating to pupils the message, "I'm too busy, come back later." The effectiveness of classroom language intervention will come to a grinding halt when such an attitude is perceived by students.

☐ Teacher versus Student Talking

Another reason that children may not be using language and communication in school may be that the teachers are doing almost all of the talking. Two studies, conducted many years apart, illustrate this point (Hoetker & Ahlbrand 1968; Rice 1895). Both studies assessed the amount of time students spend verbalizing in classroom activities as opposed to time which the teacher spoke. Rice (1895)—yes this date is not a typographical error—found that almost 85 percent of classroom instructional time was spent in teacher talking with less than 15 percent spent in student verbalizations. What followed historically in teacher preparation courses was a long period of instructing education majors about the need for student involvement, participation, and student language in school. So what did Hoetker & Ahlbrand find? Only that three quarters of a century later the percentage of teacher talking in classrooms had increased to 89 percent! In addition, the 11 percent of student verbalizations were found to consist of one or two word answers in response to direct teacher questions. Thus, it appears that students may not be using language in school because teachers are not giving them a chance to get in a word edgewise.

COPING WITH STUDENTS' LANGUAGE DEFICIENCES

☐ ☐ Related to the receptiveness of the language environment which the teacher creates in the classroom is the teacher's ability to remain tolerant of the language and communication deficiencies of handicapped students. This is particularly true of children who suffer from articulation difficulties or dysfluencies such as stuttering. A teacher who either verbally or nonverbally expresses concern or impatience over a child's speech difficulties runs the risk of causing the child to become tense and anxious about participating in speech situations. Such anxiety may lead to avoidance behavior in which the child seeks to avoid speech situations to escape unpleasant stimuli such as fear and anxiety. In such situations, not engaging in speech behavior (avoidance) becomes positively reinforcing and language participation and communication decreases dramatically. The special education teacher is not a speech pathologist trained to give specific speech therapy. However, it is the teacher who will set the psychological environment in the class which will encourage or inhibit speech usage by the speech handicapped child. In a negative classroom speech environment, language therapy by the speech pathologist will prove futile.

For dysfluent speech such as stuttering, comments such as *slow down, take your time,* and *think what you want to say before speaking,* can contribute to the dread of the stutterer speaking in social situations. Instead, the teacher who feels nervous around the stuttering child might best ask the cause for his or her own anxiety about stuttering. Once this question is satisfactorily resolved, the teacher will be in a better position to deal in a less threatening manner with the child who stutters.

Perhaps one of the best ways for the teacher to interact with children exhibiting language problems is to realize there is no magic solution to the problems of such children and language problems cannot be eliminated by force of will. This applies to both teacher and child; the teacher cannot be expected to suddenly remediate all of the child's language difficulties and the child cannot overcome difficulties simply by trying harder. Rather, the remediation of language problems will take a long time and the key word will probably be remediation not elimination. Such problems took a long time to develop; there is no reason to presuppose that they will not take an equally long time to subside and will only do so with tenderness and understanding on the part of parents, teachers, and other adults.

Regarding problems of articulation, Gearheart and Weishahn (1976) suggest the teacher make sure that the student receives adequate ear training of sounds which are produced appropriately so that the child can begin to compare misarticulations with the appropriately produced phonemes. Such ear training implies that the teacher and other adults serve as good articulation models for the child by positively reinforcing correct articulations while gently shaping incorrect articulations. Do not begin articulation intervention until the child is able to perceive appropriately the difference between correctly and incorrectly produced phonemes. Finally, Gearheart and Weishahen suggest that intervention of articulation errors in the child's running speech not be attempted until the child can correctly produce the phonemes in isolation.

SUMMARY

☐ ☐ The purpose of language is effective communication. This requires both a sender and a receiver operating in a feedback loop. In this loop, the receiver indicates understanding of the message and the sender modifies the message as needed to increase understandability. The ability to communicate effectively and to modify messages as needed is known as referential communication. The inability to take another person's perspective and thus communicate effectively is known as egocentric communication.

There are four main components to language: phonology, morphology, syntax, and semantics. Phonemes are the basic sounds of language. There are approximately forty-five phonemes in the English language. Difficulty in producing phonemes are usually classified as problems of articulation. A significant proportion of mildly mentally retarded students possess articulation difficulties. Morphemes are the smallest unit of meaningful sounds. Morphemes are usually vocabulary, root words, suffixes, and prefixes. Morpheme training should be a major part of language curriculum and instruction. Syntax, sometimes called grammar, is the rules by which words are combined in order to form messages. Although syntax does not usually effect the meaning of a message, inappropriate syntax can interfere with message understandability. Semantics is the meaning of a message. Clear and unambiguousness of messages is the goal of communication.

Two types of language are receptive and expressive. Receptive language is understanding a message and acting upon it. An example of receptive language is following directions. Expressive language represents the sending of a message in order to express one's wants and/or needs. Receptive language almost always develops before expressive language.

Language assessment is extremely important for the future schooling of mentally retarded learners. Children should go through an initial language screening with those children showing possible problems being referred for in-depth assessment. Such assessments are usually administered by the speech/language professional but can also be given by the teacher.

Setting a classroom psychological environment conducive to language usage is vital for language success especially in cases where children are demonstrating speech dysfluencies and problems in articulation. Teachers must work to set up a pleasant, unthreatening atmosphere in which the child wants to speak, feels comfortable in speaking, and feels secure in the acceptance of the teacher and other students. In a negative language classroom atmosphere, language therapy is probably useless.

There is a variety of commercial kits on the market that the teacher can use as the basis of a language and communication curriculum. In addition, it is suggested that the teacher consider using the long-term instructional unit as a basis for language instruction. Finally, there are a large number of resource materials and curriculum guides available to supply the teacher programming and material ideas.

7

Teaching Reading

Key Concepts

- [ ] Word Recognition and Decoding
- [ ] Reading Comprehension: Literal and Inferential
- [ ] Cultural Difference and the Reading Process
- [ ] Reading Readiness
- [ ] Reading Assessment: Formal and Informal
- [ ] Phonics: Analysis and Synthesis
- [ ] Look Say Word Recognition
- [ ] Eclectic Approach to Reading
- [ ] Basal Approaches to Reading
- [ ] Using the Experience Approach to Reading
- [ ] Reading and Long-term Instructional Units
- [ ] Reading Kits
- [ ] Reading Activities and Materials

Despite the amount of time and energy spent in the teaching of reading, many people cannot read. For example, as many as 40 percent of all school-age children in the United States possess reading deficiencies (Adams 1980; Goldberg & Schiffman 1972; Lipson & Wixson 1985). Unfortunately, these estimates may be misleading. Since reading is the basic tool used in mastery of other school subject areas such as social studies and science, one cannot really know the extent to which academic failure in these areas are caused, at least partially, by deficiencies in reading.

Almost every classroom teacher has encountered children who have difficulty reading. Some of these children may be limited in cognitive ability. Cognitive factors as intelligence have been shown to influence ability to learn to read (Harris & Sipay 1976; Lohnes & Gray 1972). Other factors that appear to influence the reading process are sensory functioning (Hargis 1982; Silbiger & Woolf 1965), information processing ability and memory (Perfetti 1985; Stanovich 1982), language and culture (Eisenhart & Borko 1984; Erickson 1982; McDermott 1977), and motivation (Asher 1980; Mandl, Schnotz & Tergan 1984). However, when these factors are taken into account and curriculum and instruction modified in order to optimize and individualize learning, children can learn to read. The goal of this chapter is to offer the prospective special education teacher information on processes, curriculum, instructional methods, and materials designed to improve the reading of mildly mentally retarded children.

THE READING PROCESS

☐ ☐ In order to teach reading adequately, the teacher must understand what reading is. This is not as easy as it might appear. The reading process appears to be one of those things that people often refer to as if it is universally understood, but when the surface is scratched, it often means different things to different people.

For the purposes of this text, a definition of reading will be adopted that includes both the decoding (recognizing or figuring out written symbols on the page) and then attaching meaning to those symbols (comprehension). Thus, reading is defined as:

the conversion of print into auditory equivalents and the subsequent interpretation of those equivalents into meanings based on previously learned language.

Quite a mouthful. However, taken one attribute at a time, this definition of reading becomes a succinct explanation of the reading process.

☐ Decoding

The definition of reading states the decoding process occurs when printed symbols are converted to auditory (sound) equivalents. Mature reading adults convert print to sound so quickly and effortlessly they forget they are doing it at all. Unfortunately, this is not the case for millions of school children and virtually all mentally retarded individuals. For them, the decoding process is a slow, almost painful affair which must be carried out with great effort and attention.

☐ Comprehension

The definition of reading also states that simple decoding of written symbols into sounds is not enough. The student may be the best decoder in the world, but if that child does not possess appropriate interpretation (comprehension) skills, the child is simply "barking at print." Decoding without comprehension is not reading.

The third part of the definition explains how the act of comprehension is to take place. It occurs by the reader basing the meaning of the passage on previously learned language. This means that comprehension is based on acquired language. For the child to appropriately handle written language, verbal language (or manual sign) must have been mastered.

☐ Comprehension Is Experience

Finally, the definition of reading points out that reading is experiential. It is based on the past learning experiences of the child (Chittenden 1983; Spache & Spache

1977; Spiro 1980). If a given concept is not in a child's experiential vocabulary, then the child will not be able to comprehend the concept during reading (Gentner 1975; Rosenshine 1980). Without experiential concepts already in place in the reader's memory, the comprehension of text will prove impossible.

THE COMPETENCIES OF READING

☐ ☐ Reading consists of two processes: decoding and comprehension. These processes may be further broken down into subprocesses. For example, in Figure 7.1a decoding skills are further broken down into skills of auditory and visual discrimination, word attack skills (phonetic and structural analysis), sight words, and oral reading.

Like decoding skills, the comprehension process may also be broken into subskills (Baker & Stein 1981; Barrett 1968; Stephens, Hartman & Lucas 1982). Such skills include literal comprehension (recognizing and recalling text) through the ability to make inferences and evaluations from what is read. Figure 7.1b shows a breakdown of the basic comprehension skills. Included in these comprehension skills are study and reference skills typically needed by older students for reading-related school success.

CULTURAL DIFFERENCE, LANGUAGE, AND READING

☐ ☐ Both experience and the degree of language functioning prior to the child entering school are key factors in determining a child's probable success or failure in reading (Gillespie & Johnson 1974; Zintz 1981). Such experiences include the amount and type of language used in the home as well as the life experiences, motivations, and interests which the home culture imparts on the child (Hansen & Johnson 1985; Mercer 1983; Payan 1984).

Many professionals believe the probability of reading success is heightened when experiences and language of the school curriculum matches that of the child's home culture (Cohen & Plaskon 1980; Harris 1970). Unfortunately, in the case of mildly mentally retarded learners, the experiences and language provided in the home are often quite different from the middle-class school curriculum (Alley & Foster 1979; Mercer 1974; Sattler 1982).

Although it is certainly not a given that mildly mentally retarded children will possess experiential and language deficits, there is evidence to suggest that such children are more likely to contain these deficits than average white, middle-class children. Evidence also shows that mildly mentally retarded children are more likely to come from substandard housing, possess an inadequate diet, feel alienated from school and society as a whole, and possess fewer educational and middle-class cultural materials in the home than nonretarded youngsters (Chan & Rueda 1979; Kagan 1970; Perkins 1977), and may be subject to physical

FIGURE 7.1

a. Subcomponents of Decoding Skills

Auditory Discrimination
Environmental Sounds
Rhymes
Matching Sounds
Repeating Sounds
Following Verbal Instructions

Sight Word Recognition
Preprimer
Primer
Levels 1-3

Structural Analysis
Contractions
Compound Words
Punctuation
Prefix/Suffix
Singular/Plural
Syllabication
Word Building

Visual Discrimination
Likenesses/Differences
Matching Symbols
Recognizing Letters
Repeating Visual Patterns

Phonics
Blends
Consonants (Initial and Final)
Digraphs and Diphthongs
Vowels (Long and Short)

b. Subcompetencies of Comprehension and Study Skills

Comprehension
Classifying and Categorizing
Labeling
Main Idea
Opposites
Recall
Sequencing Events
Following Written Directions
Word Meaning
Interpretation
Drawing Conclusions
Making Inferences

Study Skills
Reference
Organization
Reading Rate

Literature
Recognizing Literary Style
Recognizing Literary Techniques

abuse up to 10 times more frequently than "normal" children (Sandgrund, Gaines & Green 1974; Soeffing 1975). Furthermore, the parents of these children are less likely to take them on educational field trips, play with them in educational games, or help them with their schoolwork than children of middle-class parents (Hunt 1969; Richardson 1981).

It is crucial that teachers do everything possible to provide the culturally different child with experience with concepts and materials by engaging in

FIGURE 7.2   An Example of Black Dialectal and Standard English

SEE A GIRL
(Black English Version)
Susan say, "Hey you-all look
    down here.
I can see a girl in here.
The girl, she look like me.
Come here and look, David.
Could you see the girl?"
David, he say, "Here I come.
Let me see the girl."
David say, "I don't see no girl.
Ain't no girl in there.
I see me and my ball."
Susan, she say, "Momma, look
    in here.
David don't see no girl, and I do.
You see a girl in there?"
Momma say, "Look down there,
    David.
That little girl Susan.
Susan say, "Momma! Momma! Momma!
We can see David and me.
We can see Wiggles and a big girl.
You that big girl."

SEE A GIRL
(Standard English Version)
"Look down here," said Suzy.

"I can see a girl in here.
That girl looks like me.
Come here and look, David.
Can you see that girl?"
"Here I come," said David.
"I want to see the girl."
David said, "I do not see a girl.
A girl is not in here, Suzy.
I see me and my ball."
Suzy said, "Look in here, Mother.
David cannot see a girl.
And I can.
Can you see a girl in here?"
"Look down, Suzy," said Mother.
"Look down here, David.
That little girl is my Suzy.
"Mother! Mother!" said Suzy.
"We can see David and me.
We can see Wiggles and a big girl.
That big girl is you."

From "Toward Reading Materials for Speakers of Black English: Three Linguistically Appropriate Passages" by W.A. Wolfram and R.W. Fasold, pp. 147–149, in *Teaching Black Children to Read*, by J.C. Baratz and R.W. Shuy (Eds.), 1969, Washington, DC: Center for Applied Linguistics. Copyright 1969 by the Center for Applied Linguistics. Reprinted by permission.

such activities as field trips, hands-on activities, and bringing a variety of materials to the special education classroom. Initial reading programs for culturally different students should be written dialectally, in language and syntax that is familiar and understandable to these children (Zintz 1981). Culturally different children are often forced not only to learn to read but at the same time learn to process and use language and syntax patterns which are foreign to them (Polloway & Smith 1982). Instead of this occurring, it is suggested that beginning reading materials for these children be presented in their own dialect and syntax with the switch to standard printed English occurring only after the basic reading skills have been mastered and reading self-concept and motivation to continue reading is high (Polloway & Smith 1982; Wilg & Semel 1984). An example of dialectal reading material may be seen in Figure 7.2. In this example, a story is shown in both black dialectal and standard English (Wolfram & Fasold 1969). Initial instruction would be in the black English version. Only later, when decoding skills have been mastered, would stories in standard English be attempted.

WHERE TO BEGIN: READING READINESS

☐ ☐ What should be done for the child who is not ready for formal reading instruction? Should we simply wait until the child is ready, patiently allowing the student idly to sit in class until the time is ripe or should we force feed reading to the child, exposing him or her to the reading process in hopes that some of the instruction will eventually sink in?

Luckily, a third alternative exists. Cognitively immature children can be taught reading readiness skills. These skills consist of activities designed to strengthen cognitive, sensory-motor, and perceptual processes necessary for successful reading. The teaching of readiness skills also incudes helping the child learn a body of experientially based world knowledge and concepts which can be used to attach meaning to what is heard or read since the child who lacks relevant and important experiences and language will have little chance of understanding what she or he is reading.

In most cases, the teaching of readiness skills will pertain to relatively young children. Bearing in mind the relatively young chronological age of these students, the teacher can institute a wide variety of activities to help mentally retarded children learn the necessary readiness skills for learning reading. Some activities designed to facilitate the learning of such readiness skills are

I. *Developing Language and Vocabulary*
   A. Classify things into categories. Colors, numbers, animals, foods, people, and furniture are among the hundreds of concepts which may be classified. Play games which help the child learn to classify things by their defining attributes.
   B. Have the child learn opposites. What is the opposite of hot, of big, etc.? This is a key readiness skill.
   C. Learn and associate word pairs. What goes with *knife*? What words go with *mother*? The child needs to learn that certain words go together while other word pairs are illogical (e.g., *bed-zebra*). Learning that certain concepts do or do not go together is a reflection of experience and learning and is a key reading readiness skill.
   D. Homonyms. Many word-sounds in the English language have two meanings. Does the child understand the difference between *no* and *know*? Between *sun* and *son*? To the extent that the child has problems with homonyms, processing is occurring in the auditory modality alone rather than through visual-auditory combination. Such processing problems will almost assuredly lead to reading problems since reading is the conversion of print into auditory equivalents.
   E. Concept formation. Certain concepts are absolutely crucial to the understanding of what is being read. Does the child understand

before and *after, fast* and *slow, under* and *over?* To the extent that these and other key concepts are not part of the child's working vocabulary, they must be worked on and intentionally taught by the special education teacher.

II. *Visual Discrimination*

 A. Identifying pictorial concepts. Can the child recognize common pictures of everyday objects, or does she or he say "dog" when shown a picture of a cat? Children who mistake pictorial representations of concepts either do not have the concept in their working vocabulary or are not seeing the pictures adequately. In either case, the problem will need to be identified and remediated.

 B. Point out likenesses and differences in pictures. How are a group of pictures the same? How are they different? How do different pictures differ (along which dimensions)? The ability to discriminate likes and differences is crucial, especially in alphabet and word discrimination.

III. *Visual Memory*

 A. Can the child remember visual experiences? If shown an array of objects, how many objects are remembered? Mentally retarded learners often possess problems or deficiencies in learning and applying memory strategies.

 B. Instruction in using one's visual memory should include the training strategies of rehearsal, clustering, using memory keys, and increasing memory span. Deficiencies in memory will greatly penalize the future reader.

IV. *Auditory Discrimination and Memory*

 A. Identifying environmental sounds. How well can the child identify everyday sounds? Can the child identify a train whistle? A dog barking? A child who cannot identify the sounds of the environment either is suffering from auditory discrimination problems or lacking in the most basic experiential concepts. In either case identify and remediate the underlying problem. The teacher may wish to play tape recordings of different environmental sounds and work with the child on the identification of those sounds.

 B. Letter and word sounds. Children need to learn basic phoneme sounds of English and associate them with the graphic representations of printed letters. What sound does *D* make? How about *Z?* To the extent that the child cannot identify and discriminate letter sounds, decoding of printed words will be severely impaired. Start with the letters of the child's name, teaching the sounds of those letters and then work to other letters in the alphabet.

 C. Likewise, the child needs to gain experience in the rhyming of sounds and words. How do *sing* and *wing* differ? How about *foot* and *soot?* Auditory discrimination of words as well as their sound similarities and differences are essential for word decoding.

ASSESSING READING ABILITY

☐ ☐ One of the most important jobs that the special education teacher has is accurately assessing the reading ability of mentally retarded students. Assessment determines the child's reading strengths and weaknesses and facilitates the planning of instructional programming. As in the language and communication area, reading assessment need not be done solely by the teacher. The school system may have a reading specialist who can assist in the diagnosis of reading problems as well as offer suggestions in designing prescriptive measures to remediate reading deficiencies. However, whether or not a reading speciaist is utilized, the teacher will need to take a significant role in assessing classroom reading difficulties and evaluating the assessment information.

Reading assessment may range from formal to informal. While formal reading assessment would utilize standardized and commercially available reading tests, informal reading assessment would primarily use tests and procedures developed by the classroom teacher or school reading specialist. Regardless of the type of reading assessment used, it is strongly suggested that the assessment cover three main areas: the child's current reading level, plus a detailed analysis of decoding and comprehension skills (Carroll 1972; Howell & Kaplan 1980; Stephens, Hartman & Lucas 1982; Salvia & Ysseldyke 1985). An assessment that contains all three components will yield insight into the total reading functioning of the mentally retarded child.

TYPES OF READING ASSESSMENT

☐ Overall Reading Level

The mentally retarded child will almost always be significantly below grade level in reading and will thus be lagging behind nonretarded peers in the ability to read. The special education teacher will probably wish to know the reading level at which the mentally retarded child is operating in order to choose reading materials commensurate with the child's ability. Choose a level too high and the child will become anxious and frustrated; choose reading materials at too low a level and the child will become bored. Thus, a general knowledge of the mildly mentally retarded child's overall reading level and abilities is essential to effective teaching.

Finding the child's current reading level may be accomplished in any one of three ways: using formal survey tests, conducting an informal analysis of the child's oral reading, or constructing an informal reading inventory. Formal survey tests are commercially available achievement tests which are either totally dedicated to measuring reading achievement or which measure reading level in a subtest of a greater school achievement battery. There are a variety of these tests available; a list of the major ones is included in Table 7.1. These tests are global

TABLE 7.1 Commercially Available Global and Diagnostic Reading Achievement Tests

Test	Group or Individual	Age/Grade	Type of Referencing	Inventory of Skills
Botel Reading Inventory	Both	Gr 1-12	Diagnostic	Yes
Brigance Diagnostic Inventory	Individual	Gr K-7	Diagnostic-Criterion	Yes
California Reading Tests	Group	Gr 2.5-8.5	Norm	No
California Phonics Survey	Individual	Gr 7-12	Norm	No
Classroom Reading Inventory	Individual	Gr 1-8		Yes
Diagnostic Reading Scales	Individual	Gr 1-8	Norm	No
Doren Diagnostic Reading Test of Word Recognition Skills	Both	Gr K-6		Yes
Durrell Analysis of Reading Difficulty	Individual	Gr 1-6	Norm	No
Gates-MacGinitie Reading Test	Group	Gr K-12	Norm	No
Gates-McKillop Reading Diagnostic Tests	Individual	Gr 1-7	Norm	No
Gray Oral Reading Tests	Individual	Gr 1-12	Norm	No
Iowa Silent Reading Tests	Group	Gr 6-adult	Norm	No
Monroe Reading Aptitude Tests	Both	Gr K-1	Norm	No
Nelson Reading Test	Group	Gr 3-9	Norm	No
Phonics Knowledge Survey	Individual	All	Norm	No
Roswell-Chall	Individual	Gr 1-12	Both	No
Silent Reading Diagnostic Tests	Group	Gr 2.5-8.5	Both	No
Sipay Word-Analysis Tests	Individual	Gr K-12	Norm	No
Slosson Oral Reading Test	Individual	Gr 1-12	Norm	No
Stanford Diagnostic Reading Test	Group	Gr 1-12	Both	No
Sacher-Allred Reading Placement Inventory	Individual	Ages 5-14		Yes
Test of Reading Comprehension	Both	Gr 1-8	Norm	No
Traxler Silent Reading Test	Group	Gr 7-10	Norm	No
Woodcock Reading Mastery	Individual	Gr 1-12	Norm	No
Woodcock-Johnson Psycho-educational Battery	Individual	Age 3-Adult	Norm	No

in nature (as opposed to diagnostic in scope) and yield a general indication of the child's ability to decode and/or comprehend what is read. They also give an indication of the child's reading ability in terms of grade level, a sometimes useful piece of information if the teacher is concerned with choosing appropriate grade level reading material for the mentally retarded learner.

One of the problems with most survey level achievement tests, especially achievement level batteries which include reading subtests, is that they are group tests. In order to complete a group test successfully, the child must possess a variety of test-taking skills. These include staying-on-task, following directions, and reading. This poses an obvious problem for many mentally retarded test-takers. First, such students often do not stay on task well, nor are they particularly adroit at following directions. Second, they may be expected to possess the skill (reading) needed to take the test, but we are giving them the test because we are not sure of their reading ability. Thus, if the child does not do well on the test, is it because he or she is deficient in reading ability or did not possess the other needed skills in order to successfully complete the test? For these reasons, the informal, individualized methods of assessing reading level are suggested for mildly mentally retarded students.

□ Oral Reading

In oral reading assessment, the child is asked to read a passage. If the child has difficulty with more than five words per hundred or reads in a hesitant, word-by-word manner, the assumption is made that the particular grade level of the material which the child is reading is too high.

Some notes of caution about the informal oral reading method are in order. First, it is a test of *decoding*; it does not measure comprehension. Second it is a hit or miss proposition in that the child continues to read passages at various reading levels until the teacher hits upon the appropriate level for that child. Such a method may prove time consuming, especially when there are many students to be tested. Finally, such a method may prove threatening to the student called upon to read. The child may feel "on the spot" and that deficiencies are being exposed. Thus, the teacher must be careful to keep the atmosphere non-threatening and not even tell the children that they are in a testing situation. One teacher told the students she needed help picking out reading materials for next year's class. The students who read felt important in helping the teacher choose curricular materials. Despite the limitations of oral reading assessment, it may nevertheless prove valuable in finding the general reading level of the child.

In assessing oral reading, it is a good idea to analyze the types of errors which the student makes. There are ten error types which occur commonly in oral reading. A listing and description of these error types is in Figure 7.3.

Oral reading assessment may be conducted formally or informally. For example, Table 7.2 contains a listing of the major commercially available oral reading tests along with the types of errors which each test measures. In the

FIGURE 7.3 Common Errors Experienced in Oral Reading

1. Aid: The student hesitates for a time without making an effort to pronounce a word or appears to be attempting to pronounce the word.
2. Gross Mispronunciation: A gross mispronunciation occurs when the pupil's pronunciation of a word bears so little resemblance to the proper pronunciation that the examiner must look at the word to recognize it.
3. Omission of a Word or Group of Words: Omissions consist of skipping individual words or groups of words.
4. Insertion of a Word or Group of Words: Insertions consist of the student putting one or more words into the sentence being read.
5. Substitution of One Meaningful Word for Another: Substitutions consist of the replacement of one or more words in the passage by one or more other meaningful words.
6. Repetition: Repetition consists of repeating words or groups of words while attempting to read sentences or paragraphs. Errors due to stuttering are not repetition errors.
7. Inversion, or Changing of Word Order: Errors of inversion occur when the child changes the order of words appearing in a sentence.
8. Partial Mispronunciation: A partial mispronunciation occurs when (a) the student phonetically mispronounces specific letters, (b) the student omits part of a word, inserts elements of words, makes errors in syllabification, accent, or inversion.
9. Disregard of Punctuation: The student fails to observe punctuation. This includes not pausing for a comma, stopping for a period, or indicating by vocal inflection a question mark or exclamation point.
10. Hesitation: The student hesitates for two or more seconds before pronouncing a word. The error is recorded as a check over the word. If the examiner then pronounces the word, it is recorded as a check plus p.

informal oral reading assessment, the teacher may wish to utilize the flashcard presentation format. Such presentation is both timed (speeded) and untimed with the timed version representing word recognition skills and the untimed version representing word attack or phonics skills. The reading level at which the child falls below 90 percent accuracy in word recognition (decoding) and 50 percent in word comprehension is the level of the child's reading.

TABLE 7.2 Commercially Available Oral Reading Tests and the Types of Errors They Measure

	Gray Oral Reading Test	Gilmore Oral Reading Test	Gates-McKillop-Horowitz Reading Diagnostic Test	Durrell Analysis of Reading Difficulty
Aid	X	X		X
Gross mispronunciation	X	X	X	X
Omission	X	X	X	X
Insertion	X	X	X	X
Substitution	X	X		X
Repetition	X	X	X	X
Inversion	X		X	
Partial mispronunciation	X			
Disregard of punctuation		X		X
Hesitation		X		X

TABLE 7.3   Commercially Available Reading Tests Which Measure Word Decoding Skills

Test	Norm-Referenced	Criterion-Referenced	Age/Grade
Botel Reading Inventory	X	X	Gr 1–12
Brigance Diagnostic Inventory of Basic Skills		X	Gr K–7
Diagnostic Reading Scales	X		Gr 1–8
Doren Diagnostic Reading Test	X	X	Primary–Intermediate
Gates-McGintie Reading Test	X		Gr K–12
Roswell-Chall Diagnostic Test of Word Analysis	X	X	Gr 2–6
Stanford Diagnostic Reading Test	X	X	Gr 1–13
Woodcock Reading Mastery Test	X		Gr 1–12
Woodcock-Johnson Psycho-educational Battery	X		Ages 3–80+

☐ Word Recognition and Decoding Skills

Assessment of word-recognition and decoding skills may be accomplished by using formal or informal assessment. For example, Table 7.3 shows a number of available word-recognition/decoding tests which include measurement of the child's word attack skills needed to decode unfamiliar words. Additionally, the teacher may wish to devise her own word-recognition tests. This can be easily done by taking sample words from available word lists such as the Dolch Basic Sight Word List (1942), Fry Instant Word List (Fry 1977), or Pope (1975) List.

In conducting an informal assessment of sight word/word attack skills, the teacher would use the following process:

1. Have the child read the word using the flash card approach (assessment of sight vocabulary).
2. Have the child attempt to phonetically decode words not read correctly during the flash card assessment (decoding skills).

Whether a formal or informal word recognition test is being used, the teacher must keep in mind that only decoding and word recognition is being measured, not comprehension. Since comprehension levels are usually lower than word recognition levels, measuring the word recognition of mentally retarded students may result in placing these students at a higher reading level than they are actually functioning (Hammill & Bartel 1982; Hargis 1982; Zintz 1981).

TABLE 7.4 Commercially Available Reading Comprehension Tests

Test	Norm-Referenced	Criterion-Referenced	Grade
Botel Reading Inventory	X	X	Gr 1–12
Diagnostic Reading Scales	X		Gr 1–8
Durrell Analysis of Reading Difficulty	X		Gr 1–6
Gilmore Oral Reading Test	X		Gr 1–8
Iowa Silent Reading Tests	X		Gr 6–College
Woodcock Reading Mastery Tests	X		Gr 1–12

☐ Reading Comprehension

In addition to decoding skills, the comprehension abilities should also be assessed. Assessment of comprehension appears to be more difficult to carry out and evaluate than decoding and word recognition skills (Pearson & Dole 1985; Salvia & Ysseldyke 1985). Perhaps for this reason, there are fewer formal tests of reading comprehension available to teachers (see Table 7.4). Thus, the special education teacher who wishes to assess the comprehension of mildly mentally retarded students may be forced to construct informal comprehension instruments. To that end, an outline of procedures for designing such an informal comprehension instrument is included in Figure 7.4 (Hammill & Bartel 1982).

One method which the teacher may wish to use in informal comprehension assessment is that of the *Cloze* technique (Taylor 1953). This technique involves selecting passages of approximately 260—275 words of varying degrees of difficulty. Words are then deleted from the passages and the child is asked to write in the missing words. In order to write in these missing words, the child needs to glean contextual clues from the surrounding words and sentences in the passage. The logic is that the ability to glean such contextual meaning from surrounding phrases is a sign of reading comprehension. Figure 7.5 contains a sample passage using the Cloze technique.

The Cloze technique appears to be a valid procedure for measuring reading comprehension (Gillespie & Johnson 1974; Guszak 1972) with the technique proving useful in assessing the reading comprehension of mildly mentally retarded children (Ramanauskas 1972; Klare 1975). However, some data indicates that the technique becomes more unreliable for mentally retarded students who are operating below the fourth-grade reading level (Guszak 1972). For younger students or for students operating below the fourth-grade reading level, the use of comprehension questioning using Barrett's (Clymer 1963) comprehension taxonomy is recommended.

FIGURE 7.4   Guidelines for Construction of an Informal Reading Comprehension Assessment Instrument

1. Obtain graded copies across a multiple level basal series not currently being used in the school or school system.
2. Select two passages from the beginning of a book at each of the levels. Passage lengths should approximate:

    25-50 words for pre-primer and primer levels
    50-75 words for first-grade level
    75-125 words for second- and third-grade levels
    125-175 words for fourth- through sixth-grade levels
    200+ words for passages above the sixth-grade level

3. Designate one of each of the passage pairs at a given level for silent and oral reading, respectively. Laminate copies for student use.
4. Triple space the passages to allow room for scoring notations.
5. Develop at least five comprehension questions for each passage including examples that tap:

    a). factual recall of details (e.g., Who was the main character in the story?).
    b). sequence of events (e.g., What happened just after the door closed?).
    c). vocabulary, by defining a word from the context (e.g., What does the word "devious" mean in the first paragraph?).
    d). awareness of main idea (e.g., A good title for this story would be . . .).
    e). the ability to draw inferences (e.g., How do you think she knew that the man had been in the yard earlier in the day?).

    From E.A. Polloway & J.E. Smith, Jr. (1982).

AFTER ASSESSMENT—READING INSTRUCTION

☐ Look-Say versus Phonics: The Great Debate

After the teacher conducts a survey and an in-depth assessment of the child's pre-reading and/or reading skills and decides to go ahead with formal reading instruction, the problem becomes where to begin. Perhaps the best place to do so is at the level of the word.

A long standing controversy in the teaching of word decoding has been the issue of whether word decoding should be taught in terms of letter-to-sound correspondences or as the recognition of whole words. The letter-to-sound correspondence method, better known as the *phonics* method, teaches decoding by introducing the child to the sounds of letters and letter combinations which can be chained together to make words. By comparison, the recognition of whole words, known as word-recognition or the *look-say* method, is based on the assumption that the word is the smallest meaningful unit that the child needs in order to read successfully. Proponents of and opponents to each method abound, and the debate is of long standing. Proponents of the phonics method argue that the ability to sound out words facilitates auditory perception and provides a strategy for decoding newly encountered words (Hargis 1983; Wagner & Moyse 1984). On the negative side, opponents of the phonics approach argue that a

FIGURE 7.5 An Example of the Cloze Technique

FROM THE CLUTCHES OF DEATH

In France, about seventy-five years ago, a desperate woman brought her young _____ into the laboratory of Louis Pasteur. The boy _____ been badly bitten by a mad dog, and a terrible death from _____ was certain to follow.

Pasteur was a _____. He had saved the silk industry of France from _____ by working out a method for prevention of two diseases of _____. He had invented a process for preserving _____ by killing the bacteria contained in it and chilling it. And he _____ discovered a vaccine which protected chickens against virulent _____ of chicken cholera, and another which protected both animals and men from the feared _____ of anthrax. Pasteur had also developed a _____ which would usually prevent rabies in animals _____ by mad dogs. But the vaccine had never been _____ on man. It would be a daring experiment, but the _____ had been bitten so badly that he would surely _____ unless quick action were taken. Pasteur _____ the risk. He tried his vaccine on a human being for the first _____. The boy lived! Thus, a rabies vaccine was _____ to the world.

Today, Louis Pasteur _____ considered one of the greatest scientists of all time. Some of his _____ made possible the control of diseases that _____ cost millions of lives.

Key: (Grade level 7.0)
1. son, boy, child
2. had
3. rabies
4. scientist, doctor
5. ruin, destruction, disaster, failure, extinction, bankruptcy
6. silkworms
7. food, milk

had, also, then, alone
attacks, cases
disease, sickness
vaccine, serum
bitten
tried, used, tested
boy, child, patient
die, perish
took

time
given, known, introduced, presented, shown
is
experiments, works, discoveries
had, would('ve), might, could('ve), once, normally

From Marian J. Tonjes (1969). Evaluation of comprehension and vocabulary gains of tenth-grade students enrolled in a developmental reading program. Master's thesis, University of New Mexico. Used by permission.

strong emphasis on phonics overemphasizes decoding skills to the exclusion of comprehension, that it teaches a narrow band of skills which restrict decoding flexibility, and that it relies too heavily on rule memorization.

Likewise, there have been pros and cons advanced in favor or against the word-recognition method. On the positive side, advocates argue that it treats reading at the level of the whole word rather than letter by letter, and that it teaches reading as an integration of decoding and comprehension. However critics of the look-say method argue that the child never learns word attack skills, and consequently, never learns what to do when a new word is encountered. Critics of the whole-word method argue that when faced with new words, the child has only two choices: go to the teacher (or some other mature reader) for help or try to supply the word from context.

☐ Helping to Resolve the Conflict—The Eclectic Approach

It appears that the exclusive use of either the phonics or the word recognition approach alone will create gaps in the child's reading ability. Thus, the teacher should incorporate both approaches in the child's reading program. Known as the *eclectic* approach to teaching reading, the use of both the phonics and the word recognition approaches appears to be especially helpful with special-needs learners such as the mildly mentally retarded (Ehri & Wilce 1985; Hargis 1982; Zintz 1981). In the eclectic approach, the child would learn a basic sight vocabulary as well as the basic phonic skills needed to decode unfamiliar words. Sight words would be recruited from spoken words and concepts in the child's personal life and would be used to create a personalized reading vocabulary for each student (O'Donnel 1979; Meyen 1981; Zintz 1981). Introduce word-attack skills only after the child becomes interested in reading, and learns that reading can give expression to the relevant aspects of life. The child then needs word-attack skills to decode new words while reading and enjoying a story.

THE LOOK-SAY METHOD, EXPERIENCE STORIES, AND LONG-TERM INSTRUCTIONAL UNITS

☐ ☐ One of the best ways to encourage and teach mentally retarded children to read is by using experiences and vocabulary familiar to the individual child (Kirk, Klebhan & Lerner 1978; Meyen 1981). If words and concepts familiar to the child's speaking vocabulary are used, the vocabulary used in the child's reading instruction is guaranteed to be relevant, important to the child, and motivating, and it will thus facilitate learning. Inclusion of relevant and familiar concepts in the child's reading vocabulary also helps insure easy and relevant spin-offs into spelling and written expression.

The inclusion of those words and concepts currently part of the child's experiential life into the reading vocabulary is known as the *language experience* method of reading. In this method, the child's reading materials are not chosen in advance by the teacher but rather are stories that are created by the child and dictated to the teacher by the child. The teacher then copies down the student's stories, perhaps correcting for grammar and punctuation, and/or records the gist of the child's experience. Figure 7.6 represents a young mentally retarded child's experience story dictated to and copied down by his teacher.

Although the child's experience as dictated to the teacher is personalized and individual to the child, a set of stimulating experiences is usually provided by the teacher. These new experiences then become the basis of the child's stories. That is, the children are given highly stimulating and motivating experiences and are then asked to relate (personalize) that experience in some way to the teacher who copies down the related stories. Then, the child reads the story aloud to the class with all of the stories left on display until the next day.

The following day, the stories are copied onto a permanent chart by the teacher. The chart contains all of the children's personal stories "piggy-backed" into one larger story. The students are then helped to read the one, large story,

FIGURE 7.6 A Mentally Retarded Child's Language Experience Story

Today we went on a trip to the department store. We rode on the city bus to get there. I got to ask the driver for a transfer. At the store we saw many things. We saw dresses for girls. We saw washing machines and a refrigerator. I would like a washing machine in my house so we wouldn't have to go to the laundromat all the time! We went to the toy department. I liked looking at the video games. I would like one for Christmas.

again in sentence-by-sentence form, part from memory and part with help from the teacher to learn the configuration (shape) of the words and phrases. The goal of the exercise is to help the child recognize the whole word and phrase rather than isolated letters and letter sounds.

Stories should be duplicated and distributed to the students or they may be tape recorded and placed in a reading activity center. These duplicated stories are kept in a student notebook and referred to on a frequent, prearranged schedule. By using such a method, practice in recognizing words using a look-say approach takes place.

☐ Long-term Units and Language Experience Stories

There are two main problems inherent in the language experience method. First, the teacher faces the problem of choosing experiences to be the basis of the reading vocabulary for students. Second, many older mentally retarded students may complain that the experiences provided by the teacher (e.g., field trips to the zoo or a walk in the neighborhood) are babyish or irrelevant to their lives.

One method of overcoming these problems is to tie the language experience approach with the topics and subtopics of long-term instructional units. Recall from chapter 4 that in order to be accepted for inclusion as a unit topic, the thematic subject matter must pass the test of relevancy; it must be vital and important to the current or future life of the students for which the unit has been designed. Thus, by using the topic and subtopics of a unit currently being taught to students as the basis of those students' language experience stories, the teacher helps insure that the vocabulary of those stories will be relevant. The long-term unit approach to the reading curriculum is particularly relevant for older poor-reading students. In the language experience/long-term instructional unit approach, the student learns to read words and phrases relevant to the topic. For example, Figure 7.7 shows vocabulary relevant to two separate unit topics. Notice how the vocabulary coincides with the key concepts of the unit. The teacher introduces key vocabulary relevant to the unit topic as the unit progresses and then this vocabulary is reasserted as topic-relevant experiences are provided to learners. Thus, in this approach, key vocabulary is systematically introduced by the teacher and the relevancy of that vocabulary is reinforced by providing experiences which necessarily require the use of that vocabulary.

FIGURE 7.7   Vocabulary Included in Two Long-Term Instructional Units

1. Topic: Planning a Nutritious and Well Balanced Menu

Vocabulary

accuracy	evaluation
analyze	essential
basic	fad
caloric	fats
calories	geographical
carbohydrates	growth
category	hypothetical
combined	malnutrition
critique	measurement
deficiency	menu
deficit	nutrients
demonstrate	nutrition
development	pamphlet
diagnose	proteins
distinguish	satisfaction
evaluate	sources

2. Topic: Managing a Savings and Checking Account

Vocabulary

interest	bank teller
savings account	new account officer
checking account	check
statement savings account	deposit slip
interest checking account	deposit/withdrawal slip
checking 300 account	account register
regular checking account	loan
special checking account	safe deposit box
minimum balance	

☐ Developing Sight Vocabularies

Another method of teaching the recognition of new words is by developing and using sight vocabularies (Hargis 1983). The term sight vocabulary refers to common words that are introduced early in the child's reading, these choices being made on the basis of commonness or the frequency with which they appear in the reading materials of children. Thus, the most basic words that appear most often in children's reading would be given to children first in order to build up a core of commonly appearing words in the child's sight vocabulary.

The basic difference between the sight vocabulary and the language experience method and/or the long-term instructional unit approach is that in the language experience method the child chooses the words and concepts to appear in the reading vocabulary based on what is interesting or relevant in the child's life. Likewise, in the unit approach, the teacher chooses concepts to be read, but this is done on the basis of key relevance of the concepts in the child's current and future life even though these words may not appear often in most functional reading lists. However, in the sight word approach, the words are chosen less on their functionality and more on the frequency with which they appear in children's reading material.

In developing sight vocabularies, the key concept is *automaticity*. Students must be able to recognize a word automatically so that they can continue to move through a passage without constantly having to stop to sound out words (Cochran-Smith 1984; Juel, Griffin & Gough 1985). This means that students must overlearn words in order to recognize them on sight. Such overlearning will necessarily mean a great number of repetitions in presentations of words in order to guarantee automatic recognition (Hargis 1982). For mildly mentally retarded students, there will need to be more repetitions than for their nonre-tarded peers. For example, it appears that while a student with an IQ of 90–110 will require only 35 repetitions to automatically recognize a new word, the mildly mentally retarded child (IQ 50–70) will require 55–90 such repetitions (Hargis 1982). Thus continuous exposure to new words is an absolute requisite to sight word learning. Such continuous exposure also requires that a minimum number of new words be presented to the mentally retarded child at any one time.

☐ Choosing the Sight Word Vocabulary

How are words included in sight vocabularies chosen? That is, how can the relative frequency of words in children's reading be assessed? There are lists available which contain samples of words listed by frequency in children's reading materials. For example, Fry (1977) selected a list of 600 words which he found to be of high frequency. The first 300 words of this list contain what Fry considered to be the most essential words for inclusion in a child's initial reading vocabulary. Figure 7.8 contains an alphabetical listing of the most functional 300 words which have been broken into thirds.

For mentally retarded learners, the teacher should also choose sight words on the basis of their *survival value*. Such a list would represent those words which the child would need to be able to read to survive and function safely in society (Kirk, Klieban & Lerner 1978). Figure 7.9 contains a listing of typical survival words.

TECHNIQUES FOR TEACHING WORD RECOGNITION SKILLS

☐ Pictorial Aids

The objective in the word-recognition phase is for the child to be able to rapidly and easily recognize, read, and understand words. One method of word recognition is memorization, in which the child memorizes a large number of sight words.

FIGURE 7.8   An Alphabetical Listing of the Most Functional 300 Words Taken From the Fry Instant Word List

FIRST HUNDRED

a	at	did	had	if	man	on	so	this	what
about	be	do	has	in	many	one	some	three	when
after	been	down	have	is	me	or	take	to	which
again	before	eat	he	it	much	other	that	two	who
all	boy	for	her	just	my	our	the	up	will
an	but	from	here	know	new	out	their	us	with
and	by	get	him	like	no	put	them	very	work
any	can	give	his	little	not	said	then	was	would
are	come	go	how	long	of	see	there	we	you
as	day	good	I	make	old	she	they	were	your

SECOND HUNDRED

also	black	each	girl	left	mother	own	run	sure	upon
am	book	ear	got	let	must	people	saw	tell	use
another	both	end	hand	live	name	play	say	than	want
away	box	far	high	look	near	please	school	these	way
back	bring	find	home	made	never	present	seem	thing	where
ball	call	first	house	may	next	pretty	shall	think	while
because	came	five	into	men	night	ran	should	too	white
best	color	found	kind	more	only	read	soon	tree	wish
better	could	four	last	morning	open	red	stand	under	why
big	dear	friend	leave	most	over	right	such	until	year

THIRD HUNDRED

along	carry	don't	fat	grow	jump	off	set	stop	turn
always	clean	door	fine	hat	keep	once	seven	ten	walk
anything	close	dress	fire	happy	letter	order	show	thank	warm
around	clothes	early	fly	hard	longer	pair	sing	third	wash
ask	coat	eight	food	head	love	part	sister	those	water
ate	cold	every	full	hear	might	ride	sit	though	woman
bed	cut	eyes	funny	help	money	round	sleep	today	write
brown	didn't	face	gave	hold	myself	same	small	took	yellow
buy	does	fall	goes	hope	now	sat	start	town	yes
car	dog	fast	green	hot	o'clock	second		try	yesterday

From E.B. Fry (1977). *Elementary reading instruction*. New York: McGraw-Hill. Reprinted by permission.

However, especially for beginning mentally retarded readers, the processing demands of memorizing a large number of sight words rapidly increases to prohibitive levels and the memory system is soon overloaded. Thus, other techniques of teaching word recognition skills which do not rely solely on memorization must be utilized.

One method which may be used is using pictures to accompany text. Known as text illustrations or pictorial aids, these drawings or photographs usually appear on the same page as the corresponding text and in some way provide clues to the reader about what is happening in the story. Figure 7.10 is an example of pictorial contextual clues. As this figure shows, these illustrations do

FIGURE 7.9   Typical Survival Words

Danger
Exit
Entrance
Keep Off
Help Wanted
Go
Stop
Caution
Beware of Dog
Slippery When Wet
School
Poison
Private Property
Yield
Slow
Wet Paint
Men
Women
Police
Hot
Cold
Off/On
Doctor
Telephone

Walk
Ambulance
Open/Closed
Pull/Push
Detour
Inflammable
Nurse
Quiet
Wrong Way/Go Back
Walk/Don't Walk
Thin Ice
Gasoline
Out of Order
No Smoking
No Parking
Watch Your Step
High Voltage
Do Not Touch
Help Wanted
Vacancy/No Vacancy
No U Turn
No Passing
Look
Do Not Inhale Fumes

FIGURE 7.10   Use of Pictorial Context Cues in Reading

The fox galloped along beside the fence. He crashed under a clump of blackened brush and leaped to the top rail of the fence.

The dog went racing past.

The fox went on along the fence. The charred wood crumbled between his toes. He jumped down and raced lightly through the vineyard.

Now, far in the distance, he could hear the unhappy yelps of the dog.

Then there was silence.

Back in the barnyard, the dog trotted up, panting loudly, and the chickens scolded softly and settled down again to sleep.

The fox did not return.

From FOX AND THE FIRE by Miska Miles, illustrated by John C. Schoenherr. By permission of Little, Brown and Company, in association with The Atlantic Monthly Press.

not constitute a picture book in which text is kept to a minimum and the pictures tell the story. In the pictorial aid method, the pictures provide some contextual clues so that the child can fill the gaps of comprehension and correctly guess unfamiliar words. When using pictorial aids it is the teacher's job to help the child learn to recognize the words and move them into the child's sight vocabulary.

For older mentally retarded learners reading within a long-term instructional unit format, it is a good idea for pictures or line drawings to accompany the introduction of key unit concepts. For many learners, the concepts contained in unit topics may be abstract and/or symbolic (e.g., the concept of neighborhood or employment). Often some sort of picture cards with the word on one side of the card and a picture of the concept or action on the other will facilitate meaningful acquisition of the concept into the reading vocabulary. Such pictorial aids function to increase student motivation to read while decreasing dependence on the teacher to decode unfamiliar words. Reading self-concept and a sense of reading accomplishment are thereby increased.

One caution about the use of pictorial aids and illustrations in the learning of new words: sooner or later the pictures will need to be faded out. Real-life reading material does not come with pictorial aids designed to help the reader figure out the author's message. Thus the teacher who decides to use pictorial aids in initial stages of sight vocabulary development will need a backup method for the time that the illustrations are to be faded out and no longer used.

☐ Using Visual Configurations

Visual configurations refer to the phenomenon that some words or phrases have different shapes or configurations on the printed page. These differing visual appearances include differences in the first and last letters of words, word lengths, number of letters which fall above or below the page line, and the general shape of the overall word or phrase.

One method of highlighting the visual configurations of words is by using *perimeter maps*. This method accents both the general shape of the word as well as the degree to which letters of the word fall below the line. With a perimeter map, the most salient configuration features as well as the length of the word are emphasized. Figure 7.11 shows some perimeter maps for common reading words.

A problem with the perimeter map method is the fact that many words are quite similar in their configuration. For example, compare the configurations of *horse* and *house, ride* and *rode, fast* and *last*. For words such as these, perimeter maps which highlight word configurations may become confusing rather than helpful. Thus, the teacher must be careful to strictly control the reading vocabulary so as to guard against the introduction of words which look similar on the printed page.

☐ Rebuses

Another configuration method is one which gives cues or hints to word decoding based upon the auditory sounds found in the words. Such symbols are known as pictographic logographs or *Rebuses* (Clark 1984; Clark, Davis & Woodcock 1974). Figure 7.12 contains some words and shows how they might be depicted for the new reader based on the Rebus system. Cues are often based on phonology

FIGURE 7.11 Perimeter "Maps" of Common Words

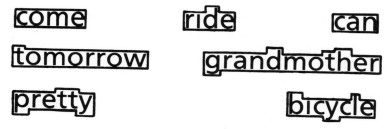

FIGURE 7.12 Sample Passage From a Rebus Reader

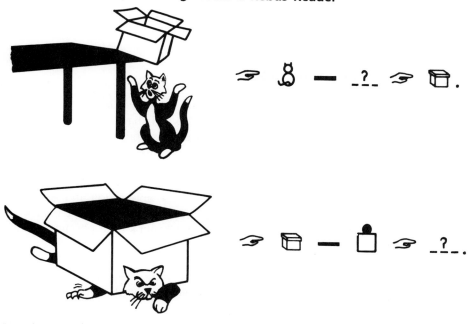

Reproduced by permission of American Guidance Service, Inc., Publishers' Bldg., Circle Pines, MN. Peabody Rebus Reading Program by Richard W. Woodcock, Charlotte R. Clark, Cornelia A. Davies. © 1979.

which treats word meanings (semantics) as if they did not exist (e.g., *eye* is used for the pronoun *I*). Pictographic logographs are useful in helping readers gain an initial sight vocabulary but they have been criticized by some for stressing cues of sound rather than cues of meaning.

PHONICS AND WORD ANALYSIS

☐ ☐ A great deal of research has been conducted on which phonics skills are most needed by students and in what order they might be best presented. There is no single definitive method for phonics instruction; nevertheless, there is some consensus on which phonics skills are needed for successful reading. These include:

1. Teaching of vowel sounds (long and short sounds)
2. Teaching of consonant sounds
3. The more common consonant sounds (*sm, sk, tr, sh* etc.)
4. Consonant digraphs (*ch, sh, th, wh*)
5. Vowel digraphs (*ay, ai, au, ee, ei*, etc.)
6. Syllables ending with vowels making the internal vowel long
7. Clues to silent letters
8. Consonants with more than one sound

☐ Nine Rules of Basic Phonics

The analysis of basic phonics skills has led to the formulation of nine basic phonics rules (Clymer 1963) which have been shown to be common to most reading vocabularies and are consistent (applicable) in at least 75 percent of phonics cases. Many reading specialists advocate that these nine rules be taught. Students are then encouraged and helped at all times to use (generalize) these rules in their decoding of new words. Of course, since mentally retarded learners have specific problems in rule application and generalization, the systematic instruction in such rule generalization must be even more greatly emphasized by the special education teacher. Clymer's nine phonics rules are

1. When the letter *c* is followed by *a* or *o*, the sound of *k* is heard.
2. When *c* is followed by *e* or *i*, the sound of *s* is heard.
3. When *c* and *h* are next to each other, they make only one (single) sound. The same applies for *sh*.
4. When two of the same consonants are side by side (double consonants), only one sound is heard (e.g., *fell*).

5. When *e* appears at the end of a word, the internal vowel of that word is long (e.g., home).
6. When there is one *e* in a word that ends with a consonant, the *e* takes the short sound.
7. When two vowels appear side by side, the word takes the sound of the first vowel.
8. When *y* is the final letter of a word, it usually has a vowel sound.
9. The letter *r* gives the preceding vowel a sound that is neither long nor short (e.g., car).

☐ Handling Exceptions to the Phonics Rules

The question may be raised as to the exceptions to phonics rules. As anyone who has struggled to learn English as a second language will readily agree, English is fraught with exceptions to the basic phonics rules. Is this not a reason to refrain from teaching phonics?

Yes and no. While it is true that English is an irregular language which contains many exceptions to phonics rules, it is also true that phonics instruction allows the child initially to attempt decoding by allowing the application of systematic rules to new words. After such an initial decoding attempt, if the rule has been found not to work for the new word in question, the child can ask for assistance. Besides, there are fewer exceptions to given rules than there are words that conform to those rules, thus increasing the probability that the child will be able to use the rule to figure out the word.

In situations where words which violate phonics rules are going to be encountered by the child, the teacher can facilitate learning and reduce confusion by adhering to two commonsense procedures:

1. Try to limit children's exposure to irregular words especially in their initial reading instruction. There will be ample opportunity to learn phonetic exceptions later when the child's reading skills are more mature and the student can handle exceptions more strategically. Delay exposure to irregular words until a later date.
2. Explain exceptions as they occur. It can only be confusing to children when the teacher attempts to list all of the exceptions to a given rule at the time that the rule is introduced. Rather, exceptions should be pointed out as they are encountered by the child with words in context rather than with words in isolation.

By using such commonsense procedures to the problem of irregular words and exceptions to phonics rules, it is anticipated that phonics instruction will remain a useful tool in the teaching of word decoding skills to mentally retarded learners.

APPROACHES TO PHONICS INSTRUCTION

☐ ☐ Within the phonics components of reading, there are two main instructional approaches: *synthesis* and *analysis*. The synthesis approach deals with the chaining or linking together of individual letters for the purpose of reading the entire word, while analysis breaks words down into their component parts.

Although the synthesis approach does have its usefulness in helping children attack and decode new words, it may be inappropriate for use with mentally retarded learners because it encourages the child to use a letter-by-letter approach to reading. Since the unit of reading for good readers is not the letter or word but rather the phrase (Golinkoff 1975), the synthesis approach is counterproductive in that it encourages the child to use a reading strategy that may not be conducive to good reading. In order to use the synthesis approach and still read well, the child must actually learn two strategies: one for decoding new words and one for reading familiar material. Since mentally retarded learners usually do not apply, discriminate, or generalize strategies well, the mildly mentally retarded learners will be hard-pressed to use the synthesis strategy appropriately.

The more facilitative phonics method in teaching mentally retarded learners phonics skills is that of analysis. In this approach, emphasis is placed on word syllables and eventual syllabication of unknown words rather than by a letter-by-letter approach. Students using the analysis approach typically would be taught to attack the whole word rather than a collection of single letters. Students would then attempt to divide the word into its component syllables and to read (and re-chain) the syllables. This approach stresses the rules between vowels and consonants rather than the sounds of individual letters.

☐ Structural Analysis

Structural analysis is a form of the analysis approach to phonics. It is a method by which parts of words which form meaningful units (morphemes) are identified within words which are not part of the student's sight vocabulary. Structural analysis includes recognizing root words, prefixes, suffixes, and components of compound words. Teachers who plan to use structural analysis in their reading instruction with mentally retarded learners should be sure to systematically point out to students how modifications can be made in words which change the meaning of the word but only slightly change the way it is read (e.g., walk, walked; knowing, unknowing). Knowing suffixes, prefixes, and root words can greatly increase the decoding and comprehension of mentally retarded learners. However, special education teachers who initiate structural-analysis instruction with mentally retarded learners must make sure that material is presented systematically and in a way that highlights the similarities in words. Immature readers cannot be expected to acquire the relatively sophisticated concept that words may contain suffixes, prefixes, and root words without well-planned instruction by the teacher.

TECHNIQUES FOR TEACHING PHONICS

☐ Color Phonics

One workable method for teaching phonics to mentally retarded learners is the *Color Phonics System* (Bannatyne 1966). This is a system where letters and letter combinations are printed on color coded cards. In this way, the child receives cues or aids in identifying each letter sound.

All vowels, consonants, and combinations possess their respective colors in this system: consonants as well as *ph* and *qu* have white lettering on a gray background; vowels, diphthongs, etc., are printed in colored letters on a white background. The color coding approach is sequenced and each phoneme can be identified from its appropriate color. Words can then be phonetically decoded by students with letter colors acting as a central cue to the decoding process.

This system has proven successful with nonreading, mildly mentally retarded children as well as with children who possess poor auditory memory. It is also systematic in its instruction for students. Of course, it should not be used with children who are suspected of possessing any type of color blindness.

☐ Glass Analysis for Decoding

The Glass Analysis approach (Glass & Glass 1978) is a system designed to teach letter/sound clusters. The Glass kit contains packs of cards which are organized into 119 letter clusters ranging in degree of difficulty from easy to complex. Students learn a given cluster and then add letters to extend that cluster. The students are trained to perceive sounds as clusters in whole words. This technique has proven particularly useful with older mildly mentally retarded students who are in need of remedial phonics drill.

☐ Syllabication

The syllabication approach to phonics is a systematic method of dividing polysyllabic words into their component syllables (Clymer 1963; Emans 1973; Bailey 1967). Syllables are then read in isolation and rechained in order to read the whole word. It has been found that six general syllabication rules can be learned and these rules will apply to approximately 80 percent of all syllabication cases (Cheek & Cheek 1980). These rules are

1. In most two-syllable words, the first syllable is accented.
2. If *a*, *in*, *re*, *de*, or *be* is the first syllable in a word, it is usually unaccented.
3. In most two-syllable words that end in a consonant followed by *y*, the first syllable is accented.

4. If the last syllable in a word ends with *le*, the consonant preceding the *le* usually begins the last syllable.
5. When the first vowel element in a word is followed by *th*, *ch*, or *sh*, these symbols are not broken when the word is divided into syllables and may go with either the first or the second syllable.
6. When the last syllable is the sound *r*, it is unaccented.

☐ A Final Note on Phonics

Like medication, phonics instruction may be helpful or harmful depending on how it is used. While appropriate phonics instruction may be beneficial in helping children to decode new words independently, too much or unsystematic phonics instructions may prove detrimental to the reading process and the mentally retarded child's motivation to read. Thus, it is suggested that the special education teacher interested in using a phonics approach keep the following considerations in mind

1. That it not be used alone but that it be incorporated with the look-say method of word recognition. Phonics is not the be-all and end-all of reading. Rather, it should be used eclectically with word-recognition techniques.
2. Students should possess the necessary prerequisite skills for phonics instruction which include adequate oral language, visual-auditory discrimination skills, and an appropriate sight vocabulary.
3. The teacher should present only those phonics rules which are necessary for the child's present decoding and reading. Present them when they are needed, not all at once.
4. Always tie in letter-sound training with their occurrence in words.
5. Develop phonics activities from meaningful reading.
6. Use sight words to demonstrate phonics applications.
7. Do not bury students with rules. Be reasonable.

Adherence to these guidelines will go far in insuring that phonics instruction for mentally retarded learners is successful, enjoyable, and meaningful.

READING COMPREHENSION

☐ ☐ People should understand what they read. There is probably not a single teacher who would disagree with this statement. Yet research done over the years indicates a sizeable proportion of children do not understand what they read (Aulls 1982; Stevens 1985).

What constitutes comprehension? That is, what processes are supposed to occur before we agree that comprehension has taken place? Davis (1968) has asserted that comprehension consists of five processes:

1. Remembering word meanings.
2. Following the structure of a passage.
3. Finding answers to questions asked explicitly in the text.
4. Recognizing a writer's purpose, attitude, tone, or mood.
5. Drawing inferences from text.

The question may be asked as to how well mentally retarded learners comprehend what they read. Unfortunately, the answer seems to be that they do not comprehend very much, even on the most basic literal levels. Several studies have investigated mentally retarded students' immediate comprehension of text (Luftig & Greeson 1983; Luftig & Johnson 1982). When literal comprehension was the test measure, the average mildly mentally retarded learner remembered less than 50 percent of the ideas of a story (even when a liberal method of scoring remembering was used). Furthermore, these pupils demonstrated significant deficiencies in answering questions of literal comprehension. Additionally, mentally retarded students showed even greater deficiencies in reorganization comprehension as demonstrated by their general inability to differentiate important from unimportant textual ideas. Thus, even in cases where mentally retarded learners can appropriately decode the words presented to them on the written page, they still experience significant difficulty in comprehending the ideas which have been decoded.

COMPREHENSION STRATEGIES

☐ ☐ In recent years, there has been a dramatic increase in interest in strategies designed to help children comprehend what they read (Baker & Brown 1985; Paris, Cross, DeBritto, Jacobs, Oka & Saarino 1984). While in the past teachers have taught comprehension by asking students pointed (usually factual) questions about what they have read, more recent instructional procedures involve having students learn and use strategies in order to enhance their own comprehension (Brown, Armbruster & Baker 1985; Paris & Jacobs 1985). These strategies include catagorizing and summarizing information, having students generate their own questions and predictions about text, and using sentence and paragraph structure to aid comprehension.

☐ Summarization Training

Summarization training is direct instruction in summarizing and paraphrasing text directly after the student has read the passage (Baumann 1984; Bean &

Steenwyk 1984). Such summarization can occur in either oral form (verbal or spoken into a tape recorder) or written summaries. Summarization and paraphrasing have been shown to be effective strategies in overcoming deficits of poor readers, particularly for older students (Paris, Cross & Lipson 1984; Taylor & Beach 1984).

Rinehart, Stahl and Erickson (1985) devised a training procedure for teaching the summarization technique. The procedure is

1. The teacher defines the summarization tasks, and explains their usefulness for reading comprehension.
2. The teacher demonstrates how to summarize individual paragraphs using a talking through technique. This is accomplished by the teacher reading a paragraph with the class and explaining the mental steps one goes through in summarizing the passage.
3. Students are told to (a) find the overall (topic) idea of the paragraph, (b) find the next most important idea in the paragraph, and (c) using as few sentences as possible, summarize the paragraph. These steps are included in checklist form in students' practice books and on a slide used in the lessons.
4. Following the teacher's talk through, students are called upon to talk through a passage using paragraphs in their practice book.
5. Students practice making short summaries of individual paragraphs and receive feedback from the teacher.

This summarization strategy operates to make impulsive readers more reflective while reading, leading to more time spent on task with better concentration. This additional time produces deeper processing of text material with better understanding of what has been read (Rinehart, Stahl & Erickson 1985).

☐ Generated Questions

In the generated question approach, students are trained to formulate questions about what they have read (Davey & McBride 1984; Gordon 1982). Such questions are generated by the students themselves rather than the teachers and it is believed that such self-generated questions involve students in active comprehension thus leading to deeper processing of text (Singer 1978).

In using the student-generated-question approach, it is a good idea to use the reciprocal questioning technique (Andre & Anderson 1979; Feldman & Risko 1985). In this method, students work in pairs, asking each other questions about what they have read. Questions may be of a literal, inferential, or predictive (what's going to happen next?) nature. The procedure for reciprocal questioning is as follows:

1. Students form dyads.
2. Student A asks a question of a partner.

3. The question is answered by the partner.
4. If the partner cannot answer the question, both students revert back to the text for the answer.
5. Roles are reversed; student B asks the question of student A.

The reciprocal questioning approach has proven especially useful and motivating with older (e.g., junior and senior high school) poor readers (Andre & Anderson 1979; Wong & Jones 1982).

☐ Central Story Problems

Central story problems involve helping students identify the central theme or main idea of a story passage (Modolfsky 1983; Stevens 1985). In this method, the student identifies the following story features:

1. The central problem of the story. What is the problem faced by the protagonist?
2. Who or what is causing the problem?
3. What was the solution to the problem.
4. How was the problem solved.

☐ Creative Questioning

Questioning by the teacher about what has happened in text is probably still the most popular comprehension instructional technique used in the classroom. However, it appears that where comprehension questions are asked by the teacher, those questions focus nearly entirely on factual and literal information (56.9 percent) and recognition questions (13.5 percent) rather than on the higher levels of comprehension (Guszak 1972). Thus, one reason mentally retarded children do not perform well at higher levels of comprehension may be that the instruction and practice which they receive in acquiring those skills is inadequate.

Types of activities which may facilitate higher level comprehension processes include

1. **Asking semantic questions:** What do you think the passage means? What was the author trying to get across?
2. **Key phrase questions:** Can you find the key words or phrases which tell you the topic of the author's message? What is important in the sentence? What can be eliminated in the passage without the loss of too much information?
3. **Divergent Questions:** In this method, the teacher asks questions which have no one right answer: How many ways can a brick be used? What could you do with coconuts if you were stranded on an island? Children

will often feel uncomfortable with divergent questions since they have been trained to look for the one right answer which will please the teacher. However, divergent questions foster both creative ability and the ability to make inferences from text.

☐ Understanding Paragraph Structure

A prose passage contains both central/important material, known as superordinate structure, and details of less important material, known as subordinate structure, (Luftig & Johnson 1982; Myer & Freedle 1984; Stephens 1985). Typically paragraphs possess the superordinate material at the beginning of the paragraph in the form of a topic sentence, with subsequent sentences containing the subordinate material. Mildly mentally retarded students typically are deficient in differentiating important from unimportant text material (Luftig & Greeson 1983; Luftig & Johnson 1982). Thus these students need instruction and practice in identifying topic sentences, outlining important material found in text, and categorizing ideas into superordinate and subordinate groups.

Ekwall and Shanker (1983) devised one way to teach paragraph structure. In this method, students are presented with a series of rectangles in which the top rectangle is the longest. The teacher explains that the main idea of the paragraph is represented by the longest rectangle while the less important ideas are represented by the lower and shorter rectangles. Teacher and students then work together orally to fill in the rectangles with the appropriate superordinate and subordinate paragraph information. Finally, students repeat the exercise alone with teacher feedback.

☐ Gaining Comprehension from Surrounding Text

One way people glean understanding from text is to use information given previously in the passage to predict what will happen next. For example, suppose you read the passage:

> John received his allowance and decided he wanted to buy a new toy. He took his money and went to the toy _____.

How would you fill in the blank? The only way you could do so intelligently would be by using contextual cues from the passage to help you fill in the missing word.

It has been demonstrated that mentally retarded children do not perform very well in using both information given in text and knowledge about how the world operates to comprehend text (Campione & Brown 1979; Luftig & Johnson 1982; Paris & Lindhauer 1974). Thus, these students need concentrated instruction and practice in using previous text to anticipate what will transpire later in a passage.

READING PROGRAMS

☐ ☐ A wide variety of reading materials and programs are available for mentally retarded learners. These programs are basically divided into five main types: basal readers, synthesis phonics basal readers, linguistic phoneme materials, individualized and/or programmed reading materials, and language experience materials.

☐ Basal Readers

Basal readers are structured, sequenced reading texts which usually include the children's reading materials, teacher's manuals, lessons, and extra materials such as workbooks and audio-visual aids. These programs are sequenced, usually from kindergarten or first grade to grades six or eight. Basal readers take the approach of introducing a sight vocabulary to students as well as providing them to a limited degree with phonics instruction. Thus, to some degree, basal readers take the eclectic approach to reading instruction. While such programs are highly sequenced, they are not individualized; they gear reading level to the typical or average child. Likewise, they may not be designed for culturally different children; many of such children may still be found in classes for mildly mentally retarded students. Thus, basal readers may prove to be unmotivating or outside of the experience of these types of learners. A brief description of commonly used basal readers designed for handicapped readers follows:

1. *Open Court*: This program is designed for direct teaching of basic phonics and reading skills. Students are taught forty-three phonemes and ninety-five spellings. Each letter of the alphabet possesses a fantasy personality and history connected with the sound it makes. The series contains eight readers ranging from grades 1–6. The program includes readers, storybooks, workbooks, and readiness materials. This program is especially popular with younger mildly mentally retarded readers.
2. *Stanwix House Reading Series*: The Stanwix Series teaches phonics and word analysis skills at a slower rate than other basal readers and is thus appropriate for use with mentally retarded learners. It consists of a series of highly motivating books and workbooks in both fictional and text form. All of the reading material is written in three parallel forms with a difficulty range that allows for individualization of assignments. This parallel form is a strong feature of this program.
3. *Caught Reading*: This program has been designed for adolescent handicapped readers. It contains stories and text written at the interest level of adolescents but at a reading level of third grade and below. Five high-interest paperbacks are included in the program along with a teacher's manual.

☐ Synthesis Basal Readers

Synthesis phonics basal readers are similar to basal readers but they emphasize the skills needed to combine sounds together to decode words and place less emphasis on sight vocabulary. The advantages and disadvantages of basal readers also apply to synthesis phonics basal readers with the added disadvantage for synthesis readers of a highly controlled vocabulary which may prove boring or unmotivating to many readers. Figure 7.13 lists popular synthesis basal readers.

☐ Linguistic Phoneme Approaches

Linguistic phoneme approaches use a highly controlled vocabulary which conforms to the sound patterns of English (e.g., *sat*, *cat*, *hat*, *fat*). They attempt to teach children to read using the common patterns of phonemes. The advantages and disadvantages of basal readers also apply to this approach. In addition, encountering new, irregular words is often difficult for children in these kinds of series. Finally, since the vocabulary is so highly controlled, it is often difficult to devise interesting stories which use these words. The linguistic phoneme approach probably should be avoided for mildly mentally retarded learners. Figure 7.13 contains a listing of popular linguistic phoneme series.

☐ Programmed Approaches

Individualized/programmed readers allow each child to read materials of personal choice at an individual pace. Words are taught to children as they are encountered. Evaluation is individualized and is accomplished either through the

FIGURE 7.13   Available Programs in Reading for Mentally Retarded Learners

1. *Basal Readers*
   American Book Co.
   Allyn & Brown, Inc.
   Ginn 720 Series
   Harper & Row
   Holt, Rinehart & Winston
   Houghton Mifflin
   Rand-McNally
   Scott, Foresman

2. *Synthesis Phonics Basal*
   DISTAR
   Lippincott Basic Reader Series
   Open Court Reading Program
   Swirl Community Skills Program

3. *Linguistic Phoneme Readers*
   Let's Read
   SRA Lift-Off to Reading
   SRA Basic
   Merrill Linguistic Readers

4. *Language Experience Approach*
   Teacher made materials

reading package or through individual student/teacher conferences. This approach appears to be highly motivating to children in getting them to read and maintain good reading habits. On the negative side, it requires much record keeping and individualized planning. However, a teacher's aide or a class parent can often aid the teacher.

☐ The Language Experience Program

In the language experience approach, children create their own vocabularies and stories based on experiences which are relevant and useful in their lives. This approach can be tied into long-term instructional units where the teacher introduces the key vocabulary needed for current and future life success. Although this approach is highly motivating to students, it provides no systematic development of materials or vocabulary. However, it does demonstrate to the child that reading is a communication process used to communicate shared experiences. It is also highly adaptive to the needs of culturally different students since they define the experiences which will become the basis of their reading.

OTHER READING PACKAGES AND PROGRAMS FOR MENTALLY RETARDED READERS

☐ The Direct Instructional System for Teaching Arithmetic and Reading (DISTAR) (Engelmann & Bruner 1974, 1975)

The DISTAR program was developed in the 1960s for use with culturally different (then more commonly known as culturally disadvantaged) children. Materials in the program range from prekindergarten readiness through the fourth grade reading level. DISTAR is a highly structured, tightly ordered sequential program which is criterion referenced and does not allow the child to move on to a new skill until current skills are mastered. The program appears to be particularly suited for mentally retarded learners, is motivating to students, and allows the student to move through the program at an individual pace.

The DISTAR program includes subprograms for symbol-action games, blending tasks, and rhyming tasks. Symbol-action games teach the basic readiness skills for success reading acquisition, while blending skills teach children to read and spell words by sounds (say it slow) and by blends (say it fast). Rhyming tasks help children learn the relationship between the auditory sounds of words and their visual counterparts.

Recently, a second program, known as the Corrective Reading Program (CRP) has been added to the DISTAR series. The CRP is a program for older students who are reading at about the second-grade level. CRP contains stories geared to the interest level of these students, who would most probably be uninterested in reading stories geared to second-grade children. Thus the CRP would be of particular use to teachers of somewhat older mentally retarded learners who are reading significantly below grade level.

☐ Edmark Reading Series

The Edmark Reading Series is a program which contains over 200 tightly constructed lessons. Materials for these lessons include storybooks, workbooks which utilize the stories presented, and a variety of other reading instruction material. The goal of the Edmark Reading Series is to teach a basic sight vocabulary. Thus, it adheres more to the word recognition than the phonics method of reading instruction. Because of this, supplemental phonics instruction may have to be given after the Edmark program has been completed. The Edmark series has been used successfully with mentally retarded students at a variety of levels.

☐ Sullivan Programmed Readers

This is an older, but still popular reading program among teachers of mentally retarded children. It is a relatively inexpensive system available at five different levels for readers of various reading abilities. Each level has its own programmed textbooks, workbooks, progress tests, and teacher manuals. The series is designed to be more of a remedial than a developmental program; consequently, the child who enters into the series should possess at least some reading skills.

☐ Hegge, Kirk & Kirk Remediational Reading Drills

Like the Sullivan Series, the Hegge, Kirk & Kirk drills are designed to be remedial. Thus the student should have at least some reading skills upon entering into the program. Although inexpensive and useful as a remedial series, the drills do not systematically and developmentally teach reading to pupils and another system should be chosen if that is the teacher's intent. Nevertheless, the program is quite useful for having students maintain newly acquired skills through practice and drill.

READING AND THE UNIT APPROACH

☐ ☐ A major tenet of this text is advocacy of the unit approach to curriculum for the mentally retarded. In this approach, the teaching of reading can be incorporated easily and comfortably. The steps to utilize in the unit approach to the teaching of reading are:

1. Identify the new vocabulary and concepts associated with the unit topic. For example, if the unit topic was "Creating and Implementing a Personal Hygiene Program," the teacher would identify new words and concepts associated with this topic.
2. Introduce these new concepts and vocabulary into the child's spoken vocabulary using the language experience method.
3. Introduce the new vocabulary and concepts into the child's reading curriculum using the language experience approach (word recognition) as well as the application of learned phonics rules used to decode new words encountered that are related to the unit theme.

Figure 7.14 contains some sample reading lesson plans taken from a long-term instructional unit.

Notice that it is imperative that the vocabulary and concepts be introduced to students and mastered as part of the spoken vocabulary before reading instruction of these words is undertaken. It must be assumed that since the curriculum unit topic is new and unfamiliar to mentally retarded students, the words and concepts related to the topic are also unfamiliar. Thus, they must become part of the child's experiential world before they are introduced as new reading materials.

FIGURE 7.14 Sample Lesson Plans for Reading from a Long-term Instructional Unit

Topic
Planning a Nutritious and Well Balanced Menu

Behavioral Objective	Activity	Materials	Evaluation
After reading chapter 1 on "Basic Nutrition Facts" in class, the student will correctly list the four basic food groups when asked to do so. 1.1	Group reading session. Individual and choral reading. Discussion time following reading will be led by the leaders of each individual section. A summary of the section's activities will be given by volunteers of each group. Each student will point to each food group and state the name of the group using the wall poster.	*Health Education & the Elementary School,* Willgoose, C. E. Saunders Co., Boston, 1969 A poster illustrating "the 4 food groups"—Florida Citrus Commission will be used paper/pencil	Each student will be orally tested on the names of the groups. Also study questions at the end of each chapter will be used for written evaluation. Accuracy will be required on the written with 100% accuracy on the oral.
When shown a list of common foods, the student will correctly choose the foods belonging in the vegetable/fruit group with 80 percent accuracy. 1.5	Students will read the stories on wheat and vegetables, followed by questions and answers. The film on food stores will then be shown. Worksheet will be handed out and completed by student.	Stories: "Plants That Feed Us" C. Fenton Stories: "Story Book of Wheat" M. Petersham	Students are tested using the list of common foods and the appropriate food group. Answers will be given with 80 percent accuracy for *both* tests administered: fruits/vegetables and bread/cereal.

Using the unit approach to teach reading frees the teacher somewhat from having to rely on word lists and formal reading series in order to set the reading curriculum. The reading curriculum is set by the topic of the unit. This method assures the relevancy and validity of the reading curriculum.

READING AND THE COMPUTER

☐ ☐ One of the greatest innovations in reading instruction for children is computer-assisted instruction (CAI). The computer can do many things educationally for mentally retarded children that fill their reading needs. For example, computers can lend novelty to the reading experiences. Many children who say they dislike reading and find reading instruction and drill boring nevertheless enjoy engaging in reading instruction when the material is presented on the computer. Computer-assisted reading instruction is also flexible and dynamic. The text presentation can be individualized and tailored to meet the needs of individual students, individualization being an important requisite in the learning of mentally retarded learners. Computers also offer to teachers sequenced, programmed instruction which progresses at the student's own pace and which instructs the student in a one-to-one relationship. Finally, computers can analyze student responses, diagnose reader mistakes, and provide remedial programming designed to attack students' reading weaknesses. (Geoffrion & Geoffrion 1983).

Computer-assisted reading instruction can assist in the areas of reading readiness, word decoding and recognition, and comprehension. Available software aids students in learning the basic concepts needed to enter reading instruction, learn phonics skills, and engage in enough practice and drill to recognize words on sight. Likewise, computer software currently exists to help students not only in literal comprehension but also in higher level comprehension processes such as making inferences and recognizing the author's purpose and message. Available programs are proliferating almost geometrically and a definitive list of available reading software will quickly become outdated. Therefore, Figure 7.15 lists the names of major educational software publishers who continue to design and market reading instructional software.

Although software is often relatively expensive, some programs are in the public domain and can be reproduced by teachers without penalty or cost. Such programs can be very useful to teachers. Figure 7.16 contains a short list of the programs available in the public domain as they relate to reading instruction. Additionally, Figure 7.17 contains a short listing of commercially available reading programs for the computer that are educationally sound as well as motivating.

SUMMARY

☐ ☐ Reading is a process by which almost all other subject matter in school is taught. Likewise, it has been shown to be a crucial skill needed for adult life success.

FIGURE 7.15   Software Publishers Who Produce Computer Assisted Reading Programs

Automated Simulations
P. O. Box 4247
Mountain View, CA 94040

Avant Associates
9 Marietta Lane
Mercerville, NJ 08619

Borg-Warner
600 W. University Drive
Arlington Heights, IL 60004

Brain Box
70 East 10th Street
New York, NY 10003

Britannica Computer-Based Learning
425 N. Michigan Avenue
Chicago, IL 60611

Educational Activities
P. O. Box 392
Freeport, NY 11520

Edu-Ware Services
P. O. Box 22222
Agoura, CA 91301

Ginn & Company
191 Spring Street
Lexington, MA 02173

Hartley Courseware
P. O. Box 431
Dimondale, MI 48821

I Discover Personalized Books
P. O. Box 170
Andover, MA 01810

L & S Computerware
1589 Fraser Drive
Sunnyvale, CA 94086

Learning Well
200 S. Service Road
Roslyn Heights, NY 11577

Merry Bee Communications
815 Crest Drive
Omaha, NE 68046

MicroPower and Light
12820 Hillcrest Road
Suite 224
Dallas, TX 75230

Minnesota Educational Computer Consortium*
3590 Lexington Ave. N.
St. Paul, MN 55126

Orange Cherry Media
7 Delano Drive
Bedford Hills, NY

Pendulum Press
Saw Mill Road
West Haven, CT 06516

Potomac Microresources
P. O. Box 277
Riverdale, MD 20737

Program Design
95 E. Putnam Avenue
Greenwich, CT 06830

Random House
201 East 50th Street
New York, NY 10022

Right On Programs
P. O. Box 977
Huntington, NY 11743

Software Productions
2357 Southway Drive
Columbus, OH 43221

Southeastern Educational Software
3300 Buckeye Road
Atlanta, GA 30341

Spinnaker Software
215 1st Street
Cambridge, MA 02142

SRA
1540 Page Mill Road
Palo Alto, CA 94303

Sublogic Communications
713 Edgebrook Drive
Champaign, IL 61820

Sunburst Communications
Pleasantville, NY 10570

*MECC has an extensive catalogue of software programs most of which are under $10. It is a very useful source of educational software for teachers.

FIGURE 7.16   Reading Programs in the Public Domain

The journal articles include BASIC programs which are adaptable for most computers.

Baker, A. What's your reading level? *Interface Age*, 1981, *6*, 27-29.

Becker, D. A. Flash Cards. *Personal Computing*, 1980, *4*.

Carlson, R. Reading level difficulty. *Creative Computing*, 1980, *6*, #4, 60-61.

Derner, R. R. A teacher for your apple. *Personal Computing*, 1980, *4*, #8, 48-49.

Fisher, M. Word Search. *Personal Computing*, 1980, *4*, #10, 34-39.

Goodman, D., & Schwab, S. Computerized testing for readability. *Creative Computing*, 1980, *6*, #4, 46-51.

Hellman, J. M. Library catalog. *Creative Computing*, 1983, *9*, #3, 216-255.

Isaacson, D. Alphabetize. *Courseware*, 1981, *2*, #2, 35-51.

Isaacson, D. Reading level. *Courseware*, 1981, *2*, #1, 11-52.

Nicastro, A. R. Extra time: Reading and comprehension tests for language arts. *Creative Computing*, 1979, *5*, #4, 62-66.

Noonan, L. Reading level: Determination and evaluation. *Creative Computing*, 1981, *7*, #3, 166-173.

Nottingham, R. B. Fog index. *Creative Computing*, 1981, *7*, #4, 152-154.

O'Connor, P., & O'Connor, L. Fog index revisited. *Interface Age*, 1982, *7*, #4, 22, 148.

Powers, D. E. Perquacky. *Creative Computing*, 1980, *6*, #4, 70-78.

Rogers, J. F. The first "R." *Creative Computing*, 1980, *6*, #4, 62.

Rugg, T., & Feldman, P. Speed reading made easy . . . via your PET. *Creative Computing*, 1979, *5*, #1, 104, 132-133.

Schlarb, K. N. Required reading. *Personal Computing*, 1980, *4*, #12, 68-71.

Schlarb, K. N. Information source for home and school. *Interface Age*, 1981, #6, 94-95, 138-140.

Schuyler, M. R. A readability formula for use in microcomputers. *Journal of Reading*, 1982, *25*, 560-591.

Smith, R. W. Speed reading with the personal computer. *Creative Computing*, 1981, *7*, #10, 162-165.

Whalen, E. A. This Johnny can run the computer. *Personal Computing*, 1980, *4*, #7.

FIGURE 7.17 Some Commercially Available Computer Reading Software

1. Reader Rabbit (Preschool-2nd) Learning Co.: This software contains four highly motivating programs designed to help students recognize letters, learn vocabulary, and use logic to match words. Very strong in graphics and sound. Highly motivating.

2. Snoopy's Reading Machine (Preschool-3rd) Random House. Uses letters as building blocks to make words. Snoopy and many other of the Peanuts characters use a magic machine to make words.

3. Fay: Word Rally (K-4th) Didatech. Fay is a woman model on this program. Uses a racetrack game to teach reading skills such as word recognition, sentence comprehension, rhyming, and phonics.

4. Stickybear Reading (K-3rd) Xerox: Uses four highly motivating games with the Stickybear family to teach word skills as well as sentence construction.

5. Word Man Series (1-4th) DLM. Actually a series of four programs: Word Man, Word Master, Word Invasion, and Word Viper (programs must be purchased separately). Teaches reading and language arts skills in a maze/puzzle format.

6. Jenny of the Prairie; Cave Girl Claire (2-7th) Addison Wesley: Uses an interactive story format to encourage reading. Jenny and Claire are in perilous situations. As the story unfolds, the reader is allowed to type in responses and the story continues based on those responses. A highly motivating reading format!

7. There is a great deal of inexpensive reading software available from the Minnesota Educational Computer Consortium (MECC), 3490 Lexington Ave., N., St. Paul, MN 55126. The price of the software and manuals are never more than $10. MECC have software available for Apple, Atari, Commodore, IBM and Radio Shack computers. Since the MECC reading catalogue is too extensive to list here, the reader is strongly encouraged to write to them for a free copy.

Thus, it is alarming that a significant proportion, if not majority, of mildly mentally retarded students possess significant reading deficiencies.

Reading is the process of converting auditory sounds into print and then making sense of that print. Thus reading is a two part process, the decoding of written symbols and the attaching of meaning to those symbols (comprehension) from experience. The interaction between the child's experiences and comprehension of what is read is particularly important in the case of culturally different children. It is crucial that the reading material of these children be related to their cultural, life experiences, and that, alternatively, the teacher provide such children with a variety of experiences from which to make sense out of what they read.

Not all children are ready to read. Reading readiness consists of possession of those key concepts and prerequisite skills needed to enter successfully into reading instruction. Reading readiness skills include developing language and vocabulary, facilitating visual and auditory discrimination and memory, and increasing motivation to read. It is suggested that children not yet ready to enter formal reading instruction receive concentrated instruction on mastering requisite readiness skills.

Assessment of reading skills is important if appropriate instruction and materials are to be designed for the mentally retarded child. Adequate assessment of reading skills keeps anxiety and frustration over the learning of the reading process to a minimum for both the child and the teacher. Reading assessment can be either formal or informal but should measure both decoding and comprehension skills.

The first step in the reading process is decoding of printed symbols. There are two main methods of decoding: word recognition, also known as the look-say method, and phonics. Since there are advantages and disadvantages to each method, it is suggested that the teacher take an eclectic approach to the teaching of reading where both methods are used.

There are a variety of techniques in the word-recognition approach. These include language-experience stories, using long-term instructional units as the basis of vocabulary selection, the use of sight vocabularies, and visual configurations and cues to facilitate word recognition. In using configurations and cues, instruction must be systematic and the teacher should keep in mind that such cues will eventually need to be faded.

There are two basic types of phonics: synthesis and analysis. Of the two, analysis phonics seems to be more germane to the reading process and helping the child to view the whole word instead of taking a letter-by-letter approach. Clymer has developed a short list of phonics rules that appear to cover over 75 percent of phonics cases. Structural analysis is also suggested for phonics instruction with mentally retarded learners.

Comprehension is very important to the reading process but less time is spent on comprehension in school than on decoding. There are different levels of comprehension ranging from literal comprehension through inferential comprehension and understanding the subtleties of the author's message. It is crucial that comprehension instruction be systematic and intentional with mentally retarded learners. Strategies for teaching comprehension include summarization and paraphrasing, generating reciprocal questions, central story problems, paragraph structure, and creative questioning.

Reading materials are of five basic types: basal readers, synthesis phonics basal readers, linguistic phoneme materials, individualized/programmed materials, and language-experience materials. Although each of these types of materials possesses advantages and disadvantages, basal readers do not possess the individualized content needed for mentally retarded students. Programmed approaches and diagnostic/prescriptive approaches may be facilitative with such students. Available reading programs which have proven to be of some success with mentally retarded readers include DISTAR; Edmark; Sullivan Programmed Readers; and Hegge, Kirk & Kirk Reading Drills.

The long-term instructional unit approach can be most helpful in designing and implementing reading instruction with mentally retarded learners. Units insure relevancy of reading material and the redundancy of the content in units helps insure enough drill to facilitate word recognition. The unit approach to reading is particularly useful with intermediate and secondary mentally retarded students.

The computer is one of the most recent aids in reading instruction and it is especially useful for mentally retarded learners. Computers help insure systematic presentation of material as well as individualization of content and presentation. Many programs are available for use in the reading instruction of mentally retarded students with the list of available programs growing monthly. There are also many programs in the public domain which can be used with little or no cost by the classroom teacher.

8

Spelling and Written Expression

Key Concepts
- ☐ Definition of the Spelling Process
- ☐ Factors Which Influence Spelling
- ☐ Channels of Spelling: Internal versus External
- ☐ Memory Channel
- ☐ Memory-Kinesthetic Detour
- ☐ Checking Channel
- ☐ Proofreading Channel
- ☐ Proofreading, Rewrite Bypass
- ☐ Diagnostic Spelling Assessment
- ☐ Error Analysis
- ☐ Linguistic Spelling
- ☐ Nature of Handwriting
- ☐ Conventional versus Creative Writing
- ☐ Components of Written Expression

We live in a culture of writing. Every day, we write hundreds, maybe thousands of words—grocery lists, letters, job applications, instructions on how to get somewhere. We write so much that we often take writing for granted—until we come across writing which is spelled so poorly, written so illegibly, or is so ungrammatical as to make us realize once again just how difficult writing is.

Writing consists of spelling, handwriting, and written expression. All three of these components must be in place for a person's writing to be legible and understandable. The purpose of writing is to convey ideas through the written word. The ability of mildly mentally retarded learners to communicate through the written word is the subject of this chapter.

☐ Spelling

For many people, spelling comes easily; they can readily spell any word that is said to them or that they wish to write. For others, spelling is a difficult, laborious task that must be constantly checked and monitored for accuracy.

But what *is* spelling, and why is it so difficult for so many people? According to the accepted definition (Boyd & Talbert 1971; Neli 1981), spelling represents the ability to arrange letters properly into words that are conventional and effective for written communication. By conventional, it is meant that the way a person spells a given word is the same way that the rest of that society or culture spells the same word.

Using this definition, spelling consists of converting phonemes (sounds) into corresponding graphemes (letter symbols) in the way that everyone else in the culture converts the phonemes to graphemes. Put in these terms, spelling sounds easy. But there's a hitch. Phonemes and graphemes are not in a one-to-one correspondence. In fact it has been demonstrated that the forty-five phonemes of English can be graphically represented 251 different ways (Feigenbaum 1958). Is it any wonder that so many English words are so often misspelled?

Another reason that students often experience difficulties in spelling is the fact that spelling is an academic area which demands 100 percent mastery. That is, each word must be spelled to absolute perfection or it is, by definition, misspelled. In addition, spelling is the one core area where creativity is absolutely not tolerated. No matter how ingenious or novel a child's spelling of a word, if it is not spelled in the exact conventional manner it is *wrong* (Lerner 1981; Smith 1974). Thus, it may be that certain children rebel against learning to spell correctly because of the high structure, rote memorization, and lack of creativity involved in the process.

FACTORS THAT INFLUENCE SPELLING ABILITY

□ □ A variety of factors influence spelling ability. These variables are generally divided into the auditory, visual, and motor skills needed for the process as well as the necessary integration abilities in these three areas (Westerman 1971). Auditory skills include auditory discrimination, and short-term (sequential) memory, as well as the ability to analyze and synthesize information in the auditory mode. Visual aspects of spelling include visual discrimination, short-term memory, and visual analysis and synthesis. Motor skills in spelling refer to the fine motor control in the fingers and hands needed for writing as well as motor control over the articulation (voice) apparatus needed to spell orally. Finally, auditory-visual (sound-symbol) and visual-motor modality integration are needed in order to spell both orally and in writing.

Based on the abilities listed above, the following prerequisite skills for success in spelling may be identified (Graham & Miller (a & b) 1983; Hasenstab & Laughton 1982):

1. Adequate visual and hearing acuity.
2. Appropriate motor skills.
3. Appropriate discrimination of visual letters.

4. Appropriate hearing discrimination of phonemes.
5. Acceptable pronunciation of words. This is important since if the word is not pronounced and thus heard correctly, it will be spelled the way it is heard.
6. Knowledge of the word meanings of words to be spelled.
7. A desire to communicate effectively.

ATTRIBUTES OF GOOD AND POOR SPELLERS

□ □ Most students who possess deficiencies in spoken language and in reading also demonstrate spelling difficulties (Cohen & Plaskon 1980). Since mentally retarded learners demonstrate marked difficulties in oral language and reading, it is not surprising to find that they also possess a greater and more serious amount of spelling problems than nonretarded learners (Polloway & Smith 1982; Stephens 1977). Stephens (1977) has identified some general spelling characteristics which apply to poor spellers. These characteristics may be summarized as follows:

1. Poor spellers usually possess lower intellectual and cognitive abilities than good spellers. This is directly applicable to mentally retarded learners who possess, by definition, intellectual and cognitive deficits.
2. Poor spellers often possess visual problems as manifested by poor visual discrimination and frequent eye regressions.
3. Poor spellers possess difficulties in devising internal (mental) images of words.
4. Poor spellers possess inadequate and/or inappropriate phonetic skills and strategies.
5. Poor spellers often mispronounce words either because of articulation errors or because of cultural/regional dialects.
6. Poor spellers overgeneralize phonetic rules and do not recognize (and learn to spell) irregular words. Thus poor spellers do not strategically apply spelling rules (experiencing problems of over- or under-generalization).
7. Poor spellers do not understand as many word meanings as good spellers.

On the other hand, competencies which distinguish good spellers have also been identified (Mangieri & Baldwin 1979; Read 1980). In general, good spellers possess the following competencies:

1. Ability to distinguish phonemes.
2. Ability to identify the graphemic options of phonemes.
3. Ability to phrase a written or spoken word into syllables.

4. Recognizes stress in words.
5. Recognizes morphemes, root words, suffixes, and prefixes.
6. Understands the rules which govern how morphemes are linked together.
7. Relates syntax and semantics to spelling.

These seven competencies are most often the exact skills which mentally retarded students lack. Thus systematic and strategic instruction in spelling for mentally retarded learners is a must.

THE PROCESS OF SPELLING

☐ ☐ The spelling process begins when the child wishes to express an idea by appropriately and conventionally writing the words of the message (Hall 1981; Personkee & Yee 1968). The child may use *internal* or *external* spelling mechanisms to correctly write down the words of the message. Internal mechanisms are those which are part of the speller and which do not require consultation with any outside source. Such processes include spelling words from memory or using phonetic rules to spell words correctly. If the speller cannot correctly spell the word using internal processes then the student must resort to external devices such as a dictionary or another individual.

This internal/external mechanism dichotomy yields five spelling channels or ways that words may be spelled (Personkee & Yee 1968).

☐ Internal Channels

1. **Memory channel:** The student creates a visual image or other internal input in order to spell the word and judge its correctness.
2. **Memory-kinesthetic detour:** The student overlearns the spelling of the word by spelling it hundreds or thousands of times (e.g., the way you spell dog, or car). In these cases, no internal image is needed and no conscious thought is necessary for correct spelling of the word.

☐ External Channels

1. **Checking channel:** The student consults an external source without attempting to use internal sources to spell the word. This involves intuitively knowing in advance that one's attempts to spell the word correctly using internal channels will prove unsuccessful.
2. **Proofreading channel:** The student writes the word using internal

channels and then immediately checks the correctness of the internal spelling using external sources.

3. **Proofreading, rewrite bypass:** The student writes the word, checks spelling by external source, and if spelling is incorrect, rewrites word correctly.

All five of these channels should be used by mildly mentally retarded students in spelling words correctly (Beers & Henderson 1977; Gentry 1977). Use of internal and external channels in the spelling process for mentally retarded learners will be discussed in greater depth later in this chapter.

ASSESSMENT OF SPELLING ABILITIES

☐ ☐ Like the other academic core areas, the spelling skills of children need to be adequately assessed to design appropriate curriculum and instruction. Traditionally, spelling assessment has tended to be purely summative (evaluative) in nature; that is, teachers judged words as being spelled either correctly or incorrectly with little regard to the kinds of errors students made in their misspellings. Today, however, spelling assessment has become more diagnostically oriented, and teachers often find it fruitful to carefully analyze students' spelling strengths and weaknesses (Edgington 1968; Hammill & Larsen 1983).

Spelling assessment for mentally retarded learners basically can be divided into two main areas: spelling achievement and diagnostic assessment of spelling errors (error analysis). Spelling achievement tests are survey in nature; they give the teacher an overall idea of the child's global spelling abilities. In-depth, diagnostic spelling assessment on the other hand, occurs when problems are indicated by the achievement tests with the purpose of precisely pinpointing the nature of the spelling difficulties. As in the other areas of academic assessment, assessment of spelling achievement and error analysis may be accomplished by using formal or informal testing instruments.

☐ Tests of Spelling Achievement

Spelling achievement tests usually measure spelling ability by one or both of two techniques: the *dictated word* or the *proofreading* method (Salvia & Ysseldyke 1985; Wallace & Larsen 1979). In the dictated-word method, the student hears a word presented orally by the tester, hears the word in a sentence, and hears the word again in isolation. The student then attempts to spell the word. In the proofreading technique, the student is presented with a list of words which are spelled correctly or incorrectly. The student's task is to identify (recognize) the misspelled words (although the student is not always required to then spell them correctly). Both of these techniques assess spelling ability in the internal channels. In fact, formal assessment instruments that measure external channel spelling abilities such as the ability to use a dictionary or thesaurus are relatively rare. Table 8.1 lists the most commonly used commercially available spelling survey tests and what they measure.

☐ Diagnostic Spelling Assessment

Once the survey assessment of spelling abilities has been completed, an in-depth, diagnostic spelling assessment should be administered. Such diagnostic assessment may be accomplished using commercially available or teacher-made instruments. In terms of choosing commercially available diagnostic spelling tests, four criteria should be met before the appropriateness of the test is decided (McLoughlin & Lewis 1986; Wallace & Larsen 1979).

TABLE 8.1 Commercially Available Achievement Tests with Survey Spelling Subtests

Test	Procedure for Assessing Spelling	Grade Levels
Test of Written Spelling (Larsen & Hammill, 1976)	Dictated-word	1–8
Comprehensive Tests of Basic Skills (CTB/McGraw-Hill, 1968)	Proofreading	2–12
California Achievement Tests (Tiegs & Clark, 1970)	Proofreading	1–12
Stanford Achievement Tests (Madden & Gardner, 1972)	Proofreading	1–9
Peabody Individual Achievement Test (Dunn & Markwardt, 1970)	Proofreading	K–12
Iowa Test of Basic Skills (Hieronymus & Lindquist, 1971)	Proofreading	1–9
Metropolitan Achievement Tests (Durost, et al., 1970)	Dictated-word Proofreading	2–4 4–9
SRA Achievement Series (Thorpe, Lefever, & Nasland, 1974)	Proofreading	1–12
The Gray-Votaw-Rogers General Achievement Tests (Gray, Votaw, & Rogers, 1963)	Dictated-word Proofreading	1–3 4–9
Wide Range Achievement Test (Jastak & Jastak, 1965)	Dictated-word	3–12
The Iowa Test of Educational Development (Lindquist & Feldt, 1959)	Proofreading	9–12
McGraw-Hill Basic Study Skills: Spelling (Raygoz, 1970)	Proofreading	9–12

From G. Wallace & S. C. Larsen (1979). *Educational Assessment of Learning Problems: Testing for Teaching.* Boston: Allyn & Bacon. Used with permission.

1. The test is published and readily available.
2. The test does not provide statistical data which makes comparisons between students (i.e., the test should be criterion-referenced).
3. The test contains spelling items selected from a wide range of word lists, basal spelling programs, and relevant language experiences to the child.
4. The test provides the teacher with diagnostic and remedial spelling information.

There are a small number of commercially available tests which meet these criteria. Such tests include the Kottmyer Diagnostic Spelling Test (Kottmyer 1970), the Test of Written Spelling (Larsen & Hammill 1983), the Gates-Russell Spelling Diagnostic Test (Gates & Russell 1940), the Lincoln Diagnostic Spelling Test (Lincoln 1962), and Spellmaster (Cohen & Abrams 1974). What these tests have in common is the ability to adequately and diagnostically assess a variety of abilities central to good spelling in the internal channel as well as yielding a spelling profile for the child. Figure 8.1 contains a sample of such a spelling profile while Table 8.2 contains a listing of each of these tests as well as an outline of their subtests.

☐ Error Analysis in Spelling Assessment

Informal spelling assessment can be of great use to the special education teacher since such an assessment yields detailed information regarding the child's specific strengths and weaknesses in a variety of spelling situations (Graham & Miller 1983a; Polloway & Smith 1982). A central approach to diagnostic spelling assessment is that of *error analysis* which is the study of trends in the child's spelling errors in order to determine possible underlying deficiencies. Error analysis requires teacher understanding of the types of spelling errors which occur most frequently. Children's spelling errors may be placed in approximately twenty-six categories, shown in Figure 8.2 (Partol 1976). By identifying the types of spelling errors which a child makes consistently (rather than just noting the number of words spelled incorrectly), the teacher can identify trends and deficiencies which may result in specific prescriptive, remedial activities.

An informal spelling assessment should contain data systematically collected from a sampling of a variety of spelling situations in which the child participates (Brueckner & Bond 1967). Figure 8.3 contains a detailed outline of the sources of spelling information for students. The use of these sources in spelling data collection will help insure validity of the ensuing error analysis and subsequent creation of a spelling profile for the mentally retarded child.

APPROACHES TO TEACHING SPELLING TO MENTALLY RETARDED STUDENTS

☐ ☐ The teaching of spelling to mentally retarded students is divided into three main areas: deciding which words to teach (the spelling curriculum), the method of

FIGURE 8.1 A Sample Spelling Profile

	AUDITORY		AUDITORY PLUS VISUAL				CONCEPTUAL	
Test Level	1	2	3	4	5	6	7	8
Avg. Grade Level	K-3	1-4	2-5	3-6	4-7	5-8	6-9	7-10
Consonants	b d f g h l m n p r t v y	s z w	c j k x qu			c: city g: germ		
Beginning Blends	dr- gr- tr- pl- fl-	sw- sp- sl- st- str- spr- spl-						
Ending Blends	-mp -nd -ft -lt -nt	-st -nt -lf -nd -mp	-nk					
Digraphs		ch sh th ng	wh					ph: phrase ch: ache
Vowels	short a e i o u	short a e i o u	ai, ay, a-e ee, ea, e-e igh, y, i-e, ind oa, ow, o-e, old	u-e: cube	u-e: rule -y: envy	ie: field ei: receive schwa (ə):*	y: system	i: stadium i: companion
Vowel Digraphs				oo: pool	oo: hood ea: ready			
Diphthongs				oi: join ou: cloud ow: down aw: claw	oy: joy ew: chew	au: sauce		
"r" & "l" control				ar, er, ir, ur er, ear are, ire, ore all				
Prefixes				un- re-	pre- en- mis- ex- a- in-	con- per- com-		Derivational Doubling immature
Suffixes		-s: chops	-s: wheels -ing -ed -es	-er -est -ly -ful -y	-tion -ive	-ent -en -ant	-ment -ous -ness -sion	-ance -ence -ible -able -fully -ally -ssion
Endings					-et: target -ic: public -al: signal -le: poodle	-ey: kidney	-us: cactus	
Syllables: ** open and closed							open: ti-ny closed: gos-sip	
Generalizations						ck-k ch-ich ge-dge		
Advanced Phonics								ti: cautious ci: social tu: future
Contractions							mustn't they've	
Rules							1. Dropping e: hope-hoping 2a. Doubling final consonants (monosyllabic): hop-hopping 3. Changing y to i: funny-funnier	2b. Doubling final consts. (polysyllabic): open-opening begin-beginner
Sample Words	lap rug flop yet mint	sang chops brush spent bathtub	mean loaded junk painting waxes	refuse smartest fired join loudly	loyal ahead expensive strangle prescribe	loosen freckle computer belief launched	skinny scaring cloudiness sympathy enormous	fortunately immortal forbidden phrase architect
Total Test Words	20	20	40	40	40	40	40	40

* The "schwa" is a neutral vowel sound in an unaccented syllable.

** Open syllable ends in a vowel making the vowel long: mo/ment, pu/pil. Closed syllable ends in a consonant making the vowel short: sad/dle, pup/py.

From C.R. Cohen & R.M. Abrams (1976). *Spellmaster.* Greenland, NH: Learnco.

FIGURE 8.2   Types of Spelling Errors

1. Consonant sounds used incorrectly (specify letters missed)
2. Vowel sounds not known
3. Sounds omitted at beginning of words
4. Sounds added at the beginning of words (e.g., a blend given when a single consonant required)
5. Omission of middle sounds
6. Omission of middle syllables
7. Extraneous letters added
8. Extraneous syllables added
9. Missequencing of sounds or syllables (transposals like "from" to "form")
10. Reve
11. Endings omitted
12. Incorrect ending substituted ("ing" for "en" or tor "ed")
13. Auditory confusion of *m/n, th/f, s/z,* or *b/d* or other similar sounds
14. Phonetic spelling with poor visual recall of word appearance
15. Spelling laborious, letter by letter
16. Poor knowledge of "demons" (e.g., one, iron, forecastle)
17. Spells, erases, tries again, etc., to no avail
18. Reversals of letter shapes *b/d, p/q, u/n,* or *m/w*
19. Spelling so bizarre that it bears no resemblance to original; even pupil cannot read his own written words
20. Mixing of upper and lower case letters
21. Inability to recall how to form either case for some letters
22. Spatial placement on line erratic
23. Spacing between letters and words erratic
24. Poor writing and letter formations, immature eye-hand coordination
25. Temporal disorientation: slowness in learning time, general scheduling, grasping the sequence of events in the day
26. Difficulty in concept formation; not able to generalize and transfer readily to abstract "the rules and the tools"

From S.F. Partoll (1976). Spelling demonology revisited. *Academic Therapy, 9,* 339–348.

TABLE 8.2   Diagnostic Spelling Tests

Test	Measures	Grade Level
Test of Written Spelling (Larsen & Hammill 1976)	Predictable and Unpredictable Words	1–8
Gates-Russell Spelling Diagnostic Test (Gates-Russell, 1940)	Spelling Ability Word Pronunciation Syllable Spelling Word Attack Reversals Auditory Discrimination	1–12
Lincoln Diagnostic Spelling Test (Lincoln, 1955)	Pronunciation Enunciation Use of Spelling Rules	K–12
Spellmaster (Cohen & Abrams, 1974)	Regular Words Irregular Words Homonyms	K–12

FIGURE 8.3   Sources of Spelling Assessment Information

A. Analysis of Written Work, Including Test Papers
   1. Legibility of handwriting
   2. Defects in letter forms, spacing, alignment, size
   3. Classification of errors in written work, letters, tests, etc.
   4. Range of vocabulary used
   5. Evidence of lack of knowledge of conventions and rules

B. Analysis of Oral Responses
   1. Comparison of errors in oral and written spelling
   2. Pronunciation of words spelled incorrectly
   3. Articulation and enunciation
   4. Dialectical and colloquial forms of speech
   5. Way of spelling words orally
      a. Spells words as units
      b. Spells letter by letter
      c. Spells by digraphs or syllables
   6. Rhythmic pattern in oral spelling
   7. Blending ability
   8. Quality and errors made in oral reading
   9. Giving letters for sounds or sounds for letters
   10. Oral responses on tests of word analysis
   11. Analysis of pupil comments as he states orally his thought processes while studying
       new words

C. Interview with Pupil
   1. Questioning pupil about methods of study
   2. Questioning pupil about spelling rules and errors in conventions
   3. Securing evidence as to attitude toward spelling

D. Questionnaire
   1. Applying check-list methods of study
   2. Having pupil rank spelling according to interest
   3. Surveying uses of written language

E. Free Observation in Course of Daily Work
   1. Evidence of improvement in the study of new words
   2. Observing extent of use of dictionary
   3. Extent of error in regular written work
   4. Study habits and methods of work
   5. Evidences of emotional and social maladjustment

F. Controlled Observation of Work on Set Tasks
   1. Looking up the meanings of given words in dictionary
   2. Giving pronunciation of words in dictionary
   3. Writing plural forms and derivatives of given words
   4. Observing responses on informal tests
   5. Observing methods of studying selected words
   6. Estimating pupil success when using a variety of methods of studying selected words

G. Analysis of Available Records
   1. Records of scores on tests in reading, spelling, language, handwriting
   2. School history
   3. Health data; physiological and sensory deficiencies and defects; and sociological data
   4. Anecdotal records

Source: Leo J. Brueckner and Guy L. Bond. *The Diagnosis and Treatment of Learning Difficulties,* ©
1955, pp. 369-370. Reprinted by permission of Prentice-Hall, Inc., Englewood Cliffs, N.J.

teaching spelling (instruction), and helping children to want to spell correctly (motivation) (Graham & Miller 1983(a); Fitzsimmons & Loomer 1977). Additionally, spelling instruction should probably include spelling in both the internal and external channels so as to help learners both overlearn the spelling of familiar words and to use dictionaries to spell unfamiliar words. It is thus suggested that the spelling program for mildly mentally retarded learners contain the triad of curriculum, instruction, and motivation as shown in Figure 8.4.

☐ Choosing the Spelling Vocabulary

For mildly mentally retarded learners, it is essential to teach a vocabulary that is functional, relevant, and useful to the child's current and future life success (Graham & Miller 1983(a); May 1980; Wilson 1979). Thus the first words that children learn to spell should be words that have meaning in their lives: places, things, and people found in their immediate environment. These words should be *functional* words that the child comes into contact with on a regular basis. To a certain extent, what is functional and relevant in the child's life will be culturally determined. Taxi may be important in the city but is not life-crucial on the farm. It is very important that the teacher be able to defend the spelling vocabulary in terms of life-relevancy for the children in the class.

There are, however, some words which appear in high frequency in most children's reading and writing and which all successful persons are expected to

FIGURE 8.4   Curriculum, Instruction, and Motivational Factors Necessary in the Spelling Program for Mildly Mentally Retarded Learners

Curriculum

1. Auditory recognition of phonemes
2. Graphemic representation of phonemes
3. Using morphemes to make structural changes
4. Devices to aid in spelling recall
5. Proofreading skills
6. Dictionary skills

Instruction

1. Various theories and techniques emphasizing internal imaging of words
2. Rules governing grapheme-phoneme relationships
3. Instruction in structural analysis
4. Instruction in using external aids

Motivation

1. Positive reinforcement
2. Games
3. Graphs
4. Simulations
5. Supplemental aids

spell correctly. A variety of high-frequency spelling lists have been developed for a variety of children including middle and lower class, urban and rural children (May 1980). Table 8.3 contains a listing of eight different vocabulary spelling lists relevant for mildly mentally retarded students, while Figure 8.5 contains a sample list of the one hundred most frequently occurring words that beginning spellers encounter in school.

☐ Spelling and the Long-Term Instructional Unit

There should be as close a link as possible between the child's reading, spelling, and writing vocabularies (Graham & Miller(a) 1983). For this reason, the long-term instructional, thematic unit is particularly useful in vocabulary selection. In such an approach, the central vocabulary and concepts (which have been chosen for their relevance and functionality to the child's present and future life success) which have become incorporated into the speaking and reading vocabulary are now adopted as the spelling vocabulary. For example, examine the key concepts and vocabulary of the long-term unit which are incorporated into the child's speaking vocabulary in Figure 8.6. These same vocabulary words would also be presented in reading lessons (see chapter 7) and would form the basis of the spelling curriculum. Notice there is a strong redundancy effect as the key words and concepts are repeated through the language arts curriculum taking place throughout the life of the thematic unit. Children speak, read, and spell the same words for a relatively long period of instructional time. This strong redundancy effect facilitates learning in all of the language-arts core areas because of over-learning, reinforcement, and increased opportunity for practice which the students receive. For this reason, it is believed that the long-term instructional unit approach aids learning in all of the language-arts core areas to the extent that the vocabulary of the unit is continuously repeated in close proximity.

TABLE 8.3 High-Frequency Spelling Lists for A Variety of School Populations

List	Population
Barnard and De bracie (1976)	K-1. Taken from eight basal readers
Dolch (1936)	Basic sight words
Hillerich (1974)	Grades 3–9
Johns (1974)	Grades 3–9
Johnson (1975)	Based upon Johns (1974)
Johnson (1971)	K–1 children's speech
Moe and Hopkins (1975)	Speech of K–2 middle-class children
Sherk & Manzo (1973)	4–6 year old lower-class children

FIGURE 8.5 The 100 Most Frequently Used Words in Children's Written Work

1. the	26. school	51. would	76. now
2. I	27. me	52. our	77. has
3. and	28. with	53. were	78. down
4. to	29. am	54. little	79. if
5. a	30. all	55. how	80. write
6. you	31. one	56. he	81. after
7. we	32. so	57. do	82. play
8. in	33. your	58. about	83. came
9. it	34. got	59. from	84. put
10. of	35. there	60. her	85. two
11. is	36. went	61. them	86. house
12. was	37. not	62. as	87. us
13. have	38. at	63. his	88. because
14. my	39. like	64. mother	89. over
15. are	40. out	65. see	90. saw
16. he	41. go	66. friend	91. their
17. for	42. but	67. come	92. well
18. on	43. this	68. can	93. here
19. they	44. dear	69. day	94. by
20. that	45. some	70. good	95. just
21. had	46. then	71. what	96. make
22. she	47. going	72. said	97. back
23. very	48. up	73. him	98. an
24. will	49. time	74. home	99. could
25. when	50. get	75. did	100. or

From S. Folger (1946). The case for a basic written vocabulary. *Elementary School Journal, 47*, 1. As found in E. DeHaven (1979). *Teaching and learning in the language arts.* Boston: Little, Brown.

FIGURE 8.6 Spelling Vocabulary Taken From Unit on "Workers in Our Community"

cook	nurse	thermostat	ruler
librarian	bookkeeper	directions	ladder
janitor	carpenter	work-study	bathroom scales
teacher	taperecorder	skills	weight
doctor	schedule	boiling	measure cup
racecar driver	calender	timer	job
boxer			

INSTRUCTIONAL METHODS FOR TEACHING SPELLING: INTERNAL CHANNELS

□ □ A variety of instructional approaches have been developed over the years to help students learn the skills and techniques needed for good internal spelling. The plethora of these spelling techniques may seem confusing; fortunately, however, a body of research exists which allows some generalizations to be made in terms of which techniques do and do not seem to work. From available research, the following implications can be made regarding the teaching of spelling to mentally retarded learners (Cohen & Plaskon 1980; Graham & Miller 1983a).

1. The most effective spelling techniques work when the student corrects spelling errors immediately after they occur.
2. Teachers should emphasize the relevance of the words to be taught in the child's current life as well as their relevance to an adult.
3. A small list of new spelling words should be presented and taught one at a time. For most mildly mentally retarded learners, the list of new words should not exceed ten.
4. Teachers should make sure that children know the meaning of new spelling words and that they can use them correctly in speaking and writing context.
5. Teachers should help children "image" or picture the correct spelling of words in their mind's eye. This can be accomplished by having students view words on the blackboard, trying to create a mental image of the correctly spelled word before attempting to write the word.
6. Teachers should provide a variety of real-life writing situations for learners in which students can practice the correct spelling of words.

It is noteworthy that two other effective spelling techniques with mentally retarded learners run counter to available research regarding children's reading. These two findings are:

1. Learning to spell words by a synthesis, letter-by-letter approach is more facilitative of learning than spelling words by syllables (an analysis approach) (Horn 1969; Humphrey 1954).
2. It is better to present new words (not already familiar words which need to be practiced) in isolation than in sentence or context form (Edwards 1953; Strickland 1951).

Taking these research findings into account, a number of relevant approaches to the teaching of spelling to mildly mentally retarded learners have been developed. These include the Fernald (1943), Horn (1969), Fitzgerald (1951), Gillingham & Stillman (1970), Gilstrap (1962), Westerman (1971), and the Cover-and-Write methods. In general, these methods have much in common in that a multimodality approach to spelling is advocated (visual, auditory, and kinesthetic) in which children see, say, and write the words. Students are also encouraged in these approaches to form mental images of the words prior to attempting a letter-by-letter spelling. A brief step-by-step description of these major spelling approaches may be seen in Figure 8.7

FIGURE 8.7 The Major Spelling Instructional Approaches

Fitzgerald Method (Fitzgerald, 1951a)

1. Look at the word carefully.
2. Say the word.
3. With eyes closed, visualize the word.
4. Cover the word and then write it.
5. Check the spelling.
6. If the word is misspelled, repeat steps 1-5.

Horn Method 1 (E. Horn, 1919)

1. Look at the word and say it to yourself.
2. Close your eyes and visualize the word.
3. Check to see if you were right. (If not, begin as step 1.)
4. Cover the word and write it.
5. Check to see if you were right. (If not, begin at step 1.)
6. Repeat steps 4 and 5 two more times.

Horn Method 2 (E. Horn, 1954c)

1. Pronounce each word carefully.
2. Look carefully at each part of the word as you pronounce it.
3. Say the letters in sequence.
4. Attempt to recall how the word looks, then spell the word.
5. Check this attempt to recall.
6. Write the word.
7. Check this spelling attempt.
8. Repeat the above steps if necessary.

Visual-Vocal Method (Westerman, 1971)

1. Say word.
2. Spell word orally.
3. Say word again.
4. Spell word from memory four times correctly.

Gilstrap Method (Gilstrap, 1962)

1. Look at the word and say it softly. If it has more than one part, say it again, part by part, looking at each part as you say it.
2. Look at the letters and say each one. If the word has more than one part, say the letters part by part.
3. Write the word without looking at the book.

Fernald Method Modified (Fernald, 1943)

1. Make a model of the word with a crayon, grease pencil, or magic marker, saying the word as you write it.
2. Check the accuracy of the model.
3. Trace over the model with your index finger, saying the word at the same time.
4. Repeat step 3 five times.
5. Copy the word three times correctly.
6. Copy the word three times from memory correctly.

(continued)

FIGURE 8.7 (continued)

Cover-and-Write Method

 1. Look at word. Say it.
 2. Write word two times.
 3. Cover and write one time.
 4. Check work.
 5. Write word two times.
 6. Cover and write one time.
 7. Check work.
 8. Write word three times.
 9. Cover and write one time.
10. Check work.

Source: S. Graham & L. Miller (1983). Spelling Research and Practice: A unified approach. In E. L. Meyer, G. A. Vergason, & R. J. Whelan (Eds.) *Promising Practices for Exceptional Children.* Denver: Love Publishing.

THE LINGUISTIC RULE (PHONICS) APPROACH TO SPELLING INSTRUCTION

☐ ☐ The linguistic approach attempts to convey the consistencies of English as they apply to spelling by pupils. In this approach, general rules which may be applied in a variety of spelling situations are taught to the child and systematic instruction is given in applying these rules.

In using the linguistic rule approach with mentally retarded learners, it is suggested that the teacher present a limited number of rules and that specific and systematic application and generalization of those rules become an intentional part of the spelling program (Hallahan et al. 1978; Borkowski & Cavanaugh 1979). More specifically, the following procedure is suggested (Brueckner & Bond 1955, 1967).

1. Select the rule to be taught. Teach one rule at a time (e.g., When two vowels go walking the first one does the talking).
2. Present a list of rules that exemplify the rule (e.g., seat, suit, loan).
3. Help students learn the generalization of the rule. If possible, help them to discover the generalization for themselves.
4. Have students immediately apply the rule. Give opportunities to practice the rule.
5. Illustrate exceptions to the rule (e.g., could, look).
6. Provide ample opportunity for continued practice in the use of the rule.

The basic linguistic/phonics spelling rules to be taught to learners are as follows:

1. The basic sounds of vowels, consonants, and letter blends.
2. The basic power phonics rules of reading (Clymer 1963) (see chapter 7).

TABLE 8.4 A Weekly Spelling Plan

Monday:	Give a pretest of spelling words to be learned. The words not mastered will become the basis of the child's spelling words for the week. Children work together or with the teacher. Words are introduced and meanings are explored. Words are used in sentences and discourse.
Tuesday:	The child begins to practice spelling the words using available techniques such as visual, auditory, and kinethestic modalities. Children continue to practice to spell the words as they are learned and used.
Wednesday:	Children continue to practice words but in a highly motivating atmosphere. Games, puzzles, spelling bees, or any activity which makes spelling fun.
Thursday:	Children continue to spell the words using the games approach. They also incorporate the words into their written products. Spelling of the words by this point should be automatic (overlearned).
Friday:	Give a mastery test (posttest). The correct spelling of the words is carried out using external sources. Place those words correctly spelled in an "I Can Spell These" notebook. Include words not mastered in next week's list.

3. Nouns made plural by the morpheme *s.*
4. Nouns ending in *s, x, sh,* and *ch* made plural by *es.*
5. If a consonant precedes the final *y,* change *y* to *i* when adding a consonant.
6. *Q* is always followed by *u.*
7. Drop the *e* at the end of a word when adding a suffix that begins with a vowel.
8. The famous rule: *i* before e except after *c* or when it sounds like an *a* as in neighbor or sleigh.
9. Form possessives by adding *'s.*

Table 8.4 contains a weekly spelling plan which may be adopted by teachers. This plan allows for systematic learning, practice, and summative evaluation of a list of spelling words.

ACTIVITIES FOR TEACHING INTERNAL CHANNEL SPELLING

☐ ☐ Because of the large amount of drill involved, spelling instruction can quickly become boring, mundane, and unmotivating for many mentally retarded students (Morsink 1984; Quandt 1983). In order to keep spelling motivation high, the teacher should use a variety of spelling games, simulations, and high-interest activities. Some such activities to help encourage internal channel spelling are in Table 8.5.

Spelling games and simulations may also become mundane and boring. In order to avoid this, the teacher must constantly change and rearrange the schedule, way, and methods by which spelling words are presented. *Be creative.* Change things around. Try new techniques and materials. Even changing the time of day the spelling lesson is usually taught can be stimulating to students. It is

TABLE 8.5 Activities for Teaching Internal Channel Spelling

See Sea the Bare Bear

Objective: To help students learn the use of different homonyms.
Materials: Newsprint for drawing. Paper for charts, crayons, pens, etc.
Procedure: Explain the nature of homonyms to students. Write several on the chart to be made as an illustration. Ask students to think of homonym pairs of their own. Give them hints such as "I use my ears to _____." List the homonym pairs the students generate. Have them illustrate their favorite pair and display the artwork around the room.

My Horse Is Hoarse

Objective: To learn spelling homonyms.
Materials: Book: *How a Horse Grew Hoarse on the Site Where He Sighted a Bare Bear* by Emily Hanlon, Delacorte Press, 1976. Index cards.
Procedure: Read the book to the class or have them read it. List specific homonym pairs from the book on the board and the sentences which they came from. Ask students to listen to the homonym and write the correct spelling on their card. Check the student's spelling. Allow a student with the correct spelling to come to the board and fill in the sentence with the correct spelling of the homonym.

Spelling Baseball

Objective: To encourage internal spelling.
Materials: None.
Procedure: Requires two teams and a pitcher (the person who pronounces the words). The batter indicates whether he wishes to try for a single, double, triple, or home run. The larger the hit, the more difficult the spelling word. The pitcher gives the spelling word and the batter spells it on the board. If it is spelled correctly, he moves to the base indicated by the hit. If he misses the word he is out. Regular baseball rules are followed.

Ringtoss Spelling

Objective: Internal spelling.
Material: Two bottles. Rings which will fall over the neck of the bottles.
Procedure: The class is divided into two teams. The teacher gives a word to a player. The student attempts to spell the word. A student who spells it correctly gets to attempt to toss a ring on the opposing team's bottle. Teams alternate getting words. The team with the most rings on the opponent's bottle at the end of the game is the winner.

Category Spelling

Objective: To encourage vocabulary generation and the correct spelling of words.
Materials: None.
Procedure: Children are given a category such as fruits, furniture, sports. They have three minutes to generate as many words as they can from that category and to spell them correctly on a piece of paper.

(continued)

TABLE 8.5 (continued)

Draw the Alien

Objective:	To correctly spell words through the internal channel as well as reinforce linguistic phonics spelling patterns.
Material:	Chalkboard and chalk.
Procedure:	Blanks are written onto the blackboard, one blank for each letter of the mystery word. Children need to try to guess the letters that go in the blank. For each wrong guess, a body part of the alien is drawn (head, trunk, one arm, two arms). The game ends when all of the blanks are filled in and the word is correctly spelled and read or when the alien is completely drawn.

important that the teacher be on guard against student apathy. Once the subject matter becomes drudgery to students, motivation and attention to spelling will drop dramatically.

TEACHING SPELLING IN THE EXTERNAL CHANNELS

☐ ☐ For older students or for those who possess higher order spelling skills, instruction in the use of external channels of spelling may be appropriate. Such skills include two processes: recognizing when a word has been misspelled or cannot be spelled correctly using internal channels (proofreading), and the correction of spelling errors using external means (i.e., the dictionary).

In terms of proofreading skills, students need systematic and intentional instruction and practice in recognizing misspelled words. In order to help accomplish this goal, Graham and Miller (1983a) argue that lists of words or prose passages be given to students which include a number of misspelled words. In initial instruction in this area, the teacher would inform the students exactly how many spelling errors are contained in the list or passage. The student's job would then be to identify the specified number of spelling errors. After the student gained proficiency in this exercise, the teacher would submit other lists or passages but no information as to the number of spelling errors. The student would then have to identify all of the errors. Finally, students would be given each other's written compositions or writing samples from another class and would be required to find all of the spelling errors.

The second part of the external channel process is correcting the spelling errors which have been identified. This second spelling strategy is often missing from the spelling behaviors of many students; however, students can be taught to identify and correct misspelled words using an external source such as a dictionary. Using a dictionary involves a variety of skills which have been summarized by Cohen and Plaskin (1980) and are included in Figure 8.8. Such skills represent a sequence from most basic to most advanced and should probably be taught in the order which they are presented.

FIGURE 8.8   Skills Needed to Use a Dictionary (Task Analysis)

1. Locate the appropriate section of the pages.
2. Determine whether the first letter of the word is before or after the page you are on.
3. Determine whether the second letter of the word is before or after the page you are on.
4. Determine whether the third or possibly the fourth letter of the word is before or after the page you are on.
5. Locate the guide words (entry words) which "enclose" the word you are looking for.
6. Locate and use the "Concise Pronunciation Key," if necessary, to determine the pronunciation of each syllable.
7. Use the diacritical marks to determine the pronunciation of certain graphemes.
8. Interpret syllabic division correctly.
9. Interpret accent marks correctly.
10. Employ knowledge of grapheme-phoneme relationships.
11. Determine whether one of the most common synonyms fits the context of a particular sentence.
12. Read some or all of the definitions.
13. Select the best definition and apply it to a particular sentence.

□ **Special Dictionaries**

Formal, adult dictionaries can be huge, intimidating affairs for mentally retarded children. For this reason, companies have produced colorful, animated, high-interest picture dictionaries. Examples are *The Cat in the Hat Beginner Book Dictionary* (1984), *The Magic World of Words* (1980), and *The Scott Foresman Beginning Dictionary* (1976). These dictionaries, rather than containing all of the words of the English language, contain the most commonly used words needed by children and contain high motivation and high stimulus materials. In addition, there are a number of beginning dictionaries designed for older, elementary students. Such dictionaries include the *Thorndike-Barnhart Beginning Diction-ary*, the *World Book Dictionary*, and *Webster's Dictionary for Boys and Girls*. Finally, there are effectively sequenced, high motivation programs available which teach dictionary skills. Such programs include *David Discovers the Dictionary, Lessons for Self Instruction*, and the *Thorndike-Barnhart Dictionary Series*. Thus, in order to keep spelling interest and motivation high, the special education teacher will need to insure that dictionaries and other external channel spelling aids are at an age-appropriate level for mentally retarded learners.

SPELLING AND THE COMPUTER

□ □ The drill-like nature of spelling, along with its letter-by-letter approach to spell-ing words correctly, make the microcomputer an excellent teaching tool in this core academic area. Computers can be extremely motivating and reinforcing to a wide variety of school-age children and have also proven successful in providing the practice needed for students to overlearn the spelling of words in the internal channel (Dickson & Raymond 1984; Geoffrion & Geoffrion 1983).

A number of spelling software programs exist for different microcomputer systems and Table 8.6 gives a brief description of some of those programs and the computers for which they are designed. Since the number of such programs

TABLE 8.6   Some Available Computer Software for Spelling

Program	Computer Compatible	Publisher	Activity
1. Flash Spell Helicopter	Apple	Microcomputer Workshop	Spelling the word correctly earns ten seconds of helicopter time. Teacher can create different dictionaries.
2. Watchwords	Apple	Micromedia	Students select or type correct spelling of 540. Wordisk Master allows teacher to create 900 word disks.
3. Hand em high	Commodore 64	DES	Spelling game. Play the computer or other children.
4. Spelling Demons, Computer Spell Down	TRS and Apple	Random House	For grades 2-adult. Spelling words increase in difficulty.
5. Word Scrambler	Commodore Pet	Gamco	Unscramble the words. How many words can you spell.
6. Blast Off 100	Commodore Pet	Gamco	Blast off into space using correctly spelled words as fuel for your rockets.
7. Customized Flash Spelling	TRS or Apple	Random House	Allows teacher to create personalized spelling flash cards.
8. Sea Speller	Commodore 64	Fisher Price	Transforms the child to a magic dolphin. Find the missing letters and letter combinations to complete words and help the submarine reach the ocean floor.
9. Spelling Bee	Apple	Edu-Ware	Uses the spelling bee format to learn new words.
10. Magic Spells	Apple, Commodore 64, IBM-PC	Learning Co.	Join a magical wizard. Spell scrambled words correctly and find the chest of gold.
11. Word Spinner	Apple, Commodore 64, IBM-PC	Learning Co.	Pick a word you know. How many new words can you create? This is word spinning.
12. Spell It!	Apple, Commodore 64, IBM-PC	Davidson	Covers over 1000 of the most commonly misspelled words. A word list game.

FIGURE 8.9 Software Manufacturers of Spelling Programs

Spinnaker
Developmental Learning (DLM)
Fisher Price
Edu-ware
Learning Company
Random House
Micromedia
Davidson

is growing rapidly, Figure 8.9 contains a list of software manufacturers involved in creating and marketing spelling educational programs. The interested teacher should keep on these company's mailing lists to receive software catalogues.

HANDWRITING

☐ ☐ On first inspection, good handwriting may not appear to be a crucial academic skill. After all, some people might even argue that poor handwriting is correlated with success in a given profession (e.g., doctors). Handwriting, however, is important, especially as it relates to effective communication between individuals. It has been called the greatest time thief in our schools, robbing instructional time as teachers and students struggle to read illegibly written assignments (Enstrom 1967). Likewise, because of illegible handwriting, over one million letters end up daily in the Post Office's dead letter file. Since we can't walk around all day with typewriters or word processors, good handwriting is important.

☐ The Nature of Good Handwriting

The goal of all handwriting instruction should be legibility (May 1980; Polloway & Smith 1982). There are five basic variables which contribute to legible handwriting. These variables are letter shape, alignment of letters on the page line, consistent letter slant, consistent letter size, and regular letter and word spacing. Figure 8.10 shows examples of deficiencies in these five areas.

HANDWRITING ASSESSMENT

☐ ☐ Before remedial handwriting instruction can be instituted, an assessment of the child's handwriting abilities must be carried out. Such an assessment will allow the following assessment questions to be answered: (*1*) whether the student possesses the requisite readiness skills to enter a program of handwriting instruction, (*2*) the level of the child's current handwriting expertise, and (*3*) which of the five handwriting areas previously described needs remediation.

FIGURE 8.10 Examples of Handwriting Deficiencies

Letter Shape

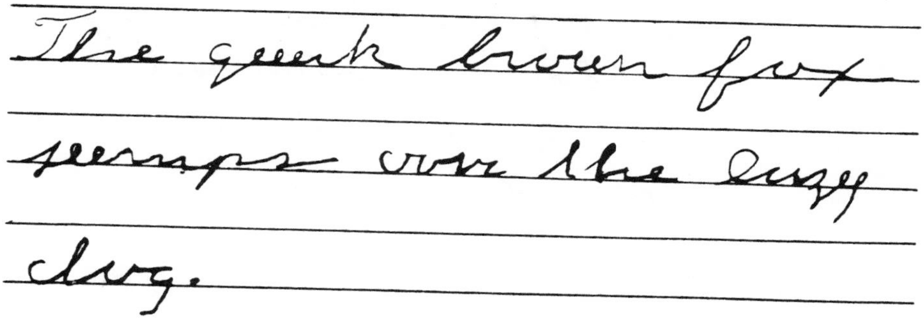

Letter Slant

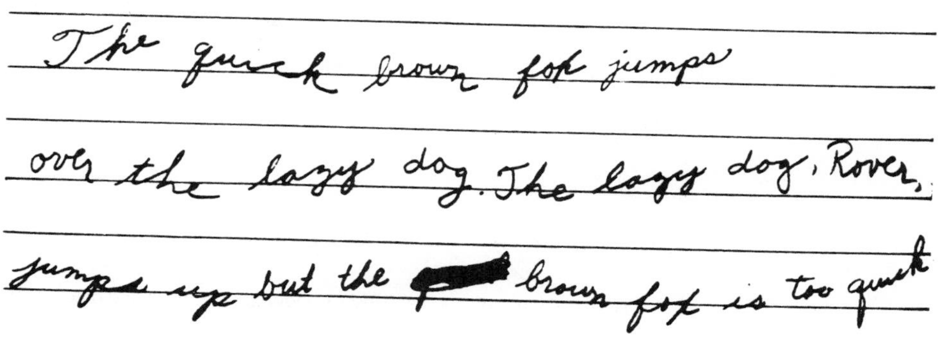

Letter Size

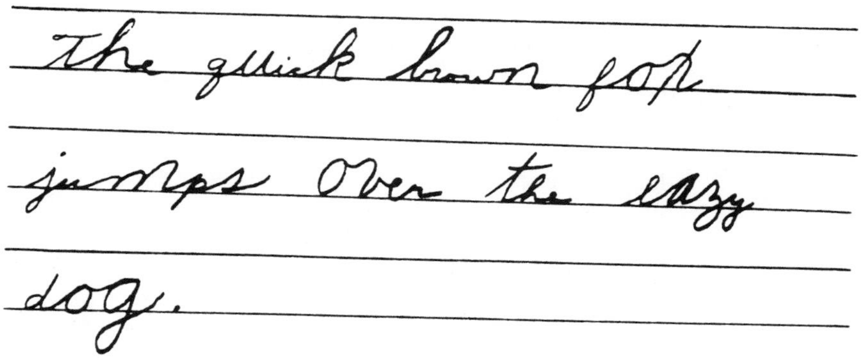

(continued)

FIGURE 8.10 (continued)

Spacing of Letters

Letter Alignment

From S. Graham & L. Miller (1983). Handwriting research and practice. In E.L. Meyen et al., *Promising practices for exceptional children.* Denver: Love.

Handwriting assessment may take place using formal or informal techniques. Since formal handwriting assessment instruments are relatively rare, the teacher will likely need to carry out informal, teacher-made handwriting assessment. However, a limited number of formal handwriting assessment tests are available to the classroom teacher. They are described in Table 8.7.

No one formal test of handwriting can completely and fully and in an indepth fashion diagnostically describe a child's handwriting abilities. Therefore, the classroom teacher should also use an informal handwriting assessment (Graham 1983). Weiner (1980) has identified the following types of handwriting errors which may be gauged in an informal handwriting assessment:

1. Heavy pencil or pen pressure on the paper.
2. Multiple or consistent erasures on the page.
3. Inappropriate upper-case and lower-case letter mix.
4. Size/space letter irregularities.
5. Off-line writing.
6. Slant or crowding of letters.

TABLE 8.7   Handwriting Assessment Tests

Test	Description	Grade Level
Thorndike Scale of Handwriting (Thorndike, 1910)	Fifteen samples of handwriting quality. Student's work is compared to these samples.	all
Ayres Scale for Measuring Handwriting (Ayres, 1912)	Measures student's handwriting against eight samples.	2–8
Bezzi Scale (1962)	Contains a series of five-step scales.	1–3
Basic School Skills Inventory (Hammill & Leigh, 1983)	Handwriting sub-test. Assesses a child's handwriting on 10 different tasks. Criterion referenced.	
Zaner-Bloser Evaluation Scale (1984)	Considers five factors of handwriting.	1–3 for manuscript. Scales 2–9 cursive.

Perhaps more than the other core areas, judgments of handwriting deficiencies by teachers is a subjective process. That is, while the judging of a misspelled word is objective (either it is or it is not misspelled), good handwriting is more in the eyes of the beholder. For this reason, attempts have been made at objectifying scoring of handwriting deficiencies. Such scoring technique includes the use of transparent overlays over samples of writing to compare the child's handwriting with that of the experts (Helwig, Johns, Norman & Cooper 1976; Salzberg, Wheeler, Devar & Hopkins 1971). Available evidence suggests that even where formal objective scoring procedures are not used, teachers often demonstrate a high degree of agreement as to what is and is not good handwriting (Otto, McMenemy & Smith 1973). Thus to a large degree, informal handwriting assessment is both a reliable and valid measure of assessment. Figure 8.11 contains a sample checklist the classroom teacher may use in analyzing children's handwriting samples.

TEACHING HANDWRITING

☐ Handwriting Readiness

Although teachers often pay less attention to handwriting readiness than to readiness in the other core academic areas, children should possess some basic requisite skills before receiving handwriting instruction (May 1980). In general,

FIGURE 8.11   Sample Checklist of Handwriting Competencies

1. *Writing Speed*
   _____ Too fast
   _____ Adequate
   _____ Too slow
   General Comments:

2. *Letter Formation*
   Capitals:
   _____ Too large
   _____ Proportionally adequate
   _____ Too small
   General Description:

   Lowercase:
   _____ Too large
   _____ Proportionally adequate
   _____ Too small
   General Description:

3. *Spacing*
   Between letters:
   _____ Too close
   _____ Adequate
   _____ Too far apart

   Between words:
   _____ Too close
   _____ Adequate
   _____ Too far apart

   Margins:
   _____ Too wide
   _____ Adequate
   _____ Too narrow
   General Description:

From S. Graham & L. Miller (1983). Handwriting research and practice. In E.L. Meyen et al., *Promising practices for exceptional children*. Denver: Love.

the teacher should assess that children possess the following abilities *prior* to beginning manuscript (print) writing:

1. Adequate eye-hand coordination
2. Adequate hand-arm coordination
3. Gross motor (large muscles) and fine motor (finger, small muscles) coordination
4. Knowledge of key concepts like up-down, left-right, around, etc.

There are a variety of activities which the child can engage in to facilitate readiness to write. For example, throwing and catching small objects like rubber balls or beanbags can help both eye-hand coordination and gross motor skills. Likewise, putting together puzzles, handling small objects with tweezers, cutting with scissors, pasting, drawing, and painting can help in fine motor coordination. In addition, it is probably a good idea to encourage children in the readiness stage of handwriting to engage in activities such as drawing circles and making vertical lines. However, if such activities are carried out, the teacher should make sure that the children make their circles counterclockwise and their vertical lines from top to bottom. If such is not the case, negative transfer may occur and the child may end up carrying over bad habits once manuscript instruction ensues.

□ Teaching Manuscript Writing

Children are usually taught to write in manuscript (print) before attempting to write in cursive (Gross & Gross 1970; May 1980). It has been argued that manuscript print is easier for children to both read and write than cursive writing and is hence easier to learn, and that positive transfer exists between reading and manuscript writing since manuscript writing closely approximates the printed page (Graham & Miller 1983b; Renaud & Groff 1966). On the negative side, it appears that many parents believe that manuscript print is babyish and wish their children to learn adult cursive writing. Additionally, many people believe that instruction in manuscript writing is a useless skill which will have to be unlearned when cursive instruction begins (Jackson 1970; Renaud & Groff 1966). Nevertheless, it is the opinion of most educational experts, especially in the field of special education, that the teaching of cursive writing before manuscript writing is too complex a cognitive and motor task for the mentally retarded child and that instruction in manuscript writing is desirable and necessary.

☐ Approaches to Teaching Manuscript Writing

There are basically two different approaches to teaching manuscript writing. Until recently, the most common approach was the *circle-line* method. In this approach, letters are formed by drawing circles, parts of circles, and/or straight lines. For example, while the letters *a*, *d*, and *b* represent circles (and straight lines), the letters *x, y, l*, and *k* represent the drawing of straight lines only. Figure 8.12a shows a sample of manuscript print using the circle-line method.

FIGURE 8.12   Samples of Manuscript Writing Using Two Handwriting Methods

a. The Circle-Line Method

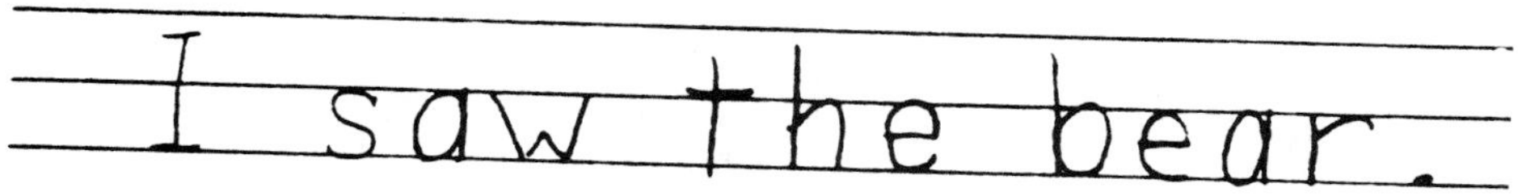

b. The D'Nealian Method

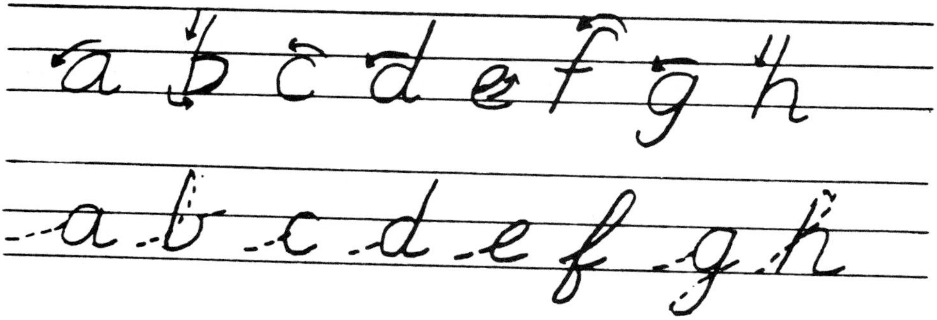

From S. Graham & L. Miller (1983). Handwriting research and practice. In E.L. Meyen et al., *Promising practices for exceptional children*. Denver: Love.

The circle-line method possesses the advantage of teaching children to write all alphabet letters with a minimal number of strokes. However, it also has the major disadvantage of having children draw letters in discrete rather than continuous strokes in which the pencil does not leave the paper (the way that cursive letters are formed) (May 1980; Thurber & Jordan 1978). For this reason, many schools have adopted the D'Nealian writing program (Thurber & Jackson 1978). The D'Nealian approach is a continuous stroke method which uses cursive forms to print manuscript letters. In this method, three techniques designed to facilitate the transition from manuscript to cursive writing are taught to the child (Thurber 1975). These techniques are

1. Letters are made with a continuous stroke.
2. Letters are slanted rather than perpendicular.
3. Letter shapes are similar in both manuscript and cursive.

Figure 8.12b shows a sample of letters in the D'Nealian format.

Since a high degree of transfer between manuscript and cursive writing is hypothesized in the D'Nealian program, this approach may be a sound one to use with mildly mentally retarded learners who often do not transfer and generalize well from one system to another. The D'Nealian program may, to a certain extent, help alleviate the problem of children having to learn two distinct handwriting systems, one of which will have to be abandoned when cursive instruction is undertaken.

☐ Teaching Manuscript Letter Formation

In teaching manuscript letter formation, it is suggested that letters be learned in isolation, that they should be practiced until they are overlearned, and that they be combined with other manuscript-acquired words only after they have been overlearned and can be reproduced from memory (Graham & Miller 1983b). Additionally, as much as possible, the special-education teacher should use external prompts and aids to help children learn the correct formation of letters. These prompts would then be faded after correct letter formations have been acquired. Such prompts and aids may include color coding, wall charts showing the correct formation of letters, dots and dashes to be traced, or specially treated paper which turns a certain color when the letter has not been formed correctly on the page (Skinner & Krakower 1968).

Given the available research on handwriting and letter formation and the above stated goals, the special education teacher should consider adopting the following instructional strategies (Graham & Miller 1983b):

1. **Modeling:** The teacher writes and names the letter as students observe.
2. **Pointing out critical attributes:** The teacher points out the key aspects and attributes of each letter. The teacher also shows how each letter is similar and different in its formation to other letters which the

student has learned to write. During this phase, it is suggested that manuscript letters be introduced in the following order to increase similarity of critical attributes:

Upper Case Letters:
L, H, T, E, F, I
J, U, P, R, B, D, K
S, Q, O, C, G
A, M, N, V, W, X, Y, Z

Lower Case Letters:
o, a, d, g, a   v, w, x, y, z
b, p   f, j
c, e, f, t, l, i, k   u
r, n, m, h   s

3. **Physical instruction:** The teacher physically moves the student's hand in forming letters correctly.
4. **Tracing:** Dots, dashes, colored lines, and specially treated paper is used to help the child trace and form the letters correctly.
5. **Copying:** Prompts are faded out. The student copies letter on paper from blackboard or wall chart.
6. **Self-verbalization:** The student copies the letter and verbalizes each step of the process by describing the letter's critical attributes and the way that the letter is formed.
7. **Writing from memory:** The student writes the letter from memory using an internal image.
8. **Repetition:** The student practices writing the letter until it is over-learned. At least forty to fifty such repetitions are usually required spaced over several sessions until most younger and/or mildly mentally retarded children can overlearn the letters.
9. **Self-correction:** The student consults an external source such as a wall chart or handwriting book and compares his or her own letters to the examples. The student corrects the letters under supervision of the teacher.

There are a variety of handwriting approaches utilizing the nine teaching suggestions listed above which may be used in handwriting instruction. Such programs include the Niedermeyer (1973), Fauke (Fauke, Burnett, Powers & Sulzer-Azaroff 1973), and the Write and See (Skinner & Krakower 1968) methods. These methods of teaching handwriting use a multimodality, multisensory approach in which visual, auditory, and kinesthetic (touch) modalities are all used in instruction. Figure 8.13 lists and briefly summarizes the major handwriting instructional approaches.

In putting letters together to form words, the natural association between handwriting, letter formation, and spelling should be utilized. That is, letters learned in handwriting should be combined to form meaningful words which are interesting, motivational, and functional in the child's life. For example, the letters of the child's name and other people central in the child's environment should probably be learned first and combined into

FIGURE 8.13 Major Approaches to Handwriting

Fauke Approach (Fauke et al., 1973)

1. The teacher writes the letter, and the student and teacher discuss the formational act.
2. The student names the letter.
3. The student traces the letter with a finger, pencil, and magic marker.
4. The student's finger traces a letter form made of yarn.
5. The student copies the letter.
6. The student writes the letter from memory.
7. The teacher rewards the student for correctly writing the letter.

Progressive Approximation Approach (Hofmeister, 1973)

1. The student copies the letter using a pencil.
2. The teacher examines the letter and, if necessary, corrects by overmarking with a highlighter.
3. The student erases incorrect portions of the letter and traces over the teacher's highlighter marking.
4. The student repeats steps 1-3 until the letter is written correctly.

Furner Approach (Furner, 1969a, 1969b, 1970)

1. Student and teacher establish a purpose for the lesson.
2. The teacher provides the student with many guided exposures to the letter.
3. The student describes the process while writing the letter and tries to write or visualize the letter as another child describes it.
4. The teacher uses multisensory stimulation to teach the letter form.
5. The student compares his or her written response to a model.

VAKT Approach

1. The teacher writes the letter with crayon while the student observes the process.
2. The teacher and student both say the name of the letter.
3. The student traces the letter with the index finger, simultaneously saying the name of the letter. This is done successfully five times.
4. The student copies and names the letter successfully three times.
5. Without a visual aid, the student writes and names the letter correctly three times.

Niedermeyer Approach (Niedermeyer, 1973)

1. The student traces a dotted representation of the letter 12 times.
2. The student copies the letter 12 times.
3. The student writes the letter as the teacher pronounces it.

Handwriting with Write and See (Skinner & Krakower, 1968)

The student traces a letter within a tolerance model on specially prepared paper. If the student forms the letter correctly, the pen writes gray; if it is incorrect, the pen writes yellow.

From S. Graham & L. Miller (1983). Handwriting research and practice. In E.L. Meyen et al., *Promising practices for exceptional children*. Denver: Love.

those meaningful words followed by other functional words central to the child. In addition, especially for somewhat older students, the key words and concepts inherent in the long-term instructional unit being taught at the time should become the vocabulary in which words taught and practiced in handwriting instruction are formed.

TEACHING CURSIVE WRITING

☐ ☐ The transition from manuscript to cursive writing is relatively straightforward when the continuous stroke method is used to teach manuscript. However, where the circle-line method has been used, transfer to cursive writing may be more problematic.

☐ Techniques of Cursive Writing

In teaching cursive writing, the teacher should focus special attention on the areas of joining or connecting letters, letter slant, dotted and crossed letters, and positioning the paper. For example, the paper should be positioned at about 30° to the left for right-handed writers and at about 20°–30° to the right for left-handed students. Likewise, the teacher should work with students in helping them slant letters slightly to the right. In terms of connecting letters, students should receive practice writing words and sentences so as to gain practice in connecting letters. Finally, students will need to learn that letters are dotted or crossed after the whole word has been written (this is different from manuscript writing where letters are dotted and crossed as they are formed). After these strategies have been learned by students, it is a good idea to teach letters which are shaped in similar ways. Figure 8.14 contains grouping of similarly formed upper and lower case letters.

☐ Activities for Teaching Cursive Writing

It is suggested that teachers adopt the following approaches when teaching cursive writing:

1. Introduce meaningful words.
2. Give an overview of the word.
3. Give students an analysis of the strokes involved.
4. Have students imitate the word.
5. Have students imitate the letters.
6. Imitate the word again.
7. Independent production of the word by students.

This can be translated into the following classroom activities (May 1980).

1. Have the students watch the teacher write the word two or three times without any analysis of the strokes. This represents an overview of the word.
2. Write the word again, this time analyzing each letter stroke by stroke.

FIGURE 8.14 Sequential Grouping of Letters for Handwriting Instruction

a. Upper Case Manuscript

ABCDEFGHI
JKLMNOPQ
RSTUVWX
YZ

LHTEFI/JU
PRBDK/AMN
VWXYZ/S
OQCG

b. Lower Case Manuscript

abcdefghij
klmnopqrst
uvwxyz

---

oadgq/bp/ce
tlik/rnmh/vw
xy/ fj/u/z/s

(continued)

FIGURE 8.14   **(continued)**

c. Upper Case Cursive

A B C D E F G H I
J K L M N O P Q
R S T U V W X Y Z

n m H K U V y w
X 2 3 / P B R / T F /
C E / Q / D / G / L / L / O /
S / J

d. Lower Case Cursive

a b c d e f g h
i j k l m n o
p q r s t u v
w x y z

i u w t j l a d
g q l n m x y v
l r s p l c l o q
l b f h k l

From Polloway et al. (1985). Sequential grouping of letters for handwriting instruction. *Strategies for teaching retarded and special needs learners* (3rd ed.). Columbus, OH: Merrill.

3. Have the children write the word as you write it—each letter stroke by stroke.
4. Have the children write each letter in the word at least three times.
5. Have children write the whole word with you—again, stroke by stroke.
6. Have the children write the word by themselves several times with the teacher monitoring the writing behavior.

It appears that teachers ought not to be concerned over details like the size of the paper, the space between the lines on the paper, or the size of the pencil that the child is using. Available research indicates that these factors make little difference in the child's cursive handwriting (Tawney 1967; Wiles 1943). Adult paper and regular sized pencils seem to work about as well as primary paper and oversized pencils. In fact, many pupils rebel against using the latter as being babyish and wish to use the implements and papers that adults use. In the primary grades, it is acceptable to use regular sized paper but have children use two lines and spaces for tall letters and skipping spaces between word lines.

THE LEFT-HANDED WRITER

☐ ☐ Take it from someone who is left-handed. The left-handed people of the world have it rough! (Do you know, for example, that the word *sinister* in Latin originally meant "toward the left"?)

Left-handed writers are in an especially precarious situation. In the past, because of beliefs that left-handedness led to illegible writing, poor academic achievement, and even stuttering, left-handed writers were often forced to become right-handed. Although this is no longer the prevailing wisdom in schools, left-handed writers are still at the distinct disadvantage of not being able to see the letters and words which they are forming. To compensate for this, many left-handed writers hook their hand in order to view their letters, which contributes to poor penmanship.

It is suggested that the special-education teacher adopt the following instructional strategies with left-handed writers (Graham & Miller 1983b; Lerner 1981):

1. Before writing instruction begins, determine the child's hand preference.
2. Left-handed children's desks should be adjusted slightly lower than the desks of right-handed children.
3. Left-handed children should be provided with left-handed desks and a left-handed writing model.
4. The teacher should have left-handed children write on the left side of the chalkboard whenever possible.
5. For left-handed writers, the paper should be positioned approximately 30° to the right.

6. The grip on the pencil should be slightly higher on the pencil than for right-handed writers. Left-handed writers should grip the pencil approximately one inch from the point.

7. The position of the hand for left-handed writers should be slightly curved with the little finger supporting the hand's weight. For inappropriate hand positions which have become habitual and resistant to change, the paper positions shown in Figure 8.15 are suggested.

SKILLS OF WRITTEN EXPRESSION

☐ ☐ Written expression is the highest form of language-arts communication (Shanklin 1982; Shanahan & Lomax 1985). That is, without the earlier acquisition of appropriate oral language, reading, and spelling skills, there is little or no chance that adequate writing skills will develop. Thus, it should not be surprising that mentally retarded children, who typically experience difficulties in oral language and reading, often also possess deficiencies in ability for written self-expression.

Good writing skills, however, are crucial for success in today's modern society. People need to write everything from letters to job applications and reports. In school, writing competence correlates highly with success in all of the language arts areas (Berieter 1980; Moran 1981), while outside of school, written expression represents a form of self-expression for people which can improve their general emotional well-being and self-concept.

For example, the author once encountered a mildly mentally retarded adolescent student who was so upset over something that had happened to him in school that he just couldn't or wouldn't speak about it. The teacher tried and tried to get the student to open up and tell what was bothering him but to no avail. Finally, the teacher asked the student to write a letter explaining what was wrong and the student agreed. At the end of the period an emotionally charged letter was placed on the teacher's desk and both the teacher and the student were able to deal with the situation based on the student's written self-expression.

CONVENTIONAL WRITING VERSUS CREATIVE WRITING: A DEBATE

☐ ☐ Should we teach children to write before they possess the conventional skills of basic grammar and punctuation? This debate has proponents on both sides. Some educators, interested in written expression primarily as a form of self-expression and creativity, argue that forcing the child to learn punctuation, capitalization, and grammar before allowing the child to write can squelch creativity (Meltzer, Fenton & Persky 1985). On the other hand, many special educators

FIGURE 8.15   Adjustments for Left-Handed Writers

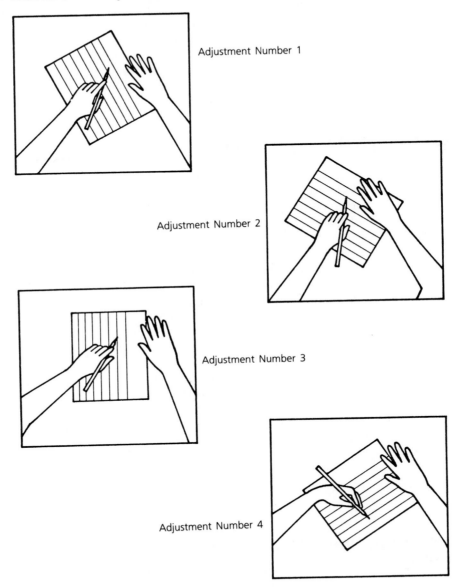

Adjustment Number 1

Adjustment Number 2

Adjustment Number 3

Adjustment Number 4

From S. Graham & L. Miller (1983). Handwriting research and practice. In E. L. Meyer, G. A. Vergason, & R. J. Whelan (Eds.) *Promising Practices for Exceptional Children.* Denver: Love Publishing. Used by permission.

involved in the education of the mentally retarded argue that behavior which differs from the norm is considered eccentric but acceptable in gifted and/or talented children but is considered deficient and deviant when exhibited by the mentally retarded (Deno, Marston & Mirkin 1982; Heigle & Sonedecker 1985). Thus, special educators argue, to increase the probability of their acceptance, mentally retarded children should learn to do things in conventional ways, including learning how to write.

In this controversy, a compromise may be possible. To force the mentally retarded student to practice, practice, and practice punctuation, capitalization, and grammar would be deadly to motivation in the classroom. In fact, probably nothing can drench the creative spark faster than the teacher who ignores the content of the child's written product and instead hones in on grammatical and punctuation shortcomings. On the other hand, even our civilization's greatest and most creative authors have had to conform to conventional form and grammar. Thus, there is no reason to believe that writing creativity and knowledge of form and grammar are mutually exclusive. Rather, both need to be emphasized in the written expression curriculum.

COMPONENTS OF WRITTEN LANGUAGE

□ □ There appear to be components or stages which must occur for written language to be effective. These stages have been termed *prewriting, writing,* and *postwriting* (Hall 1981). Prewriting represents the input which must occur before anything is written. It reflects the stimulation, experiences, and incubation of ideas. Prewriting skills include the child's life experiences, personal motivation to write, and purpose for writing (Mercer & Mercer 1981; Polloway, Patton & Cohen 1983). The writing stage represents the tools and mechanics for writing which includes handwriting, spelling, vocabulary, structure, and grammar (Polloway et al. 1983; Sink 1975). It represents the skills necessary to adequately express the ideas generated during the input stage. Finally, postwriting refers to proofreading and the creation of completed products (Alley & Deshler 1979; Krause 1983). It represents the revision of what has been written in order to form a coherent, finished whole.

ASSESSMENT OF WRITTEN LANGUAGE

□ □ The goal of written expression assessment is to identify and describe pupils who possess difficulties in written expression, especially as these deficiencies relate to the areas of prewriting, writing, and postwriting (Hogan & Mishler 1979; Jenkins & Caldwell 1985). Such an assessment gauges the child's ability to use punctuation, capitalization and form, as well as measures fluency, vocabulary and organization, proofreading, and evaluation skills.

Assessing written expression is not an easy task. This appears to be the case for a variety of reasons which include: (*1*) there is no accepted theoretical hierarchy or sequence of written expression similar to spoken language and reading, (*2*) very few formal assessment instruments of written expression exist and those that are available tend to measure mechanical aspects of writing, and (*3*) assessing written expression appears to be a highly subjective process (Jenkins & Caldwell 1985; Polloway, Patton & Cohen 1983).

☐ Formal Assessment

Despite these difficulties in assessing written expression, there are three major testing instruments which the teacher may use to measure the written language skills of students. These three tests are the Test of Written Language (TOWL) (Hammill & Larsen 1978, 1983), the Picture Story Language Test (Myklebust 1965), and the Sequential Test of Educational Progress (STEP) (Educational Testing Service, 1958). The TOWL is a norm-referenced test which assesses achievement of writing skills in seven areas: vocabulary, thematic maturity, spelling, word usage, style, thought units, and handwriting. Although the TOWL is not diagnostic and does not further break these seven subtests down into more precise diagnostic subskills, it does yield a writing profile which can indicate to the teacher general areas where the student is experiencing difficulties and where more in-depth assessment would be appropriate. Likewise, the Picture Story Language and the STEP tests assess children's writing in terms of organization, form, punctuation and grammar, and general effectiveness. However, since both of these tests possess certain problems of reliability and validity it is probably a good idea to use the results gleaned from these tests in a relatively informal manner (Hammill 1975; Wallace & Larsen 1979).

☐ Informal Assessment

Informal assessment of written expression will probably be attempted by most teachers because of the paucity of formal assessment instruments. An informal assessment in this core area should possess the following components (Jenkins 1985; Poteet 1980).

1. Punctuation and capitalization.
2. Organization of ideas.
3. Sentence and paragraph sense.
4. Vocabulary choice, usage, and fluency.
5. Purpose for writing.
6. Effectiveness of writing.

Informal assessment of writing skills would take place by having the child write a structured written assignment and then by the teacher analyzing the composition on the six criteria listed above. Such analysis would then yield in-depth knowledge about where the student is experiencing difficulties in writing. Objective scoring procedures for informal written language assessment has been created by a number of individuals (Poteet 1980; Polloway, Patton & Cohen 1983). Figure 8.16 contains Poteet's Checklist of Written Expression Skills, which informally assesses areas of penmanship, spelling, grammar, and ideation.

FIGURE 8.16 Poteet's Checklist of Written Expression Skills

Student's Name _____ *Grade Placement* _____ *Teacher* _____ *Grade* _____

	TA	A	I	R	Notes
I. PENMANSHIP					
Rating: 1 2 3 4 5					
A. Spacing on the page _____					
B. Spacing of the sentences _____					
C. Spacing of the words _____					
D. Spacing of letters _____					
E. Slant _____					
F. Letter formations _____					
G. Pressure on the paper _____					
H. Pencil grip _____					
II. SPELLING					
_____ % misspelled					
A. Miscalled rule _____					
B. Letter insertion _____					
C. Letter omission _____					
D. Letter substitution _____					
E. Phonetic spelling _____					
F. Directional confusion _____					
G. Schwa or *r*-controlled vowels _____					
H. Letter-orientation _____					
I. Sequence _____					
J. Other _____					

(continued)

FIGURE 8.16 (continued)

III. GRAMMAR	TA	A	I	R	Notes
A. *Capitalization*					
1. proper noun					
2. proper adjective					
3. first word in a sentence					
4. first word in a line of verse					
5. first word in a quotation					
6. principal words in a title					
7. personal title					
8. use of "I" or "O"					
9. personification					
10. salutation in a letter					
11. complimentary close in a letter					
12. other					
B. *Punctuation*					
1. period					
2. comma					
3. apostrophe					
4. quotation marks					
5. question mark					
6. semicolons					
7. exclamation mark					
8. colon					
9. the dash					
10. parentheses					
11. brackets					
12. the slash					
C. *Syntax*					
1. parts of speech					
a. verbs					
b. nouns					
c. pronouns					
d. adjectives					
e. adverbs					
f. prepositions					
g. conjunctions					
h. interjections					
2. agreement					
3. case					
4. pronoun reference					
5. order/position of words					
6. parallelism					
7. abbreviations/numbers					
8. the paragraph					

(continued)

FIGURE 8.16 (continued)

IV. IDEATION

    A. *Type of writing*

        1. story _____   2. poem _____   3. letter _____   4. report _____   5. review _____

    B. *Substance*

        1. Naming _____   2. Description _____   3. Plot _____   4. Issue _____

    C. *Productivity*

        1. Number of words written _____   2. Acceptable number _____   3. Too few _____

    D. *Comprehensibility*

        Easy to understand _____ Difficult to understand _____ Cannot understand _____

            _____ perservation of words   _____ illogical

            _____ perservation of ideas   _____ disorganized

    E. *Reality*

        _____ Accurate perception of stimulus or task

        _____ Inaccurate perception of stimulus or task

    F. *Style*

        1. Sentence Sense

            a. Completeness   Tallies:

                (1) complete sentences _____

                (2) run-on sentences _____

                (3) sentence fragments _____

            b. Structure

                (1) simple _____

                (2) compound _____

                (3) complex _____

                (4) compound/complex _____

            c. Types

                (1) declarative _____

                (2) interrogative _____

                (3) imperative _____

                (4) exclamatory _____

        2. Tone

            a. intimate _____ b. friendly _____ c. impersonal _____

        3. Word Choice (N = none, F = few, S = some, M = many)

            a. formality

                formal _____ informal _____ colloquial _____

            b. complexity

                simple _____ multisyllable _____ contractions _____

            c. descriptiveness

                vague _____ vivid _____ figures of speech _____

            d. appropriateness

                inexact words _____ superfluous/repetitions _____ omissions _____

Scoring Code:

TA: Too advanced for the student or not appropriate

A: Skills adequately used by student

I: Skills which need to be introduced

R: Skills which need remediation or review

From J.A. Poteet (1980). Informal assessment of written expression. *Learning Disability Quarterly, 3* (4), 88–98.

TEACHING WRITTEN EXPRESSION
TO MENTALLY RETARDED CHILDREN

☐ Prewriting

Prewriting consists of input, motivation, and purpose for writing (Hall 1981). During this stage, the key to writing instruction is to provide students with a set of stimulating, interesting experiences they will WANT to write about. For the teacher of mildly mentally retarded pupils, this may be no easy task. Such students often may be unmotivated to write and they may complain that they have nothing to say. The special-education teacher must provide relevant and meaningful opportunities for writing that motivate students to want to write.

The first step in the prewriting stage is to convince students that they have something important and worthwhile to say. Relevant conditions must persuade students they have a need for writing. Such activities include

1. Writing letters to friends who have moved away.
2. Keeping a log or diary of things happening in their lives.
3. Writing how they feel emotionally at given points in time.
4. Writing signs or posters.
5. Filling out forms.
6. Giving someone written directions (e.g., writing out a recipe).
7. Taking notes on something to be remembered.
8. Creating outlines.

Each of these activities offers students relevant reasons to write. For example, a class could converse with pen pals in a distant country or state or each student could write letters to a friend or relative. Students could create a cookbook of their favorite recipes or they could have a recipe contest where each student would enter a favorite concoction. Class members could decide to create signs and posters to advertise some upcoming class or school event. Whatever the activity, the special education teacher must make sure that it is motivating, life-like and natural to students' (as opposed to the teacher's) interests. The need and desire to write should grow naturally from the activity selected. It should not be forced or contrived.

WRITING STAGE

The writing stage consists of related tools such as handwriting, spelling, punctuation, and grammar as well as the mechanics of vocabulary, usage, sentence and paragraph structure, and organization (Hall 1981). The reader should refer to earlier sections of this chapter on handwriting and spelling.

☐ Developing Vocabulary and Usage in Written Expression

Once students have become motivated and enthused about writing a composition, the special education teacher should then pose the question: All right, you want to write something, but what exactly are you going to *say*? This is where vocabulary and word usage come into play.

First, it should be pointed out that written vocabulary does not develop and should not be taught independently of spoken and reading vocabulary. The three processes of speaking, reading, and writing are hierarchically related; oral language develops before reading which develops before writing. This means that the teacher should not expect any word or concept to be in the child's written vocabulary which is not already in his spoken and reading vocabulary.

Additionally, mentally retarded students may also experience difficulty retrieving words from speaking and reading vocabularies and effectively transferring them to the writing vocabulary. This is the cause of the famous "writer's block." You have the word in your spoken vocabulary but you just cannot recall it in order to transfer it to your written composition. In order to help facilitate this problem in mentally retarded students, the following instructional activities might prove helpful:

1. Allow the students to keep a word list which they often use in writing.
2. Keep a word box or word file of commonly used writing words in a central place for handy reference by students.
3. Keep a word wall (VanAllen 1976) which would consist of a portion of the classroom wall devoted to lists of high frequency writing words.
4. Help students arrange vocabularies by categories. This activity can be particularly adapted to the long-term instructional unit approach in which lists would be kept for each unit and subtopic covered.
5. List and discuss new words as they appear in the students' reading. Add these new words to the child's word list or to the word box if appropriate.
6. Work with students in finding synonyms and antonyms for words.
7. Have each child present a new and interesting word and definition in class. Try to incorporate these new words into the students' writings.
8. Have the class brainstorm words and concepts appropriate to a topic or assignment.
9. Allow the children to play word board games or to do crossword puzzles.
10. Give students nouns and have them generate as many adjective descriptors as they can.

By providing these opportunities for vocabulary and word generation, the teacher may be able to aid mentally retarded students in appropriately transferring and generalizing words from the spoken to the written vocabularies.

☐ Punctuation and Capitalization

Punctuation and capitalization errors are quite common and pervasive in the writing of mentally retarded students. Punctuation errors may occur frequently because children do not view punctuation as being important or because they have had insufficient opportunity for application and generalization of these punctuation rules in real-life writing situations. Likewise, punctuation may be a critical variable related to dialect and this should be taken into account when considering whether the punctuation and grammar of children's writing is correct.

Figure 8.17 contains a list of the most common punctuation rules used in the writing of English (Burns 1974; Dallman 1976). There are a variety of instructional methods which the special-education teacher may use to help teach these rules. They include

1. Prepare and dictate passages to students. Have students copy the passages. Analyze, correct, and instruct the students in the punctuation errors made.
2. Give students written passages with punctuation missing. Have students place correct punctuation in the appropriate places.
3. Develop bulletin boards and classroom wall charts about the rules of punctuation which can be referred to for help.
4. Provide many and different examples of each punctuation rule for students. Make these examples easily accessible for students at a central location in the classroom.
5. Have students tape record their written compositions. Transcribe their writings. Have them punctuate their compositions appropriately.

Like punctuation, capitalization errors are quite common among students. The confusion about when and where to capitalize may be due to the fact that typically while children learn that there are two types of letters (upper and lower case) quite early in their school careers, they do not really begin to learn why and when these letters are used differentially until they begin to write somewhat later on. For mentally retarded learners, who typically do not transfer and generalize well, such learning and adoption of capitalization rules can be doubly difficult.

There are a number of instructional activities which can be utilized by the teacher to teach capitalization procedures to mentally retarded learners. They include

1. Posting the rules of capitalization on a classroom wall and giving each child a small card with the rules printed on it for easy reference.
2. Have a capital letter scavenger hunt. Students must find all of the capital letters in a passage in a given period of time and identify the rule which governs the capital.

FIGURE 8.17   Most Common Punctuation Rules

Period
a. At the end of a sentence
b. Following a command
c. After an abbreviation
d. After numbers in a list
e. Following an initial
f. After numerals and letters in an outline

Comma
a. In dates (between the day of the month and the year)
b. In addresses (between the name of the city and state)
c. After the greeting of a friendly letter
d. After the closing of a friendly letter
e. Between words given in a series
f. To set off appositives
g. After "yes" and "no" when they are used as parenthetical expressions
h. After the name of a person being addressed
i. To separate a quotation from the explanatory part of a sentence
j. After a person's last name when it is written before the first name

Question Mark
a. At the close of a question

Quotation Marks
a. Before and after the direct words of a speaker
b. Around the title of a story, poem, or an article

Apostrophe
a. To establish a possessive noun
b. In a contraction

Exclamation Point
a. At the end of an exclamatory sentence
b. After a word or group of words showing surprise or strong feeling

Hyphen
a. In compound words
b. In compound numbers (e.g. telephone numbers)
c. Separating syllables of a word that is divided at the end of the line

Colon
a. Between the hour and minutes in the time of day.
b. After the salutation in a business letter

3. Have students dictate a story into a tape recorder. Transcribe the stories. Have students capitalize the stories appropriately.
4. Give students a passage inappropriately capitalized. For every error found, the student receives a point. Students receive an extra point for identifying the rule which governs the error.
5. Have children create works which highlight capitalization (e.g., calendars, class rosters, directory of places). Have students capitalize the works appropriately.

During the prewriting stage the teacher must create for the student an open, relaxed, and accepting attitude about writing. Now is not the time for harsh criticism of form or punctuation. Rather, the teacher needs to help the student overcome anxiety about writing and a fear of failure in writing (Petty & Bowen 1967). For many students, especially mildly mentally retarded students, attempts at written expression have led to failure and criticism (Alley & Deshler 1979; Lerner 1981). Thus, the special-education teacher must help create a non-judgmental, warm, and accepting writing environment where students will feel secure and safe in expressing themselves.

A LIFE-EXPERIENCE AND/OR UNIT APPROACH TO WRITING

□ □ One way to make writing more natural and relevant for mentally retarded students is to use a life-experience approach. In this method, the teacher uses knowledge about the child's background, environment, and culture in order to stimulate a desire to write.

The life-experience approach might begin with a one-on-one interview between the teacher and the student. What kinds of things interest the student? What events are going on in the child's life which are important (you'd be surprised how infrequently students are asked this question). What are the cultural biases (if any) for or against writing. The more information that the teacher can glean this way about the student, the better.

Next, the teacher would begin to keep a chart of the concepts and vocabulary which keep cropping up in this interview. Certain themes will keep appearing in the child's conversation (e.g., cars, food, pets, farm life, divorce) and these topics or themes will have a certain vocabulary. Could the student write something about the topic of interest using some of the words on the chart? If the student resists, could the student dictate a story to the teacher or tape record something about the topic? If this method is adopted, the teacher would then take the extra step of transcribing the student's story into print. In either case, when the child is finished writing or telling something about the topic—*voila!*— a first composition is born and the student is over that awful dreaded confrontation with a blank sheet of paper that must be filled.

The teacher may also use the theme of the long-term instructional unit in order to stimulate a desire to write. For example, a young special-education teacher in a small city was teaching a unit on the community. Wouldn't it be a good idea, she suggested to her class, if we wrote letters to various people and businesses in the city? This suggestion was promptly met with moans, groans, and assorted grunts from the students. "Boring!" they objected in unison.

But this teacher was very resourceful. First the instructor had each student write down their favorite business in the community (every student in the class chose a short-order food place; no one chose the hardware store or the mortuary). She then went to these establishments and struck up a deal. If the student would write an acceptable letter describing why this restaurant was a favorite and how good the food was, would the owner of the restaurant post the letter on the door or window where everyone could view it? And in return for this free advertising, would the owner give one food item or drink to the student for writing such a good letter? To her surprise, all of the restaurants agreed and the students worked to write literate, coherent letters, correct in form, punctuation, and grammar which would be posted on the door of the restaurant. They knew that if the teacher and the manager didn't like their letter, they wouldn't get their free food. A relevant reason for writing motivated these students.

Other unit topics can also be tied in with written composition. A unit on vehicle safety can be tied to letters sent to the Division of Motor Vehicles asking for information on mopeds and forms to be filled out for registration. A unit on living with the weather can lead to a letter to a radio or television station requesting a visit or sending a list of questions to a meteorologist. The opportunities for tying in writing with long-term instructional units are limited only by the teacher's and students' imaginations.

WRITTEN EXPRESSION AND THE COMPUTER

☐ ☐ Microcomputers have revolutionalized writing and the writing process. Word-processing systems allow the writer to write ideas, change them around, make corrections, and even delete ideas as the writer wishes. In effect, they have taken the writer's block out of writing by allowing the writer to escape the feeling that what is written is unchangeable.

There are a variety of fascinating computer programs available to help and encourage writers to generate ideas and then put those ideas into good written expressive form. These include thought processors which help generate and organize ideas, programs which allow a dialogue between the writer and the computer using the Socratic method, as well as programs designed to teach the basics of punctuation, capitalization, and grammar. Table 8.8 contains a brief listing of available programs. The special-education teacher having access to a computer should utilize it to encourage the written expression by students. Such use of the computer can help reduce writer anxiety as well as generate student interest and motivation to write.

SUMMARY

☐ ☐ Spelling is the process of converting the sounds in words into letters and then arranging those letters in a conventional way for effective written communication. Spelling is often difficult for students since there are almost five times as many ways of graphically representing phonemes as there are phonemes of English.

TABLE 8.8 Available Computer Spelling and Written Expression Software

Spelling Software

1. Sea Speller (2nd-6th) Fisher Price: (Commodore 64). Joystick required. A fast-paced adventure game which turns the student into a dolphin. The mission is to find missing letters buried at sea to spell words correctly. Difficulty level increases as the dolphin approaches the ocean floor.

2. Magic Spells (1st-5th) Learning Co.: (Apple, Commodore, IBM-PC). The magical Wizard in the Kingdom of Magic helps the student search for buried treasure. Each treasure chest is opened by spelling a target word correctly. A spelling demon lurks in the shadows to make the contest intersting!

3. Fay: The Word Hunter (3rd-adult) Didatech: (Apple, Commodore 64). Another in the Fay series. Fay helps the student learn to spell 3,000 of the most frequently used words at nine differing levels of difficulty. Gives practice opportunities as well as positive reinforcement to students for engaging in spelling activities.

4. M-ss-ng L-nks (3rd-adult) Sunburst: (Apple, Atari, Disk, Commodore 64, IBM-PC). Treats language like secret messages to be decoded. Messages appear with letters missing in the words. The students job is to spell the words correctly in order to complete and decode the message. Nine levels of difficulty.

5. Spellicopter (1st-adult) Designware: (Apple, Atari, Disk, Commodore 64, IBM-PC). A spellicopter helps students spell words correctly. A limited amount of fuel exists for the spellicopter and it can only be refueled by spelling words correctly. Lively sound effects and graphics.

6. Snoopy's Skywriter Scrambler (3rd-adult) Random House: (Apple, Commodore 64, IBM-PC Jr). Snoopy helps the student take random collection of letters and spell words. The game can be either timed or untimed and Snoopy keeps score.

Written Expression Software

1. Story Maker (3rd-adult) Scholastic: (Apple—Mouse required). Helps student create and illustrate their own stories. A gallery of sixty-five images of animals, spaceships, and robots help student create exciting stories.

2. Kidwriter (1st-5th) Spinnaker: (Apple, Commodore 64, IBM-PC). Children can choose from an array of ninety-nine characters which the computer can depict on the screen. Students use these characters to compose interesting stories. Good graphics and sound effects.

3. That's My Story (1st-adult) Learning Well: (Apple, IBM-PC). Helps children write tales of fantasy and suspense. Contains twelve story starters to help launch children's stories. A set of what if statements use the branch method to create new stories each time.

4. Story Machine (K-4th) Spinnaker: (Apple; Atari, disk and cartridge; Commodore 64, cartridge; IBM-PC). Helps create a positive attitude toward writing and written expression. Students make up words using a supplied list of forty words. High graphics.

5. Story Tree (3rd-adult) Scholastic: (Apple, Commodore 64, IBM-PC). Helps students write stories of suspense, adventure or romance. Uses the interactive/branch approach to help students write new stories. Allows for editing.

NOTE: There is a great deal of inexpensive software for spelling and written expression available from the Minnesota Educational Computer Consortium (MECC), 3490 Lexington Ave., N., St. Paul, MN 55126. The price of each piece of software with its manual and guide is usually less than $10. MECC has available programs for Apple, Atari, Commodore, IBM, and Radio Shack computers. Since the MECC catalogue is too extensive to include here, the reader is strongly encouraged to send to MECC for a free copy.

A variety of skills exist for good spelling which include ability to distinguish phonemes, knowledge of ways of graphically expressing phonemes, knowing the rules which relate to letter arrangement, and knowing the properties of structural analysis. Correct pronunciation and dialectical expression of words are also important for correct spelling.

There are two spelling processes: internal and external channels. Internal channels refer to the ability to spell words correctly without resorting to external sources such as a dictionary. External channel spelling entails the use of such external aids.

Assessment in spelling may be formal and informal. A diagnostic spelling profile can be constructed by using an error analysis procedure. Formal tests of spelling achievement also exist.

A variety of techniques exist for teaching spelling to mildly mentally retarded students. Whichever techniques are adopted, however, the spelling vocabulary should be chosen on the basis of functionality, meaningfulness, and relevancy to the lives of the learners. New spelling words should be taught in isolation rather than context.

Good handwriting is important for effective communication. Time spent deciphering a person's handwriting is time taken from understanding the writer's intended message. Five variables contribute to legible handwriting. They are letter shape, alignment, slant, spacing, and word spacing. Assessment of these variables, although often a subjective process, is possible and, in fact, should occur in order to identify the precise nature of a child's handwriting problems.

Manuscript writing is usually taught before cursive. In order to facilitate the transfer from manuscript to cursive, the continuous stroke D'Nealian approach is suggested. It is also suggested that, during manuscript instruction, letters be taught in isolation until mastered.

Cursive writing is taught after manuscript print has been mastered. Letters shaped similarly should be taught together. Letters should be grouped and written as words with letters dotted and/or crossed only after the whole word has been written. Special attention should be given to the handwriting problems of left-handed writers.

Written expression is the highest skill in the language-arts hierarchy. Good writing skills are crucial in today's modern society. There are three stages to written expression: prewriting, writing, and postwriting. Prewriting consists of the experiences, stimulation, and motivation which leads to writing. During this stage, teachers must help students want to write and have something to write about. Writing refers to the mechanics (grammar, spelling, handwriting, etc.) and the vocabulary needed to write effectively. Postwriting entails the proofreading and evaluation skills needed to judge soundly written products. It is suggested that written expression become part of the special education curriculum for mildly mentally retarded learners and that it be used in conjunction with the long-term instructional unit.

9

Arithmetic Instruction

Key Concepts

☐ Computation Skills
☐ Problem Solving
☐ Application Skills
☐ Arithmetic Algorithms
☐ Arithmetic Readiness Skills
☐ Sets and Set Membership
☐ Conservation/Centration
☐ Reversibility and Compensation
☐ Concrete/Pre-Symbolic/Symbolic Teaching
☐ Algorithms for Teaching Computational Skills
☐ Time, Money, and Measurement
☐ Fractions and Decimals

For many students, arithmetic is probably a lot like eating their vegetables; it's good for them and necessary for their growth but it's not very popular. In fact, for many learners, arithmetic is a frightening, anxiety-producing process.

Many school children, including many mentally retarded students, are fearful of math and have experienced repeated failure in this important area. Why is this so, especially when typically more time is spent on arithmetic instruction than any other academic core area except reading? A number of professionals have hypothesized why arithmetic give students so many problems. These reasons include

1. Two to three times as much instructional time is spent on language arts instruction (particularly reading) than on arithmetic processes (Bartel 1982).
2. Parents and teachers often feel that competency in arithmetic is not as important as competency in reading (Otto, McMenemy & Smith 1973).
3. Children often can hide behind knowledge of rote arithmetic behaviors which give the appearance that they understand arithmetic processes when they really do not know what they are doing (Bartel 1982).
4. Teachers appear to be less concerned about arithmetic readiness than they are about reading readiness. (Wallace & Larsen 1979; Wallace & McLoughlin 1975).

5. Many teachers have not been adequately trained in the teaching of arithmetic. Many states do not even require college coursework in teaching arithmetic in order to receive special education certification.
6. Mentally retarded students typically have difficulty in dealing with abstract concepts and are tied to concrete operations. Arithmetic, however, is often a highly abstract, symbolic process.
7. Difficulties in reading are often correlated with difficulties in arithmetic.
8. Poor motivation to learn arithmetic and negative self-concept often interact.

It is hoped that through good teaching, a solid, relevant curriculum presented in a concrete manner, and a healthy dose of success rather than failure, that arithmetic underachievement by mentally retarded students may be at least partially remedied. Arithmetic can be effectively taught to mentally retarded students (Baroody & Ginsburg 1984; Gelman 1982). The key factors in remedying these difficulties will hinge on appropriate construction of the arithmetic curriculum and the appropriate and systematic implementation of sound instructional techniques.

MENTALLY RETARDED LEARNERS AND THE ARITHMETIC CURRICULUM

□ □ What constitutes an effective arithmetic curriculum and how should such a curriculum be presented to mildly mentally retarded students? An effective arithmetic curriculum should emphasize not only the basic computational skills but also the ability to apply these skills in order to solve relevant life-like problems (Sedlak & Fitzmaurice 1981). To that end, it is suggested that children should possess competencies in the three main areas: *computational skills, problem solving,* and *application.*

□ Computational Skills

Computational skills are those abilities needed to carry out basic arithmetic processes in the four operational areas: addition, subtraction, multiplication, and division. The ability to carry out the basic arithmetic operations represents the nuts and bolts of arithmetic. Without computational skills, higher order skills such as problem solving and application cannot be accomplished.

Achieving computational competence may not be as easy as it first appears. For example, consider the problem

$$\begin{array}{r} 22 \\ +34 \\ \hline \end{array}$$

In order to solve this problem, the student must successfully carry out the following steps:

1. Perceive it as an arithmetic problem (as opposed to a problem in spelling or reading).
2. Decode the operation required ($+$, $-$, $\times$, $\div$).
3. Decode and comprehend the numbers included in the problem.
4. Retrieve the basic addition facts from memory while selectively nonattending to number facts of the other three operations.
5. Retrieve the plan or algorithm for addition so that
   a. $2 + 4 = 6$
   b. 2 (actually 20) $+$ 3 (actually 30) $= 5$ (actually 50)
   c. Answer $= 56$

One can readily see that all this is not as easy as adults sometimes consider it and it is understandable that many students experience difficulties in carrying out these "simple" operations. But hard as the mastery of these operational sequences might be, they must be mastered before any other higher order arithmetic skill can be effectively learned.

☐ Problem Solving

Problem solving refers to the ability to use computational skills to solve arithmetic problems presented in everyday terms instead of problems expressed solely in arithmetic symbols (Carpenter 1980; Mayer 1985). Problem-solving skills may be viewed roughly as being analogous to comprehension skills in reading; they represent what is done with computational abilities once these skills are mastered.

Typically, in a problem-solving situation, the individual is presented with a word problem. In order to solve the problem, the student must successfully do the following things:

1. Deduce or choose the operation which must be performed. Choosing the wrong operation will, by definition, lead to the incorrect solution of the problem.
2. Select the appropriate and relevant information while ignoring irrelevant information.
3. Convert relevant information presented via language to arithmetic symbols.
4. Calculate the answer to the problem using the correct numbers and computational algorithm (see steps 1–5 for computational skills).

The ability to use problem-solving skills involves the sophisticated use of cognitive strategies (Mayer 1985; Schoenfeld 1982). However, as we have seen, mildly mentally retarded individuals are notoriously poor in their ability to learn, retrieve, and use appropriate cognitive strategies. Thus, instruction in the area of arithmetic problem skills will require systematic instruction and constant opportunity for practice as well as strong training in and strategy usage and transfer.

☐ Application Skills

Finally, the last, and highest, process in performing effective arithmetic is use of application skills. This process is the ability to use computational and problem-solving skills such as time, money, and measurement in real-life situations (Bartel 1982). The application of arithmetic skills in real-life situations is probably, next to reading, the most important academic skill taught in school, especially as it relates to the normalization process of mildly mentally retarded learners (Thorton, Tucker, Dossey & Bazik 1983). Arithmetic application skills include

1. Acquisition of mastery of money relationships including counting money, making purchases, and making change.
2. Demonstrating skill in the areas of measurement including temperature, speed, liquid and dry measurement, and area.
3. Being able to tell time—clock time, seasons, calendar time—and knowing when it is time to do things.
4. Understanding fractions, decimals, and percentages.

The appropriate use of application skills includes the prerequisite skills of mastery of computational and problem-solving skills. In addition, application skills involves the ability to view real-life arithmetic situations as either similar and thus relevant to a given computational skill or different and irrelevant. Thus, application includes the ability to generalize as well as discriminate between different mathematical real-life situations.

PRESENTING ARITHMETIC FUNCTIONALLY: USING THE LONG-TERM INSTRUCTIONAL UNIT APPROACH

☐ ☐ Arithmetic is a means to an end. That is, arithmetic is a process used to solve problems. Thus, for arithmetic instruction to be useful and relevant for mildly mentally retarded learners, it must be functional. Functional arithmetic refers to mastery of arithmetic problems which contribute to the normalization and employment of mentally retarded students. In this framework, the arithmetic curriculum presented to mentally retarded students includes problems as they relate to the areas of vocational, consumer, social, recreational, and homemaking skills.

Before an arithmetic curriculum is considered functional, the following two questions must be answered in the affirmative: (*1*) Will the arithmetic curriculum help the child function later in life as a successful adult? and (*2*) Are the arithmetic processes being taught in such a way so as to foster transfer to real-life situations? If the answer to both of these questions is not a resounding yes, the arithmetic curriculum being taught is not functional.

Through constant instruction in functional arithmetic skills, student motivation to learn arithmetic will increase (Buffer & Miller 1976; Morsink 1984). Additionally, a functional arithmetic curriculum helps insure that the arithmetic program will be more concrete and less abstract/symbolic (Clark 1980; Vitello 1976). Finally, by tying the arithmetic curriculum to real-life situations, mildly mentally retarded students will be more attentive, will be less anxious about the subject matter, and will ultimately achieve at a higher level (Buffer & Miller 1976).

One way to insure that the arithmetic curriculum will be functional for mentally retarded learners is to teach it in conjunction with the long-term instructional unit. Recall from chapter 5 that one consideration of the unit topic before it is adopted is that it be both relevant and functional. Thus, areas necessary for survival and independent living and the component skills contained therein would be the precise curriculum topics which would form the basis of long-term instructional units. Once the topic and subtopics are developed and ascertained to be relevant and functional to the lives of mentally retarded learners the teacher need only make sure that the lesson plans in the arithmetic content area relate systematically to the unit topic.

By way of example, Figure 9.1 contains a topic and subtopics of a typical long-term instructional unit as well as math behavioral objectives and a sample lesson included within the unit. Note how the objectives are strongly related to the topic and are real-life in scope. By making sure that the topics and subtopics are relevant and functional (prior to writing even the first behavior objective), the teacher insures that the arithmetic curriculum related to the long-term unit will also be functional.

ARITHMETIC READINESS

☐ ☐ Perhaps in no other core area save for reading is the phenomenon of readiness as important as it is in arithmetic. Insufficient readiness may have a debilitating effect at any level of arithmetic functioning; appraising the child's readiness skills should be the initial step of any curriculum plan (Bartel 1982; Johnson 1979). For mentally retarded students who often possess serious deficits in possession of the introductory prerequisite arithmetic skills, assessment of readiness skills of arithmetic functioning is extremely important.

FIGURE 9.1   Topics, Subtopics and Sample Math Lesson from a Typical Long-Term Instructional Unit

Topic: Managing a Checking Account
Subtopic 1. Components of the Checking Account
Subtopic 2. Mechanics of Maintaining a Checking Account
Subtopic 3. Opening and Managing Your Own Checking Account

Topic: *Managing A Checking Account*

Core Area: Math_____   Time: 60 minutes_____

Objectives	Activities	Materials	Evaluation
A. Given a sample check register with five transactions entered on it and verbal instructions, the student will write the correct entries of the balance column as they compute the balance, using the two line entry format, making no computation errors or entry errors. B. Given the checks from objective 2J and using the two line entry method the student will enter each of the checks into a check register, omitting the balance column, making no errors.	1. The teacher will first discuss the method of filling out a register with the two line method. The students will then fill out their registers. The teacher will circulate to answer individual questions. 2. Once the students complete the above they will be given the checks they wrote for 2J. The checks will be entered, by the students, into blank check registers.	Check registers with 5 entries Pencils Checks from 2J Blank check registers	The teacher will record the number of computation errors and entry errors for objective 2A. For 2B spelling and omission errors will count as a check not entered. The number of correctly entered checks will be recorded.

Many educators have differentiated basic and secondary readiness skills (Bartel 1982; Johnson 1979). According to these individuals, basic readiness would be a requisite for those arithmetic skills taught typically in the first two years of arithmetic instruction while secondary readiness applies to skills typically taught later in the child's academic career.

It is believed that the child should possess the following basic readiness skills in order to be successful in mastering the initial arithmetic concepts and operations presented in school (Reys, Suydam & Lindquist 1984; Thornton et al. 1983):

1. Classify: The ability to distinguish one object or set of objects from another.
2. Comparisons: The ability to compare two objects for similar attributes.
3. Ability to count, recognize number symbols, and select correct number groups.
4. Sequence numbers from one to ten.
5. Seriation: Ordering objects along a given attribute or attributes.
6. Possess a knowledge of one-to-one correspondences essential for the learning of addition and subtraction.
7. Knowledge of the concept of quantity as well as the concept of sets and set membership.
8. Possess understanding and vocabulary which deal with spatial and temporal relationships.
9. Understand the concepts of reversibility and compensation.

☐ Readiness Activities

For children who do not possess these basic arithmetic readiness skills, a variety of materials and instructional activities can be devised in order to remediate readiness deficiencies. They include classification, reversibility and compensation, comparisons, counting, and seriation and conservation.

Classification
Have children sort materials by a given attribute or characteristic. For example, children can sort the objects shown in Figure 9.2a by "can eat" or "cannot eat" categories. Likewise, attribute blocks like the ones shown in Figure 9.2b can be made or purchased. For example, in Figure 9.2b, the large triangle is red, while the small square is blue. This yields three attributes along which the objects can be classified: shape, size, and color. Careful use of the attribute blocks will help the child attend to the various dimensions along which objects may be classified.

Comparisons
Making comparisons between objects and sets is extremely important during initial arithmetic instruction. In training children to make comparisons, the teacher should concentrate on placing sets in close proximity to each other, placing the members of the different sets in a one-to-one relationship, and then ascertaining which set contains more members by seeing which set has members left (i.e., members not in a one-to-one relationship with members of the other set). Thus, in Figure 9.3a, the teacher would ask: Which set has more? The answer is demonstrated by the one-to-one relationship method shown in Figure 9.3b and c.

FIGURE 9.2   Classifying Objects as a Readiness Skill

a. Classification of Edible Objects
   "Which objects are good to eat?"

b. Attribute Blocks
   "Show me all the green triangles."

Reversibility and Compensation

Reversibility is the phenomenon that things done to a set of objects can be undone simply by reversing and retracing one's steps. Thus, for example, in Figure 9.4a the child sitting on the left-hand side of the teeter-totter has caused that side to go down. This can be reversed, however, by having the child reverse his actions and get off the mechanism as shown in Figure 9.4b. Compensation, on the other hand, refers to the fact that things can often be brought back to their previous state of affairs without reversals, that is, by doing something which somehow negates or neutralizes the effects of the first action. Thus, in Figure 9.4c the teeter-totter can be placed back in the horizontal position by a child of equal weight to the first child, getting on the right-hand side of the apparatus.

Reversibility and compensation are important in addition and subtraction, especially in such areas as regrouping and carrying. For these reasons, the teacher should give the child as much experience as possible in these areas, giving hands-on practice in changing objects back to their original states both by reversing or retracing the original steps taken and by using compensatory procedures which do not include the reversal process.

FIGURE 9.3 Set Comparisons

a. There are two distinct sets of objects each set delineated by its own boundary. "Which set has more?"

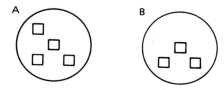

b. Boundaries between the sets are broken and set members are lined up in a 1:1 relationship.

c. The question "which set has more?" is shown by objects lined up in 1:1 relationship and bigger set has members without partners from the corresponding set.

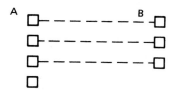

Counting

Counting set members is a crucial arithmetic skill. There are four basic components to any counting algorithm (Reys, Suydam & Lindquist 1984; Resnick 1983):

1. Each object is assigned one and only one name.
2. The numbers are used in a fixed order every time a set is counted (*1, 2, 3,* etc.).

FIGURE 9.4 Reversibility and Compensation

a. Problem. How do we make the teeter-totter balanced?

b. Reversibility. The child gets off the teeter-totter.

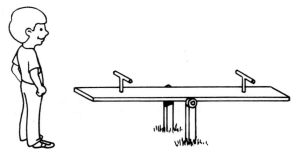

c. Compensation. Another child gets on the teeter-totter.

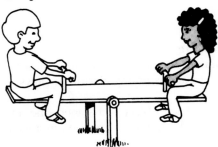

3. The order in which objects are counted does not matter.
4. The last number stated gives the number of objects in the set.

Children should count by rote (with no objects present) as well as count objects (point counting) (Petitto 1985; Resnick 1983). In point counting, it is crucial to teach that counting stops when all the objects have been enumerated. Children should also be encouraged to count backwards as well as skip counting (e.g., counting by two's, three's, etc.).

Seriation and Conservation

Figure 9.5 contains a row of blue blocks and a row of red blocks. Suppose we ask a child to count each row. The child should tell us that the number of blocks in each row is the same. Now, suppose we change the patterns of the blocks similar to that shown in Figure 9.5b and ask the child to tell us which row had more

FIGURE 9.5 Seriation and Conservation

a. Which row has more blocks?

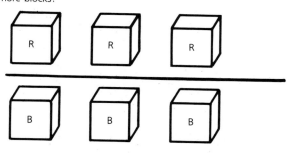

b. Which row has more blocks?

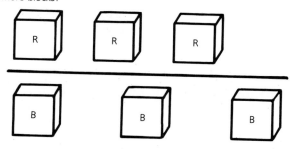

blocks. The child might tell us that the red row has more since it is bigger, even though in reality, the two rows still contain the same number of blocks.

A child demonstrating such behavior would be experiencing difficulties in seriation and conservation (Piaget 1926). The child would be centering on the length of the row rather than on the number of objects in the row. Such errors in seriation and conservation would prove serious in counting and initial arithmetic instruction. Thus, it is important that the teacher give the child continued, hands-on practice in these areas until the child learns that the length, shape, or configuration of a set are irrelevant dimensions, the only relevant dimension being set membership number.

ASSESSING ARITHMETIC ABILITY

☐ ☐ Arithmetic assessment for mentally retarded students occurs on a regular basis. Unfortunately, all too often such assessment takes the form of norm-referenced achievement testing with not enough emphasis placed on in-depth, criterion referenced diagnostic assessment of arithmetic problems. In fact, teachers interested in identifying the arithmetic problems of mentally retarded children through in-depth assessment will find only a handful of such tests available. In cases where such diagnostic instruments are unavailable or are judged inappropriate for use with the population of students in question, the teacher will have to rely on informal diagnostic assessment.

☐ Achievement (Survey) Testing

Arithmetic achievement assessment for mentally retarded learners is used to indicate that arithmetic difficulties exist for a given child and that an in-depth arithmetic assessment is in order. There are a number of arithmetic achievement survey tests appropriate for use with mentally retarded learners. Such tests usually are part of a larger achievement test battery (e.g., the California Achievement Tests or the Iowa Tests of Basic Skills). When a survey test is used, the special-education teacher should make sure that it is an individually administered rather than a group administered test and that it be appropriate for the age/grade/cognitive level of the child being tested. Table 9.1 contains a listing of the more common arithmetic achievement tests, what they measure, and the age/grade for which they are designed.

☐ Formal Diagnostic Math Assessment

In-depth, diagnostic assessment is carried out when it appears necessary to gauge the specific arithmetic deficiencies which may be contributing to the child's poor arithmetic achievement. In-depth, diagnostic assessment is more specific than

TABLE 9.1 Commonly Used Arithmetic Achievement Tests

Test	Grades	Measures
California Achievement Tests-Mathematics	3 levels; 1–9	Fundamental operations skills.
Modern Mathematics Supplement to the Iowa Tests of Basic Skills	3–9	Fundamental arithmetic. Covers new methods and materials developed since 1965.
Metropolitan Achievement Test-Mathematics	3–9	Basic arithmetic skills, problem solving.
Peabody Individual Achievement Test	K–Adult	Basic arithmetic through advanced skills such as geometry and trigonometry.
Stanford Modern Mathematics Concepts Test	5–9.1	Modern arithmetic to advanced readiness skills.
SRA Achievement Series in Arithmetic	Preschool–approx. grade 9	Counting, reading number symbols, solving oral problems and performing written computations.

arithmetic achievement testing and is also broader in scope in terms of the subskills tested.

KeyMath Diagnostic Arithmetic Test

The KeyMath Diagnostic Arithmetic Test (Connolly, Nachtman & Pritchett 1971, 1976) is a good example of a diagnostic mathematics assessment instrument. As can be seen from Figure 9.6, KeyMath assesses arithmetic abilities in fourteen skill areas taken from the arithmetic processes of *content, operations,* and *applications.* The content areas measure the basic arithmetic knowledge and concepts needed to perform operations while the operations areas measure, among other things, the ability to perform in the four basic computational areas. Finally, the application subtests assess the ability to use both content and operations in real-life situations. KeyMath yields a performance profile across the fourteen subtests and gives information as to the specific strengths and weaknesses possessed by the child in arithmetic functioning. Finally, it provides instructional objectives and suggests instructional activities designed to remedy arithmetic weaknesses.

Stanford Diagnostic Mathematics Test

Another popular diagnostic mathematics test is the Stanford Diagnostic Mathematics Test (Beatty, Madden, Gardner & Karlsen 1983, 1984). There are four levels of the SDMT, and level choice is dictated by the grade level of the child. The levels are

Red: Grades 1–3 and low achieving students in grade 4.
Green: Grades 4–5 with low achieving students in grade 6.

FIGURE 9.6   Skills Assessed in the KeyMath Diagnostic Math Test

I. *Content:*
   1. Numerations: Counting and counting set members
   2. Fractions: Answering questions about fractions
   3. Geometry and Symbols: Pointing to correct shape

II. *Operations:*
   1. Addition: Answering computational problems
   2. Subtraction
   3. Multiplication
   4. Division
   5. Mental Computation
   6. Numerical Reasoning: Child provides missing numbers in number series

III. *Applications:*
   1. Word problems: Child supplies answers after solving verbal or oral word problems
   2. Missing Elements: After being given a word problem, child tells what key information from the problem is missing
   3. Money: Child solves problems regarding money
   4. Measurement
   5. Time

Brown: Grades 6–7 and low achieving students in grades 8–9.
Blue: Grades 8–12.

Three main areas are tested in the SDMT: number systems and numeration, computations, and applications. Results are given in terms of grade norms as well as criterion-referenced progress scores which yield a diagnostic profile of the learner's mathematical strengths and weaknesses. Figure 9.7 shows the component skills tested at each level.

The Test of Mathematical Abilities (Brown & McEntire 1984).

The Test of Mathematical Abilities (TOMA) is intended for use with students in grades 3–12 or between the chronological ages of 8.6–18.11 years. It is designed to identify students who are significantly ahead or behind their age or grade peers. Thus, in this sense, the TOMA is a norm-referenced test. However, it is also criterion referenced in that it is designed to determine the child's major mathematical strengths and weaknesses. There are four major areas assessed by the test: attitude toward math, math vocabulary, computation skills, general arithmetic information, and story problems.

Diagnosis: An Instructional Aid in Mathematics (Guzaitis, Carlin & Juda 1972)

This test is designed to assess specific mathematical strengths and weaknesses as well as help the teacher plan remedial activities. In addition, it is cross-referenced to basal elementary school math curricular materials in order to help the teacher find remedial activities in the basal math series in which the child is

FIGURE 9.7 Component Skills Tested by The Stanford Diagnostic Mathematics Test

1. *Number System and Numeration*
   a. Whole numbers
   b. Decimal place value

2. *Computation*
   a. Addition facts
   b. Addition without renaming
   c. Subtraction facts
   d. Subtraction without regrouping
   e. Multiplication of whole numbers
   f. Division of whole numbers
   g. Fractions
   h. Decimals
   i. Percent
   j. Number sentences

3. *Applications*
   a. Problem solving
   b. Reading and interpreting tables and graphs
   c. Geometry
   d. Measurement

working. The test also comes with a complete set of task-sequenced instructional objectives for each skill measured by the test so that instructional objectives intended to help the child remedy mathematical weaknesses are generated for each incorrect answer given by the child.

The test consists of thirty-two probes, a diagnostic, criterion-referenced device. Each probe measures in-depth competence in a given mathematical area. Probe areas include computation, fractions, decimals, numeration, problem solving, measurement, and geometry. This is an excellent test to use.

☐ Informal Diagnostic Arithmetic Assessment

Formal standardized tests cannot always measure every skill in precisely the ways the teacher wishes. Thus the special-education teacher interested in accurate arithmetic assessment will probably need to resort to informal diagnostic assessment in order to more closely ascertain exactly which skills mentally retarded students have mastered. Such informal arithmetic assessment may take the form of work samples, checklists, rating skills, and teacher-made tests. Whichever method or methods are utilized, the teacher must make sure that the assessment tool used is both valid and reliable.

Work Samples and Error Patterns

Arithmetic work samples involve the systematic analysis of samples of the child's arithmetic behavior. This entails having the child produce written samples of math behavior via pencil and paper worksheets. The teacher then scrutinizes the child's work for evidence of systematic arithmetic errors.

A number of professionals have developed error categorization systems. For example, Moran (1978) has hypothesized three main arithmetic error types: inadequate number facts, incorrect operational behavior, and ineffective use of arithmetic strategies. A fourth error type, errors caused by incorrect usage of arithmetic algorithms or learning plans, has been added. Perhaps the most comprehensive error analysis system in arithmetic has been devised by Reisman (1978, 1982). This system consists of forty-six error types taken from the areas of number facts, operations, and algorithms. The teacher's task in this system is to match errors in the child's arithmetic behavior with the error types. Remediation is then prescribed. Figure 9.8 shows samples of Riesman's error analysis system.

Checklists

As in reading assessment, the use of arithmetic checklists may be useful in quickly noting and classifying the arithmetic difficulties of mentally retarded students. Such a checklist, for example, could be constructed from the error analysis categories of Reisman (1983) or Ashlock (1982) or may be purchased commercially (Reisman & Kauffman, 1980). Figure 9.9 contains a sample checklist which may be adopted by the special-education teacher.

BASIC APPROACHES TO TEACHING ARITHMETIC

☐ ☐ There are a variety of approaches to teaching arithmetic. All these approaches attempt to bridge the gap between the concrete and the abstract/symbolic. The next section contains a brief overview of the approaches to teaching arithmetic.

☐ Basal Math Texts

Basal math texts represent the most traditional and often used method of teaching arithmetic. Such texts usually contain pupil textbooks and workbooks as well as teacher instruction manuals. As in reading basal texts, the main disadvantage with arithmetic basals is that they are written for the average student and do not usually adapt well to the special learning needs of atypical learners. Likewise, the basal text's general orientation on drill and practice using worksheets often lead to boredom and loss of attention on the part of students. On the positive side, basal arithmetic texts are highly sequenced so that children learn skills in an ordered, sequenced, and hierarchical fashion.

☐ Comprehensive Arithmetic Programs

The last few years have seen an increase in the comprehensive math programs available. These programs usually consist of activity guides for daily lessons,

FIGURE 9.8   Examples from Reisman's (1982) Error Analysis System

Analysis   *Example*

1. Lacks mastery of basic addition facts.

$$
\begin{array}{r}
3\;\;2 \\
+4\;\;3 \\
\hline
7\;\;4
\end{array}
$$

2. Lacks mastery of basic subtraction facts.

$$
\begin{array}{r}
3\;\;8 \\
-2\;\;5 \\
\hline
1\;\;2
\end{array}
$$

3. Lacks mastery of basic multiplication facts.

$$
\begin{array}{r}
3\;\;2 \\
\times\;\;3 \\
\hline
86
\end{array}
$$

4. Lacks mastery of basic division facts.

$$35 \div 5 = 6$$

$$
\begin{array}{r}
6 \\
9\overline{)\;56} \\
-56 \\
\hline
0
\end{array}
$$

5. Subtracts incorrectly within the division algorithm.

$$
\begin{array}{r}
3)\;\;73 \text{ rem } 1 \\
70) \\
3\overline{)230} \\
-21 \\
\hline
10 \longleftarrow \\
-9 \\
\hline
1
\end{array}
$$

6. Error in addition of partial product.

$$
\begin{array}{r}
432 \\
\times 57 \\
\hline
3\;0\;24 \\
21\;6\;0 \\
\hline
24\;0\;24
\end{array}
$$

7. Does not complete addition:
   a. Does not write renamed number.

$$
\begin{array}{r}
85 \\
+43 \\
\hline
28
\end{array}
$$

   b. Leaves out numbers in column addition.

$$
\begin{array}{r}
4 \\
8 \\
2 \longleftarrow \\
+3 \\
\hline
15
\end{array}
$$

8. Rewrites a numeral without computing.

$$
\begin{array}{r}
72 \\
+15 \\
\hline
77 \\
32 \\
\times\;\;3 \\
\hline
36
\end{array}
$$

9. Does not complete subtraction.

$$
\begin{array}{r}
582 \\
-\;\;35 \\
\hline
47
\end{array}
$$

Analysis   *Example*

10. Does not complete division because of incompleted subtraction.

$$
\begin{array}{r}
1)\;\;41 \\
40) \\
7\overline{)3\;9\;7} \\
-2\;8\;0 \\
\hline
7 \\
7 \\
\hline
\end{array}
$$

11. Fails to complete division; stops at first partial quotient.

$$
\begin{array}{r}
50 \\
7\overline{)\;370} \\
350 \\
\hline
\end{array}
$$

12. Fails to complete division; leaves remainder equal to or greater than divisor.

$$
\begin{array}{r}
80 \text{ rem } 9 \\
9\overline{)\;729} \\
720 \\
\hline
9
\end{array}
$$

13. Does not complete multiplication within division algorithm.

$$
\begin{array}{r}
1)\;201 \text{ rem } 3 \\
200) \\
3\overline{)\;603} \\
600 \\
\hline
3
\end{array}
$$

14. Does not add by bridging endings—should think $5 + 9 = 14$, so $35 + 9 = 44$.

$$
\begin{array}{r}
35 \\
+9 \\
\hline
33
\end{array}
$$

15. Lacks additive identity concept in addition.

$$
\begin{array}{r}
35 \\
+20 \\
\hline
50
\end{array}
$$

16. Confuses multiplicative identity within addition operation.

$$
\begin{array}{r}
71 \\
+13 \\
\hline
73
\end{array}
$$

17. Lacks additive identity concept in subtraction.

$$
\begin{array}{r}
43 \\
-20 \\
\hline
20
\end{array}
$$

18. Confuses role of zero in subtraction with role of zero in multiplication.

$$
\begin{array}{r}
37 \\
-20 \\
\hline
10
\end{array}
$$

19. Subtracts top digit from bottom digit whenever regrouping is involved with zero in minuend.

$$
\begin{array}{r}
30 \\
-18 \\
\hline
28
\end{array}
$$

20. Confuses role of zero in multiplication with multiplicative identity.

$$7 \times 0 = 7$$

21. Confuses place value of quotient by adding extra zero.

$$
\begin{array}{r}
20 \\
30\overline{)\;60}
\end{array}
$$

22. Omits zero in quotient.

$$
\begin{array}{r}
30 \text{ rem } 3 \\
4\overline{)\;1203} \\
1200 \\
\hline
3
\end{array}
$$

(continued)

FIGURE 9.8 (continued)

Analysis	*Example*
23. Lacks facility with addition algorithm:	
a. Adds units to units *and* tens;	37 + 2 ——— 59
b. Adds tens to tens *and* hundreds;	342 + 36 ——— 678
c. Adds units to tens *and* hundreds;	132 + 6 ——— 798
d. Is unable to add horizontally: Thinks: 3 + 7 + 1 = 11; writes 1 4 + 3 = 7 (+ 1 carried) 5 = 5 May add zero to make sum greater than largest addend: 1850.	345 + 7 + 13 = 185 8 5 ——— 185
24. Does not regroup units to tens.	37 + 25 ——— 52
25. Does not regroup tens to hundreds (or hundreds to thousands).	973 +862 ——— 735
26. Regroups when unnecessary.	43 + 24 ——— 77
27. Writes regrouped tens digit in units place, carries units digit (writes the 1 and carries the 2 from "12").	② 35 + 7 ——— 51
28. When there are fewer digits in subtrahend:	
a. subtracts units from units *and* from tens (*and* hundreds);	783 −2 ——— 561
b. subtracts tens from tens *and* hundreds.	783 − 23 ——— 560
29. Does not rename tens digit after regrouping.	54 − 9 ——— 55
30. Does not rename hundreds digit after regrouping.	532 −181 ——— 451
31. Does not rename hundreds or tens when renaming units.	906 −238 ——— 778

Analysis	*Example*
32. Does not rename tens when zero is in tens place, although hundreds are renamed.	803 −478 ——— 335
33. When there are two zeroes in minuend, renames hundreds twice but does not rename tens.	5 6₁₁ 700 −326 ——— 284
34. Decreases hundreds digit by one when unnecessary.	3\7 1 −1 3 4 1/3 7
35. Uses units place factor as addend.	32 × 4 ——— 126
36. Adds regrouped number to tens but does not multiply. *7 × 5 = 35; 30 + 30 = 60	35 × 7 ——— 65*
37. Multiplies digits within one factor. *4 × 1 = 4; 1 × 30 = 30	31 × 4 ——— 34*
38. Multiplies by only one number.	457 × 12 ——— 914
39. "Carries" wrong number.	8 67 × 40 ——— 3220
40. Does not multiply units times tens.	32 × 24 ——— 648
41. Reverses divisor with dividend. * Thinks 6 ÷ 3 instead of 30 ÷ 6	2 * 6/ 30
42. Does not regroup; treats each column as separate addition example.	23 + 8 ——— 211
43. Subtracts smaller digit from larger at all times to avoid renaming.	273 −639 ——— 446
44. Does not add regrouped number.	37 × 7 ——— 219

(continued)

FIGURE 9.8 (continued)

Analysis	Example	Analysis	Example
45. Confuses place value in division:	1) 200) 201 3 /6003 6000 — 3 3 —	c. omits zero needed to show no units in quotient.	35 — 2 rem 1 3/ 61 6 — 1
a. Considers thousands divided by units as hundreds divided by units;			
b. records partial quotient as tens instead of units;	50) 100) 150 7 / 735 −700 — 35	46. Ignores remainder because: a. does not complete subtraction; b. does not *see* need for further computation; c. does not know what to do with "2" if subtraction occurs, so does not compute further.	80 7 / 562 560

Adapted from Common Errors Children Make in Elementary School Mathematics, in A GUIDE TO THE DIAGNOSTIC TEACHING OF MATHEMATICS, THIRD ED., by Fredricka K. Reisman, Copyright 1982 Merrill Publishing Company, Columbus, OH. Reprinted by permission of the publisher.

instructional objectives for those lessons, materials, and a teacher's guide—in short, everything needed to teach arithmetic. Such programs lend themselves nicely to teaching students with special needs in that lessons and materials can be easily adapted to the needs of these learners. The major disadvantage is the expense. Table 9.2 contains a listing of the major comprehensive arithmetic programs available.

□ Cuisenaire Rods and the Discovery Method

Cuisenaire Rods are a set of 291 wooden rods varying in length and color. These forms are used to help the child discover computational and algebraic relationships. For example, Figure 9.10 shows how addition may be demonstrated using the rods. The red rod (*2*) is placed next to the green rod (*3*) so that a train is formed. Various rods are placed on top of the train until the rod which precisely equals the train in length is found (the yellow rod [5]). Cuisenaire rods are an excellent tool for bridging the gap between the concrete and the abstract, especially in the areas of addition and subtraction. They also help facilitate meaningful learning by helping the child discover arithmetic relationships independently and appear to be highly motivating and interesting to students.

□ Montessori Materials

Montessori materials are designed to enhance hands-on, concrete mathematical understanding (Montessori 1964). These materials include sets of cubes, cylinders, rods, prisms, geometric shapes, counting boxes, sandpaper numbers, counting frames, and beads. The materials are sequenced to help the child acquire seriation and ordering, 1:1 correspondence, size and shape, length, volume, place value, and the four major computational operations. This method, although scien-

FIGURE 9.9 Sample Checklist for Informal Assessment of Arithmetic Ability

ADDITION: (Place a check before each habit observed in the pupil's work)

- a1 Errors in combinations
- a2 Counting
- a3 Added carried number last
- a4 Forgot to add carried number
- a5 Repeated work after partly done
- a6 Added carried number irregularly
- a7 Wrote number to be carried
- a8 Irregular procedure in column
- a9 Carried wrong number
- a10 Grouped two or more numbers
- a11 Splits numbers into parts
- a12 Used wrong fundamental operation
- a13 Lost place in column
- a14 Depended on visualization
- a15 Disregarded column position
- a16 Omitted one or more digits
- a17 Errors in reading numbers
- a18 Dropped back one or more tens
- a19 Derived unknown combination from familiar one
- a20 Disregarded one column
- a21 Error in writing answer
- a22 Skipped one or more decades
- a23 Carrying when there was nothing to carry
- a24 Used scratch paper
- a25 Added in pairs, giving last sum as answer
- a26 Added same digit in two columns
- a27 Wrote carried number in answer
- a28 Added same number twice

SUBTRACTION: (Place a check before each habit observed in the pupil's work)

- s1 Errors in combinations
- s2 Did not allow for having borrowed
- s3 Counting
- s4 Errors due to zero in minuend
- s5 Said example backwards
- s6 Subtracted minuend from subtrahend
- s7 Failed to borrow; gave zero as answer
- s8 Added instead of subtracted
- s9 Error in reading
- s10 Used same digit in two columns
- s11 Derived unknown from known combination
- s12 Omitted a column
- s13 Used trial-and-error addition
- s14 Split numbers
- s15 Deducted from minuend when borrowing was not necessary
- s16 Ignored a digit
- s17 Deducted 2 from minuend after borrowing
- s18 Error due to minuend and subtrahend digits being same
- s19 Used minuend or subtrahend as remainder
- s20 Reversed digits in remainder
- s21 Confused process with division or multiplication
- s22 Skipped one or more decades
- s23 Increased minuend digit after borrowing
- s24 Based subtraction on multiplication combination

Multiplication: (Place a check before each habit observed in the pupil's work)

- m1 Errors in combinations
- m2 Error in adding the carried number
- m3 Wrote rows of zeros
- m4 Carried a wrong number
- m5 Errors in addition
- m6 Forgot to carry
- m7 Used multiplicand as multiplier
- m8 Error in single zero combinations, zero as multiplier
- m9 Errors due to zero in multiplier
- m10 Used wrong process—added
- m11 Counted to carry
- m12 Omitted digit in multiplier
- m13 Wrote carried number
- m14 Omitted digit in multiplicand
- m15 Errors due to zero in multiplicand
- m16 Error in position of partial products
- m17 Counted to get multiplication combinations
- m18 Error in single zero combinations, zero as multiplicand
- m19 Confused products when multiplier had two or more digits
- m20 Repeated part of table
- m21 Multiplied by adding
- m22 Did not multiply a digit in multiplicand
- m23 Based unknown combination on another
- m24 Errors in reading
- m25 Omitted digit in product
- m26 Errors in writing product
- m27 Errors in carrying into zero
- m28 Illegible figures
- m29 Forgot to add partial products
- m30 Split multiplier
- m31 Wrote wrong digit of product
- m32 Multiplied by same digit twice
- m33 Reversed digits in product
- m34 Wrote tables

Division: (Place a check before each habit observed in the pupil's work)

- d1 Errors in division combinations
- d2 Errors in subtraction
- d3 Errors in multiplication
- d4 Used remainder larger than divisor
- d5 Found quotient by trial multiplication
- d6 Neglected to use remainder within problem
- d7 Omitted zero resulting from another digit
- d8 Used wrong operation
- d9 Omitted digit in dividend
- d10 Counted to get quotient
- d11 Repeated part of multiplication table
- d12 Used short division form for long division
- d13 Wrote remainders within problem
- d14 Omitted zero resulting from zero in dividend
- d15 Omitted final remainder
- d16 Used long division form for short division
- d17 Counted in subtracting
- d18 Used too large a product
- d19 Said example backwards
- d20 Used remainder without new dividend figure
- d21 Derived unknown combination from known one
- d22 Had right answer, used wrong one
- d23 Grouped too many digits in dividend
- d24 Error in reading
- d25 Used dividend or divisor as quotient
- d26 Found quotient by adding
- d27 Reversed dividend and divisor
- d28 Used digits of divisor separately
- d29 Wrote all remainders at end of problem
- d30 Misinterpreted table
- d31 Used digit in dividend twice
- d32 Used second digit of divisor to find quotient
- d33 Began dividing at units digit of dividend
- d34 Split dividend
- d35 Used endings to find quotient

From G.T. Buswell & L. John (1925). *Fundamental processes in arithmetic.* Indianapolis: Bobbs-Merrill.

TABLE 9.2 Comprehensive Arithmetic Programs

Program	Publisher	Description
Mathematics in Daily Living	Steck-Vaugh (Austin, TX)	Builds competency in basic Math skills. Good for secondary students.
Pacemaker Practical Arithmetic Series	Fearon-Pitman (Belmont, CA)	Practical problems and exercises for everyday arithmetic.
Project Math	Houghton Mifflin (Boston, MA)	Comprehensive Math program for four levels through high school.
Sequential Math	Harcourt Brace Jovanovich (New York, NY)	Useful for both readers and nonreaders. Reinforces math skills.
Target Math Series	Mafex, Inc. (Johnstown, PA)	Math Concepts needed for independent living. Especially good for older students.

FIGURE 9.10 Cuisenaire Rod Addition Program

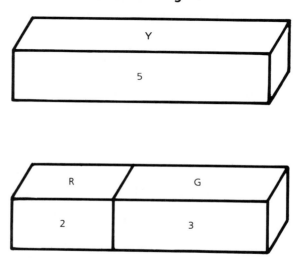

tifically unvalidated, may be useful in presenting concepts to children in a concrete, understandable fashion.

TEACHING ARITHMETIC SKILLS

□ □ Assuming that the children in your class do possess basic arithmetic readiness skills, where should instruction begin? You will recall that one reason offered for mentally retarded children's difficulties in arithmetic is the symbolic nature of the subject matter and that these students are typically tied to the concrete. Thus, it is believed that perhaps the best way to teach arithmetic to mentally retarded students is to present all material in such a way that the gap between the concrete and the abstract is adequately bridged. For this reason it is suggested that arithmetic concepts, operations, and skills be presented *concretely, presymbolically*, and *symbolically*.

Instruction in the concrete mode includes teaching with real-world, hands-on materials which can be manipulated by the child. Pre-symbolic instruction involves a transformation from manipulable, three-dimensional objects to two-dimensional representations of objects. For example, imagine using apples to describe a set. These apples represent a concrete, hands-on, manipulatable material which is easy for the child to see, handle, and understand. In short, apples are concrete. A pre-symbolical, symbolic representation of apples would be pictures of apples presented to the student or apples drawn on the chalkboard. The lesson still deals with apples, but now it really deals with representations of apples in two- rather than three-dimensions.

Finally, symbolic instruction would remove all mention of real-life objects. Rather, it includes the pure use of symbols such as numerals which have no inherent meaning in themselves but which represent abstract ideas. Symbols are one-dimensional rather than three-dimensional. They are abstract with no corresponding material in the real world.

The section on teaching arithmetic to mildly mentally retarded learners will cover the four basic operations as well as time, money, and measurement. It will also contain a section on teaching with calculators and the microcomputer. Attempts will be made to relate material to be taught in terms of concrete, presymbolically-symbolic; and symbolic instruction. Finally, instructional activities will be suggested.

TEACHING THE FOUR OPERATIONS

□ □ Teaching the four basic operations is the focus of arithmetic instruction for most elementary programs (Reys, Suydam & Lindquist 1984; Thornton et al. 1983). There are four main goals in learning each operation:

1. Conceptualization of the process (e.g., what are we doing when we add?).
2. Fact learning and mastery.
3. Learning operation algorithms.
4. Knowing when to use the operation.

☐ Addition

Set Combination

Addition is the process of joining or combining sets. Thus even before students begin to learn their addition number facts it is probably advisable to concretely present the operation of addition as a way of physically combining sets of like members.

Concrete combinations of sets can be demonstrated in the manner presented in Figure 9.11a. Notice how the child is presented with two separate sets of like objects separated by space or a physical boundary or barrier. The student counts the members in each set and records the numbers. Next, the sets are combined (the barrier or space between the sets are eliminated and the sets are "squished" together). How many members are now in the combined set? By physically combining sets, the students gain a concrete understanding of what is entailed in the operation of addition.

Set combination may also be demonstrated pre-symbolically (see Figure 9.11b). Notice how in pre-symbolic set combination, the two sets of coins are drawn on the chalkboard or placed on the feltboard and are delineated by either a chalk line border or a border of yarn which encircles each set. The membership of each set is counted and the numbers recorded. Next, the set borders are removed and the total membership of the single, new, enlarged set is counted and recorded. The problem has then been solved pre-symbolically and symbolically.

Adding

After the child learns to combine sets concretely and pre-symbolically, the next step in the addition process is to help the child learn that sets do not have to be physically combined in order for addition to take place. That is, addition can be accomplished by using numbers that symbolically represent the membership of each set. This process, of course, requires the acquisition of the basic number addition facts from 1–9. For many mentally retarded pupils, this step in the addition process causes great problems.

One reason for the difficulty many mentally retarded students have learning the basic addition number facts is that the numerical representation of those facts is highly symbolic and may appear to be meaningless. After all, number fact problems such as $4 + 2$ and $5 + 3$ do not carry a meaning of their own—they are abstract. It is important that the basic number facts in all of the operations be presented in a concrete and pre-symbolical, symbolic manner so that students understand what they are doing when they carry out the addition process.

FIGURE 9.11   Set Combination

a. Concrete Representation with Actual Coins

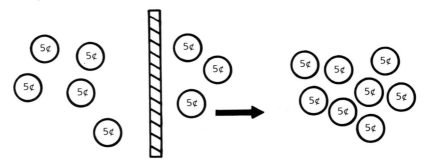

b. Pre-symbolic Representation with Cut-out Cardboard Coins on a Felt Board

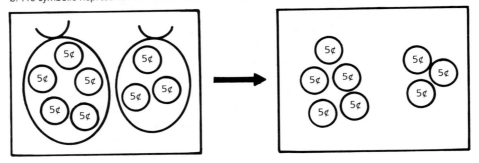

Figure 9.12a shows an addition instructional aid which can be easily constructed from a block of wood about a foot long, ten wooden dowels, and squares of latex rubber. Each of the dowels is cut to a predetermined length so that each will hold only as many squares as the numerical value of the dowel. Finally, the dowels are cemented in ascending order onto the block.

Now we have a tool that can aid in concretely demonstrating basic addition number facts. For example, in order to demonstrate 4 + 3, the student can create a group of four rubber squares and a separate group of three squares. The student's task is to find the wooden dowel just big enough to hold the two groups of squares (the pile should reach the top of the dowel without spilling over). When this is done, the child simply has to read the corresponding numeral painted on the large board near the bottom of the dowel to find that four squares plus three squares equal seven.

FIGURE 9.12 Instructional Aids For Teaching Addition

a. Teaching Addition with the Block and Dowel Instructional Aid

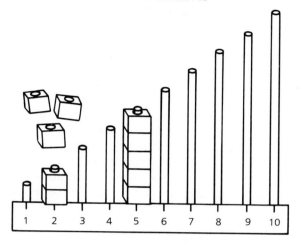

b. Teaching Addition with a Number Line

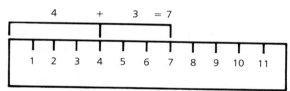

Another helpful aid for the concrete presentation of addition number facts is that of the cuisenaire rods (see Figure 9.10). Recall that these rods consist of ten different shapes and colored pieces of wood designed and measured in such a way that each next larger rod represents an increase of one unit (so that two white number *1* rods equal one red number *2* rod, etc.). To find an answer to an addition problem, the student continues to measure different sized rods until the one that equals the original rod train is found.

Pre-Symbolic Addition

Addition number facts should also be presented pre-symbolically by using devices such as the number line (Figure 9.12b). For example, to use the number line for this problem, the child would first count off four units on the line (stopping on the number four). The student would then count off the next set to be added (three) beginning from the point where counting ended, five, six, and seven, and counting would end on the number seven. Seven would then be recorded as the answer to 4 + 3.

Symbolic Addition

Once the basic addition number facts have been presented concretely and pre-symbolically, these same facts should be presented symbolically by means of numerals. To a large extent this transition should already have been taking place during concrete and pre-symbolic presentation since the numbers and number problem were always presented and the answer filled in by the pupil after the answer had been found by concrete and pre-symbolic means. During the symbolic phase of learning the addition facts, the learning aids would be faded out with the numerals and number problem format of addition facts remaining.

Once the basic one-to-ten addition number facts have been acquired, two additional adding skills remain to be learned: adding single digit numbers to sums of eighteen and adding two or more digit numbers. Adding sums to eighteen represents an extension of the learning of the basic addition facts from one to nine and may be taught concretely and pre-symbolically in much the same way as the basic number facts are taught. For example, in teaching the number facts to eighteen concretely, one might place a set of nine objects (e.g., apples) and another set of eight similar objects in close proximity to each other, remove the set boundaries (or "squish" the sets together), and count the objects in the combined set. Likewise, number facts to eighteen may be taught pre-symbolically by placing two distinct representations of set members on the chalk or felt board, erasing the borders of the set, pushing the sets together, and again counting the membership of the new combined set. Finally, the conversion from pre-symbolic to symbolic representation of the addition facts to eighteen would parallel the method used in teaching the basic addition facts.

☐ Place Value

To understand two or more digit addition, pupils must understand the concept of place value. That is, it is imperative for children to understand that the number *26* is not *2* and a *6* but rather two *10's* and six *1's*. Again, it is a good idea to teach this concept both concretely and pre-symbolically before moving into symbolic representations of the concept.

Concrete Place Value

Figure 9.13a shows how the dowel and square teaching tool can help concretely teach the notion of place value for the number sixteen. For the purpose of teaching place value, only the longest, number ten wooden dowel will be used. In the beginning of instruction the child is presented with a pile of sixteen rubber squares and told the task is to see how many groups or sets of ten

FIGURE 9.13 Teaching Place Value

a. The Dowel and Square Method

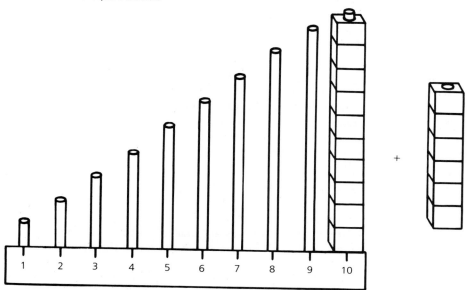

b. The Boundary Method

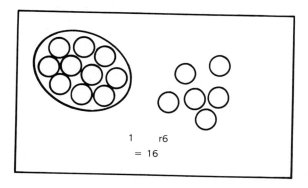

squares one can make out of the group. The child is then instructed to count off ten squares onto the large dowel. After this is accomplished the child would then remove the group of squares from the dowel, and bundle and tie up the group of ten squares (wrapping paper will do nicely here). The student is then asked: How many groups (or sets) of ten squares do we have wrapped up? (The answer is *1* but don't be surprised if the student answers *10*. If this is the case, the student has confused set membership with numbers of sets, a basic readiness skill, and this concept needs to be reviewed.)

Assuming that the student has correctly answered one bundle of ten squares, he or she would mark *1* on top of the bundle to keep track of the number of sets. Next the student would be asked to make another bundle of ten squares. This will be impossible because the six remaining squares will not fill the number ten dowel. Thus the student will be asked to write down the number of squares left which did not make a whole bundle (*6*). The student should have written the numbers *1* (one bundle of ten squares) and *6* (squares remaining).

Pre-Symbolic Place Value

The concept of place value can also be taught pre-symbolically using the boundary method shown in Figure 9.13b. For example, to teach the place value of sixteen, sixteen circles are placed on the chalk or felt board. The student is then asked to count and circle groups of ten of these representations. After a group of ten is circled a number representing the number of groups of ten counted is placed below the set. Again, since there are six representations remaining and this does not make a set of ten, the number *r6* or *6* is placed below the remaining set members.

☐ Two-Digit Addition

Once place value is learned, it is possible to begin instruction in two digit addition. Since for many students, the process of carrying over numbers from one column to the next is basically meaningless, an algorithm for two or three digit addition has been developed which keeps the place value of partial sums intact. A demonstration of this algorithm may be seen in Figure 9.14.

The concept of multiple digit addition will not be appropriate for all mentally retarded students—only for those students who have concretely, presymbolically, and symbolically mastered all of the addition skills which are below multiple digit addition in the adding hierarchy. The teacher should not force students who have not mastered the prerequisite adding skills into multiple digit addition just because the teacher feels that such an addition skill is important. Forcing the child into a process she or he is not ready for will only result in confusion and frustration. The wise special education teacher needs to assess that all of prerequisite addition skills have been mastered before multiple addition is attempted.

FIGURE 9.14   Algorithm for Two Digit Addition

a. No regrouping

```
  54
+ 32
----
  06
  80
----
  86
```

b. With regrouping

```
  54          36
+ 38        + 37
----        ----
  12          13
  80          60
----        ----
  92          73
```

☐ Subtraction

Subtraction is the inverse of addition. It involves the creation of a subgroup of members from a larger set and then counting the members of the remaining set after the new set has been carved out. As the inverse of addition, the definition of subtraction may be demonstrated concretely and pre-symbolically using Figure 9.15. A large set of objects are placed on the student's desk (e.g., ten objects). The student is asked to count the objects and record the total set membership in number form. Next the student is asked to count out and physically remove some set members (e.g., four) and record the number of objects which have been removed. Finally, the student is asked to count the number of objects remaining in the set and record the answer.

Likewise, the definition of subtraction can be represented pre-symbolically using Figure 9.15b. Representations of objects are placed on the chalk or felt board and the objects counted and recorded. A subset of objects is counted out and erased or crossed out from the original set. Finally, the set members remaining or not crossed out are counted and recorded.

Subtraction Facts

Once the concept of subtraction has been acquired concretely and pre-symbolically, it is time to symbolically teach the one-to-nine subtraction facts. This involves learning and committing these facts to memory in a similar fashion to the addition facts. As in the addition facts, it will help if these facts are presented concretely and pre-symbolically using the instructional aids such as the dowel and peg method and set bundle method. These concrete pre-symbolic aids would be faded with only the numerals in the subtraction problems remaining. An intermediate step which can also be used is that of the subtraction card shown in Figure 9.16. This is a mnemonic device designed to help in memorizing

FIGURE 9.15   Demonstrating Subtraction

a. Concrete Representation (Actual Objects Are Used)

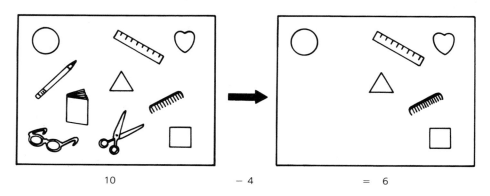

10   − 4   =   6

b. Presymbolic Representation (Pictures Are Used)

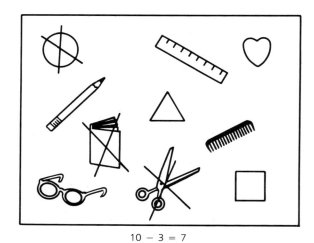

10 − 3 = 7

FIGURE 9.16   Subtraction Cards

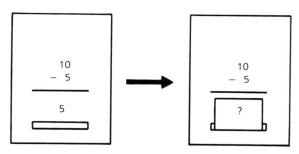

subtraction facts. As each fact is learned and memorized it is blacked out on the card until the child learns and memorizes the entire subtraction fact set.

As in addition, the basic one-to-nine subtraction facts must be practiced daily in order to be effectively learned. In order to keep up motivation and decrease drill boredom, the teacher is encouraged to develop games and activities which will stress practice of the subtraction facts while being fun at the same time. Examples of such activities are in Figure 9.17. An example is subtraction Bingo. This game follows the rules of conventional Bingo but uses subtraction facts as the stimulus items. The students have Bingo cards which have two types of problems written on them: the answer to subtraction number facts (single numbers from one-to-nine) and subtraction number fact problems (e.g., 9 − 6 = ?). The teacher has flashcards which contain either answers to subtraction problems or the problems themselves. Students must answer the problem presented by the teacher and find the answer on their Bingo cards. The first child to cover five squares in a row on a Bingo card is the winner.

Figure 9.17b shows a subtraction jigsaw puzzle. A variety of subtraction problems are cut out of tagboard as pieces of a jigsaw puzzle. The answers to the problems are cut out in such a way that only they can fit the problems in jigsaw puzzle fashion. The student then matches all of the subtraction problems with the right jigsaw puzzle answer until all of the problems have been solved.

Regrouping

A key skill in subtraction is regrouping. Understanding regrouping hinges on acquisition of the concept of set membership in units of ten. That is, in the number system of base ten, every ten objects may be bundled together and delineated as one special set. Thus, a group of twenty objects may be designated as two special sets of ten each while, conversely, two special sets of ten may be broken down into twenty individual set members.

There are a variety of ways to concretely demonstrate the concept of regrouping. For example, look at the what's-inside container shown in Figure 9.18a. A child is given a container with the number ten written in large numerals on the lid. Inside the container are ten tokens or chips. Ask how many containers the student has (one) and what the container says on its lid (ten). Then ask the student to spill out the contents of the container and count the objects (ten). Now the tokens go back into the container. Thus the special container with the label ten contains ten objects.

The concept of regrouping may also be demonstrated pre-symbolically (Figure 9.18b). For example, write the problem 17 − 8, on the chalkboard. Then depict the number seventeen as a long rectangle with the number one written above it and seven single squares. Now ask the student to subtract eight squares, impossible as there are not eight squares, only seven and a single rectangle! The teacher informs the students each rectangle always contains exactly ten squares and suggests dividing the rectangle into squares. Next, shade in or **X** out eight squares, and count the remaining squares (nine). Thus, 17 − 8 = 9. This method can also be used for regrouping in larger subtraction problems.

FIGURE 9.17   Subtraction Games

a. Subtraction Bingo

BINGO					
6 − 2	7 − 1	5 − 4	6	6 − 3	7 − 2
5	9 − 3	4 − 3	3 − 1	2	6 − 1
8 − 4	5 − 2	7 − 2	4 − 1	6 − 3	3 − 2
5 − 2	4 − 1	1	9 − 8	9	7 − 5
8 − 1	6 − 5	4 − 2	2 − 2	7 − 1	5 − 3
3	4 − 3	7 − 1	9 − 2	4	8 − 5
6 − 2	4 − 1	8 − 2	7 − 2	5 − 4	6 − 3
5 − 1̄	8	9 − 6	7 − 4	6 − 3	7

b. Subtraction Jigsaw Puzzle

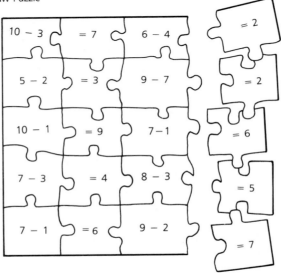

290

FIGURE 9.18   Regrouping

a. Concrete Representation

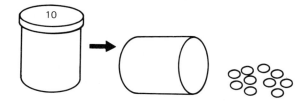

b. Presymbolic Representation

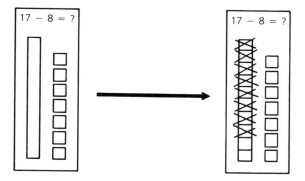

c. Symbolic Representation

1.

$$
\begin{array}{r}
53 \\
-27 \\
\hline
\end{array}
\qquad
\begin{array}{r}
(10 + 3 = 13) \\
4 + 13 \\
-2 \quad 7 \\
\hline
\end{array}
$$

2.

$$
\begin{array}{r}
67 \\
-42 \\
\hline
\end{array}
\rightarrow
\begin{array}{r}
(10 + 7 = 17) \\
5 + 17 \\
-4 \quad 2 \\
\hline
10 + 15 = 25
\end{array}
$$

Regrouping will also need to be presented symbolically so that the student can solve numerically presented subtraction problems. Figure 9.18c shows an algorithm which facilitates this process for mentally retarded learners. Consider, for example, the subtraction problem 53 − 27. In step one, the ten's column is reduced by one and the addition problem 10 + 3 = 13 is entered in subscript above the one's column. In step two, the subtraction problem of the one's column (13 − 7) is solved and written as six under the one's column. In step three, the problem 40 − 20 is solved (20) and entered as a separate line. Finally, the problem 20 + 6 = 26 is solved.

Notice the important differences between this algorithm and the one traditionally used in subtraction. First, the partial subtractions are represented with their place values intact so that the problem is represented as the partial differences of 13 − 7, and 40 − 20. Second, the same algorithm may be used both in cases where borrowing is necessary and in cases where it is not. C-2 shows this nicely (67 − 42). Here, the 67 is changed to 50 and 17 even though the borrowing is not strictly necessary. The first partial difference is represented as 17 − 2 = 15 and the second as 50 − 40 = 10. The two partial differences are then added to give a total difference score of 25. Since this subtraction algorithm of partial differences preserving place value is used for all subtraction cases rather than just those cases which "require" borrowing, strategic decision making processes of when to borrow are eliminated for mentally retarded learners. Thus the high probability of these students making the wrong decisions about when to borrow and when not to borrow is reduced.

☐ Multiplication

Multiplication is perhaps best presented as multiple addition. Thus, if the mentally retarded child has mastered the basic skills of addition, the chances are good for mastering basic multiplication. Conversely, instruction in multiplication for mentally retarded learners should probably not be attempted before addition is mastered.

The concept of multiplication as multiple addition should be presented to learners both concretely and pre-symbolically. Consider, for example, the problem 6 × 3 = 18. This may be concretely shown to the child by using tokens or buttons and telling the child that in this problem the 6 represents six columns and the 3 represents three rows. The child is to simply arrange the tokens into a 6 × 3 array. After this has been accomplished the child is then asked to count the tokens in the array (eighteen). Finally, the child completes the numerical representation of the problem such that 6 columns × 3 rows = 18 or 6 × 3 = 18.

Figure 9.19 shows how the concept of multiplication may be shown pre-symbolically. The student is given a piece of paper which is filled with an array of dots arranged in rows and columns. The student is asked to count off six columns by three rows and draw a line around the perimeter of the pattern. Next the student is asked to count all of the dots which are included in the drawn perimeter (eighteen). Finally, the student completes the numerical representation of the problem in the same fashion as was done in the concrete example.

Multiplication Facts

Symbolic multiplication involves two processes: the learning and memorization of multiplication facts from 1 × 1 to 9 × 9, and the algorithm for multiplication of multi-digit numbers. This algorithm also includes the concept of place value.

Multiplication facts are difficult; however, they are necessary. There are many multiplication facts to learn (eighty-one) so there is great opportunity for error. However, some of the memory load in learning multiplication facts can be reduced by showing the child that multiplication is communative (5 × 4 = 4 × 5) and can be reduced even further by demonstrating that any

FIGURE 9.19   Presymbolic Multiplication

6 (columns) × 3 (rows) = 18 (objects)

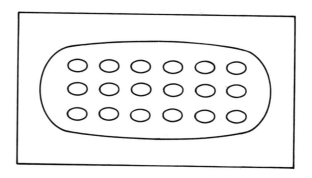

number multiplied by one yields that number. The use of a multiplication table similar to the one used for subtraction may prove to be a useful instructional aid.

Memorization of the multiplication facts entails a large amount of practice and drill. Such large amounts of drill may lead to a decrease in motivation and an increase in boredom on the part of the child. As in the case of teaching the basic addition and subtraction facts, the special education teacher will need to be innovative in devising practice techniques designed to keep motivation and interest high.

Figure 9.20 contains two sample activities which help keep drills in multiplication facts interesting. Figure 9.20a shows an activity called Secret Agent Code. Each child is given a code breaker in which each number from one to eighty-one represents an alphabet letter or a punctuation mark. The teacher then gives children number problems, the products of which will correspond to the alphabet letters of the code and which will spell out a message. The child's task is to correctly complete the problems and decode the message.

Figure 9.20b shows the game of multiplication dominoes. The teacher needs to prepare about fifty cardboard or plastic dominoes beforehand, each domino representing a multiplication problem. Each child picks five dominoes, the others remain in a pile face down. The first child can place any domino on the table. The next child's task is to calculate the answer to that problem and find another domino which presents a problem with the same product as the domino placed on the table by the first child. If the child does not have a correct domino in hand, the child draws one from the pile and either places it down on the table or passes. After a matching problem is placed on the table, the next child may lay down any domino. The process continues until all of the dominoes are expended.

An Algorithm for Multiplication

Multi-digit multiplication may be taught using an algorithm similar to the one used for addition in which place value of numbers is kept intact and the need for

FIGURE 9.20   Activities to Help Learn Multiplication Facts

a. Secret Agent Code

2 A	4 B	6 C	8 D	9 E	10 F	12 G	14 H
16 I	18 J	20 K	21 L	22 M	24 N	26 O	27 P
28 Q	30 R	32 S	33 T	35 U	36 V	38 W	40 X
42 Y	44 Z	45 °	46 '	48 ?	49 ;	50 -	52 :

b. Multiplication Dominoes

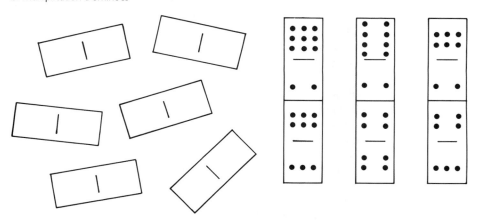

carrying numbers to the next place value column is eliminated. Figure 9.21 gives two examples of this algorithm in action. Figure 9.21a, for example, shows how the product for 27 × 16 would be calculated. First 7 × 6 would be identified as 42 (using the basic multiplication facts). Next it would be entered as 42 (not 2 carry the 4) as a partial product. Next, 6 × 2 would be calculated, but since we are dealing with the tens column, the partial product would be recorded as 120. Next, 1 (actually 10) × 7 would be entered as 70 while 1 (actually 10) × 2 (actually 20) would be entered as 200. Finally the partial products would be summed to equal 432. Likewise, Figure 9.21b shows how the algorithm would be carried out for 22 × 6 = 132.

FIGURE 9.21 Algorithm for Multiplication

a.
```
      27
      16
      42
     120
      70
     200
     432
```

b.
```
      22
     ×6
      12
     120
     132
```

□ Division

Division is multiple subtraction. While subtraction entails the one time removal of a subset of a given size from a larger set, division consists of removing that size subset over and over from the larger set until that set is completely expended. Where subtraction and division differ, however, is in the type of answer each process seeks. While subtraction asks questions about how many set members remain after a subset has been removed, division seeks to answer questions regarding the *number* of subsets which have been removed from the original set before the set was completely expended.

Concrete and Pre-Symbolic Division

As in other operations, division should be presented concretely and pre-symbolically before presented in an abstract manner. In demonstrating division concretely, the child can be presented with ten tokens and the question asked as to how many sets of two tokens can be created before the original set of ten is all gone. To answer this question, the child takes two tokens out of the set and places them on a desk. He then removes another set of two tokens and places them on another desk. He continues to remove subsets of two tokens, placing each subset on a different desk until the original set is expended. The child is then asked to count the desks which contain tokens. The answer is five.

Pre-symbolic division may be shown in a similar way which is demonstrated in Figure 9.22. Here ten vertical lines are drawn on the board and the child's task is to section them off in bundles of two. After all of the lines have been bundled (or in the case of remainders where there are not enough remaining set members to create a bundle), the bundles are counted and the answer recorded.

An Algorithm for Division

Division facts, like the number facts of the other three operations, are important and must be acquired if symbolic division is to be learned. Most of the activities described earlier in this chapter designed to facilitate practice in number facts while keeping interest high may be modified and used for practice of division number facts. As in the other operations, keeping interest and motivation high during practice sessions depends largely in part on the innovativeness of the teacher.

FIGURE 9.22   Presymbolic Division

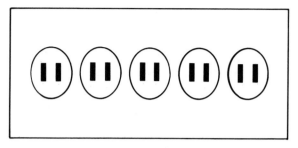

10 lines divided into bundles of 2 = 5 bundles
10 ÷ 2 = 5

FIGURE 9.23   Algorithm for Division

```
A.   6 ⌐ 27                          B.   28 ⌐ 623
        − 06      1                           280      10
        ―――                                   ―――
        121      + 1                          343     + 10
        − 06                                  280
        ―――                                   ―――
        05                                    63      + 1
        + 10                                  28
        ―――                                   ――
        0 × 5    + 1                          35      + 1
        − 06                                  28
        ―――                                   ――
        09                                    7        22    r 7
        6      + 1
        ――
        03       4   r   3
```

As in the other operations, there is an algorithm for symbolic division (Figure 9.23). The key to this algorithm is the concept of division as multiple subtraction and the counting of the number of subtractions made.

Figure 9.23a shows how this algorithm might be used in the division problem 27/6. A subset of 6 is to be constantly subtracted out of the larger set with each subtraction being enumerated. As can be seen, after four successive subtractions of 6, what remains of the original set is too small to make a fifth subtraction. Thus the answer to 27/6 is 4 remainder 2.

Figure 9.23b shows how this might be accomplished for multi-digit division. In this example we wish to successfully take subsets of 28 out of an original set of 623. We could do this, enumerating each subtraction of 28, but there is a shortcut which may be used using multiples of 10. Thus, the first grouping made is not 28 but 28 × 10 = 280. This number is subtracted from 623 and 10 28's (10) enumerated as the number of subtractions made. This can be done again with the remaining members of the original set now 63. Now 280 cannot be subtracted out of 63 but one set of 28 can (remainder 35) and done again (remainder 7). So the answer to the question as to the number of subtractions which can be made from 623 is 10 + 10 + 1 + 1 = 22, remainder 7.

APPLICATION SKILLS: TIME, MONEY, MEASUREMENT

☐ Time

There are really two processes in telling time: reading clock time and being able to know when it is time to carry out given behaviors (e.g., eat breakfast, go to school, or quit reading this book and catch a movie). Both time telling processes involve using the clock; they are discussed in this chapter.

Telling time is, of course, accomplished by reference to a clock or wristwatch. Thus it is imperative that the special education class contain a wall clock. If this is impossible, then some sort of instructional desk clock will have to do. The ability to tell clock time is dependent on the following skills:

1. To be able to read the numerals from 1–12.
2. Count to sixty by one's, five's, and ten's.
3. To understand the concept of the clock hands and what they do.
4. To be able to recite and understand the concept of *o'clock* as reflected by the relationship of the two clock hands.
5. To understand the concept of quarter and half hour.
6. To understand the relationship between numerals on the clock and five minute intervals.
7. To understand the concepts of before and after the hour depending on the minute hand's relationship to the half hour.
8. To appropriately coordinate the acquisition of the concepts of minutes, hours, and the two clock hands to appropriately read clock time.

Figure 9.24 contains some instructional aids for the telling of clock time. For example, Figure 9.24a shows an instructional aid designed to teach the concept of o'clock using the hour hand. Twelve circles are covered up by dark circles. The circles underneath have a hand indicator which indicates hour clock time. The student's task is to uncover the circle and read the correct hourly time.

Figure 9.24b contains a technique for teaching clock time with the minute hand and the relationship between the numerals on the clock and five-minute intervals of clock time. Finally, the two concepts regarding hour and minute hands are put together to tell time appropriately.

The second aspect of telling time is knowing the correct time to engage in given behavior throughout the course of the day. Knowing when to wake up, when to be at the school bus stop, when to report to work are all dependent on the person matching the current time on the clock with the time that a given chore or activity should begin. Such behavior, taken for granted as a basic skill in today's society, is not incidently acquired by many mentally retarded students, but is vitally important for normalization and vocational success.

The teacher can teach time-to-do-things by using a work roster similar to the one shown in Figure 9.25. First, each student in the class is given a copy of

FIGURE 9.24   Instructional Aids to Help in Telling Time

a. Teaching "O'Clock Time

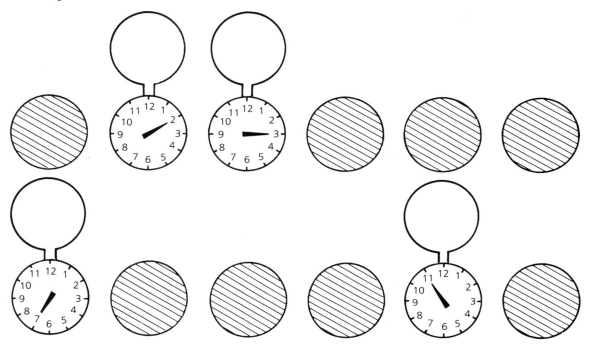

b. Telling Time with the Minute Hand

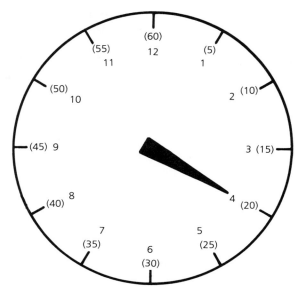

FIGURE 9.25 A Sample Job Roster for a Class

Jobs	Students	Time for Job
Sweep Floor	Steven	2:45
Arrange Books	Sally	9:30
Class Store	Robert	3:00
Help in Cafeteria	John	12:00
Clean Workshop	Susan	1:45
Collect Lunch Money	Anne	8:15

the work roster with each pupil possessing a job or series of jobs which must be completed intermittently throughout the school day. Then, students are provided with small, inexpensive wooden instructional clocks with movable hands. The clocks are set for pupils to correspond to the times that they are to begin engaging in some behavior specified by the job roster. The students' job is to check the wall clock periodically, comparing it to the time specified on their portable clocks. When the times match, it is time to engage behavior specified on the roster.

Practice at telling time and matching clock time with time to do things should be provided at every opportunity during the school day. The teacher will need to develop a class schedule for activities and encourage students to take responsibility for carrying out the activities of the day. This is in contrast to the typical classroom in which the teacher is the one who constantly tells pupils the time to do things such as to go to lunch or gym.

One variation on this theme which approximates the real-life work situation is to install a time clock and time cards in the classroom. Students are then responsible for identifying the correct time to do something (using the wall clock and their portable clocks), punching in to engage in the required job activity and punching out to return to the activity of the class.

☐ Money

In our society, the ability to handle money and monetary concepts may be summed up in the old saying "A fool and his money are soon parted." People who cannot handle money, who cannot make purchases appropriately, and who do not possess the knowledge needed to avoid getting cheated in money matters are often considered foolish. The ability to handle money appropriately is considered a key skill in the normalization and vocational process of mentally retarded learners.

Unfortunately, many mentally retarded students, especially students in the moderate retardation ranges, do not know how to handle money appropriately. It is for this reason that the application of arithmetic skills to the area of money and money management is considered vital in the special-education curriculum.

There are a variety of money skills and competencies which are needed in today's modern society in order to secure normalization and life success. They include

1. Coin discrimination
2. Coin equivalencies
3. Counting money to $1.00
4. Paper currencies (at least one and five dollar bills)
5. Purchasing items
6. Receiving correct change from purchases

It is important that in teaching the above skills, real money rather than play or bogus money be used. Using play money forces the child to deal with a meaningless monetary system that will never be used in real life. It also forces the child to transfer learning in the bogus system to real currency, but we know that mentally retarded children are notoriously poor at transfer and generalization. Also, if real money (and, of course, security measures to protect it) are used, motivation and interest will be heightened (after all, everyone, including mentally retarded children, know what real money can purchase). Thus, using real money increases interest and transfer.

Coin Discrimination
Coin discrimination is the first money skill to teach. Pennies should be the first coins introduced in this process for two reasons: they have a highly distinctive color and they are the base unit of all money. While teaching penny discrimination, it is a good idea to allow students to count pennies and to identify subsets of pennies from larger sets of cents. Such activity allows students to acquire the money skill of one-to-one relationship and teaches that the larger coins are conglomerates of pennies.

After pennies, the other coins should be taught in the order of nickels, dimes, quarters, and half dollars. Since these coins differ greatly in size, learning to discriminate among them will usually not prove to be too difficult for mildly mentally retarded students, but may be a problem for students in the moderately retarded ranges.

Coin Equivalencies
After learning coin discrimination, the student needs to acquire the values and equivalencies of coins. This is often a difficult set of concepts for mentally retarded children to handle and for this reason the concepts should be introduced both concretely and pre-symbolically. The student will need to acquire the following equivalencies in the following order:

1. 5 pennies = 1 nickel
2. 10 pennies = 1 dime
3. 2 nickels = 1 dime

4. 2 dimes + 1 nickel = 1 quarter
5. 5 nickels = 1 quarter

Once students learn the value of the various coins, it is a short step to combining coins in order to achieve sums of money. An instructional aid much like the number line but containing money amounts instead of numbers can be a useful instructional aid for helping students pre-symbolically compute money sums.

Making Purchases

Making purchases and paying for items come next in the money hierarchy. This activity is particularly appropriate for older students. Making purchases involves instruction and practice in combining coins to make $1.00 and combining coins to equal a specified sum.

Both of these skills involve picking out a subset of coins from a larger set of coins with the subset to equal either $1.00 or some specified other sum. In doing this the child will need instruction on the concept of the dollar and the kinds and combinations of coins which equal a dollar. In this area, a long-term instructional unit on making purchases wisely will prove most relevant. In addition, workbooks available on money usage will prove helpful in providing students the practice they need.

One instructional activity designed to provide practice in this area which is guaranteed to keep student motivation high is the concept of the class store. In the class store arrangement, the teacher secures different articles which may be purchased by students at different prices. The students' task is to then make appropriate purchases of items in the store using the correct monetary combinations. A teacher can even introduce the concept of money subtraction by using the idea of the layaway. Pupils who do not have enough money to purchase the item can pay it off gradually, paying on the item each day until it is completely paid for. The concept of the class store also fits in nicely with a unit on vocational education and social skills.

Making Change

The concept of making change involves the student calculating how much extra money has been given for something above and beyond the item's purchase price. This concept can be taught using the money line shown in Figure 9.26. Suppose, for example, the student wishes to purchase an item which costs 17 cents, but has only a quarter (25 cents). How much change should he or she receive?

Using Figure 9.26, the purchase price would be indicated on the appropriate point on the money line (seventeen) with the quarter being represented at the twenty-five point to the right of seventeen. To figure change, the student would need to simply count the units between seventeen and twenty-five on the money line (eight). Of course over time, the need for the money line would be

FIGURE 9.26   Making Change with a Money Line

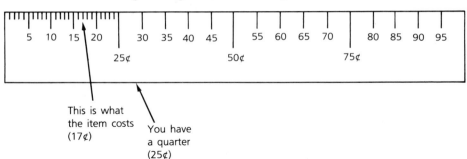

faded out and conventional subtraction utilized to figure out the amount of appropriate change from purchases.

☐ Measurement

Although there is a movement toward the metric system for measurement, it appears that the system of choice in the United States is still the English method. Until that trend changes notably, it is probably unwise to teach mentally retarded students both systems because of the problems of interference and transfer. Thus, for the time being, it may be more advisable to teach students the English system since this system will probably be used much more frequently during adulthood.

Linear Measurement

Linear measurement refers to distance. The basic concepts to be learned are inches, feet, and yards. Miles are also an important concept but ratios between feet, yards, and miles probably are not necessary. The most important aspect of teaching linear measurement is having students measure real-life objects using common instruments such as rulers, tape measures, and yardsticks. It is also advisable not to deal with fractions of inches since these concepts do not usually come up in day-to-day measurements. In teaching linear measurement, keep instruction practical, concrete, and tied to the real world as much as possible.

Volume and Weight

When teaching volume and weight, the key word should be practicality. Children should gain practice measuring real-life materials; they should weigh and measure common, everyday things found around the home and the work environment. The home economics curriculum can be very useful for instruction in weight and volume. During the preparation of food, for example, students will be required to follow recipes which will demand liquid and weight measurements. Such food preparation skills are vital for independent adult living. Figure 9.27, for example, contains two instructional objectives with accompanying activities and lessons taken from an instructional, long-term unit on food preparation and creating nutritional meals. Notice how these activities demand practice and expertise in making weight and volume measurements. Such real-life instructional activities in the measurement areas will help insure relevancy of curriculum as well as generalization and transfer to everyday, concrete situations.

FIGURE 9.27   Instructional Objectives and Activities Dealing with Measurement Taken from Long-Term Instructional Units

Core Area: Mathematics   Duration: 60 minutes

Behavioral Objective	Activity	Materials	Evaluation
After seeing the movie *The Essentials of Diet* the student will correctly select from a list of foods, two good items from each food group which are high in protein, carbohydrates or fats with 80 percent accuracy. 1.12	1. Guest lecturer: Dietitian from the local hospital or school to speak on the importance of carbohydrates, proteins, and fats. 2. Presented will be a lesson on the daily minimum requirements in grams for each nutrient. 3. (Watch film) 4. Lessons on the number of grams of carbohydrates in a food (also for fats and proteins) as demonstrated with a scale used in weighing number of grams 5. Problems on the mathematical processes: number of grams of carbohydrates, fats or proteins ingested; number of grams required daily; number of grams needed additionally to fulfill daily requirements.	A scale weighing grams. Different food items for weighing. A chart made by the teacher showing the different number of grams of each nutrient required daily for a healthy body. Film: *Essentials of Diet*—McGraw Hill Book Co.	Student will orally list the two foods from each food group which are high in carbohydrates, fats and proteins with 80 percent accuracy. This is done informally and the student may refer to the movie or to any wall charts for aids in selection.

(continued)

FIGURE 9.27 (cont.)

Core Area: Mathematics _____   Duration: 50 minutes _____

Behavioral Objective	Activity	Materials	Evaluation
Given the directions to choose one food from the four basic food groups at lunch the student will correctly do so in the school cafeteria at lunch time. 2.2	Students will read story out loud in class. Any questions will be answered by the group or the teacher if necessary. Students will then weigh themselves and record their weight on the chart in red. Each student will then be assisted by another student in measuring height and this number will be recorded on the chart in green. Each week students will weigh in and be measured and the numbers recorded. At the end of the term the amount of increase in weight and height will be totaled by the students.	Teacher made poster board charts for recording weight and height of the students. Story: *Your Food and You* H. S. Zim Scale for weighing, Tape for measuring height. Felt tip pens.	Teacher will observe during lunch if student correctly selects one food from the four food groups. Informal discussion at lunch will be held concerning this selection.

USING TECHNOLOGY IN ARITHMETIC INSTRUCTION

☐ Calculators

Should students be taught to use calculators to help with their arithmetic functioning? Should they be allowed to use them in school while they are working their math problems? To a large extent, these questions are moot. Calculators are a part of everyday life for many people and they are used throughout the day by people in a large variety of arithmetic situations. Most calculators today run on solar power, do not require expensive batteries, and are thus cheap to purchase and operate. The proliferation of calculators in our daily lives mandates that students be able to operate them if the students are to be part of the mainstream of society.

There are three main skills which need to be mastered in order to use calculators properly: key functions, counting, and operations. (Instruction in square roots, squares, logarithmic functions, etc., is probably not relevant or necessary for mentally retarded pupils.) Students will need to receive systematic instruction in all three functions as well as ample opportunity to practice in order to handle calculators properly. Various activities help children learn and practice these skill areas in calculator usage.

Counting: Calculators represent a powerful counting tool. Have students continue to push the *1* and + keys and watch the display to see that the sum always increases by one. Have the students time themselves in counting to a given number. How long will it take to count from 1–100? From 1–500, etc.?

Count backwards: This is the basis of subtraction. Begin with a number on the display. Have the students continue to hit the *1* and − keys and watch the display to see what remains after each operation. Students can fill in a worksheet on counting backwards.

Skip counting: Have students start with a given number and begin counting by a constant. For example, have them begin with *3* on their display and count by *5*'s by continuing to enter *5* and + on the keys. Skip counting is nothing more than multiplication so that this activity can be used to help learn multiplication facts.

Place value: Have students experiment with the largest one, two, three, and four digit numbers which they can find. They can do this by punching in, for example, a two digit number and then adding *1*. Does the number change to a three digit number? After experimentation, students will learn that *9*'s must fill in available place values before + *1* will add a place (e.g., 99 + 1 = 100).

The power of *1*'s the power of *10*'s: Have students punch into the display any number they choose (e.g., 34). Have them multiply the number by *1* (hitting × and *1*) on the keys. From this activity the students will learn that any number multiplied by one will be the original number. Then have the student display a number again (e.g., *28*). Multiply the number by *10*. The answer is *280*. Repeat the process with another number.

☐ Computers

The microcomputer lends itself very well to arithmetic instruction in terms of individualized tutoring, drill and practice, real-life simulations and problem solving, and learning games. Computers can give individualized, programmed instruction enabling students to advance at their own pace and allowing for learning styles. It also can make drill and practice fun and motivating. For example, one arithmetic drill game contains a magician doing magic tricks, cannons

TABLE 9.3 Arithmetic Software for the Microcomputer

Introduction to Counting (K–2). Edu-ware Company (Apple). Eight separate units teach basic counting, addition, subtraction, height, weight, shape discrimination and measurement.

Fay: That Math Woman (K–4) Didatech (Apple, Commodore 64). Uses a woman as a role model. Presents instruction on the four operations and number facts by using a pre-symbolic number line approach rather than by using abstract, symbolic memorization.

Math Maze (1–6) Designware (Apple, Commodore 64, IBM-PC & PC Jr). Uses a maze/puzzle approach for practice in the four basic math operations. Lively animation and sound. A good motivator to help students practice arithmetic facts.

Teasers by Tobbs (4–adult) Sunburst (Apple, Atari Disk, Dommodore 64, IBM-PC & PC Jr). Uses a crossword puzzle approach to help students practice their number facts and solve arithmetic in the four number operations. Difficulty level can be set by the teacher. Highly motivating.

Addition Magician (K–4) Learning Co. (Apple, Commodore 64, IBM-PC & PC Jr). A magician helps student practice number facts. Helps the student build "magic walls" in order to discover that different groups of numbers add to the same sum.

Math Blaster (1–6) Davidson & Associates (Apple, Commodore 64, IBM-PC & PC Jr). Helps student practice arithmetic facts and gain important math skills. Five levels of difficulties designed to help students build up their arithmetic "self-concept."

NOTE: There is a great deal of inexpensive arithmetic software available from the Minnesota Educational Computer Consortium (MECC), 3490 Lexington Ave., N., St. Paul, MN 55126. The price of the software and manual is always less than $10. MECC has available mathematics instructional software for Apple, Atari, Commodore, IBM, and Radio Shack computers. Since the MECC catalogue is too extensive to include here, the reader is strongly encouraged to send for the free catalogue.

going off, even exploding dynamite whenever a problem is solved correctly! Table 9.3 lists arithmetic computer programs and their publishers. The interested reader should write for company catalogues since new arithmetic programs are introduced frequently.

SUMMARY

□ □ More time is spent teaching arithmetic than almost all other subject areas. Nevertheless, many special needs learners achieve poorly in arithmetic for a variety of reasons which include poor motivation and teaching, anxiety, and the abstract/ symbolic in which material is presented.

A sound arithmetic curriculum consists of three components: computation, problem solving, and application skills. Computational skills include ability to work problems in the four operations: addition, subtraction, multiplication, and division. Problem solving refers to verbal story problems, while application skills refer to the ability to work problems in the areas of time, money, and measurement.

The arithmetic curriculum for mildly mentally retarded learners must be functional and relevant to the child's future life success. Such a curriculum must relate to the areas of consumer skills and employment. To guarantee functionality, the teacher should relate the arithmetic curriculum to the long-term instructional unit.

Arithmetic readiness is extremely important. Many children fail to achieve in arithmetic because they do not possess the prerequisite readiness skills. Thus, arithmetic readiness skills should be assessed before formal arithmetic instruction ensues. Arithmetic assessment may be formal or informal. There are a variety of diagnostic arithmetic assessment instruments available including KeyMath and the Stanford Diagnostic Mathematics Test. Informal diagnostic assessment procedures would include work samples, checklists, and error analyses.

In teaching arithmetic to mentally retarded learners, it is important that material be presented concretely, pre-symbolically, and symbolically. Concrete instruction involves using real-world, three-dimensional materials which are easily manipulated. Pre-symbolic materials are two-dimensional materials (usually pictures) of three-dimensional objects. Symbolic instruction entails using abstract symbols which are not readily tied to the real world. Concrete, pre-symbolic, and symbolic instruction should be used for instruction in operations, problem solving, and application.

There are a variety of approaches to teaching arithmetic. These include the use of basal arithmetic texts, Cuisenaire rods, Montessori materials, and individualized programs. Programs should compensate for individual differences between learners as well as be motivating, sequenced, and functional.

Technology has been a major force in innovative arithmetic instruction. The use of calculators has become an accepted way of life for many people in arithmetic computation. Thus, instruction for mildly mentally retarded learners in the use of calculators is advisable. Likewise, the microcomputer has become an important tool in instruction, motivation, and drill and can become a valuable tool for use with mentally retarded learners.

10

Social Studies and Science Instruction

Key Concepts

☐ Components of the Social Studies Curriculum: Knowledge, Values, and Social Participation
☐ Approaches to Teaching Social Studies
☐ Cognitive Dissonance in the Values Curriculum
☐ Values Clarification
☐ Inquiry and Process Approaches in Science
☐ Multisensory versus Unisensory Science Teaching
☐ Content Accessibility
☐ Process Accessibility
☐ Access to Manipulation

Social studies and science are two curricular areas not usually emphasized by teachers of mildly mentally retarded students (Keller 1983; Davies & Ball 1978). Reasons for this include beliefs about the learning characteristics of mentally retarded students as well as some preconceived, largely inappropriate ideas about what constitutes typical social studies and science curriculums in the schools. Among these beliefs are

1. Mentally retarded learners cannot adequately learn social studies and science material. The subject matter in these curricular areas is simply too abstract and difficult for such pupils to master.
2. Mentally retarded learners are not interested in social studies and science.
3. Mentally retarded learners are too cognitively unsophisticated to appropriately use and understand social studies tools (e.g., maps, charts, graphs) and science equipment.

Likewise, there are stereotypical beliefs held about what constitutes a typical social studies and science curriculum. For example, social studies have often been considered to consist of history and geography (Curtis 1974, 1978). In this type of social studies curriculum, the student would be expected to memorize a large number of historical dates and facts, and to study concepts such as the major countries and regions of the world (Curtis 1974, 1978; Engle 1974).

Stereotypic beliefs regarding the science curriculum might be along the lines of traditional lab-type experiments where students would conduct formalized scientific experiments by following a step-by-step procedure (much like the experiments included in commercially available chemistry sets). In such a curriculum, there would be little or no spontaneity in science curriculum or activities nor would there be a large measure of understanding by the students as to the underlying scientific principles upon which the experiments were based. This type of social studies and science curriculum would probably hold little or no relevance to the most mildly mentally retarded students (Keller 1983). Unfortunately, many of the social studies and science programs have been trivial and relatively meaningless to the lives of students. At the same time, many instructional methods and materials used to teach science and social studies to special-needs learners have been too abstract, symbolic, and complicated (Barr, Barth & Shermis 1978).

Fortunately, this state of affairs in social studies and science curriculum and instruction is undergoing drastic changes. As more attention is given to the mainstreaming of handicapped persons into normalized adult life, educators have come to realize that the ability to solve problems and use existing technology (science) as well as to function as a valued community member (social studies) *is* important and vital. (Jacobson & Bergman 1980; Ochoa & Shuster 1980; Taylor, Artuso & Hewett 1973).

Modification of the social studies and science curriculums and instructional methods to meet the needs of exceptional students has shown many of the myths about mentally retarded students' ability to handle social studies and science subject matter to be untrue. For example, a variety of special educators have found that mentally retarded learners are quite capable of learning scientific concepts (Corrick 1981; Keller 1983; Welliver 1980) and of applying what they have learned to solving real-life problems (Corrick 1981). Likewise, it has been demonstrated that social studies programs for the mentally retarded have been successful in preparing these students for active citizenship roles in the communities in which they live (Curtis 1974, 1978). Such programs have also been shown to help create an educational environment in which these pupils may develop interest in contemporary problems, reduce dogmatic thinking, become wiser consumers, develop problem solving skills, and improve self-concept (Corrick 1981; Jenkins, Stein & Osborn 1981). These programs have thus contributed to the normalization of special-needs students and are relevant to the future life success of these individuals when they exit school as adults. For these reasons social studies and science should be included in the academic curriculums of mildly mentally retarded learners.

THE SOCIAL STUDIES CURRICULUM

☐ ☐ Social studies is primarily concerned with the preparation of citizens who are capable of assuming responsibility for themselves and their community (Ochoa

& Shuster 1980). If upon leaving school mentally retarded learners are expected to assume this responsibility, then the special-education curriculum must provide learning experiences designed to prepare them for it. The social studies curriculum for mentally retarded learners should focus on issues and problems of the students' local community as well as provide instruction in citizenship (Osborn, Curlin & Hill 1979; Curtis 1978; Sorgman, Stout-Hensen & Perry 1979).

☐ Components of the Social Studies Curriculum

The goal of the social studies curriculum for mildly mentally retarded learners should be the same as for their nonretarded peers: to prepare students for responsible, involved citizenship in a democratic society (Curtis & Shaver 1980). In order to accomplish this goal, the learner must gain expertise in the following competency areas (Sorgman, Stout-Hensen & Perry 1979):

1. Develop full citizenship which includes participating in civic and community enterprises.
2. Gain an accurate picture of social reality in the community.
3. Gain tolerance for the individual differences of others.
4. Develop a positive, healthy, and resilient self-concept.

In order to operationalize these goals into more accessible behaviors, these goals have been partitioned into a four-part social studies curriculum (Osborne 1979). According to this model, the social studies curriculum contains four components: *knowledge, skills, values,* and *social participation.*

Knowledge
Knowledge provides for the understanding of basic social studies concepts which will allow for the eventual generalization, transfer, and application of these concepts when the other goal areas of the social studies curriculum are encountered (McKinney, Larkens, Ford & Davis 1983; Yoho 1985). Concepts to be acquired in the knowledge area include the family, neighborhood, social groups, the roles which individuals play within a social group, cooperation, interdependence of group members, social living arrangements, and handling social conflict (Ochoa & Shuster 1980). These concepts are usually introduced in the primary/intermediate school years and are reinforced and expanded upon during the secondary school social studies experience.

Skills
In the skill areas of the social studies curriculum, students are expected to acquire competence in three main areas: thinking skills, data processing skills, and human relations skills (Ochoa & Shuster 1980). Thinking skills include the ability to gather appropriate and necessary information and to form conclusions about social situations. They include

1. Asking for information, taking surveys of others, or soliciting opinions of others.
2. Separating fact from opinion and fact from fiction.
3. Forming a conclusion on the basis of data collected.
4. Operating on those conclusions in a consistent manner.

Data processing skills are skills such as map, globe, and graph skills, including the ability to orient a map and note direction, recognize map distances, locate places on maps, and read map symbols. Human relation skills involve the ability to listen, to trust and be trusted by others, to communicate effectively and to possess empathy with others. These human relation skills are extremely important in the social success of mentally retarded students in relationships with nonretarded peers (Asher, Hymel & Renshaw 1982; Asher & Renshaw 1981; Gresham 1983; Luftig 1983, c1986). Some researchers have gone so far as to suggest that these skills (rather than academic achievement or other school areas) are the greatest predictors in the success of mentally retarded students in mainstreamed settings (Gresham 1982; Luftig 1983, c1986).

Values

In order to be complete individuals and social beings, people need to possess values and make decisions that are consistent with these values (Howe & Howe 1975; Ochoa & Shuster 1980; Osborn et al. 1979). The development of values is dependent on the acquisition of a number of processes and skills, including: identifying and becoming aware of one's true feelings; using one's values to help in the decision making process; creating alternative courses of action; predicting the consequences from one's decisions and actions; and using values to justify decisions that have been made. The topic of values will be discussed further later in this chapter.

Social Participation Skills

Social participation skills are those which allow an individual to become an effective citizen. Such participation involves the taking of social action based on one's social values (Osborn et. al. 1979). In acquiring social participation skills, students typically examine actual problems in their immediate social environment and decide what to do about them. Such experiences provide opportunities for the development of leadership skills and group membership responsibilities, and allow students to learn that by their actions they can influence the social environment.

☐ Optimizing Success in the Social Studies Curriculum

How might mastery of knowledge, skills, values, and social participation be made appropriate for mildly mentally retarded learners? Ochoa and Shuster (1980) have developed some instructional "tips" for each of these goal levels. They include

Knowledge

1. Use concrete, three-dimensional, real-world instructional materials.
2. Minimize the amount of required reading.
3. Present ideas in sequenced, orderly fashion.

Skills

1. Keep tasks simple with clear, uncomplicated instructions.
2. Consider the receptive language skills in determining skills to be learned.
3. Use positive reinforcement for completion of social studies projects.
4. Use individualized teaching techniques.
5. Use modeling and role playing in the social studies curriculum.
6. Provide ample activities for practice and transfer in the social studies curriculum.

Values

1. Use the child's own environment to help define values.
2. Use meaningful social examples.

Social Participation

1. Use real-life experiences with the child.
2. Use the child's immediate environment as the basis of the social studies curriculum followed by gradual expansion of the curriculum to less familiar environments.

APPROACHES TO TEACHING SOCIAL STUDIES

☐ ☐ There are basically three approaches to teaching social studies. These are the *textbook*, the *inquiry*, and the *eclectic* approaches.

☐ The Textbook Approach

In the textbook approach, students use a commercially available text series with a predetermined social studies curriculum. While materials and lessons are provided in the textbook approach, it should be pointed out that by using texts the teacher loses the opportunity for individualizing the social studies curriculum since that curriculum is defined by the textbook author. Additionally, student success in using social studies is overwhelmingly dependent on the pupils' reading and language abilities, typical areas of deficiency for mildly mentally retarded learners (Johnson & Vardian 1973; Lundstrum 1976). In fact, even in those social studies texts that claim to have made allowances for special learners, the material contained in the texts is heavily loaded with reading materials, concepts, and vocabulary beyond the expertise of many handicapped learners (Ochoa & Shuster 1980).

Because of problems of appropriateness of social studies textbooks for mentally retarded learners in terms of content and reading level, the special-education teacher should exercise great care in choosing a textbook series. Additionally, some of the material found in social studies texts may need to be rewritten for students (Potter 1978). Whenever possible, published or teacher-made study guides, inventories, and comprehension aids should be used with social studies texts (Potter 1978; Schneider & Brown 1980). Finally, the teacher may wish to have related pictures accompany social studies text as well as present material simultaneously in the auditory and visual modes by recording social studies textbook materials (Downey 1980; Tyo 1980).

☐ The Inquiry Approach

The inquiry approach is concerned with using social studies to teach active life-relevant problem solving (Curtis & Shaver 1980; Kelly 1979). For example, using the inquiry approach, the teacher might pose a problem to students regarding a relevant neighborhood problem or issue and ask students to solve the problem using what they have learned in social studies. Students would then apply their knowledge, skills, and values in generating viable solutions to the problem.

The inquiry approach has the advantage of making social studies relevant and interesting to students. It also helps students apply the skills they have learned in real-life situations. On the negative side, there is some question as to whether mildly mentally retarded students are able to acquire the sophisticated skills and cognitive complexity needed for the inquiry approach to succeed. Nevertheless, it would seem that mentally retarded learners should be given the opportunity to use the inquiry approach. Such an approach can be successful with mentally retarded learners if the teacher is careful to structure the learning environment so as to optimize the chances for problem solving success (Curtis & Shaver 1980).

☐ The Eclectic Approach

The eclectic approach uses a combination of the textbook/lecture and inquiry methods in teaching social studies. In this approach, the teacher supplements textual and lecture materials with relevant and interesting real-life problem solving situations. One such way to supplement the social studies program is to use newspapers and other media (e.g., television and film) to develop special topics of interest to students (Gregory 1979). In using the eclectic approach, the teacher is on the constant lookout to blend techniques, content, and materials in order to make interesting lessons.

THE LONG-TERM INSTRUCTIONAL UNIT

☐ ☐ The real-life nature of social studies can lend itself easily to the long-term instructional unit. Such an approach is extremely relevant for both elementary and secondary students. In creating a long-term instructional unit to include social studies, the teacher includes activities that take in skills needed in the mastery of knowledge, values, and social participation.

Figure 10.1 contains some sample topics germane to social studies taken from long-term units. Notice how topics appropriate for both elementary and secondary students are easily generated. Figure 10.2 contains sample lesson plans from two long-term instructional units as they relate to social studies.

CONTENT IN THE SOCIAL STUDIES CURRICULUM

☐ Elementary Grades

Social studies are particularly appropriate for mildly mentally retarded learners at the elementary-school level (Chase & John 1972; Ochoa & Shuster 1980). It is

FIGURE 10.1 Sample Social Studies Long-Term Instructional Unit Topics

Topic
1. *Finding and Keeping a Job*
   Related Social Studies Topics
   > How do people in other cities, states and countries work?
   > How would I live if I lived in another country?
   > Other types of money

2. *My Family*
   Related Social Studies Topics
   > What are families like in other countries and other nations?
   > What are extended families?
   > How do other cultures treat the elderly?

3. *Your Rights as a Citizen*

4. *Getting Around Your Community*
   Related Social Studies Topics
   > Using Maps
   > Public Transportation
   > What types of transportation are there in other communities and cultures?

FIGURE 10.2   Sample Social Studies Lessons Taken from Long-Term Instructional Units

Topic: <u>Planning a Nutritious Menu</u>

Core Area: <u>Social Studies: Foods of Other Countries</u>   Duration: <u>2 hr field trip</u>

Behavioral Objectives	Activity	Materials	Evaluation
Students will identify ten foods from other countries with 100 percent accuracy. Students will correctly identify the food group of ten foreign foods without error.	Passages will be read and discussed in class. The class will then go on a field trip to a supermarket and collect foods and discuss the different kinds of foods eaten in other parts of the world. The teacher will then share some of the foreign foods that were prepared ahead of time, giving the students the opportunity to taste new and different foods.	Selected reading passage "Around the World in Eighty Dishes" (L. Blanche) Second passage: "What the World Eats" (H. H. Webster)	Criteria: primarily bringing the correct food and following directions, all of which are evaluated according to the teacher's satisfaction.

Topic: <u>Opening a Savings and Checking Account</u>

Core Area: <u>Social Studies Lesson: Money of Other Lands</u>   Time: <u>2 hours</u>

Objectives	Activities	Materials	Evaluation
Students will identify currency from five foreign countries without error.	Students will take a field trip to a local bank. The bank officer will explain how other countries have different money and show five currencies to students.	Bank Bank Officer Foreign Currency	Student identification of currency

essential, however, that the social studies curriculum be directly applicable and relevant to the personal lives of students and that the subject matter be related by direct experience to the specific environment in which they live. In fact, for young mentally retarded learners, it has been suggested that the social studies curriculum begin with materials most personal and relatable to students' lives and then work outwards toward less familiar cultures and environments (Ochoa & Shuster 1980).

FIGURE 10.3   A Framework of the Social Studies Curriculum Which Moves from Most Familiar/Personal to Less Familiar/Less Personal

Topic

1. *Local Environment*: The home, the store, service, airport, etc.
2. *Family School and Community Life*: My family, our school, neighbors, etc.
3. *Community Studies*: Community workers, public services, transportation, communication.
4. *Neighboring Communities:* Different kinds of communities, transportation and communication. Comparing our communities with other nearby communities.
5. *Our State*: Our state in early times, our state today, agriculture and industry in our area.
6. *Living in America*: Discovery and exploration of America, colonial life, pioneer life, living today in America. Rights and responsibilities of citizenship.
7. *Global Geography:* Other cultures of the world, shared humanity, tolerance of cultural differences.

From W.L. Chase & M.T. John (1972). *A guide for the elementary social studies teacher* (2nd ed.). Boston: Allyn and Bacon.

Figure 10.3 shows the framework of a social studies curriculum that follows the pattern of moving from most familiar and most personal to less familiar and less personal (Chase & John 1972). Within a given topic, the flow of material is also from concrete and known to abstract and unknown.

Notice in Figure 10.3 how the course of topics moves from the child's culture to other communities and other cultures both in the United States and in other countries. The purpose of this cross-cultural exposure is to show students that other types of families, communities, and societies exist beside the one in which the student resides. Such exposure may have the positive effect of facilitating tolerance for cultural diversity and demonstrating to students their membership in the "family of man."

Figure 10.4 shows a typical social studies unit which might be used for teaching cultural diversity at the elementary level (Chase & John 1972). Notice how each of the activities shows the similarities that bind people together as well as the rich quality of their diversity. This concept is reinforced as it is demonstrated that people in other cultures carry out the same basic roles and functions as people in the child's home community.

☐ Map and Globe Skills in the Social Studies Curriculum

The need for map and globe skills in the social studies learning curriculum has been demonstrated by a recent experiment conducted by a newspaper. Secondary students in a large metropolitan city were asked to find their city and state on a map of the United States. A sizable portion of the students could not complete this rudimentary task. Nor could they find other states and cities such as Califor-

FIGURE 10.4   A Social Studies Unit which Demonstrates Cultural Diversity

Living in an African Community

A. Location
   1. Relation to our community
      a. Direction
      b. Distance
   2. Relation to urban and rural
   3. Relation to world

There are many different communities on the earth. It takes longer to go to some than to others because of the distance and also because of the way chosen to travel.

The community is located on a revolving sphere.

The most accurate map of the whole earth is a globe. The globe shows the large and masses and the large bodies of water. Some globes show the rivers, mountains, and other physical features. Some show each country in a different color.

B. Setting
   1. Topography
      a. Effect on climate
      b. Effect on population
   2. Climate
      a. Relationship to economic activity
      b. Advantages and disadvantages
   3. Natural vegetation and animals

Topography & climate of the earth influence to some extent the way in which people live & work.

Some communities are in farming regions, some are fishing villages, some are in the forests, some in places where there are many factories.

C. Means of Earning a Living
   1. Agriculture
   2. Fishing
   3. Industry
      a. Boatbuilding
      b. Domestic
         (1) Leatherwork
         (2) Jewelry
         (3) Weaving

Customs and ways of doing things often outlive their usefulness.

Farmers, miners, fishermen, or factory workers use the earth in different ways. Some communities have not changed much for a long time. Some are changing more quickly.

D. Family Life
   1. Members
   2. Division of labor
   3. Dress
   4. Food
   5. Health & sanitation
   6. Entertainment
   7. Holidays

Different patterns of family life are found in different communities.

Human beings everywhere have similar needs and desires; their ways of meeting them differ according to their cultures. Ways of living different from our town are not necessarily worse or better than ours – they are merely different.

Customs and ways of doing things often outlive their usefulness.

Because of limited resources and man's ever-increasing needs, each community must make the wisest possible use of all its human and natural resources.

E. Education
   1. Informal
   2. Formal
      a. Primary school
      b. Middle school
      c. High school

Every community encounters problems in providing certain public services.

(continued)

FIGURE 10.4 (continued)

F. Creative Expression
   1. Music
   2. Dance
   3. Crafts

Nearly all communities provide some opportunities for the self-expression of their members and for their pleasure and satisfaction through their culture.

G. Government
   1. Tribal
   2. National

Rules and regulations are part of community life everywhere.

Local forms of government can vary from community to community within the state as well as from country to country.

Governments throughout the world vary greatly in the degree to which they provide assistance to dependent children and the aged-two groups whose members may be the victims of an inadequate distribution of income.

H. Transportation & Trade
   1. Trade
      a. Interdependence
   2. Means of transportation
      a. Land
      b. Water
      c. Air

The community gets food, clothing, and other things needed from other communities. The people of most communities trade with people of other places.

Communities in the world tend to become more closely related as transportation and communications improve.

I. Beliefs
   1. Religious
   2. Superstitious

Self-discipline enables people to live and work together in harmony, and it can be more effective than external sanctions.

From W.L. Chase & M.T. John (1972). *A guide for the elementary social studies teacher* (2nd ed.). Boston: Allyn and Bacon.

nia and Los Angeles. It was concluded that at least for the population which was tested, even the most basic map reading skills were sadly lacking.

Kohn (1953) suggests the following map and globe skills be taught to students:

1. The ability to orient a map and to note map directions.
2. The ability to recognize the scale of a map and to compute distances.
3. The ability to locate places on maps and globes.
4. The ability to express relative location on maps.
5. The ability to read map symbols.
6. The ability to compare maps and make inferences.

Each of these skills or abilities should be introduced at the readiness/ elementary level and then be extended into the secondary level with associated increases in complexity. By way of example, Ellis (1977) suggests a set of eight activities designed to teach map and globe reading skills while at the same time making learning of the subject matter fun and interesting. Each succeeding activity set represents a more sophisticated link in the map-reading hierarchy. These activities include:

1. Exploring the child's local environment from a spatial perspective.
2. Creating a traverse map.
3. Manipulating scales of maps.
4. Constructing base maps of the child's environment.
5. Hypothesizing information from map data.
6. Creating your own aerial maps of models.
7. Translating graphic data to maps.
8. Translating oral or written information to maps.

Figure 10.5 contains examples of activities which may be used to teach the eight sets of map activities. Notice the activities move from the concrete and familiar to the abstract and less familiar. Children begin by using materials and objects readily found in their environment in hands-on activities (such as signs, arrows, and cardinal directions) and then move to relatively abstract and unfamiliar ones such as maps and globes. This transition must be gradual and sequentially ordered if it is to be successful for mentally retarded learners. The special-education teacher must be careful to use as much as possible materials with which students can relate and keep within their frame of reference.

In teaching geography skills, Ochoa and Shuster (1980) suggest that whenever possible raised, graphic-relief maps be used to provide mentally retarded learners with the opportunity to concretely touch topography such as mountains, valleys, and plateaus. They also suggest that relief maps be placed on the floor so that water or other liquids can be poured on the highlands in order to demon-

FIGURE 10.5   Map Activities

A. Visualizing the Local Environment from a Spatial Perspective
   To help students to participate in the transition from reality to abstraction in representing space, you might involve them in the following progression:
   1. On a walking tour of the area surrounding the school note various landmarks, e.g., the school, businesses, houses, streets, parks.
   2. With only a camera and a roll of film, you and the students can put together a "slide tour" of the area surrounding the school in which various landmarks are portrayed.
   3. View the school area from some elevated perspective, e.g., a hill or a tall building. Take some pictures and review them in class.
   4. Make a model of the area from cardboard and paper. Again this can be done by the class or small groups can make several.
   5. Take another walk around the area. Have each student take a dittoed map. As landmarks are sighted, have students point to them on the map.
B. Plot a Traverse Map
   A traverse is a map representation of the aerial association of certain variables in a given area (e.g., houses or other buildings). For example, you could ask the question: What type and how many houses are on Wilson Street? We would then create a traverse map to answer the question.

(continued)

FIGURE 10.5 (continued)

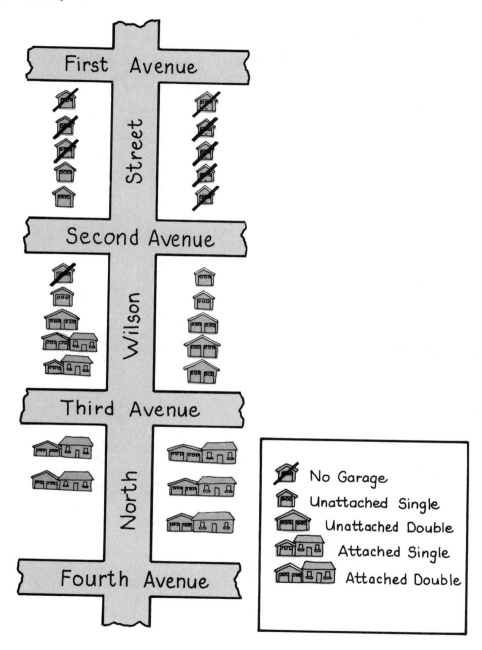

(continued)

FIGURE 10.5 (continued)

Constructing Base Maps

Students can produce original and highly accurate large-scale maps by placing tracing paper over an aerial photograph and tracing roads, cities, waterforms, wooded areas, farmland, etc.

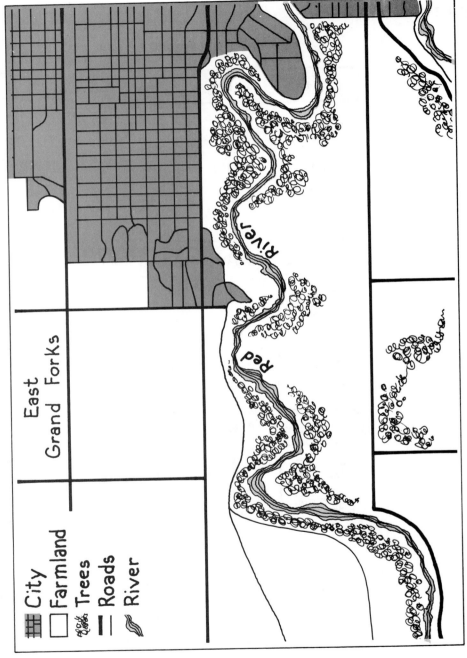

Legend:
- City
- Farmland
- Trees
- Roads
- River

East Grand Forks

Red River

(continued)

FIGURE 10.5 (continued)
Translating Oral or Written Information into a Map

This activity is designed to help students to visualize oral or written information spatially. Any story or written information that includes directions for traveling around a given space will do. Here is an example. You and your students can develop others.

> One morning Little Red Riding Hood decided to visit her sick grandmother. After she left her house, she went to the muffin man's for some muffins for her grandmother. Then she went to the flower lady's for some nice fresh flowers to take to her grandmother. Next Little Red Riding Hood entered the south entrance to the woods and walked along the path toward the woodcutter's house, which was west of her house. When she reached the woodcutter's house, she stopped for a drink of water. She then walked north to feed some squirrels, and from there she went by the most direct path to her grandmother's house.

Such a representation is shown below.

From A.K. Ellis (1977). *Teaching and learning elementary social studies.* Boston: Allyn and Bacon.

strate topography to students. In such ways, the relative representativeness of maps and topography can be made more realistic.

It may also be facilitative for students for the teacher to tie in the social studies and art programs. Maps can be constructed and cut out, and visual and kinesthetic modalities thus combined. In addition, maps can be covered with acetate and marked repeatedly with grease pens and pencils so that students can have a true hands-on relationship with maps. Finally games can be constructed or purchased (e.g., Game of the States published by Milton Bradley Inc.) in which students can learn about geographic regions on maps through a simulation approach.

SOCIAL STUDIES AT THE SECONDARY LEVEL

☐ ☐ The social studies curriculum for secondary pupils should be concerned with imparting the skills and values of citizenship in the child's culture and community, and within the larger framework of a democratic society. As such, the goals of the social studies curriculum for secondary students should include the following (Chase & John 1972; Osborne et al. 1979)

1. Awareness of the importance of meeting the basics and extending the essentials of life to all individuals.
2. Acceptance of the ideals of democracy and the putting of those ideals into practice.
3. Practicing human relations which are consistent with ideals of a democratic society.
4. Recognizing social problems and making attempts to solve them through participation in the democratic process.
5. Possessing the knowledge, skills, and abilities needed for active citizenship which will allow the student to be accepted in the community as a responsible citizen.

☐ Being a Good Citizen

Appropriate citizenship training contains four basic components (Civic Education Project-National Council for Social Studies 1980):

1. Democracy entails respect for the individual. Others should have the same rights and privileges which we claim for ourselves and all people should be allowed to develop to the best of their potential.
2. Living in a democracy entails cooperating with others. People and communities are interdependent—we need one another. Thus we must work

together for the common good, in our school, in our community, and in our nation.

3. Good citizenship means critical and logical thinking that will result in a positive approach to social action. Issues should be discussed intelligently on the basis of fact, not emotions or prejudices.

4. Citizenship entails obligations and duties as well as rights and privileges. Each individual has a duty to participate in the civic activities that contribute to a successful democratic society.

Taken together, these statements imply that such a social studies program for mentally retarded students at the secondary level should contain strong emphasis from two main areas: citizenship education and the ability to treat others fairly and without prejudice.

☐ Citizenship Training

A number of citizenship areas and activities are appropriate for students at the secondary level. Kokaska and Brolin (1985) have identified six main areas of citizenship that should be covered with mentally retarded pupils in the social studies program. These are

1. Understanding basic local government and local laws.
2. Understanding basic American government.
3. The rights and responsibilities of citizenship.
4. Registering to vote and voting in elections.
5. Selective service information.
6. The law and the citizen; handling contact and questioning by law enforcement personnel.

☐ Basic Local Government

Under the subjects of basic local government and local laws, students would learn about the various local government agencies and officials in their community. The roles of those officials and the ways that they affect the lives of individual citizens would be discussed. The people who control the schools, who run the parks, who are responsible for garbage pickup and disposal, who make local laws and who are responsible for the dozens of other community services that we have come to expect would be met, and students would learn how such decisions are made. Discussions of local laws and the relevance these laws have on the lives of students would be stimulated. Part of the curriculum would be an investigation into how local laws are made and changed. Field trips could be made to city or town council meetings to show the lawmaking process in action as well as demonstrate to students how individual citizens can have input into the making or modifying of local laws. Civic leaders in the community should be used as important resource persons who can make the lawmaking and decision-making processes of local government come alive for students. Students could write letters or otherwise have personal input to their local legislators and public servants about local issues that affect their lives.

☐ Basic American Government

Under the heading of basic American government would be the structure of the state and federal governments including the three branches of government: administrative, judicial, and legislative. Students could follow how a bill becomes law, tracing the process from the time the bill is written until it is signed into law (there is an excellent cartoon learning film entitled "I'm Just a Bill" available on this topic). Students could contact their state and federal legislators regarding the branches of government. Congresspersons for the legislative state and federal district would typically not be able to speak to a class of students, but often they will send a representative from their offices to meet with students or will at the least communicate with students in writing.

☐ Rights and Responsibilities of Citizenship

Citizenship yields not only rights; it also carries serious responsibilities. In the section on citizenship rights and responsibilities, pupils would learn and practice the responsibilities of voting, paying taxes, obeying laws, and participating as an informed citizen in the democratic process. How each of these responsibilities contributes to the social welfare would be discussed and demonstrated. Students, for example, can investigate how their tax dollars are spent, and how participation in local civic affairs can have a positive effect on the quality of life for all the citizens in the community.

Voting

Registering to vote and actually voting are subjects which are very important subcomponents to the social studies curriculum for students. Current statistics indicate that in many national elections, the percentage of eligible voters who actually vote is slightly over a majority; participation in local and so-called minor elections can fall to as low as 25 percent. This means, in effect, that in many elections 25 percent of the citizens make the decisions that will affect all of us. Thus, training students in the importance and the mechanics of responsible voting is extremely important. The League of Women Voters has available excellent learning materials on the voting process including mock voting booths and ballots. They will usually be willing to send a representative to demonstrate voting procedures for students. Mock voting can be tied in to conducting a straw election in the class to see how a given candidate would do if the students could vote. (This is fun particularly for students doing national elections, where the candidates for president have high visibility and interest.) Issues that appear on ballots would also be presented to students, who would receive instruction on how to gather information and vote on them prior to stepping into the voting booth.

Selective Service

It is currently federal law that all males register at their local post office for the selective service upon reaching their eighteenth birthday. Failure to register is a violation of federal law subject to fines and/or imprisonment. Explanation of the selective service procedure and instruction on how to register is therefore an important subcomponent for males. Additionally, during this subcomponent, information can be presented regarding the military as a career for both men and women. Trips can be made to the recruiting offices of various military branches or recruitment professionals will visit the class to meet with students.

Law Enforcement

The last subcategory is dealing with law enforcement officials. A significant number of students hold law officers in contempt. For others they evoke fear and anxiety. Much of the information which students receive regarding law enforcement comes from largely inaccurate popular television shows and movies. Thus, students need to receive relevant and accurate information as to what law enforcement officers can and cannot do. Additionally, students need to learn about their right to legal counsel when it is necessary and how they can find and engage such counsel. A variety of useful and interesting films exist on such topics as search and seizure, the Miranda laws, and the need for search warrants. Additionally, field trips to police stations and courtrooms to see the law enforcement process in action will usually prove interesting and relevant to pupils. What is important in this subcomponent is that students replace popular media-induced beliefs with accurate information about the law enforcement process.

TEACHING A VALUES AND BELIEFS CURRICULUM

☐ ☐ Most of the time when we think of curriculum we think of factual information and skills. There is, however, another type of curriculum that is hardly touched upon in school, the *affective* curriculum that deals with how the student feels about situations in life as well as the beliefs and values the individual brings into all life situations.

Values and beliefs have been shown to be an extremely strong predictor of how people will behave in many and diverse social situations (Howe & Howe 1975; Festinger 1962; Luftig 1983b). In fact, when presented with information or data which is in conflict with their belief and value system, most people will do as much as possible to close the gap between what they believe and the information presented to them—often by denying the validity of the data or information just presented (Festinger 1962). Thus the development of a healthy, realistic, objective, and non-prejudicial belief system is important in healthy emotional functioning of students and affects students' ability to participate successfully as a valuable group member in society.

A variety of educators have advocated a belief system curriculum as part of the social studies program for students, including mentally retarded pupils (Raths, et al., Harmin & Simon 1978; Howe & Howe 1975). Known as a *values clarification* curriculum, such activities are designed to help students reach the following goals (Raths, et al. 1966):

1. Encourage children to make choices freely.
2. Help them discover and examine alternatives.
3. Help students weigh the consequences of each alternative.
4. Encourage children to discover what they prize and value in their lives.
5. Give students opportunities to behave in ways consistent with their values and to judge the consequences of their actions.
6. Encourage them to behave consistently in accordance with their values.

Value clarification is not an imparting or imposing of the teacher's belief system on the child. The teacher's role is not to moralize or tell the students how they should act, even if the students' beliefs and values are personally repugnant to the teacher. Rather, value clarification allows students to get in touch with their own feelings and beliefs and helps them see the consequences of those beliefs when they are translated into behaviors.

☐ Techniques of Value Clarification

There are a variety of techniques the special education teacher can use to help students develop and/or modify their values. One such method, for example, is the *value continuum* technique. Suppose this issue arose or was presented to students:

John intensely dislikes Hispanic individuals. Juan has some tickets to the circus and he asks John to go with him. What should John do?

What follows are two poles to a continuum connected by a line:

Tell Juan he still dislikes him and tell him to stuff his tickets	————————————	Change his mind about Juan and go to the circus with him.

In the value continuum exercise, a line is drawn between the two polar responses. Students then take one of the two extreme responses or they seek a compromise response somewhere in between. The various consequences of each action are role played and/or discussed by students to explore the consequences of each action.

Another activity that may be carried out to aid value clarification is the use of value sheets. A value sheet is a piece of paper that contains provocative questions about a subject or issue like those listed in Figure 10.6. After being presented with the questions, each student answers them as honestly as possible without conferring with any other class members. The student responses are then listed and acted out and/or discussed by the group. Notice that the student

FIGURE 10.6   A Sample Value Clarification Sheet

Illegal Behavior

Directions: Write out answers to the questions below. Later, you will have a chance to discuss your answers with a small group of students. You need not reveal your answers to anyone if you choose not to do so.

New Rochelle, N.Y., Oct. 27*—When the red light turns to green and reads "Thank you" at any one of the automatic toll booths of the New England Thruway here, it does not always mean what it says. At least not if the motorist has short-changed the machine or dropped lead washers or foreign coins into it.

The state police reported today after a two-week campaign against toll cheaters that they had arrested 151 persons. They have been fined in City Court from $25 each for first offenders to $250 for multiple offenders.

Lieut. Thomas F. Darby reported that the offenders included a clergyman, a doctor, a dentist, an atomic scientist, lawyers and quite a number of engineers, advertising men and salesmen.

What the offenders did not know, the lieutenant said, was that new toll-booth glass with one-way vision prevented them from seeing watchful troopers inside.

Neither did they know, the lieutenant continued, that the license plate of each offender was recorded, along with the objects he dropped into the machine.

1. Under what circumstances would *you* try to pass a toll machine without properly paying the fee? Check the most applicable reply below.
——Only if I was certain that I would not be caught.
——If I felt I had a good chance of not getting caught.
——Never, under any circumstances.
——Only if I needed the money desperately, like for family food supplies.
——(Write any other choice that better suits you:)
2. Among the 151 persons arrested, there was only one clergyman, doctor, dentist, and atomic scientist. On the other hand, there were several lawyers, engineers, advertising men, and salesmen. Do you think this means that persons in the first group of occupations are more honest than those in the second group? Discuss.
3. Do you think that this behavior is serious? Do you think these persons are likely to be dishonest in other ways that would be more serious? Discuss.
4. Return to Question 1 and put an X by the reply that you would make to this: Under what circumstances would you keep a dime that was returned in error in a phone booth?
5. How do you account for any differences in your answers to Questions 1 and 4, if any?
6. Are you clear about how you feel about illegal behavior? Discuss.

*Date line "New Rochelle." *The New York Times*, October 28, 1961. © 1961 by The New York Times Company. Reprinted by permission.

From L. Raths, M. Harmin, & S. Simon (1978). *Values and teaching* (2nd ed.). Columbus, OH: Charles E. Merrill.

responses are elicited before they have had time to confer with each other on possible answers. Thus each student's answer to the question represents the individual's true feelings on the subject without distortion based on peer pressure—active versus passive value clarification.

Other activities designed to aid in value clarification include using forced-choice formats in which students must pick one alternative or the other, teaming up with other students in the class who hold the same beliefs and role playing and/or defending those beliefs, and analyzing the consequences of acting in accordance with one's beliefs. Simon, Howe & Kirschenbaum (1978) have identified seventy-nine strategies and activities designed to aid in value clarification, most of them applicable for use with mentally retarded students at the secondary level. The interested reader is referred to the Simon et al. text.

AVAILABLE COMMERCIAL SOCIAL STUDIES PROGRAMS

☐ ☐ There are a variety of commercially available social studies programs that can be made appropriate for use with mentally retarded learners with only slight to moderate modification. The advantage to working with such programs is that the activities, curriculum, and materials are provided to the teacher of special-needs students. In fact, much of the curriculum is stated in behavioral objective terms so that the teacher can readily assess the behavior to be mastered and can ascertain with little ambiguity whether or not such mastery has occurred. The major disadvantage to such programs is that the authors could not have possibly individualized the program for particular classes and/or special-needs learners. Thus the major responsibility of individualization and adaptation for particular mentally retarded learners will fall on the classroom teacher. In all probability these programs will not be able to be adopted in toto for every student in the class. Instead, the curriculum, activities, and materials contained in these programs will need to be carefully screened and studied by the teacher with adoption and adaptation of materials occurring on the basis of relevancy to the individual student's life environment, learning style, and developmental/cognitive level.

Multiple Activities and Projects for Social Studies   (Developmental Learning Materials, Niles, IL.) This program is a set of materials that deal with maps and globes. Students engage in a variety of experiences in which they learn geographical features, weather patterns, historical information, and cultural events of different geographic locations. The program comes with a set of twelve extremely large maps that are heavily and easily marked with key features highlighted. Students become actively involved in hands-on map activities as they work with the maps. A detailed teacher guidebook includes specific lessons and activities. Activities can be presented in such a way as to place a minimum of emphasis on requisite reading and writing skills of students, thus making it appropriate for low-reading pupils.

Target American History   (Mafex Associates, Johnstown, PA.) This is a program in workbook/worksheet form that deals with the major periods in United States history from discovery of America to the 1980s. The teacher's guide claims that the lessons and workbook materials are written in simplistic format but it appears that a moderate level of reading sophistication is needed for success on the program and that this factor must be taken into account in adopting this program for pupils. The activities included in the program are interesting and varied, ranging from crossword puzzles, word puzzles, fill-ins and other features. A time line for each historical period designed to make the concept of history more concrete for learners is included. As each historical period is studied, students cut out special markers and paste them over their time line so as to gain conceptualization of where each period fits on the continuum of history. Such a feature, while useful, will only be successful insofar as the student understands the relatively abstract concept of the time line; this conceptualization must be assessed by the classroom teacher.

Insights About America   (Opportunities for Learning, Chatsworth, CA.) This program is designed for students who possess a reading level at about the fourth to fifth grade level while possessing an interest level at the upper junior high and senior high school level. Thus it appears to be appropriate for many older individual students, but the fourth grade level prerequisite should be kept in mind when deciding on program adoption. American history is covered in three major areas: the period of the revolutionary war, the civil war, and the years of the western frontier territories. Since only the years up to the taming of the frontier west are covered, the program lacks immediate relevancy to students. A large variety of interesting materials are presented in a total of forty-eight booklets, sixteen booklets at each level and such topics as the Pony Express, the lives of major civil war leaders, and the life style of Indians are covered. Much of the conceptual material is presented in a cartoon format that may prove interesting to students. A detailed teacher's guide contains activities, follow-up activities, and stimulating discussion questions.

TEACHING SCIENCE

□ □ Traditionally, a science curriculum for mentally retarded students has been rare or even nonexistent (Keller 1983; Welliver 1980). Such exclusion has been largely based on three beliefs about mentally retarded pupils: that science is irrelevant to their lives and the normalization process, that they are incapable of benefitting from science instruction, and that they are a danger to themselves and to others when using scientific equipment (Cohen & Staley 1982; Keller 1983).

For the most part, these assumptions have been found to be untrue. Keller (1983), for example, argues that science instruction for handicapped pupils is relevant to the extent that it helps students learn how logically and systematically to solve problems. She asserts that such instruction, if handled properly, can teach students how to learn the information they need in order properly to answer relevant questions in their lives.

As for the belief that mentally retarded students cannot handle the rigor of science instruction, Davies and Ball (1978) tested the validity of this argument in a controlled experiment with 414 mildly mentally retarded students at four educational grade levels. Their results indicated that "mentally retarded children can be challenged by natural phenomena in the environment and can benefit from the experiences of observation, exploration, investigation, and problem solving." (p. 281).

Finally, a variety of educators have found that mentally retarded pupils are quite capable of appropriately using scientific equipment without endangering themselves, others, or the equipment itself (Maloney & DeLucchi 1980; Keller 1983). As we shall see, using materials and equipment that are within the life experiences of the learners, and designing equipment that is readily manipulatable by them, are keys to science instruction for the mentally retarded.

RELEVANCY OF THE SCIENCE CURRICULUM

☐ ☐ As in the other academic subject areas, the key concept in a science curriculum appropriate for mildly mentally retarded pupils is *relevancy*. This means that what is taught in science must have a direct relationship to the lives of students out of school especially as it relates to the normalization process. There is little purpose in having pupils memorize formulas and chemical symbols. Such instruction probably provides students with little useful information and ability save for being prepared for college chemistry courses. Rather, students would be much better served by systematically studying the environment in which they live and investigating the impact their actions may have upon that environment.

Grant (1975) has asserted that a sound science curriculum for mildly mentally retarded should contain the following goals:

1. It should demonstrate to the student that an individual can exert some degree of control over the immediate environment.
2. It should foster a pattern of success in pupils.
3. It should demonstrate that science can be a lifelong and interesting endeavor that can be utilized in real-life situations and can be a lifelong leisure activity or result in a career.

4. It should help foster an empathy for living things among pupils.
5. It should help the child develop a sense of responsibility for the environment and demonstrate actions designed to improve and protect it.

STRATEGIES FOR INCREASING THE RELEVANCY OF SCIENCE FOR LEARNERS

☐ ☐ In order to increase the relevancy of the science curriculum and make it more lifelike, Welliver (1980) has suggested some strategies. These include

1. Emphasize *inquiry* and *process:* Allow for individual and small-group science learning. Try to avoid large-group demonstration science projects where the teacher does all the talking and demonstrating while students are reduced to passive observers. Allow each child to investigate and explore a particular question, problem, or phenomenon, making sure that these science questions are at the ability and interest level of each student. From time to time, allow students to pool their talents in small-group activities and problems. As much as possible, allow students in the group to find answers to problems themselves, offering your help and expertise only when the group reaches an impasse in the problem-solving process.

2. Use simple materials: Try to use materials in science lessons that can be found in the child's immediate environment and which are familiar to the child. Paper towels, wax paper, foil, cardboard, candles, paper cups, styrofoam, and hundreds of other commonly found and inexpensive materials may be used in science lessons; the special education teacher is limited only by his or her imagination and creativity. The key is to look at these common objects in a new light so that aluminum foil, for example, is no longer just a vehicle for wrapping food but now becomes a vehicle for teaching science. The key problem then becomes finding ways that common household objects can be aids to scientific inquiry by students. Students will not need expensive scientific laboratory equipment in order to benefit from the science curriculum. In fact such sophisticated equipment may actually intimidate students and inhibit the science inquiry process. Figure 10.7 contains a list of commonly found materials that may be used in the science curriculum while Figure 10.8 contains a short listing of resources that outline interesting and relevant science activities using commonly found materials.

3. De-emphasize factual content. The teacher should try to avoid situations where students are overwhelmed with a large body of scientific information that must be presented and mastered before the students can engage in science activities. You probably remember from your high

school biology and chemistry classes those times in which you had to absorb large amounts of factual material and information before you were allowed to engage in a usually extremely structured and controlled laboratory experiment. This is generally not a facilitative strategy to use with mentally retarded students both because it has a tendency to destroy student motivation and for the reason that such required mastering of content may prove intimidating and difficult for the pupil. It appears that a better strategy is to use an inquiry/discovery approach in which the students (under your careful guidance) discover scientific relationships by themselves. With such an approach, a minimum of information is presented prior to the science activity, and the science lesson becomes less intimidating for students.

THE MULTISENSORY APPROACH TO SCIENCE

□ □ Malone and DeLucchi (1980) have expanded upon the work of Welliver (1980) in advocating a *multisensory* rather than a *unisensory* approach to the science curriculum for mentally retarded learners. In the multisensory approach, a maximum amount of sensory input is used with a variety of concrete, experiential, hands-on activities. Additionally, a multimodal approach is taken in which as many sense modalities as possible are used in presenting material to be learned.

This multisensory approach to teaching science contains three main processes: *content accessibility, process accessibility*, and *access to manipulation*. Content accessibility refers to experiences for pupils that are concrete and experiential rather than abstract and theoretical. Activities and investigations are constructed in such a way that students discover information and scientific rela-

FIGURE 10.7 Common Materials Which Can Be Used in Science Lessons

batteries	jars and cans	rubber bands
bell wire	iron filings	rulers
baking powder	light bulbs	rubber tubes & stoppers
buzzers	litmus paper	scissors
baking soda	lemon juice	straight pins
cardboard	microscope	screw driver
compass	milk cartons	straws
candles	magnets	salt & sugar
corks	magnifying glass	spices
cornstarch	paper clips	tacks
dishes and dish pans	popsicle stick	tape
funnels	pails	thermometers
forks and spoons	pliers	tongs
flour	prisms	wire gauge
garden hose	plaster of paris	vinegar

tionships for themselves rather than being told what is happening by the teacher. Concepts are developed through experience rather than by verbal transmission from teacher to student. In addition, verbalization through reading or lecturing is kept to a minimum while other modalities such as vision, the kinesthetic modality, taste, and smell are utilized, preferably in modality combination. For example, rather than lecture students on how plants grow and have students memorize large amounts of content material, the teacher could construct activities where students manipulate seeds and observe the plant germination and growth process, investigating by feel, smell, sight, even taste, different seeds and their resulting plants. Scientific content would not even be discussed to any great length until after the experiment was completed and the students had discovered relationships about seed growth. Content would then be discussed not as some abstract process but as a set of experiences which had occurred for students as a result of concrete, hands-on activities of investigation. Figure 10.9 contains some hands-on science activities.

Process accessibility refers to the process or actions that allow students to make scientific discoveries (Malone & DeLucchi 1980). Students would have access to experimental procedures and materials that would allow them to become independent investigators in science. Process accessibility is largely contin-

FIGURE 10.8 Resources to Find Interesting Science Activities Using Commonly Found Materials

Abrnscato, J. & Hassard (1977). *The whole cosmos: Catalogue of science activities*. Santa Monica, CA: Goodyear Publishing. A great book with many interesting ideas for teaching science. Also contains information on obtaining resources.

Allison, L. (1976). *Blood and guts: A working guide to your own insides*. Boston: Little, Brown & Co. Just the title alone will capture student's attention! An excellent book which describes how the human body works. Experiments included.

Cobb, V. (1979). *More science experiments you can eat*. NY: J. B. Lippincott Co. A great title! Describes how science is related to food, eating and the kitchen. Contains experiments which students can eat!

Goldstein-Jackson, K., Rudnick, N., & Human, R. (1978). *Experiments with everyday objects: Science activities for children, parents, and teachers*. Boston: Little, Brown & Co. A useful activity book which contains excellent, easy-to-do science activities. Discusses getting parents involved in the science curriculum.

Herbert, D. (1980). *M. Wizard's supermarket science*. NY: Random House. Relates science to supermarket consumerism. Helps make science *relevant* to student's everyday lives.

Jacobson, W. J., & Bergman, A. B. (1980). *Science for children: A book for teachers*. Englewood Cliffs, NJ: Prentice-Hall. A good activity book with topics such as plants and animals, the weather and studying ourselves.

Rights, M. (1981). *Beastly neighbors: All about wild things in the city, or why earwigs make good mothers*. Boston: Little, Brown & Co. Can nature be found in the city? In this book, students will be given activities for turning the local environment into a nature observatory. A very good sourcebook.

Strongin, H. (1976). *Science on a shoestring*. Menlo Park, CA: Addison-Wesley. Designed for teachers who do not have much money or resources to create an extensive science laboratory. Contains many activities using everyday materials.

FIGURE 10.9 Some Hands-On Science Activities

Plants and Animals

1. Growing a plant from a potato
   materials: A potato, a jar, toothpicks
   procedure: (a) place a potato in a jar of water and insert toothpick so that half of the potato is immersed in the water when the toothpick rests on the jar, (b) keep the jar and potato in a dark place for a few days. After some roots have formed, place on windowsill or other light spot.

2. *Adopt-A-Tree*
   materials: A tree situated in a convenient location
   procedure: (a) select a tree for study, make frequent visits to the tree using the Observation form below.

   First Visit
   (a) What kind of tree is it?
   (b) Where is it located?
   (c) Height? (approximately)
   (d) Describe the tree: leaves, bark, fruit, buds, branches, etc.

   Later Visits
   (a) General appearance
   (b) Changes from last visit
   (c) Changes on buds, leaves, fruit, flowers, etc.
   (d) Any effects of weather?
   (e) Any effects from insects and animals?

3. *Make a Work Mark*
   materials: A shovel, a large jar, soil with mulch and decaying leaves, commercial (food for works)
   procedure:
   (a) Obtain a large jar or container for worms
   (b) Fill three/fourths full of soil, mulch and decaying leaves
   (c) Collect a dozen worms from the soil outside the school
   (d) Put worms in container, keep soil moist
   (e) Place a handful of commercial food in container— feed twice a week
   (f) Observe the worms in the environment

You and Your Body

1. How strong are your lungs?
   materials: A large basin, pail or five gallon fish tank, a gallon plastic jug, three feet of rubber tubing, a large measuring cup
   procedure:
   (a) Fill the gallon jug with water
   (b) With a hand covering the opening, invert the jug into the larger vessel also filled with water. *Do not allow air to bubble into the jar.*
   (c) Have someone hold the jug and insert the rubber tubing up into it.
   (d) Have a child take a deep breath and blow into the other end of the tubing.
   (e) With the jug still in the large tank, remove tube and place a hand over jug opening. Remove jug.
   (f) Turn jug right-side up. Using measuring cup, fill jug again. Record amount of water needed to refill the jug. This is the volume of air that the child exhaled.

2. Teeth and Tooth Decay
   materials: A set of artificial teeth, a glass of carbonated, sugared, soft-drink
   procedure: Drop the teeth in the soft drink solution. Observe for several days. What have you observed? Discuss the effects of sugar on tooth decay.

gent on finding and using materials that are familiar and within the life experience of students but that may be used in unique ways not previously thought of by students. As Malone and DeLucchi (1980) state, "we must avoid sophisticated 'black box' tools . . . that might result in a gap in the understanding of handicapped students." (p61).

Finally, access to manipulation means that the materials given to students are of sufficient size, strength, durability, and simplicity in order to be used appropriately and successfully by students. Materials that are fragile, that are so small or so rigid as to be difficult to manipulate, or that need a great deal of prior instruction in order to be used successfully can lead to frustration on the part of pupils. Rather, the science materials used in curriculum activities for students should be those that can be used naturally without a great deal of prior instruction, that are durable, and that are of appropriate length, width, and circumference so as to be easily manipulated by students. The success of a science curriculum for mentally retarded students depends in part on the adequacy of the materials used. Those materials must lead to success and satisfaction, not frustration and anxiety. Ease of manipulation of the materials used in science activities will contribute to the motivation and interest of students in this academic area.

SCIENCE PROGRAMS AND ACTIVITIES FOR MENTALLY RETARDED LEARNERS

☐ ☐ There are a variety of science curriculums, programs, and teaching strategies appropriate for science instruction of mentally retarded learners (Grant 1975; Keller 1983; Menhusen & Gromme 1976). Although these curriculums and activities differ from one another in a variety of ways, their objectives contain a certain degree of overlap (Keller 1983; Menhusen & Gromme 1976; Ricker 1976). Such commercially available programs include:

The "Me-Now" Science Program (Hubbard Publishing Company, Northbrook, IL.) This science program was specifically constructed for mildly mentally retarded students (CA 10-13 years). It is a science and health program that focuses on helping students learn about the human body, how it works, and what can be done to help it work better. The program is divided into four units: digestion and circulation, respiration, movement and support, and human development. Little reading or writing is required. Rather, material is presented using 140 slides, posters, pictures, and film loops. The program also comes with experiments, activities, and the materials needed to complete them (e.g., stethoscope) as well as a three-foot functioning torso that demonstrates the five human systems. A detailed and comprehensive curricular guide and teacher's manual outlines experiments and activities. This appears to be a good program for use with special needs elementary and intermediate pupils who are poor readers but who possess an interest level at about the junior high school level.

The "Me and My Environment" Program (Hubbard Publishing Company, Northbrook, IL.) This is the sequel to the *Me-Now* science series published by the same company. This program is designed for mildly mentally retarded pupils a little older than those targeted by the *Me-Now* series (CA 13-16) although the cognitive/mental levels of the students would not be at such sophisticated levels. The *Me and My Environment* program goes beyond the child's body to the environment. The program deals with five units or sections: "Exploring My Environment," "Me as an Environment," "Energy Relations and My Environment," "Transfer and Cycling of Materials in My Environment," and "Water and Air in My Environment." Like the *Me-Now* program, the *Me and My Environment* system contains a minimum of reading/writing materials and a wealth of audiovisual and hands-on materials designed to facilitate learning by nonreading students. Experimental equipment is provided in the program.

Elementary Science Study (McGraw-Hill, N.Y., N.Y.) This program is designed for students who are reading at a first to eighth grade level but who possess an interest level at the junior high to senior high range. Thus, it would be useful for mildly mentally retarded students who are at a low ability level but who possess interest comparable to their age-related peers. The program contains fifty-six units which investigate a large variety of science topics including the human body, health, and the environment. The *Elementary Science Study* program, by using an inquiry/discovery approach, removes much of the need for large amounts of requisite science content which must be mastered before science activities and experiments can be attempted. Of the fifty-six units, thirty are specifically designed for children with learning problems, such as the mentally retarded. Within each unit a variety of activities allow both teacher and student to select activities and design a science curriculum on the basis of student interest, needs, and ability levels. Materials include manipulative and experimental materials, worksheets, booklets, film loops, and charts. This program is more reading oriented than the *Me-Now* and *Me and My Environment* series.

I.D.E.A.L. Science Curriculum (Opportunities for Learning, Chatsworth, CA.) This is an individualized, self-paced, self-directed program that emphasizes the human body and the human health areas. The reading level is at the fourth to fifth grade level while the material is appropriate for pupils whose interests are at the junior and senior high school levels. Thus in this respect the *I.D.E.A.L.* program is useful for adolescents with learning problems. A drawback to the program is that a significant amount of reading and writing is required of the student especially since the student does much of the work independently. Additionally, the reading level may prove to be too sophisticated for some pupils. This program is probably not appropriate for nonreading students or for those students who do not process information well through the visual (print) mode. The program comes with over 150 worksheets and self-paced activities and experiments for students.

Science for Learners with Physical Handicaps (SELPH)   (Center for Multisensory Learning) This program is appropriate for special-needs learners in grades one to ten. It is a multisensory, multimodal, hands-on program designed to teach science to students with a variety of physical and learning problems. It contains nine separate science modules ranging from measurement to energy conservation. Each module contains activity folders for each child along with a kit of teaching and instructional materials.

DEVISING YOUR OWN SCIENCE CURRICULUM

☐ ☐ Teachers of mildly mentally retarded students may choose not to use packaged science programs or may choose to use only parts of available programs and curriculum guides. Whether the teacher decides to use commercially available programs or teacher-generated topics and science materials, a variety of strategies and/or activities may prove useful in implementing a science curriculum. These strategies include the following:

1. Try to vary the science activities within any science lesson. Try not to devote one complete lesson to an experiment, another to a lecture, a third to a small group project, and so on. Especially with younger pupils it may be a good idea to vary activities within the science period so that after a few minutes at one activity (e.g., experimentation) the students can move on to another activity such as problem solving or producing an account of the results. To facilitate such movement, the teacher may want to set up science centers in which groups of children can rotate from station to station, spending some time at each activity. How such a science station or center program could be implemented in the classroom is shown in Figure 10.10. Whether or not you decide to use the science center technique, try to do everything you can to keep science activities short, crisp, and interesting.

2. Try to keep new technical scientific vocabulary and concepts to a minimum. Avoid such vocabulary items if they are not absolutely necessary to the program or relevant to the child's life experience. When introducing new vocabulary, you might wish to present the new words and concepts after students have had hands-on experiences with the concepts without necessarily knowing the technical words for what they have done during science inquiry activities. The new vocabulary and items can then be discussed after the students have concrete experiences with the concepts that the vocabulary words represent. One idea you might wish to try is having the student keep a file box of new scientific words and concepts

in a dictionary or thesaurus format. Along with entries in the file box would go pictures or concrete examples of the items. Encourage students to refer to the file box often.

3. Choose reading materials in the area of science very carefully. Science reading materials sometimes are at a higher reading level than it may appear on first glance and may contain terms and vocabulary intimidating to the student. Make sure that the science reading material is not frustrating or anxiety producing for the student. Assess frequently not only the students' ability to read the material orally but also ask comprehension questions at different levels of complexity. Do not give students large amounts of scientific reading material to absorb in one sitting. Perhaps a good rule is not to give students science reading material that they can not finish and understand in a ten minute period.

4. Use filmstrips, films, cassette recordings, and other audiovisual materials where possible, particularly with students who possess reading and language problems. Attention often will wander when material is presented through the auditory modality. Presentations for mentally retarded pupils probably should not last more than ten to fifteen minutes without a modality break or switch.

FIGURE 10.10   Using Science Stations

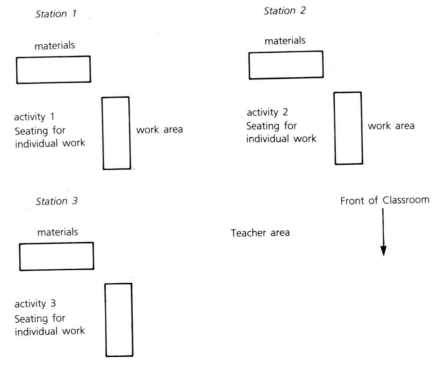

5. Use pictures, charts, posters, and concrete science instructional materials wherever possible. The more concrete, visual, and graphically stimulating, the better.

6. Use small group instructional activities allowing students to pool their scientific knowledge and problem-solving abilities. Act as a facilitator for the group, helping it when it hits an impasse. As much as possible, allow the students themselves to try to come up with methods of inquiry to solve the science problems posed.

7. Combine science with creative activities to increase the concrete and hands-on nature of instructional activities in science. Have students draw and cut maps, make posters, draw murals, sketch plants and animals, and construct mobiles. The field of science lends itself nicely to synthesis-type activities that can result in learning-type art projects.

8. Science is a sequential, ordered discipline. Make sure that your lessons and activities reflect that orderliness. Your projects and activities should be task analyzed to make sure that steps are being presented in proper sequence and that information needed to solve a problem is currently in students' response repertoire. Analyze your activities and lessons to make sure that they do not omit material or present it out of sequence, thus retarding learning.

9. Science topics should be relevant and interesting to students. They should focus on their everyday lives and environment (Turnbull & Schulz 1979). Teachers must know their students so they can ascertain what is important in their lives. Topics pertaining to health, alcohol and drug abuse, and sex education are particularly relevant but other relevant topics should also be brought into the science curriculum. Figure 10.11 contains a list of possible relevant science and health topics.

FIGURE 10.11   Relevant Science and Health Topics

1. The weather/how it effects us
2. Food and nutrition
3. Personal hygiene
4. Plants and us: Why we need them
5. Animals in our environment
6. First aid
7. CPR
8. The human body: How to take care of it
9. Responsible sexual conduct
10. Alcohol and chemical abuse
11. Taking care of the planet earth
12. Science in your home
13. Clothing
14. Gravity—who needs it?
15. Space

SUMMARY

☐ ☐ Social studies and science are two curricular areas not often emphasized in the academic programs of mildly mentally retarded students. This is unfortunate since, when presented appropriately, these two areas can prove helpful to the future life success of these learners.

Social studies is concerned with preparation of citizens who can function in democratic society in general and in their home communities in particular. The social studies curriculum contains four main components: knowledge, skills, values, and social participation. Knowledge provides for acquisition of the basic concepts that allow for later transfer, application, and generalization. Such concepts include knowledge about the family, neighborhood, social groups, and different cultures. Skills involve competence in three main areas: thinking, data processing, and human relation skills. The skill area also includes abilities to read maps and globes. Values entail the formation of a value system and action consistent with that value system. Finally, social participation includes the students' participation in a variety of social situations and social groups.

At the secondary level, the social studies curriculum consists mainly of training citizens. Students learn democratic values as well as tolerance for cultural diversity. A strong component of value clarification may also take place during this period in the students' schooling.

Science involves systematic problem solving. The goal of the science program for mentally retarded learners is to help students learn to exert systematic control over their environment, to apply systematic investigative techniques to real-life situations, and to help the students formulate empathy for all living things. For mentally retarded learners, the science program should emphasize process and discovery rather than a large body of information that must be memorized before scientific inquiry is undertaken. A multisensory, multimodal approach should be utilized that involves materials and experiences from the child's own environment. Finally, it is strongly suggested that for mentally retarded learners, the science program contain content accessibility, process accessibility, and access to manipulation in order to allow optimal access to materials and instructional methods.

11

Art and Creativity

Key Concepts
☐ Creating the Creative Environment
☐ Stages of Artistic Development
☐ Materials and Activities
☐ Art Activities for Older Students

Why are art and creativity relevant to mentally retarded learners? This question is sometimes asked by people involved with educating mentally retarded individuals. For such learners, art and creativity are often thought of as tangential subjects not really needed in their curriculum. After all, the reasoning goes, it is vitally important that the mentally retarded child learn to read, write, and do arithmetic. Why should valuable time be wasted on "nonvital" subjects such as art and creativity?

Inherent in the mindset against having art and creativity as part of the special-educational curriculum may be the belief that artistic and creative abilities are dependent on talent. Such a belief would hold that since mentally retarded persons are deficient in talent and creativity, they cannot benefit from art instruction. Furthermore, this argument, taken to its logical extreme, would also hold that art and creativity activities would ultimately prove frustrating for mentally retarded children.

WHY TEACH ART?

☐ ☐ Let us take these arguments one at a time, beginning with the belief that mentally retarded individuals are deficient in creative ability and that art experiences thus prove frustrating. Such a viewpoint takes a norm-referenced rather than a criterion-referenced view of art and creativity. That is, proponents of this view seek to compare the creative endeavors of mentally retarded persons to those of nonretarded individuals and find the artwork of the mentally retarded persons inferior in comparison. The artistic endeavors of mentally retarded persons compared against the standard of art would be judged as having little or no merit.

But what does the mentally retarded child think of her or his own artistic efforts? Does the child compare them against an objective artistic standard and find the product unacceptable? Does the mentally retarded child really find the artistic experience frustrating? One has only to observe mentally retarded school children in art class to discover that they generally look forward to art activities, that they enjoy their artistic creative time, and that it is not they who find their artistic efforts and products inferior and frustrating. In fact, since art is one of the first areas into which mentally retarded students are mainstreamed, it would appear that these learners more than hold their own with their nonhandicapped peers in enjoying their artistic endeavors (Morsink 1984; Uhlin & DeChiara 1984). Thus, it would appear that the frustration that mentally retarded learners are supposedly feeling in their artwork is more a function of certain adults who are perhaps playing the role of art critic than that of the students themselves (Lindsay 1972).

☐ Creating a Sense of Self-Worth Through Art

Art and creativity are important for mentally retarded learners because they allow them to develop a sense of self-worth and uniqueness (Clements & Clements 1984). Mentally retarded students generally have experienced a long history of failure in their academic experiences. This often leads to a general poor self-concept and an expectancy of failure. But one cannot fail in art and creativity. Whatever the child makes, draws, or creates is an outgrowth of individual experiences, feelings, and perceptions. How can what one feels be wrong? With an understanding and nonjudgmental teacher, artistic endeavors represent one curricular area in which the mentally retarded child is insulated from failure. Here, self-concept can improve as art becomes the great equalizer for handicapped students—the one area where they are on an equal footing with their nonretarded peers.

☐ Self-Expression

Art and creativity can also be used to help understand the mentally retarded child better and learn what the individual is thinking, feeling, and experiencing (James 1983; Uhlin & DeChiara 1984). Art can also help the child better achieve self-understanding (Aach 1981; Atack 1982). Often, mentally retarded children are relatively inarticulate in verbally expressing their inner feelings. This lack of verbal skills may be misinterpreted by adults to mean that the children are happy, docile, and satisfied. However, such might not be the case. There may be things that are greatly disturbing the child, things the child cannot articulate but can express through art. The author once taught a child in a primary special education class who one day came to school agitated and disturbed. This child was asked repeatedly what was wrong but he would not discuss his problem. Something, however, was greatly disturbing this child. Finally during art time he began to paint a dark picture in blacks and browns of two people, one of them wielding a knife. Who were they? It turned out that the night before the child's parents had had a quarrel and mother had wounded father with a knife in full view of this child! Thus the child's agitation and disturbance. However, once the child was able initially to express his feelings through art, he was able to open up and verbalize his feelings. Without art as a releasing mechanism, this child might have never been able to express his feelings adequately.

INTEGRATING ART AND THE CORE ACADEMIC AREAS

□ □ Art and creativity can also be used in conjunction with the daily special-education curriculum to reinforce what is being taught in the core subject areas (Clements & Clements 1984; James 1983). Many teachers have come to realize that art and creativity can be tied in with language arts, social studies, and even arithmetic activities. Likewise, it has been demonstrated that art activities can be tied in with topics in long-term instructional units. For example, creative woodworking activities may reinforce many arithmetic measurement concepts (e.g., inch, foot), while artistic topics may reinforce social skills and self-help concepts (e.g., being a friend, dressing for weather). By using art and creativity to reinforce the school curriculum in the core areas, the special-education teacher is increasing the probability that academic material will be functionally learned while making the curriculum more enjoyable and meaningful for mentally retarded children. Figure 11.1 contains an example of an art lesson plan that relates to topical content included in long-term instructional units.

GETTING READY: CREATING THE ART ENVIRONMENT

□ The Classroom

Children learn best in an atmosphere that stimulates their interest and thinking. They create best in an environment in which they feel free from the threat of tension, anxiety, and failure. This is especially true for mentally retarded learners who have learned over the years that they have a high probability of failure in many academic activities and have anxiously come to expect it. Thus, it is important that the art area of the special-education classroom be one that is stimulating to the mentally retarded child, one that the child associates with fun and success.

Professionals interested in art and creativity for mentally retarded learners suggest that a separate room or at the least a separate part of the classroom be set aside for art and creative activities (Clements & Clements 1984; Upton 1979). It is important that this area be associated with creativity and free thought. It should be an area where *divergent* thinking (no one right answer to a problem

FIGURE 11.1   Art Lesson Plan

Topic: Planning a Nutritious Menu

Code Area: Art _____   Duration: 50 minutes _____

Behavioral Objectives	Activity	Materials	Evaluation
Given a list of various sources for each food group, the student will show to the students.	Story on food is to be read first. Different pictures of foods and their sources will be drawn.	"Basketful-the Story of our Food"—J. Eberle	Student is given a work sheet every 15 minutes and asked to correctly identify one correct source for each food group (four correct answers). Two of the three work sheets must have 100 percent accuracy.
Identify one source for each food group two out of three times. 1.9	Students will draw different sources for each food group and then paste them on the appropriate food group poster board. Crayons, colored pencils, cut outs, anything may be used as long as it is clear what food source is being represented. Do three work sheets.	Construction paper, paste, colored felt tip pens, poster board, scissors, crayons.	

but many possible, creative and valuable answers exist) rather than *convergent* thinking (the one right answer to a problem) is encouraged. Upon entering the art area, the child should also be entering into a new world—one where the one "right" answer doesn't exist, only creativity and expression.

Whether a separate room or part of the special-education classroom is used, the teacher should attempt to have the area as uncluttered, airy, open, and well lit as possible. Materials should be kept out of the way but always accessible to students and teacher. Upton (1979) proposes a mobile cupboard to fulfill these requirements. The cupboard contains ample storage space and can be easily rolled out during art time. It can hold virtually all of the art materials used in class, held neatly but with high accessibility for students.

It is also important to have access to a deep sink, which would serve two purposes: it may be used for those art activities which require water (e.g., papier-mâché), as well as in cleanup. Probably nothing can kill a teacher's spontaneity and enthusiasm for an art lesson more than having to worry constantly about children making messes or having spills. This becomes a special concern to the teacher if there is no handy available water source available. Sinks should have sedimentation traps to prevent clogs and overflows.

In addition, the art center should also have the following physical equipment:

1. Long tables and chairs to facilitate group interactions and group work.
2. A painting and shellacking table.
3. Sliding drawers for holding paper, newsprint, and other consumable items.
4. A woodworking table that can take dents, holes, and other assorted punishment.
5. Brooms, mops and cleanup equipment stored in a nearby closet.
6. Handtools and a toolrack.
7. A clothing closet.
8. A display area for student's work.

The eighth environmental requisite, a display area, is especially important. Students need to see their artwork displayed. It is their work, their creations, and displaying it gives the child a sense of pride, self-fulfillment, and heightened self-worth. More discussion of how and where to display children's artwork will occur later in this chapter.

In an art center, the desks and chairs should face one another rather than the teacher. In such an arrangement, the children and their artwork become the central focus of the class instead of the teacher and the teacher's reactions and ideas. Such a setup is designed to optimize social interactions between children with the hope that such heightened interactions will serve as an impetus for artistic endeavors and creativity.

BASIC MATERIALS AND SUPPLIES

☐ ☐ The materials required for teaching art and creativity to mentally retarded students are only slightly different from those required for nonretarded children. The special education teacher differentially adapts these materials in order to teach to the developmental levels of the mentally retarded students. The teacher needs to be creative (students are not the only ones who need to be creative in art activities!) in acquiring and using "junk" or discarded materials in new ways to stimulate the creative development of mentally retarded children.

Materials that may be used in an art and creativity program for mentally retarded children can be classified into the following main categories:

1. Drawing materials and materials.
2. Paper and consumable items.
3. Paints and finishes.
4. Cutting tools.
5. Paste and glues.

6. Modeling and sculpturing materials.
7. Weaving, yarns, and twines.
8. Needlecraft.
9. Fabrics and stuffing.
10. Construction materials.
11. Collage materials.

Table 11.1 contains individual items included in these main categories (Anderson 1978).

Younger children require careful supervision in using and caring for art materials. Instruction regarding the care and maintenance of materials should therefore become part of the art curriculum. Art activities, no matter how creative and well thought out, will be doomed to failure if children are not taught to take responsibility for care of materials and equipment.

Safety procedures regarding equipment and materials must also be stressed. When used responsibly, art materials offer no threat to the safety of students. However, used in an irresponsible manner, virtually every piece of art material or equipment can become a health or safety hazard. Every child will need to take responsibility for the safe use of materials and equipment; instruction on safety should become part of the special education art curriculum. By stressing safety rules from the very beginning of art instruction, the special education teacher will avoid serious and possibly dangerous problems later on.

STAGES OF ARTISTIC DEVELOPMENT IN CHILDREN

☐ ☐ One need not observe the artistic products of children for long before discovering that children's artistic abilities differ as a function of their cognitive and physical development. For example, suppose you gave identical coloring books to a two-, four-, and eight-year-old child. What types of artistic products would you be likely to receive from each child? Probably, the two-year-old would make random scribbles on the page with the same crayon, scribbles that had little or no relationship to the topic which was supposed to be colored in. The four-year-old would probably do better at coloring; the child would probably try to color the picture but might have a difficult time staying within the lines and would not use realistic colors (e.g., the face might be colored blue). Finally, the eight-year-old child would probably stay neatly within the lines and would use colors realistically and appropriately.

These developmental differences in children's artistic behaviors have led to identification of five stages of development of artistic ability (Dennis 1984; Lowenfeld & Brittian 1975). In order of appearance these five stages are

1. *The scribbling stage:* For nonretarded children occurring between the ages of two and four. Child is interested in physically exploring the environment as well as discovering psychomotor abilities.

TABLE 11.1 Some Commonly Found Art Materials

Brushes
easel, nylon & standard
  (1", ½", ¼")
water color wash
  (#10, #7, #4, #2)
stencil
paste brush

Cutting Tools
scissors
  blunt & sharp points (L/R)
  fabric
  pinking shears
  large shears
knives
  butter
  plastic "picnic" knives
  all purpose

Fabrics & Stuffing
burlap
organdy
muslin (unbleached)
fabric scraps
Indian-head & monk's cloth
  (optional)
foam rubber
cotton batting
old stockings, etc.
  (stuffing substitute)

Collage
box of environmental materials
box of man-made materials

General Materials
rubber bands
thumbtacks
sponges
stapler
staples
paper cutter
iron
double boiler
hot plate

Paints & Finishes
tempera
tempera blocks
finger paint
water color (OH & OH semi-moist)
water pans & paint
containers
wax
decoupage antiquing materials

denatured alcohol
acrylic polymer emulsion
acrylic medium (matte & gloss)
enamel
shellac
varnish
high gloss clear plastic
turpentine

Paste & Glue
white (liquid)
school paste
rubber cement
wheat paste
epoxy
adhesive cement

**Modeling-Sculpture
Casts-Reliefs**
basic clay modeling tools
modeling clay
self-hardening clay
rolling pin (wood preferred)
styrofoam blocks
aluminum foil
plaster of paris
wheat or commercial mache paste

Construction
stone
toothpicks
counting sticks
popsicle sticks
wood scraps
pegs
jigsaw puzzle pieces
boxes, cans, paper rolls
foam rubber (blocks or pieces)
styrofoam (all types)
dowel sticks
common nails
coping saw and blades
cross-cut saw
hand drill
flat tip screw driver
screws
tin snips
wire cutters

Paper (General)
manila (18 × 24, 12 × 18)
newsprint (18 × 24, 12 × 18)
bogus (18 × 24, 12 × 18)
rough-meal (18 × 24, 12 × 18)

color construction (18 × 24,
  12 × 18, 9 × 12)
finger paint (16 × 22)
oak tag (12 × 18)
mount boards (all types—18 × 24,
  22 × 28)
block print
white (18 × 24, 12 × 18)
cardboard (corrugated & plain)
kraft (36" wide roll)
project (54" wide roll)
stencil
scratch board
tissue (bleeding & non-bleeding)
crepe
cellophane

Needlecraft
crochet hooks (lg., med., small)
embroidery needles (#18, #12, #14-S
  blunt and sharp points)
rug: latch, hook, punch
scrim (large mono-canvas &
  rug canvas)
galvanized hardware cloth
  (½" × ¼" mesh)

Yarns
worsted wool
rug yarn
sewing thread

Twine
white
hemp
fishing twine
nylon thread

Tape
masking
scotch
pliers (needle nose & blunt)
sandpaper
steelwool

Drawing Materials & Equipment
crayons (large & small wax)
crayons (kindergarten hard-pressed)
chalk (lecturer)
chalk (soft colored, white blackboard)
pastels (oil & chalk)
pencils slate
erasers (soft, rubber, kneaded)
rulers
felt tip pens (permanent/water color)

2. *The beginning symbolic and presymbolic stage:* Usually between the ages of four and seven. The student begins to realize that there is a relationship between the child's drawing and the objects seen.
3. *The symbolic and schematic stage:* Usually between the ages of seven and nine. The child develops concepts of people and objects in greater detail and this increased attention to detail is reflected in the child's artwork.
4. *Beginning realism:* Between the ages of nine and eleven. The child now possesses more self-awareness and shows more detail and realism in artwork.
5. *Beginning naturalistic and the pseudo-naturalistic stage:* From ages eleven through adult. The student now places great importance on the finished art product. Much importance is placed on making the object as real as possible.

A BRIEF DESCRIPTION OF THE DEVELOPMENTAL STAGES

☐ The Scribbling Stage

Stage one, the scribbling stage, may be viewed by some educators to be too primitive and simplistic a stage to be of educational concern. After all, what child cannot scribble? Yet there are some severely developmentally delayed children who cannot yet manipulate either their physical environment or drawing materials. These individuals, in fact, do not even have the psychomotor abilities to respond appropriately to their environment. Krone (1978) suggests that the key issue in stage one development is to help the child become aware of and respond to the physical environment. Such activities would focus on object exploration and manipulation. By way of example, Krone outlines a set of activities for exploration and manipulation for something as basic as a cardboard box in order to aid in the development of severely mentally retarded individuals. Such exploration and manipulation activities would include:

1. Visually focusing on the box.
2. Touching the box.
3. Sniffing and smelling the box.
4. Lifting the box.
5. Crawling inside.
6. Moving the box.
7. Pretending with it.
8. Imagining the box in new situations.

In stage one, the person is tied to the concrete and to the manipulation of concrete objects that may be found in the child's immediate environment. Thus, asking the stage one child to draw things would probably end up being a fruitless and possibly frustrating exercise.

☐ The Beginning Symbolic Stage

In stage two, the beginning symbolic stage, the child begins to see the relationship between objects in the physical environment and representations of those objects in artwork. In this stage, the child can recognize representations of the human face as well as show a rudimentary awareness of the human body. Expect the child to be totally self-oriented and egocentric. That is, the child in stage two of artistic development is basically uninterested in depictions of what others are feeling or experiencing.

Almost all of the basic art mediums may be introduced at stage two development. Children in the presymbolic stage are especially interested and receptive to finger paints and other materials that are kinesthetically oriented. However, other materials such as crayons and clay are also enjoyed by children at this stage. Whichever materials are used, the teacher should be careful to keep the curriculum as personal to the life of each child as possible because of the egocentrism of stage two.

☐ The Symbolic Stage

In stage three, the symbolic stage, the child moves out of egocentric perceptions and develops concepts pertaining to other people and objects in the environment. The combination of this greater sensitivity to detail in the environment coupled with the child's increased control over psychomotor functions typically leads to more realistic artistic depictions by the child. Thus, in this stage, children's artwork generally show a greater degree of accuracy and detail. Additionally, children in stage three are typically more attuned to depicting emotion in their artwork. The combination of all of these factors make the child receptive to highly creative activities and flights of imagination such as puppetry (Krone 1978).

☐ The Beginning Realism Stage

In stage four, the beginning realism stage, the child begins to show even more detail in the depiction of objects. In addition, the child begins to become aware of being a member of various groups. Group membership begins to become a part of the child's artwork, in that people are depicted in social interactions rather than alone. Students in this stage are less egocentric and need less direction from the teacher in their artwork. Thus, it is at this stage that the teacher's role begins to shift from an authority figure to a facilitator in the child's art.

In this stage, increased attention to detail makes the child a good candidate for exposure to sculpture activities using clay, papier-mâché, and other similar materials. In working with these materials, children often ask their teacher to comment on the realism of the artwork; this new job of critiquer of realism becomes an additional role for the teacher.

☐ Beginning Naturalistic Stage

Finally, in stage five, the beginning naturalistic stage, the child begins to place importance on the final product rather than just enjoyment of the artistic process. Here the child becomes greatly concerned with the artistic worth of the product and tends to judge the product accordingly. In this stage, the child places great importance on accurately depicting detail and wishes people and objects to be as real and as life-like as possible. Abstract depictions are shunned as being unreal. It is in this final stage that the child may be receptive to the realistic art mediums such as pencil and watercolor.

ART ACTIVITIES AT THE VARIOUS DEVELOPMENTAL STAGES

☐ ☐ Children who are at different developmental artistic levels should receive different art activities. It is important for the teacher to design and implement art activities commensurate with mentally retarded children's artistic developmental level to reduce frustration and optimize learning and success.

☐ Stage One: Art Readiness

In stage one, the child is engaged in cognitively and motorically exploring the environment. Formal art activities at this level probably will not be understood by the child and will lead to frustration, failure, and anxiety. Rather, "art" activities should facilitate environmental exploration. It has been suggested that artistic exploration in stage one take the following forms of art readiness: (Atack 1982; Krone 1978):

1. **Physical movement activities:** Have the child engage in the wide variety of psychomotor activities that take place in everyday life. Such activities would include but would not be restricted to running, jumping, skipping, ball-bouncing, swinging, skating, and imitating common objects such as cars and airplanes. The purpose here is to allow children to experiment with their muscles and to see how their action affects their environment. Such environmental influencing, for example, might be accomplished by having the child leave footprints in the sand or snow.

2. **Building:** Allow the child to build things using materials such as wooden blocks, tinkertoys, interlocking plastic chips, or other available materials. Encourage the child to use blocks and objects of different colors, shapes, and sizes. Allow the child to work with molds in shaping clay or wax. Any kind of creation of structures is useful and appropriate in this stage of art development.

3. **Cutting and tearing:** Allow the child to cut and tear fabrics and materials not necessarily for any artistic purpose but rather for the environmental experience. Cutting is an excellent activity for improving eye-hand coordination and fine motor control, while tearing stimulates expertise in control of the hands as they move and work in opposite directions.

4. **Shape awareness:** Shapes occur constantly in the child's everyday environment. Circles, squares, rectangles and triangles abound in almost everything we encounter visually during the day. Help the child explore the environment to discover shapes in everyday objects (e.g., a tomato, a slice of cheese, a candy bar, a piece of pie). Work with the student in discovering the similarities and differences in the shapes of commonly found environmental objects.

5. **Stringing objects:** A very useful activity for helping the child to learn about serial relationships in the environment. Objects such as beads, buttons, even dry cereal can be used to increase serial awareness.

6. **Sensory awareness:** Perhaps the most important set of curricular activities that occur in stage one of artistic development. Each of the five senses is a candidate for sensory awareness training. The child, by becoming more sensorily sophisticated, learns the cause-and-effect relationships that govern the environment as well as ways in which the child's actions can effect that environment. Table 11.2 contains some sensory awareness activities (Atack 1982).

In this stage of art development, the "sensory box" activity has proven useful with mentally retarded learners. These items are small containers, usually shoe boxes, that hold items dealing with the different sensory modalities. According to Krone (1978) a sensory awareness box may be constructed for each modality. Examples would include:

1. *A see box:* Children bring in items which are visually appealing or interesting. A given color or shape could be the color or shape of the day and criterion for inclusion of items into the box could be changed daily.

2. *A feel box:* Items of different textures and kinesthetic attributes would be included.

3. *A taste box:* Edible items of different tastes (e.g., bitter, salty, and sweet) would be included.

4. *A smell box:* Items of different smells (e.g., perfumes, sweet smelling objects, old sweat socks) would be placed in the box.

TABLE 11.2 Sensory Awareness Art Activities

Activity	Sensory Awareness
Finger painting	allow for experimentation with color spreading paints with finger and palm making circles writing
Clay or playdough	squeezing, squashing and pinching using wet, sticky clay
Squeezy Painting: Squeezing paint out of plastic squeeze bottles	traveling paint making squeeze paint paintings
Manipulate shapes of different sizes, shapes and textures	pour water in sand—mold shapes make sponge pictures with paint and water build with blocks
Cut and tear objects	cutting and pasting into a scrapbook making collages
Make sensory boxes	small box feed box see box hear box

5. *A hearing box:* Included in this box would be things which made a particular and differentiated sound when manipulated.

☐ Stage Two: Egocentric Art

Children at stage two of art development are basically egocentric—they can only deal with the *I* and the *my*. Thus, it is important to make sure that any art activities designed for stage two children be directly applicable to the personal life of each individual child. To accomplish this the teacher must become familiar with the lives of the pupils.

Figure 11.2 contains a list of possible art topics designed to motivate stage two children (Krone 1978). Notice that every topic included in this curriculum list is personal to the child. In this stage of the child's life, the art medium or materials that the teacher uses is relatively unimportant. What does make a

FIGURE 11.2   Possible Art Topics for Stage 2 Children

Me and my house (sizes)
I am brushing my teeth (teeth)
I am drinking my milk (mouth)
I wear a hat (head)
My family (emotional relationship)
I am on the swing (body)
I have a stomach ache (body)
Me and my doll (emotional relationship)
Me and my pet (emotional relationship)
I have a new dress (body)
I am walking in the grass after the rain (feet, body)
I get a birthday present (emotional relationship)
I am playing in the mud (hands, feet, body)
I am playing in the rain (body)
I am walking in the water puddles (feet)
I am rowing a boat (body actions)
I am riding in our car (body)
I am eating a banana (mouth)
I am in a rain storm
I am standing in my back yard
I visit my cousins
I am looking for a lost kitten (doll, toy)
I am climbing a hill (stairs)
I am picking apples
I am riding my bike (or tricycle)
My family at lunch
I am picking flowers (hand, arms)
I am eating breakfast (mouth)
I am blowing my nose (nose)
I hurt my knee (knee)

I am at the dentist (teeth)
I am eating an ice cream cone
I open my birthday present
I am building a snowman
I am riding on a bus
This is me kicking a ball
I have new buttons on my dress
I have new buttons on my shirt
I find a spider's web
I lie down in my bed
I see a fire engine and a fire
I see a train
I walk in a flower garden
I go to camp
I go on vacation
I watch the snow fall
The storm
My new baby sister
I got lost in the store
I can spin a top
I play dress-up
I jump a rope
I bounce a ball
I fly a kite
I go to the park
I fish
I eat candy
I hoe in the garden
I am playing on the playground

From A. Krone (1978).

difference is that the teacher makes sure that the art subject matter is particular and personal to the lives of the children involved—that it deals with each one individually. The curriculum must be personalized in order to be successful in this stage of the mentally retarded child's art development. Figure 11.3 contains some activities designed to help the stage two child explore the environment (Krone 1978; Uhlin & DeCiara 1984).

☐ Stage Three: Others-Oriented Art

In stage three of artistic development, the child is beginning to become less egocentric and more aware of other people and objects in the environment. At this stage, the child is also becoming more able to understand the perspectives of other people; that is, becoming more sensitive to the ways other individuals view the world that may be different from the child's own perspective.

FIGURE 11.3   Stage 2 Art Activities

1. Draw faces. How do people's faces differ?
2. Draw bodies and body parts.
3. Draw representations of things found in the immediate environment; animals, plants, buildings, vehicles.
4. Draw objects that express emotions. For example use favorite colors to draw favorite objects.
5. Make collages using scissors, paper, crayons, and paste.

This reduction in egocentrism allows the teacher to begin to discuss how other people live, feel, experience, and perceive; this heightened awareness to others can be reflected in the art activities of mentally retarded children at stage three development. The child is now able to move from the *I* to a perspective of *we* or *they* (Lowenfield & Brittain 1975). At this stage, topics for art activities may include items such as occupations of others, cultures different than the child's, social interactions between people, and the ways in which environment affects individuals.

Krone (1978) has suggested a variety of possible topics for mentally retarded children in stage three of artistic development. A partial list of these topics can be found in Figure 11.4. It is also posited that the child's increased psychomotor skills combined with heightened sensitivity to other people and objects in the environment will result in more sensitive and artistically accurate endeavors for these students.

☐ Stage Four: Artistic Realism

In stage four, the child shows even greater awareness of both self and others in the environment. Children in this stage of artistic development may be seen as refining those initial skills developed in earlier stages as well as heightening the awareness of others that began in stage three. Stage four children possess a high degree of psychomotor control and will thus show increased artistic realism in their artwork.

Children at stage four artistic development are particularly receptive to working in small groups rather than in isolation. This new receptiveness to small group interactions can be particularly useful in the socialization and mainstreaming process of mentally retarded children. The wise teacher will encourage social interaction between mentally retarded and nonretarded children in art activities and structure the art situations in such a way that the mentally retarded child will become an integral part of the group and be viewed positively by other group members. This may be done by structuring the project in such a way that the success of the group art project will depend in significant part on the particular artistic and creative talents of the mentally retarded students in the group. Projects at stage four often deal with the creation of some group product. Such products may include, for example, the creation of murals, dioramas, or miniatures. Figure 11.5 contains a number of possible topics that might be appropriate

FIGURE 11.4   Stage 3 Art Topics

My favorite sport
Playing football
Stockcar races
The relay race
Spring
Our family car
A visit to the pet shop
What I want to be when I grow up
This is *me*
My favorite star on TV
My father or mother at work
A bird building its nest
I make believe I'm an animal
The giant
If I were a teacher
If I could do anything I wanted to do for one day
What I liked best about camp (my vacation)
The road grader (street cleaner, excavator)
Astronauts
Men from Mars
The magic show
Preparing for blastoff
Witches in the woods
We got our new shoes covered with mud
Caged lions and tigers
I had a beautiful (horrible) dream
I saw a clown
My favorite animal
The time I was most afraid
We go to the train station (airport)
My family stays in a motel
A butterfly
I helped bake bread

We went to visit the farm
Our trip to the police department
We go on a hike in the woods
We visit a factory
We are eating in the school cafeteria
How the firemen prepare for a fire
How I come to school
We watch a parade go by
Our trip to the bakery
Playing with my friends on the school ground
Playing ball with my friends
We are climbing a mountain
I am helping plant a garden
We are sledding down a hill
We are skating on a pond
Climbing a tree
Saying goodbye as I go to school
Playing checkers with my friend
Eating breakfast across the table from my brother
Holding an umbrella in one hand and my books in another
We visit different areas of a factory
My friends and I explore a cave
My stay in the hospital
We like to play in the rain
The workmen are painting our house
Talking with my mom and dad
We are learning to swim in the pool
We are learning to bowl
Tug-of-war
A traffic jam
The view from a helicopter
Bicycle races

From A. Krone (1978).

for small group art projects. It should be pointed out that in using the group project approach in stage four, it will not be enough for the teacher to form the group, step back, and let them sink or swim. In such a situation, the group endeavor will probably fail and the mentally retarded child have a high probability of losing even more social status. Rather, the teacher will need to assume a new role of group facilitator, making sure that the group is on task, is running smoothly, and is headed toward success. Finally, the teacher will need to guide the group so that the mentally retarded child becomes an important group member, thus creating increased social ratings for that child by other group members.

FIGURE 11.5   Stage 4 Art Topics

How it would be to live in the slums
The house in which I wish to live
Helping the flood victims
Cleaning up after the storm
Firemen putting out a big fire
Fierce animals in the zoo
The city
Building a clubhouse with my friends
A policeman in five-o'clock traffic
Repairing a broken water main
A nurse taking care of the sick

Exploring the surface of Venus
Sitting around a table for dinner
Planting a garden in the spring
Watching the parade come down the street
Skating on the pond in the woods
Playing baseball on the school grounds
Looking out the window of the school bus
Sitting in the movie theater
Looking at clothes in the store window
Singing for the school assembly

From A. Krone (1978).

☐ Stage Five: The Artistic Product

In stage five, some interesting developments occur. First, the child becomes interested in the final art product rather than in just the enjoyment of the artistic process. This can sometimes prove awkward for the teacher who wishes to convey to the child that enjoyment of the artistic process is important while recognizing that the child is interested (and judges the worthiness of the entire artistic experience) by the artistic worth of the finished art product.

Second, the stage five child is now capable of dealing to some extent with abstract topics such as flights of fancy, imagination, and fantasy. Thus, stage five students can hypothesize answers to "what if" questions as well as dealing with issues of emotions, perceptions, and moods.

In contrast to this, however, the stage five child, especially the stage five mentally retarded child, will begin to show great concern over the realism of his or her work and will judge art products by such criterion. Thus, the teacher working with children in stage five will need to balance the child's ability to handle abstract variables such as emotion and mood with the child's need for artistic realism. Figure 11.6 contains a number of imaginative topics that can tap into the stage five child's heightened awareness to nuances of mood and perception.

ADDITIONAL ACTIVITIES, SUGGESTIONS, AND STRATEGIES

☐ Younger Students

1. Relate art activities into seasons and holidays. The calendar can offer a host of art ideas to the creative teacher. The book, *Arts and Crafts for*

FIGURE 11.6   Stage 5 Art Topics

Imagination
  What will happen to the world if pollution is not stopped
  The world in the year 2000
  What I will look like when I am 70 years old
  The most beautiful person in the world
  A fierce villain
  All alone on a dark, cold, night

Emotions and Expressions

Sneezes	Heat	Dizziness
Yawns	Cold	Wildness
Sadness	Anger	Sour
Joy	Fear	

Moods and Feelings
  Painting to music, showing different moods
  The way I feel today
  Sometimes I'm very happy; sometimes I'm very sad
  I look quiet and dull but my head is full of ideas and feelings about the world around me
  This is a picture of me and the things that make me happy
  A rainy day
  A sunny day

  From A. Krone (1978).

Special Education (Winsor 1972) offers excellent seasonal art ideas for younger special needs students.

2. Look for nontraditional materials that can be used in art activities. Anybody can use paper and paint! How about rice, sand, flour, syrup, beans, shaving cream, buttons, wallpaper, and styrofoam cups? The zanier the better! Be creative.

3. Collage activities are very popular and are useful for teaching spatial relationships. Collages can also teach similarities, opposites, and size. Collage materials include paper and fabrics, string, wool, beans, macaroni, and styrofoam.

4. Use nature in art activities. Take walks and collect things such as leaves, flowers, nuts, seeds, stray animals. Talk about art in nature. Tie together art, nature, and science activities.

☐ Older Students

1. Fantasy and art make a good mix. Tie in art with space, science fiction, the bizarre, and the fantastic. Surrealism can be fun!

2. Art and language arts can be related by having students create artwork for skits or plays.
3. Crafts and artwork are motivating for older students. Encourage such activities as knitting, macrame, woodcarving and jewelry making. Encourage students to try a variety of crafts activities.
4. Experiment with colors and textures. Allow students to mix colors and paint a variety of textured surfaces. The key word is *experiment*.

MOTIVATION AND THE ART CURRICULUM

☐ ☐ While it is true that motivation is somewhat easier in the art curriculum than in some of the other academic core areas (e.g., arithmetic or spelling), nevertheless the special education teacher must be careful not to respond to student's art in a way that destroys interest and motivation. Mentally retarded students are particularly susceptible to having their artistic self-concepts destroyed by harsh, unfeeling, or overly critical teachers. Such students have experienced a long, sordid history of failure in school. What they do not need is an additional, overly harsh critique of artwork indicating to them that they have also failed in this area of the school curriculum. In fact, the special education teacher should refrain from criticizing the child's final art product at all unless the child specifically asks for a critique. It is wise to emphasize the enjoyment and fulfillment that goes with the process and activity of creativity (e.g., "Did you enjoy the process?" "Was it fun?").

How a teacher praises artwork is just as important as whether or not she or he does praise. This may be surprising to teachers who believe that any praise of the child's artwork is acceptable and enhancing to motivation. Actually, some types of praise may be confusing to the child and in fact inhibit motivation and interest in art. Take for example the teacher who looks at the child's art product and says something like "very nice" or "that's good." But what's nice about it? and what's good? Unless the teacher is more specific about those areas of the project that are praiseworthy, the child could end up confused and eventually frustrated.

A much sounder strategy for the teacher is to be more specific in praise of the child's artwork. The teacher might say something like, "I like this picture because it shows me how you feel on rainy days," or "this is good because you show me that the children are happy." In other words, specific praise that indicates to the child where the art product is strong is best for enhancing motivation for art.

This does not mean that you need to praise everything that the child does in art or that you cannot offer constructive criticism of the artistic efforts of mentally retarded children. On the contrary, constructive criticism of a child's artwork can often actually motivate the child to continue or even increase artistic efforts. However, when criticism is offered, it ought to be bracketed between initial and concluding comments that contain praise. Thus, the child hears initially and leaves with a feeling of praise and self-worth. Sandwiched in the middle is how the art product or effort can be improved.

An example of this bracketing technique might be:

1. "Well, I like the way you showed the children playing together in your picture" (praise).
2. "However, you might want to show better what they are doing with their hands as well as how they are getting along" (constructive criticism).
3. "Why don't you try it again keeping up your good work in showing the children's emotions?" (praise).

By hearing such a bracketing approach, the child learns where things are wrong and what can be done about them (constructive criticism) and at the same time comes away with a good feeling that the teacher values the artistic efforts and work. Keep in mind, however, that sometimes praise should be *unconditional* rather than bracketed around constructive criticism. By offering unconditional praise once in a while, the student will be spared the "yes, but" expectancy of hearing criticism every time praise is forthcoming.

Structure (or the lack of structure) in the art lesson can also affect the child's motivation for art. An art lesson can be frightening and unmotivating if it contains either too little or too much structure. In the former case, the teacher might give the children a blank piece of paper and tell them to create whatever they want with no input, help, or guidance from the teacher. This complete lack of direction is often confusing and nonfacilitative for mentally retarded students. These children need help in reliving, visualizing, and recreating ideas and experiences in their lives. To accomplish this, the teacher will have to work with the child and serve as both a facilitator and reflector of ideas.

In the latter case, that of too much structure in the art lesson, the teacher has a set idea of what and how things in the art lesson are to be done. A child coming in with an idea of one's own would be informed, "We are not doing that today. What we are going to do is this. . . ." Such teachers typically do not allow children any creative leeway in their art products. Rather such teachers might display a finished product and have their children copy that product. Such structure is obviously stifling and destructive to the creative artistic process. All spontaneity is lost. The child becomes a copier of other people's finished artwork and the worthiness of her or his own artwork becomes a function of the accuracy of the copy.

Obviously, the type of art curriculum and lesson that proves most motivating is that which possesses some structure but does not smother creativity by refraining from withholding all choices and decisions from the child. The teacher should strive to reach a compromise between freedom and structure; allow the child to have input into what will be done in the art lesson but do not give up total control of what goes on in the classroom. What should be sought after in the art lesson, as in life, for mentally retarded students is a thinking, creative, productive individual.

SUMMARY

☐ ☐ Art and creativity programming possesses value for mentally retarded learners. It has been demonstrated that such programming is enjoyable to students, that it heightens their sense of self-worth, and eradicates some of the negative effects of school failure, and that it helps us better understand the child and helps the child better achieve self-understanding.

It is important that the teacher create the correct physical environment for art activities. A separate classroom or an art center in the existing classroom should be created. Divergent rather than convergent thinking should be encouraged in this center. The teacher also needs to have necessary art materials handy and available as well as an adequate water source. Instruction in care of materials as well as safety should be part of the art curriculum.

There are five major stages of art development. These are the scribbling, beginning symbolic, schematic, realism, and naturalistic stages. Each stage represents heightened awareness on the part of the child, less egocentric behavior, and greater emphasis on product. A variety of art activities at each stage is available.

Creating the proper psychological environment for creativity is crucial for success of the art program with mentally retarded learners. Teachers should avoid unncessary criticism of art products and should try to praise the effort rather than the product. Where criticism of the product is appropriate, the teacher should bracket that criticism between positive statements about the child's artwork.

12

Career Education Programs for the Mentally Retarded

Key Concepts

- ☐ Career Education and a Life-experience Model
- ☐ The LCCE Curriculum
- ☐ The Team Teaching Approach to Career Education
- ☐ The Role of the Family
- ☐ Community and Business Resources
- ☐ Career Awareness, Exploration, and Preparation
- ☐ The Long-term Instructional Unit Approach to Career Education
- ☐ Assessment in Career Education
- ☐ Designing a Career Educational Classroom Environment
- ☐ Components of the School Career Education Program
- ☐ Activities for Teaching the Career Educational and Life-success Curriculum

Perhaps this chapter might best be begun with a true story. Not too many years ago, a teacher was involved in training adolescent mentally retarded persons for jobs in the community. One particular student was trained to work on the assembly line of an automobile manufacturing plant. This student had been trained and tested on all of the job competencies for job success and finally he was ready for work. Surely, this was one student who would succeed!

The student began his new job. However, within a week the teacher received a telephone call from a person in the personnel office of the factory. The student was suddenly having trouble performing competently on the job, wasn't getting along with co-workers, and was in danger of being fired. What was happening?

The teacher began investigating using on-site observation and interviews. What he found was that every day at 10:00 A.M. and 2:00 P.M. coffee breaks, the workers took turn buying coffee and doughnuts for the others. The student accepted coffee and doughnuts from co-workers but when it came his turn to buy he balked. This had irked the other workers; after all, he was making a good salary and could afford to pay. After he refused to buy when his turn came around a second time, he was ostracized from the group. Now, not being able to handle or understand his sudden unpopularity, he was acting inappropriately with others and generally doing a shoddy job.

What had gone wrong? After some more thought and investigation the teacher realized that the problem originated with poor training on the part of the school vocational program. This student had received free lunch throughout his school years. He had never had to pay for his own food in a formalized setting, nor had he had to buy food for others. Now that he was out of school in a new situation, should he have been expected to acquire this new behavior on his own? If the answer was yes, then clearly he had not done so. It was apparent that somewhere along the line, instruction in the social etiquette of the job should have been taught.

This situation, unfortunately, is not unique. Throughout this country, many mentally retarded students receive either no or inadequate career education instruction. They are not taught to enter the world of work. Rather, they are expected to acquire the vast array of requisite skills and knowledge about work on their own. And ultimately, they often fail.

Do you want some proof of how bad the employment picture is for the handicapped? The United States Bureau of Education (1973) estimates that every four years approximately 2.5 million handicapped youths leave our schools. Of these students, it has been projected that only 21 percent (525,000) will be fully employed commensurate with their abilities. It is further estimated that a full 40 percent (1,000,000) will be underemployed and will be at the poverty level, 8 percent (200,000) will only be able to find part-time employment, 26 percent (650,000) will be unemployed and will be supported by the government, and 3 percent (75,000) will be totally dependent and institutionalized. Thus a full 74 percent of the handicapped population is expected to be unemployed or underemployed. Can you imagine a worse waste of human potential? Clearly, career education for handicapped students is vitally needed.

DEFINING CAREER EDUCATION

☐ ☐ At one time career education referred to training handicapped individuals for jobs. That is, career education was defined as "the totality of experience through which one learns about and prepares to engage in work" (Hoyt 1975, p. 4). However, more recent definitions of career education have expanded the concept to include teaching the totality of skills needed for successful adult living in terms of being a wise consumer, a contributing family member, homemaker, and citizen (Hoyt 1977). In short, career education is a life experience program, a program which teaches the skills needed for successful adult living in the real world (Brolin 1982; Kokaska & Brolin 1985).

Viewed in this manner, career education should be regarded as a program which strongly emphasizes the relation between what is taught in the classroom and how that content directly relates to success on the job and in day-to-day living (Brolin & D'Alonzo 1979; Clark 1980; Kokaska & Brolin 1985). More specifically, a successful career education–life experience program for mentally retarded learners should contain the following attributes:

1. Career education is an academic program where academics are intimately related to career and work. There is a theme to education; the world of work and successful adult living.
2. It is a program where students exit from school prepared for either continuing their education or productive work.
3. It is a program where a range of career options are made available to the individual.
4. In career education, self-awareness and exploration as they relate to one's life work is important. The student is helped in exploring personal strengths, weaknesses, attitudes, and interests and in forming realistic life aspirations.
5. It is a program which goes outside the school in order to involve other segments of the community in the student's career education.

These goals of career education imply that career education in school should not consist of just one academic period a day (such as shop or home economics) but rather should be a subject matter that exists throughout the school day. That is, career education should be a long-term theme in which all of the other school subject academic core areas relate. In short, for career education to be successful, it should become a life-long, long-term instructional unit topic for mentally retarded learners.

THE LIFE CENTERED CAREER EDUCATION MODEL

□ □ Over a period of time, it became evident to professionals working with handicapped students that job training alone was not enough (Brolin 1973; Brolin, Malever & Matyers 1976). After all, even a person engaged in full-time employment spends only eight hours a day on the job; the other sixteen hours are spent on avocational activities. Thus, questions began to be asked by educators as to what other skills the individual needed to master for adult life success (Bailey 1976; Brolin & Kokaska 1979).

In 1978 and again in 1983, the Council for Exceptional Children (CEC) published a Life Centered Career Education (LCCE), a curriculum designed to prepare special needs learners for adult life success. The LCCE defines twenty-two major competencies needed for successful adult living with these competencies being included in the major components of daily living, personal-social, and occupational skills. Figure 12.1 contains the twenty-two competencies as they appear in the three life areas. As can be readily seen from Figure 12.1, the LCCE curriculum provides a total life experience, educational program for handicapped learners. It provides in its complexity a lofty and relevant goal to which the special-education teacher may aspire for mildly mentally retarded learners.

FIGURE 12.1 Competencies Contained in the Life Centered Career Education Curriculum

Daily Living Skills

1 Managing family finances
1.1 Identify money and make correct change
1.2 Make wise expenditures
1.3 Obtain and use bank and credit facilities
1.4 Keep basic financial records
1.5 Calculate and pay taxes

2 Selecting, managing, and maintaining a home
2.1 Select adequate housing
2.2 Maintain a home
2.3 Use basic appliances and tools
2.4 Maintain home exterior

3 Caring for personal needs
3.1 Dress appropriately
3.2 Exhibit proper grooming and hygiene
3.3 Demonstrate knowledge of physical fitness, nutrition and weight control
3.4 Demonstrate knowledge of common illness prevention and treatment

4 Raising children—family living
4.1 Prepare for adjustment to marriage
4.2 Prepare for raising children (physical care)
4.3 Prepare for raising children (psychological care)
4.4 Practice family safety in the home

5 Buying and preparing food
5.1 Demonstrate appropriate eating skills
5.2 Plan balanced meals
5.3 Purchase food
5.4 Prepare meals
5.5 Clean food preparation areas
5.6 Store food

6 Buying and caring for clothing
6.1 Wash clothing
6.2 Iron and store clothing
6.3 Perform simple mending
6.4 Purchase clothing

7 Engaging in civic activities
7.1 Generally understand local laws and government
7.2 Generally understand the federal government
7.3 Understand citizenship rights and responsibilities
7.4 Understand registration and voting procedures
7.5 Understand Selective Service procedures
7.6 Understand civil rights and responsibilities when questioned by the law

8 Utilizing recreation and leisure
8.1 Participate actively in group activities
8.2 Know activities and available community resources
8.3 Understand recreational values
8.4 Use recreational facilities in the community
8.5 Plan and choose activities wisely
8.6 Plan vacations

9 Getting around the community (mobility)
9.1 Demonstrate knowledge of traffic rules and safety practices
9.2 Demonstrate knowledge and use various means of transportation
9.3 Drive a car

Personal-Social Skills

10 Achieving self-awareness
10.1 Attain a sense of body
10.2 Identify interests and abilities
10.3 Identify emotions
10.4 Identify needs
10.5 Understand the physical self

11 Acquiring self-confidence
11.1 Express feeling of worth
11.2 Tell how others see him
11.3 Accept praise
11.4 Accept criticism
11.5 Develop confidence in self

12 Achieving socially responsible behavior
12.1 Know character traits needed for acceptance
12.2 Know proper behavior in public places
12.3 Develop respect for the rights and properties of others
12.4 Recognize authority and follow instructions
12.5 Recognize personal roles

13 Maintaining good interpersonal skills
13.1 Know how to listen and respond
13.2 Know how to make and maintain friendships
13.3 Establish appropriate heterosexual relationships
13.4 Know how to establish close relationships

14 Achieving independence
14.1 Understand impact of behaviors upon others
14.2 Understand self-organization
14.3 Develop goal-seeking behavior
14.4 Strive toward self-actualization

15 Achieving problem-solving skills
15.1 Differentiate bipolar concepts
15.2 Understand the need for goals
15.3 Look at alternatives
15.4 Anticipate consequences
15.5 Know where to find good advice

(continued)

FIGURE 12.1 (continued)

16   Communicating adequately with others
16.1 Recognize emergency situations
16.2 Read at level needed for future goals
16.3 Write at the level needed for future goals
16.4 Speak adequately for understanding
16.5 Understand the subtleties of communication

Occupational Skills

17   Knowing and exploring occupational possibilities
17.1 Identify the personal values met through work
17.2 Identify the societal values met through work
17.3 Identify the remunerative aspects of work
17.4 Understand classification of jobs into different occupational systems
17.5 Identify occupational opportunities available locally
17.6 Identify sources of occupational information

18   Selecting and planning occupational choices
18.1 Identify major occupational needs
18.2 Identify major occupational interests
18.3 Identify occupational aptitudes
18.4 Identify requirements of appropriate and available jobs
18.5 Make realistic occupational choices

19   Exhibiting appropriate work habits and behaviors
19.1 Follow directions
19.2 Work with others
19.3 Work at a satisfactory rate
19.4 Accept supervision
19.5 Recognize the importance of attendance and punctuality
19.6 Meet demands for quality work
19.7 Demonstrate occupational safety

20   Exhibiting sufficient physical-manual skills
20.1 Demonstrate satisfactory balance and coordination
20.2 Demonstrate satisfactory manual dexterity
20.3 Demonstrate satisfactory stamina and endurance
20.4 Demonstrate satisfactory sensory discrimination

21   Obtaining a specific occupational skill (Subcompetencies will depend on the student's occupational choice.)

22   Seeking, securing, and maintaining employment
22.1 Search for a job
22.2 Apply for a job
22.3 Interview for a job
22.4 Adjust to competitive standards
22.5 Maintain post-school occupational adjustment

From C. S. Kokaska and D. E. Brolin (1985). *Career Education for Handicapped Individuals* (2nd ed.). Columbus, OH: Charles E. Merrill.

☐ Dimensions of the LCCE Curriculum

A quick glance at the LCCE curriculum reveals that all of the curricular competencies are not directly related to school. That is, while many of the competencies deal directly with school-related subjects, other competencies are best taught under the auspices of other institutions and groups such as the family or the community. Thus, a well-rounded career education curriculum should contain material found in the child's school, family, and community environments.

☐ The School

No single educational professional possesses the expertise, time, and resources to provide alone a total career education, life-experience program (Brolin 1982; Moore & Gysbers 1972; Phelps & Lutz 1977). This suggests that a team teaching approach should be instituted in which various educational professionals take responsibility for career education of the child. Such professionals would include, but would not be restricted to, the special-education and regular classroom teacher, industrial education and home economic and consumer science

TABLE 12.1 The Twenty-two LCCE Competencies and the Professionals Responsible for Their Teaching

Competency	Junior High	Senior High
Daily Living Skills		
1. Managing family finances	Business, math	Home economics, math
2. Selecting, managing, and maintaining a home	Home economics, vocational education	Home economics
3. Caring for personal needs	Home economics, health	Home economics
4. Raising children—family living	Home economics	Home economics
5. Buying and preparing food	Home economics	Home economics
6. Buying and caring for clothing	Home economics	Home economics
7. Engaging in civic activities	Social studies, music	Social studies, music
8. Utilizing recreation and leisure	Physical education, art, music, counselors	Physical education, art, music
9. Getting around the community (mobility)	Home economics	Driver's education
Personal-Social Skills		
10. Achieving self-awareness	Music, physical education, counselors	Art, music, counselors
11. Acquiring self-confidence	Art, music, physical education, home economics, counselors	Physical education, counselors, social studies, art, vocational education, music
12. Achieving socially responsible behavior	Physical education, counselors, music	Social studies, music
13. Maintaining good interpersonal skills	Counselors	Music, counselors
14. Achieving independence	Counselors	Counselors
15. Achieving problem-solving skills	Math, counselors	Science, counselors
16. Communicating adequately with others	Language arts, music, speech, physical education	Language arts, speech, music, art
Occupational Skills		
17. Knowing and exploring occupational possibilities	Vocational education, home economics,	Counselors
18. Selecting and planning occupational choices	Business, vocational education, counselors	Counselors
19. Exhibiting appropriate work habits and behaviors	Vocational education, math, home economics, art	Home economics, vocational education, music
20. Exhibiting sufficient physical-manual skills	Vocational education, physical education	Vocational education, physical education, art
21. Obtaining a specific occupational skill	Vocational education, home economics	Vocational education, home economics
22. Seeking, securing, and maintaining employment	Counselors	Counselors

From C. J. Kokaska & D. E. Brolin (1985), *Career Education for Handicapped Individuals (2nd ed.)*, Columbus, OH: Charles E. Merrill.

professionals, physical education teachers, speech and language therapists, psychologists, guidance and vocational counselors, and work-study personnel. Table 12.1 contains a listing of the twenty-two career-life competencies listed in the LCCE and the educational professionals who might take responsibility for teaching these competencies.

In the team-teaching approach, the special-education teacher operates as the leader/consultant of the team. In fact, in this approach, the teacher typically not only coordinates activities within the school components but also between the areas of family, community, and school. Thus, the special education teacher will need to be constantly aware of the child's current and projected competency levels within each of the twenty-two LCCE competencies as well as be responsible for adequately sequencing and coordinating instruction and materials from a variety of sources. The relationship between the teacher and persons from the major areas of school, family, and community are shown in Figure 12.2.

☐ The Family

The child spends more time with the family than in the school and community combined. Thus, family input into career education is vital for the success of the career education program. In fact, there is strong evidence to suggest that parental opposition or even ambivalence toward the mentally retarded child's career education program can be a powerful factor in the failure of the program (Kokaska 1968; U.S. Office of Education 1978).

In order to increase parental involvement and enthusiasm for the career education program, it is suggested that the special education teacher institute the following activities and procedures (Kokaska & Brolin 1985; Lewis et al. 1981; Razeghi & Ginyard 1980):

1. Provide information in the form of readings, reprints, and articles directly to parents. Also included can be guest speakers, mentally retarded students who have made it in the adult world, and potential employers who hire exceptional students.
2. Keep parents actively informed of the child's career education program. Give consistent and frequent feedback to the parent on how their child is progressing.
3. Conduct career workshops for parents. Include community and school persons to present aspects of the LCCE curriculum to parents.
4. Conduct field trips for parents to potential work sites, training facilities, and community agencies.

Figure 12.3 contains additional activities that parents may institute at home with the student (Kokaska & Brolin 1985; Regen 1979). By helping parents implement these suggestions, the teacher can help transform the home into a mini-vocational, life-experience center that will reinforce what is being taught in school.

FIGURE 12.2   School and Community Resources as They Relate to the Special Needs Learner

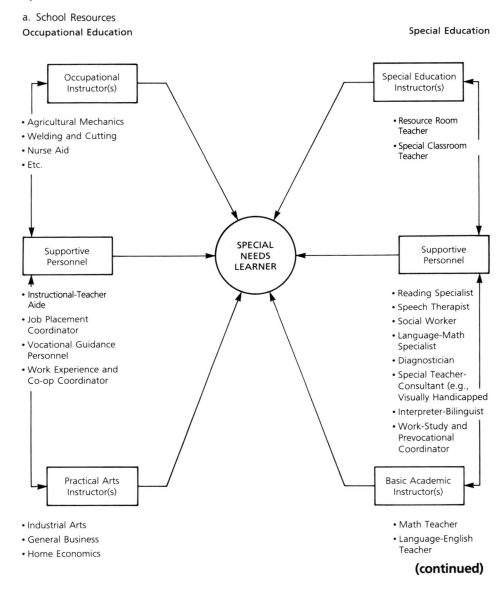

a. School Resources

Occupational Education

Special Education

(continued)

☐ **The Community**

Community resources contain a wide number of various services and opportunities: state, federal, and local rehabilitation agencies, local civic organizations,

FIGURE 12.2 (continued)

b. Community Resources

Federal and State Agencies

- Vocational Rehabilitation
- Employment Services
- Social Security Administration
- Manpower Programs (CETA)
- Mental Health
- Other Agencies

Business, Industry, and Labor Organizations

- Specialized Training Programs
- Career Speakers
- Field Trips
- Occupational Information Materials
- Other Resources

SPECIAL NEEDS LEARNER

Community Agencies and Organizations

- Chamber of Commerce
- Goodwill Industries
- Mental Health Association
- Other Organizations

Citizen and Special Interest Group Services

- Special Financial Assistance
- Prosthetic Equipment Rental
- Special Counseling (Legal, etc.)
- Other Services

From L.A. Phelps & R. Lutz (1977).

FIGURE 12.3 Suggestions for Parents in Working on Career Education Oriented Activities with Their Children

1. Emphasize activities designed to develop coordination, dexterity, balance and strength.
2. Create a home workshop with hand tools and common materials.
3. Create a job roster at home with specific chores for students to perform.
4. Visit job sites in the community. Talk about the different types of jobs performed there.
5. Discuss the types of work family members do. Don't forget homemakers!
6. Provide a variety of job projects and activities. Give children input into deciding upon these activities.
7. Encourage children to make decisions and to live with the consequences of those decisions.
8. Give positive reinforcement for work efforts.
9. Work closely with teachers and other school personnel.
10. Develop school activities such as field trips.
11. Encourage part-time work experiences.
12. Encourage parents to become involved with career education, school advisory committees.

church groups, and, of course, local businesses that operate in the child's environment.

The community resources found in the child's environment should be assessed for their potential usefulness in a systematic fashion. In doing this, the teacher may wish to begin by compiling a list of community agencies and resources from the local telephone directory or chamber of commerce. These potential resource groups may then be contacted by either telephone or mail to gain an understanding of the services performed by each group. (Many times resource agencies and groups will have printed brochures which are furnished free of charge.) The special-education teacher should be especially attuned to the interactive nature of agencies as they range from assessment and evaluation by rehabilitation agencies, through job information and placement services via state and local employment services, to actual job procurement in local community businesses. The teacher should constantly look to coordinate the services provided by community agencies and groups and weave a pattern of total career education for students. It will take considerable time and effort in order to coordinate and use these services in a systematic pattern but such interface will be well worth the effort, as needed educational, career, and life-experience services will be provided, usually free of charge, to your students. Figure 12.4 shows a brief listing of community resources available in many communities.

THE THREE STAGES OF CAREER EDUCATION

☐ ☐ A career education model for exceptional students which takes in the entire school career of students has been suggested (Kokaska & Brolin 1985; Phelps & Lutz 1977). This model begins with the child's earliest school experiences and continues until the student exits school as an adult. Such a school-long concept is quite different from more traditional models of career education (or vocational education as it is sometimes called) in which career education only becomes a limited part of the curriculum at the secondary-school level.

Career education may be divided into three phases: *career awareness, career exploration,* and *career preparation.* The components which make up each phase may be seen in Table 12.2.

Career awareness begins during the elementary school years and involves three main processes: (*a*) making students aware of what work is and why people work, (*b*) helping students learn the different types of work which people perform, and, (*c*) helping students understand levels of a given career (e.g., entry level versus management).

Career exploration typically takes place during the junior-high or middle-school years. It involves a large variety of experiences with different jobs and people who perform those jobs. Students typically meet people who perform a variety of jobs in the community, get to ask relevant questions about jobs, and

FIGURE 12.4   Commonly Found Community Resources

Business and Labor	**Service Organizations**
Chamber of Commerce Banks Credit Unions Insurance Companies Utility Company Department Stores Restaurants Grocery Stores Factories Hotels/Motels	League of Women Voters 4-H Scouts YMCA, YWCA Service Clubs Church Groups

Community Resources

Private Agencies	**Schools**
Rehabilitation Facilities Sheltered Workshops Lutheran Family Services Jewish Services Catholic Social Services	Vocational/Technical Schools Trade Schools Community Colleges

Federal and State	**National, State & Local Organizations**
Vocational Rehabilitation Services CETA Public Health Mental Health	State and Local Special Education Agencies CEC ARC United Cerebral Palsey Easter Seals

From L.A. Phelps & R. Lutz (1977).

TABLE 12.2   Phases of Career Education

Phase	Activity
Career Awareness	Self esteem and self-confidence
	Attitudes toward work
	Information about how people earn a living
Career Exploration	Career education–academic education relationship
	Pre-vocational hands-on experience in industrial arts, home economics, business, and fine arts
	Vocational educational experience in the community
	Youth activities and part-time jobs
Career Preparation	Continued emphasis in communication, language, etc.
	Vocational specialization training combined with continued and specific academic training
	Cooperative educational experience with an employer
	Successful integration of individual into the community

obtain, as much as possible, hands-on experiences with jobs. In doing this, the child gains insight into jobs of interest.

Job exploration contains four main areas: (*a*) the relationship between the academic core areas covered in school and the skills needed in the world of work, (*b*) learning specific vocationally related skills in the classroom before entering the work environment, (*c*) learning how to transfer the skills learned in the classroom to the work community, (*d*) trying out the skills learned in class in real-life work situations. In tying in academic information with career education, everything is done to give students the requisite and relevant information in the areas of language, math, social studies (including self-help and socialization), and science necessary for life success. Again, the key word is *relevancy*. If the student will not be able to use the information in adult life, it is excluded from the special-education curriculum. In the second component area, the student learns competencies in the areas of home economics and industrial education (i.e., handling tools and materials) needed for job success. The third area involves teaching students the relationship between learning skills in the classroom and using them in the community. Here the key word is *transfer*. Students simulate work situations and job roles in the classroom. They also apply their newly learned skills on job sites or various other community settings. Finally, students actually gain some limited experience on jobs working on an unpaid basis. This component is designed to stimulate transfer of information gained from the prior three components of career exploration to the actual work environment.

Career preparation takes place in high school and leads to successful job placement and employment. After job training, many students receive meaningful, relatively good-paying jobs in which they perform satisfactorily. Without adequate career educational training, the jobs would have probably been closed to them.

MAKING THE ACADEMIC CURRICULUM RELEVANT: TECHNIQUES FOR CAREER EDUCATION

☐ ☐ It is vital that academic subject matter taught to mildly mentally retarded learners be functional and *career relevant* (Kokaska & Brolin 1985; Gillet 1980). Career relevancy means that the academic core areas taught to students (e.g., reading, arithmetic) should be directly related to the real world of being a worker, consumer, and citizen. Thus, for example, teach arithmetic skills which the student needs on the job (e.g., computational skills) as well as time, money, and measurement skills which an adult needs to possess to live independently and successfully. The need for career relevancy is especially important during the high-school years in the career preparation stage, but it also should take place during the career exploration and even the career awareness stages.

There are four useful methods the teacher may employ to help insure career relevancy: (*a*) using specialized career oriented instructional material, (*b*) adopting the long-term instructional unit approach, (*c*) adopting and using existing career educational curricula, and, (*d*) instituting a work-study program for high school students. Table 12.3 lists some commercially available academic materials that directly relate core academic area content to career education.

TABLE 12.3   Career Education Materials Available Commercially

Program	Publisher	Level	Description
Be-Informed	New Readers Press	3–7	Consumer information such as paying taxes, making purchases wisely, renting or buying living quarters
Career Education for Children with Learning Disabilities	Academic Therapy Publications	LD	Career education and activities for special needs learners
Career Education for the Handicapped Child	LOVE Publishing	K–6	Activities on career education from K–6th grade
Comics Career Awareness Program	King Features	Adolescents	Fifteen career areas covered in comic book form
Pacemaker Vocational Readers	Fearon-Pitman	9–12	Ten books dealing with realistic work situations for secondary students
Math Around Us	Scott Foresman	3–7	Functional/Vocational arithmetic

THE LONG-TERM INSTRUCTIONAL UNIT APPROACH TO CAREER EDUCATION

☐ ☐ The special-education teacher may also decide to adopt the long-term instructional unit approach to work or consumer education. Long-term units relating to these topics have included, for example, such titles as "Finding and Keeping a Job," "Making Purchases Wisely," "Finding and Maintaining an Apartment," and "Buying and Caring for Clothing." All of these units typically last two to three weeks and incorporate all of the core subject matter areas. Since the topics themselves are relevant to career education and life-experience, the academic subject area content contained in the units is also career relevant. Finally, these units may also be used sequentially in interface with one another so that students move from unit to unit as material in each unit is mastered. Thus, by the time the students master all of the units, they have gained competence in the twenty-two LCCE competency areas and are ready for work and successful adult living.

Figure 12.5 shows some sample lesson plans taken from long-term instructional units on "Finding and Keeping a Job." In these lessons, each of the core areas directly relates to finding and keeping a job. Materials and assessment in the unit would also be specialized to the topic.

☐ Adopting an Existing Career Curriculum

Many large school systems have developed, adopted, and implemented career education curriculums for handicapped learners. These curriculums are readily available from university libraries, university instructional media centers, and state and county special-education resource centers. Typically, such curriculums

FIGURE 12.5   Sample Lesson Plans from the Long-Term Instructional Unit "Finding and Keeping a Job"

Curriculum Area: Language Arts   Duration: 30 minutes

Objective	Activity	Materials	Evaluation
1. Student will read want-ads in the daily newspaper and circle five jobs which the person a) is interested in and b) believes to be qualified for	Students will read the want-ads of their local, morning newspaper. Upon completion, they will circle five jobs and explain to the teacher why they are qualified for the position and why they are interested in the position	morning newspaper pen	Teacher evaluation
2. Student will telephone the place of employment and obtain information about a specific job, its duties, and pay	Students will locate the telephone number from the newspaper ad, call the job site, and obtain and write down information about the job	telephone paper pencil	

outline objectives and programs for senior high school special needs workers, but such curriculums often also include junior-high learners.

Two such curriculums are the West Allis-West Milwaukee Career Education Plan (Milwaukee, Wisconsin) and Vocational Instructional Materials for Students with Special Needs (Portland, Oregon). Both of these curriculums contain objectives, program goals, and activities designed to create the strong link of relevancy between school and work. Figure 12.6 contains samples taken from the West Allis-West Milwaukee Career Education Plan.

☐ Work Study

The work study program combines the formal academic program with on-the-job training, with the eventual goal of vocational employment (Kolstoe & Frey 1965). The key concept in work study is that the academic content taught in school is directly applicable to the vocational skills needed on the job at which the student will be working. For example, if a student is training to be a carpenter's helper, arithmetic skills taught would emphasize linear measurement and addition and subtraction computational skills.

There are three main stages to work study:

1. In-class activities in combination with on-campus (in-school) vocational-type work. Here, the students try out newly learned skills and the application of learned material in familiar environmental surroundings.
2. In-class academic instruction with half days of off-campus vocational work experience. The learner applies knowledge and learning in a closely supervised, real-world work environment.

FIGURE 12.6   Sample Activities Taken from the West Allies-West Milwaukee Career Education Plan

GOALS AND OBJECTIVES

1. To make all instructional subject matter more personally relevant through restructuring and focusing it around a career development theme when possible.
2. To provide all persons the guidance, counseling and instruction needed to (a) develop self-awareness and self-direction, (b) expand occupational awareness and aspirations, (c) develop appropriate attitudes about the personal and social significance of work.
3. To assure all persons an opportunity to gain an entry level marketable skill prior to their leaving school if termination is necessary or a desirable option.
4. To prepare all persons completing secondary school with the knowledge and skill necessary to become employed or to pursue more training.
5. To provide placement services for every person in his preparation for a career, whether it be placement assistance in employment or further education.
6. To build into the education system greater involvement and coordination of all possible resources in the community.
7. To facilitate entry and re-entry, either into the world of work or the educational system, for all persons through a flexible educational system which continually reviews and expands educational and occupational options.

(continued)

FIGURE 12.6   (continued)

Specific objectives as they relate to the implementation of the Life Centered Career Education Curriculum are presented below:

Instructional Objectives

1. To provide all students with the opportunity to develop the 22 Life Centered Career Education competencies.
2. To facilitate the integration of handicapped students into regular classes and services for career development.
3. To increase the number and kinds of hands on activities within various subject areas.
4. To encourage all teachers of handicapped students to emphasize the career implications of their subject matter and provide for career awareness, exploration, guidance, and preparation opportunities.

Community Involvement Objectives

1. To involve the family more appropriately in career education planning and services.
2. To involve community agencies more appropriately in career education planning and services.
3. To involve business and industry more appropriately in career education planning and services.

Other goals may be added as necessary since these only represent some essential goals which have been identified during the development of this curriculum.

1. Explanation of Curriculum Considerations for EEN Students

    A. *Academic Skills.*—Emphasis on functional skills (reading, writing and arithmetic) during the elementary school years establishes the foundation for subsequent learning appropriate for daily living, and occupational skills for community living and working. At the junior high school level the teaching of academic skills decreases as the teaching of specific daily living and occupation skills increases. Academic instruction at the senior high level aims to remediate those academic skills necessary for daily living and job placement.

    B. *Daily Living Skills.*—At the elementary level certain basic daily living skills can be taught in addition to the above mentioned academic skills. These skills include, but are not limited to, economic education, the need for leisure time activities, personal hygiene, and the need for local laws and government. An increased emphasis on teaching basic daily living skills plus the introduction of those subcompetencies that can be learned should occur at the junior high level. These could include information regarding personal finance, physical fitness, home and personal care, citizenship rights, and traffic laws. Senior high school students should learn as many of the subcompetencies that have not yet been taught/learned, and the procedures by which they can receive assistance for those competencies/subcompetencies they were unable to learn.

    C. *Personal-Social Skills.*—During the elementary school years students' personality development is important especially with regard to dealing with the attitudes and behaviors of other non-handicapped students. Instruction in developing self-confidence, displaying responsibility, acceptable behavior and other personal-social skills is important. Instruction in these skills should continue throughout the junior and senior high school.

    D. *Occupational Guidance and Preparation.*—Occupational development begins at the elementary level with an introduction to proper work habits, attitudes and values, and physical-manual skills. At the junior high school level occupational guidance and preparation continues with an emphasis on vocational subjects that develop pre-vocational skills and motivations. At this stage career exploration experiences in the community (e.g.; job try-outs, shadowing) assist students in their career development and decision-making.

COMPETENCY UNITS

In addition to its identification, each competency unit contains three sections: objectives, activities/strategies, and adult/peer roles, designed to assist teachers and counselors in providing students with experiences to develop and demonstrate each competency. No specific grade or developmental level is suggested for the teaching of each competency unit (subcompetency)—this is left to the discretion of the individual school and its career education plan. Obviously, some competency units could be taught during the elementary years, whereas others are more appropriate at

(continued)

FIGURE 12.6 (continued)

the junior high and senior high levels. The Competency Rating Scale (CRS) should assist educators in determining what competencies and subcompetencies have been acquired so appropriate educational programming can be done for each student. It is suggested that the Competency Rating Scale be introduced sometime during the upper elementary grades (5–6). Each section of the competency unit is discussed below:

1. *Objectives*

   Each competency unit contains suggestions for the sequencing of performance objectives for a specific subcompetency. An attempt has been made to arrange the objectives in a logical order although they can be arranged according to the instructor's evaluation of the student needs, to fit a class, or to correspond to the availability of resources. Objectives may be expanded and/or developed into smaller components to meet the specific learning abilities of the students. Additional performance objectives can be added to meet the individual needs of the learner.

2. *Activities/Strategies*

   Activities are the vehicle by which teachers, counselors, parents, administrators and community representatives shape the competencies. The suggested activities and strategies have NOT been arranged in a rigid hierarchy although some consideration has been given to difficulty levels. More appropriate activities may be inserted, depending on the characteristics of the students and available resources. The suggested activities/strategies make use of a wide assortment of resources and plans for instructions to prompt the teacher to approach the teaching task with variety. Utilization of community personnel to provide instructional activities and support is highly encouraged.

3. *Adult/Peer Roles*

   School personnel must continually attempt to bring their students into contact with community representatives—particularly role models for the demonstration of the competencies. In addition to owners of business and industries, it is recommended that the individuals who have jobs similar to those which handicapped students might later obtain should speak to the class about their work.

PROGRAM IMPLEMENTATION

The Life Centered Career Education Curriculum utilizes a competency based approach to career education. To integrate these competencies into the curriculum for handicapped students at the senior high school level, the following items have been developed:

1. RECOMMENDED FOUR YEAR PROGRAM
2. CRITERIA FOR·STUDENT ELIGIBILITY
3. ROLE/RESPONSIBILITIES OF EEN TEACHER

1. *Recommended Four Year Program*

A. Required Credits
   - 3 credits—English
   - 3 credits—Social Studies
   - 1 credit—Mathematics
   - 1 credit—Science
   - ¼ credit—Health
   - ¼ credit—Driver Education
   - ¼ credit—Pool
   - ¼ credit—Gym
   - ¼ credit—Physical Education
   - 10½ credits—Total

B. Electives
   - 1 credit—Vocational Ed I/Vocational Ed II (Course Title, Career Orientation)
   - 1 credit—Work Sample I/II
   - 3 credits—Work Experiences
   - 1 credit—Refresher/Consumer Math
   - 5 credit—Electives
   - 11 credits—Total

From C.J. Kohaska & D.E. Brolin (1985).

3. Total off-campus work experiences. Here the students receive full time, supervised instruction on the job at which they will eventually work. Since this work is unpaid, the students are allowed and expected to make mistakes from which they will learn. Close supervision and a tutorial atmosphere is maintained.

Work study is crucially important since it offers a transition from school to work. However, if the work study experience is to be successful, the teacher must make sure that

1. There is a direct and demonstrated link between academic content and the work experience.
2. This link is sequentially and systematically taught to students.
3. The transition between school and full-time work is gradual, systematic, and closely supervised.

ASSESSMENT IN CAREER EDUCATION

☐ ☐ Assessment in career education may take a variety of forms which include general aptitude batteries, assessment of occupational interests, assessment of currently possessed vocational skills, and collecting samples of a person's work behavior. Personal/social skills and life survival skills may also be assessed.

☐ Aptitude Tests

Aptitude tests measure the possession of traits and abilities needed for certain types of task success. Thus, the purpose of an aptitude test is to predict future success on a given task by measuring the person's innate or currently possessed raw abilities.

Vocational aptitude test batteries measure the possession of traits, skills, or competencies which may be needed for general job success. Such tests do not measure whether the person does or does not possess specific job competencies for a specific job, but rather tests possession of skills needed on a great variety of jobs.

☐ The General Aptitude Test Battery

The General Aptitude Test Battery (GATB, U.S. Department of Labor) was designed to test the vocational aptitude of high school students. It contains twelve subtests which measure the following nine basic vocational competencies:

1. **Intellectual-General Learning Ability:** Understanding instruction, ability to reason, and making judgments.
2. **Verbal Aptitude:** Ability to understand word meanings and associated concepts. Ability to understand sentences and phrases.
3. **Numerical Aptitude:** Perform mathematical operations.
4. **Spatial Ability:** Ability to visualize and comprehend forms and relationships in space.
5. **Form Perception:** Ability to handle pictorial or graphic material. Ability to see and understand differences and similarities in forms.
6. **Clerical Perception:** Ability to abstract out the important information contained in tabular material. Includes ability to proofread and make quick, accurate calculations.
7. **Motor Coordination:** Ability for accurate eye-hand coordination and to make quick, accurate movements.
8. **Finger Dexterity:** Ability to manipulate small objects.
9. **Manual Dexterity:** Ability to move hands in various directions with ease.

The GATB has been well validated and is probably the most popular of the vocational aptitude batteries. It has also been shown to be quite reliable. Unfortunately, it takes almost two and a half hours to administer, so students taking the tests will need frequent rests. The most damaging aspect of the GATB, however, is that it requires a great deal of reading ability to take the test. Thus, if a student performs poorly the question remains: Did the poor score occur because of poor vocational aptitude or because of overall poor reading ability?

Because of the high need for reading on the GATB, the U.S. Department of Labor devised a nonreading version of the battery known as the Non-Reading Aptitude Test Battery (NATB). This test is especially useful with nonreading, low achieving students such as mildly mentally retarded pupils. Using a nonreading format through oral vocabulary, design completion, and form matching, the NATB measures the same aptitudes as the GATB. However, the teacher intending to use the NATB should be aware that there is a possibility of inappropriateness of the test norms; the norms used for the GATB were simply transferred to the NATB. Since the populations taking the two tests will probably be quite different in terms of reading ability and academic achievement, the use of such norm transfer is questionable. Nevertheless, the NATB is a useful test to use with nonreading populations such as the mentally retarded if used with caution.

☐ Interest Inventories

Interest inventories measure interests, not abilities. Actually the relationship between interests and abilities is often rather low. Thus the teacher or counselor must help the student realize that interest in an occupation does not mean the student possesses the abilities to succeed at that job.

There are a number of occupational interest inventories available. One of the newest is the Occupational Aptitude Survey and Interest Schedule (OASIS) (Parker 1983). This test is both an aptitude survey and an interest inventory so that the purchaser of the tests gets two assessment instruments for the price of one. The instrument is appropriate for students in grades eight to twelve, including special-needs learners. The aptitude portion of the test contains subtests in the areas of vocabulary, computational skills, spatial relations, word comparisons, and making marks (manual dexterity). The interest inventory section measures the student's degree of like, dislike, or neutrality in twelve areas: artistic, scientific, nature, protection (law enforcement, etc.), mechanical, industrial, business, sales, accommodating professions (e.g., beautician), humanitarianism, leadership, and physical labor. Information obtained from these twelve scales helps guide the student into relevant and interesting occupational fields.

Other available interest inventories include the Strong Vocational Interest Blanks (SVIB), the Kuder Preference Records and Interest Survey, the California Occupational Preference Survey (COPS), the Ohio Vocational Survey (OVIS), and the Minnesota Interest Inventory (MVII). Although these tests differ in the various ways in which they endeavor to measure the student's occupational and other interests, the central goal of all is to help the individual realize what her or his interests might be. Figure 12.7 shows some sample items from the tests as well as a sample interest profile taken from the SVIB.

☐ Work Samples

In the last decade, many school systems have moved away from administering paper and pencil vocational tests which infer how a student might do in a given situation based on how he or she answers some test questions to collecting work samples which actually measure how students perform on actual work-type tasks.

FIGURE 12.7 Vocational Interest Inventories

a. Sample Item from the Kuder Interest Inventory

Punch your choices for these activities in the section at the right.

		M O L
P.	Visit an art gallery	● P ●
Q.	Browse in a library	● Q ○ ← LEAST
R.	Visit a museum ..... MOST →	○ R ●
S.	Collect signatures of famous people ..... MOST →	○ S ●
T.	Collect coins	● T ●
U.	Collect butterflies	● U ○ ← LEAST

(continued)

FIGURE 12.7 (continued)

b. Profile Score from the Strong-Campbell Interest Inventory

SCII Profile for ROMEN LENNY
Sex F Age 22 Date Scored 10/07/83
19 85 146 TWO 566236721 ◄ Sheet I.D.
Date Administered 09/28/83

Page Two
CONSULTING PSYCHOLOGISTS PRESS

COUNSELOR'S COPY

Occupational Scales

Code	Scale	Sex Norm	Standard Score
IRC	Computer Programmer	M	40
IRE	Chiropractor	F	24
IRE	Chiropractor	M	37
IE	Pharmacist	M	42
I	Pharmacist	F	28
I	Biologist	F	14
I	Biologist	M	13
I	Geographer	F	18
I	Geographer	M	24
I	Mathematician	F	3
I	Mathematician	M	16
IA	College Professor	F	20
IA	College Professor	M	32
IA	Sociologist	F	8
IA	Sociologist	M	32
IAS	Psychologist	F	15
IAS	Psychologist	M	28
AIR	Architect	F	<0
AIR	Architect	M	13
AI	Lawyer	F	9
AI	Lawyer	M	33
AE	Public Relations Director	F	6
AE	Public Relations Director	M	20
AE	Advertising Executive	F	16
AE	Advertising Executive	M	25
AE	Interior Decorator	F	<0
AE	Interior Decorator	M	19
A	Musician	F	20
A	Musician	M	27
A	Commercial Artist	F	<0
A	Commercial Artist	M	11
A	Fine Artist	F	<0
A	Fine Artist	M	3
A	Art Teacher	F	16
A	Art Teacher	M	25
A	Photographer	F	15
A	Photographer	M	20
A	Librarian	F	15
A	Librarian	M	35
A	Foreign Language Teacher	F	22
A	Foreign Language Teacher	M	41
A	Reporter	F	13
A	Reporter	M	37
A	English Teacher	F	34
AS	English Teacher	M	43
SA	Speech Pathologist	F	30
SA	Speech Pathologist	M	54
SA	Social Worker	F	26
SA	Social Worker	M	45
SA	Minister	F	32
SIE	Minister	M	38
SI	Registered Nurse	F	45
S	Licensed Pratical Nurse	M	57
S	Special Ed. Teacher	F	48
S	Special Ed. Teacher	M	74
S	Elementary Teacher	F	49
S	Elementary Teacher	M	60
SR	Physical Ed. Teacher	F	51

(similarity scale markings: 12 21 27 39 45 54 60)

Occupational Scales

Code	Scale	Sex Norm	Standard Score
SR	Physical Ed. Teacher	M	62
SRE	Recreation Leader	F	40
SRE	Recreation Leader	M	44
SE	YWCA Director	F	52
SE	YMCA Director	M	46
SE	School Administrator	F	39
SE	School Administrator	M	48
SCE	Guidance Counselor	M	54
SEC	Guidance Counselor	F	45
SEC	Social Science Teacher	F	38
SEC	Social Science Teacher	M	48
EA	Flight Attendant	F	35
EA	Flight Attendant		50
EA	Beautician	M	41
E	Beautician	F	30
E	Dept. Store Manager	F	33
E	Dept. Store Manager	M	34
E	Realtor	F	20
E	Realtor	M	25
E	Life Insurance Agent	F	26
E	Life Insurance Agent	M	27
E	Elected Public Official	F	22
E	Elected Public Official	M	28
E	Public Administrator	F	13
EI	Investment Fund Manager	M	19
EI	Marketing Executive	F	9
EI	Marketing Executive	M	16
E	Personnel Director	F	31
E	Personnel Director	M	44
E	Chamber of Commerce Exec.	M	21
E	Restaurant Manager	M	27
EC	Restaurant Manager	F	31
EC	Chamber of Commerce Exec.	F	24
EC	Buyer	F	35
EC	Buyer	M	24
EC	Purchasing Agent	F	39
EC	Purchasing Agent	M	41
ERC	Agribusiness Manager	M	23
ES	Home Economics Teacher	F	39
ECS	Nursing Home Administrator	M	52
EC	Nursing Home Administrator	F	33
EC	Dietician	F	31
ECR	Dietician	M	55
CER	Executive Housekeeper	F	48
CER	Executive Housekeeper	M	55
CES	Business Ed. Teacher	F	41
CES	Business Ed. Teacher	M	47
CE	Banker	F	48
CE	Banker	M	34
CE	Credit Manager	F	39
CE	Credit Manager	M	53
CE	IRS Agent	F	52
CE	IRS Agent	M	55
CA	Public Administrator	M	40
C	Accountant	F	19
C	Accountant	M	36
C	Secretary	F	49
C	Dental Assistant	F	48

(similarity scale markings: 12 21 27 39 45 54 60)

(continued)

FIGURE 12.7 (continued)

SCII Profile for ROMEN LENNY

Sex	Age	Date Scored
F	22	10/07/83

19 85 146 ONE 566236721 ◄ Sheet I.D.

Date Administered 09/28/83

Page One

General Occupational Themes

Theme	Std Score	Result
R – Theme	65	This is a VERY HIGH
I – Theme	54	This is a AVERAGE
A – Theme	56	This is a AVERAGE
S – Theme	66	This is a VERY HIGH
E – Theme	61	This is a MODERATELY HIGH
C – Theme	65	This is a HIGH

Administrative Indexes

Total Responses		325	
Infrequent Responses		6	
	L%	I%	D%
Occupations	56	37	8
School Subjects	47	44	8
Activities	59	31	10
Amusements	41	54	5
Types of People	25	75	0
Preferences	17	43	40
Characteristics	79	14	7
All Parts	49	41	10

Special Scales

Academic Comfort: 50

Introversion-Extroversion: 35

Basic Interest Scales

	Scale	Std Score	Result
R – Theme	Agriculture	52	This is a AVERAGE
	Nature	58	This is a MODERATELY HIGH
	Adventure	59	This is a HIGH
	Military Activities	62	This is a VERY HIGH
	Mechanical Activities	62	This is a HIGH
I – Theme	Science	50	This is a AVERAGE
	Mathematics	53	This is a AVERAGE
	Medical Science	58	This is a MODERATELY HIGH
	Medical Service	60	This is a HIGH
A – Theme	Music/Dramatics	61	This is a MODERATELY HIGH
	Art	50	This is a AVERAGE
	Writing	59	This is a AVERAGE
S – Theme	Teaching	62	This is a HIGH
	Social Service	67	This is a VERY HIGH
	Athletics	64	This is a VERY HIGH
	Domestic Arts	68	This is a HIGH
	Religious Activities	62	This is a AVERAGE
E – Theme	Public Speaking	47	This is a AVERAGE
	Law/Politics	49	This is a AVERAGE
	Merchandising	56	This is a MODERATELY HIGH
	Sales	46	This is a AVERAGE
	Business Management	60	This is a HIGH
C	Office Practices	67	This is a HIGH

Occupational Scales

Code	Scale	Sex Norm	Standard Score
RC	Air Force Officer	F	26
RC	Air Force Officer	M	31
RC	Army Officer	F	44
RC	Army Officer	M	42
RC	Navy Officer	M	46
R	Navy Officer	F	41
RE	Police Officer	F	54
RE	Police Officer	M	53
RCE	Voc Agric Teacher	M	27
RC	Farmer	F	36
R	Farmer	M	19
R	Forester	M	24
R	Skilled Craftsperson	M	24
R	Radiology Technician	F	52
RI	Radiology Technician	M	49
RI	Forester	F	24
RI	Engineer	F	26
RI	Engineer	M	19
RI	Veterinarian	M	30
RIC	Licensed Practical Nurse	F	38
RAS	Occupational Therapist	F	38
RAS	Occupational Therapist	M	47
IR	Veterinarian	F	16
IR	Chemist	F	10
IR	Chemist	M	15
IR	Physicist	F	5
IR	Physicist	M	2
IR	Geologist	F	2
IR	Geologist	M	14
IR	Medical Technician	F	31
IR	Medical Technician	M	41
IR	Dental Hygienist	F	39
IR	Dentist	F	30
IR	Dentist	M	37
IR	Optometrist	F	29
IR	Optometrist	M	32
IR	Physical Therapist	F	37
IR	Physical Therapist	M	52
IR	Physician	F	16
IR	Physician	M	27
IRS	Registered Nurse	M	57
IRS	Math-Science Teacher	M	40
IRC	Math-Science Teacher	F	39
IRC	Systems Analyst	F	27
IRC	Systems Analyst	M	28
IRC	Computer Programmer	F	31

Reproduced by special permission of the distributor, Consulting Psychologists Press, Inc., Palo Alto, CA 94306, for the publisher, Stanford University Press, from Manual for the SVIB-SCII by Jo-Ida Hansen & David Campbell. © 1985 by the Board of Trustees of Leland Stanford Junior University.

Career education professionals collect samples via a systematic and standardized procedure. Thus, work samples represent for the teacher a highly relevant and valid way of assessing work behaviors for specific job clusters.

There are a variety of commercially available work sample kits available. These systems assess a wide variety of specific work-related behaviors that are needed to perform successfully on specific job clusters. In performing on these work sample tests, students typically move through a series of stations which demand different job-related behaviors. Work sample kits available to the teacher include:

1. Jewish Employment and Vocational Services Kit (Jewish Employment and Vocational Services 1976): Includes twenty-eight hands-on work assessments organized in a hierarchy of complexity. The samples expose the worker/student to a variety of work traits listed in the *Dictionary of Occupational Titles* (DOT): Samples include assembly/disassembly, binding, clerical work, printing, housekeeping, mail handling, mechanical sorting, tailoring, and metal work.

2. MICRO-TOWER System: (Bachman 1976): Assesses student work habits, tolerance, attitudes, work speed, general motivation, and skills. Collects work samples in the areas of clerical, drawing, jewelry making, welding, mail clerk, sewing, and electronics.

3. Hester Evaluation Samples (Goodwill Industries): Measures twenty-eight independent job factors and relates them to jobs and job clusters listed in the DOT. It is appropriate for use with most populations of exceptional students including the blind.

4. Valpar Component: (Brandon, Balton, Rup & Raslter 1974): Measures sixteen work samples including small tools, size discrimination, numerical sorting, upper extremity range, independent problem solving, eye-hand-foot coordination, money use, and reading. Keyed to the DOT.

5. Comprehensive Occupational Assessment Training System (COATS) (prep 1976): Devised for mildly handicapped populations. Measures work samples, employability attitudes, and living skills. Skills are matched and keyed to the DOT.

6. Wide-Range Employment Sample Test (WREST) (Jastak & Jastak 1980): Developed for moderately mentally retarded individuals who probably will be working in a workshop setting. Measures ten work samples which include single and double folding, pasting, labeling, stuffing, stapling, bottle packaging, rice measuring, screw assembly, tag stringing, swatch pasting, collating, color matching, and pattern making. Uses industrial workshop norms acquired from a moderately mentally retarded population.

7. McCarron-Dial Work Evaluation System (McCarron & Dial 1976): Includes seventeen separate tests in five areas including verbal/cognitive ability, sensory-motor abilities, emotional coping and work activities. Designed for a moderately mentally retarded population.

It should be pointed out that work samples are not aptitude tests. Rather, they measure the current level of skill functioning for success on given jobs and job clusters. As such they are achievement tests which indicate to the teacher whether or not a student is "job ready" for a given occupation.

CREATING THE CAREER EDUCATIONAL CURRICULUM

☐ ☐ Once the vocational assessment is complete, it is time to use that information to create a curriculum of skills to be learned in order to help the student achieve occupational and independent living success. The career curriculum would contain the following components:

1. Topic, subtopic, and rationale.
2. Long-term behavioral objectives which include the concept or skill to be learned. These objectives should be spelled out in precise behavioral terms.
3. The long-term objectives written in step two above broken down into a hierarchy of subobjectives which break down the long-term objectives into its subcomponents.
4. Instructional activities for each subcomponent skill.
5. Materials and resources available for the teaching of the long-term and subobjectives.
6. A system of evaluating mastery of each subskill and each long-term objective.
7. A system of evaluating mastery of all the job skills needed for job success on a given specific job.

The first task that confronts the teacher is creation of the long-term objectives which correspond to the requisite job skills of a specific job. How is the teacher to know what specific job skills are needed for each job?

This task would be largely a hit or miss proposition if it were not for the *Dictionary of Occupational Titles* (DOT) (U.S. Department of Labor). The DOT provides descriptive information on over 22,000 occupations in fifteen job categories or clusters ranging from agriculture to transportation. For each occupation, levels of the job are described (ranging from entry level to supervisory level), and the specific competencies needed for each job are delineated. Figure 12.8a shows the fifteen job clusters contained in the DOT while Figure 12.8b shows the levels and competency descriptions for a specific occupation.

In creating long-term instructional objectives during the career preparation stage, the teacher translates the occupational competencies listed for a level of a specific occupation into instructional objective format. Recall that sound instructional objectives contain three components: an observable, measurable behavior; the conditions under which the behavior is to occur; and the criteria for master-

FIGURE 12.8   Dictionary of Occupational Titles

a. The Fifteen Job Clusters

1. Agribusiness and Natural Resources
2. Business and Office
3. Health
4. Public Service
5. Environment
6. Communication and Media
7. Hospitality and Recreation
8. Manufacturing
9. Marketing and Distribution
10. Marine Science
11. Personal Services
12. Construction
13. Transportation
14. Consumer and Homemaking
15. Fine Arts

b. Levels and Competency Descriptions in a Specific Occupation

CLUSTER RELATED INSTRUCTIONAL AREAS (Course titles and/or major instructional units)	CAREER CLUSTER: AUTOMOTIVE AND POWER SERVICE OCCUPATIONS			
Auto mechanics	Automobile mechanic helper Used car renovator	Muffler installer Automobile accessories installer Tune-up man	Automobile mechanic Transmission mechanic Automobile service mechanic	
Small engine repair		Gasoline engine repairman Power saw mechanic Outboard motor mechanic Motorcycle repairman		
Auto body repair	Automobile body repairman Helper	Painter, automobile Automobile body repairman	Shop estimator	
Heating and air conditioning	Ventilation man Furnace installer & repairman helper Air cond. installer domestic		Furnaceman	
Service station	Automobile service station attendant			
Level:	Laborer Sorter or Assistant packer Helper Loader Worker Attendant Tender	Operator Clerk Driver Installer Assembler Aide	Craftsman Supervisor Technician Inspector Complex operator	Middle manager Foreman Official

From L.A. Phelps & R. Lutz (1977).

ing the objective. Thus, the teacher's job in creating long-term career education instructional objectives is translating the job competencies listed in the DOT into sound instruction objective format.

Once the long-term objectives have been written, each objective needs to be broken down into hierarchical and sequenced subobjectives. This is a tricky task; break them down too fine and you run the risk of overwhelming and eventually boring the student with mundane detail. Make each subobjective too broad and you run the risk of confusing the student and not being systematic enough in your instruction.

Task analysis can be most helpful in breaking down objectives into subobjectives. Task analysis involves the breaking down of a work task into its component movements, materials, and responses and the subsequent re-chaining of the components back into the integrated, total task (Haines 1982; Rusch & Mithaug 1980). More specifically, task analysis consists of a three step process:

1. Deciding how to perform the total task.
2. Breaking the total task into its components.
3. Creating a task analysis data sheet which outlines training and subsequent mastery of each step (see Figure 12.9).

In order to construct a task analysis of a given skill, the teacher should implement the following procedures (Bellamy, Horner & Inman 1979):

1. Have the person doing the actual training of the task construct the task analysis. This person knows the task best.
2. Have the trainer perform the task to be taught several times exactly as the student must perform it.
3. Break the task down into *functional responses*. These responses represent the crucial, most important responses which describe the performance of the task. List the order in which these responses must be performed.
4. For each step in the chain, identify the controlling stimulus known as the discriminitive stimulus or *S* which triggers each functional response.
5. Make sure that the *S* does not also cue competing or inappropriate responses.
6. Construct the data training sheet (see Figure 12.9).

EMPLOYER CONTACTS: FINDING JOBS FOR STUDENTS

☐ ☐ Look again at the career clusters from the DOT shown in Figure 12.8. Do all of these clusters exist in your community? Probably not. For example, a community heavily involved in farming and agribusiness is not also likely to have a steel mill

FIGURE 12.9 A Sample Task Analysis Data Sheet

Auto Body Maintenance Occupational Cluster

Directions: Listed below are a series of tasks performed in one or more of the selected entry occupations identified for this cluster. For each task that is "essential or critical" for successful entry performance in the identified occupation, place an "x" in the appropriate box. For each task that is a "desirable" competency in a worker entering the identified occupation, place an "o" in the appropriate box. Add any tasks that are essential (x) or desirable (o) to successful occupational performance which are not listed.

Name of Respondent _____

Place of Employment _____

Occupation _____

No. of Years in Occupation _____

		CLUSTER OCCUPATIONS			
ID CODE	TASK INVENTORY	SHOP ESTIMATOR	AUTOMOBILE BODY REPAIRMAN	PAINTER, AUTOMOBILE	AUTOMOBILE BODY REPAIRMAN HELPER
ABM 01	Remove, overhaul, and replace trim and hardware		X	O	X
ABM 02	Perform bumping operations	X	X	O	O
ABM 03	Remove and replace body components		X	X	X
ABM 04	Prepare surface for painting		O	X	X
ABM 05	Apply masking tape and paper			X	X
ABM 06	Operate spray paint equipment			X	O
ABM 07	Perform lacquer refinishing			X	O
ABM 08	Perform enamel refinishing			X	O
ABM 09	Remove and install glass		X	O	X
ABM 10	Prepare vehicle for delivery	O	O	O	X
ABM 11	Estimate damage repairs	X	X	O	
ABM 12	Select and use appropriate materials and supplies	X	X	X	X

From L.A. Phelps & R. Lutz (1977).

389

in town. Likewise, cities not near a major port are not likely to support shipbuilding and marine biology.

Knowing what job clusters exist in the area around which you are teaching is important for the job training of the students with whom you are working. Perhaps the worst thing that can be done in career education is to prepare students for careers in which there are no jobs in the area in which they are living. While there is a chance that they could move to some distant geographical area, it is more likely that they would stay relatively close to home.

How might the appropriateness of given job clusters in a community be identified as appropriate or inappropriate? One of the best ways to accomplish this is to contact business and community leaders and use them as resources. By contacting and interviewing these persons, you can easily learn what job clusters and jobs within clusters currently exist in the community in which you are teaching as well as what jobs are likely to open as the community possibly grows and expands its business base. More specifically, these individuals will be able to give you information regarding:

1. Demands for workers with particular skills.
2. Changes in job classifications.
3. Modification of skill requirements in given jobs.
4. New local growth coming in the near future.

There are other sources which may be used in order to find out about jobs currently available in your community area. These sources include:

1. The Yellow Pages of your local telephone book
2. The Help Wanted section of your local newspaper
3. The state employment service
4. Local trade unions
5. Civil service bulletins
6. Local employment counselors

Regardless of the sources used (and the more sources used the more reliable the information will be), the central task is to find out the types of jobs that exist in the community. Armed with this information, you will be assured of training students for jobs that actually exist and those that have growth potential.

JOB PLACEMENT AND FOLLOW-UP: CONTACTING POTENTIAL EMPLOYERS

☐ ☐ Assume that you have created a career education curriculum and instructional program and that they have been an unqualified success. That is, your students have learned both job competencies and independent living skills and are ready to exit your program. What remains to be done? The answer is job placement at a meaningful, salaried job.

Sound simple? Well, it is not. Unfortunately, many prospective employers do not want to hire handicapped individuals. They often believe that such individuals are less healthy, need special working conditions, and are less cost efficient than nonhandicapped workers. It will be your job to convince them otherwise.

There are a variety of things the teacher or school vocational professional can do to better the chances of convincing a potential employer to hire special needs learners (Kokaska & Brolin 1985). These include

1. Study the employer's business, procedures or services the business provides. The more you know about the business, the more intelligently you can discuss how hiring handicapped workers would impact on that business. In short, do your homework!
2. Point out to prospective employers that the traditional stereotypes regarding handicapped workers simply do not hold up under test. Handicapped students are not a liability to themselves or their coworkers; they have demonstrated safety on the job; insurance rates do not go up when handicapped workers are hired; and they can be cost effective.
3. Decide on the most appropriate method of contact. Usually initial contact will be made by mail or by telephone followed by a face-to-face meeting.
4. Prepare a sales presentation. You're selling something of great value—your career education program!
5. Have logical arguments ready to counter resistance or stereotypical beliefs by employers.
6. Build rapport with employers.
7. Stay on the topic at hand. The employer's time is very valuable. Don't meander all over the place.
8. Speak in terms the employer can understand. However, don't talk down to employers. They are intelligent people.
9. Emphasize the effort, care, and past successes of your career education program.
10. Emphasize your availability after the initial job placement is made. Promise that you will do frequent follow-up and visitations to make sure that the student is performing well on the job. Keep this promise!

This last point is crucial both to the success of your program and the future success of placing students on jobs. You cannot simply place a student on a job and then forget about the person. Rather, you must follow-up and make sure that things are working out. Recall our example about the young man on the automobile assembly line job described at the beginning of this chapter. Part of the reason that the placement almost failed was that the teacher did not engage in adequate follow-up. Remember, the best laid plans (as well as job placements) often go astray. And such mistakes will never be corrected if appropriate and frequent job follow-up is not made.

☐ Follow-up and Evaluation

It is crucial to maintain contact with the employer after the student is placed on the job and begins work. This contact can occur through the special-education teacher or through the auspices of the school employment counselor or work-study personnel. This follow-up should not be incidental and occasional but regular and systematic, for the purpose of detailed evaluation of the worker's on-the-job progress. Such evaluation should occur in the following areas:

1. Job duties and responsibilities. What duties have been assigned to the worker? Are they performed in an acceptable manner?
2. Achievement levels. What is the level of achievement of the worker on a variety of tasks? Is the worker productive as productivity is defined by the employer?
3. Areas for improvement. Where does the employee need to improve? Is this improvement needed to meet the minimum requirements necessary to keep the job? How can the trainer help in the improvement process?
4. Communication. Does the worker communicate adequately and appropriately with supervisors and coworkers?
5. Acceptance. Is the worker accepted by supervisors and coworkers? Does the worker get along with others?
6. Overall evaluation. What is the bottom line for this worker? Is the worker successful on the job? Is the person making it?

The teacher or vocational counselor may wish to prepare a formal evaluation form for the employer and supervisor to complete periodically. Such completed forms may be kept in the worker's file (which remains with the teacher) so that progress can be periodically checked. The teacher should also periodically interview the worker to get an indication of job satisfaction and to deal with any motivational problems which may be arising. When intervention is indicated, it may be appropriate for the trainer (teacher) to work with the worker either by having the student return to the classroom environment for a short, concentrated period of time or to arrange for remedial procedures to be instituted at the job site. Wherever the remediation is to take place, it is important that it occur as soon after the inappropriate behavior is noticed and reported as possible so that the inappropriate employee behavior does not become habitual.

SUMMARY

☐ ☐ Career education is more than just training students for jobs. Rather, it is providing the training that mentally retarded learners need to become successful as workers, consumers, and citizens. In short, it is training in successful adult living.

The life-experience approach to the career education curriculum is reflected in the Life Centered Career Education Approach (LCCE). This curriculum contains twenty-two competency areas in the areas of daily living, personal social skills, and occupational training. These areas would be taught within the institutions of school, the family, and the community in which the learner resides.

Career education should not just occur during the high-school years. Rather, it should be an integrated program which encompasses the entire school career. A three-stage model of career education has been advanced which includes career awareness, career exploration, and career preparation. Career awareness is begun during the elementary-school years and involves understanding what work is and why people engage in the activity. Career exploration occurs during junior high school and involves the student investigating the different employment opportunities existing in the environment. Finally, career preparation occurs during high school and involves training for a specific job.

It is vitally important that subject matter taught in all of the core academic areas be career relevant. There are different techniques which the teacher may employ to help insure subject matter relevancy. These include adopting specialized career oriented academic materials, using the long-term instructional unit approach, adopting existing career education curricula, and operating in work-study programs.

Assessment is very important in career education. Assessment includes the use of aptitude tests, interest surveys, and work samples. Assessment yields a career education profile which may be used to help the handicapped learner find a suitable job.

In creating career educational programs the teacher may wish to use the *Dictionary of Occupational Titles* (DOT). Job roles and competencies in the DOT would be converted to long-term instructional objectives and then these objectives would be broken down into subobjectives using task analysis procedures. Mastery level of each long-term objective would be required before the student would move to later objectives in the learning sequence.

Part of the career education process is making contact with potential employers. Teachers must be prepared to overcome employer resistence to hiring handicapped learners and should be prepared to present such potential employees in a positive but realistic light. Once the student is placed on a job, follow-up is extremely important to rectify any problems which may arise on the job. A promise of periodic follow-up and evaluation by the teacher can be a major selling point to potential employers in hiring special needs students.

PART IV

Creating the Classroom Environment

13

Arranging and Managing the Classroom

Key Concepts

☐ Variables of Effective Classroom Management
    Problem Anticipation
    Overlapping Attention
    Preparedness and Momentum
    Signal Continuity
    Group Alerting
    Variety and Challenge
☐ Steps in Preparing to be an Effective Teacher
    Before the School Year Begins
    In the First Days and Weeks of Class
☐ Arranging the Classroom Environment
    Arranging the Furniture
    Using Floor and Wall Space
    Having the Right Equipment and Using It Correctly

Many prospective teachers spend the summer months prior to reporting to school reading up on educational methods, designing curriculum, and planning instructional activities. By the time the first day of school arrives and it is time to meet the new class, these first year teachers possess a relatively good idea of what and how they are going to teach and are excited and motivated about their teaching future.

Now, meet the same teachers in the new teaching assignments after the first week or two of school. Often, they are in a state of shock, perhaps even questioning why they ever entered the teaching profession in the first place. What happens in those two short weeks? Many times the teachers enter an educational environment for which they have never been trained in their college courses. Now the teachers' world has turned into a quagmire of discipline problems; of difficulties in managing the physical and psychological environment of the classroom; of questions and rebellion over homework, tests, and seating assignments; and of difficulties in record keeping and data processing. In short, the new teachers' anxiety and frustration results from daily difficulties in dealing with effective classroom management.

The next two chapters will deal with issues not often covered in the teacher preparation curriculum: arranging the physical environment of the classroom, creating a facilitative psychological environment conducive to learning, and using strategies to change inappropriate student behaviors. This chapter will deal with the first topics, effective teacher preparation and creating a physical classroom environment conducive to meaningful learning.

CLASSROOM MANAGEMENT: AN OVERVIEW

☐ ☐ In successful classrooms students appear to be on task and paying attention, and discipline problems are at a minimum. How do these classrooms differ from those in which teachers are experiencing management difficulties, where a significant proportion of time is spent on keeping students on task, and where students appear unmotivated to learn? Given these two very discrepant learning environments, can differences in teacher-student interaction patterns be identified?

Kounin (1970, 1977) investigated the characteristics of effective teachers-managers. This was accomplished by videotaping two types of classrooms. The first was exemplified by smoothness of operation—students were on task, and discipline problems were at a minimum. By contrast, the second type was extremely chaotic. It appeared to be a type of environment in which the teacher was constantly fighting to maintain order and activities were constantly suffering from frequent disruptions by students. Kounin found that the teachers in the effective classrooms engaged in certain behaviors that were different from teachers operating in the ineffective classes. These differences included:

1. **Problem anticipation:** This was labeled by Kounin as *withitness*. The effective teachers nipped classroom problems in the bud before they had the opportunity to escalate into disruption. They accomplished this by monitoring the classroom consistently and by stationing themselves so they could see all of the students in the class simultaneously. This transmitted the message to students that the teachers were aware of what was going on in the class at all times, and that they were able and likely to detect inappropriate student behavior quickly and accurately.

2. **Overlapping attention:** Effective classroom managers were able to engage in more than one activity at a time. For example, while helping a student or answering questions, the effective teacher was still able to monitor the activities of the rest of the class. Of equal importance, effective teachers appeared able to handle routine and mundane matters (e.g. collecting milk money or taking attendance) without disrupting the entire class and while keeping track of what class members were doing.

3. **Preparedness and momentum:** Effective teachers were prepared for their lessons. They knew the material they wished to teach and had their instructional materials handy. There were little or no interruptions in the

pace of the lesson caused by the teacher referring to and reading notes nor did the teacher waste time fumbling to find or set up instructional materials. In fact, many of the effective teachers did not resort to notes at all but were able to present material extemporaneously while maintaining eye contact with class members.

4. **Signal continuity:** Kounin found that effective teachers could handle minor disruptions during lesson presentation without interrupting the lesson; in fact, they could handle many potential disruptions nonverbally while continuing the lesson. Such teachers usually ignored fleeting inattention, dealing with more serious lapses of attention by moving nearer to students, using eye contact, directing a question at the inattentive student, or by making a brief lesson-related comment in the student's direction. They did not interrupt lessons with long reprimands or comments that focused attention on the disruptive student. In a variety of ways, these teachers gave clear signals about where students were to focus their attention.

5. **Group alerting and accountability:** Effective teachers used presentation and questioning techniques that kept the class alert and attending to the lesson. Techniques such as keeping students in suspense as to who would be called on next, calling upon students in random order and at unspecified times, choosing different students to respond, and challenging students that upcoming questions would be tricky or difficult. The goal of effective teachers as described by Kounin was to keep students attentive and alert that something interesting, provocative, or exciting could happen at any time, and by making them aware of the fact that it could be they who would be called upon next.

6. **Variety and challenge in seatwork:** Kounin found that students attended to tasks during seatwork when they perceived the assignment as interesting and of appropriate difficulty, not too easy to be unchallenging nor too hard to insure ultimate failure. In addition, during seatwork times, effective teachers circulated around the room instead of remaining seated at the desk making sure that students were on task and acting as a facilitator of learning.

Subsequent research conducted on what makes teachers effective classroom managers has generally supported much of Kounin's findings. For example, Kounin's withitness, anticipating disruptions before they occur, being able to do more than one task at a time, and smoothness of presentation style have all been found to be key variables in effective classroom management (Anderson, Evertson & Brophy 1979; Brophy & Evertson 1978). Likewise, it has been found that moderate levels of using group alerting techniques (as opposed to using this technique either excessively or not at all) facilitated student attentiveness and led to effective classroom control (Good & Grouws 1977). Finally, the difficulty and challenge level of independent seatwork has been found to be dependent in part on whether or not the teacher is present to act as a facilitator and answer student questions (Brophy & Evertson 1978; Gambrell, Wilson & Gnatt 1981; Fisher et al

1980). In situations where the teacher is present during seatwork assignments and is circulating around the room to help students, assignments of moderate difficulty with a success rate of 70–80 percent have been found to be appropriate for keeping student interest. However, in situations where the teacher is not present to act as a facilitator (i.e., take home assignments), a higher success rate (about 90–95 percent) is necessary.

PREPARING TO BE AN EFFECTIVE TEACHER

☐ ☐ One of the attributes of effective teaching is preparation. The effective teacher is one who possesses a thorough understanding of the material, who can deliver that material extemporaneously, who has a firm knowledge of where materials are and how to use them, and who demonstrates a knowledge of the school environment and how it operates. Clearly, the effective teacher is one who is prepared from the first day of school rather than the teacher who takes valuable days or even weeks learning the procedures and the ins and outs of school operations. Thus, according to Charles (1983), the successful teacher is one who even before the school year begins has made plans and instituted behavior in order to be organized and ready.

Charles (1983) argues that the first days and weeks of the school year are absolutely crucial for effective teaching. Thus, he suggests that the teacher spend time planning in the following areas:

Before the Year Begins
1. Getting acquainted with school facilities and personnel.
2. Planning the physical classroom environment.
3. Planning the psychological and emotional tone of the classroom.

Within the First Days or Weeks of Class
1. Preparing attendance and opening procedures.
2. Constructing seating arrangements.
3. Orienting the classroom.
4. Instituting class rules and a system of discipline.
5. Creating a daily lesson schedule.
6. Selection of student helpers and/or monitors.
7. Instituting rules for routine procedures such as bathroom, drinks, etc.
8. Establishing traffic patterns and regulations within the classroom.
9. Instituting playground and recess regulations.
10. Establishing the role of paraprofessionals such as teacher's aides.
11. Creating a schedule and establishing a procedure for substitute teachers.

The effective teacher decides and institutes crucial decisions either before the school year begins or in the first days after school opens. Such policies set the proper classroom environment for the remainder of the school year. Thus, the teacher who vacillates for days or weeks on the procedures for conducting the class runs the serious risk of losing control that may never be gained back even after classroom operating procedures are decided. Thus, the key word is *preparedness*—be ready beforehand, ideally even before the class meets for the first time. By spending time on preparation, the teacher will short circuit many problems relating to classroom management.

CREATING A BLUEPRINT

☐ ☐ One of the first things the teacher needs to do is schedule the activities of the school day. This schedule then becomes the blueprint or master plan for activities throughout the day. Scheduling can be harder than it looks. This is particularly so because there are outside factors that affect how you plan the schedule for your class. Those outside factors include curricular activities taught to your students by other school personnel; school mandated lunch, recess, and other activities; and set time periods of instruction in secondary school programs.

☐ Curricular Areas Taught by Others

Except in the smallest school districts, other teachers and professionals usually teach certain subjects such as physical education, music, art, industrial education, and home economics. The students in your class will in all likelihood either be mainstreamed into these classes with non-handicapped peers or they will be taught these subjects by school personnel in a self-contained environment. In either case, the person teaching these subjects will inform you what time your students will be receiving instruction in these areas and you will have to plan your class schedule accordingly. It will also be your responsibility to drop off and pick up your students at the appropriate classroom sites so you will need to build such travel time into your schedule.

☐ Lunch and Recess

Lunch and recess are scheduled by school administrative personnel and can sometimes pose scheduling problems for special-education teachers. For some inexplicable reason, special-needs learners often seem to be scheduled for the earliest lunch period in the school. In fact, the author has visited special education classes where students went to lunch as early as 10:30 a.m.! As can be imagined, this can make for a long afternoon for both students and teacher.

Recess is usually scheduled after lunch for a period of twenty to thirty minutes. Additionally, schools usually schedule a ten- to fifteen-minute recess during mid-morning. The teacher will need to take these recess times into account when planning the daily class schedule.

☐ Individual Periods

In secondary school programs, the unit of instruction is the individual period. These periods are usually forty-five- to fifty-five minute blocks of time which divide the school day into six to nine periods. In the secondary school program, the teacher will need to think of scheduling not in terms of the total day but rather in terms of individual periods. Thus, fifty minutes will become the crucial period of time, not the six hours that make up the normal school day. A given objective or lesson may not be completed within one day's period. In such cases, the lesson will have to be completed in the next day's period. When this occurs, it is crucial that the teacher do the following things:

Summarize: At the end of the period's activities, the teacher should summarize what has taken place and also outline how the project or lesson will be completed tomorrow. Such summarization helps to solidify what has just taken place in the lesson as well as create a set of expectations for the continuation of the activity.

Review: At the beginning of the next day's period, the teacher should review what was covered the previous day and outline what will be continued in today's lesson.

Closing activity: The closing activity comes at the completion of the total unit of instruction and represents an attempt to connect the different information and activities that have taken place across the periods of instruction.

By adopting a strategy of summarization, review, and closing, the teacher will help insure that special-needs learners see the connection between the activities that span a number of instructional periods and days. They will see that even though the lesson was not covered entirely in one instructional period, the activities covered in those periods were related and connected. Summarization, review, and closing will also help facilitate transfer and generalization.

SCHEDULING THE DAY

☐ ☐ Within the constraints of outside scheduling by other school personnel and lunch/recess periods, a typical daily class schedule might look like this:

8:00   Planning, set-up, and record keeping activities
8:15   Opening activities

9:00–9:30	Reading I
9:30–10:00	Reading II
10:00–10:15	Break or recess
10:30–11:00	Physical education
11:10–11:40	Arithmetic I
11:40–12:10	Arithmetic II
12:15–12:45	Lunch
12:45–1:05	Recess
1:15–1:45	Handwriting, language arts, spelling, etc.
1:45–2:15	Art, music, creativity, (three days/week) Science (two days/week)
2:15–2:45	Social studies, self-help
2:45–3:00	Closing activity
3:00–3:15	Clean-up
3:15	Dismissal

☐ Planning, Set-up, and Record Keeping

The first few minutes that students are in school is typically dedicated to record keeping, set-up for the day, and other relatively mundane tasks such as attendance, collecting absence notes, collecting lunch and milk money, and distributing free lunch and reduced lunch tickets. This can be a hectic time. However, the teacher can reduce chaos by instituting the following rules:

1. Children are in their seats and quiet during this period.
2. One category of activity is completed before the next record keeping activity begins.
3. Children have notes, money, tickets, and permission slips available on their desks ready to be handed in at the proper time.

It will also be important for the teacher to have envelopes, folders, pouches, and forms where the information is available and ready to use. The key is be *organized!*

☐ Opening Activities

Opening activities for younger students usually contain some kind of calendar/weather activity in which the students identify the day, date, and month and discuss the day's weather and how to dress for it. Opening activities also may involve a discussion of the day's coming events as well as student discussions of what happened after they left school yesterday. Opening activities represent an excellent time to work on counting skills (calendar) as well as self help skills such as dressing appropriately for the weather. If calendar/weather opening activities are used, it is important that such calendar words (days of the weeks, months) and weather words (sunny, rainy, etc.) be included in the child's functional vocabulary (see chapter 7 for a discussion about choosing functional sight word vocabulary). Likewise, children should be able to count to thirty-one as a prerequisite skill before engaging in calendar activities. To facilitate opening activities, teachers often use a feltboard of a calendar and another containing functional words relating to the weather, made out of stiff paperboard with a felt backing that can be attached to the feltboard. These materials can be purchased commercially or can be easily constructed by the teacher. Another teacher strategy is to have the children copy the calendar/weather information on their paper as part of handwriting practice.

Opening exercises should also be a time for sharing. Show-and-tell or just telling is appropriate here. What did the child do yesterday that was interesting or important? Allow each child to stand and relate something they consider to be important to the class. One student got up and told the class how his father and mother had had a fight the night before and the police had come and taken his father to jail. A heartbreaking story to be sure—but it was obviously important and relevant to this child's life and something he wanted to relate. It also gave the teacher some valuable insights into the child's life.

☐ Morning Activities

Most teachers use morning instructional activities to teach reading and arithmetic. Each activity typically takes an hour of instructional time. Many teachers do reading and arithmetic during the morning hours because they feel that children are freshest and most attentive at this time. Teachers also usually schedule an hour of each activity as opposed to thirty minutes in other subject areas because they believe reading and arithmetic to be most vital in children's education.

It is important that the teacher not fatigue or bore students by trying to cram too much material into the morning reading/arithmetic lessons or by having students spend long periods of time on one activity without a break. In fact, particularly with younger students, it is probably a good idea to have activities last no more than fifteen or twenty minutes without a short break.

Reading

The hourly reading activity may be thought of as having four fifteen-minute blocks (Zintz 1981). These blocks might include the following activities:

1. Teacher works with a reading group.
2. Students engage in individual set work completing exercises relating to their reading.
3. Free time reading activities.
4. Teacher checks work, completes individualized instruction/evaluation.

Table 13.1 shows how these four activities can be rotated among three

TABLE 13.1 A "Rotational" Reading Program with Fifteen-Minute Instructional Blocks

Group A		Group B	Group C
Block 1	Seatwork exercises 1. Workbooks 2. Mimeographed work 3. Practicing in pairs 4. Other	Free reading time Work at interest centers	Teacher works with reading group on direct instruction
Block 2	Free reading time Work at interest center	Teacher works with reading group on direct instruction	Seatwork exercises
Block 3	Teacher works with reading group on direct instruction	Seatwork exercises	Free reading time Work at interest centers
Block 4	Individual evaluation, diagnosis, and remediation of reading difficulties. Other children engage in a class reading assignment.		

reading groups with the fourth fifteen-minute block open for special remedial work/evaluation with one or more students. Having such a rotational reading program breaks up the reading activities from one hour straight to four fifteen-minute activities, reduces student fatigue, and keeps interest high.

Using a Reading Center

A reading center is a quiet place to read that possesses interesting, motivating reading materials. Of course, a library serves the same purpose, but the school library may not always be open or available when students wish to use it. In creating a reading center in your classroom, a table or series of tables in a quiet section of the classroom should be used. Chairs should be far enough away from one another so students will not interfere with or distract one another. There should be a variety of books, magazines, and other high interest reading materials designed to attract student attention. Unconventional literature such as brochures on automobiles and motorcycles secured from sales showrooms may be highly stimulating and interesting to junior high and secondary mentally retarded readers. Also, cassette tape recorders, headphones, and tape-recorded reading material designed to correspond with accompanying text should be included. The purpose of the center is to have students *read* during the free reading portion of the reading instructional hour. The teacher should emphasize when appropriate that this is not free time for students; it is free reading time.

Arithmetic

The arithmetic hour can also be divided into four activities:

1. Review of material and presentation of new work.
2. Seatwork and practice of arithmetic assignments.

3. The teacher and students checking seatwork and correcting student mistakes (reteaching when necessary).
4. Individual diagnosis, evaluation, and remediation for students.

Table 13.2 shows how the four main arithmetic activities may be divided into fifteen-minute blocks and rotated among three groups. The teacher may decide to have one activity (e.g., material presentation) take longer while correspondingly shortening another arithmetic activity within the arithmetic instructional block. Specific activities regarding the teaching of arithmetic to mentally retarded learners may be found in chapter 9.

□ Afternoon Activities

Afternoon activities may be scheduled in half-hour blocks and include the curricular areas of social studies, art/music/creativity, science, and other language arts activities such as spelling, written expression, and handwriting. These subjects are not necessarily taught five days per week. For example, while the language-arts program and social studies would probably occur every school day, art/music/ creativity may be two days per week with science being taught the other three days.

Since these activities last only about a half hour, they will need to be highly organized, well structured, and fast paced in order to present the material, practice, and/or experimentation. Of course activity time can be contracted or expanded as the teacher sees fit. Likewise, lessons may be carried over to the next day as long as adequate summation of the lesson and review of the previous day's activities take place. In creating the afternoon activities, the teacher needs to learn pacing—the ability not to try to pack the history of western civilization into a half-hour lesson or, alternately, not complete the lesson in ten minutes with twenty minutes left to "kill." Such effective pacing is difficult to teach; it must come with experience and in-depth knowledge of both subject matter and pupils. But for the novice and experienced teacher alike, such pacing will prove to be a key aspect to effective teaching.

□ Closing Activities

Closing activities are very important in that they summarize the child's school day. They typically represent the last school activity which the child will engage in before going home. As such, closing activities should have three goals: (*a*) a general review and/or wrapping up of the activities of the day, (*b*) giving the children a positive, warm feeling about themselves and school, and (*c*) giving the children an exciting preview of tomorrow's coming events to help them anticipate the next school day.

TABLE 13.2   Using Instructional Blocks in the Arithmetic Program

Group A		Group B	Group C
Block 1	Seatwork 1. Workbook problems 2. Individualized teacher assignments	Seatwork Teacher checks work	Teacher presents new material to group
Block 2	Teacher presents new material to group	Seatwork	Group practices newly presented material
Block 3	Group practices new material	Teacher presents new material to group	Seatwork
Block 4	Teacher checks work	Group practices newly presented material	Teacher checks work

A Review Of The Day's Activities

What did we do in school today? What did we learn? Students should be led into a discussion of what was learned and accomplished during the school day. A good idea is for the teacher to ask each child to mention something that happened during the day or tell something that was learned or accomplished. The teacher then would enter the students' responses on the chalkboard. After the children go home, the teacher can copy and mimeograph the events, and pass them out to the students the next day to be included in each child's class diary or newsletter. (Alternatively, the role of "scribe" can be created on a rotating basis with a student filling this role for the teacher.) At the end of a given period of time these diaries can be examined and the student will be pleasantly surprised to learn all that has been accomplished during a few short weeks in school. Such diaries can also be made available to parents. Such summation activities at the end of the school day will help close the day and send children home with a feeling of accomplishment.

Giving The Child A Positive Feeling

Have children in the class stand up and tell something they did well during the school day. Encourage children to praise not only themselves but other children and what they accomplished or did during the day. Display any art or creativity projects which were completed by the students making sure that all such projects are displayed, not just the ones you consider artistic or valuable. Another activity the teacher can institute is begin the sentence; "I like you because . . . ." and have all children fill in the rest of what the teacher should say about them. Children should leave school with a warm feeling about themselves, each other, and school itself. Time spent on such activities will go far in improving children's school self-concept.

Anticipation Of Tomorrow

What are we going to do tomorrow? What do we have to look forward to? This is the age old question children always seem to be asking. Do you remember how you could not wait to come to school on those days when you knew you were having a class party or field trip? The teacher should build on the natural curiosity and excitement of students in order to get them looking forward to coming to school the next day.

Such discussion of the next day's activities can be tied in with functional reading. For example, the teacher can make tagboard or magnetic cutouts of such functional words such as reading, science, arithmetic, physical education, art, lunch, recess, and special. The teacher places each word on the feltboard or blackboard and tells the class what exciting or interesting activity is going to occur tomorrow in each activity. Of course, this puts the burden of responsibility on the teacher to come up with interesting activities to excite students for the next day of school. Your goal should be to get your students to a point that they cannot wait to come to school the next day, to come to a point that they would come to school weekends and summers if they could.

MANAGING THE PHYSICAL ENVIRONMENT OF THE CLASSROOM

☐ ☐ The physical organization of the classroom has a strong influence on the quality of the learning that goes on there. The physical environment in which children learn has been shown to have a strong effect on their motivation for learning, on the amount and type of communication used in the class, and on students' classroom behavior (Borg 1979; Delefes & Jackson 1972; Gorman 1974; Sommer 1977). Unfortunately, teachers are not always aware of how improvement of the physical classroom environment can help them to reach their teaching goals (Gump 1978).

There are several considerations that should be taken into account when designing and/or rearranging your classroom (Gray 1975). These considerations include:

Correct scale: Desks, furniture and other equipment must be the right size for students. Have you ever visited a kindergarten classroom and sat in one of the desks? That feeling of physical and psychological discomfort is what children feel when they are forced to use furniture and equipment that is ill suited for them.

Personal territory: Students and teachers need their own personal territory and privacy: their desk, locker, or space which is uniquely theirs.

Spatial variation: A room should have areas of different size dimensions where groups of different numbers can meet comfortably and appropriately.

FIGURE 13.1 Physical Arrangement of the Traditional Classroom

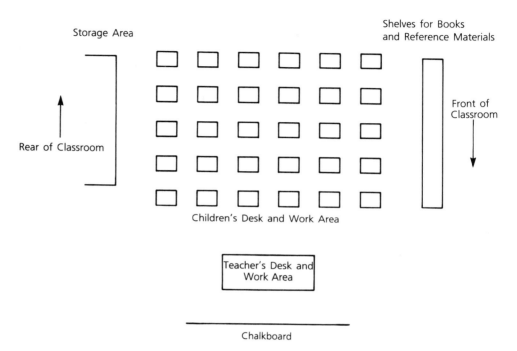

Flexibility: Materials and furniture must be easily movable and manipulatable. Likewise, equipment and furniture should be versatile, usable for a variety of activities (e.g., writing, painting, sanding). Adaptability of space is the key concept.

Wear and renewal: Furniture and equipment should be durable enough to be used, cleaned, and used again. When it finally does wear out it should be easily replaceable with a minimum of classroom disruption. All major surfaces should be washable.

ARRANGING THE CLASSROOM

☐ ☐ Close your eyes for a moment and picture the traditional classroom arrangement. What do you see? Probably something like the room pictured in Figure 13.1: rows of desks, about five or six to a row, a chalkboard at the front of the room behind the teacher's desk, and rows of reference books on bookshelves along one side of the room. This stereotypical classroom in your imagination is probably accurate for the vast majority of classrooms found in today's schools.

But how effective is such a classroom environment for facilitating both learning and communication between individuals? It has been hypothesized that while the traditional classroom is quite effective in delineating power to the teacher and encouraging one way communication from teacher to student, it is not facilitative in giving students a sense of belonging in the class or encouraging communication between students (Sommer 1977). Likewise, the class seating arrangement can affect both student attention and academic achievement. For example, studies indicate that pupils sitting across the front row and down the middle seats of the classroom do better academically than pupils sitting in the back and along the sides of the room (Adams & Biddle 1970; Daum 1972; Schwebel & Cherlin 1972). In fact, Schwebel and Cherlin (1972) found that the technique of bringing inattentive and low achieving students toward the front and middle of the classroom actually improved their attention and academic achievement. Thus, for the teacher who feels more comfortable with nondirective teaching and wishes to allow student input, a nontraditional seating arrangement that allows for small group work and that brings students to the forefront of classroom activities is suggested (see Figure 13.2).

In addition to classroom seating arrangement, Charles (1983) has suggested that five aspects of the classroom physical environment be taken into consideration when designing the classroom. They are floor space, wall space, cabinet top space, shelf space, and closet and cupboard space.

☐ Floor Space

Floor space is concerned with seating, work and activity space in the classroom, the teacher's area, and classroom traffic patterns. The traditional seating arrangement is straight rows. However, the teacher may wish to go to a clustered arrangement where seats are gathered around the chalkboard or special materials or interest center. Also, instead of rows of desks in a straight line, teachers might wish to place seats in semicircles to encourage group dynamics and interaction between students. Whichever seating arrangement is used, teachers should remain flexible in using a variety of seating arrangements throughout the day, adapting the seating arrangement to meet the demands of individual lessons and activities.

☐ Work and Activity Space

Work and activity space refers to the amount of usable and functional work space that there is in the classroom. There are some classroom activities that require relatively little workspace (i.e., seatwork or pencil and paper assignments) while other activities require more work room (e.g., science and/or art projects). For this reason, the teacher should consider the reciprocal relationship between the classroom seating arrangement and the amount of available workspace in the

FIGURE 13.2 Physical Classroom Arrangement Designed to Facilitate Two-Way Communication and Student Interactions

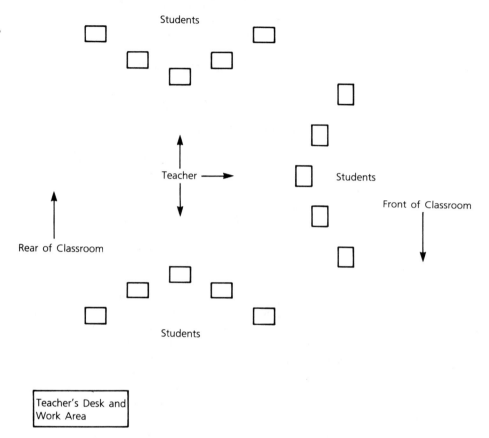

room. For those activities where more functional workspace is regularly needed, the classroom seating arrangement should probably be more compact. In such an arrangement, seats should be out of the center of the room and off to the side, thus opening up a large central work area. Conversely, in a classroom where seatwork predominates and the teacher wishes to closely monitor individual students' work, less central workspace is necessary and a more liberal seating arrangement can be utilized.

In addition, the often wasted space at the rear and the sides of the classroom should be made functional. For example, such areas at the rear may be used for interest or small group activity centers, areas where students can work quietly on projects, either alone or in pairs. Such interest centers can be built around a given theme or topic: science, music, current affairs, maps, etc. They can also be directly related to the long-term thematic unit currently being taught. One special-education classroom had a corner of the room as a stamp collecting center in which students traded stamps of the world and played stamp lotto. Such activities would not have been possible and would have interfered with ongoing activities occurring in the mainstream of the classroom if the peripheral areas such as the rear and sides of the room had not been used. Figure 13.3 shows how the seating arrangement and the workable space of the classroom can be utilized to institute such interest and activity centers (Reyes & Post 1973).

The teacher's station is the area where the teacher's desk and personal equipment are located. One of the first decisions concerning the classroom physical environment that must be made is where the teacher's area will be located. In the majority of classrooms, the teacher's desk is found in the front of the room with all students' desks facing the teacher's area. However, this need not be the case. For example, Figure 13.4 shows a classroom arrangement where the teacher's station is pushed off to a relatively peripheral corner of the room with the space at the front of the classroom being used either for small group activities or for class focus on a small group of class members (Reyes & Post 1973). Wherever the teacher's station is located, it should be an area in which students are welcome and to which they want to come. Thus, this area should be warm, colorful, and human rather than intimidating, colorless, and businesslike. A classroom where the children are not allowed to approach the teacher's desk without raising their hand and seeking formal permission intimidates students. This quickly leads to an "us versus the teacher" attitude which leads to behavior problems. A better attitude for the teacher to take is that the teacher's station is a shared space for both teacher and students. To that end, a teacher may place a special soft chair near the desk to be used by students during conferences or other one-to-one interactions with the teacher.

The seating and floor arrangement should also take into consideration the traffic patterns of the classroom. For example, do not situate the room in such a way that anyone needing to go to the classroom door has to weave around virtually every other child in the class. This floor arrangement would disrupt individual seatwork and small group activities. Likewise high traffic usage areas like the pencil sharpener or the paper supply should be located away from the center of student work areas. Such attention to classroom traffic patterns can reduce significantly the number of distractions caused by these high volume, much traveled centers.

☐ Wall Space

Generally, there are five major uses of available classroom wall space: bulletin boards, chalkboards, display areas for student work, classroom reference materials, and class rules, slogans, reminders, or schedules. The chalkboard is of course a very important and often used teaching aid. Usually, the teacher will have little say about where the chalkboard is located since it was bolted in place when the

FIGURE 13.3 Using the Workable Space in the Classroom to Optimal Advantage

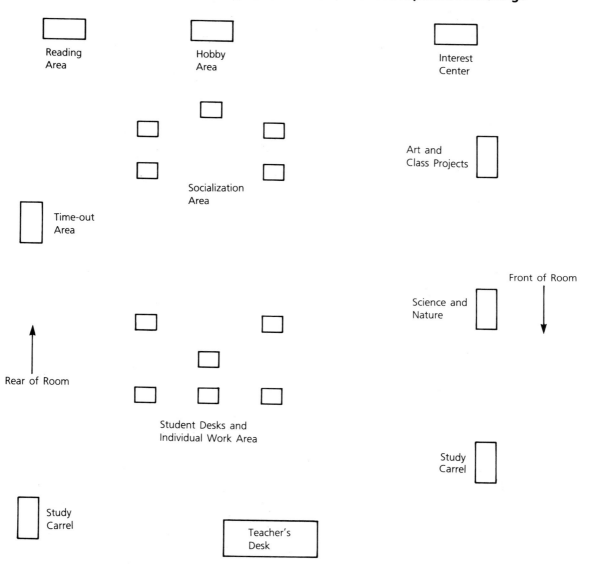

classroom was originally constructed. Thus, in order to use the chalkboard effectively, the class needs to have movable seats and desks that can be turned toward or away from the chalkboard as appropriate. The teacher should keep in mind that the chalkboard is not only a useful tool for the teacher's use but it can be a valuable learning tool for the students and can be used by them to demonstrate skills in virtually all of the core academic areas.

FIGURE 13.4   Arranging the Classroom to Optimize Small Group Interaction

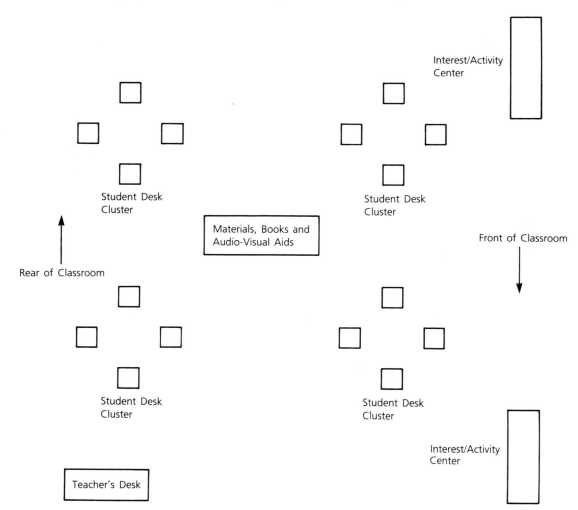

Bulletin boards are an important part of the classroom environment. The general purpose of these displays is both instructional and effective. They can be quite useful as attention getters, motivators, or setters of the mood of the classroom. Bulletin boards are often used to demonstrate themes varying from holidays to some special activity being learned or carried out by the class. By using bulletin boards in this way, the teacher of mentally retarded pupils can emphasize the theme of the long-term instructional unit currently being taught.

Perhaps two mistakes that teachers most often make regarding bulletin boards is that they do not change them frequently enough and that they do not allow student input in conceptualizing and creating the displays. One of the chief educational values of bulletin boards is their stimulation and interest value for students. If the displays remain up for an excessively long period of time, they may become boring to students. Likewise, many teachers feel that they need to construct their bulletin boards after school so that when the children come to school the next morning, a new bulletin board will have mysteriously appeared. However, many students enjoy having input into what will go on bulletin boards as well as actually creating the displays. Student participation can go a long way toward keeping student interest strong in a thematic long-term unit topic, stimulating interest, reinforcing learning, and fostering student creativity.

Displaying Student Work

Wall space allocated to displaying students' work should be an integral part of the physical classroom environment. It is highly reinforcing for children to see their work displayed on the wall, and this phenomenon is especially rewarding for mentally retarded students who, perhaps because of their relative lack of academic success or quality of their work, have not often had the opportunity to see their work shown. Children take great pride in seeing their work displayed, and displays are also facilitative for helping parents, many of whom have experienced negative school experiences themselves, to realize that their children can have positive experiences in school. Children also greatly enjoy showing their displayed work to parents and siblings in open house or similar school events.

Two very important principles should be kept in mind, however, in exhibiting student work. First, this should not be a competitive endeavor among students. That is, students should not have to compete among themselves with the best work of the winners being displayed. For example, the author once visited a class where the teacher displayed a chart showing how many books each child in the class had read. A gold star was placed next to the name of the child for each completed book. On the surface, this might have seemed like a good idea, but consider what happened. Every child's name appeared on the chart. Next to some names there was a long string of stars and next to some other names only a few stars. In addition, the teacher also had decided to give a prize to the student who had read the most books. So what did this teacher end up with? Simply a large number of frustrated students who realized early that no matter how hard they tried, they had no chance of catching the star readers.

The other rule that should be followed is that each child's best work should be periodically displayed; there should not be a classwide minimum success level that children need to master before they get to see their work displayed. All children should systematically get their work displayed, not just those pupils who do well. Thus, children get rewarded for trying and doing their best, not living up to an external standard. Adoption of such a philosophy will go far in improving the academic self-concept, eradicating the stigma of defeat for mentally retarded children.

OTHER EQUIPMENT AND INSTRUCTIONAL AIDS

☐ Reference Materials

Maps, globes, charts, dictionaries, books, and other reference materials are an important part of the classroom. Some classes have letters, number facts, phonics rules, and common spelling demons displayed around the class as well as standard maps and charts available to students. Such reference aids can be particularly useful for mentally retarded learners in the areas of spelling, arithmetic, and reading. However, these aids will only be of use if students can easily see them and can refer to them often. Placed in the back of the room where students have to make a 180° turn to see them or hidden behind the hamster's cage, these learning aids will not do students much good. Reference aids should be in the direct line of sight of students, especially when those subject matters are being taught. Finally, the teacher of mentally retarded students cannot expect that such learning aids will be used by students without systematic instruction on what these aids are and how they are to be used effectively. Nor can the teacher expect that mentally retarded students will use these materials spontaneously without prompting. Rather, it is probably true that such materials will not be appropriately used by mentally retarded pupils and might even be completely ignored without prompting from the teacher.

☐ Cabinet and Closet Space

Cabinet, shelf, and closet space are important factors in the organization of the classroom. All three space areas must be utilized to keep the room uncluttered and neat. Also, the more materials that are lying around the room, the less space there is for students to use the classroom for learning experiences. Thus, a cardinal rule is: when not in use, materials should be put away!

This rule, however, can be carried too far. For example, things should not be packed away so tightly that they cannot be easily reached without removing dozens of other materials first. Likewise, students should feel that they can have easy access to stored materials. Such materials should not be stored away in places in which students have to be constantly bothering the teacher to get them. After all these are educational materials there for the students' use. As such, students should be able to reach them easily and use them independently. Finally, the proverb "out of sight, out of mind" may be true here. If materials are packed away or hidden from students' view they may forget about them and fail to use them. Whenever possible, materials should be safely stored but visibly accessible to students. They should be able to see them, remember them, and thus consider using them. Hidden away they may be in excellent condition five years after purchase because they have never been used! The best materials are perhaps those well worn from use.

□ Study Carrels

Study carrels are small, isolated cubicles that allow for independent work by students. Such carrels are designed to significantly limit the amount of outside stimulation received by the person in the carrel and to identify a specific, quiet place in the classroom where work may be completed.

Study carrels come in all shapes and sizes. They can be made out of cardboard, wood, plastic, virtually anything that will keep out noise and distractions. Some teachers even use folding screens or curtains with a chair enclosed as a study carrel. Whatever the construction, the carrel should effectively keep out visual, and, if possible, auditory outside stimuli. In cases where outside noise is a particular problem for a student, headphones may be used to keep out sound.

Carrels can become a special place for independent study or a quiet place to read or think. For other students, such carrels can become their own little office, a place to go for privacy while studying. It is suggested that the special-education classroom contain at least one study carrel for every eight to ten students and that these carrels be located in out-of-the-way and relatively untraveled places in the room.

□ Time-Out Area

The time-out area is an isolated, nonstimulating place to which a child who is exhibiting inappropriate behavior is sent or where the child can go of his or her own volition. Unlike the study carrel, the time-out area is completely nonstimulating. While there, the child is not to engage in any academic or other activity.

The key concept in the time-out procedure is to remove the child from an environment that may be reinforcing inappropriate behavior (Gast & Nelson 1977; Nelson & Rutherford 1983). As such, the time-out area should be a quiet, isolated, and completely unstimulating area of the classroom separated from all other classroom activities. The time-out area is a place where students cool off their inappropriate or overstimulated behavior. However, it is important to emphasize that the time-out area is not a punishment box.

Time-out areas are not for all children and all classrooms. Therefore it is not being suggested that a time-out area become standard equipment in every special-education classroom. Rather, the special education teacher will need to give careful consideration to whether or not a time-out area is appropriate for a particular class. More on the time-out procedure as a vehicle for behavioral change is included in chapter 14.

SUMMARY

□ □ Some classrooms seem to be effective and work while others appear to be ineffective and chaotic. Investigations have characterized effective teachers and effective classrooms. Effective teachers appear to be those individuals who display the ability to spread their attention, who are prepared and have momentum, who possess signal continuity, who use group alerting techniques, and who challenge and motivate students with a variety of teaching techniques.

In preparing to be an effective teacher, the individual should set the necessary groundwork before school even begins and during the first few days and weeks of class. For example, before the school year begins, the teacher should get acquainted with facilities and personnel, and plan for the physical and psychological environment of the classroom. Likewise, during the first days of class, the teacher should set the operating rules of the class, create schedules, and orient students to the classroom environment.

Scheduling the school day is very important. Outside factors which will affect a teacher's scheduling include curricular areas taught by other school personnel, lunch and recess times, and individual period blocks in secondary programs. Outside of those constraints, the teacher is relatively free to schedule the class day.

A typical class schedule includes planning, setup and record keeping, opening activities, morning reading and arithmetic periods, afternoon curricular activities, and closing activities. Reading and arithmetic typically last one hour each and occur in the morning when children are fresher. The teacher can schedule reading and arithmetic activities into fifteen-minute blocks with the teacher rotating between ability groups.

The physical arrangement of the classroom is important for effective learning. Variables that affect the arrangement of the class include the seating arrangements, furniture and equipment, and the use of floor and wall space.

The traditional seating arrangement of rows of desks all facing the teacher may not be conducive for two-way communication between teacher and students and among students. Rather, the more viable arrangement may be to have seats facing each other where children can interact as well as have areas of the classroom such as interest centers where movement and noise can be tolerated. Individual students should also be allowed their own private area or special space.

Wall space can be used to post reference materials for students such as spelling/reading rules or arithmetic facts. It can also display class work. However, in displaying class work, the teacher should not foster a competitive situation showing only the best work but rather should display all work.

Furniture, equipment, and cabinet space should be adequate for children's needs. Furniture and materials should be on the right scale for students and should be durable and versatile. There should be enough cabinet and closet space so that the classroom does not appear cluttered, but materials should not be packed away so tightly so that they are inaccessible to students.

The teacher may wish to use study carrels and a time-out area in the classroom. The time-out area is not a punishment box. Rather, it is a place for students to cool off. In addition, a time-out area may not be facilitative for all classrooms and all students.

14

Creating the Classroom Psychological Environment and Managing Student Behavior

Key Concepts

☐ Teaching Styles: Authoritarian, Democratic, and Laissez-faire
☐ Glasser's Eight Behaviors for Effective Teaching
☐ Student Responsibilities to the Teacher and to Each Other
☐ Theories of Managing Behavior: Behavior Modification and Social Learning, Group Management Theory, Power Theory
☐ Methods of Increasing Student Behavior: Shaping, Modeling, Contingency Contracting, Token Economies
☐ Methods of Decreasing Student Behavior: Extinction, Time-out, Satiation, Punishment, Reinforcement of Incompatible Behaviors, Desensitization
☐ Group Management Techniques and Learner Accountability
☐ Power Systems: The CMTP Model, Assertive Discipline

In the not too distant past, if you asked educators what constituted classroom management, you probably would have received a one word answer: discipline. For years, teachers, school administrators and parents have been extremely concerned about the issue of classroom discipline. For example, for every year in which the Gallup Poll on education has been conducted since 1969, the primary concern among parents, teachers, administrators, and even students themselves has been discipline (Charles 1983; Tanner 1980).

The results of the polls were reinforced by a study (Luftig 1979). College students who had completed student teaching but not yet graduated from college, first-year teachers, and school principals were interviewed regarding their greatest job-related concerns. For the prospective teachers who were not yet working, instructional materials, curricular design, and planning considerations ranked as chief concerns. However, for the first-year teachers (average time on the job, three months), the greatest concern was classroom discipline and control. As it turned out, these concerns were accurate; principals interviewed also named classroom control as one of the most important criteria for rehiring teachers for the second year.

In spite of the public's concern with matters of classroom control and discipline, it is surprising to find that these topics have traditionally not been a high priority for educational research nor have they been strongly stressed in preparation courses taken by university education majors (Charles 1983; Tanner 1980). Tanner (1980) writes: "Discipline is not mentioned in many educational methods books. Discipline is linked historically with poor methodology and is therefore an uninviting, if not unrespectable, pursuit for educational theorists (p 9–10)."

One aspect of the topic of classroom control and discipline that has evolved in recent years is the expansion of the discussion from the single topic of discipline to the larger area of effective classroom management. The discussion has grown from one of controlling classroom interruptions and behavior problems to the larger arena of conducting a well organized and well managed classroom (Brophy 1983). As such, the topic of classroom management includes the study of how effective classrooms work in terms of physical, psychological, and interpersonal dynamics. It includes areas of classroom that create psychological environments conducive to communication and human interaction, making students feel secure and safe, and protecting the rights of teacher and students through mutual respect. In short, creating the proper psychological environment for meaningful learning is more than just discipline and student control; it deals with human respect and human caring.

THE PSYCHOLOGICAL ENVIRONMENT IN THE CLASSROOM

☐ ☐ Teaching is an interactive process. It requires social interactions among people, usually between teachers and students. Social interaction proceeds in two phases: first a stimulus message is sent (from teacher to student or from student to teacher) that elicits a response from the other person engaged in the interaction. Then the response of the second person elicits or stimulates a response from the original speaker.

The social interactions that go on between teacher and student are not neutral; they do not occur in a psychological vacuum. Rather, they occur in an environment in which the social participants set the emotional and psychological ground rules for their interactions. They judge, evaluate, and transmit unspoken messages that create a psychological atmosphere in which all future messages between the individuals will occur.

The school is no different from any other social environment in which social interactions take place. Teachers and pupils create a psychological and emotional classroom climate in which social interactions are to occur (Sapon-Shevin, Sametz & Kaczala 1985; Rossetti 1985). This psychological tone then becomes the environment in which future messages and interactions will be judged unless changed or modified by teacher and students. Unfortunately, while it is true that both teacher and students are responsible for creating a positive psychological classroom climate, it is nevertheless also true that the teacher possesses proportionately greater power in setting the psychological atmosphere and transmitting that atmosphere to students (Mosley & Sullivan 1984; Pallak, Costomiris, Sroka & Pittman 1982).

THREE TYPES OF TEACHING STYLES: AUTHORITARIAN, DEMOCRATIC, AND LAISSEZ-FAIRE

□ □ How can teachers contribute to the psychological climate of the classroom? A variety of studies indicate that teachers use several different communication styles with children, each style transmitting a clear message to students about how the teacher expects social interactions between teacher and pupils to proceed (Helton & Oakland 1977; Lippitt & White 1958; Silberman 1971; Spock 1984). For example, Spock (1984, p. 28) writes that teachers traditionally have taken one of two philosophical approaches toward students;

> . . . One (view) might be labeled 'authoritarian' or 'coercive' (and) rests on an assumption that children are by nature irresponsible and lazy and will do their schoolwork only if they are penalized for poor performance. The opposite view might be labeled 'progressive' or 'democratic.' It rests on the assumption that children who are brought up with love, trust, and clear but kind leadership are eager to grow up and be like their parents. . . . they are eager to learn, master skills, and take on responsibility; they need guidance but not sternness or punishment.

According to Lippitt and White (1958) these outlooks on children and the schooling process have yielded three main teaching styles: *authoritarian, democratic*, and *laissez-faire*. The authoritarian teacher is one who sets all rules and policies in the classroom. Information, procedures, and processes are communicated by the authority figure/teacher and no divergence from prescribed procedures is tolerated. Flow of information is one way—from teacher to student, with the student's sole role being compliance.

The democratic teacher, on the other hand, actively seeks and allows input from students, especially in allowing input into creating the rules and procedures under which the class will operate. However, the democratic teacher does not abrogate authority. Rather the teacher views the students as partners in the educational process while making sure that no one's (including the teacher's) rights are violated and that procedures and rules, once created, are followed.

Finally, a laissez-faire teacher is one who plays a passive role in the class. This type of teacher believes students can resolve all of their own problems and that it is the teacher's job to give students the least amount of direction as possible. Such a nondirective teacher does not take the initiative in running the class but rather acts as a facilitator of the group, supportive rather than directive.

The laissez-faire teacher is almost the complete opposite of the teacher who adopts the authoritarian style.

A COMPARISON OF THE EFFECTIVENESS OF THE THREE TEACHING STYLES

☐ ☐ Which type of teaching style is the most effective? Lippitt and White (1958) conducted a social experiment in which the three types of leaders oversaw a group cooperative work task completed by a matched set of boys. The investigators found that the children who worked under the authoritarian leader completed the most work. However, there was not a strong feeling of group cohesiveness, the students depended on the leader for nearly everything, and the group's work and attention dropped drastically whenever the leader temporarily left the room.

The students who worked under the democratic leader did not produce as much work as those who were in the authoritarian leader group. However, these boys worked better on their own, were more independent, and seemed to have more group spirit and cohesiveness. Finally, in the laissez-faire leader group, the boys were generally unproductive both when the leader was present and when he was absent. In fact, the children actually worked better when the leader was absent! Very little work actually was accomplished and there was little, if any, group cohesiveness.

☐ Implications for Special-Education Teachers

What implications does all this have for the teachers of mentally retarded children as they begin to design their teaching style to improve the psychological climate of their class? That depends on what the teachers' goals are for the children with whom they will be working. For example, it was certainly true that the children who worked under the authoritarian leader were more productive than the children who worked under the two other leader types. Thus, one could conclude that since mentally retarded students possess so many academic deficits and have so much information to learn in order to be able to function as independent adults, that, for mentally retarded learners, the authoritarian approach is best. But even though the authoritarian group accomplished much, the group's interpersonal skills were weak, motivation was poor, and the group members did not work well independently. If you believe that children should feel good about what they accomplish, that interpersonal relationships are as important as product, and that a goal of education is to help children work independently, then the democratic outlook is probably the teaching style to adopt for mentally retarded pupils.

Finally the results from the laissez-faire group indicate that the nonleading, nondirective teacher is, if anything, a disturbing, negative factor. Effective teaching is not abdicating leadership in the class and going along with anything the class desires. Rather, the teacher is the leader of the group and brings to class special levels of expertise which the group needs in order to learn and mature. Perhaps in time, it will be appropriate for teachers to relinquish leadership; in fact, this should be the goal for our students as they approach adulthood. However, during the formative years of school, completely relinquishing leadership is inappropriate.

WHAT TYPES OF CLASSROOM ENVIRONMENTS DO STUDENTS WANT?

☐ ☐ If students could structure the psychological environment of the classroom in any way they wished, what variables would they wish to increase and which would they wish to decrease or eliminate? Barry Fraser and his associates (Fraser 1984; Fraser & Fisher 1983) have shed some light on this subject. Fraser developed an assessment instrument entitled *My Classroom Inventory* (MCI) which he administered to a large number of students and teachers at a variety of grade levels. From the MCI, Fraser isolated five psychological classroom factors which seemed to be on the minds of both students and teachers alike: *class cohesiveness, satisfaction, friction, competition, and difficulty of academic material.* Figure 14.1 shows what students and teachers wanted in their classrooms as opposed to what they were actually experiencing. For example, Figure 14.1 indicates that both students and teachers wanted classes high in cohesiveness (togetherness) that were satisfying to be in. They also wanted classes low in friction and competition with academic material of intermediate difficulty. This, however, was not what they were finding in reality.

The implications of Fraser's work with the MCI should be clear. Students do not want to feel that they are in competition with one another. When competition is appropriate, the teacher should strive to make it intrapersonal competition in which each student attempts to better himself or herself rather than compete against others. Students also wish the class to be cohesive with few or no cliques or "in" groups. Whenever possible, the teacher should strive to enhance a class spirit rather than reinforce individual social groups. Finally, it is clear from the MCI that students want their classes to be satisfying with the academic material not so easy as to bore them but not so difficult that it "blows them away."

STEPS IN CREATING A WARM CLASSROOM ATMOSPHERE

☐ ☐ In order to create such a warm classroom environment, Glasser (1969) has advanced that the teacher exhibit the following behaviors:

1. **Being friendly:** This means not just feeling friendly toward students but behaving in such a way that is interpreted by students as friendly. As

FIGURE 14.1   The Perceived and Desired Classroom Environments For Students and Teachers

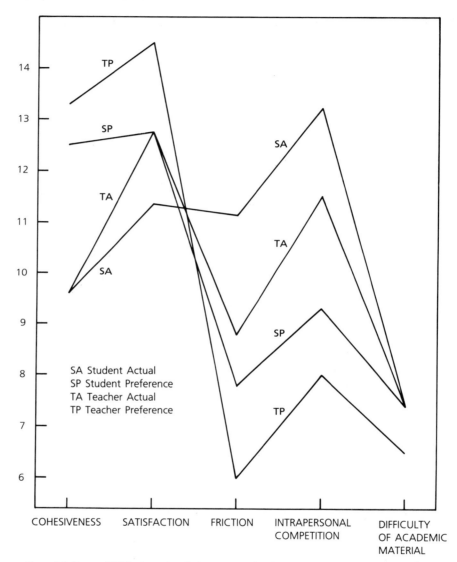

From B.J. Fraser (1954). A study of elementary school students' perceptions of the classroom psychosocial environment. (Paper presented at the annual meeting of the American Educational Research Association, New Orleans.)

Glasser points out, this is not as easy as it might seem, especially with students whom we don't particularly like or who we perceive as a threat.

2. **Taking a positive stance in interpersonal relationships:** This means being optimistic, upbeat, and seeking positive and viable solutions to classroom and interpersonal problems as opposed to being pessimistic, backbiting, fault finding, or negative.

3. **Ability to listen:** Not just hearing but actively listening to students. Teachers who actively listen to students accomplish three important interpersonal goals. First, they demonstrate to the students that they are genuinely interested in the student as an individual. Second, active listening shows students that their opinions and ideas are of value. Finally, active listening opens up communication from a one-way (teacher-to-student) pattern to a two-way flow of ideas. It creates dialogue instead of monologue.

4. **Giving students regular and personalized attention:** Good teachers are those who find the time to talk to and get to know their students even on matters not directly related to school. These teachers take the time on a regular basis to talk to all their students, not just those having problems or those doing exceptionally well. For example, one inner-city elementary school has behavioral problems and vandalism significantly lower than the other inner-city schools located in the same city. Why has this occurred? One possible explanation is that the principal in this school has taken the time to learn the names and recognize every pupil in the school, and he speaks to them on a regular, almost daily basis. In addition, this principal pops into every class, every morning to say hello to each class. Needless to say, he is a very popular educator with students, many of whom do not get much personalized attention either at school or at home.

5. **Regular verbal and behavioral reinforcers:** Most often, this means verbal praise. However, many teachers who implement a program of praise with behaviorally disruptive students are disappointed to find that the students' behavior has not significantly improved. They conclude that the principles of positive reinforcement do not work. Available research indicates, however, that praise must be appropriately given, genuine, and earned for it to be meaningful to students (Dreikurs and Gray 1972; Gordon 1972; Ginott 1972). For example, in one college class, a professor consistently commented on every student's remark in a positive fashion (e.g., "That's a good idea." "You're really onto something there!") as a way of eliciting more student responses. However, one day one of the students blurted out, "Look every idea cannot be a good idea. Some things we say are just plain dumb!" The teacher then realized that his praise was being recognized for what it really was—insincere praise designed with an ulterior motive rather than for actually rewarding student performance.

6. **Continual willingness to help:** Teachers who transmit to students that they wish to help—that that is what they are in the classroom for—will

have students gravitating to them and feeling good about them. Conversely, those teachers who transmit the unspoken message that they really would rather not be bothered will, in fact, get their wish. This is particularly true for mentally retarded students who, while needing help desperately both in their academic learning and their interpersonal lives, are, at the same time, wary of adult help, especially teachers' help, as a result of years of rejection.

7. **Modeling in practicing courtesy, respect, and interpersonal skills:** Studies conducted by Bandura and his associates (Bandura 1965, 1977, 1978; Bandura & Kupers 1964), show that students model what they see. If a child has been exposed to violence she or he will act in an aggressive manner. Likewise, children who have been treated inconsiderately will act rudely toward others. There is probably nothing that "turns off" students faster than the hypocritical teacher who sets up rules of courtesy and consideration that students are expected to follow but that the teacher violates at almost every opportunity. "Do as I say, not as I do" is inappropriate in the classroom, especially with mentally retarded students who so often must learn by concrete example.

8. **Leading and following:** Democratic teachers both lead *and* follow. At appropriate times, the democratic teacher sets the leadership role for the class and is quite directive. At other times, the democratic teacher should be a follower, respecting what the class has decided and following their lead. This, of course, does not mean completely giving up the leadership role, that is, adopting the laissez-faire model that has been shown to be educationally ineffective. Rather, the democratic teacher works toward achieving the shared goals designed by both the teacher and the class members.

By instituting these eight attributes, the teacher of mentally retarded children can, perhaps for the first time, give children the feeling of a measure of control over what goes on in their lives, of warmth and belonging in the classroom, and of self-worth. Such feelings are very important; in fact, some would argue that they are as important as the attainment of academic skills. For long after they exit the special educational environment, mentally retarded learners carry into their adult lives what they think and believe about themselves and others. Such is the normalization process.

DISCIPLINE IN THE CLASSROOM

☐ ☐ Discipline and classroom control are a necessity of educational life. No matter how hard the teacher tries, there will simply be some students who are unresponsive to all efforts, who are disruptive, and who do not conform to class rules. And just as the teacher has certain responsibilities to the class for creating an effective physical environment and a warm, supportive psychological climate, students have responsibilities to the teacher and to themselves. These responsibilities include:

1. **Learning:** Despite what some educators argue (and what some students would like to believe), the goal of school is learning. This is especially true for mentally retarded students who, by definition, come into educational situations with severe academic and social learning deficits and who must have these deficits significantly remediated if the normalization process is to occur successfully when school is exited. Students have a responsibility in the learning process; it is not solely the teacher's job to teach. Rather, students must make active responses such as completing assignments, paying attention, etc., that will significantly contribute to their learning.

2. **Making a contribution:** Students are expected to make a contribution to the well-being of the class. This is accomplished by helping with the duties of the class, by helping themselves and others, and by helping the teacher when appropriate. The key concept is not that they are being the teacher's pet by contributing but that they are contributing to the common good.

3. **Being considerate:** Just as it is expected that the teacher will be considerate and responsive to students' feelings, it is expected of students that they will be considerate of each other and of the teacher. This includes being friendly, courteous and fair as well as respecting the rights of others. Perhaps one of the biggest points of contention in the classroom is the resolution between a person's desires and the infringement of those actions on another individual's rights. Since the classroom is a social system, students must realize the consequences of their own actions on other individuals and temper their acts accordingly.

4. **Accepting consequences:** Students need to learn that they are responsible for the consequences of their behavior. That is, students need to realize that behaving in certain ways will result in related consequences and that negative consequences can be avoided or positive consequences achieved by alternative student behaviors. Although the relationship between behavior and consequences should be obvious, students are often heard to comment "the teacher 'gave' me a *b*" or "the teacher 'gave' me detention." But in reality, the teacher did nothing of the sort. Rather, the student behaved in such a way as to make a given set of consequences inevitable.

☐ When Students Misbehave

When students do not actively participate in the learning process, do not contribute to the common good, are not considerate of other people's rights and feelings, and do not accept the consequences of their actions, behavior change is in order.

In the past, "behavior change" conjured up images of dicipline, coercion, and punishment. That is, when students misbehaved, they were usually punished in a variety of ways which included corporal (physical) punishment, exposure to unpleasant stimuli (staying in after school, cleaning the room, doing extra assignments) or expulsion and/or exclusion from school. Over the years these methods of discipline have either fallen into disfavor with educators or have been found to be illegal and/or unconstitutional. For example, many states specifically prohibit corporal punishment and those states that do permit paddling of students define exact and precise conditions under which corporal punishment may occur. Likewise, suspension and expulsion from school have often been found to be unconstitutional. For example, before any child can be excluded from school, a detailed due process hearing must be conducted, proving conclusively that the student's rights have not been violated by denying the individual educational access or due process (Duke, Donmoyer & Farman 1980). For exceptional students, the issue of suspension from school becomes even cloudier with some special-education advocates arguing that the provisions of PL 94–142 specifically prohibit the exclusion of handicapped students from school for any reason (Winborne & Stainback 1983; Lichtenstein 1980).

For these reasons, the concept of discipline, especially for exceptional students, has changed from a punishment model to one of management and rehabilitation (Winborne & Stainback 1983; Wiles & Rockoff 1979). In this model, the goal of the teacher is to rehabilitate the students to get them to accept their responsibilities to themselves and to the general welfare of the class instead of punishing them for inappropriate behavior. Thus, the current model contains more interactive and counseling techniques than the older conceptualization of discipline and is less dependent on coercion and punishment.

There is a large number of theories of discipline and classroom management; each theory has attracted a number of advocates over the years. Basically, however, theories of classroom management may be divided into three main areas: behavior management/social learning theory, group management techniques, and power theories. These theories, which can be of particular usefulness to the classroom teacher, are discussed next.

BEHAVIOR MANAGEMENT AND SOCIAL LEARNING THEORY

□ □ The learning models of classroom management include behavior modification as well as social learning theory (Charles 1983; Martin 1981). In the behavior modification approach, the paired relationship between the stimulus (behavior) emitted by the student and the resulting responses of the environment is all-important (Axelrod 1977; O'Leary & O'Leary 1977; Skinner 1968). In its simplest terms, the behavior modification model asserts that student behaviors occur because such behavior is rewarded (reinforced) by the environment. Thus, if a teacher wishes to change student behavior through behavior modification techniques, the teacher rewards the new (desirable) student behavior while selectively ignoring (or in extreme cases punishing) the inappropriate behavior. The new behavior is thus strengthened while the old, inappropriate behavior is extinguished.

According to Walker and Shea (1984), there are five basic principles needed for effective behavior management programs. These are:

1. Reinforcement must be dependent on the child exhibiting the target behavior. Simply put, no appropriate behavior, no reinforcement.
2. Reinforcement should be administered immediately (or as soon as possible) after the target behavior occurs. Waiting hours to reinforce the child will prove confusing to the student and will also be counterproductive. Be alert to when the target behavior occurs and reinforce immediately!
3. During the initial stages of the behavior management process, reinforce the target behavior each time it occurs. You can reinforce intermittently later. In the beginning, reinforce every time.
4. Only after the newly acquired target behavior is learned by the child should the teacher use intermittent reinforcement.
5. If you give a tangible reinforcer, *always* accompany it with a social reinforcer (e.g., praise, a hug, etc.). The goal of behavior management is to wean students off tangible reinforcers and have the behavior appear for social and intrinsic rewards.

☐ A Word on Reinforcers

In using behavior modification techniques, one of the most important keys to success lies in the teacher discovering the particular reinforcers (rewards) that are important to the student. For example, how many students do you think would do their work for the reward of listening to the teacher's opera records? On the other hand, students have been known to complete schoolwork and adhere to classroom rules for the privilege of listening and dancing to the latest rock and roll records. Christian (1983) has identified a hierarchy of reinforcers appropriate for use with mentally retarded students. These reinforcers range from physical contact to tangible reinforcer to internal self-reward (see Table 14.1). This hierarchy is tied to the child's developmental and cognitive levels, as well as the child's personal preference for certain reinforcers.

It is believed that use of Christian's hierarchy of reinforcers will be of use to teachers of mentally retarded children who wish to use behavior modification as a technique of classroom management. One such method might be to actually pass Christian's list of reinforcers to students in the class and allow them to choose which ones they would like to receive for appropriate behavior. Remember, however, whichever reinforcers are used, tangible rewards should always be linked with intangible (secondary) reinforcers.

TABLE 14.1   Christian's Hierarchy of Reinforcers

	A	B	C	D	E	F	G
	⟨ · · · · · · · · · · · · · · · · · *Concreteness*				*Abstractness* · · · · · · · · · · · · · · · ⟩		
Consequence Level	Infantile Physical Contact	Food	Toys	School Implements	Privileges	Praise	Internal Self-Reinforcement
Examples	Hugs, Pats, Physical Proximity	Milk, Raisins, Crackers, Gum	Balloon, Marble, Kite, Clay	Eraser, Ruler, Notepad, Crayon	Free Time, Errands, Collect Papers	Verbal Comments, Grades, Certificate	"I did well!" "My work's all complete."

From B. T. Christian (1983). A practical reinforcement hierarchy for classroom behavior modification. *Psychology in the Schools, 20,* 83–85. Used by permission.

METHODS FOR INCREASING BEHAVIOR

☐ Shaping

Shaping entails sequential, systematic reinforcement of successive approximations of target behavior until that behavior is reached. For example, suppose Bobby is a child in your class who is a loner; he does not interact with other children and will not enter into play activities with his peers. You wish to institute a behavior management program to have Bobby play with his classmates. (For the purposes of a true behavior management program this target behavior would need to be defined much more behaviorally and precisely but for the purposes of this discussion the definition of the target behavior will suffice.) If you waited until Bobby entered a group, spoke with classmates, and played with peers before reinforcing this target behavior, you would be waiting a long time indeed! Instead, it might help to reinforce Bobby for successive approximations of the target behavior. You could reinforce him for coming within five feet of the group, then three feet, then entering the proximity of the group. Then he could receive reinforcement for making eye contact with group members, for touching toys, for vocalizing, and finally for playing. Notice that with each successive approximation, we are pushing Bobby closer and closer to our target behavior of playing with the other children.

There are six main steps that should be followed in shaping behavior (Neisworth, Deno & Jenkins 1969; Walker & Shea 1984).

1. Select the target behavior in precise and behavioral terms.
2. Obtain baseline data on how often the target behavior is occurring in the natural environment.

3. Select appropriate reinforcers.
4. Reinforce successive approximations.
5. Reinforce the target behavior each time it occurs.
6. At the appropriate time, reinforce the target behavior on an intermittent schedule.

☐ Modeling and Social Learning

The social learning/modeling theory is based on the notion of *vicarious reinforcement* (Bandura 1969, 1977; Bandura & Walters 1963; Rosenthal & Zimmerman 1978). Vicarious reinforcement refers to the idea that it may be reinforcing for students to watch other students gaining reinforcement even though the observer receives no direct reinforcement himself or herself. This can work two ways in the classroom in regards to classroom management: students may receive vicarious reinforcement watching other students get rewarded for appropriate behavior or they may receive vicarious reinforcement as a student is inadvertently rewarded by the environment for inappropriate behavior (e.g., the class clown). It would then not be surprising to have other students in the class, who were not directly reinforced by the teacher for inappropriate behavior, begin to behave in exactly the same disruptive ways as the child who had received the teacher's attention. Thus, the teacher who is having trouble with a class clown could suddenly face an entire classroom of clowns. For this reason, it is important for the teacher to keep in mind that because of the vicarious reinforcement, more is at stake in rewarding behavior then just one student's actions. The entire class may gain reinforcement by what the teacher does in the classroom in terms of classroom management with individual students.

Vicarious reinforcement presumes that children will model or imitate others (Bandura 1969; Clarizio & Yelon 1967). There are at least two techniques the teacher can use in implementing a modeling procedure:

1. **Peer modeling and peer tutoring:** Students can learn appropriate classroom behaviors by viewing and subsequently modeling other students in the class whom they like and respect. Students can work with the models in private sessions and then institute a program where the models work with other students providing feedback on the adequacy of their behavior.
2. **Buddy systems:** Students who regularly engage in inappropriate behavior can be paired with students who consistently engage in appropriate behavior. The students then work together as a team to modify the inappropriate behavior. The students receive their reinforcement for the appropriate behavior as a team. This pair/team approach has been shown to be a powerful social modifier of behavior. However, the teacher should be on guard against one member of the team becoming dominant and overly influencing the more passive pair member.

Before utilizing a modeling program, however, the teacher should carefully consider the following four factors in order to decide whether such an approach is a good idea for the class:

1. Is the child developmentally and cognitively prepared to imitate a model?
2. Will the child be extrinsically rewarded for appropriate modeling? It is probably unrealistic to expect the child to begin to model for intrinsic reasons.
3. Is the model appropriate? We do not want students modeling inappropriate behaviors. Having the child model the wrong behavior is an invitation to disaster!
4. Is the model acceptable to the child? Does the child like and respect the model? Children model whom they like, not dislike. The social status of the model will need to be taken into account for modeling to work.

☐ Contingency Contracting

When you work on your job you expect reinforcement (i.e., pay). Put another way, when you work you enter into a contract (either written or verbal) with your employer which states that you will receive some reinforcement for behaving appropriately (working) and/or rendering services. Contingency contracting represents an agreement (either written or oral) between teacher and student in the form of

"Exhibit the target behavior, and you will receive the reinforcement which we agreed upon" (Premack 1965).

In contingency contracting, the target behavior as well as the reinforcement type and amount is individualized for each student. For example, examine the four contingencies for the following students:

Bobby: Complete one workbook page and receive reinforcement.
Sally: Complete three workbook pages and receive reinforcement.
Tim: Stay in your seat for five minutes and receive reinforcement.
Bozo: Stop being the class clown and receive reinforcement.

In the case of Bobby and Sally, the target behavior is the same (completing workbook pages) but Sally must complete more pages than Bobby to receive her reinforcement. At first, this may seem unfair but it really is quite appropriate. If Bobby is more distractable than Sally or is a slower worker, he should not have to live up to Sally's standard to receive his reinforcement. Bobby should be compared to himself not to Sally. Likewise, Sally should not be concerned with what Bobby must do to receive his reinforcement. All she has to do is fulfill the terms of her contract and reinforcement will be forthcoming.

In the case of Tim and Bozo, these two students are to engage in different behaviors to gain reinforcement. Again, the contracts of these two students are individualized. However, in Bozo's case, the probability of his ceasing to be a clown is quite low.

In writing and negotiating contracts with students, there are some basic rules or guidelines which should be followed (Homme et al. 1969; Walker & Shea 1984). These include:

1. The contract payoff should occur immediately after the contract is fulfilled.
2. In the beginning of the program, contracts should call for successive approximations of desired behavior.
3. Contracts should call for frequent payoffs in small amounts rather than one large payoff in the distant future.
4. The contract must be fair to both parties, must be clear and straightforward, and must be stated positively.
5. The contracting program must be an integral part of the classroom program and be used on an ongoing basis rather than being used as a one-shot procedure.
6. The contract must specifically state the desired achievement or productivity level.
7. The reinforcer must be delivered in accordance with the terms of the contract.
8. Terms of the contract should include dates for periodic contract review and renegotiation.

There are many types of contracts which can be drawn up by teachers and students. Some are elaborate, artistic affairs, others are just bare bones standard contracts. Figure 14.2 contains two samples of contracts taken from classrooms.

☐ Token Economies

For some children, verbal reporting of progress toward a goal by the teacher is not sufficient motivation to continue a behavior management program. That is, many children simply cannot wait a long period of time for their reward. In addition, for some children, social rewards are not yet motivating; they need something tangible that they can see, feel, and manipulate to indicate progress toward their goal. For such children, a token economy may be a valuable tool for motivating behavior.

A token is a tangible and usually intrinsically worthless item that may be exchanged for a variety of desirable rewards. Tokens may include poker chips, macaroni, beads, point cards, and even money. (Yes, money is a token. In itself it has no reward value. It is what money can buy that makes it valuable.)

A token economy is one where students receive tokens for appropriate behavior that can be exchanged for tangible rewards, privileges, or activities (see Table 14.2 for a menu of possible rewards and activities for which tokens may be exchanged). The basic idea behind a token economy is that the tokens are saved until the child has earned enough to purchase a desired item or activity.

Walker and Shea (1984) have identified some basic rules for establishing a classroom token economy:

1. Select the target behavior for each child.
2. Present the target behavior to children in terms they can understand.
3. Post the rules for receiving tokens and review them frequently with students.
4. Select an appropriate token. It should not be one that is easily forged or duplicated, one that is expensive to distribute to students, or one that is edible.
5. Establish the rules under which tokens may be exchanged.
6. Develop a reward menu and post it in the classroom where children can refer to it easily.
7. Implement the token economy. Start small and on a limited basis and build on a firm foundation.

FIGURE 14.2 Sample Contingency Contracts

Let it be understood that I, _____, will work at the following rules of my class, or that I will not receive the privileges of being a senior at _____ School.

The rules I will work on are as follows:
1. I will behave like an adult, *not* like a baby.
2. I will not bother my teachers or my classmates by acting silly or causing trouble.
3. I will raise my hand to talk.
4. I will work harder on my diet.

If I do not follow these rules, I understand that Mr. Keyes, as my teacher, has the right to refuse any of the following senior privileges:
1. Free time
2. Records and music in the room
3. Extra lunch
4. Juice bar and pop on Friday
5. Jazzercise
6. Dances and senior group activities
7. Holiday and classroom parties
8. Extra sports—cheerleading, baseball, etc.
9. Projector and screen set-up for movies
10. Field trips—e.g. King's Island

Because I am an adult, older than a child, and am old enough to know how to behave correctly, I promise to work on these goals, and will follow the rules of the class.

_____
Pupil's Signature

Teacher _____
Principal _____
Parent _____

FIGURE 14.2 (continued)

I WILL PLOW THROUGH, and if

_____

_____

_____

by _____
    (date)

then _____

_____

_____

Contractor   Contractee   Witness

From P. Kaplan & A. Hoffman (1981). *It's absolutely groovy.* Denver: Love.

TABLE 14.2 A Sample Menu of Items and Activities Which Can Be Purchased With Tokens

Reward	Time Allowed	Cost
Magazine	—	5 points
Penny candy	—	4 points
Candy Bar	—	15 points
Ten Baseball Cards	—	20 points
Costume Jewelry	—	20 points
Kite	—	30 points
Action Figure	—	50 points
Free Time	10 minutes	20 points
Watching TV	30 minutes	40 points
Listening to Records	15 minutes	20 points
Playing with Toys	15 minutes	20 points
Playing a Game	30 minutes	40 points

8. At first, provide immediate reinforcement for acceptable behavior. Give tokens as soon as appropriate behavior occurs. You may also wish to allow immediate token exchange. Gradually, you can move token exchange to designated times during the day.

9. Gradually change from a continuous to an intermittent reinforcement giving of tokens.

10. Revise the reward menu often. Do not let children become bored with the program.

Instead of using actual tokens, the teacher may wish to use a *point card*. Such a card contains spaces for the teacher's initials or other distinguishing mark, each mark equaling one point. Points, like tokens, can then be exchanged for rewards or activities. When using a point card, however, the teacher should make sure that the points cannot be easily duplicated or forged by the child. Figure 14.3 contains a sample point card.

A technique sometimes used in classes that has proved successful is that of the *layaway* procedure. Students who wish to purchase a high-cost item but do not have the necessary tokens or points may reserve the item by putting it on layaway as in a department store. Each day, the child exchanges her or his tokens or points and pays off the desired item (with no interest) until the item is paid in full by the student. Such a layaway procedure has proven popular with students who do not have enough tokens to purchase an item but nevertheless do not wish to lose it to someone else.

METHODS OF DECREASING BEHAVIOR

☐ ☐ Many times you may wish not that children increase certain behavior, but rather that they decrease inappropriate behavior. Inappropriate behaviors are usually disruptive to the class, counterproductive, and/or dangerous either to the child

FIGURE 14.3 A Sample Point Card

Point Tally Form

Child _____ Date _____

Monday											
Tuesday											
Wednesday											
Thursday											
Friday											

TOTAL

Monday	
Tuesday	
Wednesday	
Thursday	
Friday	
Week	

or to other children. Hall, Lund & Jackson (1968) in an early article describing behavior management procedures to eliminate inappropriate behaviors in the classroom described some student classic classroom misbehaviors. They visited inner-city elementary classes with an average class size of forty pupils. The teachers in the classes simply could not handle student misbehaviors any longer. Such behaviors included:

> Robbie: Engaged in inappropriate behavior 75 percent of the time. Behaviors included snapping rubber bands, playing with toys from his pocket, talking and laughing, and slowly and loudly drinking the half-pint of milk served earlier in the morning.
>
> Rose: 70 percent inappropriate behavior. Included laying head on desk, taking off her shoes, and being out of seat.
>
> Ken: Inappropriate behavior 60 percent of the time. Playing with toys from his desk and pockets, rolling pencils on the floor and desk, and wiggling and jiggling in his seat.
>
> Gary: 57 percent inappropriate behavior. Behaviors included beating his desk with a pencil, chewing and licking the pages of his book, moving his chair back and forth in unison with classmates, blowing bubbles in his milk, and punching holes in the full milk carton and letting the milk flow onto the floor!

These students were not in a special-education class for behaviorally disordered children. They were normal third grade children who were obviously off the track and behaving inappropriately 60–80 percent of the school day.

What can be done to eliminate such inappropriate behaviors? Obviously yelling and scolding by the teacher had not worked. Punishment had been unsuccessful. There are a variety of different techniques which the teacher may wish to use in order to eliminate inappropriate student behaviors. These include (*a*) extinction, (*b*) punishment, (*c*) time-out, (*d*) satiation, and (*e*) reinforcement of incompatible behaviors.

☐ Extinction

Behavior modification theory holds that all behavior occurs because it is reinforced. If a given student's behavior is not reinforced or rewarded, it will not occur. Sometimes, punishing or at least not positively reinforcing inappropriate behavior may in fact be rewarding it at a strong rate. For example, consider the child who does not do very well academically in school and is constantly out of her seat. The teacher may not pay much attention to the girl when she is in her seat. However, when she is out of her seat, she is scolded, reprimanded, and told to sit down. In short, she is getting attention for her inappropriate behavior. This is negative attention, but to an ignored child even negative attention is better than no attention at all.

Extinction is the withholding of a reinforcer for a behavior that previously has been reinforced. It is the ignoring of inappropriate behavior formerly given attention. For example, let us return for a moment to our students in the Hall et al. (1968) study who were misbehaving so badly and frequently. Hall analyzed that a major reason that these students were acting so badly was that they were getting attention in the form of teacher comments and the teacher moving closer to the child when he or she misbehaved. Hall and his associates devised a program where the teacher moved away from misbehaving students when they acted inappropriately and closer to students when they behaved in an appropriate manner. Within the relatively short time of a month, the inappropriate behavior for each student dropped to almost zero with time on appropriate behavior increasing to almost 100 percent. In short, the extinction process had instituted a major behavioral change.

To be effective, teachers must be consistent in the extinction process. To sometimes ignore the behavior and sometimes reinforce it will actually be creating an intermittent reinforcement schedule for the child that will powerfully increase inappropriate behavior. Additionally, in the initial stages of the extinction process, you can expect the magnitude of inappropriate behavior to increase as the child tries harder and harder to regain reinforcement for inappropriate behavior. Stick to your guns! Continual nonreinforcement will eventually lead to extinction. However, to speed up the process, make sure you offer reinforcement for appropriate behavior as you are nonreinforcing incorrect behavior.

☐ Punishment

Punishment is probably the most used form of behavior management for decreasing inappropriate behavior. There are actually two forms of punishment: addition of an aversive stimulus for unacceptable behavior (e.g., a spanking or verbal abuse) or subtraction of something the child wants or has earned (being grounded, loss of television, staying up late). Sometimes, subtraction punishment is called *response cost*.

Does punishment work? There is evidence to suggest that in the short run, punishment can be very effective in reducing inappropriate behavior (Azrin & Holz 1966; Feshback 1970; Johnston 1972). However, in the long run, punishment has been shown to produce some negative consequences (Clarizio & Yelon 1967). These consequences include the findings that punishment:

1. Often does not eliminate but merely suppresses inappropriate behavior. Inappropriate behavior may return at even higher levels when punishment is removed.
2. It does not provide information or a model on what constitutes appropriate behavior.
3. That it offers a model of aggression to the child.

4. That it contains emotional byproducts such as stress, anxiety, or anger. We usually do not think very warm thoughts about people who punish us.
5. That the emotional byproducts caused by punishment may lead to other types of deviant behavior.

In short, before punishment is used other techniques of behavior modification should be employed. If the teacher does decide to use punishment techniques, it is suggested that the following guidelines be followed (Good & Brophy 1980; Walker & Shea 1984):

1. Specifically communicate to children punishable behavior by use of posted classroom rules. Post the rules where children can refer to them frequently and review the rules frequently with students.
2. Provide models of acceptable behavior.
3. Punishment should be threatened before it is actually used. Students should know that they are getting a warning and will be punished on the next offense.
4. When used, punishment should be applied systematically, deliberately, and in a noncapricious manner. It should not be applied when you are angry or emotional.
5. The punishment should be as short and as mild as possible but unpleasant enough to motivate students to change their behaviors.
6. Punishment should be applied with positive statements about rules and what the child should be doing to gain positive reinforcement.

□ Time-Out

As mentioned earlier, time-out is the removal of a child from a reinforcing or stimulating setting to a nonreinforcing, nonstimulating environment for a specific period of time (Lewellen 1980). Basically, there are three types of time-out: *observational, exclusion*, and *seclusion*.

In observational time-out a child is withdrawn from a reinforcing activity by being placed on the perimeter of the activity, by having materials taken away, or by being told to place his or her head on the desk. In this type of time-out the child can observe what the other children are doing but cannot participate.

Exclusion time-out occurs when the child must leave a reinforcing situation but is allowed to stay in the classroom. The student is not, however, allowed to observe the group. Typically, in exclusion time-out the child is separated from the activity by a screen or other opaque object.

Seclusion time-out occurs when the child is removed not only from the activity but from the classroom itself. In this situation the child is removed to an extremely nonreinforcing, nonstimulating area for a designated period of time.

When time-out procedures are used, the teacher should make efforts to insure that the following procedures or techniques are followed:

1. Time-out should be administered consistently and systematically, not capriciously. Nonconsistent administration of time-out will only lead to stress, confusion, and anxiety on the part of children.
2. Students should clearly understand the rules of behaviors which will lead to time-out. Rules should be posted, explained, and frequently reviewed.
3. Scolding, reprimanding, or punishment does not occur before or after time-out. Such teacher behavior can be positively reinforcing to the child. The key concept in time-out is to remove the child from the reinforcing situation, not provide another one.
4. Time-out becomes less effective as the duration in time-out increases. Time-out should probably last two to three minutes after the child has calmed down. A child should never remain in time-out more than ten minutes. The purpose of time-out is not to get a child out of your hair. To remind you that you have a child in time-out, a timer with an alarm or bell should be used.

☐ Satiation

Satiation involves the decrease of an unacceptable behavior as a result of strong and increased reinforcement of that behavior (Krumboltz & Krumboltz 1972; Walker & Shea 1984). During satiation, the person receives so much reinforcement for the behavior that it soon ceases to be attractive. An example of satiation occurred when the author worked in a bakery as a youth. The bakery owner, a wise man, told his new employees to eat as much baked goods as they liked, free. This was like a dream come true! For two days on the job, employees ate cakes and cookies until ready to burst. By the third day, however, they were satiated on baked goods. From that day on, they never ate on the job. They had become satiated.

To be effective, the teacher should employ the following strategies when employing the satiation technique (Good & Brophy 1980; Krumboltz & Krumboltz 1972).

1. The activity should be reinforced on a fixed rather than variable schedule. This means that reinforcement should not occur randomly but after every or nearly every correct response.
2. That each reinforcement be powerful and plentiful. Now is not the time to be stingy. Reinforce in full.
3. That it not be used in situations where strong repetition of the behavior is dangerous to the child or to other children.

☐ Reinforcement of Incompatible Behaviors

In this technique, the teacher reinforces a behavior that precludes an inappropriate behavior from occurring simultaneously. For example, suppose you had a pupil who kept getting out of his or her seat to get a drink of water. You may wish to reward heavily this child for working on an arithmetic workbook. Even though you are not dealing directly with the out-of-seat behavior, one cannot be out of one's seat getting a drink and in-seat working on arithmetic problems at the same time. The two behaviors are incompatible.

Reinforcement of incompatible behaviors is useful in that they can extinguish inappropriate behavior while simultaneously rewarding appropriate behaviors. However, the teacher must make sure that the two behaviors in question are, in fact, incompatible. If it is possible for two behaviors to occur at the same time (e.g., doing workbook pages and talking in class), the inappropriate behavior will not necessarily be extinguished when this behavior change technique is used.

GROUP MODELS OF CLASSROOM MANAGEMENT

□ □ There are a number of models of group management but one of the most relevant to classroom control is Kounin's Group Managerial Approach (1977). Basically, Kounin asserts that by projecting an image of being in charge in the classroom as well as effectively managing lessons and the transitions between lessons, teachers can prevent much disruptive behavior before it begins. More specifically, Kounin suggests that teachers react to student disruptive behaviors in the following ways:

1. **Desist:** Teachers may simply and firmly tell pupils to cease deviant and off-task behaviors. However, for this technique to be effective, such admonitions must be timely; they must come early when the behavior is first beginning and before it gets more serious. If the teacher waits until the behavior is too advanced, simple admonitions to desist will probably not be effective.
2. **Suggest alternative behavior:** Often, the student engaging in disruptive behavior does not know any alternative behavior to demonstrate. This is often the case when students crave the teacher's attention but do not know socially acceptable ways to gain it. In such cases, the teacher can offer alternative behaviors to the student that may solve the student's problem and at the same time be acceptable and appropriate.
3. **Concurrent praise:** This represents the behavior modification approach. If much disruptive behavior occurs for the purpose of gaining the teacher's attention, then the teacher technique of reinforcing other students' appropriate behavior while ignoring inappropriate behavior should extinguish the disruptions. This technique is quite useful when combined with the strategy of telling students what alternative behaviors would gain the teacher's approval and attention. Especially for mentally retarded students, a teacher cannot ignore inappropriate behavior and expect students to guess what might constitute behavior that would gain

the teacher's approval. For this reason the concurrent strategy of ignoring inappropriate behavior and informing students of their alternative behavioral options (as well as modeling the appropriate behavioral options) is highly facilitative.

4. **Description of desirable behavior.** The teacher has the off-task student describe the inappropriate behavior the child is currently demonstrating, the behavior the child should be displaying, and the difference between the two. Such a method allows the child to paraphrase the teacher's instructions for appropriate behavior as well as put into her or his own words descriptions of acceptable alternative behaviors

DISCOURAGING INAPPROPRIATE STUDENT BEHAVIOR BEFORE IT BEGINS

☐ ☐ A major goal of Kounin's model is to avoid disruptive behavior before it even begins. In order to do this, he advises that the teacher use *learner accountability* techniques to keep students on task and away from disruptive activity. The teacher can institute these learner accountability strategies by using the following teaching behaviors:

1. **Goal directed prompts:** The teacher asks questions that focus on the students' goals by asking the pupils about work plans for a given period of time—what they are hoping to accomplish and how they are planning on accomplishing it. Such a technique helps the student to focus on the task at hand and offers students a means for achieving their classwork goals.

2. **Work showing:** The teacher holds students accountable for their work by having them demonstrate what they have accomplished in a given period of class time. The belief is that students will work harder and complete assignments if they know that they will be held accountable. Here, the teacher's goal is not to grade student work on quality but rather to reward time on-task, judging whether work has been completed in a given period of time.

3. **Peer involvement:** The teacher involves students in commenting on other students' work or helping their peers. This technique can be tricky, however, especially when used with mentally retarded pupils, and the teacher must be sure that student critiques are given and taken positively by pupils. Again, the key is not the quality of the student's work but rather whether or not the student has stayed on-task and has accomplished productivity goals.

The Kounin model is less a system of discipline and more one of classroom management; it helps the teacher to avoid classroom control problems. Thus, it must be used and presented by the teacher from the first day of class to give the appearance the teacher is in control. It is probably not a useful system to use when things have already gotten out of hand and highly disruptive behaviors are already firmly in place. When that occurs, other systems of classroom control and management will probably need to be used.

POWER THEORIES

☐ ☐ One of the problems with management theories such as Kounin's is that they do not deal well with handling disruptive behavior once it has occurred and is firmly in place. Rather, it is aimed at avoiding disruptive behavior before it occurs. Recently two systems have been advanced which allow teachers to deal quickly and efficiently with disruptive behavior as it occurs rather than ignoring it or taking valuable class time to extinguish it. These theories have been labeled power management systems because they are designed to help teachers deal quickly and powerfully with class disruptions.

☐ The Classroom Management Training Program

The Classroom Management Training Program (CMTP) is a power system developed by Frederick Jones (1979). Jones spent ten years investigating the problems often encountered by teachers and found some surprising results. For example, Jones found that while teachers most feared crisis situations in the classroom such as violent challenges to their authority, such open and violent challenges actually occurred quite rarely, even in difficult, hard-to-manage classes. Rather, Jones found that approximately 80 percent of student misbehaviors consisted of students talking to their peers in class at inappropriate times and on inappropriate topics, while the remaining 20 percent of student misbehaviors consisted of students walking and moving about the classroom at inappropriate times. However, Jones found that disciplining these two relatively "harmless" student behaviors often robbed teachers of as much as 50 percent of available instructional time. Jones found that through four basic behaviors and processes, the teacher could recover this lost instructional time and extinguish many cases of such disruptive student behaviors. These processes were identified as:

1. **Limit setting:** This procedure encompasses the creation of rules which behaviorally define the boundaries separating acceptable from unacceptable behavior. These rules are not a list of do's and dont's. Rather the rules behaviorally outline how students act (i.e., what constitutes appropriate work behavior), what to do when materials and supplies are needed, what students should do when they are stuck on a problem and do not know how to proceed, and what to do when assigned work is finished.

2. **The use of body language:** Jones found that class rules could often be enforced using body language that eliminates the necessity of taking instructional time to chastise students verbally for inappropriate behavior. The attributes of effective body language include physical proximity to students, body position, facial expression, tone of voice, and eye contact.

3. **Incentive systems:** Incentive systems refer to a phenomenon known as the Premack Principle (sometimes called "Grandma's law") which allows students to engage in a desired activity as a reward for appropriately participating in activities that they do not consider very popular or entertaining. For example, with the incentive system, a student would be allowed to play a game or listen to pop music after completing arithmetic seatwork. In the CMTP system, preferred activities occur for the class instead of individual students, and Jones describes two techniques for motivating students to stay on-task and complete their work in exchange for collective class time in popular activities. The first method is the *stopwatch* technique. In this procedure, the teacher uses a large stopwatch that can be clicked on and off. Whenever a misbehavior occurs by any class member, the clock is clicked on; it is clicked off only when the misbehavior ends. The total elapsed time on the watch represents time subtracted from the total time spent on a preferred activity for the entire class. Jones comments that student peer pressure is often enough to get students to end their misbehavior quickly. The second procedure, called *omission training*, is the opposite of the subtraction technique of taking away time from preferred activities for misbehaviors. In omission training, the class can have time added to preferred activities as an incentive for spending time on task and behaving appropriately. Again, peer pressure works to the teacher's advantage as students, who once gained attention by misbehaving, now can gain status by behaving appropriately and earning extra time for the class on preferred activities. This second process would seem to hold special potential for adding to the status of mentally retarded children in mainstreamed situations— situations where mentally retarded pupils have been known to suffer from status deficits and who consequently may try to increase their status by misbehaving in class and gaining peer and teacher attention for their misdeeds.

☐ Learned Helplessness and the Special-Needs Learner

The last technique Jones suggests for teachers is that of giving help to students more effectively. Jones argues that teachers often give help to students who are not suffering from academic learning difficulties on their assignments but rather who are acting disruptive and or are displaying *learned helplessness*—defined as habitual student surrender, lack of effort, and requests for teacher assistance—in order to gain the teacher's attention and help (Dweck 1975; Dweck & Wortman 1982; Reynolds & Miller 1984, 1986). Jones believes that teachers can give help more efficiently to those students who really need it, reduce learned helplessness, and stop reinforcing off-task behavior with personalized attention by providing detailed and graphic instructions as to what is to be done in children's seatwork, by commenting positively on student effort and student accomplishments, by telling the student in the individualized help situation exactly what is to be done next, and by not staying to watch that the student has appropriately accomplished what the teacher has said to do next. This last step is a way of transmitting to the student that the teacher has confidence in the student's ability to carry out the teacher's detailed instruction without the teacher looking over the student's shoulder. In this setting, students who act helpless get proportionately less attention from the teacher while students who make an effort to put into practice the teacher's instruction receive praise and personalized attention. Such a strategy provides help for the learner who really needs it while at the same time fosters independence and reduced helplessness in others.

☐ A Summary of Suggestions for Teachers Using the CMTP Approach

In summary, Jones suggests the following teacher behaviors for the CMTP model of classroom management:

1. Establish a set of work-related rules that the class is to follow.
2. Arrange the room seating pattern so that the teacher can circulate among the students easily and can reach any student quickly and effortlessly.
3. Use body language while teaching rather than stopping to deal verbally with students' disruptions.
4. Use incentive systems, especially those that add status to children for behaving appropriately.
5. Give help efficiently, especially by extinguishing learned helplessness and reinforcing initiative and motivation to try.

The CMTP model can be especially relevant for mentally retarded learners. First, it can help add to the status of low-achieving, disruptive students by making them responsible for time on preferred tasks spent by the entire class. This avenue for increasing status often offers the low-status child a means for increasing popularity by appropriate means rather than by acting as the class clown. Second, it is a method of extinguishing the planned helplessness which is often exhibited by many mentally retarded students and for rewarding motivation to learn, staying on task, and trying. This will help to extinguish the behavior of those children who are paralyzed by fear of failure since they are being reinforced for trying although not necessarily succeeding. The teacher also displays confidence in the student by not monitoring everything the student does while the student is working. Of course, some mentally retarded students will need some monitoring so they are not learning and practicing inappropriate academic content. The special-education teacher, now free from much of the time spent on correcting disruptive and learned helplessness behaviors, can give those students the individualized instructional time they need.

ASSERTIVE DISCIPLINE

□ □ The last system to be discussed is assertive discipline (Canter 1976). This system is very popular in schools and has been adopted in many special-education classrooms. Canter sets four major principles of education and the need for discipline in the schools. They are:

1. Firm classroom control is not inhumane. In fact it is highly humane because it gives all students the opportunity to learn.
2. Teachers have basic rights. They include a safe and effective teaching environment, appropriate behavior from students, and support from parents and other school staff.
3. Students also have basic rights. These include an orderly learning environment, the right to receive educational help when needed, and positive support for their learning efforts.
4. Given 1–3 above, teachers need to resolve that they will not tolerate violation of either their own or students' rights.

□ Techniques in the Assertive Discipline Program

The assertive discipline model begins by creating a clear set of expectations as defined in nonambiguous classroom rules. Students can and should have input into forming these rules, but once the rules have been set they are to be followed by everyone. Students need to learn that if they choose to violate the rules, they must accept the consequences of their actions. The teacher's job is to let students know rule violations will not be tolerated, to believe that students possess the ability to act in an acceptable manner, and to treat lapses in such behavior fairly and consistently.

Canter believes that student rule violations need to be dealt with quickly, efficiently, and in a straightforward manner with as little emotion as possible. He suggests a consistent program of dealing with student misbehaviors that escalates in severity as student misbehavior persists. Such a program might include the following sanctions:

1. First offense of the day: name on chalkboard.
2. Second offense: check by name which means fifteen minute loss of privileges.

3. Third offense: a second check, thirty minute loss of privileges.
4. Fourth offense: another check and trip to principal's office.
5. Fifth offense: same as 1–4 above plus student calls parent on the telephone to explain offense.
6. Sixth offense: parent is called and must come immediately to school to meet with principal and teacher.
7. Implement a system to reward students for appropriate behavior.

☐ Suggestions for Teachers Using Assertive Discipline

Advocates of assertive discipline suggest that the classroom teacher engage in some pragmatic and systematic actions that will help with classroom control. These suggestions include:

1. Establishing a minimum set of rules (no more than five) and enforcing the rules strongly. The rules should be posted in clear view of students and teacher as a continual reminder and should be alluded to when necessary.
2. Praising students in public but chastising them in private whenever possible. Negative comments to students should be handled in private meetings and should remain as nonemotional as possible.
3. Be consistent with deadlines, announcements, and sanctions for missing deadlines. Following through on sanctions for missed deadlines.
4. Give detailed oral and/or written instructions and expect that those instructions will be followed.

Proponents of assertive discipline maintain that when these techniques are instituted and followed, a shift of responsibility for appropriate behavior and consequences for inappropriate behavior occurs from teacher to student. In this way, responsibility for behavior and the consequences of such behaviors become part of a training in independent living, a key concept in the education of mentally retarded individuals. Finally, advocates argue that classroom rules can be easily learned by all students and implemented easily and fairly by teachers with a minimum of classroom instruction time utilized. Students know beforehand what the consequences of inappropriate behavior will be and, if they choose to engage in that behavior, they know what will happen. Finally, proponents of the system argue that assertive discipline is an appropriate method to use for both mentally retarded and nonretarded learners in that it can be easily understood by both groups of students and does not discriminate against a child because of intellectual handicap.

SUMMARY

☐ ☐ Classroom management deals not only with discipline but also with the effective handling of student behavior before that behavior becomes problematic. It also refers to the handling of student inappropriate behavior in ways that are not aversive or anxiety producing for the student. Research indicates that classroom control and behavior management is of primary concern to teachers, administrators, parents, and even students themselves. Nevertheless, many college teaching-preparatory programs contain only a cursory discussion of classroom management.

There appear to be at least three types of classrooms: democratic, authoritarian, and laissez-faire. Children in democratic classrooms appear to produce less work than children in authoritarian classrooms but work better on their own—a key goal for the schooling of mentally retarded learners. Laissez-faire classrooms seem to be extremely ineffective.

Glasser (1969) outlined steps for creating a warm, safe classroom environment for students. These steps include being friendly, taking a positive stance toward interpersonal relationships, listening to students, giving personalized attention, giving regular positive reinforcement, being willing to help, modeling respect, and leading and following. By instituting these steps, it is believed that special-needs learners can feel that they have some control over their educational lives.

Students have reponsibilities to the teacher and to teach each other. These responsibilities include actively learning, making a contribution to the class, being considerate of others, and accepting the consequences of their actions. When students do not live up to these responsibilities and obligations, behavior change is in order.

There are a number of theories of discipline and behavior change. These include behavior modification and social learning, group management techniques, and power theories. Within behavior modification theories there are two types: increasing appropriate behaviors and decreasing inappropriate behaviors. Among the techniques for increasing behavior is social learning/modeling, reinforcement for successive approximations, contingency contracting, and token economies. Methods for decreasing inappropriate behaviors include extinction, punishment, time-out, satiation, and reinforcement of incompatible behaviors.

Group management techniques have been formalized by Kounin (1977). He asserts that teachers should use the following techniques in dealing with student inappropriate behavior: telling them firmly to desist, using concurrent praise, suggesting alternative behaviors, and describing appropriate behaviors. In order to avoid disruptive student situations, Kounin suggests that the teacher engage in the following activities: use goal directed prompts, use work showing, and encourage peer involvement.

There are two main power theories: the CMTP approach and Assertive Discipline. In the CMTP approach there are four basic processes: limit setting, using body language, using incentive systems, and giving hope appropriately. Teachers must give help to students in the right ways at the appropriate times in order to discourage learned helplessness, a real problem among special-needs learners.

The assertive discipline model is based on the idea that students must receive clear instruction as to what is expected of them and when those expectations are not met, sanctions ought to be forthcoming. By using assertive discipline, it is believed that responsibility and consequences for inappropriate behavior shifts from the student to the teacher.

Appendix

A SAMPLE INSTRUCTIONAL UNIT: PLANNING AND MAINTAINING A NUTRITIOUS MENU

☐ I. Population Parameters

The class where this unit is to be implemented is an EMH/DH class ranging in age from 12 to 14 years old. The mean age is 13.2. There are twelve students in the class—seven girls and five boys. Their chronological age places them between the sixth to eighth grade level but their mental ages are approximately at the fourth to sixth grade level (C.A. 9–12 yrs.). The students' IQ's range between 53 and 67, with the mean at 60.1. Two of the students also have mild behavior problems.

The students are all from middle to lower class socioeconomic families, with many of their parents working blue collar jobs at the nearby factory in the city. Five students come from one-parent homes, three students have one original parent who is either remarried or living with a boyfriend/girlfriend. The other four students live with both original parents. None of these students are the only child; the mean number of children in each family is 3.6.

The school is a junior high school for grades six through eight. There are approximately 325 students in the school. The socioeconomic status of the students varies widely from lower to upper-middle class. This is the only EMH/DH class in the school, although there is an LD resource room in the school.

The city is mainly supported by industry along with professional offices, stores, etc. Many of the students are bussed into the school from outlying regions of the city.

☐ II. Topic and Subtopics

Topic: Planning and maintaining a nutritional diet.
Subtopic: Knowledge of the four food groups and the six basic nutrients.
Subtopic: Planning and preparing a well-balanced meal.
Subtopic: Planning and maintaining a nutritional diet.

☐ III. Rationale

"You are what you eat." This phrase sums up the need for a person to maintain a healthy diet or nutritional program. The foods we eat determine a large factor of our health. Students have many established eating habits and yet are still developing new ones. For these students in this particular age group, they are beginning to feel the tug of independence, especially those students whose parent's time is limited and they are unable to fix breakfast, lunch, afterschool snacks, or dinner. They are beginning to make decisions as to what they will eat and when they will eat it. On a long term basis, these students will eventually be responsible for their own family's nutrition. What is learned now can also be used later in life. Proper diet and eating patterns affect behavior and total physical, mental, and social health.

A varied, well-balanced, nutritious diet is derived from the selection of foods from the four food groups. It is important that these foods contain a recommended amount of daily essential nutrients also. This knowledge is important and useful for the second subtopic of planning and preparing a well balanced meal. Knowledge of the proper daily caloric intake is important when planning both daily meals and weekly menus. Many junior high students whose bodies are beginning to develop may also be having weight problems. Social and peer acceptance is very important at this age, so it is important that students be aware of calories and the effects of too many calories on their bodies.

Finally, regular nutritional eating is the only way to keep a healthy body. This consistency is to be emphasized in the last subtopic by having the student plan and follow a weekly nutritional menu. This will be implemented within the school also in case a home situation is uncooperative or unable to provide the planned meals.

A general awareness of the importance of nutrition and maintaining a nutritional diet will hopefully be continued independently by the student after the completion of this unit.

☐ IV. Prerequisite Skills

The students will need to possess the following prerequisite skills.

In math, the students will need to recognize and count numbers up to 3000. They will learn subtraction with borrowing, multiplication of two-digit numbers, addition with decimal places, and will demonstrate the concept of money values. These skills will be tested through teacher observations and tests. During math lessons, the teacher will mentally assess the students' preparedness for the unit. The teacher also will develop several test/worksheets on these skills and assess the students' work.

For reading, the students have to read to the point where they can follow step-by-step directions. Teacher-made tests are also used to assess the students' skill in this area. The language arts plans include verbal tasks where the students need listening and communicating skills.

Many of the lessons are also done in groups. Therefore, the students should have proper social interaction skills to work in groups of four. They should also be able to work independently as a part of a group. Teacher observations are used to assess the student's social readiness by observing the student in various classroom situations.

☐ **V. Behavioral Objectives**

I. Knowledge of the four food groups and the six basic nutrients.
   A. After teacher instruction, the student will state the four food groups with 100 percent accuracy. (Knowledge)
   B. After a class review, the student will recite three examples of foods from the meat group with 100 percent accuracy. (Knowledge)
   C. After a class review, the student will recite three examples of foods from the milk and dairy group with 100 percent accuracy. (Knowledge)
   D. After a class review, the student will recite three examples of foods from the fruit and vegetables group with 100 percent accuracy. (Knowledge)
   E. After a class review, the student will recite three examples of foods from the bread and cereal group with 100 percent accuracy. (Knowledge)
   F. Given the name of the meat group and a worksheet with pictures of various foods on it, the student will select five food items which belong in the meat group with 100 percent accuracy. (Comprehension)
   G. Given the name of the milk and dairy group and a worksheet with pictures of various foods on it, the student will select five food items which belong to the milk and dairy group with 100 percent accuracy. (Comprehension)
   H. Given the name of the fruit and vegetables group and a worksheet with pictures of various foods on it, the student will select five food items which belong to the fruit and vegetables group with 100 percent accuracy. (Comprehension)
   I. Given the name of the bread and cereal group and a worksheet with pictures of various foods on it, the student will select five food items which belong to the bread and cereal group with 100 percent accuracy. (Comprehension)
   J. After teacher instruction, the student will state how many items from each food group should be eaten every day, with 100 percent accuracy. (breads-4, fruits-4, milk-3, meat-2) (Knowledge)
   K. After teacher instruction, the student will state the six basic nutrients found in foods with 100 percent accuracy. (carbohydrates, fats, protein, minerals, vitamins, and water) (Knowledge)

L. After teacher instruction, the student will state the use of each nutrient in daily diets with 100 percent accuracy. (Knowledge)

M. When given the name carbohydrates, the student will select three food sources of that nutrient with 100 percent accuracy. (Comprehension)

N. When given the name fats, the student will select three food sources of that nutrient with 100 percent accuracy. (Comprehension)

O. When given the name protein, the student will select three food sources of that nutrient with 100 percent accuracy. (Comprehension)

P. When given the name minerals, the student will select three food sources of that nutrient with 100 percent accuracy. (Comprehension)

Q. When given the name vitamins, the student will select three food sources of that nutrient with 100 percent accuracy. (Comprehension)

R. When given the name water, the student will select three different food sources of that nutrient with 100 percent accuracy. (Comprehension)

S. After teacher instruction, the student will state the amount of each nutrient required for the U.S. Recommended Daily Allowance with 100 percent accuracy. (Knowledge)

T. Given a restaurant menu (or facsimile), the student will select a well balanced meal (one containing the four food groups and basic nutrients) to the satisfaction of the teacher. (Comprehension)

U. After teacher instruction, the student will state what a calorie is (energy) with 100 percent accuracy. (Knowledge)

V. Given the name or picture of certain food items, the student will state if they are high or low in calories with 100 percent accuracy. (Knowledge)

W. Given the categories "high in calories" and "low in calories," the student will choose food items which belong in each category with 100 percent, accuracy. (Comprehension)

X. Given the categories "high in calories" and "low in calories," the student will choose food items which belong in each category with 100 percent accuracy. (Comprehension) suggested experimental error from losing heat). (Application)

Y. Given an equation and the child's weight, the student will determine his recommended daily caloric intake with 95 percent accuracy. (Application)

II. Planning and preparing a well-balanced meal.
   A. Given a one-day chart, the student will record the foods he eats in a twenty-four hour period to the teacher's satisfaction. (Application)

B. After a review of the four food groups, foods within each group, and the recommended daily number of servings from each group and from the nutrients, the student will categorize (according to food group and nutrients) those foods eaten during the twenty-four hour period with 90 percent accuracy. (Analysis)

C. Given this categorized list, the student will compare his list of food groups and nutrients with the recommended daily servings with 90 percent accuracy. (Analysis)

D. Using a standard calorie chart, the student will determine the number of calories consumed during the charted twenty-four hour period and the difference from his ideal intake, with 90 percent accuracy. (Application)

E. Given the group assignment of planning one daily meal, the students will select a proper menu for that meal including foods from the four food groups and the six basic nutrients, to the teacher's satisfaction. (Analysis)

F. Given the meal they have selected, the student will calculate the caloric intake of the meal with 90 percent accuracy. (Application)

G. Given a recipe cookbook, the students will find appropriate recipes for the meal they have selected to the teacher's satisfaction. (Application)

H. Given the meal and recipes they have selected, the students will construct a shopping list of the foods they will need to purchase to prepare the meal with 100 percent accuracy. (Synthesis)

I. Given the shopping list, a budget, and a newspaper ad from a local grocery store, the student will collect coupons and sale item prices to be used for the shopping trip and determine an estimated total price within the given budget to the teacher's satisfaction. (Application)

J. Given a trip to the store, the student will collect and purchase the correct food items on his list, using the coupons, staying within the allotted budget, and receiving the correct amount of change with 100 percent accuracy. (Application)

K. Given the recipe and ingredients for the planned meal the students will prepare and serve the selected meal following all directions, to the teacher's satisfaction. (Application)

III. Planning and maintaining a nutritional diet.
   A. Given a daily menu of three meals, the student will put the foods into their respective food groups with 100 percent accuracy. (Analysis)
   B. Given a daily menu of three meals, the student will chart the nutrients found in the foods with 90 percent accuracy. (Analysis)
   C. Given a daily menu of three meals, and a calorie chart, the student will determine the number of calories eaten in that day with 100 percent accuracy. (Analysis)

D. Given choices of different dishes for breakfast, lunch, and dinner, the student will develop a daily menu fulfilling the daily requirements of the food groups and basic nutrients with 90 percent accuracy. (Synthesis)

E. Given this menu (F) developed by the student, he will determine the number of calories in his daily menu with 100 percent accuracy. (Application)

F. Given the assignment to develop a school lunch menu, the student will interview four students outside his classroom to determine what foods other students like to eat, to the satisfaction of the teacher. (Synthesis)

G. Given other students' ideas about school lunches, the student will develop a school lunch menu for one week which would fulfill the needed requirements and students' choices with 90 percent accuracy. (Synthesis)

H. Given a seven-day chart, the student will select three meals for each day for seven days to maintain for one week straight which fulfills daily requirements of food groups, nutrients, and personal caloric intake, with 100 percent accuracy. (Synthesis)

I. Given an empty chart, the student will chart his actual eating habits during his "maintaining" week with 100 percent accuracy. (Application)

J. Given recipes for a variety of meals (from home or from school), the student will select one favorite recipe from each meal (breakfast, lunch, and dinner). (Application)

K. After viewing "Nutrition: Food and Health" Part Two, the students will discuss the American eating habits from positive and negative viewpoints to the teacher's satisfaction. (Evaluation)

L. After listening to foreign students discuss the eating habits and nutritional diets of their countries, the student will recognize difference between American eating habits and other cultures and choose one particular culture as one they would like to live by, to the teacher's satisfaction. (Evaluation)

☐ VI. Concepts and Vocabulary Introduced in Unit

food groups	coupon
nutrients	well-balanced
carbohydrates	Recommended Daily Requirement
minerals	menu
fats	budget
proteins	recipe
vitamins	nutrition
calorie	vocabulary of foreign foods

Specification Chart

Topic

Subtopic	Knowledge	Comprehension	Application	Analysis	Synthesis	Evaluation
Subtopic 1 Knowledge of the four food groups and the six basic nutrients	ABCDEJKLSUV	FGHIMNOPQRTW	XY			
Subtopic 2 Planning & preparing a well-balanced meal			ADFGIJK	BCE	H	
Subtopic 3 Planning and maintaining a nutritional diet			IJ	ABCE	DFGH	KL

Lesson Plans

Core Area: Science/Health   **Time: 15 minutes**

Behavioral Objective	Activities	Materials	Evaluation
I. F-I Given the name of the meat, milk & dairy, fruits & vegetables, & breads & cereals, and a worksheet with pictures of various foods on it, the student will select five food items which belong to that group w/100% accuracy.	1. Discuss what belongs in which group. 2. Give worksheet w/25 pictures of foods from various 4 food groups. 3. Have a guide on top of the paper. Meat-red Dairy-blue F&V-green B&C-orange 4. Have the students circle 5 appropriate foods from that food group with appropriate color crayon. 5. After completion, the teacher names 1 food group to each student & he states which foods he circled.	worksheets colored crayons	Circled the correct foods with the correct color and stated them when asked.

Core Area: Math   **Time: 10-15 minutes**

Behavioral Objective	Activities	Materials	Evaluation
I. J After teacher instruction, the student will state how many items from each food group should be eaten every day w/100% accuracy. (breads-4 fruits-4 milk-3 meat-2)	1. Discussion of amount eaten each day. 2. Worksheets similar to other lesson w/pictures of different foods on it and lines underneath. 3. Student will look at picture and determine how many of that group should be eaten in one day (not the specific food). 4. The student will write the name of the food group and the number of daily servings on the line.	worksheets pencils	Correct amount written for each picture 4 b&c 4 f&v 3 milk 2 meat

Core Area: Art   **Time: 20-25 minutes**

Behavioral Objective	Activities	Materials	Evaluation
I. M-R When given the name of a nutrient, the student will select three food sources of that nutrient w/100% accuracy.	1. Class review of what foods contain what nutrients. 2. Given 1 piece of posterboard divided into six parts student writes name of a nutrient in each box. 3. Using magazines, the student will find pictures of foods containing that nutrient and glue them in the appropriate box (3 in each). 4. Hang posters in room.	posterboard markers magazines scissors glue	Correct food in each box

Core Area: Math   **Time: 10-15 minutes each day for 3-4 days**

Behavioral Objective	Activities	Materials	Evaluation
I. S After teacher instruction the student will state the amount of each nutrient required for the U.S. Recommended Daily Allowance w/100% accuracy.	1. Discuss Recommended Daily Allowance of each nutrient using an example chart. 2. Worksheets w/6 charts on them w/one item's amount missing on each chart (different for each). 3. Reduce amount of information given each day until chart is empty & student must fill in without prompts.	example chart worksheets pencils	On last sheet student should have correct number for each nutrient in the charts

Core Area: Social Studies   Time: **done throughout unit so every child can interview**

Behavioral Objective	Activities	Materials	Evaluation
III. F Given the assignment to develop a school lunch menu, the student will interview 4 students outside his classroom to determine what foods other students like to eat for lunch, to the satisfaction of the teacher.	1. During a student's free time he is allowed to enter a nearby class to interview students about school lunch. 2. The students will develop 3 questions to ask the other students and have them written on paper. 3. Using the tape recorder he will interview 4 students w/his 3 questions. 4. Afterwards, he will listen to the tape recording & write his results to be added to the other students.	paper pencil tape recorder w/tape microphone	Teacher sees the student's suggestions written on his interview sheet

Core Area: Science/Health   Time: **30-45 minutes**

Behavioral Objective	Activities	Materials	Evaluation
III. G Given other students' ideas the student will develop a school lunch menu for one week which would fulfill the needed requirements and students' choices. 90%	1. Teacher will read the suggestions made by other students. 2. During class discussion led by the teacher, as a group they will develop the weekly menu. 3. The teacher will write it on a master sheet to be turned to the kitchen staff.	master menu student responses	Menu fulfills daily nutritional requirements and students' choices

Bibliography

Aach, S. (1981). Art and the IEP. In L. N. Kearns et al. (Eds.), *Readings: Developing arts programs for handicapped students*. Harrisburg, PA: Pennsylvania State Department of Education.

Adams, M. J. (1980). Failures to comprehend and levels of processing in reading. In R. Spiro, B. Bruce, & W. F. Brewer (Eds.), *Theoretical issues in reading comprehension*. Hillsdale, NJ: Lawrence Erlbaum.

Adams, R. & Biddle, B. J. (1970). *Realities of teaching: Explorations with videotape*. New York: Holt, Rinehart & Winston.

Algozzine, B. (1979). *The disturbing child: A validation report (Research Report No. 8)*. Minneapolis: University of Minnesota, Institute for Research on Learning Disabilities.

Algozzine, B., Ysseldyke, J., & Christenson, S. (1983). An analysis of the incidence of special class placement: The masses are burgeoning. *Journal of Special Education, 17*, 141–147(a).

Algozzine, B., Ysseldyke, J., & Christenson, S. (1983). The influence of teachers' tolerances for specific kinds of behaviors on their ratings of a third grade student. *Alberta Journal of Educational Research, 29*, 89–87(b).

Alley, G. & Deshler, D. (1979). *Teaching the learning disabled adolescent: Strategies and methods*. Denver, CO: Love Publishing Co.

Alley, G. & Foster, C. (1978). Nondiscriminatory testing of minority and exceptional children. *Focus on Exceptional Children, 9*, 1–14.

Anastasiow, N. J. & Hanes, M. L. (1974). *Sentence repetition task*. Bloomington, IN: Institute for Child Study.

Anderson, F. E. (1978). Mainstreaming art as well as children. *Art Education, 28*(8), 26–27.

Anderson, L., Evertson, C., & Brophy, J. E. (1979). An experimental study of effective teaching in first-grade reading groups. *Elementary School Journal, 79*, 193–223.

Anderson, P. S. & Groff, P. J. (1968). *Resource materials for teachers of spelling*. Minneapolis, MN: Burgess.

Andre, M. E. & Anderson, T. H. (1979). The development and evaluation of a self-questioning study technique. *Reading Research Quarterly, 14*, 605–623.

Armbruster, B. B., Echols, C. H., & Brown, A. L. (1982). The role of metacognition in reading to learn: A developmental perspective. *Volta Review, 84*, 45–56.

Asher, S. (1980). Topic interest and children's reading comprehension. In R. J. Spiro, B. C. Bruce, & W. F. Brewer (Eds.), *Theoretical issues in reading comprehension*. Hillsdale, NJ: Lawrence Erlbaum.

Asher, S. R., Hymel, S., & Renshaw, P. D. (1982). Loneliness in children. Paper presented at the annual meeting of the American Educational Research Association, Montreal.

Asher, S. R. & Renshaw, P. D. (1981). Children without friends: Social knowledge and social skill training. In S. R. Asher & J. M. Gottman (Eds.), *The development of children's friendships*. New York: Cambridge University Press.

Atack, S. M. (1982). *Art activities for the handicapped*. Englewood Cliffs, NJ: Prentice Hall.

Atkinson, R. C. & Shiffrin, R. M. (1969). Human memory: A proposed system and its control processes. In K. W. Spence & J. T. Spence (Eds.), *The psychology of learning and motivation: Advances in research and theory* (Vol. 2). New York: Academic Press.

Aulls, M. W. (1982). *Developing readers in today's elementary schools*. Boston: Allyn & Bacon.

Ausubel, D., Montemayor, R., & Svajian, P. (1977). *Theory and problems of adolescent development* (2nd ed.). New York: Grune & Stratton.

461

Axelrod, S. (1977). *Behavior modification for the classroom teacher*. New York: McGraw-Hill.

Ayres, L. (1912). *A scale for measuring the quality of handwriting of schoolchildren*. New York: Russell Sage Foundation.

Azrin, N. H. & Holz, W. C. (1966). Punishment. In W. K. Honig (Ed.), *Operant behavior: Areas of research and application*. New York: Appleton-Century-Crofts.

Bachman, R. (1976). *Micro-Tower*. New York: MICRO-TOWER, Institutional Services.

Bailey, L. J. (1976). *Career & vocational education in the 1980's: Toward a process approach*. Carbondale: Southern Illinois University.

Bailey, M. H. (1967). The utility of phonic generalizations in grades one through six. *The Reading Teacher, 20*, 413–418.

Baine, D. (1982). *Instructional design for special education*. Englewood Cliffs, NJ: Educational Technologies Publications.

Baird, J. R. & White, R. T. (1984). *Improving learning through enhanced metacognition: A classroom study*. Paper presented at the annual meeting of the American Education Research Association, New Orleans.

Baker, L. & Brown, A. L. (1985). Metacognition skills in reading. In D. Pearson (Ed.), *Handbook of reading research*. New York: Longman.

Baker, L. & Stein, N. L. (1981). The development of prose comprehension skills. In C. M. Santa & B. L. Hayes (Eds.), *Children's prose comprehension*. Newark, DE: International Reading Association.

Bandura, A. (1965). Influence of models' reinforcement contingencies on the acquisition of imitative responses. *Journal of Personality and Social Psychology, 1*, 589–595.

Bandura, A. (1969). *Principles of behavior modification*. New York: Holt, Rinehart & Winston.

Bandura, A. (1978). The self-esteem in reciprocal determinism. *American Psychologist, 33*, 344–358.

Bandura, A. (1977). *Social learning theory*. Englewood Cliffs, NJ: Prentice-Hall.

Bandura, A. & Kupers, C. J. (1964). Transmission of patterns of self-reinforcement through modeling. *Journal of Abnormal and Social Psychological, 69*, 1–9.

Bandura, A. & Walters, R. H. (1963). *Social learning and personality development*. New York: Holt, Rinehart & Winston.

Bannatyne, A. D. (1966). *Psycholinguistic color system*. Urbana, IL: Learning System Press.

Balthazar, E. E. (1975). *General programs for the mentally retarded*. (Monograph No. 3 of Pro-grams for the developmentally disabled: A multidisciplinary approach.) Wisconsin: State of Wisconsin Department of Health and Social Services.

Balthazar, E. E. (1971). *Balthazar scales of adaptive behavior: Section 1: The scales of functional independence*. Champaign, IL: Research Press.

Barclay, C. B. (1979). The executive control of mnemonic activity. *Journal of Experimental Child Psychology, 27*, 262–276.

Baroody, A. J. & Ginsburg, H. P. (1984). *TMR and EMR children's ability to learn counting skills and principles*. Paper presented at the annual meeting of the American Educational Research Association, New Orleans.

Barr, R., Barth, J. L., & Shermis, S. S. (1978). *The nature of social studies*. Palm Springs, CA: ETC Publications.

Barrett, T. C. (1968). *Taxonomy of cognitive and affective dimensions of reading comprehension*. Unpublished paper, Madison, WI.

Bartel, N. R. (1982). Problems in mathematics achievement. In D. D. Hammill and N. R. Bartel (Eds.) *Teaching children with learning and behavior problems* (3rd ed.). Boston: Allyn & Bacon.

Baumann, J. F. (1984). The effectiveness of a direct instruction paradigm for teaching main idea comprehension. *Reading Research Quarterly, 20*, 93–115.

Baumeister, A. A. & Brooks, P. H. (1981). Cognitive deficits in mental retardation. In J. M. Kauffman & D. P. Hallahan (Eds.), *Handbook of Special Education*. Englewood Cliffs, NJ: Prentice-Hall.

Bean, T. & Steenwyk, F. L. (1984). The effect of three forms of summarization instruction on sixth graders' summary writing and comprehension. *Journal of Reading Behavior, 16*, 297–307.

Beatty, L. S., Madden, R., Gardner, E. G., & Karlsen, B. (1983, 1984). *Stanford Diagnostic Mathematics Test*. New York: Psychological Corp.

Becker, W. C., Engelmann, S., & Thomas, D. R. (1971). *Teaching: A course in applied psychology*. Chicago: Science Research Associates.

Beers, J. & Henderson, E. A. (1977). Study of developing orthographic concepts among first grade children. *Research in the Teaching of English, 11*, 133–148.

Bellack, A. A. (1976). *Studies in the language of the classroom*. Paper presented at the First Invitational Conference on Research on Teaching, Memorial University of Newfoundland, St. Johns.

Bellamy, G. T., Horner, R. H., & Inman, D. P. (1979).

Vocational habilitation of severely retarded adults. Baltimore: University Park Press.

Belmont, J. M. & Butterfield, E. C. (1969). The relations of short-term memory to development and intelligence. In L. P. Lippsitt & H. Reese (Eds.), *Advances in child development and behavior* (Vol. 4). New York: Academic Press.

Belmont, J. M. & Butterfield, E. C. (1971). Learning strategies as determinants of memory deficiencies. *Cognitive Psychology, 2,* 411–420.

Belmont, J. M. & Butterfield, E. C. (1977). The instructional approach to developmental cognitive research. In R. Kail & J. Hagen (Eds.) *Perspectives on the development of memory and cognition.* Hillsdale, NJ: Erlbaum.

Bellugi-Klima, U. (1968). *Evaluating the child's language competence.* (ERIC Document Reproduction Service No. Ed 019 141).

Bensberg, G. J. & Sigelman, C. K. (1976). Definitions and prevalence. In L. L. Lloyd (Ed.) *Communication assessment and intervention strategies.* Baltimore, MD: University Park Press.

Berdine, W. H. (1985). Mental retardation. In W. H. Berdine & A. E. Blackhurst (Eds.). *An introduction to special education* (2nd Ed.). Boston: Little, Brown and Company.

Berieter, C. (1980). Development of writing. In M. L. W. Gregg & E. R. Steinber (Eds.), *Cognitive processes in writing.* Hillsdale, NJ: Erlbaum.

Berieter, C. & Engelmann, S. (1966). *Teaching disadvantaged children in preschool.* Englewood Cliffs, NJ: Prentice-Hall.

Berko, J. (1958). The child's learning of English morphology. *Words, 14,* 150–177.

Berko, J. (1961). The child's learning of English morphology. In S. Saporta (Ed.), *Psycholinguistics.* New York: Holt, Rinehart & Winston.

Berndt, T. J. (1981). Relations between social cognition, nonsocial cognition and social behavior: The case of friendship. In J. H. Flavell & L. Ross (Eds.), *Social cognitive development.* Cambridge, MA: Cambridge University Press.

Bezzi, R. (1962). A standardized manuscript scale for grades 1, 2, and 3. *Journal of Educational Research, 55,* 339–340.

Binet, A. & Simon, T. (1916). *The development of intelligence in children* (E. S. Kite, Trans.) Baltimore: The Williams and Wilkins Co.

Birch, H. R., Richardson, S. A., Baird, D., Horobin, G., & Illsley, R. (1970). *Mental abnormality in a community: A clinical and epidemiological study.* Baltimore: Williams & Wilkens.

Blackburn, J. & Powell, W. (1976). *One at a time all at once: The creative teacher's guide to individualized instruction without anarchy.* Pacific Palisades, CA: Goodyear Publishing Co.

Blake, K. A. (1976). *The mentally retarded: An educational psychology.* Englewood Cliffs, NJ: Prentice-Hall.

Blatt, B., Ozdin's, A., & McNally, J. (1979). *The family papers: A return to purgatory.* New York: Longman.

Block, J. H. (Ed.). (1971). *Mastery learning.* New York: Holt, Rinehart & Winston.

Block, J. H. & Burns, R. B. (1976). Mastery learning. In Lee S. Shulman (Ed.), *Review of research in education, 4.* Itasca, IL: F. E. Peacock.

Bloom, B. S. (1968). Learning for mastery. *Evaluation Comment, 1, No. 2.* Los Angeles: University of California Center for the Study of Evaluation.

Bloom, B. S., Engelhort, M. B., Furst, E. J., Hill, W. H., & Krathwohl, D. R. (1956). Taxonomy of educational objectives: The classification of educational goals. *Handbook I: Cognitive domain.* New York: Longmans Green.

Borg, W. (1979, March). Time and school learning. *Beginning Teacher Evaluation Study Newsletter.*

Borkowski, J. G. & Cavanaugh, J. C. (1979). Maintenance and generalization of skills and strategies by the retarded. In N. R. Ellis (Ed.), *Handbook of Mental Deficiency* (2nd ed.), Hillsdale, NJ: Erlbaum.

Borkowski, J. G., Johnston, M. B., & Reid, M. K. (in press). Metacognition, motivation, and the transfer of control processes. In S. J. Ceci (Ed.), *Handbook of cognitive, social and neuropsychological aspects of learning disabilities.* Hillsdale, NJ: Erlbaum.

Borkowski, J. G. & Krause, A. J. (1985). Metacognition and attributional beliefs. *In the Proceedings of the XXIII International Congress of Psychology.* Amsterdam: Elsoever Publishers.

Borkowski, J. C., Levers, S. R., & Gruenenfelder, T. M. (1976). Transfer of mediational strategies in children: The role of activity and awareness during strategy acquisition. *Child Development, 47,* 779–786.

Borkowski, J. G. & Wanschura, P. B. (1974). Mediational procesess in the retarded. In N. R. Ellis (Ed.), *International review of research in mental retardation* (Vol. 7). New York: Academic Press.

Bowerman, M. (1976). Semantic factors in the acquisition of rules for word use and sentence construction. In D. Morehead & A. Morehead (Eds.), *Directions in normal and deficit child language.* Baltimore: University Park Press.

Boyd, G. A. & Talbert, E. G. (1971). *Spelling in the elementary school.* Columbus, OH: C. E. Merrill.

Brandon, T., Balton, D., Rup, D. & Raslter, C. (1974). *Valpar Component*. Tuscon: Valpar Corporation.

Bray, N. (1979). Strategy production in the retarded. In N. R. Ellis (Ed.), *Handbook of mental deficiency* (2nd ed.). Hillsdale, NJ: Erlbaum.

Bray, N. W. (1985). *An overview of strategy deficiencies: A case for production anomalies and strategy competence*. Paper presented at the Gatlinburg Conference on Research and Theory in Mental Retardation and Developmental Disabilities, Gatlinburg, TN.

Bray, N. W., Goodman, M. A., & Justice, E. M. (1982). Task instructions and strategy transfer in the directed forgetting performance of mentally retarded adolescents. *Intelligence, 6*, 187–200.

Broadbent, D. E. (1958). *Perception and Communication*. New York: Pergamon Press.

Broadbent, D. E. (1970). Stimulus set and response set: Two kinds of selective attention. In D. I. Mostofsky (Ed.), *Attention: Contemporary theory and analysis*. New York: Appleton-Century-Crofts.

Broadbent, D. E. & Gregory, M. (1965). On the interaction of S-R compatibility with other variables affecting reaction time. *British Journal of Psychology, 56*, 61–67.

Broadbent, D. E. & Gregory, M. (1963). Division of attention and the decision theory of signal detection. *Proceedings of the Royal Society, 158*, 222–231.

Brolin, D. E. (1973). Career education needs of secondary educable students. *Exceptional Children, 39*, 619–624.

Brolin, D. E. (1982). *Vocational preparation of persons with handicaps* (2nd ed.). Columbus, OH: C. E. Merrill.

Brolin, D. E. & D'Alonzo, B. J. (1979). Critical issues in career education for handicapped students. *Exceptional Children, 45*, 246–253.

Brolin, D. E. & Kokaska, C. J. (1979). *Career education for handicapped children and youth*. Columbus, OH: C. E. Merrill.

Brolin, D. E., Malever, M., & Matyers, G. (1976). *PRICE needs assessment study* (Project PRICE Working Paper 7). Columbia, MO: University of Missouri-Columbia.

Brophy, J. E. (1983). Classroom organization and management. *Elementary School Journal, 83*, 265–285.

Brophy, J. E. & Evertson, C. (1978). Context variables in teaching. *Educational Psychologist, 12*, 310–316.

Brown, A. L. (1977). The role of strategic behavior in retardate memory. In N. R. Ellis (Ed.), *International review of research in mental retardation* (Vol. 7). New York: Academic Press.

Brown, A. L. (1978). When, where and how to remember: A problem of metacognition. In R. Glaser (Ed.), *Advances in instructional psychology* (Vol. 1). Hillsdale, NJ: Erlbaum.

Brown, A. L., Armbruster, B. B., & Baker, L. (1985). The role of metacognition in reading and studying. In J. Orasanu (Ed.), *A decade of reading research: Implications for practice*. Hillsdale, NJ: Erlbaum.

Brown, A. L., Campione, J. C., Bray, N. W., & Wilcox, B. L. (1973). Keeping track of changing variables: Effects of rehearsal training and rehearsal prevention in normal and retarded adolescents. *Journal of Experimental Psychology, 101*, 123–131.

Brown, F. (1979). The SOMPA: A system of measuring potential abilities. *The School Psychology Digest, 8*, 37–46.

Brown, R. (1973). *A first language: The early stages*. Cambridge, MA: Harvard University Press.

Brown, V. & McEntire, E. (1984). *Test of mathematical abilities*. Austin, TX: Pro-Ed.

Brueckner, L. & Bond, G. (1955). *Diagnosis and treatment of learning difficulties*. New York: Appleton-Century-Crofts.

Brueckner, L. J. & Bond, G. L. (1967). *The diagnosis and treatment of learning difficulties*. New York: Appleton-Century-Crofts.

Bruininks, R. H. & Clark, C. R. (1972). Auditory and visual paired associate learning in first grade retarded and nonretarded. *American Journal of Mental Deficiency, 76*, 561–567.

Buffer, J. J. & Miller, P. W. (1976). The effects of selected industrial arts activities on educable mentally retarded students' achievements and retention of metric linear concepts. *Journal of Industrial Teacher Education, 15*, 7–16.

Burns, P. C. (1974). *Diagnostic teaching in the language arts*. Itasca, IL: F. E. Peacock.

Butterfield, E. C. & Belmont, J. M. (1977). Assessing and improving the cognition of mentally retarded people. In I. Bialer & M. Sternlicht (Eds.), *Psychology in mental retardation: Issues and Approaches*. New York: Psychological Dimensions.

Butterfield, E. C. & Ferretti, R. P. (1985). Toward a theoretical integration of cognitive hypotheses about intellectual differences among children. In J. G. Borkowski & J. D. Day (Eds.), *Memory and cognition in special children*. Norwood, NJ: Ablex.

Butterfield, E. C., Wambold, C., & Belmont, J. M. (1973). On the theory and practice of improving short-term memory. *American Journal of Mental Deficiency, 77*, 654–669.

Cain, L. F., Levine, S., & Elzey, F. F. (1963). *Manual for the Cain-Levine Social Competency Scale*. Palo Alto, CA: Consulting Psychologists Press.

Campione, J. E. & Brown, A. L. (1977). Memory and metamemory development in educable retarded children. In R. V. Kail, Jr. & J. W. Hagen (Eds.), *Perspectives on the development of memory and cognition.* New York: Erlbaum.

Campione, J. E., Brown, A. L., & Ferrara, R. A. (1982). Mental retardation and intelligence. In R. J. Sternberg (Ed.), *Handbook of human intelligence.* Cambridge, MA: Cambridge University Press.

Canter, L. (1976). *Assertive discipline: A take-charge approach for today's educator.* Seal Beach, CA: Canter & Associates.

Carpenter, T. P. (1980). Heuristic strategies used to solve addition and subtraction problems. In R. Karplus (Ed.), *Proceedings of the fourth international conference for the psychology of mathematics instruction.* Berkeley: University of California.

Carroll, J. B. (1972). Defining language comprehension: Some speculations. In R. O. Freedle & J. B. Carroll (Eds.), *Language comprehension and the acquisition of knowledge.* New York: John Wiley & Sons.

Carrow, W. E. (1973). *Test for auditory comprehension of language.* Austin, TX: Learning Concepts.

The Cat in the Hat Beginning Book Dictionary (1984). New York: Random House.

Caton, R. (1985). Visual impairments. In W. H. Berdine & Blackhurst, A. E. (Eds.), *An introduction to special education* (2nd Ed.). Boston: Little Brown.

Cattell, R. B. (1950). *Culture fair intelligence test: Scale 1.* Champaign, IL: Institute for Personality and Ability.

Cattell, R. B. & Cattell, A. K. (1960). *Culture fair intelligence test: Scale 2.* Champaign, IL: Institute for Personality and Ability Testing.

Cattell, R. B. & Cattell, A. K. (1963). *Culture fair intelligence test: Scale 3.* Champaign, IL: Institute for Personality and Ability Testing.

Cegelka, W. J. (1978). Educational materials: Curriculum guides for the mentally retarded: An analysis and recommendations. *Education and Training of the Mentally Retarded, 13,* 187–188.

Chan, K. S. & Rueda, R. (1979). Poverty and Culture in education: Separate but equal. *Exceptional Children, 45,* 422–428.

Charles, C. M. (1980). *Individualizing instruction.* St. Louis, Mosby.

Charles, C. M. (1980). *Individualizing instruction.* St. Louis: Mosby.

Chase, W. L. & John, M. T. (1972). *A guide for the elementary social studies teacher* (2nd ed). Boston: Allyn & Bacon.

Cheek, M. C. & Cheek, E. H., Jr. (1980). *Diagnostic-Prescriptive reading instruction.* Dubuque, IA: Wm. C. Brown.

Cherkes-Julkowski, M. C., Gertner, N., & Norlander, K. (1985). *Differences in cognitive processes among handicapped and average children: A group learning approach.* Paper presented at the Gatlinburg Conference on Research and Theory in Mental Retardation and Developmental Disabilities, Gatlinburg, TN.

Chittenden, E. A. (1983). *Styles, reading strategies and test performance: A follow-up study of beginning readers.* Princeton, NJ: Educational Testing Service.

Chomsky, N. (1985). *Aspects of the theory of syntax.* Cambridge, MA: M.I.T. Press.

Chomsky, N. (1957). *Syntactic structures.* The Hague. Mouton Publishers.

Chomsky, N. (1975). *Reflections on language.* New York: Pantheon Books.

Christian, B. T. (1983). A practical reinforcement hierarchy for classroom behavior modification. *Psychology in the Schools, 20,* 83–85.

Clarizio, H. F. & Yelon, S. L. (1967). Learning theory approaches to classroom management: Rationale and intervention techniques. *Journal of Special Education, 1,* 267–274.

Clark, C. R. (1984). Close look at the standard Rebus system and Blissymbolics. *Journal of the Association for the Severely Handicapped, 9,* 37–48.

Clark, C. R., Davies, C. O., & Woodcock, R. W. (1974). *Standard Rebus glossary.* Circle Pines, MN: American Guidance Service.

Clark, G. M. (1980). Career education: A concept–a challenge. In S. E. Schwartz (Ed.), *Institute on career education for the handicapped.* Huntsville, AL: University of Alabama: Project Retool.

Clark, H. & Clark, E. (1977). *Psychology and language: An introduction to psycholinguistics.* New York: Harcourt Brace Jovanovich.

Claus, C. K. (1968). *The fuzzy, goofy, fifty-five.* Paper presented at the National Council on Measurement and Education. Chicago (9).

Claus, C. K. (1968). *The functional, forceful, four hundred, fifty-five.* Paper presented at the National Council on Measurement and Education (b).

Clements, C. B. & Clements, R. D. (1984). *Art and mainstreaming.* Springfield, IL: Charles C. Thomas.

Clymer, T. (1963). Utility of phonics generalizations in the primary grades. *Reading Teacher, 16,* 252–258.

Cochran-Smith, M. (1984). *The making of a reader.* Norwood, NJ: Ablex.

Cohen, C. & Abrams, R. (1974). *Spellmaster.* Exeter, NJ: Learnco.

Cohen, H. & Staley, F. (1982). Integrating with science: One way to bring science back into the elementary school day. *School Science and Mathematics, 82,* 565–572.

Cohen, S. B. & Plaskon, S. B. (1980). *Language arts for the mildly handicapped.* Columbus, OH: C. E. Merrill.

Committee on the Status of Racial Minorities (1983). Social dialects: Position paper. *American Speech, Hearing, and Language Association, 25,* 23–24.

Conolly, A. J., Nachtman, W., & Pritchett, E. M. (1971, 1976). *Key Math diagnostic arithmetic test.* Circle Pines, MN: American Guidance Service.

Cooper, C. R. (1972). Training inquiry behavior in young disadvantaged children. Unpublished doctoral dissertation, University of Minnesota.

Corrick, M. E., Jr. (Ed.). (1981). *Teaching handicapped students science.* Washington, DC: National Education Association of the U.S.

Crystal, D., Fletcher, P., & Garman, M. (1976). *The grammatical analysis of language disability.* New York: American Elsevier.

Curtis, C. K. (1974). Social studies for the slow learner. *The Clearing House, 48,* 456–460.

Curtis, C. K. (1978). *Contemporary community problems in citizenship education for slow-learning secondary students* (Vol. 1 and 2). Ogden, Utah: Utah State University.

Curtis, C. K. & Shaver, J. P. (1980). Slow learners and the study of contemporary problems. *Social Education, 44,* 302–309.

Dallman, M. (1976). *Teaching the language arts in the elementary school* (3rd ed.). Dubuque, IA: Wm. C. Brown.

Daum, J. (1972). *Proxemics in the classroom: Speaker-subject distance and educational performance.* Paper presented at the annual meeting of the Southeastern Psychological Association.

Davey, B. & McBride, S. (1984). *The effects of question-generation on comprehension question performance.* Paper presented at the annual meeting of the American Educational Research Association, New Orleans.

David discovers the dictionary. Chicago: Coronet Learning Programs.

Davies, J. M. & Ball, D. W. (1978). Utilization of the elementary science study with educable mentally retarded studies. *Journal of Research in Science Education,* 281–286.

Delefes, P. & Jackson, B. (1972). Teacher-pupil interaction as a function of location in the classroom. *Psychology in the Schools, 9,* 119–123.

Dennis, S. I. (1984). *Stages in the development of children's drawing.* Paper presented at the annual meeting of the American Educational Research Association, New Orleans.

Deno, E. (1973). *Instructional alternatives for exceptional children.* Reston, VA: Council for Exceptional Children.

Deno, S., Marston, D., & Mirkin, P. (1982). Valid measurement procedures for continuous evaluation of written expression. *Exceptional Children, 48,* 368–370.

Deno, S. L. & Jenkins, J. L. (1967). Semantic generalization of a voluntary response: Effects of responding in training and rate of presentation. *Journal of Verbal Learning & Verbal Behavior, 6,* 300–302.

Detterman, D. K. (1979). Memory in the mentally retarded. In N. R. Ellis (Ed.), *Handbook of Mental Deficiency* (2nd ed.). Hillsdale, NJ: Erlbaum.

de Villiers, J. G. & de Villiers, P. A. (1978). *Language acquisition.* Cambridge, MA: Harvard University Press.

Diaz, R. M. (1984). *The union of thought and language in children's private speech: Recent empirical evidence for Vygotsky's theory.* Paper presented at the annual meeting of the International Congress of Psychology, Acapulco, Mexico.

Dickson, W. & Raymond, M. W. (1984). *Language arts computer book.* Reston, VA: Reston Publishing.

Diener, C. I. & Dweck, C. W. (1978). An analysis of learned helplessness: Continuous changes in performance strategy, and achievement cognitions following failure. *Journal of Personality and Social Psychology, 36,* 451–462.

Dinkmeyer, D. D. (1972). *Developing understanding of self and others.* Circle Pines, MN: American Guidance Service.

Di Vesta, F. J. (1974). *Language learning and cognitive processes.* Monterey, CA: Brooks/Cole.

Dolch, E. W. (1942). *Dolch Basic Sight Word Test.* Champaign, IL: Garrard Publishing Co.

Doll, E. A. (1953). *A manual for the Vineland Social Maturity Scale.* Minneapolis: Educational Testing Service.

Donahoe, J. W. & Wessells, M. G. (1980). *Learning, language and memory.* New York: Harper & Row.

Donmoyer, R. & Kidd, S. (1984). *Language acquisition research: Implications for curriculum design.* Paper presented at the annual meeting of the American Educational Research Association, New Orleans.

Downey, M. T. (1980). Pictures as teaching aids: Using the pictures in history textbooks. *Social Education, 44,* 93–99.

Drelikurs, R. & Grey, L. (1972). *Discipline without tears.* New York: Hawthorne.

Dugas, J. (1975). Effects of stimulus familiarity on the rehearsal strategies transfer mechanism in retarded and nonretarded individuals. *American Journal of Mental Deficiency, 80,* 349–356.

Duke, D. L., Donmoyer, R., & Farman, G. (1980). Emerging legal issues. In E. H. Weiner (Ed.), *Discipline in the classroom* (2nd ed.). Washington, DC.: National Educational Association.

Dunn, Horton, K. B., & Smith, J. O. (1967). *Peabody language development kit, Level P.* Circle Pines, MN: American Guidance Service.

Dweck, C. S. (1975). The role of expectations and attributions in the alleviation of learned helplessness. *Journal of Personality and Social Psychology, 31,* 674–685.

Dweck, C. S. & Wortman, C. B. (1973). Learned helplessness, anxiety and achievement motivation: Neglected parallels in cognitive, affective, and coping responses. In H. W. Krohne & L. Laux (Eds.), *Achievement, stress, and anxiety.* New York: Hemisphere Publications.

Dyer, H. S. (1967). The discovery and development of educational goals. *In proceedings of the 1966 invitational conference on testing problems.* Princeton, NJ: Educational Testing Service.

Eckwall, E. E. & Shanker, J. L. (1983). *Diagnosis and remediation of the disabled reader.* Boston: Allyn & Bacon.

Edgar, E., Maser, J., Smith, D., & Haring, N. (1977). Developing an instructional sequence for teaching a self–help skill. *Education and Training of the Mentally Retarded, 10*(1), 42–50.

Edgington, R. (1968). But he spelled them right this morning. In J. I. Arena (Ed.), *Building spelling skills in dyslexic children.* Belmont, CA: Academic Therapy Publications.

Edwards, M. (1953). *An evaluation of the Casis school instructional program in spelling.* Unpublished master's thesis, University of Texas.

Ehri, L. C. & Wilce, L. S. (1985). Movement into reading: Is the first stage of printed word learning visual and phonetic? *Reading Research Quarterly, 20,* 163–179.

Eisenhart, M. & Borko, H. (1984). *What makes a difference in children's success at learning to read in school.* Paper presented at the annual meeting of the American Educational Research Association, New Orleans.

Ellis, A. K. (1977). *Teaching and learning elementary social studies.* Boston: Allyn & Bacon.

Ellis, N. R. (1970, March). *Memory processes in retardates and normals: Theoretical and empirical considerations.* Paper presented at the Gatlinburg Conference on Research and Theory in Mental Retardation, Gatlinburg, TN.

Ellis, N. R. & Meador, D. M. (in press). Forgetting in retarded and nonretarded persons under conditions of minimal strategy use. *Intelligence.*

Ellis, N. R. (1979). Introduction. In N. R. Ellis (Ed.), *Handbook of mental deficiency* (2nd ed.). Hillsdale, NJ: Erlbaum.

Emans, R. (1973). Linguistics and phonics. *The Reading Teacher, 26,* 477–482.

Engelmann, S. (1967). Teaching reading to children with low mental ages. *Education and training of the mentally retarded, 2,* 193–201.

Englemann, S. & Bruner, E. (1974, 1976). *DISTAR Reading.* Chicago: Science Research Associates.

Englemann, S. & Osborn, J. (1972, 1976). *DISTAR Language.* Chicago: Science Research Associates.

Enstrom, A. (1967). Improving handwriting. *Improving College and University Teaching, 15,* 168–169.

Erickson, F. (1982). Taught cognitive learning in its immediate environments: A rejected topic in the anthropology of education. *Anthropology and Education Quarterly, 13,* 149–180.

Evans, R. A. & Bilsky, L. H. (1979). Clustering and categorical list retention in the mentally retarded. In N. R. Ellis (Ed.), *Handbook of mental deficiency: Psychological theory and research* (2nd Ed.). Hillsdale, NJ: Erlbaum.

Fauke, J., Burnett, J., Powers, M., & Sulzer-Azaroff, B. (1973). Improvement of handwriting and letter recognition skills: A behavior modification procedure. *Journal of Learning Disabilities, 6,* 25–29.

Feigenbaum, L. H. (1958). For a bigger better alphabet. *High Points, 40,* 34–36.

Feldman, N. & Risko, V. J. (1985). *Teaching remedial readers to generate questions about their reading.* Paper presented at the annual meeting of the American Educational Research Association, Chicago.

Fernald, G. M. (1943). *Remedial techniques in basic school subjects.* New York: McGraw-Hill.

Ferretti, R. P. & Butterfield, C. C. (1983). *Testing the logic of instructional studies.* Paper presented at the Gatlinburg Conference on Mental Retardation, Gatlinburg, TN.

Feshback, S. (1970). Aggression. In P. Mussen (Ed.), *Carmichael's Manual of Child Psychology* (3rd ed., Vol. 2). New York: Wiley.

Festinger, L. (1962). Cognitive dissonance. *Scientific American, 207.*

Fisher, C., Berliner, D., Filby, N., Marliave, R., Cahen, L., & Dishaw, M. (1980). Teaching behaviors, academic learning time, and student achievement: An overview. In C. Denham & A. Lieberman (Eds.), *Time to learn.* Washington, DC: National Institute of Education.

Fisher, M. A. & Zeaman, D. (1973). An attention-retention theory of retardate discrimination learning. In N. R. Ellis (Ed.), *International review of mental retardation* (Vol. 6). New York: Academic Press.

Fitzgerald, J. A. (1951). *A basic life spelling vocabulary*. Milwaukee: The Bruce Publishing Co.

Fitzsimmons, R. & Loomer, B. (1977). *Spelling research and practice*. Iowa State Department of Public Instruction and University of Iowa.

Flavell, J. H. (1970). Developmental studies in mediated memory. In H. W. Reese & L. P. Lipsett (Eds.), *Advances in child development and behavior* (Vol. 5). New York: Academic Press.

Flavell, J. H. (1977). *Cognitive development*. Englewood Cliffs, NJ: Prentice-Hall.

Flavell, J., H., Beach, D. R., & Chinsky, J. M. (1966). Spontaneous verbal rehearsal in a memory task as a function of age. *Child Development, 37,* 283–299.

Flavell, J. H., Botkin, P. T., Fry, C. L., Wright, J. W., & Jarvis, P. E. (1975). The development of role-taking and communication skills in children. New York: John Wiley & Sons (reprinted by Robert E. Krieger Publishing Company, Huntington, NY).

Flavell, J. H. & Wellman, H. M. (1977). Metamemory. In R. V. Kail, Jr., & J. W. Hagen (Eds.), *Perspectives on the development of memory and cognition*. Hillsdale, NJ: Erlbaum.

Fokes, J. (1976). *Fokes sentence builder*. New York: Teaching Resources Corp.

Foxx, R. M. & Azrin, N. H. (1973). *Toilet training the retarded: A rapid program for day and nighttime independent toileting*. Champaign, IL: Research Press.

Frank, A. R. (1973). Breaking down learning tasks: A sequential approach. *Teaching Exceptional Children, 6,* 16–19.

Fraser, B. J. (1984). *A study of elementary school student perceptions of classroom psychosocial environment*. Paper presented at the annual meeting of the American Educational Research Association, New Orleans.

Fraser, B. J. & Fisher, D. L. (1983). Use of actual and preferred classroom environment scales in person-environment fit research. *Journal of Educational Psychology, 75,* 303–313.

Freides, D. (1974). Human information processing and sensory modality. *Psychological Bulletin, 5,* 284–310.

Friedman, P. G. (1978). *Listening processes: Attention, understanding, evaluation*. Washington, DC: National Education Association.

Fristoe, M. & Lloyd, L. L. (1979). Nonspeech communication. In N. R. Ellis (Ed.), *Handbook of mental deficiency, psychological theory and research* (2nd ed.). Hillsdale, NJ: Lawrence Erlbaum Associates.

Fry, E. B. (1977). The instant words. *Elementary reading instruction*. New York: McGraw-Hill.

Gagné, R. M. (1964). The implications of instructional objectives for learning., In C. M. Lindvall (Ed.), *Defining Educational Objectives*. Pittsburgh: University of Pittsburgh Press.

Gagné, R. M. (1977). *The conditions of learning* (3rd ed.), New York: Holt, Rinehart & Winston.

Gambrell, L., Wilson, R., & Gnatt, W. (1981). Classroom observations of task-attending behaviors of good and poor readers. *Journal of Educational Research, 74,* 400–405.

Gamlin, P. J. & Bountrogianni, M. (1985). *The assessment of the potential to learn: A multicultural perspective*. Paper presented at the annual meeting of the American Educational Research Association, Chicago.

Garguilo, R. & Pigge, F. (1979). Perceived competencies of elementary special education teachers. *The Journal of Educational Research, 72,* 339–343.

Gast, D. L. & Nelson, C. M. (1977). Legal and ethical considerations for the use of time-out procedures in special education settings. *Journal of Special Education, 11,* 457–467.

Gates, A. I. & Russell, D. (1940). *Gates-Russell spelling diagnostic test*. New York: Columbia University Press.

Gearheart, B. R. & Weishahn, M. W. (1976). *The handicapped child in the regular classroom*. St. Louis: C. V. Mosby Co.

Gelman, R. (1982). Basic numerical abilities. In R. J. Sternberg (Ed.), *Advances in the psychology of intelligence* (Vol. 1). Hillsdale, NJ: Erlbaum.

Gentner, D. (1975). Evidence for the psychological reality of semantic components: The verbs of possession. In D. A. Norman & D. E. Rumelhart (Eds.), *Explorations in cognition*. San Francisco: Freeman.

Gentry, J. (1977). *A study of orthographic strategies of beginning readers*. Unpublished doctoral dissertation, University of Virginia.

Geoffrion, L. D. & Geoffrion, O. P. (1983). *Computers and reading instruction*. Reading, MA: Addison-Wesley.

Gerber, M. M. & Semmel, M. I. (1984). Teacher as imperfect test: Reconceptualizing the referral process. *Educational Psychologist, 19,* 137–148.

Gillespie, P. H. & Johnson, L. (1974). *Teaching reading to the mildly retarded child*. Columbus, OH: C. E. Merrill.

Gillet, P. (1980). Career education in special and elementary education program. *Teaching Exceptional Children, 13*(1), 17–21.

Gillingham, A. & Stillman, B. (1960, 1968, 1970). *Re-*

medial teaching for children with specific disability in reading, spelling, and penmanship. Cambridge, MA: Educator's Publishing Service.

Gilstrap, R. (1962). Development of independent spelling skills in the intermediate grades. *Elementary English, 39*, 481–483.

Ginott, H. (1972). *Teacher and child*. New York: MacMillan.

Ginsburg, H. & Opper, S. (1969). *Piaget's theory of intellectual development*. Englewood Cliffs, NJ: Prentice-Hall.

Glass, E. W. & Glass, G. G. (1978). *Glass analysis for decoding only*. New York: Easier to Learn.

Glasser, W. (1969). *Schools without failure*. New York: Harper & Row.

Glidden, L. M. (1979). Training of learning and memory in retarded persons: Strategies, techniques and teaching tools. In N. R. Ellis (Ed.), *Handbook of Mental Deficiency* (2nd ed.). Hillsdale, NJ: Erlbaum.

Glucksberg, S., Krauss, R. M., & Higgins, T. (1975). The development of communication skills in children. In F. Horowitz (Ed.), *Review of child development research* (Vol. 4). Chicago: University of Chicago Press.

Goh, D. S. & Hanson, J. M. (1984). *Relationship between conservation concept development and academic achievement in learning disabled children*. Paper presented at the American Educational Research Association, New Orleans.

Goldberg, H. K. & Schiffman, G. R. (1972). *Dyslexia: Problems of reading disabilities*. New York: Grune & Stratton.

Goldman, R. & Fristoe, M. (1972). *Test of articulation*. Circle Pines, MN: American Guidance Service.

Goldstein, H. (1975). Importance of social learning. In J. M. Kauffman & J. S. Payne (Eds.), *Mental retardation: Instruction and personal perspectives*. Columbus, OH: C. E. Merrill.

Golinkoff, R. M. (1975). A comparison of reading comprehension processes in good and poor comprehenders. *Reading Research Quarterly, 11*, 623–659.

Good, T. L. & Brophy, J. E. (1980). *Educational Psychology: A realistic approach*. New York: Holt, Rinehart & Winston.

Good, T. & Grouws, D. (1977). Teaching effects: A process-product study in fourth-grade mathematics classrooms. *Journal of Teacher Education, 28*, 49–54.

Goodman, J. F. (1979). Is tissue the issue? A critique of SOMPA's models and tests. *The School Psychology Digest, 1*, 47–62.

Gordon, B. (1982). Teach them to read the questions. *Journal of Reading, 26*, 126–132.

Gordon, T. (1974). *Teacher effectiveness training*. New York: Peter H. Wyden.

Gorman, A. H. (1974). *Teachers and learners* (2nd ed.). Boston: Allyn & Bacon.

Graham, S. (1983). Measurement of handwriting skills: A critical review. *Diagnostique, 8*, 32–42.

Graham, S. & Miller, L. (1983). Spelling research and practice: A unified approach. In E. L. Meyer, G. A. Vergason, & R. J. Whelan (Eds.), *Promising practices for exceptional children: Curriculum implications*. Denver: Love Publishing (a).

Graham, S. & Miller, L. (1983). Handwriting research and practice: A unified approach. In E. L. Meyer, G. A. Verguson, & R. J. Whelan (Eds.), *Promising practices for exceptional children: Curriculum implications*. Denver: Love Publishing (b).

Grant, W. D. (1975). Me now and me and my environment: Science for the exceptional student. *Science Education, 59*, 249–254.

Gray, G. (1975). Education service delivery. In W. J. Cegelka (Ed.), *Educating the 24-hour retarded child*. National Training Meeting on Education of the Severely and Profoundly Mentally Retarded. Arlington, TX: National Association for Retarded Citizens.

Gray, J. & Wedderburn, A. (1960). Grouping strategies with simultaneous stimuli. *Quarterly Journal of Experimental Psychology, 12*, 180–184.

Gray, R. A. (1978). *The relationship of oral language proficiency in five and six year old preschoolers to readiness for school success*. Unpublished doctoral dissertation, University of Texas at Austin.

Greenspan, S. (1979). Social intelligence in the retarded. In N. R. Ellis (Ed.), *Handbook of mental deficiency: Psychological theory and research* (2nd ed.). Hillsdale, NJ: Erlbaum.

Gregory, G. P. (1979). Using the newspaper in the mainstreamed classroom. *Social Education, 43*, 140–143.

Gresham, F. M. (1982). Misguided mainstreaming: The case for social skills training with handicapped children. *Exceptional Children, 48*, 422–433.

Gresham, F. M. (1983). Social skills assessment as a component of mainstreaming placement decisions. *Exceptional Children, 49*, 331–336.

Gross, R. & Gross, B. (1970, May 16). A little bit of chaos. *Saturday Review*, pp. 71–73.

Grossman, H. J. (Ed.). (1983). *Classification in mental retardation*. Washington, DC: American Association on Mental Deficiency.

Gump, P. (1978). School environments. In I. Altman & J. Wohlwill (Eds.), *Children and the environment*. New York: Plenum.

Guszak, F. J. (1972). *Diagnostic reading instruments in*

the elementary school. New York: Harper & Row.

Guzaitis, J., Carlin, J. A., & Juda, S. (1972). *Diagnosis: An instructional aid (mathematics).* Chicago: Science Research Associates.

Hagan, J. W. & Stanovich, K. G. (1977). Memory: Strategies of Acquisition. In R. V. Kail, Jr. & J. W. Hagen (Eds.), *Perspectives on the Development of Memory and Cognition.* New York: John Wiley & Sons.

Haines, R. R. (1982). *Project useful hands.* Renton, WA: Renton School District #403, Department of Special Education.

Hall, J. K. (1981). *Evaluating and improving written expression: A practical guide for teachers.* Boston: Allyn & Bacon.

Hall, R. V., Lund, D., & Jackson, D. (1968). Effects of teacher attention on study behavior. *Journal of Applied Behavior Analysis, 1,* 1–12.

Hallahan, D. P. & Kauffman, J. M. (1982). *Exceptional children.* Englewood Cliffs, NJ: Prentice-Hall.

Hallahan, D. P., Tarver, S. G., Kauffman, J. M., & Graybeal, N. L. (1978). A comparison of the effects of reinforcement and response costs on the selective attention of learning disabled children. *Journal of Learning Disabilities, 11,* 430–438.

Hammill, D. D. (1975). Problems in writing. In D. D. Hammill and N. Bartel (Eds.), *Teaching children with learning and behavior problems.* Boston: Allyn & Bacon.

Hammill, D. D. & Bartel, N. R. (1982). *Teaching children with learning and behavior problems* (3rd ed.). Boston: Allyn & Bacon.

Hammill, D. D. & Larsen, S. C. (1978). *Test of written language.* Austin, TX: Pro-Ed.

Hammill, D. D. & Larsen, S. C. (1983). *The test of written language.* Austin, TX: Pro-Ed.

Hamill, D. D. & Leigh, J. (1983). *Basic school skill inventory-diagnostic.* Austin, TX: Pro-ed.

Hansen, D. A. & Johnson, V. A. (1985). *School year and summer influences on auditory vocabulary and text comprehension.* Paper presented at the annual meeting of the American Educational Research Association, Chicago.

Hargis, C. H. (1983). Word recognition development. In E. L. Meyen, G. A. Vergason, & R. J. Whelan (Eds.), *Promising practices for exceptional children.* Denver: Love Publishing.

Hargis, C. H. (1982). Word recognition development. *Focus on exceptional children, 14,* 3–6.

Hargis, C. H. (1982). *Teaching reading to handicapped children.* Denver, CO: Love Publishers.

Harrell, M., Bowers, J. W., & Bacal, J. P. (1973). Another stab at meaning: Concreteness, iconicity, and conventionality. *Speech Monographs, 40,* 199–207.

Harris, A. J. (1970). *How to increase reading ability* (5th ed.). New York: David McKay Co.

Harris, A. J. & Sipay, E. R. (1976). *How to increase reading ability* (6th ed.). New York: David McKay Co.

Hart, B. M. & Risley, R. R. (1974). Using preschool materials to modify the language of disadvantaged children. *Journal of Applied Behavior Analysis, 7,* 243–256.

Hasenstab, M. S. & Laughton, J. (1982). *Reading, writing and the exceptional child.* Rockville, MD: Aspen.

Hayden, A. H. & Dmitriev, V. (1975). The multidisciplinary preschool programs for Down's syndrome children at the University of Washington Model Preschool Center. In B. Z. Friedlander, G. M. Sterritt, & G. E. Kirk (Eds.), *Exceptional Infant, Vol. 3: Assessment & Intervention.* New York: Brunner/Mazel.

Hayden, A. H., Morris, K., & Bailey, D. (1977). *The effectiveness of early education* (Final report to the Bureau of Education for the Handicapped, USOE) Model Preschool Center for Handicapped Children, Seattle, WA.

Hayes, J. (1977). Annual goals and short-term objectives. In S. Torres (Ed.), *A primer on individualized education programs for handicapped children.* Reston, VA: The Foundation for Exceptional Children.

Heber, R. (1959). *A manual for terminology and classification in mental retardation.* Willimantic, CT: The American Association on Mental Deficiency.

Heigle, D. R. & Sonedecker, J. W. (1985). *Writing across the content areas.* Paper presented at the annual meeting of the American Educational Research Association, Chicago.

Helton, G. B. & Oakland, T. D. (1977). Teachers' attitudinal responses to differing characteristics of elementary school students. *Journal of Educational Psychology, 69,* 261–265.

Helwig, J. J., Johns, J. D., Norman, J. E., & Cooper, J. O. (1976). The measurement of manuscript letter strokes. *Journal of Applied Behavior Analysis, 9,* 231–236.

Hoetker, J. & Ahlbrand, W. P., Jr. (1969). The persistance of the recitation. *American Educational Research Journal, 6,* 145–167.

Hogan, T. P. & Mishler, C. J. (1979). Judging the quality of students' writing: Where and how. *Elementary School Journal, 79,* 142–146.

Homme, L. E., Csanyi, A. P., Gonzales, M. A., & Rechs, J. R. (1969). *How to use contingency contracting in the classroom.* Champaign, IL: Research Press.

Hopkins, C. D. & Antes, R. L. (1978). *Classroom measurement and evaluation.* Itasca, IL: F. E. Peacock.

Horn, T. (1969). Research critiques. *Elementary English, 46,* 210–212.

Houssiadas, L. & Brown, L. B. (1967). The coordination of perspectives by mentally defective children. *Journal of Genetic Psychology, 110,* 211–215.

Howe, L. W. & Howe, M. M. (1975). *Personalizing education: Values clarification and beyond.* New York: Hart.

Howell, K. W. & Kaplan, J. S. (1980). *Diagnosing basic skills: A handbook for deciding what to teach.* Columbus, OH: C. E. Merrill.

Howell, K. W., Kaplan, J. S., & O'Connell, C. Y. (1979). *Evaluating exceptional children.* Columbus, OH: C. E. Merrill.

Hoyt, K. B. (1975). *An introduction to career education: A Policy paper of the U.S. Office of Education.* Washington, DC: Office of Education.

Hoyt, K. M. (1977). Community resources for career education. *Monographs on career education.* Washington, DC: U.S. Office of Education.

Humphrey, M. (1954). *The effect of a syllabic presentation of words upon learning to spell.* Unpublished master's thesis, University of Texas.

Hunt, J. McV. (1969). *The Challenge of incompetence and poverty.* Urbana, IL: Ronald Press.

Inhelder, B. & Piaget, J. (1958). *The growth of logical thinking from childhood to adolescence.* New York: Basic Books.

Jackson, A. (1970). *A comparison of speed and legibility of manuscript and cursive handwriting of intermediate grade pupils.* Unpublished doctoral dissertation, University of Arizona, Tucson.

Jacobson, W. J. & Bergman, A. B. (1980). *Science for children: A book for teachers.* Englewood Cliffs, NJ: Prentice-Hall.

James, P. (1983). *Teaching art to the special student.* Portland, MA: J. Weston Walch.

Jastak, J. F. & Jastak, S. R. (1980). *Wide range employability sample test.* Wilmington, DE: Jastak Associates, Inc.

Jenkins, F. (1985). *Defining general classroom writing ability.* Paper presented at the annual meeting of the American Educational Research Association, Chicago.

Jenkins, J. R., Stein, M. L., & Osborn, J. R. (1981). What next after decoding? Instruction and research in reading comprehension. *Exceptional Education Quarterly, 2,* (1) 27–39.

Jenkins, J. & Caldwell, J. (1985). *The direct assessment of writing: The effect of essay features and task conditions.* Paper presented at the annual meeting of the American Educational Research Association, Chicago.

Jensen, A. R. & Frederickson, J. (1973). Free recall of categorized and uncategorized lists: A test of the Jensen hypothesis. *Journal of Educational Psychology, 3,* 304–314.

Jewish Employment and Vocational Service (1976). Jewish employment and vocational service work sample system. Philadelphia: Vocational Research Associates.

Johnson, R. & Vardian, E. R. (1973). Reading readability and the social studies. *The Reading Teacher, 26,* 483–488.

Johnson, S. W. (1979). *Arithmetic and learning disabilities.* Boston: Allyn & Bacon.

Johnson, W., Brown, S. F., Curtis, J. E., Edney, C. W., & Keaster, J. (1967). *Speech handicapped school children.* New York: Harper & Row.

Johnston, J. M. (1972). Punishment of human behavior. *American Psychologist, 27,* 1033–1054.

Jones, F. (1979, June). The gentle art of classroom discipline. *National Elementary Principal,* 1–5.

Jones, J. & Collins, A. (1966). *Educational programs for visually impaired children.* Washington, DC: U.S. Government Printing Office.

Jordan, T. E. (1976). *The mentally retarded* (4th ed.). Columbus, OH: C. E. Merrill.

Juel, C., Griffin, P. & Gough, P. (1985). *A longitudinal study of the changing relationships of word recognition, spelling, reading, comprehension, and writing from first to second grade.* Paper presented at the annual meeting of the American Educational Research Association, Chicago.

Justice, E. M. (in press). Metamemory development in the mentally retarded: Research and implications. In N. R. Ellis & N. W. Bray (Eds.), *International Review of Research in Mental Retardation* (Vol. 13). New York: Academic Press.

Kachuck, B. (1978). Black English and reading: Research issues. *Education and Urban Society, 10,* 385–398.

Kagan, J. (1970). On class differences and early development. In V. Deneberg (Ed.), *Education of the infant and young child.* New York: Academic Press.

Karnes, M. B. (1972). *Game oriented activities for learning.* Springfield, MA: Milton Bradley Co.

Karnes, M. B. (1976). *Karnes' early language activities.* Champaign, IL: Gem Materials Enterprises.

Kauffman, J. M., Snell, M. E., & Hallahan, D. P. (1976). Imitating children during imitation training. Two experimental paradigms. *Education and Training of the Mentally Retarded, 11,* 324–332.

Kellas, G., Ashcraft, M. H., & Johnson, N. S. (1973). Rehearsal processes in the short-term memory performance of mildly retarded adolescents. *American*

Journal of Mental Deficiency, 77, 670–679.

Keller, W. D. (1983). Science for the handicapped. In E. L. Meyen, G. A. Vergason, & R. J. Whelan (Eds.), *Promising practices for exceptional children.* Denver: Love Publishing.

Kelly, E. J. (1979). *Elementary school social studies instruction: A basic approach.* Denver: Love Publishing.

Keppel, G. & Underwood, B. J. (1962). Proactive inhibition in short-term retention of single items. *Journal of Verbal Learning and Verbal Behavior, 1,* 153–161.

Kintsch, W. & Bates, E. (1977). Recognition memory for statements from a classroom lecture. *Journal of Experimental Psychology: Human Learning and Memory, 3,* 150–159.

Kirk, S. A., Klebhan, J. M., & Lerner, J. W. (1978). *Teaching reading to slow and disabled learners.* Boston: Houghton Mifflin.

Klare, G. (1975). Assessing readability readability. *Reading Research Quarterly, 10,* 62–102.

Klatzky, R. L. (1981). *Human memory: Structures and processes* (2nd Ed.). San Francisco: Freeman.

Klausmeier, H. J. & Ripple, R. E. (1975). *Learning and human abilities: Educational psychology* (4th ed.). New York: Harper & Row.

Klein, E. S. (1981). Communication dysfunctions. In R. M. Smith & J. T. Neisworth, *Exceptional child: A functional approach.* New York: McGraw-Hill.

Kohn, C. F. (1953). Interpreting maps and globes. In *Skills in social studies, 24th Yearbook.* Washington, DC: National Council for the Social Studies, National Educational Association.

Kokaska, C. J. (1968). *The vocational preparation of the educable mentally retarded.* Ypsilanti, MI: Eastern Michigan University Press.

Kokaska, C. J. & Brolm, D. E. (1985). *Career education for handicapped individuals* (2nd Ed.). Columbus, OH: C. E. Merrill.

Kolstoe, O. P. & Frey, R. M. (1965). *A high school work-study program for mentally subnormal students.* Carbondale, IL: Southern Illinois University Press.

Kottmyer, W. (1970). *Teacher's guide for remedial reading* (2nd ed.). New York: McGraw-Hill.

Kounin, J. S. (1970). *Discipline and group management in classrooms.* New York: Holt, Rinehart & Winston.

Kounin, J. S. (1977). *Discipline and group management in classrooms.* New York: Kriegar.

Krause, L. A. (1983). Teaching the second "R". *The Directive Teacher, 5*(1), 30.

Krone, A. (1978). *Art instruction for handicapped children.* Denver: Love Publishing.

Krumboltz, J. & Krumboltz, H. (1972). *Changing children's behavior.* Englewood Cliffs, NJ: Prentice-Hall.

Krupski, A. (1981). An interactional approach to the study of attention problems in children with learning handicaps. *Exceptional Education Quarterly, 2,* 1–12.

Larsen, S. C. & Hammill, D. D. (1983). *Test of written spelling.* Austin, TX: Empiric Press.

LaCrosse, E. L. (1976). The contribution of the nursery school. In R. Koch & J. C. Dobson (Eds.), *The mentally retarded child and his family* (2nd Ed.). New York: Brunner/Mazel.

Lakeoff, A. (1971). On Generative semantics. In D. Steinberg & L. Jakobovits (Eds.), *Semantics.* London: Cambridge University Press.

Lambert, N. M., Windmiller, M. B., Cole, J. J., & Figueroa, R. A. (1975). *AAMD Adaptive Behavior Scale: Public School Version.* 1974 version. Washington, DC: American Association on Mental Deficiency.

Lamberts, F. (1979). Describing children's language behavior. In D. A. Sabatino & T. L. Miller (Eds.), *Describing learner characteristics of handicapped children and youth.* New York: Grune & Stratton.

Lancy, D. F., Goldstein, G. I., & Rueda, R. S. (1984). *Concept acquisition in language handicapped populations.* Paper presented at the annual meeting of the American Educational Research Association, New Orleans.

Lazarus, P. (1985). *The relationship of oral language features to reading achievement.* Paper presented at the annual meeting of the American Educational Research Association, Chicago.

Lefley, H. (1975). Differential self-concept in American Indian children as a function of language and examiner. *Journal of Personality and Social Psychology, 31,* 36–41.

Leiter, R. G. (1948). *Leiter international performance scale.* Chicago: Stoelting Co.

Lenneberg, E. H. (1967). *Biological foundations of language,* New York: John Wiley & Sons, Inc.

Lerner, J. (1981). *Learning disabilities: Theories, diagnosis, and teaching strategies* (3rd ed.). Boston: Houghton-Mifflin.

Lessons for self-instruction. Los Angeles: California Test Bureau.

Lewellen, A. (1980). *The use of quiet rooms and other timeout procedures in the public school: A position paper.* Matoon, IL: Eastern Illinois Area of Special Education.

Lewis, M. J., Rimal, C., DiPalma-Meyer, F., & LaFevre, K. (1981). *Training parents in career education* (preliminary report). New York: Teachers College, Columbia University, New York.

Lichtenstein, E. (1980, March). Suspension, expulsion

and the special education student. *Phi Delta Kappan*, pp. 459–461.

Life Centered Career education: A competency-based approach. (1978, 1983). Reston, VA: Council for Exceptional Children.

Lincoln, A. L. (1962). *Lincoln Primary Spelling Tests.* Indianapolis: Bobbs-Merrill.

Lindsay, Z. (1972). *Art and the handicapped child.* New York: Van Nostrand.

Lippitt, R. & White, R. (1958). An experimental study of leadership and group life. In E. Maccoby (Ed.), *Readings in social psychology.* New York: Holt, Rinehart & Winston.

Lipson, M. Y. & Wixson, K. K. (1985). *Reading disability research: An interactionist perspective.* Paper presented at the annual meeting of the American Educational Reseach Association, Chicago.

Lloyd, L. L. (1973). Mental retardation and hearing impairment. In A. G. Norris (Ed.), *PRWAD Deafness Annual* (Vol. 3). Washington, DC: Professional Rehabilitation Workers with the Adult Deaf.

Lohnes, P. R. & Gray, M. M. (1972). Intelligence and the cooperative reading studies. *Reading Research Quarterly*, 7(3), 466–476.

Lorsbach, T. C. & Gray, J. W. (1985). *Item identification speed and memory span performance in learning disabled children.* Paper presented at the annual meeting of the American Educational Research Association, Chicago.

Lovaas, O. I., Schreibman, L., Koegel, R., & Rehmn, R. (1971). Selective responding by autistic children to multiple sense output. *Journal of Abnormal Psychology*, 77, 211–222.

Lowenfeld, V. & Brittain, L. W. (1975). *Creative and mental growth* (6th Ed.). New York: MacMillan.

Luftig, R. L. (1979). *What are first year teachers concerned about? Control and discipline in the schools.* Unpublished manuscript.

Luftig, R. L. (1983). Variables influencing the learnability of individual signs and sign lexicons. *Journal of Psycholinguistic Research*, 12, 361–376(a).

Luftig, R. L. (1983). Effects of peer labeling on the metamnemonic estimates of mentally retarded and nonretarded children. *American Journal of Mental Deficiency*, 87, 522–527(b).

Luftig, R. L. (1983). Evaluation, interpretation, and acceptance of defense mechanistic behavior by mentally retarded and nonretarded children. *American Journal of Mental Deficiency*, 87, 514–521(c).

Luftig, R. L. (1986). *The social loneliness of mentally retarded children.* Manuscript submitted for pubication.

Luftig, R. L., Gauthier, R. A., Freeman, S. A., & Lloyd, L. L. (1980). Modality preference and facilitation of learning using mixed and pure sign, oral, and graphic inputs. *Sign Language Studies*, 28, 255–266.

Luftig, R. L. & Greeson, L. E. (1983). Effects of structural importance and idea saliency on discourse recall of mentally retarded and nonretarded pupils. *American Journal of Mental Deficiency*, 87, 414–421.

Luftig, R. L. & Johnson, R. E. (1982). Identification and recall of structurally important units in prose by mentally retarded learners. *American Journal of Mental Deficiency*, 86, 495–502.

Lundstrum, J. P. (1976). Reading in the social studies: A preliminary analysis of recent research. *Social Education*, 40, 10–17.

The Magic World of Words (2nd Ed.). (1980). New York: MacMillan.

Malone, L. & DeLucchi, L. M. (1980). Multisensory science education—meeting special challenges. In M. E. Corrick, Jr. (Ed.), *Teaching handicapped students science.* (ERIC Document Reproduction Service No. ED 213220).

Mandl, H., Schnotz, & Tergan (1984). *On the function of examples in instructional texts.* Paper presented at the 1984 annual meeting of the American Educational Research Association, New Orleans.

Mangieri, J. & Baldwin, R. (1979). Meaning as a factor in predicting spelling difficulty. *Journal of Educational Research*, 72, 285–287.

Mann, L., Davis, C. H., Boyer, C. W, Jr., Metz, C. M., & Wolford, B. (1983). LD or not LD, that was the question: A retrospective analysis of child service demonstration centers' compliance with the federal definition of learning disability. *Journal of Learning Disabilities*, 16, 14–17.

Maratsos, M. P. (1973). Nonegocentric communication abilities in preschool children. *Child Development*, 44, 697–700.

Martin, J. (1981). Models of classroom management. Calgory, Alberta: Detselig Enterprises Ltd.

May, F. B. (1980). *To help children communicate.* Columbus, OH: Merrill.

Mayer, R. E. (1985). *Learnable aspects of problem solving.* Paper presented at the annual meeting of the American Educational Research Association, Chicago.

McCall, R. B., Appelbaum, M. I., & Hogarty, P. S. (1973). Developmental changes in mental performance. *Monographs of the Society for Research in Child Development*, 38, Serial No. 150.

McCarron, L. T. & Dial, S. G. (1976). *McCarron-Dial evaluation system.* Dallas: Common Market Press.

McDermott, R. P. (1977). The ethnography of speaking and reading. In R. W. Shuy (Ed.), *Linguistic theory:*

What can it say about reading? Newark, DE: International Reading Association.

McKinney, C. W., Larkins, A. G., Ford, M. J., & Davis, J. C. III (1983). The effectiveness of three methods of teaching social studies concepts to fourth-grade students: An aptitude-treatment interaction study. *American Educational Research Journal, 20,* 663–670.

McLean, J. E. (1976). Articulation. In L. L. Lloyd (Ed.), *Communication assessment and intervention strategies.* Baltimore: University Park Press.

McLoughlin, J. A. & Kelly, D. (1982). Issues facing the resource teacher. *Learning Disability Quarterly, 5,* 58–64.

McLoughlin, J. A. & Lewis, R. B. (1981). *Assessing special students.* Columbus, OH: Merrill.

McLoughlin, J. A. & Lewis, R. B. (1986). *Assessing special students: Strategies and procedures* (2nd Ed.). Columbus, OH: Merrill.

Meador, D. M. & Ellis, N. R. (1985). *Automatic and effortful components of semantic priming effects in mentally retarded and nonretarded persons.* Paper presented at the Gatlinburg conference on Research and Theory in Mental Retardation and Developmental Disabilities, Gatlinburg, TN.

Meltzer, L. J., Fenton, T., & Persky, S. (1985). *A developmental study of the components of written language in children with and without learning difficulties.* Paper presented at the annual meeting of the American Educational Research Association, Chicago.

Menhusen, B. R. & Gromme, R. O. (1976). Science for handicapped children—Why? *Science and Children, 13,* 35–37.

Menyuk, P. (1963). A preliminary evaluation of grammatical capacity in children. *Journal of Verbal Learning and Verbal Behavior, 2,* 429–439.

Menyuk, P. (1964). Comparison of grammar of children with functionally deviant and normal speech. *Journal of Speech and Hearing Research, 7,* 109–121.

Merbler, J. B., Jr. (1978). A simple method for estimating instructional time. *Education and Training of the Mentally Retarded, 13,* 397–399.

Mercer, C. D. & Algozzine, B. (1977). Observational learning and the retarded: Teaching implications. *Education and Training of the Mentally Retarded, 12,* 345–353.

Mercer, C. D. & Mercer, A. R. (1981). *Teaching students with learning problems.* Columbus, OH: C. E. Merrill.

Mercer, C. D. & Snell, M. E. (1977). *Learning theory research in mental retardation.* Columbus, OH: C. E. Merrill.

Mercer, J. R. (1973). *Labeling the mentally retarded.* Berkeley, CA: University of California Press.

Mercer, J. R. (1973). The myth of the 3% prevalence. In R. K. Eyman, C. E. Meyers, & G. Tarian (Eds.), *Sociobehavioral studies in mental retardation: Papers in honor of Harry F. Dingman. Monographs of the American Association on Mental Deficiency, 1,* 1–18.

Mercer, J. R. (1973). *Labeling the mentally retarded.* Berkeley, CA: University of California Press.

Mercer, J. R. (1974). A Policy statement on assessment procedures and rights of children. *Harvard Educational Review, 44,* 125–141.

Mercer, J. R. (1975). Sociocultural factors in educational labeling. In M. J. Begab & S. A. Richardson (Eds.), *The mentally retarded and society: a social science perspective.* Baltimore: University Park Press.

Mercer, J. R. (1983). Issues in the diagnosis of language disorders in students whose primary language is not English. *Topics in Language Disorders, 3,* 46–56.

Mercer, J. R. & Lewis, J. F. (1977). *Adaptive behavior inventory for children, parent interview manual: System of multicultural pluralistic assessment.* New York: The Psychological Corp.

Mercer, J. R. & Lewis, J. F. (1978). *System of multicultural pluralistic assessment.* New York: The Psychological Corp.

Meyen, E. L. (1978). *Exceptional children: An introduction.* Denver: Love.

Meyen, E. L. (1981). *Developing instructional units* (3rd ed.). Dubuque, IA: Wm. C. Brown.

Meyer, B. J. (1975). Identification of the structure of prose and its implications for the study of reading and memory. *Journal of Reading Behavior, 7,* 7–74.

Meyer, B. J. & Freedle, R. O. (1984). Effects of discourse type on recall. *American Educational Research Journal, 21,* 121–143.

Miller, G. A. (1956). The magical number seven plus or minus two: Some limits on our capacity for processing information. *Psychological Review, 63,* 81–97.

Mims, H. A. & Camden, C. T. (1984). *Comparison of a sentence completion test and spontaneous conversation as measures of nonstandard dialect grammatical usage.* Paper presented at the annual meeting of the American Educational Research Association, New Orleans.

Minskoff, E. H., Wiseman, D. E., & Minskoff, J. G. (1972). *MWM program for developing language abilities.* Ridgefield, NJ: Educational Performance Association.

Minsky, S. K., Spitz, H. H., & Besselieu, C. L. (1985).

Maintenance and transfer of training by mentally retarded young adults on the Tower of Hanoi problem. *American Journal of Mental Deficiency, 490,* 190–197.

Modolfsky, P. B. (1983). Teaching students to determine the central story problem: A practical application of a schema theory. *The Reading Teacher, 36,* 740–745.

Monson, L. B., Greenspan, S., & Simeonsson, R. J. (1976, May). *Egocentrism and personal-social competence in retarded children.* Paper presented at the annual meeting of the American Association of Mental Deficiency, Chicago.

Montessori, M. (1964). *The Montessori Method: Rome, 1912.* Cambridge, MA: Bentley, Inc.

Moore, E. J. & Gysbers, N. C. (1972). Career development: A new focus. *Educational Leadership, 30,* 1–8.

Moran, M. (1978). *Assessment of the exceptional learner in the regular classroom.* Denver: Love Publishing.

Moran, M. R. (1981). Performance of learning disabled and low achieving secondary students on formal features of a paragraph-writing task. *Learning Disability Quarterly, 4,* 271–280.

Morsink, C. V. (1984). *Teaching special needs students in regular classrooms.* Boston: Little, Brown & Co.

Mosley, M. L. & Sullivan, H. J. (1984). *Teacher comments, student attitudes, and continuing motivation.* Paper presented at the annual meeting of the American Educational Research Association, New Orleans.

Mowrer, D. (1978, January). Speech problems: What you should do and shouldn't do. *Learning Magazine.*

Myers, P. & Hammill, D. D. (1976). *Methods for learning disorders* (2nd ed.). New York: John Wiley.

Myklebust, H. P. (1965). *Development and disorders of written language.* New York: Grune & Stratton.

National Center for Health Statistics (1982). Unpublished data from the 1980 National Health Survey.

Neef, N., Walters, J., & Egel, A. (1984). Establishing generative yes/no responses in developmentally disabled childen. *Journal of Applied Behavior Analysis, 17,* 453–460.

Neisser, U. (1967). *Cognitive psychology.* New York: Appleton-Century-Crofts.

Neisworth, J. T., Deno, S. L., & Jenkins, J. R. (1969). *Student motivation and classroom management: A behavioristic approach.* Newark, DE: Behavior Technics.

Neli, E. (1981). Teaching spelling and writing skills in the mainstreamed elementary classroom. In *Toward a research base for the least restrictive envi-ronment. A collection of papers.* Lexington, KY: University of Kentucky Dean's Grant.

Nelson, C. M. & Rutherford, R. M. (1983). Guidelines for its use in special education. *Special Education Quarterly, 3*(4), 56–67.

Nelson, F. H. (1982). A simultaneous equation model of the provision of services to handicapped children at the school district level. *American Educational Research Journal, 19,* 579–597.

Niedermeyer, F. (1973). Kindergarteners learn to write. *Elementary School Journal, 74,* 130–135.

Nihira, K., Foster, R., Shellhaas, M., & Leland, H. (1974). *AAMD Adaptive Behavior Scale, 1974 Revision.* Washington, DC: American Assocation on Mental Deficiency.

Norman, C. A., Jr. & Zigmond, N. (1980). Characteristics of children labelled and served as learning disabled in school systems affiliated with child service demonstration centers. *Journal of Learning Disabilities, 13,* 546–547.

Oakland, T. (1979). Research on the adaptive behavior inventory for children and the estimated learning potential. *The School Psychology Digest, 8,* 63–70.

Ochoa, A. S. & Shuster, S. K. (1980). *Social studies in the mainstreamed classroom, K–6.* Boulder, CO: Social Science Education Consortium.

O'Donnel, M. P. (1979). *Teaching the stages of reading progress.* Dubuque, IA: Kendall/Hunt.

O'Leary, K. D. & O'Leary, S. G. (1977). *Classroom management: The successful use of behavior modification.* New York: Pergamon Press.

Otto, W., McMenemy, R. A., & Smith, R. J. (1973). *Corrective and remedial teaching* (2nd ed.). New York: Houghton Mifflin.

Orazco, C. (1980). *The classroom environment and the development of oral expression.* A report prepared at California State University, Fresno, CA. (ERIC Document Reproduction Service No. ED 189603).

Osborn, J. (1968). Teaching a teaching language to disadvantaged children. In M. A. Brottman (Ed.), *Language remediation for the disadvantaged preschool child. Monographs of the Society for Research in Child Development, 33* (8, 26–48, Serial No. 124).

Osborn, R. et al. (1979). NCSS social studies curriculum guidelines. *Social Education,* 261–278.

Otto, W., McMenemy, R. A., & Smith, R. G. (1973). *Corrective and remedial teaching.* Boston: Houghton Mifflin.

Pallak, S. R., Costomiris, S., Sroka, S., & Pittman, T. S. (1982). School experience, reward characteristics, and intrinsic motivation. *Child Development, 53,* 1382–1391.

Paris, S., Cross, D., DeBritto, A. M., Jacobs, J., Oka, E., & Saarino, D. (1984). *Improving children's metacognition and reading comprehension with classroom instruction*. Paper presented at the annual meeting of the American Educational Research Association, New Orleans.

Paris, S. G., Cross, D. R., & Lipson, M. Y. (1984). Informed strategies for learning: A program to improve children's reading awareness and comprehension. *Journal of Educational Psychology, 76,* 1239–1252.

Paris, S. G. & Jacobs, J. E. (1985). The benefits of informed instruction for children's reading awareness and comprehension skills. *Child Development*.

Paris, S. G., Newman, R. S., & McVey, K. A. (1982). Learning the functional significance of mnemonic actions: A microgenetic study of strategy acquisition. *Journal of Experimental Child Psychology, 34,* 490–509.

Parker, R. M. (1983). *Occupational aptitude survey and interest schedule*. Austin, TX: Pro-Ed.

Patton, J. R., Payne, J. S., & Beirne-Smith (1986). *Mental retardation* (2nd ed.). Columbus, OH: Merrill.

Payan, R. (1984). Language assessment for bilingual exceptional children. In L. M. Baca & H. T. Cervantes (Eds.), *The bilingual special education interface*. St. Louis: Times/Mirror/Mosby.

Pearson, P. D. & Dole, J. A. (1985). *Explicit comprehension instruction: The model, the research, and the concerns*. Paper presented at the annual meeting of the American Educational Research Association, Chicago.

Perfetti, C. A. (1985). *Reading ability*. New York: Oxford Press.

Perkins, S. A. (1977). Malnutrition and mental development. *Exceptional Children, 43,* 214–219.

Perrone, V. (1977). *The abuses of standardized testing* (2nd ed.). New York: McGraw-Hill, 1976.)

Personkee, C. & Yee, A. H. (1968). The situational choice and the spelling program. *Elementary English, 45,* 32–27, 40.

Peterson, L. R. & Peterson, M. J. (1959). Short-term retention of individual verbal items. *Journal of Experimental Psychology, 58,* 193–198.

Petitto, A. L. (1985). *More on the developing concept of mathematical concept development: Number line and measurement concepts*. Paper presented at the annual meeting of the American Educational Research Association, Chicago.

Petty, W. T. & Bowen, M. E. (1967). *Slithery snakes and other aides to children's writing*. New York: Appleton-Century-Crofts.

Phelps, L. A. & Lutz, R. J. (1977). *Career exploration and preparation for the special needs learner*. Boston: Allyn & Bacon.

Phillips, G. M., Dunham, R. E., Brubaker, R., & Butte, D. (1970). *The development of oral communication in the classroom*. Indianapolis, IN: Bobbs-Merrill.

Piaget, J. (1968). *On the development of memory and identity*. Barre, MA: Clark University Press and Barre Publishers.

Piaget, J. (1926). *The language and thought of the child*. New York: Harcourt Brace.

Piaget, J. (1952). *The origins of intelligence in children*. New York: International Universities Press.

Piaget, J. & Inhelder, B. (1969). *The psychology of the child*. New York: Basic Books.

Piaget, J. & Inhelder, B. (1973). *Memory and intelligence*. New York: Basic Books.

Polloway, E. A., Patton, J. R., & Cohen, S. B. (1983). Written language for mildly handicapped students. In E. L. Meyen, G. A. Vergasson, & R. J. Whelan (Eds.), *Promising practices for exceptional children: Curriculum complications*. Denver: Love Publishing.

Polloway, E. A. & Smith, J. E., Jr. (1982). *Teaching language skills to exceptional learners*. Denver: Love Publishing.

Polloway, E. A. & Smith, J. E., Jr. (1982). *Teaching language skills to exceptional learners*. Denver, CO: Love Publishing.

Pope, L. (1975). Sight words for the seventies. *Academic Therapy, 10,* 285–289.

Popham, W. J. (1979). *Criterion-referenced measurement*. Englewood Cliffs, NJ: Prentice-Hall.

Poplin, M., Gray, R., Larsen, S., Banikowski, A., & Mehring, T. (1980). A comparison of components of written expression abilities in learning disabled and non-learning disabled children at three grade levels. *Learning Disability Quarterly, 3,* 46–53.

Poteet, J. A. (1980). Assessment of written expression. *Learning Disability Quarterly, 3,* 88–98.

Potter, S. (1978). Social studies for students with reading difficulties. *The Social Studies, 69,* 56–64.

Premack, D. (1965). Reinforcement theory. In D. LeVine (Ed.) *Nebraska symposium on motivation: 1965*. Lincoln, NE: University of Nebraska Press.

Prep Inc. (1976). *Comprehensive occupational assessment and training system*. Trenton, NJ.

Pressley, M., Borkowski, J. G., & O'Sullivan, J. T. (1984). Memory strategy instruction is made of this: Metamemory and durable strategy use. *Educational Psychologist, 19,* 94–107.

Punch, J. (1983). Prevalence of hearing impairment. *American Speech, Hearing & Language Association, 25,* 27.

Quandt, I. J. (1983). Language arts for the child. Englewood Cliffs, NJ: Prentice-Hall.

Ramanauskas, S. (1972). Oral reading errors and cloze comprehension of mentally retarded children. In J. Cawley, H. Goldstein, & W. H. Burrow (Eds.), *The slow learner and the reading problem*. Springfield, IL: Charles C. Thomas.

Raths, L. E., Merrill, H., & Simon, S. B. (1975). Values and valuing. In D. A. Read & S. B. Simon (Eds.), *Humanistic education sourcebook*. Englewood Cliffs, NJ: Prentice-Hall.

Raths, L., Harmin, M., & Simon, S. (1978). *Values and teaching* (2nd ed.). Columbus, OH: Charles E. Merrill.

Razeghi, J. A. & Ginyard, E. J. (1980). *Resource guide for parents: Career education and vocational education rights and opportunities for disabled students and youth*. Washington, DC: American Coalition of Citizens with Disabilities.

Read, C. (1980). Preschool children's knowledge of English phonology. In M. Wolf, M. McQuillan, & E. Radwin (Eds.), *Thought and language/language and reading. Harvard Educational Review Reprint Series #14*. Cambridge, MA: Harvard University Press.

Regen, M. K. (1979). The parent's role in vocational education starts early. *Perceptions, 1*(7), 4.

Reisman, F. K. (1982). *A guide to the diagnostic teaching of arithmetic* (3rd ed.). Columbus, OH: C. E. Merrill.

Reisman, F. K. & Kauffman, S. H. (1980). *Teaching mathematics to children with special needs*. Columbus, OH: C. E. Merrill.

Reitman, J. S. (1971). Mechanisms of forgetting in short-term memory. *Cognitive Psychology, 2*, 185–195.

Renaud, A. & Groff, P. (1966). Parent's opinions about handwriting styles. *Elementary English, 43*, 873–876.

Resnick, L. B. (1983). A developmental theory of number understanding. In H. P. Ginsburg (Ed.), *The development of mathematical thinking*. New York: Academic Press.

Reyes, R. & Post, T. (1973). *The mathematics laboratory: Theory into practice*. Boston: Prindle, Weber & Schmidt.

Reys, R. E., Suydam, M. N., & Lindquist, M. M. (1984). *Helping children learn mathematics*. Englewood Cliffs, NJ: Prentice-Hall.

Reynolds, W. M. & Miller, K. L. (1984). *Development and validation of a scale to measure learned helplessness*. Paper presented at the annual meeting of the American Educational Research Association, New Orleans.

Reynolds, W. M. & Miller, K. L. (in press) (1986). Depression and learned helplessness in mentally retarded and nonretarded adolescents: An initial investigation. *Applied Research in Mental Retardation*.

Rice, J. M. (1983). *The public school system of the United States*. New York: Century.

Richardson, S. A. (1981). Family characteristics associated with mild mental retardation. In M. J. Begab, H. C. Haywood, & H. L. Garber (Eds.), *Psychosocial influences in retarded performance: Strategies for improving competence Vol. II*. Baltimore: University Park Press.

Ricker, K. S. (1976). A review of Me Now and Me and My Environment. *Science and Children, 13*, 37.

Rinehart, S. D., Stahl, S. A., & Erickson, L. G. (1985). *The effects of summarization training on reflective and impulsive sixth graders*. Paper presented to the annual meeting of the American Educational Research Association, Chicago.

Robinson, N. M. & Robinson, H. B. (1976). *The mentally retarded child: A psychological approach* (2nd ed.). New York: McGraw-Hill.

Rosenshine, B. V. (1980). Skill hierarchies in reading comprehension. In R. Spiro, B. Bruce, & W. Brewer (Eds.), *Theoretical issues in reading comprehension*. Hillsdale, NJ: Erlbaum.

Rosenthal, T. L. & Zimmerman, B. J. (1978). *Social learning and cognition*. New York: Academic Press.

Rossetti, R. (1985). *Teacher tolerance and its relationship to teacher traits and disciplinary effectiveness*. Paper presented at the annual meeting of the American Educational Research Association, Chicago.

Roth, R. (1984). *Language learning and the practical use of language in school*. Paper presented at the annual meeting of the American Educational Research Association, New Orleans.

Rubin, K. H. & Orr, R. R. (1974). Spatial egocentrism in nonretarded and retarded children. *American Journal of Mental Deficiency, 79*, 95–97.

Rusch, F. & Mithaug, D. (1980). *Vocational training for mentally retarded adults*. Champaign, IL: Research Press.

Sachs, J. S. (1967). Recognition memory for syntactic and semantic aspects of connected discourse. *Perception and Psychophysics, 2*, 437–442.

Safer, N. & Hobbs, V. (1979). Developing, implementing, and evaluating individualized education programs. *JWK, International*.

Salvia, J. & Ysseldyke, J. E. (1985). *Assessment in spe-*

cial and remedial education. Boston: Houghton Mifflin.

Salzberg, B. H., Wheeler, A. J., Devar, L. T., & Hopkins, B. L. (1971). The effect of intermittent feedback and intermittent contingent access to play on printing of kindergarten children. *Journal of Applied Behavior Analysis, 4,* 153–171.

Sandgrund, A., Gaines, R. W., & Green, A. H. (1974). Child abuse and mental retardation: A problem of cause and affect. *American Journal of Mental Deficiency, 79,* 327–330.

Sapon-Shevin, M., Sametz, L., & Kaczala, C. (1985). *What makes teachers fair? Children's evaluation of differential teacher treatment.* Paper presented at the annual meeting of the American Educational Research Association, Chicago.

Sass-Lehrer, M. (1983). Competencies critical to teachers of hearing-impaired students in two settings. *American Annals of the Deaf, 128,* 867–872.

Sass-Lehrer, M. & Wolk, S. (1984). Underlying dimensions and correlates of the perceived importance of teacher competencies for special education. *Teacher Education and Special Education, 7,* 188–197.

Sass-Lehrer, M. & Wolk, S. (1985). *Teachers in special education settings: What are the critical competencies?* Paper presented at the annual meeting of the American Educational Research Association, Chicago.

Sattler, J. M. (1974). *Assessment of children's intelligence.* Philadelphia: W. B. Saunders.

Sattler, J. M. (1982). *Assessment of children's intelligence and special abilities* (2nd ed.). Boston: Allyn & Bacon.

Schneider, D. O. & Brown, M. J. (1980). Helping students study and comprehend their social studies textbook. *Social Education, 44,* 105–112.

Schoenfeld, A. H. (1982). Some thoughts on problem solving research and mathematics education. In F. K. Lester & J. Garofalo (Eds.), *Mathematical problem solving.* Philadelphia: Franklin Institute Press.

Schwebel, A. & Cherlin, D. (1972). Physical and social distancing in teacher pupil relationships. *Journal of Educational Psychology, 63,* 543–550.

Scott Foresman Beginning Dictionary (1976). New York: Doubleday.

Sedlak, R. A. & Fitzmaurice, A. M. (1981). Teaching arithmetic. In J. M. Kauffman & D. P. Hallahan (Eds.), *Handbook of special education.* Englewood Cliffs, NJ: Prentice-Hall.

Sequential test of educational progress (1958). Palo Alto, CA: Educational Testing Service.

Serapiglia, T. (1980). Language. In K. W. Howell & J. S. Kaplan (Eds.), *Diagnosing basic skills: A handbook*

of deciding what to teach. Columbus, OH: C. E. Merrill.

Serwatka, T., Venn, J., & Shreve, A. (1984). Single vs multiple certification for teachers of hearing-impaired students. *American Annals of the Deaf, 129,* 424–430.

Shanahan, T. & Lomax, R. G., (1985). *An analysis and comparison of theoretical models of the reading-writing relationship.* Paper presented at the annual meeting of the American Educational Research Association, Chicago.

Shanklin, N. K. (1982). *Relating reading and writing: Developing transactional theory of the writing process.* Bloomington, IN: Indiana University School of Education.

Sherwin, J. S. (1969). *Four problems in teaching English: A critique of research.* Scranton, PA: International Textbook.

Shriner, T. H. (1971). Economically deprived: Aspects of language skills. In L. E. Travis (Ed.), *Handbook of speech pathology and audiology.* Englewood Cliffs, NJ: Prentice-Hall.

Shuy, R. W. (1972). Speech differences and teaching strategies: How different is enough? In R. E. Hodges and E. H. Rudorf (Eds.), *Language and learning to read.* Boston: Houghton-Mifflin.

Siegel, E. & Siegel, R. (1977). *Creating instructional sequences.* San Rafel, CA: Academic Therapy Press.

Siegel, P. A. (1979). Incentive motivation and the mentally retarded. In N. R. Ellis (Ed.), *Handbook of mental deficiency* (2nd ed.). Hillsdale, NJ: Erlbaum.

Silpola, E. M. & Hayden, S. D. (1965). Scoring eidetic imagery among the retarded. *Perceptual and Motor Skills, 21,* 275–286.

Silberman, M. L. (1971). Teachers' attitude and actions toward their students. In M. L. Silberman (Ed.), *The experience of schooling.* New York: Holt, Rinehart & Winston.

Silbiger, F. & Woolf, D. (1965). Perceptual difficulties associated with reading ability. *College Reading Association Proceedings, 6,* 98–102.

Simon, H. A. (1974). How big is a chunk? *Science, 183,* 482–488.

Simon, S. B., Howe, L. W., & Kirschenbaum, H. (1978). *Values clarification: A handbook of practical strategies for teachers and students* (2nd ed.). New York: Hart.

Sindelar, P. T., Smith, M. A., Harriman, N. E., & Hale, R. L. (1985). *Teacher effectiveness in special education programs.* Paper presented at the annual meeting of the American Educational Research Association, Chicago.

Singer, H. (1978). Active comprehension: From answering to asking questions. *The Reading Teacher, 31*, 901–908.

Sink, D. M. (1975). Teach-write/write-teach. *Elementary English, 52,* 175–177.

Skinner, B. F. (1968). *The technology of teaching.* New York: Appleton-Century-Crofts.

Skinner, B. F. (1971). *Beyond freedom and dignity.* New York: Knopf.

Skinner, B. F. (1980). The experimental analysis of operant behavior: A history. In R. W. Rieber & K. Salzinger (Eds.), *Psychology: Theoretical-historical perspectives.* New York: Academic Press.

Skinner, B. F. & Krakower, S. (1968). *Handwriting with write and see.* Chicago: Lyons & Carnahan.

Slobin, D. I. (1979). *Psycholinguistics* (2nd ed.). Glenview, IL: Scott Foresman & Co.

Smith, R. M. (1974). *Clinical teaching: Methods of instruction for the retarded.* New York: McGraw-Hill.

Snell, M. E. (1983). *Systematic instruction of the moderately and severely handicapped* (2nd ed.). Columbus, OH: Merrill.

Soeffing, M. (1975). Abused children are exceptional children. *Exceptional Children, 42,* 126–133.

Sommer, R. (1977). Classroom layout. *Theory into Practice, 16,* 174–175.

Sorgman, M., Stout-Hensen, S., & Perry, M. L. (1979). "The least restrictive environment": Social studies goals and practices. *The Social Studies, 70,* 108–111.

Snell, M. E. (Ed.) (1983). *Systematic instruction of the moderately and severely handicapped* (2nd ed.). Columbus, OH: C. E. Merrill.

Snell, M. E. (1981). Daily living skills. In J. M. Kauffman & D. P. Hallahan (Eds.), *Handbook of special education.* Englewood Cliffs, NJ: Prentice-Hall.

Snell, M. E. & Gast, D. L. (1981). Applying time delay procedures to the instruction of the severely handicapped. *The Journal of the Association for the Severely Handicapped, 6,* 3–14.

Spache, G. D. & Spache, E. (1977). *Reading in the elementary school,* (4th ed.). Boston: Allyn & Bacon.

Sperling, G. (1960). The information available in brief visual presentations. *Psychological Monographs, 74* (Whole No. 11).

Spiro, R. (1980). Constructive processes in prose comprehension and recall. In R. Spiro, B. Bruce, & W. Brewer (Eds.), *Theoretical issues in reading comprehension.* Hillsdale, NJ: Lawrence Erlbaum.

Spiro, R. J., Bruce, B., & Brewer, W. F. (1980). *Theoretical issues in reading comprehension.* Hillsdale, NJ: Lawrence Erlbaum.

Spitz, H. H. (1979). Beyond field theory in the study of mental deficiency. In N. R. Ellis (Ed.), *Handbook of Mental Deficiency* (2nd ed.). Hillsdale, NJ: Erlbaum.

Spitz, H. H. (1973). Consolidating facts into the schematized learning and memory system of educable retardates. In N. R. Ellis (Ed.), *International review of research in mental retardation* (Vol. 6). New York: Academic Press.

Spitz, H. H. & Webreck, C. A. (1972). Effects of spontaneous vs externally cued learning on the permanent storage of a schema of retardates. *American Journal of Mental Deficiency, 7,* 163–168.

Spock, B. (1984, April). School reform: Coercion in the classroom won't work. *Atlantic, 253,* No. 4, pp. 28–35.

Stanovich, K. E. (1982). Individual differences in the cognitive processes of reading. II. Text level processes. *Journal of Learning Disabilities, 15,* 549–554.

Stengel, N. (1985). *Non-testing techniques of student assessment.* Paper presented at the annual meeting of the American Educational Research Association, Chicago.

Stephens, B. & McLaughlin, J. A. (1974). Two-year gains in reasoning by retarded and non-retarded persons. *American Journal of Mental Deficiency, 79,* 116–126.

Stephens, T. M. (1977). *Teaching skills to children with learning and behavior disorders.* Columbus, OH: C. E. Merrill.

Stephens, R. J. (1985). *The effects of strategy training on the identification of the main idea of expository passages.* Paper presented at the annual meeting of the American Educational Research Association, Chicago.

Stephens, T. M., Hartman, A. C., & Lucas, V. H. (1982). *Teaching children basic skills* (2nd ed.). Columbus, OH: C. E. Merrill.

Strickland, R. (1951). *The language arts in the elementary school.* Boston: D. C. Heath.

Sulzer-Azaroff, B. & Mayer, G. R. (1977). *Applying behavior-analysis procedures with children and youth.* New York: Holt, Rinehart & Winston.

Switzky, H. N., Haywood, H. C., & Rotatori, A. F. (1982). Who are the severely and profoundly retarded? *Education and Training of the Mentally Retarded, 17.*

Tanner, L. N. (1980). A model of school discipline. In E. H. Weiner (Ed.), *Discipline in the classroom* (2nd ed.). Washington, DC: National Education Association.

Tarjan, G., Wright, S. W., Eyman, R. K., & Keeran, C. V. (1973). Natural history of mental retardation: Some aspects of epidemiology. *American Journal of Mental Deficiency, 77,* 369–379.

Tarver, S. G., Hallahan, D. P., Kauffman, J. M., & Ball, D.

W. (1976). Verbal rehearsal and selective attention in children with learning disabilities: A developmental lag. *Journal of Experimental Child Psychology, 22*, 375–385.

Tawney, S. (1967). An analysis of the ball point pen versus the pencil as a beginning handwriting instrument. *Elementary English, 44*, 59–61.

Taylor, B. M. & Beach, R. W. (1984). The effects of text structure instruction on middle grade student's comprehension and productive of expository text., *Reading Research Quarterly, 19*, 132–146.

Taylor, F. D., Artuso, A. A., & Hewett, F. M. (1973). *Exploring our environment: Science tasks for exceptional children in special and regular classrooms.* Denver: Love Publishing.

Taylor, W. L. (1953). Cloze procedure: A new tool for measuring reliability. *Journalism Quarterly, 30*, 415–433.

Telford, C. W. & Sawrey, J. M. (1981). *The exceptional individual* (4th ed.). Englewood Cliffs, NJ: Prentice-Hall.

Terman, L. M. & Oden, M. H. (1959). *The gifted group at mid-life. Genetic studies of genius, V.* Stanford, CA: Stanford University Press.

Thorndike, E. (1910). Handwriting. *Teachers College Record, 11*, 83–175.

Thorndike-Barnhart Beginning Dictionary. (1952). Chicago: Scott Foresman & Co.

Thorndike-Barnhart Dictionary Series. Chicago: Scott Foresman & Co.

Thornton, C. A., Tucker, B. F., Dossey, J. A., & Bazik, E. F. (1983). *Teaching mathematics to children with special needs.* Menlo Park, CA: Addison-Wesley.

Thurber, D. N. (1975). *D'Nealian manuscript: A continuous stroke print.* (ERIC Document Reproduction Service, No. ED 169 533).

Thurber, D. N. & Jordan, D. R. (1978). *D'Nealian Handwriting.* Glenview, IL: Scott, Foresman & Co.

Tiedt, S. & Tiedt, I. (1978). *Language arts activities for the classroom.* Boston: Allyn & Bacon.

Torgesen, J. K. (1981, November). The relationship between memory and attention in learning disabilities. *Exceptional Education Quarterly*, 51–57.

Turnbull, A. P. & Schulz, J. B. (1979). *Mainstreaming handicapped students: A guide for the classroom teacher.* Boston: Allyn & Bacon.

Turnbull, A. P., Strickland, B. B., & Brantley, J. C. (1978). *Developing and implementing individualized education programs.* Columbus, OH: Merrill.

Turner, L. A. & Bray, N. W. (in press). Spontaneous rehearsal in mildly mentally retarded children and adolescents. *American Journal of Mental Deficiency.*

Turnure, J. E., Larsen, S. N., & Thurlow, M. L. (1976). Outerdirectedness in retarded children as a function of sex of experimenter and sex of object. *American Journal of Mental Deficiency, 80*, 460–468.

Tymitz, B. L. (1981). Teacher performance on IEP instructional planning tasks. *Exceptional Children, 48*, 258–260.

Tyo, J. (1980). An alternative for poor readers in social science. *Social Education, 44*, 309–310.

Uhlin, D. M. & DeChiara, E. (1984). *Art for exceptional children* (3rd ed.). Dubuque, IA: Wm. C. Brown.

Upton, G. (Ed.). (1979). *Physical and creative activities for the mentally handicapped.* London: Cambridge University Press.

United States Bureau of Education for the Handicapped (1973). *Selected career education programs for the handicapped.* Washington, DC: U. S. Government Printing Office.

United States Office of Education (1978). *Helping children make career plans: Tips for parents.*

VanAllen, R. (1976). *Language experiences in communication.* Boston: Houghton-Mifflin.

Vellutino, F. R. (1979). Toward an understanding of dyslexia: Psychological factors in specific reading disability. In A. L. Benton & D. Pearl (Eds.), *Dyslexia.* New York: Oxford University Press.

Vernon, P. E. (1960). *The structure of human abilities.* London: Methuen Press.

Vitello, S. J. (1976). Quantitative abilities of mentally retarded children. *Education and training of the mentally retarded, 11*, 125–129.

Wagner, J. & Moyse, E. (1984). *The effects of redundancy on the visual word learning performance of children.* Paper presented at the annual meeting of the American Educational Research Association, New Orleans.

Walker, J. E. & Shea, T. M. (1984). *Behavior management: A practical approach for educators* (3rd ed.). St. Louis: Times Mirror/Mosby.

Wallace, G. & Larsen, S. C. (1979). *Educational assessment of learning problems: Testing for teaching.* Boston: Allyn & Bacon.

Wallace, G. & McLoughlin, J. A. (1975). *Learning disabilities: Concepts and characteristics.* Columbus, OH: C. E. Merrill.

Webster's dictionary for boys and girls. (1971). New York: American Book Co.

Weed, K., Ryan, E. B., & Day, J. (1984). *Motivational and metacognitive aspects of strategy use and transfer.* Paper presented at the annual meeting of the American Educational Research Association, New Orleans.

Wehman, P. & McLoughlin, P. J. (1981). *Program devel-*

opment in special education. New York: McGraw-Hill.

Weiner, E. S. (1980). Diagnostic evaluation of writing skills. *Journal of Learning Disabilities, 13*, 43–48.

Welliver, P. W. (1980). Strategies for stimulating scientific inquiry for all students. In M. E. Corrick, Jr. (Ed.), *Teaching handicapped students science*. (ERIC Document Reproduction Service No. ED 213220.)

Wepman, J. M. (1975). *Auditory discrimination test*. (Revised). Palm Springs, CA: Research Associates.

Westerman, G. (1971). *Spelling and writing*. San Rafel, CA: Dimensions Press.

Westerman, G. S. (1971). *Spelling and writing*. Sioux Falls, SD: Adapt Press.

Westling, D. L. & Koorland, M. A. (1979). Some considerations and tactics for improving discrimination learning. *Teaching Exceptional Children, 11*, 97–100.

Wheldall, K. (1976). Receptive language development in the mentally handicapped. In P. Berry (Ed.), *Language and communication in the mentally handicapped*. Baltimore, MD: University Park Press.

Wiig, E. H. & Semel, E. (1984). *Language assessment and intervention for the learning disabled* (2nd ed.). Columbus, OH: Charles E. Merrill.

Wiles, D. & Rockoff, E. (1979). Problems in achieving rehabilitation and punishment in special school environments. *Journal of Law and Education, 7*, 165–176.

Wiles, M. (1943). The effect of different sizes of tools upon the handwriting of beginners. *Elementary School Journal, 43*, 412–414.

Williams, R. L. (1972). *The BITCH (Black intelligence test of cultural homogeneity)*. St. Louis: Williams and Associates.

Williams, W. & Gotts, E. A. (1977). Selected considerations on developing curriculum for severely handicapped students. In E. Sontag, J. Smith, & N. Certo (Eds.), *Educational programming for the severely and profoundly handicapped*. Reston, VA: Council for Exceptional Children.

Wilson, S. (1979). Beyond the spelling book. *Instructor, 89*, 128–130.

Winborne, C. R. & Stainback, G. H. (1983). The new discipline dilemma. *Educational Forum, 47*, 435–443.

Winsor, M. T. (1972). *Arts and Crafts for Special Education*, Belmont, CA: Fearon Press.

Wolfensberger, W. (1976). The origin and nature of our institutional models. In R. B. Kugel & A. Shearer (Eds.), *Changing patterns in residential services for the mentally retarded* (revised ed.).

Washington, DC: President's Committee on Mental Retardation.

Wolfensberger, W. (1972). *The principle of normalization in human services*. Toronto: National Institute on Mental Retardation.

Wolfram, W. A. & Fasold, R. W. (1969). Toward reading materials for speakers of Black English: Three linguistically appropriate passages. In J. Baratz & R. Shuy (Eds.), *Teaching Black Children to Read*. Washington, DC: Center for Applied Linguistics.

Wong, B. & Jones, W. (1982). Increasing metacomprehension in learning disabled and normally achieving students through self-questioning training. *Learning Disabilities Quarterly, 5*, 228–239.

Wood, B. S. (1976). *Children and communication: Verbal and nonverbal language development*. Englewood Cliffs, NJ: Prentice-Hall.

Woodward, W. M. (1979). Piaget's theory and the study of mental retardation. In N. R. Ellis (Ed.), *Handbook of Mental Deficiency* (2nd Ed.). Hillsdale, NJ: Lawrence Erlbaum.

The World Book Dictionary (1970). Chicago: Field Enterprises Educational Corporation.

Worthen, B. R. & Sanders, J. R. (1973). *Educational evaluation: Theory and practice*. Worthington, OH: Charles A. Jones Publishing Co.

Yap, K. O. (1984). *Evaluation of a bilingual test: Adding the consumer's point of view*. Paper presented at the annual meeting of the American Educational Research Association, New Orleans.

Yoho, R. F. (1985). *Effectiveness of four concept teaching strategies on social studies concept acquisition and retention*. Paper presented at the annual meeting of the American Educational Research Association, Chicago.

Ysseldyke, J. E., Pianta, R., Christenson, S., Wang, J., & Algozzine, B. (1983). An analysis of pre-referral interventions. *Psychology in the Schools, 20*, 184–190.

Ysseldyke, J. E. & Salvia, J. (1974). Diagnostic-prescriptive teaching: Two models. *Exceptional Children, 41*, 181–185.

Ysseldyke, J. E. & Thurlow, M. L. (1984). Assessment practices in special education: Adequacy and appropriateness. *Educational Psychologist, 9*, 123–136.

Zaner-Bloser evaluation scales (1984). Columbus, OH: Zaner-Bloser Inc.

Zeaman, D. & House, B. J. (1963). The role of attention in retarded discrimination learning. In N. R. Ellis (Ed.), *Handbook of Mental Deficiency*. New York: McGraw-Hill.

Zeaman, D. & House, B. J. (1979). A review of attention theory. In N. R. Ellis (Ed.), *Handbook of men-*

tal deficiency (2nd ed.). Hillsdale, NJ: Lawrence Erlbaum.

Zigler, E. (1973). The retarded child as a whole person. In D. K. Routh (Ed.), *The experimental psychology of mental retardation*. Chicago: Aldine.

Zigmond, N., Vallercorsa, A., & Silverman, R. (1983). *Assessment for instructional planning in special education*. Englewood Cliffs, NJ: Prentice-Hall.

Zintz, M. V. (1981). *Corrective Reading* (4th ed.). Dubuque, IA: W. C. Brown.

Index